Social Structure
and
Social Personality

Social Structure
and
Social Personality

JEROLD M. STARR
University of Pennsylvania

LITTLE, BROWN AND COMPANY
Boston   Toronto

For Judy

Preface

Never before have I had to encompass such a tremendous range of material as is offered here. To do so in a way comprehensible and relevant to students, I have developed an overview that is presented in the systemic diagram contained in the Introduction. The diagram outlines the structure and process of socialization and provides the rationale for the book's organization. An introduction to each section of the book summarizes and integrates the principal research in the area, discusses the social and theoretical importance of key issues, and places the readings which follow in proper context. The readings are contemporary and interesting to intelligent laymen, as well as to specialists.

The book focuses on the interaction between social structure and social personality, especially underlining the effect of institutions on individuals. Individuals are viewed as members of social aggregates exposed to different but characteristic social conditions and socializing experiences. Although I emphasize the contemporary American scene, historical and cross-cultural comparisons are drawn to make the student aware that many broader theoretical issues can only be addressed meaningfully in the broadest of contexts.

This book improves on various conventional treatments of the subject. Unlike anthropological studies, it stresses that a nation's culture is not uniform, nor is it experienced alike by everyone in the society. Rather, it is interpreted, transmitted, and selectively received by persons performing social roles in institutions. Unlike conventional psychological treatments, this book avoids the less generalizable aspects of personality and examines instead those facets of personality that membership in social aggregates most directly influences. And unlike those sociological treatments that become preoccupied with the academic discipline, the subject of society and personality is kept in sight. I have avoided confusing jargon; sociological concepts are invoked only when they clarify the discussion and can be adequately defined and illustrated.

Although I consider man an active agent in the historical process, I deal primarily with the impact of institutions on individuals. That is because I wish to emphasize that people must define themselves and their environment in terms and on conditions, as Marx has said, "not of their own choosing." In order to implement change, one must first understand those forces which impede change. This is a book for people interested in social change. However, above all, this is a book for the young student of social structure and social personality. It is a book for those interested in the nature of people and institutions — for those who desire new perspectives on the important problems confronting contemporary man.

Acknowledgments

Preparing this anthology on social structure and social personality turned out to be a much more time-consuming, energy-depleting, and intellectually complicated task than I originally imagined. The sheer volume of research material to be reviewed, digested, and integrated was enormous. When one considers that there are more than a dozen sections, each of which has been the exclusive subject of other books or anthologies, the problem readily becomes apparent. So let me make it clear here that the task would have been even more difficult were it not for the invaluable bibliographic and secretarial assistance of a handful of very competent undergraduate students at the University of Pennsylvania. Patricia Sze, Donald Whitten, Ruth Rovinsky, Alan Light, Robert Long, and, especially, William Flynn Martin all made the work not only bearable, but interesting and pleasant.

Special thanks are also due Professor Alex Inkeles, probably the most distinguished authority in this field of study, for his insights and suggestions over the entire period in which the organizing model was constructed, the essays selected, and the introductions written for this book.

Also, the people at Little, Brown — Chris Hunter, Milton Johnson, and Frank Graham — deserve acknowledgment for their confidence, encouragement, and good judgment through it all. Last, but not least, my colleagues Jan Smith and Frank Furstenberg must be recognized for offering me much needed criticisms and recommendations on some of the more difficult sections.

Contents

Social Structure
and
Social Personality

INTRODUCTION

Biologically speaking, human beings are animals. They are a species of the genus primate (which also includes apes, monkeys, marmosets, and lemurs) in the mammal family (any of the highest class of vertebrates that nourish their young with milk). However, human beings are very peculiar in the animal world because practically none of their behavior is instinctive, or the product of genetically determined inborn drives. In fact, almost all human behavior is learned throughout life from other human beings. While human beings have such biological drives as sex, hunger, thirst, temperature control, pain avoidance, and waste elimination, the form and object of behavior motivated by these drives are not predetermined. As Erikson (1963, p. 95) states: "Man's 'inborn instincts' are drive fragments to be assembled, given meaning, and organized during a prolonged childhood by methods of child training and schooling which vary from culture to culture and are determined by tradition."

The wide variation across cultures in values, customs, and tastes relating to courtship, marriage, and family life (sex), food and drink (hunger and thirst), clothing and shelter (temperature control), risk-taking and medicine (pain avoidance), and sanitation (waste elimination) provides abundant evidence of the plasticity of these basic drives.

Cultural Influences on Behavior

This plasticity makes man the only animal that, in the most fundamental sense, must learn through personal experience to be what he is. Though all human behavior — for example, the ability to read and write — must be genetically based, it only exists in a potential state and requires specific environmental stimulation before it can be actualized. Man is able to compensate for his instinctual poverty because he is the only animal capable of constructing a culture — that vast storehouse of language, knowledge, values, and customs which provides people with a design for living and is symbolically transmitted

1

and acquired across generations within human groups. In fact, man is the only creature that no longer adapts himself to his natural environment by the relatively slow and inefficient process of natural selection, but by deliberately adapting his environment to himself. The social cooperation required for such a complicated enterprise can only be achieved because of the existence of culture.

Human beings are able to build and sustain cultures because of their unique capacity to engage in highly complex forms of interaction with each other. Some other animals manifest primitive forms of social organization; some teach their young certain patterns of behavior in the earliest stages of maturation. This, however, hardly compares with man's ability to learn sophisticated modes of symbolic communication and to even further enrich interaction with empathy, the developed ability to see things as others see them.

These faculties make it possible for human beings to share a range of knowledge and feeling far beyond the comprehension of other animals. The unique and characteristically human capacity for empathic behavior also allows human beings to experience self-consciousness; to make themselves an object unto themselves in an effort to see themselves as others see them. The self gradually emerges out of interaction with significant others in infancy and childhood and thereafter functions as the conscious, governing agent of the personality.

Human beings become persons by being socialized into a culture. The term *socialization* also refers generally to any learning process necessary to assuming membership in any group. Those few famous cases of children raised by animals or otherwise shut off from almost all contact with other human beings — for example, Singh and Zingg (1942) and Davis (1940, 1947) — have vividly illustrated the essential role of the socialization process in molding human beings into persons. When discovered, the children did not manifest any patterns of thought, emotion, or behavior which we would characterize as human. In effect, they had not learned to become persons.

Although all human beings are socialized into a culture and become persons, they don't all necessarily become the same kind of persons. As Kluckhohn and Murray (1953) say, every man is in certain respects like all other men, like some other men, and like no other man. All men are like all other men in the sense that they are subject to the basic needs of the human organism and the demands of the larger society and must experience crucial events and processes like birth, maturation, and death. At the other extreme, every human being's biological heredity and social experience is sufficiently distinct to make him like no other man.

It is the problem of how and why every man is like some other men which has most occupied social scientists. Their research attempts to puzzle out the many factors influencing personality development — the process whereby human beings become certain kinds of persons. This problem is also the central issue in this book. More particularly, we are interested in the impact of the social structure on social personality.

Personality refers to the total organization of all the biologically rooted drives, socially acquired needs, and learned behavior patterns that characterize an individual. *Social personality* refers to those fundamental aspects of personality which are shared by members of major social aggregates as a consequence of their similar life circumstances and experiences. In this sense we can talk about the social personality of classes, races, religions, and nations without considering the more particular, idiosyncratic differences between people within such aggregates. In social psychological research, social personality is usually measured by the patterns of attitude and behavior manifested by aggregates of people distinguished by certain sociological criteria.

Social structure, on the other hand, is the whole complex of organized social relationships that binds people together in any given society. This concept is premised on the fact that people in society are tied by bonds of law, custom, and mutual interest. In fact, the very notion of society means that people live out their lives within complex networks of association that connect individuals with each other in systematic ways.

The articles in this volume examine the similarities in life conditions and regularities in socialization experiences that various aggregates of people in society share and the consequences this has for their personality development and change. One implication of this orientation is that everyone in society is not exposed to or influenced by the general or official culture (that is, the culture which directly reflects the institutionalized historical experience of the traditional elites in the society) in the same way. It would be more precise to propose that culture is interpreted, transmitted, and selectively received by individuals performing particular social roles located in different institutions.

Institutional Influences on Behavior

Institutions can be thought of as organized systems of collective behavior oriented to the performance of functions which serve certain needs of the larger collectivity or society. Some examples of institutions would be the *economy,* the organization of the production and distribution of goods and services, and the *polity,* the organized distribution of power for the purpose of making decisions which are binding on all members of the society. Thus, institutions are not to be confused wth mere physical plants or even particular formal organizations, but include all forms of social organization which are tied together by a common function. Although General Motors and the Department of Public Welfare may seem to be very different organizations in terms of their authority structure, resources, and operational goals, they both participate in the production and distribution of goods and services in American society and, thus, constitute component parts of our particular economy.

All institutions are structured in terms of statuses or positions. To each status are attached roles. According to Gerth and Mills (1953, p. 10), the concept of role refers to "(1) units of conduct which by their recurrence stand out as regularities and (2) which are oriented to the conduct of other actors." Role can also represent the pattern of behavior characteristically associated with a particular status. Thus, the status "father" refers to a particular position within the institution of the family, whereas the role "father" refers to behavior one would normally expect from someone occupying that status.

To each status are attached different degrees of power and prestige. To each role are attached *norms* (that is, general rules and standards of conduct) that regulate the behavior of the role occupant, thus making his relationships with others more predictable and continuous. The notion of different roles means that people have different rights, privileges, and obligations toward each other depending on their status. The individual's self-image or identity is constructed out of his evaluation of the appraisals of his self communicated by others during role interaction. Thus, the roles assigned to or chosen by the individual have important consequences for his perception of himself and his general feeling of self-worth.

Gerth and Mills's definition of role is especially useful because it establishes that (1) what is actually observed are certain recurrent patterns of interaction which we infer must require some common frame of reference and from which we induce the theoretical construct of role. Also, (2) roles are not solitary units, but only exist in relation to each other. No role can exist in isolation just as no person can engage in social interaction by himself. Roles are situated in systems of interaction of varying degrees of scope and complexity.

Of course, even the fact that social behavior is organized by roles does not mean that everyone performs the same role in the same way. Differences in personality express themselves in different performances of the same role by different social actors. Just as every man is like no other man so is every role performance like no other role performance. But behavior by persons occupying identical statuses has sufficient basic similarities to establish the validity of the concept of role. Ultimately, as Goffman (1961) suggests, it is probably most fruitful to think of role performances as (1) *ideal,* (2) *typical,* and (3) *actual,* by which we mean role performances which (1) are in strict accord with cultural norms, (2) occur most frequently, and (3) are observed in any particular instance.

Perspectives of Book

Most of an individual's life can be thought of as membership in different social aggregates and, in particular, as the enactment of roles attached to statuses within institutions. This is certainly not the only way to view human life, but it is a perspective in which to organize a great variety of social activity comprehensively and systematically. Despite the growing popularity of sociology in America, however, many students still find this view somewhat distasteful.

The values of rugged individualism, unlimited opportunity, and ceaseless progress are still powerful forces in American culture. American history has been charted by the assault on new frontiers and the great achievements of common men. Clearly, many young people today are less enthralled with our territorial acquisitiveness and even our achievements in the exploration of outer space. However, they still strive to expand the barriers of individual consciousness and to experiment with institutional alternatives with a sense of mission very similar to that of their forefathers. And each generation still inherits both the burden and privilege of improving on the last.

The increasing sociological sophistication of young Americans is reflected in their use of concepts like identity, status, role, class, and the system, among others, to make sense of their social environment and personal experience. To acknowledge the extent to which such concepts have a social reality which influences one's choice of personal values and goals and limits the range of one's occupational and life-style alternatives is still understandably difficult for many, however.

Almost all relevant evidence indicates that patterns and regularities in human behavior result from similar kinds of social conditioning. Not only is man in society, but society is in man. After all, what do we really mean by the "authentic individual"? Lindesmith and Strauss (1950, p. 591) ask, "Do not cultural roles and internalized norms connected with them (e.g., sex roles) influence the 'authentic individual'?" Could you imagine some special, remote "inner self" without any gender identification? Yet sexual behavior is role behavior. The renewed interest in the nature and dynamics of sex-role learning aroused by the Women's Liberation Movement has reminded us how much even the most rudimentary patterns of male and female behavior are culturally learned and vary according to society. In criticizing educators who speak about the "full development of the personality," Sprott (1958, p. 28) states:

> They speak as though there were in each of us a little seed called the "personality" which must be carefully tended and allowed the maximum freedom for it to grow. Nothing could be more mistaken. A permissive social environment produces one sort of personality, an authoritarian one produces another. Permission is not the *removal* of social influence so that the "natural" personality can have a chance to develop, it merely replaces one kind of social influence for another.

This emphasis on environmental influence does not imply that the individual is a tabula rasa — a blank slate — to be written on by others in the society. In fact, drives or basic human needs will be examined in the section on heredity. Nor does it mean that the individual is a helpless dependent buffeted about by the omnipotent winds of social forces. Individuals can and do achieve self-consciousness which enables them to mobilize resources for achieving personal goals. And individuals, particularly when organized into groups, can measurably affect the circumstances of their existence. Ultimately, all social action is the function of social actors evaluating alternatives and making decisions which have real consequences.

Rather, the justification for the particular selection and organization of articles in this book rests on a conviction that, to be an effective social actor in the sense just discussed, people must become aware in a realistic and meaningful way of the nature of those circumstances which affect the decisions which they make. Though many anthologies have assembled various reflections on the relationship between the general culture and the basic personality, very few have carefully scrutinized the role of the social structure which, by establishing certain conditions for social behavior, both nourishes and deprives the biological organism and reflects and refracts the general culture.

By now, the careful reader should realize that the concept of the individual in social theory is as much an abstraction as the concept of the social structure. Prior to the Renaissance and the Protestant Reformation, Western culture had no concept of the individual — as a being with potentialities and rights independent of his membership in certain social groups like the family. During the Industrial Revolution — a period of rapid social change and great personal mobility — the individual came to be considered the basic unit of society. Only recently have we achieved the maturity to appreciate the interdependence and interaction between the individual and the collectivity in creating social reality.

Influences of Social Structure on Social Personality

The social structure influences the social personality of the individual in many ways. To illustrate, I have sketched a diagram (Figure 1), which describes the relationships of the principal influences on personality development to each other and to the individual. The units in the model parallel the headings of the parts and chapters of this book. Like any diagram attempting to depict linguistic conceptualizations of social behavior spatially, precision and subtlety are sacrificed to help establish the essential ideas under consideration.

At the top of the diagram there is the *culture* which exists in a relationship of mutual influence with the *social structure,* as indicated by the double arrow. Quite simply, this means that the organization of social relationships is closely related to the values that people hold and changes in one tend to produce changes in the other. For example, Ogburn, Wheelis, and others have argued that the diffusion of scientific ideas and, more importantly, their application in

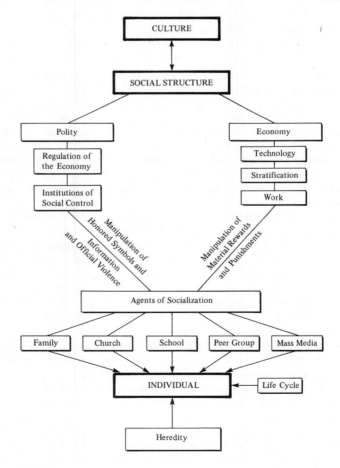

FIGURE 1

Detroit: Please order an examination copy for
my course in Personality & Social Structure. Top priority.

✓

rec
ordered
2-7-75

STARR, Jerold, ed., <u>Social Structure and Social Personality</u> (34 Beacon St., Boston,
02106: Little Brown & Co, College Div, April 1974),

economic production have led to changes in cultural values as well as in the structure and relative social influence of other institutions. Obversely, other studies, discussed in the introduction to Chapter 5 have shown how certain cultural values and practices have encouraged, if not caused, changes in the level of economic technology.

The social structure itself is composed of many different institutions, not all of which are included in the diagram. Two institutions already referred to in this introduction are the *polity* and the *economy*. The economy, in turn, is broken down into several principal factors that are often used to distinguish among different types of economies: the kind and level of *technology* utilized in production; the kind of *stratification*, or social ranking, which emerges as a result of the status structure of the economy and differential access to such positions; and the kind of *work* that people can or must do to survive.

Though many other factors may distinguish different economies, technology, stratification, and work appear to relate most directly to the organization of the social structure and seem to influence most profoundly individual personality development. Many articles in this volume are investigations of the impact of such factors as social class, race, and occupation on the social personalities of their members.

Also included in the diagram is a special class of institutions called "agents of socialization": the family, church, school, peer group, and mass media. Their primary function is to instruct the individual in the ways of the society and to motivate him to strive toward certain culturally defined goals. Obviously, not all these agents of socialization can be found in every society throughout history. In fact, the mass media, public school, and age-graded, heterosexual peer group have come into being only in advanced industrial societies. In less technologically developed societies information is conveyed by word of mouth, most education takes place in the early years of childhood within the context of the extended family, and children play primarily with family members under the supervision of kinship authorities. This diagram is most applicable to understanding the impact of social structure on social personality in modern Western society. This is appropriate insofar as almost all research on the subject, including that presented in this book of readings, has been done on that kind of society, particularly the United States.

In contradistinction to the social functions which such agents of socialization may perform, the explicit goals of these various institutions may be defined differently by institutional leaders. Mass media entrepreneurs may say their business is to entertain, religious leaders may say their mission is to save souls, family heads may emphasize their responsibility to provide for the physical and emotional well-being of their children, educators may differ profoundly on methods and objectives, and, for many, peer groups are just friends informally organized for the purpose of companionship and recreation. Nevertheless, as the essays either cited or reprinted here demonstrate, all these institutions are experienced directly and contribute in important ways to the personality development of the individual. They are, in effect, the agencies through which human beings learn to become certain kinds of persons.

Consistent with our definition of social structure, the various parts of the whole are integrated. The role differentiation and life style of the family, for example, are mainly a product of the occupational role of the family head which, in turn, is both cause and consequence of his social class identification. For example, the son of a blue-collar worker is much more likely to become a blue-collar worker himself than is the son of a professional and, if he does, the ways in which he and his wife define their mutual responsibilities and expectations, spend their leisure, and raise their children will differ from the family of the professional. Their children will, in turn, reflect their social milieu, particularly as experienced in the family setting, in the distinctive patterns of attitudes and behavior which describe their personalities. Similarly, the kind and amount of schooling required of or permitted a child, for the most part, will vary according to his or her race and social class.

At the bottom of Figure 1 is the *individual* whose personality is shaped, in great measure, through the interaction of his biological drives, limitations, and potentialities with the demands imposed upon him by persons acting on behalf of "society." This relationship is not static. The individual's biological properties as well as the societal demands placed upon him tend to vary systematically according to age. Each culture, with varying degrees of formality, divides the individual *life cycle* into various stages. As age, like sex, is a status and role, to each stage are assigned different rights, privileges, obligations, and standards of behavior. So, in a sense, the individual is always being socialized; his personality is always, to some extent, changing and developing.

Certainly, many roles an individual can and must play vary according to life-cycle stage and, at least to that extent, so must his personality. According to Inkeles (1968), the individual undergoes two principal "waves" of socialization. The first wave consists of his child or primary socialization. In the second wave (secondary socialization), according to Inkeles (p. 92),

> The individual not only learns the detailed role contents socially necessary to acting in accord with earlier acquired basic predispositions, but he also acquires new dispositions and social skills which he could not appropriately learn in infancy and early childhood. Many aspects of heterosexual relations, much of the orientation and behavior appropriate to work and to political allegiance and action exemplify those realms in which, perforce, socialization must come mainly after the early years.

The diagram also shows the mechanisms (that is, types and sources of power) that other people, particularly institutional authorities — ranging all the way from family heads to political leaders — use to limit the degree of individual deviance from group norms. The issue of the *social control* of *individual deviance* is particularly relevant to the perspective used to organize the selections in this book and is dealt with on three levels: internalized controls, interpersonal controls, and institutional controls.

Everyone, to some extent, is involved in controlling and being controlled by other people during daily human interaction. Most often it is a question of whose or which definition of the situation will prevail at any time. Some concede, some compromise, some seduce, some outwit, and others overpower, but we're all involved in the complicated process of transacting meanings and sentiments and arbitrating conflicting values and interests.

A great many institutional roles in modern society (for example, policeman, teacher, clergy, counselor, social worker, psychiatrist) influence the behavior of individuals. This does not imply that a vast conspiracy exists to keep everyone in line. Many efforts at social control are uncoordinated and agreement among authorities, especially in modern societies, is much less than perfect as to what constitutes proper behavior. However, some institutions exclusively function to promote social control. Whether this is for the good of the whole or a few elite is debatable, but all societies do use various mechanisms of social control.

In all societies throughout history one can find examples of both deviance and conformity and ours is certainly no exception. However, most evidence indicates that societies change slowly, that almost all people conform to social expectations almost all the time, and that this orientation to the existing social structure is both internalized early and actively reinforced throughout the life of the individual.

In some sense, socialization may be thought of as persuading people to want to do what they must do. Societies which are not very successful at this cannot be expected to last very long. This doesn't mean the end of the people themselves, but of the particular ways in which they behave and are organized. If certain forms of deviant behavior become accepted by most people, they may come to be redefined as normative and eventually institutionalized. The basic malleability of presocialized human beings makes possible a tremendous range of behavior and forms of social organization. As I said, human beings are very peculiar animals.

References

Davis, Kingsley
    1940   "Extreme Social Isolation of a Child." *American Journal of Sociology* 45 (January):554–64.
    1947   "Final Note on a Case of Extreme Isolation." *American Journal of Sociology* 50 (March):432–37.
Erikson, Erik H.
    1963   *Childhood and Society*, 2d ed. New York: Norton.
Gerth, Hans and C. Wright Mills
    1953   *Character and Social Structure: the psychology of social institutions*. New York: Harcourt, Brace and World.
Goffman, Erving
    1961   *Encounters: Two Studies in the Sociology of Interaction*. Indianapolis: Bobbs-Merrill.
Inkeles, Alex
    1968   "Society, Social Structure and Child Socialization." Pp. 73–129 in John A. Clausen (ed.), *Socialization and Society*. Boston: Little, Brown.
Kluckhohn, Clyde, and Henry A. Murray
    1967   "Personality Formation: The Determinants." Pp. 53–67 in Clyde Kluckhohn, and Henry A. Murray with David M. Schneider (eds.), *Personality in Nature, Society, and Culture*. New York: Knopf.
Lindesmith, Alfred, and Anselm L. Strauss
    1950   "A Critique of Culture-Personality Writings." *American Sociological Review* 15 (October):587–600.
Singh, J. A. L., and Robert M. Zingg
    1942   *Wolf-Children and Feral Man*. New York: Harper.
Sprott, W. J. H.
    1964   *Human Groups*. London: Penguin.

I

Individual Organism

1

HEREDITY

In every society some value assumptions are so widely shared and consistently reinforced that they become "common knowledge." Much of this common knowledge relates to suppositions about human nature and provides convenient explanations for recurrent patterns of behavior. These colloquial notions of common knowledge and human nature implicitly deny any possibility of individual or collective choice, let alone any concept of social influence.

The notion of human nature in American society, as in many others, is invoked especially when describing the pursuit of personal survival (the "law of survival") or material gain achieved at the expense of others. In a sense, it allows others in the society to disavow any responsibility for the behavior of the offender, blaming it on the mysterious, primitive nature of man which lurks beneath the thin veneer of civilization imposed upon him by others. This theme can be found frequently in some of the best literature (such as Conrad and Golding) as well as in the most popular fiction of Western man.

This cultural pattern is dangerous precisely because it denies the influence of culture as well as of social structure. It dismisses the possibility that these established patterns of behavior could express values particular to a given culture or be influenced by the organization of institutional relations particular to a given society. The popular notion of human nature does not recognize that human beings are unique in that only they can have culture. Having culture means that people learn values and having values makes people capable of truly selfless behavior even when such behavior could result in their own destruction. Individuals learn to value some people, ideas, or things more than others—perhaps even more than their very selves.

Instinct for Survival

The dangerous tenacity of this common knowledge about human nature, perhaps, is no better exemplified than in the obvious unwillingness or inability

13

of many Americans to understand the nature of our long drawn-out war in Indochina. Many of our political leaders have shown themselves to be embarrassingly ignorant of the fundamental facts of human nature and human being. When, in desperation, some Senate doves invited a contingent of social scientists to lecture their more hawkish fellows on these issues (apparently in a vain attempt to persuade them to see the exasperating persistence of the "enemy" in a more understanding light), the network news treated the event like a delightful spectacle, focusing their cameras on the beleaguered old war horses who dozed placidly in their chairs while the intellectuals pontificated.

"But doesn't it all boil down to the law of survival?" thundered one Southern senator (an advocate of saturation bombing). The social scientists, pathetically encumbered in academic terminology, tried to explain otherwise, but to no avail. Ironically the front page of the *Washington Post* that day carried a story about a courageous American GI who had thrown himself on a hand grenade to save his three comrades. His behavior was hailed as heroic, rather than perplexing, but the lesson was obviously lost on the policy makers.

Instinct for Aggression

When public disillusionment with the Indochina war began to grow, an epidemic of books by popular ethnologists broke out in bookstores all over the country. Human beings were portrayed as naked apes living in human zoos desperately pursuing their territorial imperatives. The puerile speculation that complex societies engage in modern warfare because of "man's instinct for aggression" became vogue in many circles. The political and economic motives, plans, and purposeful behavior of institutional authorities responsible for conducting the war were reduced, in many minds, to sophisticated elaborations on basic animal behavior. After all, "man's inhumanity to man" was "common knowledge" (that is, a matter over which human beings had no control).

We are not in a position to determine conclusively whether or not human beings have an instinct for aggression. We do know, however, that the form and object of human instincts are culturally learned and vary according to society. Accordingly, the level and expression of aggression are peculiar to the cultural values, socialization practices, and institutional constraints of the social environment. Unfortunately, our ignorance of social practices in other cultures permitted us for many years to believe that it was "natural" for all human beings to respond with physical aggression to the frustration of any impulse or goal achievement. We have known better for some time, however.

Thirty years ago, John Whiting (1944) formulated several propositions about human responses to frustration. First, although the "innately dominant emotional reaction to frustration" is some kind of "indeterminate visceral response," such responses "may be modified by learning, so that frustration may result in anger, in fear, in a combination of the two, or in neither of them." In fact, physiologists often have difficulty in distinguishing between these various emotional states. Second, although the "innately dominant overt response to frustration" in infants takes the form of "violent thrashing muscular movements of the arms, legs, and torso, loud crying, and holding the breath," these responses are gradually modified and replaced by "culturally defined responses."

Third, overt reactions to frustration may include submission, dependence, and avoidance in addition to aggression. Fourth, which response is invoked "depends upon the culturally defined context, and particularly upon the social relationship between the frustrated person and the frustrator." Fifth, "the idealized reaction to frustration is correlated and integrated with other aspects of the culture" (for example, who has primary responsibility for social control).

Sixth, if "the anger-aggression sequence has been established, and then inhibited," the aggression is often displaced onto some person other than the frustrator. Finally, "aggression, submission, dependence, and avoidance will be likely to be specified as proper responses to frustration in given contexts in all societies."

In discussing the socialization of aggression in the formerly warlike Sioux Indians, Erikson (1963, p. 156) emphasizes the importance of the old customs governing the nursing of infants. He explains:

> Sioux child training forms a firm basis for this system of centrifugality [i. e., the decentralization or dispersion of tribal bands, extended family tension, technology and property and the diversion of aggression toward prey and outgroup] by establishing a lasting center of trust, namely the nursing mother, and then by handling the matter of teething, of infantile rage, and of muscular aggression in such a way that the greatest possible degree of ferocity is provoked, channelized socially, and finally released against prey and enemy. We believe that we are dealing here, not with simple causality, but with a mutual assimilation of somatic, mental, and social patterns which amplify one another and make the cultural design for living economical and effective.

Hallowell (1940) provides an interesting contrast to the Sioux case in his study of aggression among the Saulteaux Indians of North America. The Saulteaux have never engaged in war with whites or other Indian tribes, suicide is unknown, and there are no official records of murder. Even theft is extremely rare. On the surface, the people are cooperative, patient, and self-controlled. Disapproval, open contradiction, ridicule, and insults of any kind are carefully avoided. After long study, however, Hallowell discovered strong undercurrents of aggression.

In analyzing the culturally sanctioned channels for hostility, Hallowell found that one channel was the prevalence of gossip which allowed people to say unpleasant and even scandalous things about each other without face-to-face confrontation. The other channel was the sincere belief in sorcery and magic as a means of inflicting harm on someone. Even in the few cases where overt aggression occurred it was "almost immediately displaced to the level of sorcery (fantasy) for the showdown."

Any sickness, death, or even failure in hunting that occurred to anyone in the tribe was attributed to the ill will of some injured party exacting his revenge through sorcery. Consequently, avoiding offense was clearly a matter of self-defense. Sorcery and magic were used frequently as instruments of covert aggression and, although this led to a rather pervasive anxiety among the tribe, overt physical aggression with direct and real consequences was avoided. In the Chapter 3 introduction, another example of avoidance is shown in Sechrest's description of the distinctive cultural patterns that contribute to the relative infrequency of interpersonal aggression in the Philippines. However, in this particular case, the extreme emphasis on interpersonal harmony, in combination with other factors, paradoxically produces an all or nothing pattern of aggression which results in a very high rate of homicide.

Henry and Short (1954) and Martin Gold (1958), among others, have analyzed the sociological and psychological factors affecting the rates of homicide vs. suicide among different social aggregates (for example, males vs. females, middle class vs. working class, whites vs. blacks) in the United States with some interesting results. According to Gold, the primary factor in determining a preference for suicide vs. homicide is "the manner in which children are socialized, as indicated by the way in which they are punished."

Gold explains the greater preference for suicide vs. homicide among whites, females, and the middle class because, compared to blacks, males, and the working class, they are much more likely to be punished psychologically rather than physically. As a result it is more difficult to clearly identify the punisher and to "tell where one's hurt feelings are coming from. Their source is more likely to seem inside" one than outside. If there is to be a target for aggression, then, the physically punished child has an external target readily available. Also the physically "punishing parent serves as a model" for the child, identifying the "approved behavior when one is hurt or angry."

Basic Human Needs

Of course, the question of whether or not human beings have an instinct for aggression and, if so, whether and how it is modified by cultural conditioning is not the only question we may ask about the larger issue of human nature. Many social scientists have proposed the existence of many instincts or basic human needs other than aggression.

W. I. Thomas (1966) proposed basic needs for security, new experience, recognition and response. Freud (1949 edition) wrote of instincts for sex and aggression. Fromm (1965) listed basic human needs for relatedness, transcendence, rootedness, a sense of identity, and a frame of orientation and devotion; and Horney (1939) for safety and satisfaction. The list could be extended, but it would add little to our understanding of the core issues. Some theorists refer to needs as organizing principles or motives for behavior, others use them in different combinations to describe various personality types, still others use them to examine contradictions in the nature of man and in his relationship to society (for example, the conflict between individualism and autonomy vs. collectivism and conformity).

There really isn't any dispute over whether people think and act as if they had certain needs. Rather, the controversy is whether such needs are innate or acquired, constitutive or culturally derivative. Psychologists have been more inclined to posit the existence of basic needs than anthropologists and sociologists.

In criticizing some of his more purist colleagues, sociologist Dennis Wrong (1961) has pointed out that much modern sociology assumes an "oversocialized conception of man" in which individuals are motivated by the desire to maximize favorable evaluations by others through conformity to shared norms in a highly integrated social system. Wrong calls for greater attention to autonomous bodily drives and energies (like sex and aggression), which, although socialized, may still not always be congruent with the demands of society, thus contributing to conflict within the individual.

More recently, Etzioni (1968, p. 871) has advanced this theme by considering such distinctly human needs as those for "affection and recognition," which "have attributes of their own which are not determined by the social structure, cultural patterns, or socialization processes." Such an assumption, Etzioni argues, would allow us to construct a universal index of the psychic costs (for example, frequency of ulcers or suicide) of socialization to role networks which are differentially "responsive" to the satisfaction of such basic needs. According to him, we would then be in a better position to systematically evaluate different societies' "responsiveness" to individuals, the dynamic relationship between types of deviance and means of social control, and the genesis of various movements for social change. An important premise that Wrong and Etzioni share is that happiness is not necessarily equivalent to adjustment and that individuals may have needs which are in conflict with certain demands of a given society.

On the other hand, according to anthropologist Dorothy Lee (1948), there is no such thing as a basic need. All needs are acquired as a result of socialization practices that express cultural values. She speculates that the very concept of basic need in social science may simply reflect Western cultural values, particularly the religious idea that man was born in sin and its Freudian equivalent of antisocial instincts. Thus, the concept of a good or healthy society becomes one which removes evil or relieves tension. She finds such a conception inferior to a gestalt orientation in which the individual achieves a meaningful understanding of the total social reality of which he or she becomes an integral part.

Underlying this controversy are two fundamentally different conceptions of the human condition: the dualist conception of Freud and others of basic human nature in conflict with the requirements of civilization, and the integrationist conception of more sociologically and anthropologically oriented psychologists of basic human nature being totally a product of the experience of civilization. At the risk of oversimplifying a complicated matter, much of the debate is over whether man, at base, is an antisocial, partly social, or completely social animal.

Those upholding the existence of basic needs keep open the possibility of ultimately being able to establish general propositions about the nature of man that would explain certain similarities in behavior observed in different societies despite quite diverse cultural traditions and social structures. Those who reject the idea of basic needs assume the essential plasticity of the human organism and are less likely to selectively ignore important differences between people raised in different societies. They are also more likely to search for explanations for similarities in social practices between peoples believed to have been isolated from each other in new discoveries about historical migrations and cultural borrowing.

Nature and Nurture

In addition to the question of basic human nature, another issue is the old nature vs. nurture controversy, which is now formulated in terms of *interaction*, rather than conflict, between genetic and environmental factors in the determination of individual personality.

Insofar as the first selection by John Clausen provides a sophisticated review of many major issues and studies of biology and personality, any further discussion is unnecessary. The second selection, on sex differences in socialization by Barry, Bacon, and Child, is a classic discussion of a contemporary controversy which also has important political implications.

Their cross-cultural survey of 110 cultures concludes that many behavioral traits traditionally identified as male or female are the result of differential socialization rather than biological determinism. This does not mean that there are not basic biological differences between men and women which would make one more suited than the other for the performance of a particular role under certain circumstances. Rather, it means that the degree to which such differences might be relevant to the sexual division of labor in society (and, consequently, entail differential primary socialization) seems to be socially determined, varying according to the structure of the economy and the family among other variables. This implies, of course, that the sex-role behavior considered appropriate for males and females, behavior which encompasses a great deal of the individual's basic personality, is defined by some interaction between biological properties and societal needs and opportunities.

The resolution, through continued research, of theoretical issues such as these is not only of interest to scholars. The political implications of such debates should be apparent. We live in an age of social change and social planning. Demands for change must be evaluated in light of the realistic possibilities for change and the consequences such change would bring. The controversy over whether and what genetically determined differences exist between whites and blacks, males and females — and the relevance of any differences which might exist to the current division of labor — inevitably intrudes itself into conflicts over the inequitable distribution of positions of power and prestige in society. We have discovered that much less behavior than was previously supposed can be attributed to the influence of "human nature." How much is a question which has yet to be resolved.

References

Eckland, Bruce
   1967   "Genetics and Sociology: A Reconsideration." *American Sociological Review* 32 (April):173–94.
Erikson, Erik H.
   1963   *Childhood and Society.* New York: Norton.
Etzioni, Amitai
   1968   "Basic Human Needs, Alienation, and Inauthenticity." *American Sociological Review* 33 (December):870–85.
Freud, Sigmund
   1949   *An Outline of Psychoanalysis.* Authorized translation by James Strachey. New York: Norton.
Fromm, Erich
   1965   *The Sane Society.* Greenwich, Conn.: Fawcett.
Gold, Martin
   1958   "Suicide, Homocide, and the Socialization of Aggression." *The American Journal of Sociology* 13 (May):651–61.

Gotesman, Irving
 1966 "Genetic Variance in Adaptive Personality Traits." *Journal of* chology and Psychiatry 7:199–208.
Hallowell, A. Irving
 1940 "Aggression in Saulteaux Society." *Psychiatry* 3:395–407.
Henry, A. F., and J. F. Short, Jr.
 1954 *Suicide and Homicide.* New York: The Free Press.
Horney, Karen
 1939 *New Ways in Psychoanalysis.* New York: Norton.
Jost, Hudson, and Lester W. Sontag
 1944 "The Genetic Factor in Autonomic Nervous-System Function." *Psycho-somatic Medicine* 6:308–10.
Lee, Dorothy
 1948 "Are Basic Needs Ultimate?" *Journal of Abnormal and Social Psychology* 43:391–95.
Mead, Margaret
 1957 "Anthropological Data on the Problem of Instinct." Pp. 115–18 in Clyde Kluckhohn and Henry A. Murray, *Personality in Nature, Society, and Culture.* New York: Knopf.
Sanford, R. Nevitt
 1967 "Physical and Physiological Correlates of Personality Structure." Pp. 100–104 in Kluckhohn and Murray, *Personality in Nature.*
Thomas, W. I.
 1966 *On Social Organization and Social Personality: Selected Papers.* Ed. Morris Janowitz. Chicago: The University of Chicago Press.
Whiting, John
 1944 "The Frustration Complex in Kwoma Society." *Man* 44 (115).
Wrong, Dennis H.
 1961 "The Oversocialized Conception of Man in Modern Sociology." *American Sociological Review* 26 (April):183–93.

JOHN A. CLAUSEN

The Organism and Socialization

Until quite recently, sociologists have not been seriously concerned with individual differences among the organisms that make up a society, nor have they been much interested in the nature of man's biological development. Although few sociologists would deny that organisms differ in capacities, proclivities and vulnerabilities, such variations have not been regarded as having direct consequences for sociological analysis. Indeed, any suggestion that physical or psychological charac-

Reprinted by permission from *Journal of Health and Social Behavior* 8 (1967). A revised version of a paper presented at the meetings of the American Sociological Association, Miami, Florida, August 30, 1966. The longitudinal research referred to in this paper was supported in part by a grant from the National Institute of Mental Health, MH-5300.

teristics of the organism may influence social processes is still likely to give rise to accusations of "reductionism" in some sociological circles. To a far greater degree than anthropologists and psychologists, sociologists have disembodied man and ignored relationships between characteristics of the organism and social behavior.

Yet in the formative years of sociology, around the end of the last century, "social thought was almost completely dominated by biological concepts and points of view," according to E. B. Reuter.[1] Sociologists were not less impressed with evolutionary theory than were other members of the academic community. Among the manifestations of the evolutionary-biological point of view that appealed to at least some sociologists were theories which proposed that progress and civilization are marks of superior biological stock; instinct theories, explaining social behavior in terms of presumed innate dispositions; and preoccupation with the definition of physical and mental traits as a basis for understanding relationships between racial and ethnic groups. With the development of understanding of cultural differences and the beginnings of research on social processes, however, the influence of such theories and preoccupations largely disappeared from American sociology.

Indeed, sociologists helped to demolish the elaborate structures built on instinct theory[2] and to bring to the study of race a new dimension, a concern not with racial traits but with the circumstances leading to the imputation of traits and to the development of attitudes toward members of other ethnic groups. In thus combatting what came to be seen as patently invalid attempts to explain social and cultural phenomena (such as crime, delinquency and poverty) in terms of biological processes, sociologists inevitably became less receptive to giving any place to biology in their thinking. This rejection was undoubtedly strengthened by revulsion to Nazi race theory. From evidence that the differences in physical and intellectual ability between races were far less than differences within races, some sociologists not only inferred that racial differences are non-existent but also that individual differences in capacity are negligible.[3]

Both biologists and social scientists now generally accept the view that heredity and environment interact and that it is meaningless to try to establish the greater absolute importance of one or the other. Nevertheless, to a very large extent, we have been content to let *ceteris paribus* take care of the biological contribution. The sociologist who is impressed with the genetic contributions to schizophrenia may still find a few of his associates muttering that he has "sold out" to the geneticists. One who suggests that social differentiation and stratification may be influenced by heredity is likely to be viewed by at least some of his peers as antidemocratic.

In general, conservatives have been more likely to emphasize the importance of genetic differences, while liberals have traditionally emphasized the importance of human educability. In a sense this would seem to be a logical philosophical linkage, except that, as Dobzhansky has noted, it is based on a sheer confusion as to the meaning of heredity. Human populations contain an enormous genetic diversity. Nevertheless,

the genetic endowment of *homo sapiens* guarantees the development in all individuals which belong to the adaptive norm of the species of such capacities as educability, symbolic thinking, communication by symbolic language. It is perhaps justified to say that human evolution has been dominated by a stabilizing selection for these capacities, and for a consequent destabilization of the overt observable behavior. This is responsible for the illusion that man at birth is a *tabula rasa* as far as his prospective behavioral development is concerned. In reality, the educability goes hand in hand with a genetic diversity.[4]

Developments in the fields of population genetics and of behavior genetics during recent decades have brought a marked increase in the interest of many biologists in social and cultural phenomena. Psychologists and anthropologists have been closer to such developments than sociologists. Relatively few sociologists have had a sufficient grounding in the biological sciences to keep abreast of these recent developments in genetics, nor have they been *au courant* with the comparably important contributions of ethology, developmental and comparative psychology and psychosomatic medicine. The fact that sociology has been almost exclusively concerned with mature man and not with the maturational process has made it possible for us to remain largely ignorant of knowledge of developmental processes which may significantly influence the development of the person as well as of the organism. In the following pages, I wish to highlight some of the characteristics of the organism and its development that seem to me to merit sociological attention in research on socialization.

The Nature of Socialization

Primary socialization within the family entails demands upon parents and upon offspring, with each having to put out effort if the child is to achieve levels of control, skill, orientation and need-satisfaction which will permit him to participate with others outside the family. The infant's very survival is, of course, dependent on the provision of nurturance; his development of a sense of trust and security is equally dependent on provision of a reasonably stable source of nurturance and affection. The infant early learns to adapt his bodily movements to those of his caretaker. Failing such adaptation, either because of biological deficits in the child or anxiety and tension in the caretaker, a great deal of frustration will result for both infant and caretaker.

Within the family the child learns control of impulses and the acceptable channels for satisfaction of physiological needs. He learns to fit his behaviors to situational demands. He develops a variety of skills — motor, perceptual, cognitive, relational — linked to maturation and to parental expectations and demands. With language, and in the light of evaluations by others, he acquires criteria for evaluating his performances and achieves a sense of self. His learning and development of skills and controls will, of course, be influenced by his capacities or deficits as an organism.

The individual acts upon his environment, carving out experiences for himself, and is acted upon by others. His activity level, his patterns of sleeping and of eating are themselves influences upon his caretakers. His ability to meet their expectations and his physical stimulus value help to define and stabilize relationships with other persons as well. As he moves outside the family, he must meet demands and expectations of others and at the same time satisfy his own quest for experience and meaning. He must fit his behaviors to the guidelines that define social roles. He must cope with tendencies of others to deal with him in stereotypic terms.

Socialization is an ongoing process with many phases, many changing tasks to be accomplished. Goals change, in accordance with age and social position. But insofar as we can speak of an ultimate goal, it is that the individual be prepared to deal with the requirements of full adult participation in his society. It is this goal that should be kept in mind as we consider some of the specific ways in which biological features may make a difference.

Biological Factors in Behavioral Development

Donald Hebb,[5] who has contributed so much to the study of psychology as a biological discipline, notes six classes of factors influencing behavioral development: (1) genetic, that is, properties of the fertilized ovum; (2) prenatal chemical factors which exercise nutritive or toxic influence in the uterine environment; (3) post-natal chemical influences, which may be endogeneous to the organism, such as endocrine balance, or exogenous, such as diet, drugs, etc.; (4) sensory experiences which are normally inevitable for all members of the species (for example, contact between mother and offspring in the case of all mammals); (5) sensory experiences that vary from one member of the species to another; and (6) traumatic events. A sociologist might well subdivide classes 4 and 5 to deal with experiences that are culturally prescribed for all persons of a given age and sex, those that are prescribed for certain categories of persons, those that are accepted alternatives and those that are culturally proscribed or devalued. Hebb's other classes could undoubtedly be subdivided and enlarged upon also. The list is a useful reminder of the variety (and potential interaction) of influences upon behavioral development. We may note that genetic, chemical and traumatic events may themselves be responsible for the individual's having experiences that vary from those of other members of the species. It is equally true that experiences in the socialization of the individual can influence not only such biologically relevant behaviors as dietary intake and intake of other chemicals, but also internal biochemical processes and the likelihood that the individual will be exposed to various types of trauma or injury.[6]

Genetic Factors

Theoretical statements of the interrelationships of heredity and environment in various circumstances (genetic pools and environments) have been available for several decades. Geneticists like Dobzhansky[7] have given us formulations of the problem that show high sophistication in the treatment of social and cultural variables as well as in the realm of genetics. A whole field of behavioral genetics, relating primarily to infrahuman species, has evolved and has produced impressive evidence on the nature of the interaction between heredity and environmental experience.[8] The existence of critical periods during which certain types of learning must occur if that learning is to be effective has been clearly documented for a number of species. For example, Harlow's research on rhesus monkey infants, reared in isolation from age-mates, demonstrated conclusively that deprivation of early experience with peers irrevocably destroyed the heterosexual capabilities of these monkeys in adulthood.[9] Scott generalizes that "every highly social animal has a short period early in life in which the formation of primary social relationships takes place." [10] The development of sensory modalities and of particular skills which entail learning to use the senses effectively is also closely scheduled for many species. Moreover, experimental studies have demonstrated that for a variety of species the effects of early experience are influenced by genotype or biological variations.[11]

With humans, such experimental studies are not possible. We cannot manipulate genetic make-up, nor can we identify genotypes. Only in instances of genetically transmitted diseases or deformities are we able to put a genetically relevant label on an individual at birth. Some approach to valid labeling is essential if we are to study closely the interaction between genetic potentiality and socialization processes. Yet the tremendous number of gene combinations with which one deals in man may render infeasible any attempt to work with genotypes except as these are manifest in gross behavioral effects, at least until further advances are made in methodology. Our ability to go further in studying this particular aspect of the relationship between the organism and socialization may have to rest on crude approximations to labeling through (1) twin and family geneology studies or (2) our finding behavioral and temperamental tendencies or sensitivities that are manifest very early and that can serve as indicators of biological make-up.

Studies of monozygotic and dizygotic twins reveal a number of psychological characteristics whose variance is markedly greater for dizygotic twins[12] but unfortunately we have almost no data on the ongoing socialization process in their families. Indeed, one of the major deficits in our knowledge derives from the fact that research has overwhelmingly dealt with outcome variables and not with how the outcomes came about. Sociologists have been prone to argue that identical twins are more likely to be reared alike than fraternal twins; some geneticists have denied this and others have attempted to estimate the effects of rearing by analyzing separately their data on same-sex and opposite-sex fraternal twins. We badly need a sophisticated formulation and conceptualization of the kinds of socialization experiences that may make a difference and the application of such concepts in longitudinal studies of families with twins.

Systematic research on early differences in temperament and sensitivity is still in its infancy. There is evidence of a variety of differences between males and females in skin sensitivity and responsiveness in the neonatal period.[13] Individual differences within the sexes are greater than mean differences between the sexes in this respect, and it seems reasonable to predict that such variations influence caretaking practices and attitudes as well as the response of the infant to such practices. Girls appear to many parents to be much more pliant to the early demands put upon them by the imposition of training disciplines, though available research does not support the existence of clear differences in conformity at early ages.[14]

Another lead to the possibility of differences in responsiveness of the child comes from recent research on "cuddlers" and "non-cuddlers" — children who like to be held and cuddled and those who respond by kicking and crying when they are held. It appears that such differences are in part related to the mother's enjoyment of sensual contact, but they are also significantly related to the sleeping patterns of the children ("cuddlers" sleep much longer), to the child's enjoyment of soft, cuddly toys and to reactions to any kind of physical restraint.[15]

Studies of infant conditioning[16] and of autonomic responses[17] have also revealed individual differences which may have significance for socialization experience. A critical methodological problem is posed by the high lability of responses in the neonate (making reliable measurement of response tendencies extremely difficult) and the very rapid development of learned responses which depend on environmental and socialization influences.

Behavioral Correlates of Morphology

Another approach to the identification of constitutional attributes that may influence socialization and behavior is afforded by the study of body build. Sheldon's classification of components or varieties of physique as endomorphic (soft, fat), mesomorphic (muscular, tough) and ectomorphic (thin, fragile) has been carefully developed and standardized.[18] His classification of personality components or varieties of temperament — viscerotonic, somatotonic and cerebrotonic — is less well accepted, and his attempts to demonstrate relationships between the two[19] have been rejected as methodologically indefensible by most psychologists and social scientists who have reviewed his work. Personality ratings are inevitably influenced by the rater's presuppositions as to what goes with what; Sheldon's ratings could hardly have failed to confirm his expectations. Yet there have been enough indications that somatotypes do have some relationship to behavior to merit further consideration. Gardner Lindzey notes five classes of mechanisms which might mediate relationships between morphology and behavior:[20] (1) experiential events that influence both morphology and behavior or personality (as in the influence of certain types of maternal overprotectiveness on both overeating and timidity); (2) the facilitation of certain performances by physical characteristics such as height, strength and stride; (3) the recruitment or selection of individuals for social roles and activities on the basis of physical characteristics; (4) related to (2) and (3), the existence of cultural expectations as to the behavior or temperament of persons of given physique ("lean and hungry" types, "jolly fat people," etc.), regardless of the validity of the underlying rationale for the expectation, and (5) joint biological determinants of both behavior and physique, as brought about, for example, by genetic determinants or by endocrinological function. Sociologists have in general been willing to contemplate the first four of these mechanisms but have boggled at the fifth.

The data on relationships between physique and behavior available from independent assessments of the two realms do establish that there are significant correlations. If they are less high than the correlations reported by Sheldon, they are nevertheless not appreciably less than correlations between behavior and many variables of socialization experience presumed by social scientists to be important influences on adult personality. But the data thus far available do not permit us to establish what mechanisms account for the correlations between physique and behavior. Perhaps each accounts for some part of the relationship.

One's physique is certainly determined in large part by his heredity. It does not appear, however, that body type is inherited as a unit. For physique and temperament to be jointly determined by heredity would require that these complexes of traits be inherited as units through the operation of linked groups of genes. The one available study on the heritability of Sheldon's components, based on somatotyping of fraternal and identical twins by Osborne and DeGeorge,[21] found higher heritability coefficients for females than for males, but even for females the correlation was less than would be expected if somatotype were inherited as a unitary trait.

Nevertheless, it does appear that there are linkages between somatotype and other aspects of physical development. For example, body build is related to rate of maturing sexually, especially for girls, with mesomorphic girls maturing earlier and becoming more amply endowed while their ectomorphic peers are growing taller but less curvy.[22] Despite relationships between physique and the attainment of sexual maturity, we shall defer consideration of personality and behavioral differences associated with early or late maturing since the social significance of this event may entail different social implications than does body build.

How might somatotype modify socialization influences? Consider Sheldon's hypothesis that a *mesomorph* should tend toward *somatotonic* temperament, which he characterizes as high in aggressiveness, activity, need for power by dominance and low in sensitivity to others. As yet unpublished analyses of data from the Oakland Growth Study, by Glen Elder and the writer, give at least partial confirmation of Sheldon's hypotheses, especially among males. Somatotypes were ascertained by Sheldon from body photographs taken periodically through adolescence. Personality data were secured from self-report inventories, peer-ratings and staff ratings (made before the publication of Sheldon's formulations) for this group of subjects who were intensively studied during their high school years in the 1930's. Boys high in mesomorphy were seen by their peers as getting into fights ($r = .63$), "active" ($r = .57$) and "daring" ($r = .58$), but these correlations vary somewhat by social class and by height above or below the median.

There seems but little doubt that in Western society physiques high on the mesomorphic component are regarded as most attractive, despite the recent trend to ectomorphic models in the world of fashion. Among the higher correlations found in our data between components of physique and social or psychological attributes of the individual are the .55 between mesomorphy and attractiveness (factor score derived from ratings in adolescence by adult observers). The differing correlations between somatotype and psychological characteristics among middle-class and working-class subjects suggest that the social meaning of the somatotype rather than genetic constitution accounts for a good deal of the variance. It remains to be seen whether further analysis, in longitudinal perspective, will reveal changing correlations by age groups as well.

Early vs. Late Maturing

Linked with morphology are such characteristics as stature and rate of maturing. The age at which the organism approaches full stature or reaches sexual maturity is somewhat influenced by diet and the conditions of life, but research on twins suggests that up to 90 per cent of the variance in height is attributable to heredity and a large proportion of the variance in rate of maturing seems likewise to be genetically determined.[23] In general, the child who is tall or short relative to his peers at the time of entrance into school will tend to maintain this position in adulthood; correlations between height at age eight and height at maturity average about .8 in various longitudinal studies, though the correlation drops a bit during puberty.[24] Early maturers achieve their maximum height at a younger age than do late maturers but they tend to be no taller at maturity than their late-maturing peers. Indeed, among females, late maturers tend to grow taller, and, as already noted, to be more ectomorphic.

Among males in the Oakland Growth Study at the Institute of Human Development, University of California, early maturers were most likely to make a favorable impression as to physique and to exhibit leadership and assurance in adolescence, according to analyses by Mary Jones.[25] Significant psychological differences between early and late maturers persist at least into the thirties. The early maturers, who appear to have acquired substantial social skills and assurance along with sexual maturity, scored higher at age 32 on C.P.I. scales of dominance, responsibility and desire to make a good impression, for example, while later maturers scored higher on flexibility, psychological mindedness and psychoneurotic tendencies. We cannot yet be certain whether these differences are largely the consequence of the adaptation of the early and late maturers to their social stimulus values in adolescence, or whether the organisms also differ in temperament (especially as a consequence of endocrinological differences) and other respects. The groups do *not* differ in tested intelligence.

Body build, height, weight and strength certainly affect the individual's choice of activities and his selection or recruitment for certain roles. This is equally true of attractiveness and of manifestly high intelligence, but sociologists have not attempted to examine the different developmental pathways of the homely and the beautiful, the very bright and the dull child, except as intelligence is related to school attainment.[26] The interactions of a biological attribute and a social behavior with important consequences for health are revealed in an examination of the relationships between cigarette smoking and various physical, psychological and social attributes of the subjects of the Oakland Growth Study. Early maturers were *less* likely to become smokers and late maturers *more* likely to become smokers than their peers, especially among males. The late maturers were more often smoking before they finished high school (in 1938–39), and more of them became heavy smokers subsequently.[27] One is tempted to interpret their smoking as evidence of a compensatory striving to appear mature, but the large number of other attitudinal and behavioral correlates suggests caution in offering interpretations.

Aberrant Development

Most of the research that has been directly concerned with investigating the effects of biological variation on socialization has dealt with instances of gross pathology, deficit, or consequences of illness or injury. For the study of influences on socialization, it is often irrelevant whether such deficit or disorder has come about through genetic mutation, prenatal influences, birth injury or subsequent illness. Among prenatal conditions that leave many infants impaired are the mother's contracting rubella in the first trimester of pregnancy, the effects of drugs like thalidomide or the use of hormone treatments during pregnancy. Premature birth and the process of birth itself account for a substantial amount of neurological damage. Early blindness, deafness or crippling as a consequence of various diseases of childhood account for additional instances of aberrant physical development. With notable exceptions, sociologists have been interested in the influences of such conditions primarily as they lead to stereotyping or, to use a term that has become increasingly fashionable, "stigmatization." The person whose morphology is grossly variant from population norms, the person with an obvious sensory defect, the brain-injured child with his emotional lability, short attention span and disordered behavior, are all subject to labels that stigmatize. In some instances, the attribute that leads to stereotypic responses from others will have trivial influence on ability to master the tasks of normal development; in others, those tasks will be made much more difficult and problematic of attainment. Stigmatization inevitably affects identity to some degree, but the nature of the social matrix surrounding the individual at crucial developmental phases may make an enormous difference on whether a physical deficit becomes the core of identity or merely one attribute among many.

The past decade has produced evidence of a much greater prevalence of neurological damage in surviving infants than had hitherto been suspected.[28] Such children show various limitations in adaptive capacity or learning ability, ranging from highly circumscribed deficits to generalized depression of intelligence. Quite clearly they need learning environments that can make maximal use of sensorimotor channels that are relatively unimpaired, while bypassing those in which the child is most deficient.[29]

We know from a number of studies that parental attitudes toward a child that is early perceived as vulnerable or defective will be different from parental attitudes toward normal offspring. As Eisenberg notes, "Parental behavior may be so skewed as to induce in the child the very patterns of behavior we would have recognized as psychogenic had the presence of brain damage not preempted our attention."[30] He goes on to raise a number of highly pertinent questions for research. For example, what kind of parental socialization practices are most successful in dealing with the outbursts of seemingly uncontrollable behavior manifested by such children? Eisenberg suggests that: "Such children plead for external controls upon their behavior; permissive childrearing practices multiply the problem and increase the [child's] burden of guilt."[31]

Whether or not they recognize the nature of the child's needs, parents of children who are congenitally impaired appear to respond more protectively and intrusively to these children than do parents of normal children. Many of the parental behaviors which appear to be implicated in the etiology of schizophrenia, duodenal ulcer, asthma and a number of other psychiatric and psychosomatic disorders are also found *in response to* deficits of clearly biological origin.[32] This is not to say that the theories of psychogenic origin are necessarily invalid, but rather that the interactions between parental socialization behavior and the nature of the particular organism being socialized must be studied with a recognition that causal influences work in both directions.

Parental overprotection may take place even when impairment is very minor. Stephen Richardson has noted how a single functional impairment may jeopardize the child's opportunity to gain experiences necessary for his socialization.[33] He cites research indicating, for example, that a normally intelligent child with mild cerebral palsy (leading to motor impairment of the legs) is less likely than a child without such motor impairment to be given increasing responsibility with increasing age, to be liked by his peers, and to be permitted to explore his environment.

Sex Differences

Students of socialization research have been especially interested in the learning of sex identity and sex-appropriate behaviors. Maccoby's recent volume, *The Development of Sex Differences*, summarizes theory and research on this topic from biological, psychological, social and cultural perspectives. In all societies, males and females differ not merely in primary sex characteristics but also in secondary sex attributes such as height, musculature and body hair. The degree of sexual dimorphism can be influenced by both genetic and cultural factors.[34] In all human populations, men tend to be taller, heavier and stronger than women, but the relative differences between the sexes in height, weight and strength vary substantially from one population to another. Both sexual selection and social roles play a part in determining the size of such differences. Yet we have very little research that relates to the process of achieving sex identity or, for that matter, to socialization for sexual competence.

Studies of persons born with sexual anomalies that rendered original sex assignment ambiguous (most often females with congenital adrenal hyperplasia) suggest that the gender role assigned in the first three years is more important than chromosomal, gonadal or hormonal sex in determining the individual's sexual identification in later life.[35] In other words, "labeling" of sex can to a large extent determine how the individual will be regarded, and will regard himself, even when such labeling is erroneous. That erroneous labeling is likely to lead to severe social disabilities and psychological problems for the individual is obvious.

The Labeling of Bodily Processes

Sociologists have, as noted above, been much concerned with the effects of stigmatizing labels. We have devoted less attention to the way in which the individual comes to label his own feelings and bodily states. Zborowski's insightful analysis of cultural components in responses to pain contained a number of hypotheses as to how socialization agents teach the child to label his feelings and actions when hurt or sick.[36] One would like to have direct observational data bearing on such hypotheses. Does the child reared in a family of Christian Scientists come to label his discomforts differently than one who receives prompt medical attention when ill with diarrhea or bronchitis?

Recent research by Schacter has demonstrated the importance of the labeling of bodily states in determining response to injections of epinephrine.[37] Even more impressive is his research on obesity. Starting with Hilde Bruch's[38] hypothesis that obese persons have not been taught in childhood to discriminate between hunger feelings and such states as fear, anger and anxiety, Schacter has conducted experiments which document that the obese do not label as "hunger" the same set of bodily symptoms as do normals.[39] Unlike normal subjects, the obese ate as much on a full stomach as on an empty stomach, and whereas normals ate appreciably less when in a fear-inducing situation, the obese ate somewhat more in this situation than in a less threatening one.

A Plea for Observational Study

Study of the interaction of biological make-up and socialization experience requires direct repeated observation of the socialization process as well as repeated assessment of the individuals undergoing socialization. The past two decades have witnessed a tremendous advance in knowledge of the nature of the infant's behavioral repertoire, largely because of the very great increase in systematic observation by physiologists, psychologists and pediatricians. Sociologists have seldom engaged in such observation. Sociological surveys reveal attitudes and reported socialization practices and experiences but they cannot answer such crucial questions as: (1) In what situations or circumstances do behaviors of children with particular biological attributes or deficits call forth different responses from the environment? and (2) Under what conditions do the same environmental influences produce quite different effects in the child? I am aware that "the same influences" are never *really* the same. Unique meanings are evolved, which is precisely the process that needs to be studied.

There are many basic questions begging for investigation. What are the consequences for parents with low energy level of having a child with an inordinately high energy level? Or the reverse? Parents with unrealistically high or unrealistically specialized expectations for their children often apply pressures for performance that lead to rebellion or to frustration for both parent and child. But what happens when the child *is able to meet* those expectations? The life histories of a number of outstanding scholars and athletes suggest that sometimes unusual excellence results. Can we learn how to maximize the fit between what is biologically given and what is to be done in the course of socialization?

Conclusion

Recent developments relevant to the topic of this paper have been so varied as to make even a summary difficult. Studies of primate behavior in natural habitats and in experimental settings have added new dimensions to comparative research on learning.[40] Careful studies of species-specific behavior by ethologists with backgrounds in zoology, psychology and anthropology have given new and scientifically respectable meaning to the term instinct.[41] Neurophysiological and biochemical processes mediating behavior in stressful situations are under study.[42] The emergence of medical sociology and the increasing participation of sociologists in research teams containing physicians and physiologists have created opportunities for sociologists to become more knowledgeable about the nature of man as an organism. Publications of the proceedings of the ongoing series of conferences on biological aspects of behavior sponsored by the Russell Sage Foundation and the Rockefeller University will help to make available to sociologists some of the crucially important recent developments in other fields.[43] There is an opportunity for major advances if we can incorporate some of this recently acquired knowledge in research on the development of the person in society.

Notes

1. E. B. Reuter, "Racial Theory," *American Journal of Sociology,* 50 (May, 1945), p. 454.
2. See, for example, Ellsworth Faris, "Are Instincts Data or Hypotheses?" *American Journal of Sociology,* 27 (1921), pp. 184–196.
3. An example of this tendency, which equated belief in the inheritance of mental ability with belief in racial theories is found in Paul A. Witty and Harvey C. Lehman, "The Dogma and Biology of Human Inheritance," *American Journal of Sociology,* 35 (January, 1930), pp. 548–563.
4. Theodosius Dobzhansky, "On Types, Genotypes and the Genetic Diversity in Populations," in James N. Spuhler (Ed.), *Genetic Diversity and Human Behavior,* Viking Fund Publications in Anthropology, No. 45, Chicago: Aldine Publishing Company, 1967.
5. Donald O. Hebb, *A Textbook of Psychology,* Philadelphia: W. B. Saunders Company, 1958.
6. For evidence on the relationship of maternal attitudes and child personality to children's accident experience, see D. I. Manheimer and G. D. Mellinger, "Personality Characteristics of the Child Accident Repeater," *Child Development,* 38 (June, 1967), pp. 497–513.
7. Theodosius Dobzhansky, "The Biological Concept of Heredity as Applied to Man," in *The Nature and Transmission of the Genetic and Cultural Characteristics of Human Population,* New York: Milbank Memorial Fund, 1957, pp. 11–19. See also Theodosius Dobzhansky, *Mankind Evolving,* New Haven, Conn.: Yale University Press, 1962.
8. See John L. Fuller and William R. Thompson, *Behavior Genetics,* New York: John Wiley & Sons, 1960.
9. Harry F. Harlow and Margaret K. Harlow, "The Affectional Systems," in A. M. Schrier, H. F. Harlow and F. Stollnitz (ed.), *Behavior of Nonhuman Primates,* New York: Academic Press, 1965, Vol. II, pp. 287–334.
10. J. P. Scott, "The Process of Primary Socialization in Canine and Human Infants," *Monographs of the Society for Research in Child Development,* 28 (1963), No. 1, p. 4.
11. Fuller and Thompson, op. cit.
12. Steven G. Vandenberg, "Hereditary Factors in Psychological Variables in Man, with a Special Emphasis on Cognition," in James H. Spuhler (Ed.), *Genetic Diversity and Human Behavior,* Viking Fund Publications in Anthropology, No. 45, Chicago: Aldine Publishing Company, 1967.
13. For a brief summary of relevant studies see David A. Hamburg and Donald T. Lunde, "Sex Hormones in the Development of Sex Differences in Human Behavior," in Eleanor E. Maccoby (ed.), *The Development of Sex Differences,* Stanford, Calif.: Stanford University Press, 1966, p. 18.
14. For a summary of the literature on sex differences in conformity see Maccoby, op. cit., pp. 329–330.
15. H. R. Schaffer and P. E. Emerson, "Patterns of Response to Physical Contact in Early Human Development," *Journal of Child Psychology and Psychiatry,* 5 (June, 1964), pp. 1–13.
16. Hanus Papousek, "Genetics and Child Development," in James H. Spuhler (ed.), *Genetic Diversity and Human Behavior,* Viking Fund Publications in Anthropology, No. 45, Chicago: Aldine Publishing Company, 1967.
17. Wagner H. Bridger and Morton F. Reiser, "Psychophysiologic Studies of the Neonate: An Approach Toward the Methodological and Theoretical Problems Involved," *Psychosomatic Medicine,* 21 (1959), pp. 265–276.
18. William H. Sheldon (with the collaboration of S. S. Stevens and W. B. Tucker), *The Varieties of Human Physique: An Introduction to Constitutional Psychology,* New York: Harper, 1940.
19. William H. Sheldon (with the collaboration of S. S. Stevens), *The Varieties*

of Temperament: A Psychology of Constitutional Differences, New York: Harper, 1942.

20. Gardner Lindzey, "Morphology and Behavior," in James H. Spuhler (ed.), *Genetic Diversity and Human Behavior,* Viking Fund Publications in Anthropology, No. 45, Chicago: Aldine Publishing Company, 1967.

21. R. H. Osborne and F. V. DeGeorge, *Genetic Basis of Morphological Variation,* Cambridge, Mass.: Harvard University Press, 1959.

22. David McNeill and Norman Livson, "Maturation Rate and Body Build in Women," *Child Development,* 34 (March, 1963), pp. 25–32.

23. See Benjamin S. Bloom, *Stability and Change in Human Characteristics,* New York: John Wiley & Sons, 1964, p. 34.

24. Ibid., pp. 18–32.

25. Mary Cover Jones, "Psychological Correlates in Somatic Development," *Child Development,* 36 (1965), pp. 899–911.

26. An excellent review of research on intelligence and school attainment which explores a number of aspects of behavioral genetics is contained in Bruce K. Eckland, "A Sociologist's Perspective on Behavior Genetics," *American Sociological Review,* 32 (April, 1967), pp. 173–194.

27. J. A. Clausen, "Smoking in Longitudinal Perspective," *Social Science and Medicine,* 1 (December, 1967).

28. Benjamin Pasamanick and Hilda Knobloch, "Retrospective Studies on the Epidemiology of Reproductive Casualty: Old and New," *Merrill-Palmer Quarterly,* 12 (1966), pp. 7–26.

29. Leon Eisenberg, "Behavioral Manifestations of Cerebral Damage," in H. G. Birch (ed.), *Brain Damage in Children: The Biological and Social Aspects,* Baltimore: The Williams and Wilkins Company, 1964, pp. 61–73.

30. Ibid., p. 70.

31. Ibid.

32. Some of the relevant evidence is presented by Richard Q. Bell, "The Effect on the Family of a Limitation in Coping Ability in the Child: A Research Approach and a Finding," *Merrill-Palmer Quarterly,* 10 (April, 1964), pp. 129–142. Bell also discusses a methodological strategy for attempting to resolve alternative interpretations of the observed correlations between family patterns and child disorders.

33. Stephen A. Richardson, "The Social Environment and Individual Functioning," in Birch, op. cit.

34. See Roy D'Andrade, "Sex Differences and Cultural Institutions," in Maccoby, op. cit.

35. John Hampson and Joan Hampson, "The Development of Gender Role," in Frank Beach (ed.), *Sex and Behavior,* New York: Holt, Rinehart & Winston, 1965.

36. Mark Zborowski, "Cultural Components in Responses to Pain," *Journal of Social Issues,* 8 (1952), pp. 16–30.

37. Stanley Schacter, "The Interaction of Cognitive and Physiological Determinants of Emotional State," in P. H. Leiderman and David Shapiro (eds.), *Psychobiological Approaches to Social Behavior,* Stanford, Calif.: Stanford University Press, 1964.

38. Hilde Bruch, "Transformations of Oral Impulses in Eating Disorders: A Conceptual Approach," *Psychiatric Quarterly,* 35 (1961), pp. 458–481.

39. Stanley Schacter, "Cognitive Effects on Bodily Functioning: Studies of Obesity and Overeating," in David C. Glass and Carl Pfaffman (eds.), *Biology and Behavior: Neurophysiology and Emotion,* New York: Rockefeller University Press and Russell Sage Foundation, 1967.

40. See, for example, Irven DeVore (ed.), *Primate Behavior: Field Studies of Monkeys and Apes,* New York: Holt, Rinehart & Winston, 1965, and the volumes cited in footnote 9, *Behavior of Non-human Primates.*

41. Good examples are: Claire H. Schiller (ed. and transl.), *Instinctive Behavior,*

New York: International Universities Press, 1957; Harriet Rheingold (ed.), *Maternal Behavior in Mammals,* New York: John Wiley and Sons, 1963; and Peter Marler and W. J. Hamilton, *Mechanisms of Animal Behavior,* New York: John Wiley and Sons, 1966.

42. See, for example, Leiderman and Shapiro, op. cit., and Glass and Pfaffman, op. cit.

43. In addition to the volume cited in reference 39, see David C. Glass, "Genetics and Social Behavior," *Items,* 21 (March, 1967), pp. 1–5.

HERBERT BARRY III
MARGARET K. BACON
IRVIN L. CHILD

A Cross-Cultural Survey of Some Sex Differences in Socialization

In our society, certain differences may be observed between the typical personality characteristics of the two sexes. These sex differences in personality are generally believed to result in part from differences in the way boys and girls are reared. To the extent that personality differences between the sexes are thus of cultural rather than biological origin, they seem potentially susceptible to change. But how readily susceptible to change? In the differential rearing of the sexes does our society make an arbitrary imposition on an infinitely plastic biological base, or is this cultural imposition found uniformly in all societies as an adjustment to the real biological differences between the sexes? This paper reports one attempt to deal with this problem.

Data and Procedures

The data used were ethnographic reports, available in the anthropological literature, about socialization practices of various cultures. One hundred and ten cultures, mostly nonliterate, were studied. They were selected primarily in terms of the existence of adequate ethnographic reports of socialization practices and secondarily so as to obtain a wide and reasonably balanced geographical distribution. Various aspects of socialization of infants and children were rated on a seven-point scale by two judges (Mrs. Bacon and Mr. Barry). Where the ethnographic reports

From Herbert Barry III, Margaret K. Bacon, and Irvin L. Child, "A Cross-Cultural Survey of Some Sex Differences in Socialization," *Journal of Abnormal and Social Psychology* 55 (1957), pp. 327–332. Copyright 1957 by the American Psychological Association. Reprinted by permission. Footnotes have been renumbered.

permitted, separate ratings were made for the socialization of boys and girls. Each rating was indicated as either confident or doubtful; with still greater uncertainty, or with complete lack of evidence, the particular rating was of course not made at all. We shall restrict the report of sex difference ratings to cases in which both judges made a confident rating. Also omitted is the one instance where the two judges reported a sex difference in opposite directions, as it demonstrates only unreliability of judgment. The number of cultures that meet these criteria is much smaller than the total of 110; for the several variables to be considered, the number varies from 31 to 84.

The aspects of socialization on which ratings were made included:

1. Several criteria of attention and indulgence toward infants.
2. Strength of socialization from age four or five years until shortly before puberty, with respect to five systems of behavior; strength of socialization was defined as the combination of positive pressure (rewards for the behavior) plus negative pressure (punishments for lack of the behavior). The variables were:
   (a) Responsibility or dutifulness training. (The data were such that training in the performance of chores in the productive or domestic economy was necessarily the principal source of information here; however, training in the performance of other duties was also taken into account when information was available.)
   (b) Nurturance training, i.e., training the child to be nurturant or helpful toward younger siblings and other dependent people.
   (c) Obedience training.
   (d) Self-reliance training.
   (e) Achievement training, i.e., training the child to orient his behavior toward standards of excellence in performance, and to seek to achieve as excellent a performance as possible.

Where the term "no sex difference" is used here, it may mean any of three things: (a) the judge found separate evidence about the training of boys and girls on this particular variable, and judged it to be identical; (b) the judge found a difference between the training of boys and girls, but not great enough for the sexes to be rated a whole point apart on a seven-point scale; (c) the judge found evidence only about the training of "children" on this variable, the ethnographer not reporting separately about boys and girls.

Sex Differences in Socialization

On the various aspects of attention and indulgence toward infants, the judges almost always agreed in finding no sex difference. Out of 96 cultures for which the ratings included the infancy period, 88 (92 per cent) were rated with no sex difference by either judge for any of those variables. This result is consistent with the point sometimes made by anthropologists that "baby" generally is a single status undifferentiated by sex, even though "boy" and "girl" are distinct statuses.

On the variables of childhood socialization, on the other hand, a rating of no sex difference by both judges was much less common. This finding of no sex difference varied in frequency from 10 per cent of the cultures for the achievement

TABLE 1
Ratings of Cultures for Sex Differences on Five Variables
of Childhood Socialization Pressure

Variable	*Number of cultures*	*Both judges agree in rating the variable higher in*		*One judge rates no difference, one rates the variable higher in*		*Percentage of cultures with evidence of sex differences in direction of*		
		Girls	*Boys*	*Girls*	*Boys*	*Girls*	*Boys*	*Neither*
Nurturance	33	17	0	10	0	82%	0%	18%
Obedience	69	6	0	18	2	35%	3%	62%
Responsibility	84	25	2	26	7	61%	11%	28%
Achievement	31	0	17	1	10	3%	87%	10%
Self-reliance	82	0	64	0	6	0%	85%	15%

variable up to 62 per cent of the cultures for the obedience variables, as shown in the last column of Table 1. Where a sex difference is reported, by either one or both judges, the difference tends strongly to be in a particular direction, as shown in the earlier columns of the same table. Pressure toward nurturance, obedience, and responsibility is most often stronger for girls, whereas pressure toward achievement and self-reliance is most often stronger for boys.

For nurturance and for self-reliance, all the sex differences are in the same direction. For achievement there is only one exception to the usual direction of difference, and for obedience only two; but for responsibility there are nine. What do these exceptions mean? We have reexamined all these cases. In most of them, only one judge had rated the sexes as differently treated (sometimes one judge, sometimes the other), and in the majority of these cases both judges were now inclined to agree that there was no convincing evidence of a real difference. There were exceptions, however, especially in cases where a more formal or systematic training of boys seemed to imply greater pressure on them toward responsibility. The most convincing cases were the Masai and Swazi, where both judges had originally agreed in rating responsibility pressures greater in boys than in girls. In comparing the five aspects of socialization we may conclude that responsibility shows by far the strongest evidence of real variation in the direction of sex difference, and obedience much the most frequently shows evidence of no sex difference at all.

In subsequent discussion we shall be assuming that the obtained sex differences in the socialization ratings reflect true sex differences in the cultural practices. We should consider here two other possible sources of these rated differences.

1. The ethnographers could have been biased in favor of seeing the same pattern of sex differences as in our culture. However, most anthropologists readily perceive and eagerly report novel and startling cultural features, so we may expect them to have reported unusual sex differences where they existed. The distinction between matrilineal and patrilineal, and between matrilocal and patrilocal cultures, given prominence in many ethnographic reports, shows an awareness of possible variations in the significance of sex differences from culture to culture.

2. The two judges could have expected to find in other cultures the sex roles which are familiar in our culture and inferred them from the material on the cultures. However, we have reported only confident ratings, and such a bias seems less likely here than for doubtful ratings. It might be argued, moreover, that bias has more opportunity in the cases ambiguous enough so that only one judge reported a sex difference, and less opportunity in the cases where the evidence is so clear that both judges agreed. Yet in general, as may be seen in Table 1, the deviant cases are somewhat more frequent among the cultures where only one judge reported a sex difference.

The observed differences in the socialization of boys and girls are consistent with certain universal tendencies in the differentiation of adult sex role. In the economic sphere, men are more frequently allotted tasks that involve leaving home and engaging in activities where a high level of skill yields important returns; hunting is a prime example. Emphasis on training in self-reliance and achievement for boys would function as preparation for such an economic role. Women, on the other hand, are more frequently allotted tasks at or near home that minister most immediately to the needs of others (such as cooking and water carrying); these activities have a nurturant character, and in their pursuit a responsible carrying out of established routines is likely to be more important than the development of an especially high order of skill. Thus training in nurturance, responsibility, and, less clearly, obedience, may contribute to preparation for this economic role. These consistencies with adult role go beyond the economic sphere, of course. Participation in warfare, as a male prerogative, calls for self-reliance and a high order of skill where survival or death is the immediate issue. The childbearing which is biologically assigned to women, and the child care which is socially assigned primarily to them, lead to nurturant behavior and often call for a more continuous responsibility than do the tasks carried out by men. Most of these distinctions in adult role are not inevitable, but the biological differences between the sexes strongly predispose the distinction of role, if made, to be in a uniform direction.[1]

The relevant biological sex differences are conspicuous in adulthood but generally not in childhood. If each generation were left entirely to its own devices, therefore, without even an older generation to copy, sex differences in role would presumably be almost absent in childhood and would have to be developed after puberty at the expense of considerable relearning on the part of one or both sexes. Hence, a pattern of child training which foreshadows adult differences can serve the useful function of minimizing what Benedict termed "discontinuities in cultural conditioning"(1).

The differences in socialization between the sexes in our society, then, are no arbitrary custom of our society, but a very widespread adaptation of culture to the biological substratum of human life.

Variations in Degree of Sex Differentiation

While demonstrating near-universal tendencies in direction of difference between the socialization of boys and girls, our data do not show perfect uniformity. A study of the variations in our data may allow us to see some of the conditions which are associated with, and perhaps give rise to, a greater or smaller degree of this difference. For this purpose, we classified cultures as having relatively large or small sex difference by two different methods, one more inclusive and the other more selective. In both methods the ratings were at first considered separately for each of the five variables. A sex difference rating was made only if both judges made a rating on this variable and at least one judge's rating was confident.

In the more inclusive method the ratings were dichotomized, separately for each variable, as close as possible to the median into those showing a large and those showing a small sex difference. Thus, for each society a large or a small sex difference was recorded for each of the five variables on which a sex difference rating was available. A society was given an over-all classification of large or small sex difference if it had a sex difference rating on at least three variables and if a majority of these ratings agreed in being large, or agreed in being small. This method permitted classification of a large number of cultures, but the grounds for classification were capricious in many cases, as a difference of only one point in the rating of a single variable might change the over-all classification of sex difference for a culture from large to small.

In the more selective method, we again began by dichotomizing each variable as close as possible to the median; but a society was now classified as having a large or small sex difference on the variable only if it was at least one step away from the scores immediately adjacent to the median. Thus only the more decisive ratings of sex difference were used. A culture was classified as having an over-all large or small sex difference only if it was given a sex difference rating, which met this criterion on at least two variables, and only if all such ratings agreed in being large, or agreed in being small.

We then tested the relation of each of these dichotomies to 24 aspects of culture on which Murdock has categorized the customs of most of these societies[2] and which seemed of possible significance for sex differentiation. The aspects of culture covered include type of economy, residence pattern, marriage and incest rules, political integration, and social organization. For each aspect of culture, we grouped Murdock's categories to make a dichotomous contrast (sometimes omitting certain categories as irrelevant to the contrast). In the case of some aspects of culture, two or more separate contrasts were made (e.g., under form of marriage we contrasted monogamy with polygyny, and also contrasted sororal with nonsororal polygyny). For each of 40 comparisons thus formed, we prepared a 2×2 frequency table to determine relation to each of our sex-difference dichotomies. A significant relation was found for six of these 40 aspects of culture with the more selective dichotomization of over-all sex difference. In four of these comparisons, the relation to the more inclusive dichotomization was also significant. These relationships are all given in Table 2, in the form of phi coefficients, along with the outcome of testing significance by the use of χ^2 or Fisher's exact test. In trying to interpret these findings, we have also considered the nonsignificant correlations with

TABLE 2

Culture Variables Correlated with Large Sex Differences in Socialization, Separately for Two Types of Sample

Variable	*More selective sample*		*More inclusive sample*	
	ϕ	N	ϕ	N
Large animals are hunted	.48 [a]	(34)	.28 [a]	(72)
Grain rather than root crops are grown	.82 [b]	(20)	.62 [b]	(43)
Large or milking animals rather than small animals are kept	.65 [a]	(19)	.43 [a]	(35)
Fishing unimportant or absent	.42 [a]	(31)	.19	(69)
Nomadic rather than sedentary residence	.61 [b]	(34)	.15	(71)
Polygyny rather than monogamy	.51 [a]	(28)	.38 [b]	(64)

Note: The variables have been so phrased that all correlations are positive. The phi coefficient is shown, and in parentheses, the number of cases on which the comparison was based. Significance level was determined by χ^2, or Fisher's exact test where applicable, using in all cases a two-tailed test.

[a] $p < .05$.
[b] $p < .01$.

other variables, looking for consistency and inconsistency with the general implications of the significant findings. We have arrived at the following formulation of results:

1. Large sex difference in socialization is associated with an economy that places a high premium on the superior strength, and superior development of motor skills requiring strength, which characterize the male. Four of the correlations reported in Table 2 clearly point to this generalization: the correlations of large sex difference with the hunting of large animals, with grain rather than root crops, with the keeping of large rather than small domestic animals, and with nomadic rather than sedentary residence. The correlation with the unimportance of fishing may also be consistent with this generalization, but the argument is not clear.[3] Other correlations consistent with the generalization, though not statistically significant, are with large game hunting rather than gathering, with the hunting of large game rather than small game, and with the general importance of all hunting and gathering.

2. Large sex difference in socialization appears to be correlated with customs that make for a large family group with high cooperative interaction. The only statistically significant correlation relevant here is that with polygyny rather than monogamy. This generalization is, however, supported by several substantial correlations that fall only a little short of being statistically significant. One of these is a correlation with sororal rather than nonsororal polygyny; Murdock and Whiting (4) have presented indirect evidence that co-wives generally show smoother cooperative interaction if they are sisters. Correlations are also found with the presence of either an extended or a polygynous family rather than the nuclear family only; with the presence of an extended family; and with the extreme contrast between maximal extension and no extension of the family. The generalization is also to some extent supported by small correlations with wide extension of incest taboos, if we may presume that an incest taboo makes for effective unthreatening cooperation within the extended family. The only possible exception to this generalization, among substantial correlations, is a near-significant correlation with an extended or polygynous family's occupying a cluster of dwellings rather than a single dwelling.[4]

In seeking to understand this second generalization, we feel that the degree of social isolation of the nuclear family may perhaps be the crucial underlying variable. To the extent that the nuclear family must stand alone, the man must be prepared to take the woman's role when she is absent or incapacitated, and vice versa. Thus the sex differentiation cannot afford to be too great. But to the extent that the nuclear family is steadily interdependent with other nuclear families, the female role in the household economy can be temporarily taken over by another woman, or the male role by another man, so that sharp differentiation of sex role is no handicap.

The first generalization, which concerns the economy, cannot be viewed as dealing with material completely independent of the ratings of socialization. The training of children in their economic role was often an important part of the data used in rating socialization variables, and would naturally vary according to the general economy of the society. We would stress, however, that we were by no means using the identical data on the two sides of our comparison; we were on the one hand judging data on the socialization of children and on the other hand using Murdock's judgments on the economy of the adult culture. In the case of the second generalization, it seems to us that there was little opportunity for information on family and social structure to have influenced the judges in making the socialization ratings.

Both of these generalizations contribute to understanding the social background of the relatively small difference in socialization of boys and girls which we believe characterizes our society at the present time. Our mechanized economy is perhaps less dependent than any previous economy upon the superior average strength of the male. The nuclear family in our society is often so isolated that husband and wife must each be prepared at times to take over or help in the household tasks normally assigned to the other. It is also significant that the conditions favoring low sex differentiation appear to be more characteristic of the upper segments of our society, in socioeconomic and educational status, than of lower segments. This observation may be relevant to the tendency toward smaller sex differences in personality in higher status groups (cf. Terman and Miles, 8).

The increase in our society of conditions favoring small sex difference has led some people to advocate a virtual elimination of sex differences in socialization. This course seems likely to be dysfunctional even in our society. Parsons, Bales, et al. (5) argue that a differentiation of role similar to the universal pattern of sex difference is an important and perhaps inevitable development in any social group, such as the nuclear family. If we add to their argument the point that biological differences between the sexes make most appropriate the usual division of those roles between the sexes, we have compelling reasons to expect that the decrease in differentiation of adult sex role will not continue to the vanishing point. In our training of children, there may now be less differentiation in sex role than characterizes adult life — so little, indeed, as to provide inadequate preparation for adulthood. This state of affairs is likely to be especially true of formal education, which is more subject to conscious influence by an ideology than is informal socialization at home. With child training being more oriented toward the male than the female role in adulthood, many of the adjustment problems of women in our society today may be partly traced to conflicts growing out of inadequate childhood preparation for their adult role. This argument is nicely supported in extreme form by Spiro's analysis of sex roles in an Israeli kibbutz (7). The ideology of the founders of the kibbutz included the objective of greatly reducing differences in sex role. But the economy of the kibbutz is a largely nonmechanized one in which the superior average strength of men is badly needed in many jobs. The result is that, despite the ideology and many attempts to implement it, women continue to be assigned primarily to traditional "women's work," and the incompatibility between upbringing or ideology and adult role is an important source of conflict for women.

Note on Regional Distribution

There is marked variation among regions of the world in typical size of sex difference in socialization. In our sample, societies in North America and Africa tend to have large sex difference, and societies in Oceania to have small sex difference. Less confidently, because of the smaller number of cases, we can report a tendency toward small sex differences in Asia and South America as well. Since most of the variables with which we find the sex difference to be significantly correlated have a similar regional distribution, the question arises whether the correlations might better be ascribed to some quite different source having to do with large regional similarities, rather than to the functional dependence we have suggested. As a partial check, we have tried to determine whether the correlations we report in Table 2 tend also to be found strictly within regions. For each of the three regions for which we have sizable samples (North America, Africa, and Oceania) we have separately plotted 2 × 2 tables corresponding to each of the 6 relationships reported in Table 2. (We did this only for the more inclusive sample, since for the more selective sample the number of cases within a region would have been extremely small.) Out of the 18 correlations thus determined, 11 are positive and only 3 are negative (the other 4 being exactly zero). This result clearly suggests a general tendency for these correlations to hold true within regions as well as between regions, and may lend further support to our functional interpretation.

Summary

A survey of certain aspects of socialization in 110 cultures shows that differentiation of the sexes is unimportant in infancy, but that in childhood there is, as in our society, a widespread pattern of greater pressure toward nurturance, obedience, and responsibility in girls, and toward self-reliance and achievement striving in boys. There are a few reversals of sex difference, and many instances of no detectable sex difference; these facts tend to confirm the cultural rather than directly biological nature of the differences. Cultures vary in the degree to which these differentiations are made; correlational analysis suggests some of the social conditions influencing these variations, and helps in understanding why our society has relatively small sex differentiation.

Notes

1. For data and interpretations supporting various arguments of this paragraph, see Mead (2), Murdock (3), and Scheinfeld (6).
2. These data were supplied to us directly by Professor Murdock.
3. Looking (with the more inclusive sample) into the possibility that this correlation might result from the correlation between fishing and sedentary residence, a complicated interaction between these variables was found. The correlation of sex differentiation with absence of fishing is found only in nomadic societies, where fishing is likely to involve cooperative activity of the two sexes, and its absence is likely to mean dependence upon the male for large game hunting or herding large animals (whereas in sedentary societies the alternatives to fishing do not so uniformly require special emphasis on male strength). The correlation of sex differentiation with nomadism is found only in nonfishing societies; here nomadism is likely to imply large game hunting or herding large animals, whereas in fishing societies nomadism evidently implies no such special dependence upon male strength. Maximum sex differentiation is found in nomadic nonfishing societies (15 with large difference and only 2 with small) and minimum sex differentiation in nomadic fishing societies (2 with large difference and 7 with small difference). These findings further strengthen the argument for a conspicuous influence of the economy upon sex differentiation.
4. We think the reverse of this correlation would be more consistent with our generalization here. But perhaps it may reasonably be argued that the various

nuclear families composing an extended or polygynous family are less likely to develop antagonisms which hinder cooperation if they are able to maintain some physical separation. On the other hand, this variable may be more relevant to the first generalization than to the second. Occupation of a cluster of dwellings is highly correlated with presence of herding and with herding of large rather than small animals, and these economic variables in turn are correlated with large sex difference in socialization. Occupation of a cluster of dwellings is also correlated with polygyny rather than monogamy and shows no correlation with sororal vs. nonsororal polygyny.

References

1. Benedict, Ruth. 1938. Continuities and discontinuities in cultural conditioning. *Psychiatry* 1: 161–67.
2. Mead, Margaret. 1949. *Male and female.* New York: Morrow.
3. Murdock, G. P. 1937. Comparative data on the division of labor by sex. *Social Forces* 15: 551–53.
4. Murdock, G. P., and J. W. M. Whiting. 1951. Cultural determination of parental attitudes: The relationship between the social structure, particularly family structure and parental behavior. In M. J. E. Senn (ed.), *Problems of infancy and childhood: Transactions of the Fourth Conference,* March 6–7, 1950. New York: Josiah Macy, Jr. Foundation. Pp. 13–34.
5. Parsons, T.; R. F. Bales; et al. 1955. *Family, socialization and interaction process.* Glencoe, Ill.: Free Press.
6. Scheinfeld, A. 1944. *Women and men.* New York: Harcourt, Brace.
7. Spiro, M. E. 1956. *Kibbutz: Venture in utopia.* Cambridge, Mass.: Harvard University Press.
8. Terman, L. M., and Catherine C. Miles. 1936. *Sex and personality.* New York: McGraw-Hill.

2

LIFE CYCLE

Any proper understanding of an individual's personality must be placed within the context of his life cycle. In the sociologist's view age is an important variable because it not only imposes omnipresent role norms on the individual's behavior, but it also establishes the criteria for incumbency in other statuses in the society. Neugarten, Moore, and Lowe, the authors of the first selection, establish that in "all societies, age is one of the bases for the ascription of status and one of the underlying dimensions by which social interaction is regulated."

In modern societies, the life cycle is conventionally broken down into infancy, childhood, adolescence, young adulthood, middle age, and old age. In all societies, resources, like power and prestige, are distributed differentially across age groupings. However, different societies may organize the life cycle of the individual into different stages and define the rights, privileges, obligations, and norms of behavior appropriate to individuals at each stage differently. For example, the very slow rate of cultural change in traditional societies lends authority to the opinions of those with greater experience in living. Thus, the elderly occupy positions of power and prestige they could not occupy in a change-oriented modern society.

To understand the interaction of age and personality, biological maturation must be distinguished from social psychological development. The organism, allowing for differences in diet and other conditions, matures at a relatively constant rate among all human beings. However, the cultural meaning attached to this maturation and the consequences it has for the behavior expected of the individual may vary markedly from one society to the next.

Adolescence

This distinction between biological maturation and social psychological development is especially important in understanding adolescence. In Freudian theory, the "storm and stress" typically associated with adolescence was believed to be a consequence of certain physiological changes resulting from the onset of puberty. Freud saw the individual as evolving through different stages of psychological development which were determined by different biologically rooted drive systems. Margaret Mead, gathering data by studying adolescence in traditional rather than modern societies, was the first to effectively challenge this view with the publication of *Coming of Age in Samoa* in 1949. According to Mead, adolescence as a growth period of personality is a function of the complexity of society, not merely of the human life cycle. In Samoa children were given many duties and responsibilities within the context of an extended family, experienced a smooth transition from child to adult status, and ceased participating in their age-graded peer group before puberty.

Qualitative differences in complexity do exist between traditional and modern societies. Among other things, industrialization usually leads to increasing institutional specialization, greater diversity in cultural values, and greater vertical mobility for individuals within the social structure. According to Kingsley Davis (1940), these conditions have tended to foster conflict between the generations, a phenomenon by now so familiar that it has been labelled the "generation gap."

Other social theorists like Erikson (1968), Friedenberg (1959), Goodman (1956), Keniston (1971), and Riesman (1953) have also discussed the dilemma of contemporary youth in numerous books and articles. Erikson (1965; pp. 3–4) writes:

> The evidence in young lives of the search for something and somebody to be true to is seen in a variety of pursuits more or less sanctioned by society. It is often hidden in a bewildering combination of shifting devotion and sudden perversity, sometimes more devotedly perverse, sometimes more perversely devoted. Yet, in all youth's seeming shiftiness, a seeking after some durability in change can be detected. . . . This search is easily misunderstood, and often it is only dimly perceived by the individual himself, because youth, always set to grasp both diversity in principle and principle in diversity, must often test extremes before settling on a considered course. These extremes, particularly in times of ideological confusion and widespread marginality of identity, may include not only rebelliousness but also deviant, delinquent, and self-destructive tendencies. However, all this can be in the nature of a moratorium, a period of delay, in which to test the rock-bottom of some truth before committing the powers of body and mind to a segment of the existing (or a coming) order.

The alienation and rebelliousness of many adolescents and young adults have been attributed to a wide variety of factors: the difficulty of establishing some continuity of identity between one's self and one's rapidly changing environment; the increasing irrelevance of adult role models to the needs and problems of youth; the increasing discrepancy between the adolescent and young adult's biological maturity and his prolonged social dependence through more and more years of formal education; the increasingly salient discrepancy between the universalistic ethic of modern industrial society and the age-ascriptive basis of most positions of institutional authority, producing for many an acute sense of normlessness; the absence of any purpose or vital idealism in the society at large because of the weakening of old cultural values as a result of modernization; the frightening uncertainty over occupational opportunities in an economy where access to gainful employment is often controlled by impersonal bureaucratic authorities; the exacerbation of anxiety about employment by the additional pressure to achieve success in order to earn the social approval upon which much of one's self-esteem is based; and even the omnipresence of a threatening world situation, purveyed through the mass media, lending even greater uncertainty about the shape of the future and the relevance of contemporary planning and sacrifice.

All these conditions, peculiar to the advanced technobureaucratic society, exacerbate the gap between child and adult statuses and problems which is common to any social order. Such conditions tend to make the individual's transition to adulthood painful and difficult, to set youth apart. The youth culture which emerges as a stabilizing force evolves its own fads and fashions, heroes and villains, values and institutions. According to Keniston (1963, p. 81), this "special set of anti-adult values and institutions" allows young people to "at least temporarily negate the feared life of the adult." It represents what Erikson has termed a "psycho-social moratorium" which, while it may itself prolong and intensify the difficulty of the uncertain transition to adult status, is often an essential waiting period in the growing process — allowing young people the opportunity to examine and experiment with different alternatives before making any important commitments. This, of course, makes the peer group, with its more egalitarian status structure and contemporary cultural norms, a major vehicle for adolescent personality development in modern society. This shift in the influence of socializing agents can permit the individual to achieve an increasingly greater degree of independence from his family until he is ready to assume adult status.

In contradistinction to this view, Joseph Adelson, in "The Mystique of Adolescence" included in this chapter, argues that the peer group does not encourage the "growth and differentiation of the self." Taking issue with the authorities already cited, Adelson presents the provocative thesis that the "typical" adolescent does not achieve "an unusual degree of independence from the family," manifest much "discontent with the social order," or adopt "radical solutions to that key problem of adolescence, the task of ego synthesis." Rather, according to him, "there is more commonly an avoidance of inner and outer conflict, premature identity consolidation, ego and ideological constriction, and a general unwillingness to take psychic risks" (p. 2). Moreover, it is precisely the peer group, with its emphasis on the "learning and display of sociability and social skills" which "more often than not acts to hinder differentiation and growth" (p. 4).

Adelson's approach is primarily psychoanalytic and his method is clinical. His essay was written in 1964 and, since that time, a new youth stereotype, in addition to the "fool," the "visionary," and the "victimizer," may have been added to the list: the "radical activist," combining the perceptiveness and moral precocity of the visionary with the aggressive sadism of the victimizer. Despite the spate of books and films examining, criticizing, or celebrating the "counterculture," Adelson's observations still offer a fresh counterpoint to conventional thinking about youth.

It must also be recognized that the ideological disaffection of some youth may represent more than a temporary adjustment to the strains of their marginal status. It may reflect the development of a new historical consciousness expressed in the form of new values and ideas about what society is and should be. In this context, the decreasing rate of socialization which universally characterizes the human life cycle is a constant factor in making social change possible. In addition, the effects of major sociopolitical events (such as war, depression, revolution) differ according to one's stage in the life cycle, increasing the probability of ideological differences between age groups.

Aging

Age also may be considered an ontogenetic factor in personality in that it interacts in specific ways with the individual organism to produce different behavior over time. The maturation of the organism makes the actualization of certain biological potentialities more or less possible at different ages. Generally, the infant and child must experience the gradual development of certain cognitive and motor skills before being able to expand the range of his intellectual and physical activity. Obversely, the elderly person may be compelled to restrict his activity as declining age is accompanied by a gradual deterioration of the organism. Although the vitality of the organism influences the individual's social behavior at various stages of the life cycle, social factors may in turn have their effect on the health and development of the organism. For example, in *The Family Life of Old People* (1962, pp. 338–39), Peter Townsend compares the death rates of single, married and widowed men and women in modern societies and concludes, "Biological, physiological and health factors aside, one would expect, on the rather limited evidence from the present study, that old women and, to a lesser extent, old men who are at the center of a secure family live longer than those who are socially isolated or desolated [suffer the loss of their spouse], particularly the latter." Townsend's argument infers physical well-being from psychological well-being and psychological well-being from social integration (that is, the relative involvement of the individual in a system of roles which provide structure and purpose to his existence).

The last selection in this chapter is a provocative contrast in tone and emphasis to the conventional literature on old age. The gerontologist Otto Pollak presents a lucid overview of the process of aging and the problem of retirement. Rather than considering only the pains and losses of the elderly in modern society, he also points out their pleasures and attainments. Pollak concludes by applying this more comprehensive perspective to all stages in the life cycle of modern man.

References

Benedict, Ruth
   1938   "Continuities and Discontinuities in Cultural Conditioning." *Psychiatry* 1(2):161–67.
Davis, Kingsley
   1940   "The Sociology of Parent-Youth Conflict." *American Sociological Review* 5 (August):525–35.

Erikson, Erik H.
    1965   "Youth: Fidelity and Diversity." Pp. 1–28 in Erik H. Erikson (ed.), *The Challenge of Youth*. New York: Doubleday.
    1968   *Identity: Youth and Crisis*. New York: Norton.
Friedenberg, Edgar Z.
    1959   *The Vanishing Adolescent*. New York: Beacon.
Goodman, Paul
    1956   *Growing Up Absurd*. New York: Random House.
Keniston, Kenneth
    1963   "Alienation and the Decline of Utopia." Pp. 79–117 in Hendrik M. Ruitenbeek (ed.), *Varieties of Modern Social Theory*. New York: Dutton.
    1971   *Youth and Dissent: The Rise of a New Opposition*. New York: Harcourt, Brace, Jovanovich.
Kimball, Solon
    1963   "Cultural Influences Shaping the Role of the Child." Pp. 268–83 in George D. Spindler (ed.), *Education and Culture: Anthropological Approaches*. New York: Holt, Rinehart and Winston.
Mead, Margaret
    1949   *Coming of Age in Samoa*. New York: New American Library.
    1958   "Adolescence in Primitive and Modern Society." Pp. 341–9 in Eleanor E. Maccoby, Theodore M. Newcomb, and Eugene L. Hartley (eds.), *Readings in Social Psychology*, 3d ed. New York: Holt, Rinehart and Winston.
Riesman, David, with Nathan Glazer and Reuel Denney
    1953   *The Lonely Crowd: A Study of the Changing American Character*. Garden City, N. Y.: Doubleday-Anchor.
Townsend, Peter
    1962   "Isolation, Loneliness and the Hold on Life." Pp. 326–46 in Eric and Mary Josephson (eds.), *Man Alone: Alienation in Modern Society*. New York: Dell.

BERNICE L. NEUGARTEN
JOAN W. MOORE
JOHN C. LOWE

Age Norms, Age Constraints, and Adult Socialization

In all societies, age is one of the bases for the ascription of status and one of the underlying dimensions by which social interaction is regulated. Anthropologists have studied age-grading in simple societies, and sociologists in the

Reprinted by permission of the author and publisher, the University of Chicago Press, from *American Journal of Sociology* 70:6, pp. 710–716. Copyright © 1965 by the University of Chicago. Adapted from a paper presented at the annual meeting of the American Sociological Association, September 1963. This study has been financed by research grant No. 4200 from the National Institute of Mental Health. Some footnotes omitted.

tradition of Mannheim have been interested in the relations between generations; but little systematic attention has been given to the ways in which age groups relate to each other in complex societies or to systems of norms which refer to age-appropriate behavior. A promising group of theoretical papers which appeared twenty or more years ago have now become classics,[1] but with the exceptions of a major contribution by Eisenstadt and a provocative paper by Berger,[2] little theoretical or empirical work has been done in this area in the two decades that have intervened, and there has been little development of what might be called a sociology of age.

The present paper deals with two related issues: first, with the degree of constraint perceived with regard to age norms that operate in American society; second, with adult socialization to those norms. Preliminary to presenting the data that bear upon these issues, however, a few comments regarding the age-norm system and certain illustrative observations gathered earlier may help to provide context for this study.

Background Concepts and Observations

Expectations regarding age-appropriate behavior form an elaborated and pervasive system of norms governing behavior and interaction, a network of expectations that is imbedded throughout the cultural fabric of adult life. There exists what might be called a prescriptive timetable for the ordering of major life events: a time in the life span when men and women are expected to marry, a time to raise children, a time to retire. This normative pattern is adhered to, more or less consistently, by most persons in the society. Although the actual occurrences of major life events for both men and women are influenced by a variety of life contingencies, and although the norms themselves vary somewhat from one group of persons to another, it can easily be demonstrated that norms and actual occurrences are closely related. Age norms and age expectations operate as prods and brakes upon behavior, in some instances hastening an event, in others delaying it. Men and women are aware not only of the social clocks that operate in various areas of their lives, but they are aware also of their own timing and readily describe themselves as "early," "late," or "on time" with regard to family and occupational events.

Age norms operate also in many less clear-cut ways, and in more peripheral areas of adult life as illustrated in such phrases as "He's too old to be working so hard" or "She's too young to wear that style of clothing" or "That's a strange thing for a man of his age to say." The concern over age-appropriate behavior is further illustrated by colloquialisms such as "Act your age!" — an exhortation made to the adult as well as to the child in this society.

Such norms, implicit or explicit, are supported by a wide variety of sanctions ranging from those, on the one hand, that relate directly to the physical health of the transgressor to those, on the other hand, that stress the deleterious effects of the transgression on other persons. For example, the fifty-year-old man who insists on a strenuous athletic life is chastised for inviting an impairment of his own health; a middle-aged woman who dresses like an adolescent brings into question her husband's good judgment as well as her own; a middle-aged couple who decide to have another child are criticized because of the presumed embarrassment to their adolescent or married children. Whether affecting the self or others, age norms and accompanying sanctions are relevant to a great variety of adult behaviors; they are both systematic and pervasive in American society.

TABLE 1
Consensus in a Middle-Class Middle-Aged Sample Regarding
Various Age-related Characteristics

	Age range designated as appropriate or expected	Per cent who concur	
		Men (N = 50)	Women (N = 43)
Best age for a man to marry	20–25	80	90
Best age for a woman to marry	19–24	85	90
When most people should become grandparents	45–50	84	79
Best age for most people to finish school and go to work	20–22	86	82
When most men should be settled on a career	24–26	74	64
When most men hold their top jobs	45–50	71	58
When most people should be ready to retire	60–65	83	86
A young man	18–22	84	83
A middle-aged man	40–50	86	75
An old man	65–75	75	57
A young woman	18–24	89	88
A middle-aged woman	40–50	87	77
An old woman	60–75	83	87
When a man has the most responsibilities	35–50	79	75
When a man accomplishes most	40–50	82	71
The prime of life for a man	35–50	86	80
When a woman has the most responsibilities	25–40	93	91
When a woman accomplishes most	30–45	94	92
A good-looking woman	20–35	92	82

Despite the diversity of value patterns, life styles, and reference groups that influence attitudes, a high degree of consensus can be demonstrated with regard to age-appropriate and age-linked behaviors as illustrated by data shown in Table 1. The table shows how responses were distributed when a representative sample of middle-class men and women aged forty to seventy[3] were asked such questions as: "What do you think is the best age for a man to marry? . . . to finish school?" "What age comes to your mind when you think of a 'young' man? . . . an 'old' man?" "At what age do you think a man has the most responsibilities? . . . accomplishes the most?"[4]

The consensus indicated in the table is not limited to persons residing in a particular region of the United States or to middle-aged persons. Responses to the same set of questions were obtained from other middle-class groups: one group of fifty men and women aged twenty to thirty residing in a second midwestern city, a group of sixty Negro men and women aged forty to sixty in a third midwestern city, and a group of forty persons aged seventy to eighty in a New England community. Essentially the same patterns emerged in each set of data.

The Problem and the Method

Based upon various sets of data such as those illustrated in Table 1, the present investigation proceeded on the assumption that age norms and age expectations operate in this society as a system of social control. For a great variety of behaviors, there is a span of years within which the occurrence of a given behavior is regarded as appropriate. When the behavior occurs outside that span of years, it is regarded as inappropriate and is negatively sanctioned.

The specific questions of this study were these: How do members of the society vary in their perception of the strictures involved in age norms, or in the degree of constraint they perceive with regard to age-appropriate behaviors? To what extent are personal attitudes congruent with the attitudes ascribed to the generalized other? Finally, using this congruence as an index of socialization, can adult socialization to age norms be shown to occur as respondents themselves increase in age?

The Instrument

A questionnaire was constructed in which the respondent was asked on each of a series of items which of three ages he would regard as appropriate or inappropriate, or which he would approve or disapprove. As seen in the illustrations below, the age spans being proposed were intended to be psychologically rather than chronologically equal in the sense that for some events a broad age span is appropriate, for others a narrow one.

A woman who feels it's all right at her age to wear a two-piece bathing suit to the beach:

> When she's 45 (approve or disapprove)
> When she's 30 (approve or disapprove)
> When she's 18 (approve or disapprove).

Other illustrative items were:

> A woman who decides to have another child (when she's 45, 37, 30).
> A man who's willing to move his family from one town to another to get ahead in his company (when he's 45, 35, 25).
> A couple who like to do the "Twist" (when they're 55, 30, 20).
> A man who still prefers living with his parents rather than getting his own apartment (when he's 30, 25, 21) .
> A couple who move across country so they can live near their married children (when they're 40, 55, 70).

The thirty-nine items finally selected after careful pretesting are divided equally into three types: those that relate to occupational career; those that relate to the family cycle; and a broader grouping that refer to recreation, appearance, and consumption behaviors. In addition, the items were varied systematically with regard to their applicability to three periods: young adulthood, middle age, and old age.

In general, then, the questionnaire presents the respondent with a relatively balanced selection of adult behaviors which were known from pretesting to be successful in evoking age discriminations. A means of scoring was devised whereby the score reflects the degree of refinement with which the respondent makes age discriminations. For instance, the respondent who approves of a couple dancing the "Twist" if they are twenty, but who disapproves if they are thirty, is placing relative age constraint upon this item of behavior as compared to another re-spondent who approves the "Twist" both at age twenty and at age thirty, but not at age fifty-five. The higher the score, the more the respondent regards age as a salient dimension across a wide variety of behaviors and the more constraint he accepts in the operation of age norms.[5]

The Sample

A quota sample of middle-class respondents was obtained in which level of education, occupation, and area of residence were used to determine social class. The sample is divided into six age-sex cells: fifty men and fifty women aged twenty to thirty, one hundred men and one hundred women aged thirty to fifty-five, and fifty men and fifty women aged sixty-five and over. Of the four hundred respondents, all but a few in the older group were or had been married. The great majority were parents of one or more children.

The only known bias in the sample occurs in the older group (median age for men is sixty-nine; for women seventy-two) where most individuals were members of Senior Citizens clubs and where, as a result, the subsample is biased in the direction of better health and greater community involvement than can be ex-pected for the universe of persons in this age range. While Senior Citizens is a highly age-conscious and highly age-graded association from the perspective of the wider society, there is no evidence that the seventy-year-old who joins is any more or any less aware of age discriminations than is the seventy-year-old who does not join.[6] The older group was no more or less homogeneous with regard to religious affiliation, ethnic background, or indexes of social class than were the other two age groups in this sample.

Administration

To investigate the similarity between personal attitudes and attitudes ascribed to the generalized other, the questionnaire was first administered with instructions to give "your personal opinions" about each of the items; then the respondent was given a second copy of the questionnaire and asked to respond in the way he believed "most people" would respond.[7]

In about half the cases, both forms of the instrument were adminstered con-secutively in personal interviews. In the remainder of the cases, responses on the first form were gathered in group sessions (in one instance, a parents' meeting in a school), and the second form was completed later and returned by mail to the investigator.

The two types of administration were utilized about evenly within each age-sex group. No significant differences in responses were found to be due to this difference in procedure of data-gathering.

Findings

The findings of this study can be read from Figure 1. The figure shows a striking convergence with age between the two sets of attitudes.

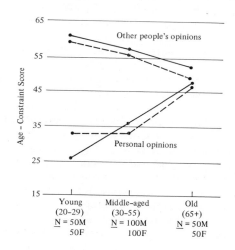

FIGURE 1 Perception of age constraints in adulthood, by age and sex. An analysis of variance for the data on "personal opinions" showed that age was a highly significant variable (F is statistically reliable beyond the .001 level); and the interaction between age and sex was significant (F is reliable at the .05 level). For the data on "other people's opinions," age alone is a significant variable (F is reliable beyond the .001 level). Dotted line, women; solid line, men.

1. Age trends within each set of data are opposite in direction. With regard to personal opinions, there is a highly significant increase in scores with age — that is, an increase in the extent to which respondents ascribe importance to age norms and place constraints upon adult behavior in terms of age appropriateness.

2. With regard to "most people's opinions" there is a significant decrease in scores with age — that is, a decrease in the extent to which age constraints are perceived in the society and attributed to a generalized other.

3. Sex differences are minimal with the exception that young women stand somewhat outside the general trend on "personal opinions," with scores that differentiate them from young men but not from middle-aged women.

Discussion

The difference shown in these data between personal attitudes and attitudes attributed to the generalized other (a finding that holds true for all but the oldest respondents) implies that age norms operate like other types of norms insofar as there is some lack of congruence between that which is acknowledged to be operating in the society and that which is personally accepted as valid. It is noteworthy on the one hand, that age norms are uniformly acknowledged to exist in the minds of "most people." While the data are not shown here, on each one of the thirty-nine behavioral items some 80 per cent or more of all respondents made age discriminations when asked for "most people's opinions." In other words, general consensus exists that behaviors described in the test instrument are age-related. On the other hand, respondents uniformly attributed greater stricture to age norms in the minds of other people than in their own minds. This difference was reflected in the scores for every respondent as well as in the mean scores.

These findings indicate that there is an overriding norm of "liberal-mindedness" regarding age, whereby men and women consistently maintain that they hold more liberal views than do others. In many ways this situation is reminiscent of the phenomenon of pluralistic ignorance, in which no respondent's personal view of the attitudes of others is altogether correct.[8] In other ways, however, this may be a situation in which respondents tend to exaggerate, rather than to misconstrue, the opinions of others. A young person who says, in effect, "I am not strict about age norms, but other people are," is indeed correct that other people are stricter than he is (as shown in these data on "personal opinions"); but he exaggerates, for other people are not so strict as he thinks. Similarly, when an old person says, in effect, "I think this is the norm, and other people think so, too," he is also partly correct that other old people agree with him, but he ignores what *young* people think.

These partial misconceptions have at least two implications: first, when a person's own opinions differ from the norms he encounters, he may exaggerate the differences and place the norms even further away from his own opinions than is warranted. Second, it may be that in considering age norms, the individual gives undue weight to the opinions of persons who are older or stricter than himself and ignores the opinions of others who are younger or less strict. In both instances, the norm image is not the average of all opinions encountered but the image of the "ideal" norm. In the case of age norms, the "ideal" norms may well be those held by older persons.

The findings of this study are also of interest when viewed within the context of adult socialization. Cross-sectional data of this type must be interpreted with caution since the differences between age groups may reflect historical changes in values and attitudes as much as changes that accompany increased age itself. Still, the findings seem congruent with a theory of adult socialization: that personal belief in the relevance and validity of social norms increases through the adult life span and that, in this instance, as the individual ages he becomes increasingly aware of age discriminations in adult behavior and of the system of social sanctions that operate with regard to age appropriateness. The middle-aged and the old seem to have learned that age is a reasonable criterion by which to evaluate behavior, that to be "off-time" with regard to life events or to show other age-deviant behavior brings with it social and psychological sequelae that cannot be disregarded. In the young, especially the young male, this view is only partially accepted; and there seems to be a certain denial of age as a valid dimension by which to judge behavior.

This age-related difference in point of view is perhaps well illustrated by the response of a a twenty-year-old who, when asked what he thought of marriage between seventeen-year-olds, said, "I suppose it would be all right if the boy got a good job, and if they loved each other. Why not? It isn't age that's the important thing." A forty-five-year-old, by contrast, said, "At that age, they'd be foolish. Neither one of them is settled enough. A boy on his own, at seventeen, couldn't support a wife, and he certainly couldn't support children. Kids who marry that young will suffer for it later."

Along with increased personal conviction regarding the validity of age norms goes a decreased tendency to perceive the generalized other as restrictive. The over-all convergence in the data, a convergence which we have interpreted in terms of adult socialization, may reflect status and deference relationships between age groups in American society, where high status is afforded the middle-aged and where social enforcement of norms may generally be said to be vested in the mature rather than the young. The young person, having only recently graduated from the age-segregated world of adolescents, and incompletely socialized to adult values, seems to perceive a psychological distance between himself and "most people" and to feel only partially identified with the adult world. This is evidenced by the fact that when asked, "Whom do you have in mind when you think of 'most people'?" young adults tended to answer, "Older people."

Only for old people is there a high degree of congruence between personal opinions and the opinions ascribed to others. This may reflect not only the accumulated effects of adult socialization and the internalization of age norms, but also a certain crystallization of attitudes in the aged. Older respondents volunteered the most vehement and the most opinionated comments as they moved from item to item, as if to underscore the fact that their attitudes with regard to age and age-related behaviors are highly charged emotionally. Under these circumstances, there is likely to be a blurring of distinctions between what the respondent himself regards as right and what he thinks other people would "naturally" regard as right.

With regard to sex differences, the fact that young women perceive greater constraints regarding age-appropriate behavior than do young men is generally congruent with other evidence of differences in socialization for women and men in our society. Young women are probably more highly sensitized to the imperatives of age norms than are young men, given the relatively more stringent expectations regarding age at marriage for women.

It should be recalled that the present study is based upon quota samples of middle-class respondents and that accordingly the findings cannot be readily generalized to other samples. Nevertheless, the findings support the interpretation that age norms are salient over a wide variety of adult behaviors and support the view that adult socialization produces increasingly clear perception of these norms as well as an increasing awareness that the norms provide constraints upon adult behavior.

Notes

1. Following the classic article by Karl Mannheim ("The Problem of Generations," *Essays on the Sociology of Knowledge* [New York: Oxford University
   Press, 1952], pp. 276–322), these include Ralph Linton's discussion in *The
   Study of Man* (New York: Appleton-Century, 1936); Ruth Benedict, "Continuities and Discontinuities in Culture Conditioning," *Psychiatry,* I (1938),
   161–67; Kingsley Davis, "The Sociology of Parent-Youth Conflict," *Ameri-
   can Sociological Review,* V (1940), 523–35; and Talcott Parsons, "Age and
   Sex in the Social Structure of the United States," *American Sociological Re-
   view,* VII (October, 1942), 604–16. Anthropological classics include Arnold
   Van Gennep (1908), *The Rites of Passage* (Chicago: University of Chicago
   Press, 1960); Robert H. Lowie (1920), *Primitive Society* (New York: Harper
   & Bros., 1961). More recently, A. H. J. Prins, *East African Age-Class Systems*
   (Groningen: J. B. Wolters, 1953) has presented a critical analysis of concepts
   and terms in use among anthropologists.
2. S. N. Eisenstadt, *From Generation to Generation* (Glencoe, Ill.: Free Press,
   1956); and Bennett M. Berger, "How Long Is a Generation?" *British Journal
   of Sociology,* XI (1960), 10–23.
3. The sample was drawn by area-probability methods (a 2 per cent listing of
   households in randomly selected census tracts) with the resulting pool of cases
   then stratified by age, sex, and socio-economic status. Using the indexes of occupation, level of education, house type, and area of residence, these respondents were all middle class. The data were gathered in connection with the
   Kansas City Studies of Adult Life, a research program carried out over a
   period of years under the direction of Robert J. Havighurst, William E.
   Henry, Bernice L. Neugarten, and other members of the Committee on Human
   Development, University of Chicago.
4. For each item in the table, the percentages that appear in the third and fourth
   columns obviously vary directly with the breadth of the age span shown for
   that item. The age span shown was, in turn, the one selected by the investigators to produce the most accurate reflection of the consensus that existed in
   the data.
   The way in which degree of consensus was calculated can be illustrated on
   "Best age for a man to marry." Individuals usually responded to this item in
   terms of specific years, such as "20" or "22" or in terms of narrow ranges,
   such as "from 20 to 23." These responses were counted as consensus within
   the five-year age range shown in Table 1, on the grounds that the respondents
   were concurring that the best age was somewhere between twenty and twen-
   ty-five. A response such as "13 to 20" or "any time in the 20's" was outside
   the range regarded as consensus and was therefore excluded.
5. For each item of behavior, one of the ages being proposed is scored as the
   "appropriate" age; another, the "marginal"; and the third, the "inappropriate"
   (the age at which the behavior is usually proscribed on the basis of its transgression of an age norm). A response which expresses disapproval of only
   the "inappropriate" age is scored 1, while a response which expresses disapproval of not only the "inappropriate" but also the "marginal" age receives a
   a score of 3. The total possible score is 117, a score that could result only
   if the respondent were perceiving maximum age constraint with regard to
   every one of the thirty-nine items. A response which expresses approval or
   disapproval of all three ages for a given behavior is scored zero, since for that
   respondent the item is not age-related, at least not within the age range being
   proposed.
   The "appropriate" age for each item had previously been designated by
   the investigators on the basis of previous findings such as those illustrated on
   Table 1 of this report. That the designations were generally accurate was cor-
   roborated by the fact that when the present instrument was administered to the
   four hundred respondents described here, more than 90 per cent of respon-

dents on successive test items checked "approve" for the "appropriate" one of the three proposed ages.

6. On the other hand, members of Senior Citizens are more likely to be activists and to regard themselves as younger in outlook than persons who do not join such groups. If this is true, the age differences to be described in the following sections of this paper might be expected to be even more marked in which samples are more representative.

7. The problem being studied here relates problems of conformity, deviation, and personal versus public attitudes. As is true of other empirical research in these areas, the terms used here are not altogether satisfactory, in part because of the lack of uniform terminology in this field. For example, while age norms are in some respects related to "attitudinal" and "doctrinal" conformity as posed by Robert K. Merton ("Social Conformity, Deviation, and Opportunity Structures: A Comment on the Contributions of Dubin and Cloward," *American Sociological Review*, XXIV [1959], 177–189), these data do not fit that analytical framework because age norms are less clear-cut than the norms Merton discusses, and the realms of attitudinal and doctrinal conformity are less prescribed. . . .

8. Floyd H. Allport, *Social Psychology* (Boston: Houghton Mifflin Co., 1924).

JOSEPH ADELSON

The Mystique of Adolescence

In recent years the adolescent has come to weigh oppressively on the American consciousness. Just a few years ago he was of little substance in our collective imaginings, in fiction, and in the mass media. He was represented as a figure of fun: callow, flighty, silly, given to infatuations, wild enthusiasms, and transient moodiness. His prototype was Andy Hardy, Henry Aldrich. Or he was sometimes seen as a latter-day and rather harmless Werther: sensitive, emotionally afflicted, overly sentimental. In either case the figure was seen as lovable, though sometimes exasperating, and not to be taken too seriously. He would get over it — whatever *it* might be — in time. I shall call this type the adolescent as Fool.[1] The Fool exists outside the world of adult happenings; he is blessedly innocent of complication, guilt, or responsibility. He is a fool not in being duped, but because he is unrelated to the intrigues and corruptions, or the moral seriousness, of adulthood. He inhabits an Eden of preresponsibility.

These days two new images, weightier and more ominous, have superseded the Fool figure, and between them they divide the contemporary sense of the adolescent. One of these I shall call the adolescent as Visionary. He is distinguished by

Reprinted by special permission of the William Alanson White Psychiatric Foundation, Inc., from *Psychiatry* 27 (1964), pp. 1–5, copyright by William Alanson White Psychiatric Foundation, Inc. This paper was originally read at the American Psychological Association meetings, September 1, 1961.

a purity of moral vision which allows him to perceive or state the moral simplicity hidden by adult complication. In the way of prophets, he is also a Victim. He is betrayed, exploited, or neglected by the adult world. His needs go unrecognized by adults too busy in their own affairs; or as an innocent bystander he may be victimized by adult corruption. The prototypes here are J. D. Salinger's adolescents, Holden Caulfield or Franny Glass. Whereas the Fool is essentially unrelated to the adult world, the Visionary-Victim is connected to it in being passive and powerless. Perceptive, articulate, morally precocious, his only resources are insight and knowledge, and the strength which may eventually accrue from them.

The antitype to the Visionary is the newest and most disturbing representation of the adolescent, as Victimizer. Leather-jacketed, cruel, sinister, and amoral, he is the nemesis-hero of a new genre of fiction and film. Here, as one example, is the plot of a typical fiction of the genre. A man accidentally incurs the hatred of some hoodlum youths who threaten to kill him. He appeals to the police for protection, but they are impotent to help him. The story ends as the night closes in, and the man, alone and helpless, awaits his death at the hands of the youths. The story's mood is paranoid; the adolescent is the persecutor, the killer. This adolescent stands in utter contrast to the Visionary; one is innocent, the other evil; one is powerless, the other omnipotent.

The emergence of these images makes it clear that the adolescent occupies a peculiarly intense place in American thought and feeling.[2] As prophet and victim he joins and replaces the child-innocent who once played these roles exclusively. As victimizer, he is the carrier of the society's projections; sadistic and sexual motives are imputed to him, and he joins or replaces the gangster, the Negro, and other projective enemies. Nor is it only in our dark imaginings that these adolescent types hold so central a place. A good deal of recent social thought sees in the adolescent's character and situation the key to our moral and social pathology. Curiously, it is in their response to the adolescent that the social criticism of the Left is joined by the social criticism of the Right. Both see our youth as reflecting what is most ignoble and most portentous in our time.

I have stressed this mystique of adolescence because it has influenced both work and thought in the social sciences. The attention of social scientists has been captured by two conspicuous but atypical enclaves of adolescence, drawn from extreme and opposing ends of the social-class continuum, and representing exceptional solutions to the adolescent crisis. The victimizer corresponds, of course, to the delinquent. The visionary-victim corresponds — though this may not be apparent at first — to the sensitive, articulate, intense, intelligent type of upper-middle-class adolescent on whom the psychoanalytic theory of adolescence is almost exclusively based.

Now in most ways these two adolescent types could not be more dissimilar. The estranged lower-class youngster relies largely on alloplastic solutions to the adolescent crisis, living out mutely, in urgent yet aimless acts of violence or bravado, a sullen resentment against the middle-class world and its values. The estranged upper-middle-class youngster is largely autoplastic in response, subject to acute intrapsychic upheavals which are expressed in neurotic symptoms, affect storms, character eccentricities, and a general value ferment. Paradoxically, these two extremes are alike, and their alikeness is in being different from the normative adolescent — that is, the socially modal adolescent. The extremes are alike in showing an unusual degree of independence from the family; they are alike in disaffection, in acting out or thinking out a discontent with the social order; they are alike, above all, in their adoption of radical solutions to that key problem of adolescence, the task of ego-synthesis. I want to suggest that one cannot generalize these processes to the adolescent population at large. The adolescent at the extremes responds to the instinctual and psychosocial upheaval of puberty by disorder, by failures of ego-synthesis, by a tendency to abandon earlier values and object-attachments. In the normative response to adolescence, however, there is more commonly an avoidance of inner and outer conflict, premature identity consolidation, ego and ideological constriction, and a general unwillingness to take psychic risks.[3]

Now having stated my thesis, let me pause here to say something about its origins. These conclusions derive from a national survey of adolescent boys and girls.[4] A colleague and I studied, by means of a rather extensive semistructured interview, 3,000 youngsters, including about 1,000 boys between 14 and 16, and about 2,000 girls between 12 and 18. Let me say at once that we were very much aware of the limitations of this sort of interview; one must write questions suitable for the lowest common denominator, and the interview setting is one which maximizes cautious, shallow, and platitudinous responses. But we were, if anything, hypersensitive to these problems, and mined the questionnaire with a great number and variety of projective items. Thanks to IBM technology we were buried in data; but I want to bypass a discussion of specific findings and approach these interviews as personal documents, to consider them impressionistically, discursively, clinically. The great advantage of this kind of project is that it permits study of those adolescents who make up the middle majority, who evoke neither grief nor wonder, and who all too often escape notice. When one looks at the normative forms of the adolescent experience, one is led to think twice about the received version of adolescence.

Let me begin with the question of autonomy and conflict. Many writers take the position that at puberty the child is under great pressure to detach himself from the family emotionally, to find a pattern of disengagement. The instinctual revival brings with it a return of Oedipal dangers and temptations. The home is a hothouse and the youngster must discover a way out, a means of escaping his dependent status in the family, and even more urgently, the dimly recognized drives and feelings toward his parents. The psychosexual irritation pushes the child from home, leading him to negotiate or battle with the parents for greater freedom. The conflict of generations is joined. Theorists add to this the psychosocial pull of the child's need to be his own man, to forge an individual identity — those needs which draw him toward the future. These forces give the adolescent peer group its critical importance. Peer group and culture supplant the family as the locus of authority and the giver of norms. Through his immersion in the peer group, through the incorporation of peer ideals and values, the youngster gains the support he needs to win autonomy from the family. And the peer group provides a haven in which the delicate task of self-exploration and self-definition can be accomplished.[5]

This view of adolescence has a good deal to recommend it, but my reading of the interviews suggests that it needs revision in some important particulars. It exaggerates the degree of conflict between parent and child; it wrongly estimates the autonomy issue; and it misinterprets the role of the peer group. The normative adolescent tends to avoid overt conflict with his family. This is not to say that conflict is not present, but it is largely unconscious conflict — undersurface resentments which do not necessarily liberate or enlarge the personality, but which, paradoxically, increase the child's docility toward his parents. Even when one does find overt conflict one senses that it has an *as if* quality to it, that it is a kind of war game, with all the sights and sounds of battle but without any bloodshed. More often than not the conflicts center on trivia, on issues of taste — clothing, grooming, and the like. It can be argued that these issues are trivial only to the adult, that they are of great symbolic importance in the adolescent's quest for autonomy. True; but one can reply that parent and child play out an empty ritual of disaffection, that they agree to disagree only on token issues, on teen issues, and in doing so are able to sidestep any genuine encounter of differences.

Much of the same is true of autonomy. There are autonomies and autonomies. The American adolescent asks for and is freely given an unusual degree of behavioral freedom — the right to come and go, to share in setting rules, and so on. But it is far more problematic whether he asks for or achieves a high degree of emotional autonomy, and it is even more doubtful whether he manages much in the way of value autonomy. Indeed, the ease with which the adolescent acquires behavioral freedom may tend to interfere with the achievement of emotional and ideological freedom, for reasons I will mention in a moment. As to the peer group, its supposed functions — as an arena for the confrontation of the self, for the testing and trying out of identities — are present for many adolescents, but for many more the peer group is used for the learning and display of sociability and social skills. The peer culture is all too often a kind of playpen, designed to keep children out of harm's way and out of parents' hair. It may not work out this way; the children may begin throwing toys at each other, or — what is worse — may begin throwing them at the grown-ups in the living room. But generally it does work out just this way. The peer group, with its artificial amusements and excitements, more often than not acts to hinder differentiation and growth.

This is especially evident in the area of values and ideology. The traditional idea of the adolescent experience holds that the youngster becomes involved in an intense concern with ethics, political ideology, religious belief, and so on. The moral parochialism of early childhood was thought to be smashed by the moral fervor and incipient cosmopolitanism of adolescence. The youngster's need to detach himself from the family and its view of the moral and social order, his need to redo the ego-superego constellation, his need to find new and more appropriate ego ideals, his need to use ideology as a solution for instinctual problems — all these needs came together, so it was thought, to produce a value crisis somewhere in the course of the adolescent career. This pattern can be found in adolescence, but it is found in a bold, sometimes stubborn, often unhappy minority. Our interviews confirm a mounting impression from other studies that American adolescents are on the whole not deeply involved in ideology, nor are they prepared to do much individual thinking on value issues of any generality. Why is this so? I would guess because to think anew and differently endangers the adolescent's connection to the community — his object attachments — and complicates the task of ego synthesis.

Let me sum up in the language of personality theory. The inherent tensions of adolescence are displaced to and discharged within the matrix of peer-group sociability. Intrapsychically the defenses and character positions adopted are those which curtail experience and limit the growth and differentiation of the self — repression, reaction-formation, and certain forms of ego restriction. These modes of dealing with inner and outer experience join to produce a pseudo-adaptive solution of the adolescent crisis, marked by cognitive stereotypy, value stasis, and interpersonal conformity. It is a solution which is accomplished by resisting conflict, resisting change, resisting the transformation of the self. It settles for a modest, sluggish resynthesis of the ego that closely follows the lines of the older organization of drives, defenses, values, and object-attachments. It is characterized by an avoidance of identity-diffusion through identity-coarctation.

One is left to wonder whether this form of adolescence is a new thing in this country, or whether Americans have always been falsely bemused by one or another mystique of adolescence. Of course we cannot know; if, as this paper has suggested, today's adults have egregiously misunderstood the adolescents they see before their very eyes, then it would be prudent, to say the least, to avoid generalizations about historically earlier patterns of adolescence. In all likelihood, the degree of tension and disorder has always been more apparent than real. It is always more likely that passion, defiance, and suffering will capture the fancy, and that the amiable, colorless forms of adaptation will be ignored.

And yet — and yet — one feels, nevertheless, that the contemporary modes of adolescence do involve something new, that Friedenberg,[6] among others, is correct in saying that adolescence is disappearing as the period during which the individual can achieve a decisive articulation of the self. If this is so — and granting how large an *if* this is — then perhaps one important reason that can be singled out is the extraordinary attenuation of today's adolescence. Given the long preparation required for advanced technical training, given the uselessness of the adolescent in the labor market, parent and child settle down for a long, long period of time during which the child will, in one way or another, remain a dependent being. Traditionally, adolescence has been the age in which the child readied himself to leave home; accounts of adolescence in the earlier part of this century often describe a decisive encounter between father and son, a decisive testing of wills, in which the son makes a determined bid for autonomy, either by leaving home, or threatening to do so, and meaning it. The adolescent then had little of the freedom he has today; he was kept under the parental thumb, but he used his captivity well, to strengthen himself for a real departure and a real autonomy. Nowadays the adolescent and his parents are both made captive by their mutual knowledge of the adolescent's dependency. They are locked in a room with no exit, and they make the best of it by an unconscious *quid pro quo,* in which the adolescent forfeits his adolescence, and instead becomes a teen-ager. He keeps the peace by muting his natural rebelliousness, through transforming it into structured and defined techniques for getting on people's nerves. The passions, the restlessness, the vivacity of adolescence are partly strangled, and partly drained off in the mixed childishness and false adulthood of the adolescent teen culture.

Notes

1. Compare Orrin E. Knapp, *Heroes, Villains, and Fools: The Changing American Character;* Englewood Cliffs, N. J., Prentice-Hall, 1962.

2. Yet this is not to say that these motifs have been restricted either to American thought, or to the representation of adolescence. The themes of saintliness and violence have been endemic in recent European writing as well, and have also figured in the depiction of postadolescent prototypes — for example, the Beats as "holy barbarians." An interesting variation is seen in the effort to fuse saintliness and violence, as in the writings of Jean Genet, Norman Mailer, and William Burroughs.

3. It should be clear that I am speaking here of institutionalized patterns, rather than voluntaristic "choices."

4. A full report on this research, in co-authorship with Elizabeth Douvan, will be published shortly by John Wiley. A report on one aspect can be found in Douvan and Adelson. "The Psychodynamics of Social Mobility in Adolescent Boys," *J. Abnormal and Social Psychol.* (1958) 56:31–44.

5. A full yet succinct review of this general position can be found in Leo Spiegel, "A Review of Contributions to a Psychoanalytic Theory of Adolescence: Individual Aspects," in *Psychoanalytic Study of the Child* 6:375–393; New York, Internat. Univ. Press, 1951.

6. Edgar Z. Friedenberg. *The Vanishing Adolescent;* Boston, Beacon, 1959.

OTTO POLLAK

Catching Up: A Retirement Role Set

In a dynamic society anything which suggests an end rather than a process, a standstill instead of movement, or a late stage of development rather than a beginning has the implication of failure and misfortune. It is in this mood that retirement is frequently discussed. It puts an end to employment, it decreases income, it interrupts the routine of an ordered time schedule and it suggests the nearness of death. At best, it suggests completion of development. In that sense, Erik H. Erikson has discussed maturity as the last of the "eight ages of man" and has tried to trace dignity of accomplishment in decline. He has seen ego integrity which permits being a follower as well as a leader as the ultimate attainment of this last stage of development. It is interesting, however, to note that his examples are "a wise Indian, a true gentleman, and a mature peasant." [1] Since our society contains very few people who would fall into any one of these categories, the failure to come up with a more representative example should give the student of aging and retirement some pause.

In the wisdom of religion, aging is frequently seen as a transitory stage, as a phase in a process leading to eternal life. The idea of ending, of completion, is

Reprinted and substantially revised by permission from "Unfinished Life Tasks in Retirement," *Proceedings of the Eighth Annual Volunteer Venture Conference,* Connecticut State Department of Health, 1969.

thus avoided and the idea of an endless process affirmed. In the secular perspective, the idea of process also opens up more realistic, more meaningful, and, ultimately, more gratifying aspects for the later stages of life rather than the concept of completion. When life is seen as a process, life tasks remain persistent motives and supportive guideposts of the human existence. They furnish energy as well as direction on the conscious as well as on the unconscious level.

Life tasks are never completed. They see the person through to the end. As a matter of fact, our current society forces most of us to live without the experience of completion. Americans are a busy people. This can be seen in the fact that most American men do more than one job. From the Supreme Court judge, whose right to accept speaking engagements is now questioned, to the garage mechanic who takes on a few gardening jobs for the weekend, moonlighting is a regular aspect of earning a living. From the woman whose name appears in the Social Register and who needs a secretary to run the parties which she thinks she has to give, to the ADC mother who cannot fit waiting time at a clinic into the multiplicity of chores required in running a household with too many children, every woman in the United States, barring a few exceptions, is too busy and overscheduled. If the overdemand on her time should subside because all her children have attained school age, she frequently has to recreate it in community work, education for a second career, or hobbies.

Our high standard of living produces, in many instances, such an accumulation of possessions that their maintenance and care alone represents a life task. Under such conditions, it is almost impossible to attain retirement stage without a backlog of uncompleted tasks.

Marriage after retirement may renew demands which have been left unfulfilled under the pressures and exhaustion of one or two working lives. Friendships that one has not cultivated enough may still be available for revival and intensification, church attendance which one has let slide may become a new source of comfort or, at least, a new source of superego pleasure. There are books that one always wanted to read but never found the time to do so, there are cities that one has not seen, flowers which one has not grown, tears in clothing that one has not mended. All this leaves the whole realm of unconscious motivation still untouched.

Unconscious thought, although frequently disturbing, can also become socially useful and give meaning to life in retirement if one finds for it a socially acceptable outlet and accepts the child within oneself. Whether one wants to please one's mother at the age of sixty-five or to compete with one's brother at the age of seventy-two; whether one wants to play with trains at the age of eighty-three or express an anal arrest in gardening; play the stock market or learn how to do pottery, as long as nobody is hurt and as long as one can accept these longings in one's self, unconscious motivation will remain a source of meaning and aid in the use of time in retirement.

Many uncompleted life tasks require human interaction, meaningful encounters, or at least repeated contacts with service and sales people. It is difficult to visualize, therefore, how loneliness and an empty life can come about in old age unless it has been predetermined by alienating people before retirement and by nonresponsiveness to the stimulation and challenges which life in modern civilization so abundantly provides. Jeremy Tunstall, an English sociologist, studied a random sample of persons age 65 and over and found only 9 per cent to declare themselves as often lonely and 25 per cent as sometimes lonely, permitting him to speak of an "alone minority." [2]

One of the most important uncompleted life tasks to which aging people must address themselves is learning a practice of recreation which is not the counterpoint to gainful work. A retired business executive who owned a ranch in California which was a little paradise, once made this point by saying that it was one thing to come to this ranch for a weekend after five days in the office downtown and a completely different thing to live on the ranch seven days a week. [3]

Recreation means to create anew or to create something which has been lost. Re-creating that part of the self which has been depleted in gainful work is something that we practice every evening and every weekend. This, however, is not the recreation of the retired person. To make recreation meaningful for him we have to give the concept two different dimensions, one larger and one smaller than the one to which we are normally accustomed. The longer dimension has the perspective of a life span. We want to re-create the self that has been depleted by a lifetime of employment. The smaller dimension is the re-creation of the aging self that has been depleted by the demands of everyday living such as fixing breakfast, cleaning the apartment, going to a clinic for a checkup, going to the bank to deposit checks, going to the supermarket to shop.

What younger people frequently overlook is the meaning of wisdom and the meaning of fatigue. Wisdom means having a larger perspective. Fatigue in the aged means the need for recreation two or three times a day. People who are trained to think of recreation in terms of arts and crafts, listening to music, learning new skills, gardening, etc. have not yet experienced the re-creation which comes from recuperation after exertion, resting after fatigue. To learn these things is one of the never-finished life tasks of the aged.

Old age has been called "second childhood." Although the phrase is frequently used to express a negative judgment, it is perfectly possible that in the wisdom of Shakespeare, to whom we owe this phrase, it really refers to a person to whom old age has given an opportunity to express interests which he has maintained since childhood and which permits him to revisit his youth toward the end of his physiological existence. "Second childhood" in that sense may be an important means of avoiding fears of death and existential anxiety. [4] It gives the man with little future a renewed grip on his past. For this reason, social workers and psychiatrists have found that reminiscing gives older patients and clients a significant chance of recovery from morbid disengagement. [5] For this leads us into the problem of role theory with regard to living after retirement. As is widely known, there are three types of such theories. The disengagement theory proposed by Elaine Cummings and William E. Henry, [6] the social adjustment theory of Robert J. Havighurst, [7] and the "new role" theory or "activity within disengagement" theory formulated by Gordon F. Streib and Clement J. Schneider. [8]

According to the disengagement theory, both the individual and society demand that social roles in aging be discontinued, that social contacts be decreased and that the life space of the individual become smaller. Mutual withdrawal is inevitable although not necessarily synchronized and results in decreased interaction between older people and their younger associates. If individual and social expectations of disengagement coincide, disengagement is likely to be successful. If there is conflict between society and the individual about disengagement, there will be dissatisfaction both on the part of the individual and his associates and demoralization and alienation are likely to result.

It is not sufficiently stressed in this theory that disengagement is a means of life maintenance for the individual and of effectiveness maintenance for society. Physical energy declines with age, the body and brain of an aging person cannot support the full load of activity that he carried in middle years. As was pointed out by C. K. Yang[9] for China, in which the traditional prestige of the aged was probably stronger than it ever was in Western civilization, rapid social change and great technological advances make obsolescence in occupational and professional skills an unavoidable by-product of the aging process. Continued employment of obsolete personnel produces just as much of a strain on societal functioning as overload and over-demand puts upon the individual aging organism. Disengagement is, therefore, to be seen as an adaptive role change and as an opportunity for the performance of new roles and activity within disengagement. To learn disengagement skills and disengagement attitudes is, in and by itself, an unfinished life task which will occupy people in retirement whether they want it or not.

People who are active in a wide variety of social roles are likely to have a large number of options for partial disengagement and for gradual disengagement than people whose life space has been structured in terms of only very few social roles. Important to note is also the impact of modern medicine on the role set of the aged. Frequent check-ups, isometric exercises to control hypertension, finger exercises in arthritis, hydrotherapy, and sustaining contacts with physicians facilitated by Medicare, have the making of a geriatric sick role which older people are beginning to find meaningful, time-consuming, and moving into the center of their life space.

In the social adjustment theory the assumption is usually made, but not expressly stated, that older persons maintain a desire for role continuation and interactions without change. It is assumed that old people remain, in vitality and attitude towards others, the same people which they were in their forties. Energy is assumed to remain constant but requiring redistribution when retirement closes customary outlets by taking the work role away. In consequence, it is felt that role flexibility is a requirement of successful social adjustment in old age.

Perhaps more important than the new life tasks of disengagement and role flexibility are tasks of reorientation which accompany the last stages of the life cycle. These tasks of reorientation follow roughly three directions and have been searchingly and beautifully elucidated by Robert Peck[10] who presents them under the following headings:

Ego Differentiation vs. Work Role Preoccupation
Body Transcendence vs. Body Preoccupation
Ego Transcendence vs. Ego Preoccupation

After retirement an individual can and probably must be able to assess his self-image and his meaning to others in terms separate from the work that he did before retirement. If he cannot do that, retirement approaches psychological and social dying. A person must retain or acquire sufficient activities different from those which composed his work role, in order to be able to love himself and be

rs in spite of the fact that he does not go to the office or the shop
: must be able to consider himself a worthwhile person in spite of his
me and must, therefore, be able to assess himself separately from
f money that he now receives.

ie need to separate one's self-perspective from work and income, it is
an unfulfilled life task in old age to learn to live with chronic diseases, with declining vitality, and with the nearness of physical death. Decline in such perceptive powers as hearing, vision, and the sense of smell parallel the appearance of
such recurring pains as the proverbial backache, rheumatic pains, and lesions in
skin texture. He who anchors his self-image in his physical appearance, in his
bodily well-being, and in his fantasies of immortality, is likely to have a miserable
old age.

Ultimately, he who is concerned with himself more than with others is betting
on a losing proposition. The basis of his existence is slipping away from him, the
returns from himself as a place for his investment are likely to be diminishing and
he will have to end in existential despair because life inevitably runs its course
away from him. He, however, who puts his concerns and investments into others
will be fortified against losing himself because others, people, issues, and ideas,
are likely to survive him and if he connects his existence with them, he will have
attained a measure of immortality.

In sum total, the unfinished life tasks of the aged person represent a system of
morality, of conduct norms, and think work which, if the aged learn to practice it,
will make it easier for a younger person to face aging. That is the ultimate meaning of unfinished life tasks in old age and the one most likely to bring results.

Such a morality, which is altruistic and in a very distinctive sense parental,
is not fully spelled out in our society. The development of such a morality in
detail will be, at least in part, the task of the helper. The development will probably have to occur on a case-by-case basis. Like all morality, it will imply control
of impulse in the service of a long-range goal. Helping older people to develop a
conduct of life which is not only good for them but also good for their younger
associates, particularly their children who very soon may brush against the experience of aging and retirement themselves, is a matter of social urgency. It is
likely to give volunteers and professionals a very significant part in the continued
development of our civilization and a challenge which may well compensate for
the unavoidable anxieties which serving the aged frequently stimulates.

Any task of helping, whether it be volunteer effort or professional intervention,
works with criteria of success. The helper wants to see improvement in the person
to be helped. Frequently we equate such improvement with happiness. This is a
dangerous criterion which is likely to disappoint the helper.

Successful aging, like any other successful developmental phase, cannot be
equated with happiness. Development always means loss as well as attainment.
The toddler loses the unconditioned care of the mother but gains a measure of
independence, mobility in space, and the power of initiative in playing, in association with other children, and in the management of his own body. The adolescent loses the relative peace and equanimity of the latency period while attaining
the power of sexuality, choice of occupation, and of being heard on social issues.
The adult loses the freedom of experimentation granted to the adolescent, but
gains the experiences of marriage, of income, of parenthood. Similarly the aging

person loses reproductive powers, income, structure for the use of his time, and the status of employment. He gains, however, freedom of choices, freedom from excessive demands on his vitality, freedom to pursue interests without competitive claims on his time, and freedom from the tribulations and burdens of child-rearing.

Happiness is an evaluative experience which depends on the circumstances of the individual in relation to his needs. He who helps people to respond adequately to the challenge of a new phase of development will always encounter ambivalence unless the individual operates with the mechanism of denial. It is important, therefore to arrive at a definition of successful aging where the unhappiness over loss is compensated for by happiness over gains. It is in this respect that encouragement and assistance in pursuit of unfulfilled life tasks will help the aged.

Notes

1. Erik H. Erikson, *Childhood and Society* (New York: Norton, 1950), p. 232.
2. Jeremy Tunstall, *Old and Alone* (London: Routledge and Kegan Paul, 1966), p. 3.
3. Otto Pollak, *Positive Experiences in Retirement,* Pension Research Council (Homewood, Ill.: Richard D. Irwin, 1957), p. 39.
4. Jacques Choron, *Modern Man and Mortality* (New York: Macmillan, 1964), p. 153.
5. Judith Liton and Sara C. Olstein, "Therapeutic Aspects of Reminiscence," *Social Casework,* vol. 50, no. 5 (May 1969): 263–268.
6. Elaine Cumming and William E. Henry, *Growing Old* (New York: Basic Books, 1961), p. 293.
7. Robert J. Havighurst, "Flexibility and the Social Roles of the Retired," *American Journal of Sociology,* LIX (1954), pp. 309–311.
8. Gordon F. Streib and Clement J. Schneider, *Retirement in American Society* (Ithaca and London, Cornell University Press, 1971), pp. 171–191.
9. C. K. Yang, "Crumbling of the Age Hierarchy," *The Chinese Family in the Communist Revolution* (Cambridge, Mass.: Technology Press of M.I.T. and Harvard University Press, 1959), pp. 86–104.
10. Robert Peck, "Psychological Developments in the Second Half of Life," *Psychological Aspects of Aging,* ed. John E. Anderson (Washington, D.C.: American Psychological Association, 1956), pp. 42–53.

II

Patterning of Personality

3

CULTURAL CONDITIONING

Culture was defined in the Introduction as that vast storehouse of language, knowledge, values, and customs which provides people with a design for living and is transmitted across generations in human groups. Values, which may be considered the basic building blocks of culture, may be defined as formulations and selections of what is considered desirable in any society. Thus, values represent more than just criteria for choosing between alternative goals or courses of action; values define the very nature of the goals or courses of action from which the individual might choose.

If meaning depends upon the existence of a set of consensually validated symbols, then individuals can only interact meaningfully after they learn the symbols of interaction (for example, language, object referents) shared by others in their society. It is therefore essential that human beings internalize the fundamental categories of perception and affect shared by members of their society in the process of primary socialization before they can think, feel, and act like people.

In this sense, the culture internalized by the individual functions like a special set of lenses, focusing on those aspects of any situation which have been defined as meaningful and excluding those which haven't. Only through this special set of lenses can the myriad sensory impressions received by the organism be screened, organized, and transformed into cognitive perceptions. This means, of course, that culture also functions like a set of blinders, obscuring or completely ignoring aspects of the total reality which have not been defined as meaningful by one's own society, but might well be by other societies.

This unique and characteristic faculty of human beings for acquiring culture distinguishes them from all the other animals and enables only people to act intelligently, to draw on the distilled experiences of those before them and to apply proven solutions to conventional problems. At the same time, this faculty of human beings for acquiring culture enables only people to act stupidly; to fail

69

to perceive the uniqueness of a situation and to attempt to apply conventional solutions to novel problems. Other animals act instinctively, which sometimes results in their destruction, but they could never be said to act stupidly. People can act stupidly because their commitment to certain cultural values ofen prevents them from learning different interpretations of and devising new modes of response to the reality they encounter even when the learning of such responses is obviously within the intellectual capacity of human beings.

In the same way, culture can be thought of as both potentiating and constraining the individual. Culture may provide people with the means to develop capabilities and achieve experiences which would not otherwise be possible. However, it may also restrain the development of certain capabilities and prevent people from achieving certain experiences regardless of the consequences for the individual. In short, it may cultivate (as with certain finer aesthetic experiences) or it may control (as with the suppression of certain sensibilities defined as threatening to the maintenance of order within the group).

Cultural Variations in Nonverbal Behavior

Although their reasoning processes may be identical, the concept of different cultures implies that people make deductions from different sets of learned basic assumptions about the world. And, as Weston LaBarre illustrates in the first article, these value assumptions are not only learned and expressed verbally, but extend into the realm of posture, gestures, and general bodily movement. The anthropologist Edward Hall has devoted two books to the examination of how basic perceptions and uses of time and space, the "silent languages" and "hidden dimensions" of experience, vary markedly between cultures.

Both Hall's books are filled with unusual insights into the largely subconscious definitions of time and space which characterize different cultures. Many Americans know that we have a more elaborate and binding sense of time than people in most other cultures. It may be less obvious how radically our culturally patterned sense of space may vary from that of other cultures. Hall (1959, p. 164) gives one illustration:

> In Latin America the interaction distance is much less than it is in the United States. Indeed, people cannot talk comfortably with one another unless they are very close to the distance that evokes either sexual or hostile feelings in the North American. The result is that when they move close, we withdraw and back away. As a consequence, they think we are distant and cold, withdrawn and unfriendly. We, on the other hand, are constantly accusing them of breathing down our necks, crowding us, and spraying our faces.

Even attitudes toward the use of the basic senses are culturally determined. Among Arabs, for example, olfaction plays a much more prominent part in interpersonal relations than among Americans. Hall (1969, pp. 159–60) explains:

> To the Arab good smells are pleasing and a way of being involved with each other. To smell one's friends is not only nice but desirable, for to

deny him your breath is to act ashamed. Americans, on the other hand, trained as they are not to breathe in people's faces, automatically communicate shame in trying to be polite.

One implication of this is that effective cross-cultural communication can be unintentionally undermined by mutual ignorance of the nature and extent to which behavior is culturally patterned. Another is that even the development of basic sensory perception is a function of cultural values. Extending this theme, Hall (1969, p. 81) states that art is "a system of communication which is historically linked with language." This point rests on the assertion that "vision is not passive but active, in fact, a transaction between man and his environment in which both participate" (p. 82). In his popular book, *Understanding Media: The Extensions of Man* (1965), Marshall McLuhan provides an interesting illustration of this phenomenon. According to McLuhan, observations of Nigerian students at American Universities have demonstrated that, like medieval man, they do not perceive space as something homogeneous, containing various objects. For them, each thing makes its own space. Consequently, they are unable to predict in which direction an object in sunshine will cast a shadow, since this requires a three-dimensional perspective in which sun, object, and observer are related rather than independent.

Cultural Variations in Abnormal Behavior

Just as different cultures provide their own solutions to problems encountered by group members, so do different cultures create their own problems for group members. As normal behavior tends to vary characteristically according to culture, so does abnormal or pathological behavior tend to vary characteristically according to culture.

In his study of mental disorder in the Philippines, Sechcrest (1963, p. 201) states that all cases appear to be "exaggerations of tendencies prevalent in the culture." According to Sechcrest's analysis, the extremely high rate of homicide in the Philippines (over six times that of the United States and almost forty times that of England) represents an exaggerated form of such culturally patterned personality factors as the tendency to blame others for failure or misfortune (based on a fatalistic orientation toward life), low impulse control (as a result of high group dependence and the use of shame rather than guilt as the primary means of social control), weak self-esteem, an exaggerated concern for public face, and the all-or-nothing character of aggression (caused by the extreme emphasis on interpersonal harmony to protect extended family and barrio cohesion).

Sechcrest also found that extreme regression, depression, guilt, and delusions of guilt, nihilism, and death were extremely low. The low rate of such regressive behavior as "urinary and bowel incontinence, eating or smearing feces and the like would seem due to the relatively low concern for the acquisition of sphincter control on the part of Filipino mothers." These functions, therefore, do not become charged with any particular emotional significance and are not used as a means of expressing defiance against authorities. As opposed to American patients whose paranoid delusions usually consist of imagined threats from large, faceless organizations like the Communist party or the FBI, Filipino patients, raised in a personalized society, "almost always mention either family members or neighbors as those intending to kill them" (p. 201). Sechcrest explains:

> Perhaps the difference between the "enemies" of the Americans and the Filipinos indicates something about the pressures within the two societies, the American fighting to survive in an impersonal, large society that threatens to deny his existence, but satisfied in having no quarrel with his immediate neighbors; the Filipino little worried about society in general but preoccupied with the question of how to maintain smooth interpersonal relations with those persons living around him (pp. 201–2).

Eaton and Weil (1953) have discovered that, relative to other societies, manic depression is more common than schizophrenia among the Hutterites, a small German sect which migrated from southern Russia and settled in South Dakota between 1874 and 1877, because their social lives are organized around submission to a strong religious community. Consequently, their antisocial and aggressive impulses are effectively repressed, but at the cost of self blame, remorse and psychosomatic symptoms. Schizophrenia, on the other hand, is more prevalent among people living relatively isolated social lives.

Zola's research (1966) has shown that, even within the same city, there may be strong cultural differences between ethnic groups in such things as their perception of symptoms (for example, the location and intensity of pain) and the implications of their illness for their general functioning and interpersonal relations. Thus, not only normality but abnormality — not only health but illness — are determined by the standards and stresses of one's own culture.

Subcultural Variations in Behavior

Variations from the general culture which are themselves institutionalized within certain social aggregates are called "subcultures." Unlike cultures, which may differ qualitatively in their world view, subcultures differ from the general culture primarily in the relative emphasis placed on different values. This divergence manifests itself in relatively different normative expectations with respect to institutional role performance. John Gillin (1955, p. 110) describes the concept of regional subcultures or regionalism in American society as "an 'orchestration of diversity' within a total national cultural unity."

Gillin explains regional differences primarily as differences in the "adaptive and exploitative aspects of culture" which have emerged because of "natural" differences in climate, topography, resources, and the like and historical differences in modes of adaptation to natural conditions. It can be inferred from Gillin's analysis that the magnitude of regional diversity should decline in relation to the degree to which man-made conditions become more salient than natural conditions in the social environment of the nation's people. Moreover, environmental homogenization is mainly a function of the degree of integration in the social structure. As national corporations continue to industrialize the South, one may then expect some decline in traditional North-South cultural differences.

Subcultural variations based on such factors as social class and race may provide members with effective solutions to the special problems which such aggregates face. Individual patterns of attitude and behavior which conform to the established subcultural norms within such aggregates are precisely what is meant by "social personality." Whether none, some, or all these more distinctive patterns are actually internalized in the personality system of the individual, or whether they simply represent relatively self-conscious adaptations to particular structural conditions remains a major controversy among social scientists.

Like cultures, subcultures also tend to produce relatively characteristic forms of abnormality. Hollingshead and Redlich (1958) have demonstrated that rates and types of mental illness tend to vary systematically along class lines even within the same community, just as the norms which define acceptable sexual and aggressive behavior vary between classes.

In the second selection in this chapter, Harold Christensen compares premarital coitus and postmarital infidelity sex norms between students in Denmark and the United States. In his analysis, he uses a sample of Midwestern American students as "representative" of the general culture and a sample of Mormon students representing a distinct subcultural variation of the general American culture. Christensen not only compares sex norms in these different groups, but the rates and consequences of deviations from the norm in an attempt to construct some preliminary formulation of the relationship between the organism's needs and the culture's demands.

References

Eaton, Joseph, and Robert Weil
  1953 *Culture and Mental Disorders.* Glencoe, Ill.: The Free Press.
Gillin, John
  1955 "National and Regional Cultural Values in the United States." *Social Forces* 39 (December):107–13.
Hall, Edward T.
  1959 *The Silent Language.* Greenwich, Conn.: Fawcett.
  1969 *The Hidden Dimension.* Garden City, N. Y.: Doubleday-Anchor.
Hollingshead, August B., and Fredrich C. Redlich
  1958 *Social Class and Mental Illness.* New York: Wiley.
Klineberg, Otto
  1938 "Emotional Expression in Chinese Literature." *The Journal of Abnormal and Social Psychology* (October):517–20.
Kluckhohn, Florence Rockwood
  1958 "Variations in the Basic Values of Family Systems." *Social Casework* 34 (February-March):63–72.
McLuhan, Marshall
  1965 *Understanding Media: The Extensions of Man.* New York: McGraw-Hill.
Mead, Margaret, and Martha Wolfenstein
  1955 *Child Rearing in Contemporary Cultures.* Chicago, Ill.: Phoenix.
Sechcrest, Lee
  1963 "Symptoms of Mental Disorder in the Philippines." *Philippine Sociological Review* 3–4 (July-October):189–206.
Zola, Irving Kenneth
  1966 "Culture and Symptoms — An Analysis of Patients' Presenting Complaints." *American Sociological Review* 31 (October):615–30.

WESTON LA BARRE

The Cultural Basis of Emotions and Gestures

Psychologists have long concerned themselves with the physiological problems of emotion, as for example, whether the psychic state is prior to the physiological changes and causes them, or whether the conscious perception of the inner physiological changes in itself constitutes the "emotion." The physiologists also, notably Cannon, have described the various bodily concomitants of fear, pain, rage, and the like. Not much attention, however, has been directed toward another potential dimension of meaning in the field of emotions, that is to say the *cultural* dimension.

The anthropologist is wary of those who speak of an "instinctive" gesture on the part of a human being. One important reason is that a sensitivity to meanings which are culturally different from his own stereotypes may on occasion be crucial for the anthropologist's own physical survival among at least some groups he studies, and he must at the very least be a student of this area of symbolism if he would avoid embarrassment.[1] He cannot safely rely upon his own culturally subjective understandings of emotional expression in his relations with persons of another tribe. The advisability and the value of a correct reading of any cultural symbolism whatsoever have alerted him to the possibility of culturally arbitrary, quasilinguistic (that is, noninstinctual but learned and purely agreed-upon) meanings in the behavior he observes.

A rocking of the skull forward and backward upon its condyles, which rest on the atlas vertebra, as an indication of affirmation and the rotation upon the axis vertebra for negation have so far been accepted as "natural" and "instinctive" gestures that one psychologist at least [2] has sought an explanation of the supposedly universal phenomenon in ascribing the motions of "yes" to the infant's seeking of the mother's breast, and "no" to its avoidance and refusal of the breast. This is ingenious, but it is arguing without one's host, since the phenomenon to be explained is by no means as widespread ethnologically, even among humans, as is mammalian behavior biologically.

Indeed, the Orient alone is rich in alternatives. Among the Ainu of northern Japan, for example, our particular head noddings are unknown:

> the right hand is usually used in negation, passing from right to left and back in front of the chest; and both hands are gracefully brought up to the chest and gracefully waved downwards — palms upwards — in sign of affirmation.[3]

The Semang, pygmy Negroes of interior Malaya, thrust the head sharply forward for "yes" and cast the eyes down for "no." [4]

> The Abyssinians say "no" by jerking the head to the right shoulder, and "yes" by throwing the head back and raising the eyebrows. The Dyaks of Borneo raise their eyebrows to mean "yes" and contract them slightly to mean "no." The Maori say "yes" by raising the head and chin: the Sicilians say "no" in exactly the same manner.[5]

A Bengali servant in Calcutta rocks his head rapidly in an arc from shoulder to shoulder, usually four times, in assent; in Delhi a Moslem boy throws his head diagonally backward with a slight turning of the neck for the same purpose; and the Kandyan Singhalese bends the head diagonally forward toward the right, with an indescribably graceful turning in of the chin, often accompanying this with a cross-legged curtsey, arms partly crossed, palms upward — the whole performance extraordinarily beautiful and ingratiating. Indeed, did my own cultural difference not tell me it already, I would know that the Singhalese manner of receiving an object (with the right hand, the left palm supporting the right elbow) is not instinctive, for I have seen a Singhalese mother *teaching* her little boy to do this when I gave him a chunk of palm-tree sugar. I only regretted, later, that my own manners must have seemed boorish or subhuman, since I handed it to him with my right hand, instead of with both, as would any courteous Singhalese. Alas, if I handed it to a little Moslem beggar in Sind or the Punjab with my *left* hand, he would probably have dashed the gift to the ground, spat, and called me by the name of an animal whose flesh he had been taught to dislike, but which I have not — for such use of the left hand would be insulting, since it is supposed to be confined to attending to personal functions, while the right hand is the only proper one for food.

Those persons with a passion for easy dominance, the professional dog-lovers, must often be exasperated at the stupidity of a dog which does not respond to so obvious a command as the pointed forefinger. The defense of man's best friend might be that this "instinctively" human gesture does not correspond to the kinaesthesias of a nonhanded animal. Nevertheless, even for an intelligent human baby, at the exact period when he is busily using the forefinger in exploring the world, "pointing" by an adult is an arbitrary, sublinguistic gesture which is not automatically understood and which must be *taught*. I am the less inclined to berate the obtuseness to the obvious of either dog or baby, because of an early field experience of my own. One day I asked a favorite informant of mine among the Kiowa, old Mary Buffalo, where something was in the *ramada* or willow-branch "shade" where we were working. It was clear she had heard me, for her eighty-eight-year-old ears were by no means deaf; but she kept on busying both hands with her work. I wondered at her rudeness and repeated the request several times, until finally with a puzzled exasperation which matched my own, she dropped her work and fetched it for me from in plain sight: she had been repeatedly pointing with her lips in approved American Indian fashion, as any Caucasian numbskull should have been able to see.

Some time afterward I asked a somewhat naive question of a very great anthropologist, the late Edward Sapir: "Do other tribes cry and laugh as we do?" In appropriate response, Sapir himself laughed, but with an instant grasping of the point of the question: In which of these things are men alike everywhere, in which different? Where are the international boundaries between physiology and culture? What are the extremes of variability, and what are the scope and range of cultural differences in emotional and gestural expression? Probably one of the most learned linguists who have ever lived, Sapir was extremely sensitive to emotional and sublinguistic gestures — an area of deep illiteracy for most "Anglo-Saxon" Americans — and my present interest was founded on our conversation at that time.

Smiling, indeed, I have found may almost be mapped after the fashion of any other culture trait; and laughter is in some senses a geographic variable. On a map of the Southwest Pacific one could perhaps even draw lines between areas of "Papuan hilarity" and others where a Dobuan, Melanesian dourness reigned. In Africa, Gorer noted that

> laughter is used by the negro to express surprise, wonder, embarrassment and even discomfiture; it is not necessarily, or even often a sign of amusement; the significance given to "black laughter" is due to a mistake of supposing that similar symbols have identical meanings.[6]

Thus it is that even if the physiological behavior be present, its cultural and emotional functions may differ. Indeed, even within the same culture, the laughter of adolescent girls and the laughter of corporation presidents can be functionally different things; so too the laughter of an American Negro and that of the white he addresses.

The behaviorist Holt "physiologized" the smile as being ontogenetically the relaxation of the muscles of the face in a baby replete from nursing. Explanations of this order may well be the case, if the phenomenon of the smile is truly a physiological expression of generalized pleasure, which is caught up later in ever more complex conditioned reflexes. And yet, even in its basis here, I am not sure that this is the whole story: for the "smile" of a child in its sleep is certainly in at least some cases the grimace of *pain* from colic, rather than the relaxation of pleasure. Other explanations such as that the smile is *phylogenetically* a snarl suffer from much the same *ad hoc* quality.

Klineberg writes:

> It is quite possible, however, that a smile or a laugh may have a different meaning for groups other than our own. Lafcadio Hearn has remarked that the Japanese smile is not necessarily a spontaneous expression of amusement, but a law of etiquette, elaborated and cultivated from early times. It is a silent language, often seemingly inexplicable to Europeans, and it may arouse violent anger in them as a consequence. The Japanese child is taught to smile as a social duty, just as he is taught to bow or prostrate himself; he must always show an appearance of happiness to avoid inflicting his sorrow upon his friends. The story is told of a woman servant who smilingly asked her mistress if she might go to her husband's funeral. Later she returned with his ashes in a vase and said, actually laughing, "Here is my husband." Her White mistress regarded her as a cynical creature; Hearn suggests that this may have been pure heroism.[7]

Many in fact of these motor habits in one culture are open to grave misunderstanding in another. The Copper Eskimo welcome strangers with a buffet on the head or shoulders with the fist, while the northwest Amazonians slap one another on the back in greeting. Polynesian men greet each other by embracing and rubbing each other's back; Spanish-American males greet one another by a stereotyped embrace, head over right shoulder of the partner, three pats on the back, head over reciprocal left shoulder, three more pats. In the Torres Straits islands "the old form of greeting was to bend slightly the fingers of the right hand, hook them with those of the person greeted, and then draw them away so as to scratch the palm of the hand; this is repeated several times." [8] The Ainu of Yezo have a peculiar greeting; on the occasion of a man meeting his sister, "The man held the woman's hands for a few seconds, then suddenly releasing his hold, grasped her by both ears and uttered the Aino cry. Then they stroked one another down the face and shoulders." [9] Kayan males in Borneo embrace or grasp each other by the forearm, while a host throws his arm over the shoulder of a guest and strokes him endearingly with the palm of his hand. When two Kurd males meet, "they grasp each other's right hand, which they simultaneously raise, and each kisses the hand of the other." [10] Among the Andaman Islanders of the Gulf of Bengal:

> When two friends or relatives meet who have been separated from each other for a few weeks or longer, they greet each other by sitting down, one on the lap of the other, with their arms around each other's necks, and weeping or wailing for two or three minutes till they are tired. Two brothers greet each other in this way, and so do father and son, mother and daughter, and husband and wife. When husband and wife meet, it is the man who sits in the lap of the woman. When two friends part from one another, one of them lifts up the hand of the other towards his mouth and gently blows on it. [11]

Some of these expressions of "joy" seem more lugubrious than otherwise. One old voyager, John Turnbull, writes as follows:

> The arrival of a ship brings them to the scene of action from far and near. Many of them meet at Matavai who have not seen each other for some length of time. The ceremony of these meetings is not without singularity; taking a shark's tooth, they strike it into their head and temples with great violence, so as to produce a copious bleeding; and this they will repeat, till they become clotted with blood and gore.

The honest mariner confesses to be nonplussed at this behavior.

> I cannot explain the origin of this custom nor its analogy with what it is intended to express. It has no other meaning with them than to express the excess of their joy. By what construction it is considered symbolical of this emotion I do not understand. [12]

Quite possibly, then, the weeping of an American woman "because she is so happy" may merely indicate that the poverty of our gamut of physiological responses is such as to require using the same response for opposite meanings. Certainly weeping does not obey social stereotypes in other cultures. Consider old Mary Buffalo at her brother's funeral: she wept in a frenzy, tore her hair, scratched her cheeks, and even tried to jump into the grave (being conveniently restrained from this by remoter relatives). I happened to know that she had not seen her brother for some time, and there was no particular love lost between them: she was merely carrying on the way a decent woman should among the Kiowa. Away from the grave, she was immediately chatting vivaciously about some other topic. Weeping is *used* differently among the Kiowa. Any stereotypes I may have had about the strong and silent American Indian, whose speech is limited to an infrequent "ugh" and whose stoicism to pain is limitless, were once rudely shattered in a public religious meeting. A great burly Wichita Indian who had come with me to a peyote meeting, after a word with the leader which I did not understand (it was probably permission to take his turn in a prayer) suddenly burst out blubbering with an abandon which no Occidental male adult would permit himself in public. In time I learned that this was a stereotyped approach to the supernatural powers, enthusiastic weeping to indicate that he was powerless as a child, to invoke their pity, and to beseech their gift of medicine power. Everyone in the tipi understood this except me.

So much for the expression of emotion in one culture, which is open to serious misinterpretation in another: there is no "natural" language of emotional gesture. To return a moment to the earlier topic of emotional expression in greetings: West Africans in particular have developed highly the ritual gestures and language of greeting. What Gorer says of the Wolof would stand for many another tribe:

> The gestures and language of polite intercourse are stylized and graceful; a greeting is a formal litany of question and answer embracing everyone and everything connected with the two people meeting (the questions are merely formal and a dying person is stated to be in good health so as not to break the rhythm of the responses) and continuing for several minutes; women accompany it with a swaying movement of the body; with people to whom a special deference is due the formula is resumed several times during the conversation; saying goodbye is equally elaborate.[13]

But here the sublinguistic gesture language has clearly emerged into pure formalisms of language which are quite plainly cultural.

The allegedly "instinctive" nature of such motor habits in personal relationships is difficult to maintain in the face of the fact that in many cases the same gesture means exactly opposite, or incommensurable things, in different cultures. Hissing in Japan is a polite deference to social superiors; the Basuto applaud by hissing, but in England hissing is rude and public disapprobation of an actor or a speaker. Spitting in very many parts of the world is a sign of utmost contempt; and yet among the Masai of Africa it is a sign of affection and benediction, while the spitting of an American Indian medicine man upon a patient is one of the kindly offices of the curer. Urination upon another (as in a famous case at the Sands Point, Long Island, country club, involving a congressman since assassinated) is a grave insult among Occidentals, but it is part of the transfer of power from an African medicine man in initiations and curing rituals. As for other opposite meanings, Western man stands up in the presence of a superior; the Fijians and the Tongans sit down. In some contexts we put on more clothes as a sign of respect; the Friendly Islanders take them off. The Toda of South India raise the open right hand to the face, with the thumb on the bridge of the nose, to express respect; a gesture almost identical among Europeans is an obscene expression of extreme disrespect. Placing to the tip of the nose the projecting knuckle of the right forefinger bent at the second joint was among the Maori of New Zealand a sign of friendship and often of protection;[14] but in eighteenth-century England the placing of the same forefinger to the right side of the nose expressed dubiousness about the intelligence and sanity of a speaker — much as does the twentieth-century clockwise motion of the forefinger above the right hemisphere of the head. The sticking out of the tongue among Europeans (often at the same time "making a face") is an insulting, almost obscene act of provocative challenge and mocking contempt for the adversary, so undignified as to be used only by children; so long as Maya writing remains undeciphered we do not know the meaning of the exposure of the tongue in some religious sculptures of the gods, but we can be sure it scarcely has the same significance as with us. In Bengali statues of the dread black mother goddess Kali, the tongue is protruded to signify great raging anger and shock; but the Chinese of the Sung dynasty protruded the tongue playfully to pretend to mock terror, as if to "make fun of" the ridiculous and unfeared anger of another person.[15] Modern Chinese, in South China at least, protrude the tongue for a moment and then retract it, to express embarrassment at a *faux pas*.

Kissing, as is well known, is in the Orient an act of private loveplay and arouses only disgust when indulged in publicly: in Japan it is necessary to censor out the major portion of love scenes in American-made movies for this reason. Correspondingly, some of the old *kagura* dances of the Japanese strike Occidentals as revolting overt obscenities, yet it is doubtful if they arouse this response in Japanese onlookers. Manchu kissing is purely a private sexual act, and though husband and wife or lovers might kiss each other, they would do it stealthily since it is shameful to do in public; yet Manchu mothers have the pattern of putting the penis of the baby boy into their mouths, a practice which probably shocks Westerners even more than kissing in public shocks the Manchu.[16] Tapuya men in South America kiss as a sign of peace, but men do not kiss women because the latter wear labrets or lip plugs. Nose-rubbing is Eskimo and Polynesian, and the Djuka Negroes of Surinam[17] show pleasure at a particularly interesting or amusing dance step by embracing the dancer and touching cheek to cheek, now on one side, now on the other — which is the identical attenuation of the "social kiss" between American women who do not wish to spoil each other's makeup.

In the language of gesture all over the world there are varying mixtures of the physiologically conditioned response and the purely cultural one, and it is frequently difficult to analyze out and segregate the two. The Chukchee of Siberia, for example, have a phenomenal quickness to anger, which they express by showing the teeth and growling like an animal — yet man's snout has long ceased being functionally useful in offensive or defensive biting as it has phylogenetically and continuously retreated from effective prognathism. But this behavior reappears again and again: the Malayan pagans, for example, raise the lip over the canine tooth when sneering and jeering. Is this instinctual reflex or mere motor habit? The Tasmanians stamped rapidly on the ground to express surprise or pleasure; Occidentals beat the palms of their hands together for the same purpose ordinarily, but in some rowdier contexts this is accompanied by whistling and a similar stamping of the feet. Europeans "snort" with contempt; and the non-Mohammedan primitives of interior Malaya express disgust with a sudden expiration of the breath. In this particular instance, it is difficult to rid oneself of the notion that this is a consciously controlled act, to be sure, but nevertheless at least a "symbolic sneeze" based upon a purely physiological reflex which does rid the nostrils of irritating matter. The favorite gesture of contempt of the Menomini Indians of Wisconsin — raising the clenched fist palm down up to the level of the mouth, then bringing it swiftly downwards, throwing forth the thumb and first two fingers — would seem to be based on the same "instinctual" notion of rejection.

Notes

1. The notorious Massey murder in Hawaii arose from the fact that a native beach boy perhaps understandably mistook the Occidental "flirting" of a white woman for a *bona fide* sexual invitation. On the other hand, there are known cases which have ended in the death of American ethnographers who misread the cultural signs while in the field.
2. E. B. Holt, *Animal drive and the learning process* (New York, 1931), p. 111, and personal conversations.
    The idea is originally Darwin's, I believe (Charles Darwin, *The expression of the emotions in man and animals,* New York, 1873) but he himself pointed out that the lateral shake of the head is by no means universally the sign of negation. . . .
3. A. H. Landor, *Alone with the Hairy Ainu* (London, 1893), pp. 6, 233–234.
4. W. W. Skeat and C. O. Blagden, *Pagan races of the Malay Peninsula* (London, 1906; 2 vols).
5. Otto Klineberg, *Race differences* (New York, 1935), p. 282.
6. Geoffrey Gorer, *Africa dances* (New York, 1935), p. 10.
7. Lafcadio Hearn, The Japanese smile, in *Glimpses of unfamiliar Japan* (New York, 1894; 2 vols.), quoted in Klineberg, op. cit.
8. *Report on the Cambridge expedition to the Torres Straits,* ed. A. C. Haddon (Cambridge, 1904; 5 vols.), IV, p. 306; Thomas Whiffen, *The North West Amazons* (London, 1905), p. 259.
9. R. Hitchcock, The Ainos of Yezo, in *Papers on Japan,* pp. 464–465. See also Landor, op. cit., pp. 6, 233–234.
10. J. Perkins, Journal of a tour from Oroomish to Mosul, through the Koordish Mountains, and a visit to the ruins of Nineveh, *Journal of the American Oriental Society,* 1851, *2*, 101; Charles Hose & William MacDougall. *The pagan tribes of Borneo* (London, 1912; 2 vols.), *1*, 124–125.
11. A. R. Radcliffe-Brown, *The Andaman Islanders* (Cambridge, 1922), p. 117 and p. 74, n. 1.
12. John Turnbull, *A voyage round the world* (London, 1813), pp. 301–302.
13. Gorer, op. cit., p. 38. Cf. Hollis, *The Masai, their language and folklore* (Oxford, 1905), pp. 284–287; E. Torday & T. A. Joyce, *Notes ethnographiques sur les peuples communément appelés Bakuba, ainsi que sur les peuplades apparentées, les Bushonga* (Brussels, 1910), pp. 233–234, 284, et passim. West Africans have developed the etiquette and protocol of greeting to a high degree, adjusting it to sex, age, relative rank, relationship degrees, and the like. Probably there is more than a trace of this ceremoniousness surviving in American Negro greetings in the South.
14. Klineberg, op. cit., pp. 286–287, citing J. Lubbock, *Prehistoric times* (New York, 1872); E. Best, *The Maori* (Wellington [N. Z.], 1924, 2 vols.); R. H. Lowie, *Are we civilized?* (New York, 1929); and A. C. Hollis, *The Masai, their language and folklore* (Oxford, 1905), p. 315.
15. *Chin P'ing Mei* (Shanghai, n. d.), Introduction by Arthur Waley. The sixteenth-century Chinese also had the expressions to act "with seven hands and eight feet" for awkwardness, and "to sweat two handfuls of anxiety."
16. S. M. Shirokogoroff, *Social organization of the Manchus* (Extra Vol. III, North China Branch, Royal Asiatic Society, Shanghai, 1924), pp. 122–123.
17. M. C. Kahn, Notes on the Saramaccaner Bush Negroes of Dutch Guiana, *Amer. Anthrop.,* 1929, *31,* 473.

HAROLD T. CHRISTENSEN

Scandinavian and American Sex Norms: Some Comparisons, with Sociological Implications

It is the fashion these days for popular writers to exploit the subject of sex, due to the intrinsic interest it holds. Perhaps partly as a reaction against this kind of sensational journalism, certain academicians tend to look down their noses at colleagues who deal with sex as a subject of professional interest. Nevertheless, no social scientist worth his salt is willing to be greatly influenced by either type of pressure: to jump on the bandwagon for the sake of popularity, or to dodge real issues at stake in order to protect his image. Science, almost by definition requires its workers to pursue all available data that are relevant to the solutions of their research problems, and, secondly, to keep their generalizations within the limits of their data. When the scientist goes beyond his data, as he sometimes must, it is proper that his pronouncements be labeled something like "speculations" or "interpretations."

This paper uses the scientific frame of reference to analyze the subject of sex viewed in cross-cultural perspective. Sex is a sensitive phenomenon, not only in the public view, but also as a research focus for pointing up differences across cultures. This latter fact was a major consideration in selecting it as the substantive side of a project which sought to compare normative systems.[1] The analysis to follow draws upon the writer's cross-cultural research in recent years (see reference list, items 5 through 13); but it differs from the previous articles in that this is more a discussion of issues than a formal reporting of research. It therefore attempts to interpret the generalizations in terms of dominant issues which are of social import.[2]

The concern here moves beyond sexual understanding at the descriptive level, though that too is important in its own right. The concern also transcends simple juxtaposition of the sexual cultures of several societies; as interesting as that would be, the presentation would still remain at the level of description, and, if the reader were left there, he might be tempted to ask, "so what?" Relationships among factors must be tested, most especially the relationship between behavior and behavioral consequences and the normative systems of the societies studied. In other words, for genuine understanding one needs to move from questions of "what" to those of "how" and "why." [3]

Nevertheless, the focus here is upon the contemporary sex norms of Scandinavia and America; and even this focus is further narrowed to *selected aspects of the sex norms,* and to the subcultures of *Denmark* in Scandinavia, and the *Midwestern Region* and so-called *Mormon Country* (Utah and parts of surrounding states) in

Reprinted from *Journal of Social Issues* 22:2 (1966), pp. 60–75 with the permission of the Society for the Psychological Study of Social Issues. Some footnotes omitted.

America.[4] The selection of these three subcultures for research provided a convenient range of norms and practices useful for the testing of hypotheses having both particular and general interest: particular, in seeking additional understanding of the sexual phenomenon in specified areas; general, in suggesting wider applicability of the findings and in reaching for a theory of normative systems.

Description of the Norms

The sex norms of Denmark are known to be highly permissive; those of Midwestern United States, moderately restrictive; and those of Mormon Country, highly restrictive. In Denmark — which is broadly typical of all of Scandinavia — sexual intercourse during the engagement is a tradition that goes back three or four centuries at least, and in recent years the practice has spread to include the "going steady" relationship; now as earlier, many Danes tend to wait for pregnancy before going ahead with the wedding (1, 2, 3, 14, 15, 18, 22, 23). In the United States, including the Midwestern Region — which may be taken as a fair cross-section of the whole — chastity is the code; and this prescription, though frequently violated and though undergoing considerable liberalization in recent decades, is still the dominant norm, backed heavily by a strong Judaeo-Christian tradition (16, 20). In Mormon Country — which, of course, is part of the United States, but, because of the particular religious culture which pervades it, unique in many respects — chastity is a highly institutionalized norm supported by strong positive and negative sanctions. With orthodox Mormons, "breaking the law of chastity" is among the most serious of sins (7, 10).

Since norms tend to be internalized within the personality structures of those who make up the society, one would expect to see cross-cultural differences, similar to those just reported, in expressions of personal attitude. This is exactly what was found. Questionnaire returns from samples of university students revealed that Danish respondents, in comparison with others:

1. Gave greater approval to both premarital coitus and postmarital infidelity (5, pp. 128–131; 12, p. 31).
2. Approved earlier starting times, in relation to marriage, of each level of intimacy — necking, petting, and coitus (12, pp. 32–35).
3. Thought in terms of a more rapid progression in intimacy development from its beginnings in necking to its completion in coitus (12, pp. 32–35).
4. Scored significantly higher on a Guttman-type scale, which combined ten separate attitudinal items into a measure of "Intimacy Permissiveness" (13, pp. 67–68).

Furthermore, since a person's behavior tends to line up with his values (including internalized norms), it follows that behavioral items can be used as indicators of the norms which lie back of them. This approach also gave support to the differing cultural patterns previously described; specifically, Danish subjects, more than others:

1. Participated in premarital coitus (13, pp. 68–69).
2. Went on to coitus from petting; that is, fewer of them engaged in *terminal petting* (13, p. 69, footnote 9).

3. Confined premarital coitus to one partner, and had first experience with a "steady" or fiancé(e); hence, were less promiscuous (13, p. 69. This generalization holds for males only).

4. Gave birth to an illegitimate child (7, p. 33).

5. Conceived the first legitimate child (postmarital birth) premaritally (6, p. 277; 7, p. 33; 9, p. 121).

6. Postponed further conception following the wedding; hence, showed a low proportion of early postmarital conceptions (6, p. 277; 9, pp. 121ff.).

In virtually all of the above attitudinal and behavioral measures, as well as with most others to be cited below, Mormon Country fell at the opposite or restrictive end of the continuum from Denmark, with Midwestern United States in between — though closer to the Mormon than to the Danish, which is why we have labeled it "moderately restrictive."

Generally speaking, the normative system of the United States includes early, frequent, and random dating; with a gradual narrowing of the field, a gradual development of intersex intimacy, the delaying of coitus until after the wedding, and the strong expectation of marital fidelity. These patterns differ, of course, from one subgroup to another, and the Mormon segment is known to be among the strongest adherents to convention and chastity. Individual variability is great, however, and the trend over time is toward liberalization. Especially noticeable is an increase of coitus during the engagement, which is an alteration in the direction of Scandinavian practice.

The Danish system stands in sharp contrast to the American. There, dating (which is a relatively recent innovation) starts later, is less widely practiced, and is more likely to begin with a "going steady" arrangement and an expectation of marriage to follow. Furthermore, all levels of sexual intimacy are accepted once the relationship becomes firmly established; and the progression to complete intimacy is relatively rapid. As a matter of fact, the Danes do not draw a sharp line to set off technical chastity (as do Americans), but rather regard petting and coitus as belonging together, and see them both as appropriate in a relationship based on love and oriented toward marriage. Today, this kind of a relationship is most apt to be established with "going steady" in Denmark but not until the engagement in America (Cf. 12, p. 31). Actually, in Denmark both "going steady" and engagement mean more in terms of commitment and privileges than they do in America, and the wedding probably means less — relatively speaking. It is to be noted, therefore, that the greater sexual permissiveness in Denmark (and all of Scandinavia for that matter) does not necessarily imply greater looseness or higher promiscuity; intimacy is simply made more a part of the courting and marrying processes. Nevertheless, it must be additionally observed that there seems to have been a spreading or generalizing of this marriage-oriented permissiveness to non-marital situations, for the Danes gave greater approval to *all* of our propositions regarding intimacy (12, pp. 31–35) and also showed higher rates of illegitimacy (7, p. 33). Finally, though the trend in recent years is toward the adoption of American dating patterns, and though the cultures on both sides of the Atlantic are moving toward convergence, differences in sex norms are still striking enough to give illumination to certain vital issues.

Analysis of the Issues

Attention is now turned to four basic questions, which pinpoint major issues in the sex problem that can be approached via cross-cultural research. Since the majority of readers will be American, the questions are phrased in terms of *effects of restrictiveness*.

1. How does restrictiveness affect deviation from the norm? Norms have been taken to mean the prescriptions or rules of conduct that a society imposes upon its members, whether formally or informally. They are reflected in the verbalizations and overt behaviors of the people. Nevertheless, though behavior may be taken as an index of a norm, it is not the norm itself, and, most importantly, it will usually vary somewhat from the norm. Only rarely, if ever, is the fit between prescription and performance a perfect one. Yet discrepancies of this sort lead to tension and disorganization in the systems involved.

As has been seen, the performance measures of sexual behavior did tend to line up broadly with expectation within each of the three normative systems, though this told us nothing of *specific deviations*. To get at the latter, we compared for each culture percentages who approved premarital coitus with percentages who actually had experienced it (13, pp. 70–72). Here are the results:

1. For Denmark, substantially more approved than had had experience.
2. For the two American samples, the reverse was true: substantially more had had experience than approved.
3. Of the American samples, this discrepancy between experience and approval was greater for Mormon Country.

Explanation for the Danish pattern probably lies in the permissive norms of that culture, coupled with the youthfulness and hence lack of marriage orientation of many of the respondents. (Recall that premarital intercourse in Denmark is more frequently tied in with love and commitment to marry; many hadn't yet reached that stage, though they approved of coitus for those who had.) Explanation for the American patterns, and most especially that of Mormon Country, probably lies in the restrictiveness of the culture, coupled with biological and social pressures upon individuals to violate the norms.

But whatever the explanations, the conclusion that norm violation varies directly with norm restrictiveness seems almost inescapable.

Yet, it must be emphasized that we are now speaking of deviation from *internalized norms* — the case in which the individual violates his own standards. The suggestion that this kind of norm violation is proportionately greater in restrictive societies in no sense contradicts the earlier conclusion that societies with restrictive norms also have higher proportions showing restrictive behavior; United States in contrast to Denmark, and Mormon Country in contrast to the Midwest, were disproportionately high in *both* respects. Thus it can be said, tentatively at least, that sex norm restrictiveness elicits greater conformity *to the prescribed goal* (e.g., chastity) than does sex norm permissiveness, but at the same time results in greater non-conformity *assimilated to the value structure* of the people: the relationship specified will be relative to whether one is thinking of a nominal category (first instance) or an internalized value system (second instance).

2. How does restrictiveness affect the Consequences of norm deviation? Even more important to our theory than deviation from norms is the question of consequences. We are interested in knowing the effects of norm violation and how these compare across cultures. Following are some summary points taken from the research:

1. Of the males and females who had experienced premarital coitus, proportionately more from Mormon Country did so out of coercion and/or felt obligation, and experienced guilt and other negative feelings subsequent to the event. Danish respondents were lowest on these reactions (13, pp. 69–70).
2. Of those who became premaritally pregnant, the tendency in Mormon Country was to marry even before confirming the pregnancy; in the Midwest, to marry immediately after the pregnancy was definitely known, or about 2 months after conception; and in Denmark, to not let pregnancy pressure them into hurrying the wedding — most of these Danish marriages took place about 5 months after conception (6, pp. 275–278; 7, pp. 35–36).
3. Percentage differences by which divorce rates in the premarital exceeded those in the postmarital pregnancy groups, were highest in Mormon Country and lowest in Denmark (6, p. 278; 7, pp. 36–38; 9, pp. 123–126).

Admittedly these three measures of consequences do not exhaust the possibilities; yet they deal with crucial points and at least suggest what the outcome of a more comprehensive analysis might be. Here it is seen that the most permissive culture (Denmark) shows the least negative effects from both premarital coitus and premarital pregnancy: guilt and kindred feelings are at a minimum; there is little pressure to advance the wedding date; and the influence of these intimacies upon subsequent divorce is relatively small. Conversely, negative effects are in each instance greater in the most restrictive culture (Mormon Country), with the more moderate culture (Midwestern) showing in-between effects.

It would seem that the negative consequences[5] of norm deviation tend to vary directly with norm restrictiveness — probably because deviation in the more restrictive societies represents a larger gap between norms and behavior; and, hence, constitutes a greater offense.

3. How does restrictiveness affect patterns of Subcultural variation? In building normative theory, it would be important to know if there is any relationship between the strength of norms and the homogeneity of culture. The following findings from the author's research are relevant to this question.

1. The two extremes on our permissiveness-restrictiveness continuum, that is, Denmark and Mormon Country, showed the greatest convergence of male and female *attitudes*. Furthermore, proportionately more respondents from these cultures, and especially from the Danish, believed in a single standard of sexual morality (5, pp. 129–132, 134–137; 12, p. 32; 13, p. 74).
2. When it comes to behavior, however, only the permissive culture (Denmark) showed a strong convergence of male and female patterns.[6] As a matter of

fact, the most restrictive (Mormon Country) tended to be the most divergent in this respect — a fact which, when combined with attitudinal homogeneity between the sexes, means, as pointed out earlier, that disproportionately large numbers there fail to practice what they profess (5, p. 135, footnote 2; 13, pp. 68–74).

3. An incomplete testing[7] of cross-cultural differences in homogeneity of sex attitudes according to certain other variables — age, education, residence, social class, church attendance, et cetera — revealed Mormon Country with the fewest and Denmark with the most intrafactor significant differences. For example, high versus low church attendance differentiated attitudes toward marital infidelity in a statistically significant way in Denmark, but not in Mormon Country (5, pp. 132–137).

Though explanations are not clearly visible within the data, there are some which seem plausible. As to attitude, we would hypothesize that the male-female convergence in Denmark is due to a freeing or liberalizing of the female, whereas in Mormon Country it is due to a taming or conventionalizing of the male — through stress on authority, conformity, and participation within the church, all of which are reinforced by a lay priesthood involving most male members twelve years of age and over. As to behavior, we would hazard the guess that in Denmark, where there is little stigma attached to premarital sex activity, behavior tends to follow the norms, and hence male-female similarity in attitude becomes male-female similarity in behavior also; whereas, in Mormon Country, where the standards set by the church may be somewhat utopian in nature, a stronger sex urge among males,[8] plus a persuasive double standard in the general culture, causes more males than females to violate the norms, which in turn increases the gap by which the two sexes diverge. As to the third finding, which describes the prominence of certain other subcategories as differing across our three normative systems, we would tentatively suggest the following: in permissive Denmark, sexual codes are more flexible and the resulting wider range of tolerance permits greater development of the subgroups; whereas, in restrictive America, and especially in Mormon Country, there is a greater rigidity of the codes and a narrower range of tolerance, which discourage deviation and the development of subgroups and subcultures.

4. Can sex norms and their consequences be generalized across cultures? Science looks for uniformities in nature; out of analysis comes synthesis and general theory. In the spirit of science, sociology and kindred disciplines search for principles of human behavior that can be generalized over time and across cultures. But the social sciences also see the peculiarities of each culture and, recognizing this, tend to adhere to a theory of cultural relativism. In the preceding pages we have observed ways in which sexual attitudes and behaviors and behavior consequences are relative to cultural norms. Nevertheless, _not everything is relative_. Here are some phenomena in our research which were found to apply to each of the three cultures studied — though not always in the same degree:

1. Most sexual intimacy and reproductive pregnancy occur within the institutional bounds of marriage.
2. The modal timing of first _postmarital conception_ is approximately one month after the wedding (6, p. 273).

3. Patterns of sexual behavior are strongly correlated with personal attitudes and social norms; permissive thinking tends to beget permissive behavior and restrictive thinking, restrictive behavior (13, pp. 70–71).

4. Approval of non-marital coitus, as applied to the premarital period, increases with each specified advance in involvement and/or commitment between the couple; but, as applied to the postmarital period, the reverse is true (5, pp. 130–131; 12, p. 31).

5. Females are more conservative in sexual matters than are males, almost without exception and regardless of the measure used or whether it measures attitudes or behavior (5, pp. 131–132; 12, pp. 31–35; 13, pp. 68–72).

6. Females who engage in premarital coitus are more likely than males to do so because of pressure of felt obligation, and also more than males to have as a partner either a "steady" or a fiancé(e) (13, p. 70).

7. There is a suggestion — though the testing was inconclusive — that persons who have premarital coitus are disproportionately low on satisfaction derived from their courtships (13, pp. 72–73).

8. Premaritally pregnant couples subsequently experience higher divorce rates than the postmaritally pregnant (6, p. 276; 9, pp. 123–126).

9. Of the premarital pregnancy couples, higher divorce rates are found for the "shotgun" type, that is, those who wait for marriage until just before the child is born, than for those who marry soon after pregnancy (7, p. 39; 9, pp. 123–126).

10. Of the postmarital pregnancy couples, higher divorce rates are found for the early conceivers than for those who wait a few months before starting their families (6, p. 276; 9, pp. 126–127).

11. Premarital pregnancy is greater among young brides and grooms in contrast to older ones, among those who have a civil wedding in contrast to a religious one, and among those in a laboring line of work in contrast to the more skilled and professional occupations (6, pp. 274–275; 7, pp. 34–35; 8, pp. 39–40; 9, p. 121).

To repeat, each of the above statements is applicable to all three of the cultures studied: Danish, Midwestern, and Mormon Country. Though these items do not apply in equal strength to each of the samples, they do represent significant regularities that can be generalized.

Toward a Theory of Normative Morality

The term *morality* is used commonly to designate conduct that is considered "good" or "right," frequently conceived in terms of absolutes. But questions of ultimates and absolutes lie outside the reach of science, and the best the scientist can do with them — in fact, all he can do as scientist — is to maintain suspended judgment and apply objective analysis. Assertion without evidence is the essence of dogmatism and the scientist as well as the religionist can be dogmatic, though to do so puts him beyond his data.

What, then, can science add to the field of morals; and, if anything, at what points can it contribute? Can there be a sociological basis for decisions on proper behavior? If by "proper" is meant something that is intrinsically or eternally right, the answer to this last question is "no," but if the meaning is simply that the behavior lines up with group norms, and hence escapes the consequences of negative group sanctions, the answer is "yes." Though the sociologist cannot decide what is best in an absolute sense, he can determine what is most functional to the systems involved [9] — and hence help decide what is best in a relative sense.

It should be evident, then, that the task of the scientist is not to actually set up or affirm a moral system, not, in other words, to take a moral position — even one based upon empirical evidence — but only to determine cause and effect relationships which can aid the non-scientist (including the scientist in his non-scientist role as a citizen) in choosing criteria for moral decision. The scientist, being confined to empirical data, cannot touch questions of absolutistic morality; nor can he, while in his professional role, make choices among the alternatives of relativistic (normative) morality. But he can clarify the alternatives and thus contribute *something* to moral questions.

Normative morality is defined here as any code of right and wrong that is founded upon the operations of normative systems. It is more, however, than the particular systems standing by themselves; for only by knowing the ways in which these interrelate, how personal behaviors deviate from social prescriptions, and what the consequences of such deviations are, can there be any rational basis for moral decision. Thus, normative morality is relativistic rather than absolutistic. It attempts to put science in place of polemics and to see questions of right and wrong in terms of the measurable and variable consequences of the behavior involved. At this stage of inquiry, we can only speak of *moving toward* such a theory, for the crucial hypotheses are only now being formulated and their testing is as yet but meager and exploratory.

Though the social scientist, as scientist, cannot make value judgments, he is entitled to study values as data. As a matter of fact, this is more than his privilege, it is his obligation. The values people hold tend both to shape their behavior and to determine the effects of this behavior upon themselves, upon others, and upon society at large. Values are intervening variables which, for any genuine understanding, must be taken into account.

One small attempt at preliminary testing and theory formulation is the cross-cultural research summarized above. This has focused upon the sex side of the question — with the realization, of course, that morality is concerned with more than sexual behavior; but, also, with the accompanying belief that any increased understanding of even a small part of a phenomenon is likely to give some illumination to the whole.[10] In the following concluding paragraphs let us further speculate as to what may have been accomplished and what the next steps might be.

We have demonstrated for the three cultures studied that sex patterns show both regularities and variabilities. If *everything* were regular, that is, generalizable across cultures, one could look to these universals as bases for a uniform morality; or, if *everything* were culture bound, one could conclude that nothing is fixed and morality is entirely relative. The truth of the matter seems to lie between these two conditions.

Many of the regularities found (suggestive of universals) seem to be the kinds of things one would expect to be functional to personality systems and/or social systems *per se:* confining reproduction, for the most part, to marriage; maintaining a reasonable alignment between beliefs and practices; females being more conservative re sex beliefs and practices than males; divorce being greater than average among the premaritally pregnant, and especially among those of the "shotgun marriage" variety; et cetera.

Logical explanations for these regularities are not difficult to find. To give but two brief examples: (1) females everywhere tend to be more conservative in sexual matters than males because by nature they are tied more closely to the productive process, which, disproportionally for them, increases the hazards of unprotected intimacy (men can't get pregnant); and also because most cultures hold a double standard, which places the female offender under greater social condemnation. (2) Premarital pregnancy is regularly associated with disproportionately high divorce rates, both because some divorce-prone individuals are pressured into marriage, though love and/or adequate preparation may be lacking, and because in all cultures (though more in certain ones than others) there will be some of the premaritally pregnant who will harbor feelings of guilt or blame which can frustrate their personalities and disrupt their relationships. In other words, the explanations seem to lie in both selection and causation; and we would hypothesize that both of these operate to some extent in all cultures. If space permitted, it would be possible to extend these arguments and also to speculate concerning other factors. Nevertheless, for any general theory of morality based upon the regularity of consequences, it will be necessary to go beyond logic and to carry out research on these and related points.

But a general morality may not be possible — at least not without severe qualification — simply because the consequences of sexual acts are not always the same; they differ in degree, if not in kind, depending upon the cultural milieu in which they occur. For example, regarding the case of premarital pregnancy and divorce just cited, though the relationship between these two factors was regular (in the same direction) in all three of the cultures studied, it was also relative to each culture: *divorce rate differentials* between premarital and postmarital conceivers were lowest in Denmark and highest in Mormon Country, suggesting that negative effects vary directly with the restrictiveness of the normative system.

A relativistic (normative) sexual morality would judge acts in terms of their varying consequences. In the research dealt with here, we have found for the premaritally intimate in Mormon Country (the most restrictive of the samples) not only higher divorce rate differentials but also greater guilt and a stronger tendency to seek escape from conscience and social condemnation by hurrying up the wedding. Two additional items pertaining to Mormon culture seem relevant at this point. First, of the three cultures studied, this one showed the highest percentage of respondents engaging in *terminal* petting, which suggests that its very strict proscription against premarital coitus may be resulting in an excess of precoital activity carried out for its own sake; at least there seems to be a tendency there, more than in the other cultures and especially the Danish, to draw the line separating moral and immoral sexual behavior just short of chastity. The second item to be mentioned (though not part of the research previously cited in this paper) is that age at marriage shows up as disproportionately low in Mormon Country; as a matter of fact, in recent years Utah has been among the highest of the reporting states in percentage of teen-age marriages (11, pp. 29, 33, footnote 6). Explanations for this cultural difference probably lie in the severity of the religious sanctions in support of the chastity norm, plus heavy romantic-sexual stimulants in the general culture, reinforced by church teaching on the importance and sacredness of marriage, and church programs bringing young people together at early ages and somewhat continuously — plus the petting pattern just noted. All of this would seem to leave boys and girls charged emotionally and/or stimulated sexually, yet without socially approved modes of release except marriage. But the matter needs to be researched.

We have used Mormon culture in our analysis in order to accentuate the contrasts. It must be kept in mind, however, that the average or more typical American culture has these same differences compared with Scandinavia, though to a lesser degree, and the explanations might be expected to be similar: the United States has more terminal petting, younger ages at marriage, more guilt associated with premarital coitus, a greater tendency to hurry the wedding when caught with pregnancy, a disproportionately higher divorce rate associated with premarital pregnancy, and so on. Some of the writer's Danish acquaintances have, in defense of their system, even gone further than these research points and suggested that the restrictiveness of American culture — including its emphasis upon technical chastity while at the same time permitting petting — is resulting in larger proportions of such "pathologies" as cheesecake publications, hardcore pornography, prostitution, and homosexuality. Whether or not these asserted differences would hold up under research remains to be seen; they do make interesting hypotheses.

What, then, can be said about the relative merits of the Scandinavian and American sexual systems? Certainly nothing by way of ultimate judgment (unless one abandons science and accepts the tenets of transcendental morality). Seen in terms of behavioral consequences, which is the view of normative morality, there are both functional and dysfunctional practices within both cultures — some of which have been outlined above. But when a thing is recognized as dysfunctional, this judgment is only with reference to the normative system in which it exists; and whether, in order to obtain equilibrium one should change the behavior to fit the system, or the system to fit the behavior, or some of both, is a question for the religionist or the philosopher, not the scientist.

In recent years, American sexual practices have been moving in the direction of the more liberal Scandinavian norms. Some people argue that this will be the solution to our problems. It must be remembered, however, that consequences are relative to the systems within which the behavior takes place. The functionality or dysfunctionality of *American sex practices* must be seen against *American sex norms*, and unless the latter have been liberalizing as rapidly as the former there will have been *an increase* of strains (dysfunction) within the personalities and the relationships involved. There is at least a suggestion that this may be happening. It could be, for example, that the increasing rates of personal and marital disorganization of recent decades are due in part to an enlarging sex freedom in the face of a lagging sex ethic. But whether or not the gap separating prescription from practice actually is getting larger, at least it exists, and its existence calls for objective investigation and analysis — as background for decision and adjustment.

Within the framework of normative morality, an act is "good" if it succeeds and "bad" if it fails in terms of meaningful criteria. For the scientist, the most meaningful criterion appropriate to moral judgment is the action's nearness of fit to the values or norms which govern the behavior. There has been little research relating nonmarital sexual behavior to its measurable consequences, which may be presumed to exist. Of the existing objective studies (as well as causal speculations) on this problem some have been solely concerned with possible effects upon *the individual*, his mental health and adjustments; others with possible effects upon *the pair relationship*, whether it is made mutually reinforcing or enduring; and still others upon possible effects upon *the community or society*, whether there are interconnections between sexual controls and societal stability. It is our contention that a theory of normative morality, if it is to be built, must draw upon culturally relevant research relating to all of these effect levels.

Notes

1. The project's aim was to discover evidences of how normative systems affect behavior and — what was thought even more important — affect the outcomes of behavior (see discussion below). To do this, we needed to compare social phenomenon cross-culturally. Since sexual behavior is generally accompanied by strong feelings and sanctions, it was thought that cross-cultural differences would be greater in this than in many other areas of social action. At least a suggestion of support for this notion was found in the research itself: premarital coitus was seen to differ cross-culturally in much greater magnitude than premarital petting, and the latter in much greater magnitude than premarital necking; in other words, the more intimate the behavior the more accentuated the behavioral differences among normative systems (8, p. 32).

2. Though methodological details may be found in the reports published earlier, and listed at the end of this paper, the following brief description will help orient present readers. Two types of data were gathered for each of the three cultures studied (Denmark, Midwest American, and Mormon American). The first was from questionnaires administered in the spring of 1958 to selected students from three universities, one from within each culture; it tapped attitudes and practices in the area of premarital sexual intimacy. The second was from record-linkage; marriage records for selected years were matched with birth and divorce records, to yield data on child spacing and associated factors. Cross-cultural comparability was approached but not fully achieved, especially in the record-linkage data; identical years and lengths of search were not always maintained. Nevertheless, the cross-cultural pictures derived from these two complementary sets of data were so consistent and, in most cases, the differential so dramatic as to lend support to the theory being tested.

3. As will be evident from the discussion to follow, we do not here mean "why" in terms of ultimate meanings or supernatural explanations, for these are beyond the reach of the scientist, but only "why" in the sense of establishing causal connections, and hence finding plausible explanations within the limits of empirical data and testable relationships.

4. In focusing upon these three subcultures, we make no pretense of describing *all* of the United States and Scandinavia. Nevertheless, Mormon Country is known to be among the most sexually conservative sections of the United States; the Midwest, aside from being somewhat centrally located, has many bio-social characteristics that fall close to national averages; and Denmark is very much a part of Scandinavia, which, taken as a whole, manifests a considerable amount of cultural homogeneity. Concerning this last point, and with special attention to the sexual phenomenon, we should point out that our own questionnaire was administered separately to a university sample in Sweden with results remarkably similar to those of Denmark (analysis as yet unpublished). For research data on other Scandinavian countries than Denmark, and for additional evidences of sex norm homogeneity among them all, see references at the end of this paper (especially 4, 15, 17, 19, 21, 22, 23)....

5. Though we use the terms "effects" and "consequences" it is recognized that

association is not the same thing as causation and that the latter has not actually been established. . . .

6. There is still a further evidence that permissiveness makes for homogeneity
   at the behavioral level: just as the most permissive of the cultures (Denmark) showed the smallest male-female difference, so the more permissive of
   the sexes (males) showed the smallest cross-cultural differences in premarital
   coitus (13, p. 68, Table 2).

7. So far, the tests have been confined to attitudes toward marital infidelity, and
   have not included attitudes toward premarital practices, nor any of the behavior patterns.

8. Though the existence of male-female differences in *biological* sex drive is
   open to some question and is in need of further research, there can be little
   doubt but that in our culture most males have stronger *learned* sexual desire
   than do females.

9. According to the structural-functional school, human activities tend to become organized into *intra-* and interdependent *systems,* which perpetuate
   themselves only by maintaining necessary degrees of balance or equilibrium.
   There are personality systems and social systems — and subsystems of each
   — all interrelated. When an activity is in harmony with, and helps to maintain, a system it is said to be *functional;* when the reverse is true, *dysfunctional.*

   It is thus possible to use system maintenance as the criterion against which
   the propriety of behavior is decided. This essentially is what we mean by a
   normative morality.

10. It is also realized that present generalizations are based upon samples from
    a very limited number of cultures, and even within these samples the phe-
    nomenon has been only preliminarily explored. Furthermore, not all of the
    summary points given in this paper were found to have statistical significance.
    (For details on this and other matters, the reader is referred to the original
    publications given in the reference list.) Nevertheless, it is felt that the find-
    ings are sufficiently reasonable and consistent to provide guidelines for fu-
    ture research and theory building.

References

1. Anderson, Robert T. and Anderson, Gallatin. "Sexual Behavior and Urbanization in a Danish Village." *Southwestern Journal of Anthropology,* 1960, 16,
   93–109.

2. Auken, Kirsten. "Time of Marriage, Mate Selection and Task Accomplishment in Newly Formed Copenhagen Families." *Acta Sociologica,* 1964, 8,
   138–141.

3. Auken, Kirsten. *Unge Kvinders Sexuelle Adfaerd.* Copenhagen: Rosenkilde
   og Bagger, 1953. English summary, pp. 389–402.

4. Birgitta, Linner. *Society and Sex in Sweden.* Stockholm: Swedish Institute for
   Cultural Relations, 1955. Pamphlet, 37 pp.

5. Christensen, Harold T. "A Cross-Cultural Comparison of Attitudes Toward
   Marital Infidelity." *International Journal of Comparative Sociology,* 1962, 3,
   124–137.

6. Christensen, Harold T. "Child Spacing Analysis via Record Linkage: New
   Data plus a Summing up from Earlier Reports." *Marriage and Family Living,* 1963, 25, 272–280.

7. Christensen, Harold T. "Cultural Relativism and Premarital Sex Norms."
   American Sociological Review, 1960, 25, 31–39.

8. Christensen, Harold T. "Selected Aspects of Child Spacing in Denmark."
   Acta Sociologica, 1959, 4 ,35–45.

9. Christensen, Harold T. "Timing of First Pregnancy as a Factor in Divorce:
   a Cross-Cultural Analysis." *Eugenics Quarterly,* 1963, 10, 119–130.

10. Christensen, Harold T. "Value Variables in Pregnancy Timing: Some Intercultural Comparisons." In N. Anderson (Ed.), *Studies of the Family,* Vol. 3, Gottingen: Vandenhoeck & Ruprecht, 1958, 29–45.
11. Christensen, Harold T. and Cannon, Kenneth L. "Temple versus Nontemple Marriage in Utah: Some Demographic Considerations." *Social Science,* 1964, 39, 26–33.
12. Christensen, Harold T., and Carpenter, George R. "Timing Patterns in the Development of Sexual Intimacy." *Marriage and Family Living,* 1962, 24, 30–35.
13. Christensen, Harold T., and Carpenter, George R. "Value-Behavior Discrepancies Regarding Premarital Coitus in Three Western Cultures." *American Sociological Review,* 1962, 27, 66–74.
14. Croog, Sydney H. "Aspects of the Cultural Background of Premarital Pregnancy in Denmark." *Social Forces,* 1951, 30, 215, 219.
15. Croog, Sydney H. "Premarital Pregnancies in Scandinavia and Finland." *American Journal of Sociology,* 1962, 57, 358–365.
16. Ehrmann, Winston. "Marital and Nonmarital Sexual Behavior." In H. T. Christensen (Ed.), *Handbook of Marriage and the Family.* Chicago: Rand McNally, 1964, 585–622.
17. Eliot, Thomas D., et al. *Norway's Families: Trends, Problems, Programs.* Philadelphia: University of Pennsylvania Press, 1960. See especially Chapter 12, "Non-Wedlock Situations in Norway," 240–280.
18. Hansen, George. *Saedelighedsforhold Blandt Landbeforkningen i Denmark i det 18 Aarhundrede.* Copenhagen: Det Danske Forlag, 1957.
19. Jonsson, Gustav. "Sexualvanor hos Svensk Ungdom." In *Ungdomen Möter samhället.* Stockholm: K. L. Beckmans Boktryckeri, 1951, 160–204.
20. Reiss, Ira L. *Premarital Sexual Standards in America.* Glencoe, Ill.: Free Press, 1960.
21. Sturup, Georg K. "Sex Offenses: The Scandinavian Experience." *Law and Contemporary Problems,* 1960, 25, 361–375.
22. Svalastoga, Kaare. "The Family in Scandinavia." *Marriage & Family Living,* 1954, 16, 374–380.
23. Wikman, K. Robert. *Die Einleitung der Ehe.* Aabo, Finland: Acta Academiae Aaboensis, 1937, XI.

4

MECHANISMS OF SOCIAL CONTROL

Despite crucial differences, the major theories of personality development (that is, Freudian psychoanalytic theory in its orthodox and revisionist forms, learning theory, and symbolic interactionism) share several fundamental assumptions about human beings. These assumptions are that human beings (1) are born with biological drives that require gratification; (2) are born into society in a state of physical and cognitive immaturity, making them dependent upon others for instinctual gratification; (3) are acted upon and influenced by others who use rewards and punishments to manipulate behavior; (4) develop empathy, the ability to take roles, and self-consciousness; (5) establish commitments to certain role models and values; (6) experience anxiety when they deviate from such commitments; and (7) rarely deviate because the experience of anxiety is so unpleasant.

Freudian theory examines subconscious instincts and early childhood experiences in adult personality formation. Learning theory is more concerned with the reward or punishment of responses to social cues in learning behavior which will satisfy primary drives. And symbolic interactionism concentrates more on the development of empathy in primary groups and the learning of social roles. Nevertheless, all accept the basic ideas that sensitivity to the expectations of others and the capacity for self-control (to adjust one's behavior accordingly) are developed early and remain throughout life as distinctively human attributes.

The social control of individual deviance can be conceptualized on three distinct levels: internalized controls, interpersonal controls, and institutional controls. Internalized controls are those restraints on the gratification of biological drives which are experienced in primary socialization and, as a consequence, incorporated into the individual's personality.

Internalized Controls

Individuals internalize self-control in the sense that drives are channeled in certain directions and attached to certain social objects through cultural conditioning before the individual is capable of envisioning alternatives. With respect to drives like sex, childhood socialization molds instincts into impulses, or situational reflexes, which are so much a part of the individual's personality they are largely below the level of consciousness. For example, Victorian ladies were trained to blush, or even faint, in response to sexual overtures which a modern woman might consider a harmless flirtation. Thus, behavior is socially controlled at the most primary level through the mechanism of tension management to avoid disruptive anxiety caused by deviation from internalized normative restraints.

The first article in this chapter, by Sears, Maccoby, and Levin, is about the socialization of aggression. The authors note that all animals use physical attack as a means of defense, but the techniques of defense and the forms of injury inflicted are most varied and subtle in human beings. For example, injury can be construed as anything ranging from physical attack, to painful assaults on one's self-esteem, to frustrations of one's impulses.

Also, in human society the closeness of group members (that is, the degree of physical and emotional interdependence) has a direct correlation to the degree of prohibition of in-group fighting. To safeguard the complex and delicate forms of interdependence out of which social institutions like the family are formed, the primitive rage and direct aggression of the infant and young child must be modified and channelled by significant others in the process of socialization.

The authors examine the extent to which children learn to control aggression as a result of differential socialization experiences, considering two variables in their analysis: (1) the mother's attitude toward the child's aggression (classified according to low or high permissiveness), and (2) how much aggression or physical punishment the mother herself uses in attempting to control the child's behavior (also dichotomized in the analysis). Thus, they analyze the interaction between the form and the content of the behavior of the child's primary socializing agent. The results of this very interesting research may surprise you.

Interpersonal Controls

On the interpersonal level, other individuals and groups exercise interpersonal control over deviant behavior by manipulating rewards and punishments. Individuals grow to require certain kinds and levels of emotional support which others can threaten to withdraw should they be perceived to violate their "social contract" to uphold the norms of the group. Expressions of approval or disapproval may reassure or threaten the individual's sense of belonging or affection. And because self-esteem rests, in large measure, on positive feedback from significant others, our very sense of self-worth is intimately related to conformity with the demands and expectations of others.

The second selection, by Stanley Milgram, further advances his now classic research on individual obedience by introducing the variable of small-group influence on the willingness of an individual to inflict physical pain on another person. It is one of the most imaginative, revealing, and even terrifying pieces of social psychological research ever conducted.

Institutional Controls

In traditional societies, because they are composed primarily of small, rural communities where residents are known and bound to each other in various ways, interpersonal influence can function as a very effective method of social control. On the other hand, modern societies are composed primarily of large, ethnically heterogeneous urban centers where people lead highly mobile lives, mutual obligations are weak, value consensus is low, privacy is valued, and anonymity is prevalent. In such societies more formal mechanisms of external control have been instituted.

The first modern police force was founded by Robert Peale during the Industrial Revolution in England in 1829. This is the etymology for the name "Bobby" which is still popularly applied to police officers in England. The first police force in the United States was established in 1844. Previously, private citizens had volunteered to "watch and ward." The increasing jeopardy and ineffectiveness of such assignments made the change imperative. Since then, modern societies have instituted asylums for the "mentally disturbed" in addition to elaborate police, court, and prison systems (distinguished by jurisdiction, and sex and age of inmates) to maintain order by isolating lawbreakers, punishing them, and occasionally even attempting more sophisticated methods of reform or rehabilitation (that is, resocialization into culturally acceptable behavior). In many societies today the military performs domestic peace-keeping operations in the absence of a modern police force. Even a high technology society, such as the United States, may resort to military organizations, such as the National Guard, when the threat to public safety appears to exceed the containment capacity of the police.

Authorities in institutions have many resources for the prevention and control of deviance. As the diagram in the Introduction indicates, political authorities may maintain control by manipulating the informational environment of the individual or whole society through methods such as withholding information or lying on the individual level and media censorship or propaganda on the societal level.

People are either denied information they need to decide realistically on a course of action or they are given false information upon which to base their decision. Authorities may also use propaganda to strengthen the internalized control of people by appealing to their consciences; they claim to represent certain culturally valued symbols and traditions to which people have been taught to defer.

A more extreme level of control, usually reserved for those not adequately contained by such methods, may be achieved by manipulating goods. Individuals may be promoted, given salary increases or cuts, demoted, fired, and even blacklisted depending on how their behavior is viewed. Interest groups and institutions may be rewarded with grants, deprived of existing aid, or otherwise controlled by such methods as tokenism (that is, the practice of making minor material concessions to quell protest addressed to larger social reforms).

Institutional authorities can also use official violence. Ultimately, the people provide the means of violence for the authorities to use when they feel their position is threatened. The possibilities for social change (involving maybe not only a change of authorities but possibly a more basic redistribution of power) hinge, of course, on whether most people continue to view the authorities as legitimate and whether they are willing or able to act on their views if they do not.

Our final paper by Adamek and Dager represents one attempt to isolate and measure individual and organizational variables affecting the degree of social personality change in a correctional institution. Their attempt is interesting, but the assumed worthiness of the goal to be achieved should not distract the student from a critical intellectual and ethical examination of the structure of the institution and the techniques of personality change which are employed. The operational model of this institution for delinquent girls may be fruitfully compared to other institutional models that attempt to initiate similar personal change processes toward different ends, such as Army basic training camps, Chinese POW camps during the Korean War, to some extent Nazi concentration camps, slave plantations, and even some secret societies and retreat movements.

References

Asch, Solomon E.
    1952   *Social Psychology*. New York: Prentice-Hall.
Cooley, Charles Horton
    1964   *Human Nature and the Social Order*. New York: Schocken.
Freud, Sigmund A.
    1960   *General Introduction to Psychoanalysis*. Authorized English translation of the revised edition by Joan Riviere. New York: Washington Square Press.
    1949   *An Outline of Psychoanalysis*. Authorized translation by James Strachey. New York: Norton.
Goffman, Erving
    1959   *The Presentation of Self in Everyday Life*. Garden City, N. Y.: Doubleday-Anchor.
    1961   *Asylums: Essays on the Social Situation of Mental Patients and Other Inmates*. Garden City, New York: Doubleday Anchor Books.
Gold, Martin
    1958   "Suicide, Homicide and the Socialization of Aggression." *American Journal of Sociology* 13 (May):651–61.
Mead, George Herbert
    1964   *On Social Psychology*. Ed. Anselm Strauss. Chicago: The University of Chicago Press.
Miller, Neal E., and John Dollard
    1941   *Social Learning and Imitation*. New Haven: Yale University Press.
Paul, Benjamin D.
    1962   "Mental Disorder and Self-Regulating Processes in Culture: A Guatemalan Illustration." Pp. 147–59 in Bartlett H. Stoodley (ed.), *Society and Self: A Reader in Social Psychology*. Glencoe, Ill.: The Free Press.

ROBERT R. SEARS
ELEANOR E. MACCOBY
HARRY LEVIN

The Socialization of Aggression

Aggression, as the term is commonly used, means behavior that is intended to hurt or injure someone. Most human adults have quite a repertory of acts that fit this definition. Some of these are bold and violent, others sly and attenuated. Some are accompanied by rage or annoyance; others are done coldly and seemingly, to the perpetrator, without emotion. The complexity and subtlety of adult aggression is the end product of two or three decades of socialization by the individual's parents and peers, however, and bears little resemblance to the primitive quality of the infant's action patterns, from which it is developed.

To understand the problem of aggression in child rearing, one does well to remind himself firmly that man is a mammal and that there are certain kinds of behavior which characterize all mammals. The two that are most relevant to the problem of aggression are fighting and the *expression of rage*.

From the lowest quadruped to the highest biped, physical attack is used for defense. Techniques vary, depending on the sharpness of hooves, the strength of jaws, and the presence of specialized weapons like antlers. Man, being the most intelligent and inventive of all, makes use of many of the other species' techniques and adds a host of new ones that, happily, no other animal has ever dreamed of.

Physical fighting is not the commonest form of human aggression. *Injury* is a broad term, and the socialization process develops many motives that can be thwarted. Interference with any of these motives causes pain or anguish and if this was the intention, the interfering act was truly aggressive.

Defensive fighting is usually accompanied by expressions of rage. The older child or adult, who can report his feelings, may recognize his desire to hurt and be very aware of his angry emotion. But this quality of aggression is attenuated, too, in the process of socialization, and there are many forms of hurt that an adult inflicts with little emotional arousal.

In a civilized society adults are rarely beaten or knifed or lashed. More often, they are hurt by attacks on their pride or status, their desire for social approval, or their feelings of affection for their families and friends. These kinds of hurt can be far more serious and more prolonged than most physical hurts. The withholding of affection by a loved spouse, for example, can have the meaning of pain that goes far beyond that from broken legs or crushed fingers. Nor do injuries that come through sheer accident, the vagaries of nature, hurt like injuries to self-esteem.

Not all injuries are so great as these, of course. There are the little obstinacies in one's friends and the noncooperative indifferences of one's working associates. There are the irritants of family living — a tired and sassy child, a grumpy and complaining husband, a daughter who dawdles. Since all these cause discomfort, they *can* be forms of aggression. Whether they are in fact, however, depends on whether the discomfort they engender was *designed* by the perpetrator to hurt someone else.

Not all acts that hurt are intended to do so. Even sophisticated and sensitive adults sometimes fail to anticipate the effects of what they do. The unanswered letter can seem a slight; the unasked question can be interpreted as indifference. With children, the problem is especially noticeable in the manipulation of physical forces. A child's innocently swinging stick only too easily turns into a painful club, the experimental bombing into a brother's broken toys.

Since these hurts are obviously unintentional, they do not qualify as *aggression* in the technical sense of the word. There are certain borderline examples, however, that are hard to be sure about. There are acts that sometimes are and sometimes are not aggressive. Most mothers consider obedience of some importance, for they use much verbal guidance in instructing and controlling their children. The children know their mothers want compliance with directions and, hence, willful disobedience is widely recognized as a form of aggression. Now if a child has been told to pick up his clothes a dozen times and if he has remembered to do this the last half-dozen times, his mother may look suspiciously at his motives if he forgets the thirteenth time. Did he just forget? Or was he angry and disobedient? People differ considerably in the degree to which they perceive an aggressive intent in the behavior of others and what one mother calls carelessness another will call disobedience.

If we disregard borderline cases and accidents, however, there is still a great deal of human behavior that is designed to hurt. Such activity develops early in life and is a disrupting influence on family living. Later it becomes a problem for the peer group.

Control of Aggression

All human societies, even all colony-living subhuman primates, have rules to limit the kinds and direction of aggression that may be expressed. The most fundamental of these is the high degree of prohibition on in-group fighting. The closer together people live, the more interdependent they are, the less they dare be aggressive toward one another. Free fighting and antagonism within the household — whether it be a nomad's hut or a suburbanite's four-bedrooms-and-two-baths — could only lead to wreckage of the family unit. Hence, all societies require that only very attenuated forms of aggression be expressed among family members and that, within the parent-child relationship, aggression be expressed only downward. One mother described this principle with great clarity[1]:

I. How do you handle it (if he strikes you)?
M. I don't allow it. I slap him and punish him for it, and explained that

he was never to raise his hand to anyone older than himself, that he must respect older people — his mother and father especially. Never! But they do attempt it, of course; but I do think it should be checked right away.

I. How did you handle this?

M. I would just put him right in his room. Just take hold of him right at the moment and put him right in his room, and say "You mustn't do that! You never should hit your mother and father, ever; they're always right." I always make a big issue out of it.

I. That your mother and father are always right?

M. Always right; "You must never raise your hand to your mother or father."

Not all mothers felt as strongly as this one did, and different societies have different degrees of tolerance for in-family aggression, but the prohibition exists in some degree in all known societies.

Outside the family, limitations are less severe in most societies. The mothers in this present study were less concerned — more permissive — about fighting between their own children and neighbor youngsters than about sibling quarrels. There were a number of instances in which mothers felt children must be encouraged to fight, to protect their own interests. Even so, there is still a good deal of necessary restriction on the more severe forms of aggression, no matter toward whom they are directed.

To insure the firm establishment of these rules many mothers feel they must begin the control of aggression very early in the child's life. A newborn infant is not particularly dangerous, even to himself, but he represents a potential threat nevertheless. The family, indeed the whole society, has a delicate balance; the forces of aggression are being kept in check, and cooperation and love outweigh noncooperation and hate. The baby is an alien who does not know the rules. He must be taught them if he is to be an acceptable member of society.

Methods of Control

Aggression, being a frustration to its object, has a strong tendency to evoke counteraggression or punishment. This built-in relationship between the aggressor and his victim has an important consequence. It means that every child grows up with the experience of being punished in some degree for his aggressive behavior. The extent and severity of such punishment differs greatly from one child to another, of course, depending on the tolerance of his parents and siblings. It is our impression, however, that the average child in our sample received more actual *punishment* (as distinguished from *nonreward*) for aggressive behavior than for any other kind of change-worthy action.

One significant effect of punishment is the production of anxiety. If the punishment is repeated many, many times through early childhood, situations that provoke aggressive feelings gradually come to arouse anxiety, too — anxiety over the danger of being punished for aggression. Eventually, the aggression itself or the accompanying feeling of being angry becomes sufficient to arouse anxiety. In such cases the anxiety may properly be called aggression-anxiety.

The formation of such a reaction has two kinds of consequences that are relevant to the socialization process. One is the uneasiness and discomfort that become connected with the arousal of aggressive impulses. By and large, adults in our culture do not tolerate aggression comfortably, neither their own nor that displayed by others. It evokes too much anxiety; this may be reflected in feelings of worry, dislike, avoidance, guilt, or moral disapproval. They cannot feel fully comfortable when they are angry. They are in conflict — ambivalent — about their own impulses. The carrying through of an aggressive act is often followed not simply by the catharsis or satisfaction that one would expect from a successful action (assuming the action accomplished the intended results), but also by feelings that arise from the undercurrent anxiety. These may be shame, embarrassment, guilt, regret, self-deprecation, or even just plain fear of retaliation. A mother's uneasiness and conflict often make difficult a calm use of reason in deciding how to handle a child's aggressive actions.

A second consequence of punishment and its ensuing anxiety is the development, by the child, of techniques for avoiding punishment. The child who is consistently punished for swearing is likely to cease the practice in his parents' presence. This does not necessarily mean he will stop swearing, for punishment seems usually to have a rather localized inhibiting effect. The impulse to be aggressive is not reduced but only the overt aggressive act that was punished. The total impulse to aggression is made stronger than ever, for the punishment is itself an additional frustration.

Measures of Mothers' Behavior

We can turn now to the findings from our interviews. We will describe first the ways in which the mothers handled aggression, with respect to both permissiveness and punishment. Then we will examine the relation between these child-rearing practices and the mothers' own reports of their children's aggressiveness to discover what procedures seemed to influence such behavior.

In the discussion so far we have talked of aggression as a change-worthy form of behavior, particularly that directed toward the parents. This is a generalization, however, that hides a multitude of individual differences among the mothers. As might easily be predicted from what has been said of aggression-anxiety, parents differ greatly from one another in the amount of aggression they can tolerate. Some set great store by a completely nonaggressive child; others accept the inevitability of a certain amount of aggression even as late as age five; a few believe aggression is such a natural quality of early childhood behavior that they simply ignore all but the most violent episodes.

In our interviews, the mothers described the ways in which children got on adult nerves, found ingenious devices for expressing annoyance or getting revenge, and in general created the social and emotional havoc that goes with anger. They also expressed their own attitudes toward their children's aggression and gave descriptions of how this change-worthy behavior was handled. With respect to aggression of children toward their parents, the mothers were asked:

> Sometimes a child will get angry at his parents and hit them and kick them or shout angry things at them. How much of this sort of thing do you think parents ought to allow in a child of (his, her) age? How do you handle it when (child's name) acts like this?

Following are examples of the kinds of statements parents made in answer to these questions.

Case A

M. I think he's at the age right now where you're apt to get quite a lot of it. I think as they get a little bit older, you can stop and reason with them, but right now I think that they get pretty angry at times and they do say things. And afterwards they're sorry for it, so I let him say it and it's over with, and afterwards I might say, "You weren't very nice to Mummy," and he'll generally admit it.

Case B

I. In what ways do you get on each other's nerves?

M. I think our mutual tempers, as much as anything, as he has one, and so have I. I attempt to control it, so for instance I can understand things that he does. He gets very angry and he goes upstairs and throws things, and I can understand that perfectly. I don't know whether I was ever allowed to or whether I ever did throw things, but I wanted to, so that heaving things into the closet, I can easily understand; so that kind of thing doesn't aggravate me the way it would somebody else, and the same way with getting very angry at me. I never mind that as much, because I also get angry at him, and if I am going to, he has got to be allowed that privilege also.

Case C

M. Well, she'll say, "I don't like you." She seldom says, "I hate you." or "I don't like you anymore," or something like that. I have let her go up to now because I feel she's just getting it out of her system. If it isn't too loud, or if she isn't too angry about it, I just let it go. If it's something that I can't turn my back on, if it's something that she's so angry about that she won't stop, then I speak to her. Otherwise she'll say, "Well, I don't like you." And I say, "Well, that's all right," or something like that. I don't pay too much attention to it because I know that she doesn't actually mean it. She means it because she isn't getting what she wants, and she doesn't mean it actually.

If she kicked me or if she slapped me, I'd slap her back. I just told her that it doesn't feel good to get slapped. If she didn't want to get slapped herself, not to slap other people. The reaction would be the same in anyone that got slapped — they wouldn't like it.

Case D

M. They never should allow him to hit them back. If he hits them, they should hit him right back. If you let him get away with it once he will always want to get away with it.

I. How do you handle it when he acts like this?

M. If he hits me I hit him back twice as hard, and if he does it again, I just get my paddle I have, and I give it to him again, and then he stops.

I. How do you handle it if he is deliberately disobedient?

M. I take off his clothes and he's in for the day and he's not to play with anything — not even his toys or anything that belongs to him — he's not to touch anything — he's to leave things alone and stay in bed.

Case E

M. That is something I will not tolerate — my child has never done it. I mean, they have done it once in a while, both of them, but I would absolutely not tolerate it.

I. How did you teach them not to do this?

M. I don't know — I guess I just told them once, in no uncertain terms, that it was something that was never done, and I have never had any trouble with it; and if I did, I don't know just how I would cope with it, because I wouldn't stand for it.

I. How much of this sort of thing do you think a parent ought to allow?

M. I don't think they should allow it at all. I think a child should be allowed to express himself, and all that, but I don't think there is ever an exception for a child to hit his parents.

Responses of these kinds, together with much other relevant material elsewhere in the interview, enabled us to rate each mother on two dimensions: (1) her *permissiveness* for aggression directed by the child toward herself and (2) the amount (and severity) of *punishment* she had administered to the child for such aggression. Under the heading of permissiveness we included not only the mother's stated values as to whether aggression should be allowed but also her behavior toward the child, i.e., whether she actually *did* allow it or whether she always tried to take measures to prevent or stop it.

As might be expected, the two scales were correlated. That is, the mothers who were permissive about aggression, tended to use little punishment, while the non-permissive mothers used quite a bit. But the correlation was only —.46, a low enough value to warrant considering the two dimensions separately. The two scales did not correlate more closely because there were a number of mothers who did not permit aggression from their children, but stopped it by other means than punishment. Surprisingly, there were also a number whom we rated both quite permissive and highly punishing. In this latter group were some mothers who felt they *should* allow their children to display aggression; but they could restrain their own impulses to suppress the child's aggression only so long, and then they would blow up. When the punishment came, it was likely to be severe.

In this sample of 379 normal mothers, we found that a majority were most accurately rated at the *nonpermissive* end of our permissiveness scale. The social norm prevailing in these families was one of little tolerance about parent-directed aggression from children, although there was considerable variation in the severity with which this value was enforced.

It is of some interest to note that parents allowed somewhat more aggression from their sons than from their daughters, and that working-class parents were less permissive about aggression than parents at the middle-class level.

Effects on Children's Aggression

We turn now to a consideration of the child's aggressiveness, and will then address ourselves to the question: Does the amount of overt aggression a child displays at home have any relation to the values parents hold about aggression and the techniques they have employed in dealing with the child's aggression?

Measure of Aggression

Among these youngsters, there were a few whose mothers could recall almost no angry behavior around home, but this was not the case for most of them. In spite of the general aura of prohibition, the majority of the youngsters had displayed many varieties and combinations of angry emotional response. Some children were more aggressive toward one parent than the other, some quarreled mainly with siblings and were pleasant toward the parents, some expressed themselves openly, and some relied chiefly on non-cooperation for their expression.

Nearly all the mothers gave fairly detailed reports of the typical forms of aggression their children displayed. It was thus possible to make a rating of *amount of aggression exhibited in the home* (excluding that toward siblings).

These ratings can be compared with the mothers' reports of child-rearing practices to discover what characteristics of the latter were associated with high or low degree of reported aggression by the child.

The measures of the mothers' practices and the children's reactions were not independent. Both came from the mother herself. We cannot be certain in any particular case, therefore, that we have secured an unbiased report of the child's actual behavior. It is possible that some quality in a given mother — for instance, a sense of despair about her effectiveness as a child rearer — might lead her to give an exaggerated report about her child's aggressiveness. If we find, as we do, that mothers who felt little confidence in themselves had more (reportedly) aggressive children, we cannot tell whether this finding results from exaggerated reports by these mothers, or whether there was actually something about their behavior toward children that evoked more child aggressiveness. It would not be surprising if both were true, for the same qualities of her personality that influence her perception of the child may also induce a characteristic set of responses in him.

Permissiveness and Punishment

There is a constant tug of war in a child's behavior between the instigation and the inhibition of aggression. On the one hand there are frustrations, threats, or other stimulating situations that tend to evoke aggressive action; on the other, there are warnings that inhibit aggression and there are instigators to competing responses that the mother finds more desirable than aggression. One of the major research problems in the investigation of the socialization process is the discovery of just what kinds of maternal behavior fall into these classifications. What does the mother do that excites aggression in her child? What does she do that inhibits it?

The two scales of *permissiveness for aggression* and *severity of punishment for aggression* are obviously relevant dimensions to examine. What should we expect of their relation to the reported amount of aggression the child shows in the home? Permissiveness, by definition, is an expression of the mother's willingness to have the child perform such acts. A simple and straightforward prediction is that children with permissive mothers will be more aggressive than children with non-permissive mothers. Similarly with punishment: if we assume that this method of discipline establishes in the child a fear of behaving aggressively, then the more punitive the mother is, the more the child should avoid being aggressive. These two predictions fit together nicely. As we noted above the scales for *permissiveness* and *punishment* are correlated —.46; that is, to some degree the more permissive mothers tended to be less severe in their punishment.

In point of fact, however, one of the predictions is right and the other is wrong. It is true that high *permissiveness* is associated with high aggression. The correlation is +.23. But *punishment* works just the other way: the more severe the punishment, the more aggression the child showed. The correlation is +.16. Both these correlations are small, but they are significant and they are artificially reduced by the negative correlation between the permissiveness and punitiveness scales. Their true importance is substantially greater as may be seen in Table 1.

TABLE 1

Percentage of Highly Aggressive Children in Subgroups [a]

	Highly aggressive [b]			
	Boys		Girls	
Subgroup	Percentage	N	Percentage	N
Low permissiveness, low punishment	3.7	27	13.3	30
Low permissiveness, high punishment	20.4	51	19.1	47
High permissiveness, low punishment	25.3	81	20.6	63
High permissiveness, high punishment	41.7	36	38.1	22

[a] Divided according to whether mother was in upper or lower half of the distribution on permissiveness and severity of punishment for aggression toward parents.

[b] By "highly aggressive" is meant that the child was rated in one of the two highest levels of aggression on a 5-point rating scale.

We interpret these findings in this way. When a mother adopts a permissive point of view about aggression, she is saying to her child, in effect, "Go ahead and express your angry emotions; don't worry about me." She gives few signals in advance that would lead the child to fear to be aggressive. On the contrary, her attitude is one of expectancy that he *will* be and that such behavior is acceptable. It is scarcely surprising that the child tends to fulfill her expectations. The non-permissive mother, however, does something quite different. She has an attitude that aggression is wrong, that it is not to be tolerated, and an expectancy (often very subtly expressed) that the child will not behave in such undesirable ways. When he is aggressive, she does something to try to stop it — sometimes by punishment, sometimes by other means. He, also, fulfills his mother's expectations. This dimension of permissiveness, then, is a measure of the extent to which the mother prevents or stops aggression, the nonpermissive extreme being the most common.

Punishment is apparently a somewhat different matter. It is a kind of maternal behavior that occurs *after* the child's aggression has been displayed. The child has already enjoyed the satisfaction of hurting or of expressing anger — and so has had a reinforcement for aggressive action. But then he gets hurt in turn. He suffers further frustration. This should, and on the average does, incite him to more aggression. If the punishment is very severe, he may gradually learn to fear the consequences of his own actions and the particular acts that get most repeatedly punished may be inhibited. But the total frustration is increased and hence the total amount of aggression displayed in the home is higher. The dimension called *severity of punishment for aggression towards parents,* then, is one measure of the amount of painful frustration that is imposed on the child without direct guidance as to what would be a more acceptable form of behavior.

It is evident from this analysis that the mothers who were most permissive but also most severely punitive would have the most aggressive children; those who were most nonpermissive but least punitive would have the least aggressive ones. As may be seen in Table 1, this was the case for both sexes. The children of mothers in the other two groups were in between.

These findings are similar to those of an earlier study[2] in one respect. In that research, 40 children were observed in nursery school. The amount of aggression they showed there was compared with their mothers' reports of the severity of punishment for aggression that they suffered at home. In that study, too, high aggression was found to be associated with severe punishment, especially in the boys. There was some indication that the *most* severely punished girls had become quite passive and inhibited. They displayed little activity of any kind, including aggression. When activity level was taken into consideration, they tended to be more like the boys, i.e., the more severely punished girls were *relatively* more aggressive than the less severely punished. It is interesting to note the similarity between the present findings and the earlier study, because in that research the measure of child aggression was entirely independent of the measures of child-rearing practices.

A word of caution must be said here about the interpretation of our results. We have shown that the mothers who punished their children most severely for aggression tended to report that their children displayed more than the average amount of aggression toward their parents. We have implied in our discussion that the maternal behavior *caused* the child behavior. It is entirely possible, of course, that the correlation could be explained as a parental response to the child's pre-existing temperament. That is, some children may have been born with a higher level of aggressive impulses than others, and the more aggressive the child naturally was, the more his parents may have been forced to punish him for aggression. We have chosen to interpret the matter the other way around: that punishment by the mother bred counter-aggression in the child. Our reason is that permissiveness was also associated with aggression and we cannot see why aggression in the child should elicit permissiveness in the mother.

Our interpretation must be tentative, however, for the other explanation of the results cannot be ruled out without further research. It is quite possible, of course, that a circular process develops: the parent's punishment makes the child aggressive, this aggression leads to further punishment, and so on. Which came first, to set the whole thing in motion, is a problem we cannot solve with our existing information.

Our findings suggest that the way for parents to produce a nonaggressive child is to make abundantly clear that aggression is frowned upon and to stop aggression when it occurs, but to avoid punishing the child for his aggression. Punishment seems to have complex effects. While undoubtedly it often stops a particular form of aggression, at least momentarily, it appears to generate more hostility in the child and lead to further aggressive outbursts at some other time or place. Furthermore, when the parents punish — particularly when they employ physical punishment — they are providing a living example of the use of aggression at the very moment they are trying to teach the child not to be aggressive. The child, who copies his parents in many ways, is likely to learn as much from this example of successful aggression on his parents' part as he is from the pain of punishment. Thus, the most peaceful home is one in which the mother believes aggression is not desirable and under no circumstances is ever to be expressed toward her, but who relies mainly on non-punitive forms of control. The homes where the children show angry, aggressive outbursts frequently are likely to be homes in which the mother has a relatively tolerant (or careless!) attitude toward such behavior, or where she administers severe punishment for it, or both.

These conclusions will certainly not astonish anyone who has worked professionally with children and their parents, but they will not find ready acceptance by many other people. There are two reasons.

First, *punishment is satisfying* to the parent. When a child aggresses toward his mother, he angers her, interferes with what she is doing, with her peace of mind, with her dignity and self-respect. Aggression hurts. It is meant to. And it produces in the mother the appropriate stimulation to retaliate in kind. Combined with her sense of obligation to rear her child properly, this retaliation comes out in a way she thinks of as "punishment" — that is, a form of aggression designed to have a good *training* effect on its recipient. Many mothers have developed strong beliefs that punishment is a helpful method of control. (Sometimes it is, too.) These beliefs are essential to the peace of mind of such mothers. Without the conviction that "punishment is *good* for my child," these mothers would be forced to view their own behavior as retaliatory, aggressive, childish — in short, contemptible. This would not long provide a tolerable self-image. It is to be expected, then, that our demonstration of the deleterious effect of severe punishment of aggression will not be an easy finding for many people to swallow.

A second matter has to do with permissiveness. The difficulty grows out of the problem of punishment. During the last three decades there has developed, among the more literate and sensitive part of the American people, an uneasy recognition that punishment sometimes eliminates a few specific responses but leaves a strongly hostile drive bottled up within the child. There is evidence to support this belief. With this consideration in mind and an urgent desire to provide better mental hygiene for their children, not a few parents have developed what almost amounts to a cult of being permissive about aggression. They seem to have assumed (we think wrongly) that if they are to avoid punishing their children for aggression, they must allow the children's aggression to go unchecked. Their aim is to avoid repression, to permit the child easier and freer expression of his impulses, and thus to prevent the development of aggression-anxiety, with its accompanying displacements, projections, and sometimes uncontrollable fantasies.

This aim is good, both for the children and the society they will compose, but whether it can be achieved by a high degree of permissiveness for expression of aggression toward the parents is a question. Does a permissive attitude, with the consequent freer expression of aggression help the child to "get his aggression out of his system" and thus decrease the strength of projective fantasies? There is no indication in our own data that it does. Each of the children in the present study was tested with two 20-minute sessions of doll play. The children of the more nonpermissive half of the group of mothers showed little if any more fantasy aggression under these circumstances than the children of the more permissive half. It seems, therefore, that the parents' refusal to permit aggression had not produced a "bottled-up" aggressive force in the children that sought expression in fantasy. This finding is in sharp contrast to that with respect to punishment; the children of the more severely punishing mothers displayed quite significantly more fantasy aggression than the children of the less severely punishing ones.[3]

Permissiveness does not seem to decrease fantasy indications of aggressive impulses. Permissiveness *does* increase the amount of aggression in the home, however, and it is worth considering what this does to the child himself. An angry child is not usually a happy child nor is he one who receives affection and willing companionship from others. He is a source of discomfort to family and peers and probably receives a certain amount of retaliation. He upsets his siblings, raises the level of frustration imposed on his parents, and inevitably has an increase, to some extent, of his own aggression-anxiety. There seems little advantage in all this, either to the child himself or to his parents.

One cautionary point: we are not suggesting that parents should band together in omnipotent suppression of every justifiable angry response the child makes. The right to be angry without fear or guilt is as inalienable as any other, and more important than some. But since anger interferes with constructive action in the face of many, if not most, problem situations that the child and his family face, parents are understandably anxious to keep it within reasonable bounds; and our interest has been in showing what parental actions are likely to have the desired effects and what actions are likely to have undesired side-effects.

Notes

1. In these excerpts from interviews, *I* designates the questions put by the interviewer and *M* the replies of the mother.
2. R. R. Sears, J. W. M. Whiting, V. Nowlis, and P. S. Sears, "Some Child-rearing Antecedents of Aggression and Dependency in Young Children," *Genet. Psychol. Monogr.,* 1953, XLVII, 135–234.
3. H. Levin and R. R. Sears, "Identification with Parents as a Determinant of Doll Play Aggression," *Child Devel.,* 1956, XXVII, 135–153.

STANLEY MILGRAM

Group Pressure and Action against a Person

A great many variations of a paradigm provided by Asch (1951) show that there is an intelligible relationship between several features of the social environment and the degree to which a person will rely on others for his public judgments. Because it possesses merits of simplicity, clarity, and reconstructs in the laboratory powerful and socially relevant psychological processes, this paradigm has gained widespread acceptance as a basic technique of research on influence processes.

One feature that has been kept constant through the variations on Asch's work is that verbal judgment has been retained as the end product and basic index of conformity. More generally, a *signal* offered by the subject as representing his judgment has been the focus of study. Most often the signal has taken the form of a verbal pronouncement (Asch, 1956; Milgram, 1961), though mechanical devices which the subject uses to signal his judgment have also been employed (Crutchfield, 1955; Tuddenham and MacBride, 1959).

A distinction can be made between *signal conformity* and *action conformity* in that the immediate consequence of the former is purely informational; the subject states his opinion or reports on his perception of some feature of the environment. Action conformity, on the other hand, produces an immediate effect or alteration in the milieu that goes beyond a contribution of information. It refers to the elicitation of a *deed* by group forces, the induction of an act that is more than communicative in its effect. The act may be directed toward the well being of another person (e.g., a man is induced by group pressure to share bread with a beggar) or it may be oriented toward nonsocial parts of the environment (a delinquent is induced by gang pressure to throw a rock at a shop window).

There is little reason to assume a priori that observations made with regard to verbal conformity are automatically applicable to action. A person may pay lip service to the norms of a group and then be quite unwilling to carry out the kinds of behavior the group norms imply. Furthermore, an individual may accept and even promulgate a group standard at the verbal level, and yet find himself *unable* to translate the belief into deeds. Here we refer not to the distinction between overt compliance and private acceptance, but of the relationship between a genuinely accepted belief and its transformation into behavior.

From Stanley Milgram, "Group Pressure and Action against a Person," *Journal of Abnormal and Social Psychology* 69 (1964), pp. 137–143. Copyright © 1964 by the American Psychological Association. Reprinted by permission. Footnotes renumbered. This research was supported by Grant NSF G-17916 from the National Science Foundation.

The main point of the present experiment is to see if a person will perform acts under group pressure that he would not have performed in the absence of social inducement. There are many particular forms of action that can be inserted into a general group-pressure experimental design. One could study sorting IBM cards, or making paper cutouts, or eating crackers. Convenience makes them attractive, and in several valuable experiments investigators have used these tasks to good advantage (Frank, 1944; French, Morrison, and Levinger, 1960; Raven and French, 1958). But eventually social psychology must come to grips with significant behavior contents, contents that are of interest in their own right and are not simply trivial substitutes for psychologically meaningful forms of behavior. Guided by this consideration, a relatively potent form of action was selected for shaping by group pressure. We asked: Can a group induce a person to deliver punishment of increasing severity to a protesting individual? Whereas Asch and others have shown in what manner group pressure can cause a person to pronounce judgments that contradict his thinking, the present study examines whether group pressure causes a person to engage in acts at variance with his uninfluenced behavior.

Method

The details of subject recruitment, subject composition, experimenter's introductory patter, apparatus, and learning task have been described elsewhere (Milgram, 1963) and need only be sketched here.

Subjects consisted of eighty male adults, ranging in age from twenty to fifty years, and distributed in equal numbers, ages, and occupational statuses in the experimental and control conditions.

Procedure for Experimental Condition

General. The basic experimental situation is one in which a team of three persons (including two confederates) tests a fourth person on a paired-associate learning task. Whenever the fourth party makes a mistake the team punishes him with an electric shock. The two confederates suggest increasingly higher shock levels; the experimenter observes in what degree the third member of the team (a naive subject) goes along with or resists the confederates' pressure to increase the voltage levels.

Details. Four adults arrive at a campus laboratory to participate in a study of memory and learning. On arrival each subject is paid $4.50. The experimenter explains that a variety of roles must be performed in the experiment, and that to make role assignments fairly, subjects are to draw printed slips from a hat, each slip designating a particular experimental role. Actually, three of the adults are confederates, and only one naive subject is tested each hour. The drawing is rigged so that the naive subject is always assigned the position, Teacher 3, and Confederate B is always the Learner. The role assignments, which the subjects read from the drawn slips, are as follows:

Role title	Participant	Task
Teacher 1	Confederate C	First, you will read word pairs to the learner. Then you will read a stimulus word along with four possible answers.
Teacher 2	Confederate A	When the learner gives his answer, your task is to indicate whether he is correct or incorrect. When he has erred you will provide him with the correct answer.
Teacher 3	Naive subject	Whenever the learner gives an incorrect answer, you will administer punishment by activating a shock generator.
Learner	Confederate B	Your task will be to learn a list of word pairs read to you by Teacher 1.

The experimenter explains that the purpose of the experiment is to study the effects of punishment on memory in a contest of "collective teaching." Confederate B is taken to an adjoining room and in full view of the others is strapped into an electric-chair apparatus. The experimenter explains the nature of the learning task to the Learner and, passing over a remark made by the Learner concerning a mild heart condition, takes the three teachers to the main experimental room.

They are seated before an imposing shock generator whose essential feature is a horizontal line of thirty lever switches, labeled 15–450 volts, in 15-volt increments. Verbal designations are spread along the line of switches reading: Slight Shock, Moderate Shock, Strong Shock, Very Strong Shock, Intense Shock, Extreme Intensity Shock, and Danger: Severe Shock.

The experimenter restates that the Learner is to be tested on a paired-associate learning task (see Milgram, 1963, for details). Teachers are told that the Learner must be shocked each time he errs in the learning task. The experimenter explains how the level of shock is to be determined:

> Now the amount of punishment given on any trial is decided by the teachers themselves. Each of you will suggest a shock level. And the shock actually administered will be the lowest level suggested by any of the three teachers. In order to keep the experiment running smoothly, give suggested levels in this order: Teacher 1, submit your bid first; Teacher 4, submit your bid second; and teacher 3, submit your bid third. Remember you can stick to one level or raise or lower your level as you desire, but on any trial, the punishment administered will be the lowest level suggested by any teacher on that trial.

Thus the naive subject finds himself in a position in which, on any trial, he can effectively control the maximum shock administered to the Learner, e.g., the ground rules of the experiment would permit him to hold the shock level down to 15 volts throughout the laboratory session. On the other hand he may go along with or move in the direction of the group choice. It is the naive subject who actually adminsters the shock by depressing the appropriate lever on the generator (i.e., he always emerges from the rigged drawing as Teacher 3).

The three teachers each have their roles spelled out for them again, and there remains only the task of giving each a sample shock from the generator before the experiment gets under way.

Behavior of Teachers 1 and 2 (Confederates). According to a prearranged schedule the two confederates at the shock generator call for a one-step increase in the shock level each time the Learner errs. On the first error they both call for Shock Level 1 (15 volts); on the twentieth error they both call for Shock Level 20 (300 volts), and so forth. Their constant unanimity is rendered credible by having Teacher 1 play a somewhat domineering, and Teacher 2 a somewhat submissive type. The confederates, played by adult actors, appear indifferent to the complaints of the Learner.

Behavior of the Learner. According to a prearranged schedule the Learner responds to the learning task by providing answers in the proportion of three wrong answers to each correct one. There are a total of forty trials, thirty of them being critical (occasions when the Learner answers incorrectly).

The Learner's responses are not limited to providing answers. As the shocks administered to him become stronger, he grunts, protests, and demands to be let out of the experiment. Each complaint of the Learner is, in fact, prerecorded on magnetic tape, and is coordinated to a specific shock level. The protests and expressions of discomfort follow spontaneously the administration of an electric shock.

The Learner indicates no discomfort until the 75-volt shock is administered, at which time there is a slight grunt in response to the punishment. Similar reactions follow the 90- and 105-volt shocks, and at 120 volts the Learner shouts to the experimenter that the shocks are becoming painful. Painful groans are heard on the administration of the 135-volt shock, and at 150 volts the Learner cries out that he wants to be released from the experiment, complaining of a heart disturbance. Cries of this type continue with generally rising intensity, so that at 180 volts, the Learner cries out "I can't stand the pain," and by 285 volts his response to the shock is clearly an agonized scream. At 300 volts the victim shouts in desperation that he will no longer provide answers to the memory test, and so forth through 450 volts. In other words, increases in shock level are met by increasingly severe reactions from the person being punished.

It is to be remembered that this is merely a *potential* series of responses. If a shock no higher than the 75-volt level is administered, only a grunt is heard. As a point of procedure, protests were not repeated at the same shock level, e.g., after the first grunt was used in response to Shock Level 75, no further complaints were introduced until and if a higher shock level were used.

Experimental Measures. The principal experimental measure, therefore, is the level of shock administered by the subject on each of the thirty critical trials. The shock levels were automatically recorded by an Esterline-Angus event recorder wired directly into the shock generator, providing us with a permanent record of each subject's performance.

Postexperimental Session. An interview and debriefing session were held immediately after each subject's performance. A variety of background measures was obtained, as well as qualitative reactions to the experimental situation.

Control Condition

The purpose of the control condition is to determine the level of shock the naive subject administers to the Learner in the absence of group influence. One naive subject and one confederate (the Learner) perform in each session. The procedure is identical to that in the experimental condition, except that the tasks of Confederates A and C are collapsed into one role handled by the naive subject. References to collective teaching are omitted.

The naive subject is instructed to adminster a shock each time the Learner errs, and the naive subject is told that as teacher he is free to select any shock level on any of the trials. In all other respects the control and experimental procedures are identical.

Results

Figure 1 shows the mean shock levels for each critical trial in the experimental and control conditions. It also shows a diagonal representing the stooge-groups suggested shock level on each critical trial. The degree to which the experimental function moves away from the control level and toward the stooge-group diagonal represents the effects of group influence. Inspection indicates that the confederates substantially influenced the level of shock administered to the Learner. The results will now be considered in detail.

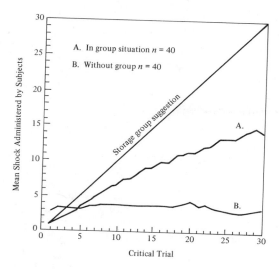

FIGURE 1 Mean Shock Levels in Experimental and Control
Conditions over Thirty Critical Trials

In the experimental condition the standard deviation of shock levels rose regularly from trial to trial, and roughly in proportion to the rising mean shock level. However, in the control condition the standard deviation did not vary systematically with the mean through the thirty trials. Representative mean shock levels and standard deviations for the two conditions are shown in Table 1. Hartley's test for homogeneity of variance confirmed that the variances in the two conditions were significantly different. Therefore a reciprocal-of-the-square root transformation was performed before an analysis of variance was carried out.

TABLE 1
Representative Mean Shock Levels and Standard Deviations
in the Experimental and Control Conditions

Trial	*Experimental condition*		*Control condition*	
	Mean shock level	*SD*	*Mean shock level*	*SD*
5	4.03	1.19	3.35	2.39
10	6.78	2.63	3.48	3.03
15	9.20	4.28	3.68	3.58
20	11.45	6.32	4.13	4.90
25	13.55	8.40	3.55	3.85
30	14.13	9.59	3.38	1.89

As summarized in Table 2, the analysis of variance showed that the overall mean shock level in the experimental condition was significantly higher than that in the control condition ($p < .001$). This is less interesting, however, than the differing slopes in the two conditions, which show the group effects through the course of the experimental session.[1] The analysis of variance test for trend confirmed that the slopes for the two conditions differed significantly ($p < .001$).

Examination of the standard deviations in the experimental condition shows that there are large individual differences in response to group pressure, some

TABLE 2
Analysis of Variance of Shock Levels Administered
in the Experimental and Control Conditions

Source	df	SS	MS	F
Total between individuals	79	966,947.1	12,239.8	
Between experimental conditions	1	237,339.4	237,339.4	25.37 [a]
Between individuals	78	729,607.7	9,353.9	
Within individuals	2,320	391,813.5	168.9	
Between trials	29	157,361.7	5,426.3	96.04 [a]
Trials × Experimental conditions (trend)	29	106,575.4	3,675.0	65.04 [a]
Remainder	2,262	127,876.4	56.5	

[a] $p < .001$.

subjects following the group closely, others resisting effectively. Subjects were ranked according to their total deviation from the confederates' shock choices. On the thirtieth critical trial the most conforming quartile had a mean shock level of 27.6, while the mean shock level of the least conforming quartile was 4.8. Background characteristics of the experimental subjects were noted: age, marital status, occupation, military experience, political preference, religious affiliation, birth-order information, and educational history. Less educated subjects (high school degree or less) tended to yield more than those who possess a college degree (x^2 $_{df = 1} = 2.85$, $p < .10$). Roman Catholic subjects tended to yield more than Protestant subjects (x^2 $_{df = 1} = 2.96$, $p < .10$). No other background variable measured in the study was associated with amount of yielding, though the number of subjects employed was too small for definite conclusions.

The shock data may also be examined in terms of the *maximum* shock administered by subjects in the experimental and control conditions, i.e., the highest single shock administered by a subject throughout the thirty critical trials. The information is presented in Table 3. Only two control subjects administered shocks beyond the tenth voltage level (at this point the Learner makes his first truly vehement protest), while twenty-seven experimental subjects went beyond this point. A median test showed that the maximum shocks administered by experimental subjects were higher than those administered by control subjects (x^2 $_{df = 1} = 39.2$, $p < .001$).

The main effect, then, is that in the experimental condition subjects were substantially influenced by group pressure. When viewed in terms of the mean shock level over the thirty critical trials, as in Figure 1, the experimental function appears as a vector more or less bisecting the angle formed by the confederates' diagonal and control slopes. Thus one might be tempted to say that the subject's action in the experimental situation had two major sources: it was partly determined by the level the subject would have chosen in the control condition, and partly by the confederates' choice. Neither one nor the other entirely dominates the average behavior of subjects in the experimental condition. There are very great individual differences in regard to the more dominant force.

Discussion

The substantive contribution of the present study lies in the demonstration that group influence can shape behavior in a domain that might have been thought highly resistant to such effects. Subjects are induced by the group to inflict pain on another person at a level that goes well beyond levels chosen in the absence of social pressure. Hurting a man is an action that for most people carries considerable psychological significance; it is closely tied to questions of conscience and ethical judgment. It might have been thought that the protests of the victim and inner prohibitions against hurting others would have operated effectively to curtail the subject's compliance. While the experiment yields wide variation in performance, a substantial number of subjects submitted readily to pressure applied to them by the confederates.

The significance of yielding in Asch's situation is sometimes questioned because the discriminative task is not an issue of self-evident importance for many subjects (Bronowski).[2] The criticism is not easily extended to the present study. Here the subject does not merely feign agreement with a group on a perceptual task of undefined importance; and he is unable to dismiss his action by relegating it to the status of a trivial gesture, for a person's suffering and discomfort are at stake.

TABLE 3
Maximum Shock Levels Administered in Experimental
and Control Conditions

| Verbal designation and voltage indication | Number of subjects for whom this was maximum shock | |
	Experimental	Control
Slight shock		
15	1	3
30	2	6
45	0	7
60	0	7
Moderate shock		
75	1	5
90	0	4
105	1	1
120	1	1
Strong shock		
135	2	3
150	5	1
165	2	0
180	0	0
Very strong shock		
195	1	0
210	2	0
225	2	0
240	1	0
Intense shock		
255	2	0
270	0	0
285	1	0
300	1	0
Extreme intensity shock		
315	2	0
330	0	0
345	1	0
360	2	0
Danger: severe shock		
375	0	1
390	0	0
405	1	0
420	2	0
XXX		
435	0	0
450	7	1

The behavior observed here occurred within the framework of a laboratory study presided over by an experimenter. In some degree his authority stands behind the group. In his initial instructions the experimenter clearly legitimized the use of any shock level on the console. Insofar as he does not object to the shocks administered in the course of the experiment, his assent is implied. Thus, even though the effects of group pressure have been clearly established by a comparison of the experimental and control conditions, the effects occurred within the context of authoritative sanction. This point becomes critical in any attempt to assess the relative effectiveness of *conformity* versus *obedience* as means of inducing contravalent behavior (Milgram, 1963). If the experimenter had not approved the use of all shock levels on the generator, and if he had departed from the laboratory at an early stage, thus eliminating any sign of authoritative assent during the course of the experiment, would the group have had as powerful an effect on the naive subject?

There are many points of difference between Asch's investigation and the procedure of the present study that can only be touched upon here.

1. While in Asch's study the *adequate* response is anchored to an external stimulus event, in the present study we are dealing with an internal, unbound standard.

2. A mispoken judgment can, in principle, be withdrawn, but here we are dealing with action that has an immediate and unalterable consequence. Its irreversibility stems not from constraints extrinsic to the action, but from the content of the action itself: once the Learner is shocked, he cannot be unshocked.

3. In the present experiment, despite the several sources of opinion, there can be but a single shock level on each trial. There is, therefore, a competition for outcome that was not present in the Asch situation.

4. While in the Asch study the focus of pressure is directed toward the subject's judgment, with distortion of public response but an intermediary stage of influence, here the focus of pressure is directed toward performance of action itself. Asch's yielding subject may secretly harbor the true judgment; but when the performance of an action becomes the object of social pressure, there is no comparable recourse to a covert form. The subject who performed the act demanded by the group has yielded exhaustively.

5. In the Asch situation a yielding subject engages in a covert violation of his obligations to the experimenter. He has agreed to report to the experimenter what he sees, and insofar as he goes along with the group, he breaks this agreement. In contrast, in the present experiment the yielding subject acts within the terms of the "subject-experimenter contract." In going along with the two confederates the subject may violate his own inner standards, and the rights of the Learner, but his relationship with the experimenter remains intact at both the manifest and private levels. Subjects in the two experiments are faced with different patterns of social pressure and violate different relationships through social submission.

Notes

1. On the first four trials the control group has a higher mean shock than the experimental group; this is an artifact due to the provision that in the experimental condition the shock actually administered and recorded was the lowest sug-

gested by any member of the group; when the subject called for a shock level higher than that suggested by the confederates, it was not reflected in the data. (This situation arose only during the first few critical trials.) By the fifth critical trial the group pressure begins to show its effect in elevating the mean shock level of the naive subjects.

2. J. Bronowski, personal communication, January 10, 1962.

References

Asch, S. E. 1951. Effects of group pressure upon the modification and distortion of judgment. In H. Guetzkow (ed.), *Groups, leadership, and men.* Pittsburgh: Carnegie Press.

Asch, S. E. 1956. Studies of independence and conformity: I. A minority of one against a unanimous majority. *Psychological Monographs* 70: (9, Whole No. 416).

Crutchfield, R. S. 1955. Conformity and character. *American Psychologist* 10: 191–98.

Frank, J. D. 1944. Experimental studies of personal pressure and resistance. *Journal of General Psychology* 30: 23–64.

French, J. R. P., Jr., H. W. Morrison, and G. Levinger. 1960. Coercive power and forces affecting conformity. *Journal of Abnormal and Social Psychology* 61: 93–101.

Milgram, S. 1961. Nationality and conformity. *Scientific American* 205: 45–51.

Milgram, S. 1963. Behavioral study of obedience. *Journal of Abnormal and Social Psychology* 67: 371–78.

Raven, B. H., and J. R. P. French. 1958. Legitimate power, coercive power, and observability in social influence. *Sociometry* 21: 83–97.

Tuddenham, R. D., and P. MacBride. 1959. The yielding experiment from the subject's point of view. *Journal of Personality* 27: 259–71.

RAYMOND J. ADAMEK
EDWARD Z. DAGER

Social Structure, Identification, and Change in a Treatment-Oriented Institution

In recent years, sociologists have focused a good deal of attention on what Goffman (1961) has called the "total institution," and especially on correctional institutions. As these studies have accumulated, our knowledge of the complexity of such institutions and their related subsystems have increased. Earlier studies, such as those of Clemmer (1958), McCorkle and Korn (1958), and Sykes (1958),

Reprinted by permission from *American Sociological Review* 33:6 (1968), pp. 931–944.

described what came to be known as the "solidary opposition" model of inmate culture, with inmates aligned almost as one body against the formal organization and its goals. Newcomers to the inmate world were soon socialized into this inmate culture, and the process of "prisonization" was thought to increase with length of incarceration. Wheeler's (1961) study, however, indicated that inmate values tended to follow a U-shaped pattern, being most conventional at the beginning and end of one's sentence. He suggested that those nearing the end of their sentence were experiencing anticipatory socialization which would prepare them for life in the outside world. Garabedian (1963) noted a similar pattern in his study, but also noted that not all prisoners' values changed in the same manner. The type of role one adopted during his incarceration determined in part the extent and point of greatest impact of the prison culture on his initial values.

The relatively simple "solidary opposition" model of inmate culture has now been replaced by a more complex model which finds inmate organization dependent in large part upon the location of the institution's primary goals along a custodial-training-treatment continuum. This development owes much to the work of Vinter and Janowitz (1959), Grusky (1959), Street (1965), and Berk (1966), and has culminated in a volume by Street, Vinter, and Perrow (1967) which reports the results of these and related studies which examine the effect of organizational goals not only on inmate culture, but also on staff-inmate relations, staff-staff relations, staff-parent organization relations, and institution-local community relations.

All of the aforementioned studies have dealt with institutions serving males. Until recent years, comparatively few sociological studies have been made of institutions for females. The work of Heffernan (1964), Ward and Kassebaum (1965), and Giallombardo (1966), however, serves to close this gap. Studying three different institutions serving adult females, they all find pseudo-family and homosexual ties to be an important aspect of inmate social organization, although Heffernan especially notes two other major adaptations to prison life, relating prison roles to criminal career prior to incarceration. Kosofsky and Ellis (1958) and Konopka (1966), among others, note similar patterns in institutions serving adolescent females.

The particular appeal of the correctional institution for the sociologist, of course, is not only that it is a society-in-miniature, whose structure and functioning he may describe, but also that it is what Vinter (1963) has called a "people-changing organization." Such organizations, he points out, "are usually concerned with effecting new and diffuse modes of behavior, new self-images or personalities" in the people who come to it. This they attempt to do by deliberately structuring staff-client relations in a manner intended to permit realization of this goal. Such organizations are, therefore, engaged in the business of socialization, a process of major interest to the sociologist. How successful institutions are at this business will depend not only on their major goal-orientation, but in large part first, upon how aware they are of inmate-inmate relations, and second, upon how successful they are in mobilizing these relations to support the achievement of staff goals. Ohlin and Lawrence (1959) and Vinter (1963) point out the perils of ignoring the inmate culture if treatment goals are to be achieved, and the work of Blum (1962), Fisher (1961), and Polsky (1962) in institutions serving male delinquents lends empirical support to their papers. Cressey (1955), Grosser (1958), and

Vinter and Janowitz (1959), among others, have suggested principles which might be followed in order to successfully involve the inmate culture in assisting the staff in the task of socializing the individual inmate. These principles have been put into practice to varying degrees, and have met with more or less success at Northways (Miller, 1964), at Highfields (McCorkle et al., 1958), and in the Provo Experiment (Empey & Rabow, 1961).

Identification

One important factor in understanding why some institutions are able to mobilize inmate support for staff goals, and why some inmates are effectively socialized by their institutional experience, while others are not, is the social-psychological process of identification. Unless the inmates come to accept staff members as significant others, unless they come to feel a part of the institution so that its goals become their goals, we can hardly expect the staff to enlist the aid of the inmate culture, or to be successful in its task of people-changing.[1]

We may distinguish at least three types of identification: personal, positional, and institutional. Following Winch's (1962) analysis of the first two types, personal identification signifies that type in which the model becomes a significant other to the identifier, who feels positive affection and admiration for the model, takes on his norms and values, and defines the model's direct control over him as legitimate. Effective socialization within the institution then, would be facilitated if an inmate personally identified with a staff member, or with another inmate who was himself effectively socialized by the institution.

Positional identification is that which results from one individual being placed in a role relationship with another, in which relations are reciprocal, e.g., teacher/student or staff-member/inmate, are governed by norms, and in which the model probably has control over resources valuable to the identifier, and is superior in status to the identifier. The identifier will feel admiration and respect for the model, but not necessarily affection or emotional warmth. Again, a staff member or another inmate might serve as the model for positional identification.

Finally, we may speak of institutional identification, by which we mean that an individual comes to feel a part of an organization, has primarily positive attitudes toward it, and in general has accepted its goals, values, and norms as his own. Institutional identification is closely related to positional identification, since the individual comes into contact with the "institution" through the roles he plays in that institution relative to others within it. It differs in that it is somewhat less dependent upon a specific model in the form of a single individual, and is broader in scope.

The degree to which an individual identifies with a particular organization is not entirely beyond the organization's control, as Etzioni (1961) has pointed out. By focusing on various types of control and reward mechanisms, varying degrees of commitment to the organization may be obtained. Moreover, such factors as the clarity of organizational structure and role expectations, the length of time an individual anticipates membership in an organization and actually spends in the organization, the number of alternative reference groups available to the individual, the degree to which the individual is allowed to participate in organizational activities, and the degree to which it is possible for him to increase his organizational status, all have a bearing on the likelihood that identification will take place, and are, in fact, amenable to control by the organization.[2]

Identification with other persons or groups implies that these persons become significant others to ego, and that these groups become his reference groups. As the individual identifies, therefore, he becomes more amenable to social influence. He looks to those with whom he identifies to define role expectations for him, is sensitive to the sanctions they impose, and receives gratification from pleasing them. They become the primary audience to which he plays his roles. Their norms and values are utilized as criteria for judging his behavior, and in time are adopted as his own.

In view of the foregoing discussion, we hypothesize that both institutional identification and identification with staff members in correctional institutions are directly related to the amount and type of change inmates experience during their incarceration. Further, we suggest that relatively clear organizational structure and role expectations, long length of anticipated and actual stay, few alternative reference groups, high organizational participation, and readily available channels for organizational mobility are conducive to identification with the institution.

Procedure and Data

A treatment-oriented,[3] closed institution for delinquent girls provided the setting in which we were able to "test" these hypotheses. The institution is located in a large midwestern city, and is operated by the Sisters of the Good Shepherd, who operate some 48 similar institutions in the country. Together, these institutions are said to serve one-fourth of our delinquent female population (Engh, 1966). An official brochure describing the institution notes, "The environment [the institution] offers shields the girl from her former associates and from a prejudicial society. It provides opportunities to acquire new ideals and constructive habits that will reestablish her in society." The staff attempts to provide what is felt most of the girls have lacked in their past life — love (a concern for the individual's welfare, and interest in that individual as a person), and firm direction.[4]

Responsibility for the day-to-day management of the institution rests upon the shoulders of one of the nuns, who serves as Directress of Girls and Co-Director of the Diagnostic Center. Two psychiatrists, a psychologist, several doctors and dentists, and a nurse serve on a part-time basis. A full-time Director of Social Service, a part-time social worker, a part-time administrative assistant, and two secretaries round out the diagnostic center staff. The institution also maintains an accredited, four-year high school, staffed by eight nuns and four lay women. Four nuns, including the Directress, serve as "group mothers" to the four school classes, and conduct weekly group meetings, to be described below. The group mothers are in contact with the girls more than any other staff member, and sleep in private rooms within the girls' dorms.

Data on the institution and the girls were gathered by questionnaire, an extensive search of institutional records, informal conversations with staff, structured interviews with 50 of the girls, and non-participant observation in the institution. The principal author spent 55 days at the institution over an eight-month period, including eight days observing the girls in their daily routine. He also attended several special institutional functions, e.g., graduation ceremonies.

The Delinquents

The girls resident at the institution (the normal population is between 80–105) are committed by the Courts. Admission, however, is selective. Only those girls are admitted who are over 13 years of age, have completed at least eight years of schooling, and who are judged by the staff, on the basis of referral material, to indicate a potential for benefiting from the program. In addition, girls who have severe emotional problems are not admitted, nor are those who are known to have had homosexual experiences.

The 119 girls who were residents sometime between May and October of 1966 comprise the population of the present study.[5] They are predominantly white (86.8 per cent) Protestants (59.7 per cent). One girl is Jewish, 28.6 per cent are Catholic, and 10.9 per cent indicate no religious preference. On the basis of father's occupation, the girls come from predominantly lower-middle and upper-lower class families. Of those whose fathers' occupations were known (information was lacking for 20 girls), approximately 33 per cent were skilled manual workers, 25 per cent were operatives and semi-skilled workers, and 16 per cent were unskilled laborers. Ten per cent of the girls had fathers with occupations above that of clerical worker.

Forty-nine per cent of the girls were admitted to the institution between the ages of thirteen and fifteen-and-a-half, and 51 per cent were older at admission. Their primary offenses were rather typical of female delinquents. Sixteen per cent were specifically charged with ungovernability, 22 per cent with runaway, 7 per cent with truancy, 2 per cent with sex delinquency, and 45 per cent with a combination of these offenses. Five per cent of the girls were charged with stealing, and three per cent were apparently committed to protect them from an undesirable home atmosphere. The girls' records indicated that 40 per cent had no official police contact prior to admission, 27 per cent had one such contact, and 28 per cent had two or more contacts.

Measures of Identification

During the course of a case study of the institution, the senior author administered questionnaires which contained two measures of identification and five measures of change. Identification of the girls with staff members was measured by the Interpersonal Check List (ICL) (Leary, 1956, 1957). This instrument contains 128 adjectives or phrases which the respondent may signify as descriptive of his "real" self, his "ideal" self, or other persons. An individual is said to identify with another if his real-self description is similar to his description of that person. Leary (1956) presents the procedure by which an "identify" or "does-not-identify" decision may be made. In utilizing the ICL, we are assuming that a person who is perceived as similar to oneself is a significant other who will be able to influence one's norms and behavior. The work of Fiedler (1953) and Jourard (1957) lends some support to this assumption.

Identification with the institution was measured by a 35-item Likert scale adapted from a longer scale developed by Eshleman et al. (1960). Sample items from this scale include the following: "I'm glad I came to (institution)," "I feel I really belong to (institution)," and "Anyone who accepts the values of (institution) simply does not think for herself." Utilizing the mean-difference method suggested by Edwards (1957), we found all items discriminated satisfactorily. The corrected split-half reliability of the scale was 0.96. With a possible range of scores from 35 to 175, the actual range for our respondents was 46 to 175. Respondents were divided into three numerically equal groups, and classified as high (score 148 and above), medium (122 to 147), and low (121 and below) identifiers.

As a partial validity check on our measures of identification, we analyzed the relationship between identification and two other variables, leadership and conformity, reasoning that identification with a staff member and with the institution should be positively related to being a leader, and to being high on conformity to institutional norms.[6] The results generally support our expectations. While 35.1 per cent of those ($N = 57$) who identify with staff are leaders, only 17.2 per cent of those ($N = 29$) who do not identify are leaders. Since age at entrance to the institution was related to identification with staff members, age differences might have accounted for this finding. However, even when we control for age, those who identify with staff are more likely to be leaders than those who do not identify. Similarly, while 50.0 per cent of those ($N = 32$) with high *institutional* identification are leaders, leaders comprise only 25.0 per cent of those ($N = 28$) with medium, and 10.7 per cent of those ($N = 28$) with low institutional identification. Leaders are more likely to have high institutional identification than non-leaders, even when we control for length of stay, which was found to be significantly related to institutional identification.

Girls who identify with staff, and who are high on institutional identification are also more likely to be high on conformity than those who do not identify. Thus, while 37.5 per cent of those ($N = 56$) who identify with staff are high conformers, this is true of 23.3 per cent of those ($N = 30$) who do not identify. The trend is maintained when we control for age at entrance. Of those high on institutional identification ($N = 33$), 54.5 per cent are high on conformity, 39.4 per cent are medium, and 6.1 per cent are low. Of those ($N = 27$) low on institutional identification, 33.3 per cent are high on conformity, 37.0 per cent are medium, and 29.6 per cent are low. The direction of the relationship is maintained when we control for length of stay.

Measures of Change

The ICL, the Minnesota Multiphasic Personality Inventory (MMPI), and the IPAT Anxiety Scale are administered to the girls by the staff as part of normal intake processing. It was therefore decided to readminister these tests to provide a longitudinal measure of change. In view of the institution's goals, and the means it utilizes to reach these goals, we expected that the girls would "improve" on these measures to the extent that they identified with the staff and/or institution.

Besides providing a measure of identification with other persons, the ICL provides a measure of self-esteem, defined operationally as a low-self/ideal-self discrepancy score. Respondents were rated as having increased, remained the same, or decreased in self-esteem on the basis of the amount of change in these scores from first to second administration. Those whose discrepancy score increased 0.5 standard deviations (SD) or more, from first to second administration, were considered to have decreased in self-esteem, those whose discrepancy score decreased 0.5 SD or more were considered to have increased in self-esteem, and those whose discrepancy score neither increased nor decreased by at least 0.5 SD were considered to have remained the same in self-esteem.

The MMPI is a widely used measure of psychological and behavioral adjustment (Dahlstrom and Welsh, 1960). Results on this test are usually interpreted by plotting the scores of ten clinical scales on a standard form, and noting the configuration of the resulting profile. After plotting the profiles of our respondents for the first and second administration of the MMPI, we presented them to eight clinical psychologists (two with Ph.D.s and considerable experience, and six advanced graduate students), and asked them to rate the respondents as improved or not improved from first to second administration. The judges agreed unanimously on 52.5 per cent of the profiles, and at least five of eight judges agreed on 97.5 per cent. In two cases, only four of eight judges agreed, but, since these included the more experienced judges, these profiles were retained.

The IPAT Anxiety Scale is a 40-item scale designed to measure "free floating anxiety," a high degree of which the authors suggest is a common element in all forms of mental disorder, and a low degree of which indicates mental health (Cattell and Scheier, 1963). A respondent was categorized as having decreased in anxiety from first to second administration if her second administration score was 0.5 SD lower than her first administration score, to have increased if it was 0.5 SD higher, and to have remained the same if it was neither 0.5 SD above or below her first administration score.

Finally, two other scales were utilized to determine the degree to which the institution was successful in attaining its goal of people-changing. These were two Guttman scales developed by Rosenberg (1965) to measure faith in people and self-esteem. These scales were administered only once, and thus utilized in cross-sectional analysis. They were chosen for several reasons. Utilizing the theory of differential opportunity systems, Morris (1964) has suggested that the differential rate of delinquency among males and females, and the different types of offenses committed by them are related to different sex role objectives and access to these objectives provided by our society. Her dissertation provides evidence which supports the theory that male delinquency is largely a response to problems related to the achievement of status goals, while female delinquency is largely a response to problems related to the achievement of "relational goals" (the ability to establish close and harmonious relationships with others). Faith in people, we suggest, is one prerequisite for the achievement of such goals. Furthermore, several authors (Hersko, 1964; Konopka, 1966; Kopp, 1960) have noted that delinquent girls are characterized by low self-esteem. Morris' (1964) finding that delinquent girls seem particularly careless about personal grooming when compared to nondelinquent girls or boys, and even to delinquent boys, would seem to support these observations. If we accept Morris' explanation that female delinquency is a response to frustrated attempts to attain relational goals, we can better understand the association of low self-esteem and female delinquency. In his study of over 5,000 high school juniors and seniors, Rosenberg (1965) presents rather convincing evidence that persons with low self-esteem have a good deal of difficulty in interpersonal relations. In light of these studies, we reasoned that if the institution were going to change the girls so that they might function effectively on the outside, its program should serve to increase their faith in people, and their self-esteem. The institution does, in fact, consciously attempt to accomplish this through its program.

After slight modification, both scales yielded a coefficient of reproducibility of 0.92, and a minimal marginal reproducibility of 0.68, utilizing the Cornell Technique. On the basis of profile types, the respondents were classified as having low, medium, or high faith in people, and as being low, medium, or high in self-esteem.

The relationship of change in the girls to five variables other than identification was also investigated, utilizing chi-square analysis. These variables were intelligence quotient, social class, religion, age at entrance, and length of stay in the institution. None of the first three variables were significantly ($p < 0.05$) related to any of the measures of change or of identification. Since we found both length of stay and age at entrance to be significantly related to change and identification, however, we controlled for these two variables in our analyses.[7]

Results

As Table 1 indicates, those girls who identify most highly with the institution are most likely to have high faith in people, and least likely to have low faith in people. The relationship holds both for girls admitted prior to and after age 15½ ($N = 48$ and 54, respectively) with approximately the same strength (gamma = 0.52 and 0.64, respectively).[8] The relationship between institutional identification and faith in people also holds for those ($N = 57$) resident 0–12 months, and for those ($N = 45$) resident over 12 months, although it is considerably stronger for the latter (gamma = 0.42 and 0.71, respectively). The concern for others exhibited by the staff, the training the girls receive in group sessions, and the general norm of "be thy brother's keeper" which is part of the institutional culture, would seem to result in a generally high faith in people, especially for those girls who identify with the institution, and are long-term residents.

TABLE 1
Faith in People by Institutional Identification

Faith in people	Institutional identification		
	High *(N = 34)*	*Medium* *(N = 33)*	*Low* *(N = 35)*
High	35%	21%	11%
Medium	56	52	51
Low	9	27	37
Total %	100	100	99

Gamma = .43.

As is seen in Table 2, there is only a slight relationship between institutional identification and self-esteem as measured by Rosenberg's scale for the total sample. The results for short-term residents (gamma = 0.18), long term residents

TABLE 2
Self-esteem by Institutional Identification

Self-esteem	Institutional identification		
	High (N = 34)	Medium (N = 33)	Low (N = 35)
High	44%	42%	31%
Medium	44	42	49
Low	12	15	20
Total %	100	99	100

Gamma = .17.

(gamma = 0.08), and older girls (gamma = − 0.06) were of the same magnitude. For younger girls, however, there was a relatively strong, positive relationship (gamma = 0.52) between institutional identification and self-esteem. Identification was also more strongly related to favorable change for the younger girls on the MMPI and the Anxiety scale. In addition, length of stay was more strongly related to change on four of the five measures for the younger girls. The apparently greater impact of the institution on younger girls may be attributable to their greater impressionability and willingness to conform to the institution's somewhat authoritarian atmosphere. Of course, it may be that maturation, aside from any institutional effect, accounts for much of the change observed in the younger girls, but we could not effectively control for this variable.

As indicated in Table 3, self-esteem as measured by the ICL is positively related to identification with a staff member. The relationship was also maintained with approximately the same strength when we controlled for age and length of residence (gamma ranging between 0.48 and 0.59 in the four control tables). In describing staff members on the ICL, the girls were particularly likely to picture them as somewhat managerial and autocratic. Comparison of the girls' real and ideal-self descriptions at entrance to the institution and then at second administration of the ICL revealed a general movement toward the managerial-autocratic octant for their own profiles. Apparently, as the girls see themselves becoming more like staff members, their self-esteem increases.

TABLE 3
Self-esteem by Identification with Staff

Self-esteem	Identify with staff (N = 67)	Do not identify (N = 33)
Increased	36%	15%
Remained same	46	39
Decreased	18	46
Total %	100	100

Gamma = .51.

Table 4 indicates that improvement in the girls' psychological-behavioral adjustment is positively related to institutional identification. Controlling for length of stay, however, we find that for short term residents $(N = 52)$, institutional identification is only slightly related to improvement on the MMPI (gamma = 0.14). For long term residents $(N = 27)$, the relationship is relatively strong (gamma = 0.43). The relationship is also stronger for younger girls $(N = 32)$ than it is for those $(N = 47)$ older at entrance (gamma values were 0.58 and 0.25, respectively).

TABLE 4

Improvement on MMPI by Institutional Identification

	Institutional identification		
MMPI status	*High (N = 19)*	*Medium (N = 31)*	*Low (N = 29)*
Improved	42%	32%	21%
Not improved	58	68	79
Total %	100	100	100

Gamma = .32.

Finally, Table 5 shows there is a slight relationship between institutional identification and improvement on the IPAT Anxiety Scale. High identifiers are most likely to improve, but equally as likely as low identifiers to grow worse. As was true for the MMPI, when we control for length of stay, the relationship between identification and improvement is stronger for long term residents $(N = 31,$ gamma = 0.55) than it is for short term residents $(N = 51,$ gamma = 0.04), and stronger for those girls admitted prior to age 15½ $(N = 33,$ gamma = 0.59) than it is for those admitted after this age $(N = 49,$ gamma = −0.04).

TABLE 5

Change in Anxiety by Institutional Identification

	Institutional identification		
Anxiety	*High (N = 25)*	*Medium (N = 28)*	*Low (N = 29)*
Decreased	48%	18%	24%
Remained same	28	50	52
Increased	24	32	24
Total %	100	100	100

Gamma = .16.

In summary, five "tests" of the hypothesis that identification (institutional identification in four instances, and identification with staff in one) is positively related to the amount and type of change experienced by inmates in a correctional setting yielded results in the expected direction for the total population, although the relationship was rather weak in two instances. Even in these instances, however, a strong relationship between identification and change was found for girls who entered the institution at a relatively young age. We would conclude, therefore, that people-changing institutions will attain their goal to the extent that their programs foster identification. We now turn to an analysis of some of the mechanisms by which the institution under study was able to do this.

The Development of Identification

We suggest that identification is facilitated by a relatively structured social environment — i.e., an environment in which behavior is predictable, norms and behavior expectations are clear, and conforming behavior is rather consistently rewarded while non-conforming behavior is consistently punished.

Because of its highly structured program, the institution in question is apparently rather successful in fostering identification with individual staff members and with institutional norms and values. Of the 100 girls for whom we have complete data, 67 identified with the staff member they described on the ICL. This compares favorably with the girls' identification with their parents as indicated by the initial administration of the ICL upon their admission to the institution. At that time, 48.6 per cent of 105 girls for whom we have data identified with their mothers, and 50.5 per cent of 104 girls identified with their fathers.[9]

On the basis of a cross-sectional analysis of Institutional Identification Scale scores (see Table 6), and interviews with the girls, we would also conclude that institutional identification was fostered by the institution's program. We have suggested that one of the factors conducive to identification is the clarity of institutional social structure and role expectations. Just as important for identification as the degree to which a social system is structured, of course, is the nature of the social interaction which takes place within that system. Many closed institutions present highly structured programs for their inmates, but do not foster identification with staff members or with the institution itself. The girls identify not only because the institution presents a structured environment, but also because staff and peers exhibit genuine concern for their welfare. Mindful of the girls' position, the staff does attempt to treat them as individuals, and is predisposed to be reasonable, loving, and supportive, within the limits set by the rules and nature of the institution. Given these necessary preconditions, a highly structured setting becomes the sufficient condition facilitating identification.

TABLE 6
Institutional Identification by Length of Stay

Institutional identification	Length of stay in months		
	17 & over (N = 39)	7–16 (N = 36)	0–6 (N = 28)
High	62%	19%	11%
Medium	33	31	36
Low	5	50	54
Total %	100	100	101

Gamma = .64.

Several mechanisms of social control are employed by the institution which serve to structure social relations in a definite pattern, so that behavioral and attitudinal norms flow primarily from staff to inmates, and from older, staff-oriented inmates to newer inmates. One of these mechanisms is the rule of silence. Girls are expected to maintain silence for all but approximately two hours per day. The rule of silence is enforced most strictly in the dormitory, where the girls are also expected not to "pay attention" to one another. That is, they are expected to avoid even eye contact with one another. Officially maintained as a means of instilling self-discipline, the rule of silence has the obvious effect of facilitating verbal control over a large group of teenage girls, and of focusing their attention on the tasks at hand. More importantly, it also serves to reduce peer interaction, and to channelize it into those time periods and those places where it can best be supervised. The development and maintenance of a deviant peer subculture under these conditions is thus made very difficult.

In general, our data indicate that the peer subculture is primarily staff-oriented. One indication of this is the results obtained by an analysis of peer identification. Besides asking the girls to describe a staff member on the second administration of the ICL, we also asked them to describe, "the girl here at (institution) who is the most important and meaningful to you." Of the 67 girls named, only four received four or more nominations. Three of these four girls were seniors, and one was a junior who was a resident for over two years. All four had acted in the capacity of group leader three or more times, all had high institutional identification scores, and all identified with the staff member they described on the ICL. Three were high conformers to institutional norms, and one was a medium conformer. In all, 43 of 115 girls were identified with by one or more of their peers. As Table 7 indicates, compared to those who are not identified with, these girls are more likely to be long-term resident upper-classmen who identify with the staff and the institution, are group leaders, and relatively high conformers to the institutional norms.

Another important mechanism of social control is the demerit, pink slip, and gold star system. This system of punishment and reward is the chief means by which a daily record of the girls' activities as individuals, and as class groups, is recorded. For minor infractions of institutional norms, demerits are issued by the staff, while major infractions merit a pink slip. At the end of each day, the list of

TABLE 7
Characteristics of Girls Who Are and Are Not
Identified with by Peers

Characteristics	Girls identified with		Girls not identified with	
	%	(Total N)	%	(Total N)
Leaders	48	(42)	24	(58)
Low conformers	16	(43)	35	(57)
High institutional identification	41	(39)	25	(60)
Identify with staff	77	(43)	63	(67)
Resident 0–6 months	14	(43)	32	(72)
Seniors or juniors	46	(43)	36	(72)

demerits and pink slips, the name of the girl involved, and the nature of the in-fraction, is read to all the girls assembled in a large study hall. Individual and class ratings of "excellent" to "poor" are also given during these sessions, based upon the girls' performance in their classrooms for the day. The major effect of either the demerit or the pink slip is that they take away a girls' gold star for the month, the latter being a symbol of perfect conduct. Girls who accumulate a given number of gold stars are eligible for various outings held during the year, and for other privileges. Gold stars are officially awarded only four or five times a year, in a ceremony presided over by the Directress of Girls.

The girls' conduct, then, is constantly being observed and evaluated. The con-ference at the end of the day is a structually imposed examination of conscience. Whether or not a particular girl has received a mark that day, she is reminded of the rules and of what the staff considers acceptable or unacceptable behavior. Since the honor system is employed, girls do report themselves during conference for rule infractions which went unnoticed or unheeded by others.

For many of the girls, participating in a social system in which rules of conduct are clearly stated, repeated frequently, and enforced is a relatively new experience. Asked "Considering your life at home, and your life here at (institution), what things would you say are most different?," the modal responses of the fifty girls interviewed fell into two categories. First, they noted, there was more discipline at the institution, that is, one had to do what one was told to do, and second, there was more of a set routine, or "planned and guided rules." The institution's program did appear to have a greater impact on those girls coming from a more unstruc-tured social background. We divided our respondents into two groups on the basis of the number of family constellations they had lived in prior to coming to the institution.[10] Those girls ($N = 41$) who lived in two or fewer constellations were considered to have structured backgrounds, and those ($N = 78$) who lived in three or more were considered to have unstructured backgrounds. While girls from struc-tured and unstructured backgrounds were about equally likely to identify with staff, and to have high institutional identification scores, identification was more strongly related to change for girls coming from unstructured backgrounds. The re-sults of our analysis are summarized in Table 8. As indicated by the values for

TABLE 8
Impact of Identification [a] on Girls from Structured
and Unstructured Backgrounds

	Structured		Unstructured	
"Change" variable	*N*	*Gamma (ID × Change)*	*N*	*Gamma (ID × Change)*
Faith in people	35	.25	68	.52
Self-esteem (Rosenberg)	35	−.02	67	.30
Self-esteem (ICL)	33	.32	67	.59
MMPI	24	.19	55	.30
Anxiety	28	−.34	54	.38

[a] Identification for the ICL is identification with staff member. For all other variables it is institutional identification.

gamma, identification is more strongly related to positive change (improvement) on each of the five measures of change for girls from unstructured backgrounds. These results suggest that a relatively structured environment is important both for identification, and for effective socialization, i.e., for people-changing.[11]

The Directress of Girls estimates that it takes three to six months for a girl to adjust to the institution (during which time she is somewhat rebellious), six months to "find herself," and six months during which she becomes an active, contributing member of the organization. Our observation suggests that, in order not to be won over to staff values and goals, a girl must remain isolated both from staff and from peers. Since this is a closed institution, in which the girls' entire existence is lived, such isolation is difficult to maintain. Again and again in the interviews, the girls cited the inescapable fact that they would be in residence for 18 to 24 months (the normal length of stay before a girl is considered for release) as a reason for a change in behavior and attitudes. To "fight the system" for this period of time would require an heroic effort, especially when one must do it without general peer support.

The absence of alternative reference groups also contributes to the girls' institutional identification. Since this is a closed institution, staff and inmates are the only immediate reference groups available to the girls. As we have indicated, the staff is in rather complete control of the institutional culture, and peer culture offers no effective alternative to staff norms. There are few other groups to which a girl may turn to support anti-staff norms. Parental visits are limited to one per month, and the girls are counseled not to dwell on institutional experiences at these times. Incoming and outgoing mail is censored, so that the girls are also isolated from contrary norms from other outside sources.

Besides the somewhat negative mechanisms of social control outlined above, there are several other mechanisms which more positively involve the girls in the staff's norm and value system. One of these is the monitor system. A system of monitorship is employed in many correctional institutions, including those at the custodial and treatment ends of the continuum. At its worst, it involves corruption and the exploitation of one inmate by another. At its best, it is an effective tool for rehabilitation, since it places the inmate in the staff member's position, and allows him to play a staff role. Staff attitudes and values are thus more readily understood and assimilated as one's own.

Even more than the monitor system, the use of group leaders serves to place inmates in staff roles. Each of the school classes, from Freshman to Senior, meets once a week under the supervision of one of the nuns, known as a group mother. The group mother is assigned to a class for one year, and is assisted in her duties by two girls, titled the group leader and assistant group leader. These girls are elected each month by their peers from a list of those who have indicated their willingness to serve in this capacity. The list is subject to the approval of the Directress of Girls. Once elected, the group leader is responsible for everything her group and its individual members do or fail to do. Her duties involve doing what she can to help her girls "keep their marks down," getting them to the right place at the right time, seeing that any special activities assigned to or planned by the group are carried out, keeping the group's morale high, and getting them to function as a unit. Above all, she is expected to set the example of good attitude and conduct for the girls under her charge. Charged with enforcing the institution's rules, with setting the example of proper behavior for her peers, and with assisting them to live up to staff expectations, a group leader finds it difficult not to accept staff norms and values. A majority of the girls do serve as group leader at least once during their stay.

The group meetings themselves contribute to the girls' identification with the institution. While they are used to disseminate staff directives and information regarding program scheduling, and so forth, the girls also use them to plan various group projects and extracurricular activities. The primary purpose of the meetings, however, is to focus on the group's behavior during the week, as indicated by its record of demerits and pink slips, and to work out ways to improve this record. The meetings also focus on the behavior of individuals. A girl who has been troublesome during the week may be called upon by the group leader to explain her behavior. Group members may then comment upon this behavior, analyzing the reasons behind it, and suggesting ways of improving it. Numerous studies of small groups have indicated that group discussion is important in fostering individual commitment to group goals, and that it is more effective in changing norms than other forms of persuasion, such as lectures or directives (Hare, 1962). By involving each girl in planning for class activities, and in an attempt to keep the group's "marks" down and "build the group up," the meetings contribute to the girls' identification with staff values, and with the institution itself.

Finally, the staff utilizes work assignments (called charges) to permit the girls to increase in status during their stay. The interview material indicates that the girls are aware of a charge hierarchy, and of what one must do to be assigned to a desired charge. The charge system provides a means by which a girl may advance during her stay from responsibility over things to responsibility over people, and from relatively little to relatively great autonomy and trust.

The mechanisms of social control we have outlined above describe a somewhat authoritarian, though benevolent, social system. Newer inmates generally rebelled against these mechanisms, but long-term residents generally were favorable to them, and some even enthusiastic about them. While we have suggested that these mechanisms fostered identification, they are not without dysfunctional potentialities. While the gold star system provided an incentive to many to "prove themselves" and to win staff approval and other rewards by good behavior, it was cited by some as the reason they stopped trying to live up to staff expectations, since gold stars were too easily lost for minor rule infractions which the girls themselves did not define as wrong. Group meetings could and sometimes did deteriorate into sessions in which a girl's ego was "torn down." The situation and responsibilities of monitors and group leaders could lead to discouragement and disillusionment when peers did not cooperate, and in spite of the prestige and privileges which attached to these positions, some girls shunned them. In general, however, these mechanisms did appear to be effective in fostering identification, both with staff members and with the institution.

Summary and Discussion

We have suggested that the degree to which individuals are changed by correctional institutions is related to the extent to which they identify with staff members, and with the institutional program. Data from a treatment-oriented institution serving delinquent females lend support to this hypothesis.

139

LITTLE, BROWN AND COMPANY

34 BEACON STREET
BOSTON, MASS. 02106

PAGE 1

00126-71-15

QUANTITY	AUTHOR	TITLE	CODE
1	STARR	SOC STRUCT CL	810924

CHECKER	PACKER	DATE	POSTAGE

We have further suggested that correctional institutions may exercise a great deal of control over the extent to which their inmates identify. Given a setting in which administration and staff are benevolent and mindful of inmate status, such factors as clear organizational structure and role expectations, long length of anticipated and actual stay, few alternative reference groups, high organizational participation, and readily available channels for organizational mobility are conducive to identification. A brief description of several mechanisms of social control employed by the study institution served to illustrate these points.

It should be noted, however, that the same highly structured program would not necessarily be equally successful with other populations, and that other types of programs might be equally successful. The Highfields program (McCorkle et al., 1958), and particularly the Provo Experiment (Empey and Rabow, 1961), achieve similar results by thrusting the delinquent into a relatively *unstructured* social system, placing the responsibility for rehabilitation, from the beginning, on the individual himself. These programs serve delinquent males. Perhaps it is precisely because of the difference in male and female psychology and socialization that these different programs appear to result in equal success. The study institution's program of total environmental control would perhaps meet with much stronger opposition from a delinquent male population. Likewise, we suspect its attempts to isolate dissident inmates from one another and to prevent the development of a deviant peer subculture would be less successful in an institution serving males. Studies of institutions serving females reveal an inmate subculture composed primarily of couples, and an underlying lack of trust, or at least an expectation of "betrayal" on the part of fellow inmates. This type of inmate social structure is more amenable to staff control than the more pervasive inmate social structure which appears to be characteristic of institutions serving males, and is thus more responsive to a highly structured program.

Finally, we must note that the factors considered conducive to identification were isolated on the basis of a review of varied literature and the empirical study of but one organization. Further research will be necessary to determine to what extent and under what conditions these factors are operative in other organizations.

Notes

1. Grusky (1962) has indicated that authoritarian immates in a treatment-oriented correctional camp were most effectively indoctrinated by the staff. Authoritarianism may well be one personality variable which facilitates identification in such settings although we have not as yet explored this relationship in the present study.
2. For a fuller discussion of the factors conducive to positional identification and a review of some of the pertinent literature, see Adamek (1965).
3. As will be clear from the description to be given later in the text, the study institution might more accurately be termed a training institution in the Street et al. (1967) sense. However, since it does utilize individual and group counseling sessions which aim at increasing inmates' insight into their behavior, the treatment-oriented label is felt to be appropriate.
4. For a discussion of the treatment philosophy and program of the Sisters of the Good Shepherd, see Thompson (1961).
5. Because of missing data, the N's reported below vary from this total. In particular, 14 girls were released from the institution early in the study before proper coordination could be effected, and most data are missing for these girls.

6. Girls were classified as leaders if they had served at least once as official group leaders (see text below). A measure of conformity to institutional norms was obtained by dividing the number of gold stars (see text below) a girl had been awarded by the number of months she had resided in the institution. Girls who received 60 per cent or more of their possible gold stars were classified as high conformers, those receiving 30–59 per cent were classified as medium conformers, and those receiving 29 per cent or less were classified as low conformers. These data include only girls resident at the institution for four months or more, since girls were not usually permitted to serve as group leaders before this period, and this was felt to be the minimum time in which a girl could establish a meaningful pattern of conformity.

7. Originally, we had intended to test the relationship of both identification with staff and with the institution to each of the five measures of change in the inmates. However, because of a procedural error, we administered the measure of staff identification to a majority of the girls three months prior to the other instruments. Since several of the girls might have identified or disidentified with the staff in that time, we felt it unwise to test the relationship between identification with staff and four of the measures of change.

8. To avoid analying tables with very small Ns in the cells, institutional identification was dichotomized into high and low in the control tables. It should be noted, therefore, that the gamma values for these tables are not strictly comparable to those in the main tables.

9. Data from the girls' records and interviews indicate that, compared to their institutional experience, the girls' home life was relatively unstructured, being characterized by a plurality of parents and pseudo-parents who issued few or contradictory behavior directives. A gross indicator of the girls' chaotic home life is that 25.2 per cent had lived in five or more family constellations prior to coming to the institution, and 65.5 per cent had lived in at least three.

10. A "family" constellation was defined to be any living situation (including institutional) which a girl experienced for a period of at least one month, and in which she was supervised by one or more adults. Thus, if a girl lived with both natural parents for ten years, with only one natural parent for one year, with a parent and step-parent for six months, and in a mental institution for six months, she was classified as having lived in four family constellations.

11. Some caution would be wise in evaluating these findings. The number of cases considered is small. Moreover, our measure of the relative "structuredness" of a girl's background was rather crude, taking into account primarily the number of family constellations reported in her case record (or self-reported in a few instances where no data were available in the record). No precise measure of the length of time in each constellation, nor the nature of social interaction within each of these constellations could be taken into account. Finally, the greater amount of improvement exhibited by the "unstructured" girls on Rosenberg's Self-Esteem Scale and on the MMPI may in part be an artifact of their initially poorer scores on these instruments. There were, however, no initial differences between the two groups on any of the other scales.

References

Adamek, R. J. 1965. The positional identification of adults. Mimeographed.

Berk, B. B. 1966. Organizational goals and inmate organization. *American Journal of Sociology* 71:522–34.

Blum, A. 1962. Peer group and a child's verbal accessibility in a treatment institution. *Social Service Review* 36:385–95.

Cattell, R. B., and I. H. Scheier. 1963. *Handbook for the IPAT anxiety scale questionnaire*. Champaign, Ill.: Institute for Personality and Ability Testing.

Clemmer, D. 1958. *The prison community*. New York: Rinehart.

Cressey, D. R. 1955. Changing criminals: The application of the theory of differential association. *American Journal of Sociology* 61:116–20.

Dahlstrom, W. G., and G. S. Welsh. 1960. *An MMPI handbook.* Minneapolis: University of Minnesota Press.

Edwards, A. L. 1957. *Techniques of attitude scale construction.* New York: Appleton-Century-Crofts.

Empey, L. T., and J. Rabow. 1961. The Provo experiment in delinquency rehabilitation. *American Sociological Review* 26:679–96.

Engh, J. 1966. New hope for girls in trouble. *U.S. Catholic* 31:37–42.

Eshleman, J. R.; A. E. Havens; and H. R. Potter. 1960. Construction of an identification scale. Unpublished paper. Columbus: The Ohio State University.

Etzioni, A. 1961. *A comparative analysis of complex organizations.* New York: The Free Press.

Fiedler, F. E. 1953. The psychological-distance dimension in interpersonal relations. *Journal of Personality* 22:142–50.

Fisher, S. 1961. Social organization in a correctional residence. *The Pacific Sociological Review* 4:87–93.

Garabedian, P. G. 1963. Social roles and processes of socialization in the prison community. *Social Problems* 11:139–52.

Giallombardo, Rose. 1966. *Society of women: A study of a women's prison.* New York: Wiley.

Goffman, E. 1961. *Asylums.* Garden City, N. Y.: Anchor Books, Doubleday.

Grosser, G. H. 1958. The role of informal inmate groups in change of values. *Children* 5:25–29.

Grusky, O. 1959. Organizational goals and the behavior of informal leaders. *American Journal of Sociology* 65:59–67.

Grusky, O. 1962. Authoritarianism and effective indoctrination: A case study. *Administrative Science Quarterly* 7:79–95.

Hare, A. P. 1962. *Handbook of small group research.* New York: The Free Press of Glencoe.

Heffernan, Sister M. Esther. 1964. Inmate social systems and sub-systems: The square, the cool, and the life. Ph.D. dissertation. Washington, D. C.: Catholic University of America.

Hersko, M. 1964. Community therapy in an institution for delinquent girls. *Federal Probation* 28:41–46.

Jourard, S. M. 1957. Identification, parent cathexis, and self-esteem. *Journal of Consulting Psychology* 21:375–80.

Konopka, Gisela. 1966. *The adolescent girl in conflict.* Englewood Cliffs, N. J.: Prentice-Hall.

Kopp, Sister Mary Audrey. 1960. Anomic pressure and deviant behavior. *The Sociological Quarterly* 1:226–38.

Kosofsky, S., and A. Ellis. 1958. Illegal communication among institutionalized female delinquents. *The Journal of Social Psychology* 48:155–60.

Leary, T. 1957. *Interpersonal diagnosis of personality.* New York: Ronald Press.

Leary, T. 1956. *Multilevel measurement of interpersonal behavior.* Berkeley: Psychological Consultation Service.

McCorkle, L. W.; A. Elias; and F. L. Bixby. 1958. *The Highfields story.* New York: Holt.

McCorkle, L. W., and R. Korn. 1954. Resocialization within the walls. *The Annals of the American Academy of Political and Social Sciences* 293:88–89.

Miller, D. 1964. *Growth to freedom.* London: Tavistock.

Morris, Ruth R. 1964. Female delinquency and relational problems. *Social Forces* 43:82–89.

Ohlin, L. E., and W. C. Lawrence. 1959. Social interaction among clients as a treatment problem. *Social Work* 4:3–13.

Polsky, H. 1962. *Cottage six.* New York: Russell Sage Foundation.

Rosenberg, M. 1965. *Society and the adolescent self-image.* Princeton, N. J.: Princeton University Press.

Street, D. P. 1965. Inmates in custodial and treatment settings. *American Sociological Review* 30:40–55.

Street, D. P.; R. D. Vinter; and C. Perrow. 1967. *Organization for treatment.* New York: The Free Press.

Sykes, G. M. 1958. *The society of captives.* Princeton, N. J.: Princeton University Press.

Thompson, Dorothy J. 1961. The psychology of the Good Shepherd nuns in the re-education of the emotionally disturbed. M.A. thesis. San Antonio: St. Mary's University.

Vinter, R. D. 1963. Analysis of treatment organizations. *Social Work* 8:3–15.

Vinter, R. D., and M. Janowitz. 1959. Effective institutions for juvenile delinquents: A research statement. *Social Service Review* 33:118–30.

Ward, D. A., and G. C. Kassebaum. 1965. *Women's prison: Sex and the social structure.* Chicago: Aldine.

Wheeler, S. 1961. Socialization in correctional communities. *American Sociological Review* 26:706–11.

Winch, R. F. 1962. *Identification and its familial determinants.* Indianapolis: Bobbs-Merrill.

III

Economy and Personality

5

TECHNOLOGY

The relationship between the economy, the culture, and social personality is complex. Technology is one aspect of the economy which has received the most attention. In the broadest sense, it is the uniquely human faculty for designing and utilizing tools to perform tasks. The development of primitive digging instruments some 10,000 or so years ago made it possible for men to begin cultivating the soil for food. The ensuing settlement of agricultural communities is generally characterized as the beginning of civilization.

According to Lewis Mumford (1971) the "new wave" in technology can be traced as far back as the eleventh century. The invention of the mechanical clock, which was a powerful thrust to further technical development, dates to the fourteenth century. Nevertheless, technology is usually defined more narrowly to mean the application of science to industry over the past two hundred or so years. This period, known as the Industrial Revolution and its aftermath, marks the shift from stone, wood, copper, and bronze as the dominant raw materials used, to iron and steel and from men and beasts as the sources of power used, to coal and steam, gas and electricity, and, finally, atomic energy. Probably the quintessence of this new period, however, is the reorganization of labor around machine production.

Numerous studies have been done on the impact of technological innovation on the social structure and culture. Such works have postulated the following ramifications, particularly in the United States:

1. The shift in place of work from the family farm, shop, or store to the corporate office or factory.
2. The concomitant migration of large segments of the population from rural to urban centers.
3. The consequent breakdown of the extended family into its component

139

nuclear units to facilitate geographic mobility, urban settlement, and adjustment to wage labor.

4. The redefinition of the husband's role as family breadwinner, using the concept of the "job" to re-establish the link between the family and the economy.

5. A basic transformation in the structure of the economy involving the mechanization of unskilled and semiskilled labor to increase the standardization and volume of production; the division of labor into increasingly more narrow and technical tasks leading to greater occupational specialization involving particularized training; and the emergence of a broader and more complex integration of all facets and phases of gathering and processing raw materials and manufacturing and marketing finished goods.

6. New and greater opportunities for individual status mobility based on occupational achievement, a development leading to an even further weakening of extended family ties.

7. An increase in the living standard caused by the proliferation of mass-produced, inexpensive household technology. This development has also diminished some more conspicuous life-style distinctions between families of different social status and, more importantly, liberated the housewife from many of her more demanding traditional obligations.

8. The erosion of the reverence for tradition, hierarchy, and mysticism in religious and secular life caused by the diffusion of the rational, instrumental orientation embodied in technology.

9. An increasing value emphasis on youth, change, individual choice, and achievement.

10. The emergence of specialized educational and recreational institutions to supplement the family in the socialization of the child.

11. The emergence of other institutions to fulfill needs for physical and material security previously provided for by the extended family.

12. The development of high-speed transportation and mass communication facilities which has made possible the increasing centralization of political power and administration. These developments have also contributed to the increasing standardization of institutional structures and homogenization of life styles across the continent while greatly expanding the awareness, experience, and frame of reference of the average citizen.

The technological revolution has greatly increased the number and size of cities in the modern world. In the United States the proportion of the population living in urban areas increased from 5 per cent in 1790, to 21 per cent in 1870, slightly under 40 per cent in 1900, 56 per cent in 1930, to over 70 per cent today. This has meant a tremendous increase in the proportion of the population affected by the ecology, structure, and culture of the city.

Some principal characteristics of this "urban way of life," according to Wirth (1938), are: higher population density (over 70 per cent of the United States' population lives on less than 1 per cent of the land space); greater diversity in racial and ethnic composition, but a high degree of residential segregation according to ethnicity, race, and class; an undermining of such traditional bases for social solidarity as family and community; the centralization of the means for communication and social control in formal institutions; a greater number of secondary (one-dimensional, utilitarian) rather than primary (holistic) contacts; greater sophistication, rationality, and freedom from personal controls, but more superficiality and anonymity in human affairs; sensitivity to the world of artifacts and removal from nature; and fluid population shifts and an inability to conceptualize the whole community and one's place in it. These and other factors have all contributed to a higher rate of loneliness, mental breakdown, suicide, delinquency, crime, corruption, and disorder.

On the other hand, improved technology has produced greater material abundance for most Americans. Between 1950 and 1970 the purchasing power of the median family income almost doubled. By 1970 the average household head had a high school diploma (representing an increase in three years of formal education), the husband was more likely to be in a skilled occupation, and the family lived in a larger home than twenty years ago. By 1970, almost 65 per cent of American families owned a home which was almost sure to have complete plumbing facilities and central heating, a telephone and several radios. Nearly 30 per cent of U.S. families owned two cars, almost 40 per cent owned a color television set, 17 per cent a dishwasher, and 40 per cent a clothes dryer. Although little or no progress may have been made in such areas as the availability of medical care (the proportion of physicians to population declined 25 per cent between 1930 and 1970), the average life expectancy has increased by eighteen years since 1900. In a world where two-thirds of all people go to bed hungry, this standard of living is impressive even for a country as large and rich in natural resources as the United States.

Social Psychological Consequences of Technological Development

Despite or because of this singular emphasis on industrial production and improvement in material life style, however, the emotional malaise of contemporary, urban, industrial society proliferates. This is not to imply that people in primitive or traditional societies live lives filled with the peace and joy of simple brotherhood. As Foster's article on the traditional rural community makes clear, the emphasis on personalized relationships and family unity and the complex forms of cooperative interdependence which prevail in such communities are opposed by antagonistic forces toward mutual suspicion and envy, quarrelsome rivalry, and a pervasive fear of exploitation by fellow villagers, urban merchants, and officials.

Curiously, Foster's explanation of the dynamics of such peasant villages postulates the *lack of technology* and the scarcity mentality that this entails as the critical link between the social structure and social personality. It is difficult to judge whether this reflects a modern parochial outlook which is very difficult to transcend or whether he has accurately depicted the gestalt of such communities.

In modern society, according to Wheelis (1958), the *instrumental process* of applied reason embodied in technological innovation has greatly diminished the traditional authority of the *institutional process*. The more limited but objectively real security obtained by applied reason is rapidly replacing the grander but purely subjective security provided by institutional myths (such as magic and religion). According to Wheelis, some secondary effects of technological change have been "the loss of eternal verities and the fixed order, the weakening of traditions and institutions, the shifting values, the altered patterns of personal relationships" (p. 82). Moreover, these changes, continuous with the instrumental process, mold the emergent social personality. As a result, people tend to "ape models" to adjust to changing mores or customs rather than "abstract principles" to acquire a permanent morality. Wheelis (pp. 18–19) states:

> Our grandparents had less trouble than we do in finding themselves. . . . Sooner rather than later one found his calling; and having found it, failure did not readily cause one to reconsider, but often it was a goad to greater effort. The goal was achievement, not adjustment, the young were taught to work, not to socialize. Popularity was not important, but strength of character was essential. Nobody worried about rigidity of character; it was supposed to be rigid. If it were flexible you couldn't count on it.
>
> Change of character was desirable only for the wicked. . . . During the past fifty years there has been a change in the experienced quality of life, with the result that identity is now harder to achieve and harder to maintain.

Wheelis's distinction parallels Riesman's discussion (1953) of the modern American evolution from the "inner-directed" man with a fixed set of principles enforced by guilt and a "gyroscopic" orientation to people and situations to the "other-directed" man with a "diffuse anxiety" regarding acceptance and a "radar screen" sensitivity to changing mores. Erikson (1963, p. 279) adds, "The patient of today suffers most under the problem of what he should believe in and who he should — or, indeed, might — be or become; while the patient of early psychoanalysis suffered most under inhibitions which prevented him from being what and who he thought he knew he was."

Like Wheelis, Erikson studies the transition from the Victorian era, characterized by rigid superego repression and hysterical symptom formation, to the modern era, characterized by strong ego control and general character disorder. Keniston (1967) calls this new mechanism of impulse control the "technological ego." He states (p. 366):

> The virtues of our technological society require a dictatorship of the ego rather than a good government. The self-denying potential of the ego is minimized: playfulness, fantasy, relaxation, creativity, feeling, and synthesis take second place to problem-solving, cognitive control, work, measurement, rationality, and analysis. The technological ego rarely relaxes its control over the rest of the psyche, rarely subordinates itself to other psychic interests or functions. Though its tyranny is seldom obvious, it is firm and unrelenting. Although apparently benevolent and reasoning, seeming to "understand" the motivations it regulates, ignoring the pangs of conscience when it can (and when it cannot, seeking to undermine their claims), the technological ego still dominates rather than governs well.

All these scholars postulate empirical interaction resulting in structural parallelism between the relative force of tradition and change in the culture and the relative strength of the superego and ego in the personality. The alienation of modern man figures prominently in all their works. Probably the most careful analysis of the concept of alienation, as it has been variously employed in social psychological literature, has been done by Seeman (1959). He distinguishes five variants of alienation based on particular applications of the concept by different theorists. The variants are:

1. Powerlessness, defined as "the expectancy or probability held by the individual that his own behavior cannot determine the occurrence of the outcomes, or reinforcements, he seeks."
2. Meaninglessness, used when "the individual is unclear as to what he ought to believe — when the individual's minimal standards for clarity in decision-making are not met" leading to a "low expectancy that satisfactory predictions about future outcomes of behavior can be made.
3. Normlessness, characteristic of the "anomic situation" in which there is "a high expectancy that socially unapproved behaviors are required to achieve given goals."
4. Isolation, typical of those who "assign low reward value to goals or beliefs that are typically highly valued in the given society."
5. Self-estrangement, which can mean "to be insecure, given to appearances, conformist" and also refers to "the inability of the individual to find self-rewarding . . . activities that engage him."

Wheelis, a practicing psychiatrist, has examined the relative "meaninglessness" of contemporary society, a situation which he proposes leads to "self-estrangement." He seems primarily concerned with the problems of the educated middle-class youth with whom he, undoubtedly, is the most familiar. In recent years, increasingly these youths also have been experiencing greater "isolation" from what they perceive to be the goals and beliefs of the larger society, and have sought to institutionalize such rejection in what has been termed the "counterculture," described in numerous books by Roszak (1969), Mead (1970), Flacks (1971), and others. Wheelis is not ostensibly concerned with the "normlessness" of the lower classes and racial minorities striving to achieve culturally valued goals where legitimate opportunities for success are few.

In contrast, Slater, in the next selection, stresses the sense of "powerlessness" that omnipresent and seemingly omnipotent technological change has engendered in modern man. Slater asserts that Americans have become slaves to the "mysterious, impersonal, and remote mechanisms" of modern technology, that this has made us feel confused and helpless, so that "our preference for violence at a distance," such as in the widespread bombing of Indochina, is "both an expression of and a revenge against this process."

Cultural and Sociological Consequences of Technological Development

Technology has been a powerful force in reshaping American culture. It has influenced our language, habits, and modes of thought. Machines serve as often as the model for human beings as do human beings for machines. Edward Shoben, Jr. (1964–65) cites both Greg Walter's working assumption that the human nervous system behaves essentially like a computer, the electronic analogy utilized by behavior science information theorists, and the machine-like model of man which underlies Skinner's theory of operant conditioning as examples of this phenomenon.

Certainly our popular language betrays this influence. In attempting to communicate with one another, individuals try to "connect" or "tune in" on the same "wave length" to avoid "static" so as to be able to "process data" more efficiently. Institutions look for "high-powered" individuals who can get "geared up" to perform the tasks they set for them while others implore such individuals to "turn on, tune in, and drop out" when such tasks begin to "turn them off."

On the other hand, Gerth and Mills (1953) point out that technology is not autonomous or self-determining. "To be part of history" technology must be institutionalized in the economic, military, or political orders. Thus, it is not really a question of the effects of some abstract force, but of the particular kinds of technology designed by men in positions of authority in specific institutions. Slater acknowledges this when he says that essentially "the nature of our current relationship to the technological order" is at issue. In so doing, he effectively elaborates on a position long advocated by Lewis Mumford. Almost forty years ago, Mumford (1934) was decrying the fact that "in the translation of technical improvements into social process ... the machine has undergone a perversion: instead of being utilized as an instrument of life, it has tended to become an absolute." To illustrate, Mumford observes (p. 282):

> Railroads may be quicker than canalboats, and a gas lamp may be brighter than a candle; but it is only in terms of human purpose and in relation to a human and social scheme of values that speed and brightness have any meaning. If one wishes to absorb the scenery, the slow motion of a canalboat may be preferable to the fast motion of a motor car, and if one wishes to appreciate the mysterious darkness and the strange forms of a natural cave, it is better to penetrate it with uncertain steps, with the aid of a torch or lantern than to descend into it by means of an elevator, as in the famous caves of Virginia, and to have the mystery entirely erased by a grand display of electric lights — a commercialized perversion that puts the whole spectacle upon the low dramatic level of a cockney amusement park.

Unlike Slater, but like Fromm (1955), Mumford is especially concerned with the use of technology in a capitalist economy. Harnessed to the goals of production and profit, he has seen technology convert skilled work into meaningless labor and sensual human beings into passionless consumers; they are consumed by their own consumption and possessed by their own possessions without meaningful improvement in the quality of their lives.

Modern technology has increased the sense of powerlessness of most Americans in four other important ways. First, the organization of production around power machinery has meant that considerable capital is required for those who wish to manufacture goods — a change from when most consumer goods, like shoes, clothing, and furniture were produced by hand or, at least, by human-powered mechanical contrivances.

Most aspiring entrepreneurs have simply not been able to accumulate enough capital to compete successfully against large manufacturers who mass-produce relatively inexpensive (although less distinctive or durable) goods for large markets. This relative monopoly on heavy machinery, along with the mechanization of agriculture, has been primarily responsible for the severe reduction in the proportion of self-employed in the nation's work force from about 80 per cent in the early nineteenth century to slightly over 40 per cent in 1870, 18 per cent in 1940, and less than 10 per cent today (over half of which are farmers). Continued evolution of this trend has led us to the current situation in which, as Mintz and Cohen (1971) point out, the two hundred largest corporations do most of the government's business and control two-thirds of all manufacturing.

This development means that most Americans work for a wage or salary in giant bureaucracies under the supervision and control of remote, impersonal employers primarily concerned with organizational efficiency rather than worker satisfaction or job security. The direct consequences that technological change has had on the division of labor and the demand for various skills has caused concern on the part of the unprotected American worker, *powerless* (except through infrequent and almost random union obstructionism) to control the forces which may one day rob him of his means of survival.

A second important ramification of this concentration of the means of production into fewer and fewer hands is that, contrary to the impression created by the increased standard of living brought about by improved technology, the real distribution of wealth and power in the United States has not changed in this century. According to Kolko (1962) the top 10 per cent of the population received more annual income than the bottom 50 per cent throughout the 1950's, just as they had done in the 1910–18 period. At the same time the proportion of national personal income for the bottom 50 per cent actually declined from 27 per cent in 1910 to 23 per cent in 1959.

In 1959, according to Williams, the top 4 per cent received 18 per cent of the nation's income and the bottom 31 per cent just 10 per cent. And income figures do not reveal the true disparity in wealth between strata in the United States. According to Andrew Greeley, while the top 5 per cent earned 25 per cent of the annual income in 1971, the top 1 per cent owned more than one-third of the nation's total assets. When one translates such wealth differentials into political power, achieved in capitalist democracies through extravagant lobbying, campaign financing, and effectively influencing the media through the control of advertising revenue, it becomes quite apparent that if people in this country haven't become slaves to technology, they have or might well become slaves to the people who control the technology.

The pollster Louis Harris, who periodically measures public attitudes toward government officials, has found evidence for a diminishing confidence in the American polity. By the end of 1971, he found 59 per cent to 81 per cent of his cross-section sample agreeing with statements that, although initially motivated by a desire to serve others, most politicians make false promises, are not appointed on the basis of merit, are in politics to make money for themselves, and take graft. He found that the margin of public distrust had increased from 12 per cent to 16 per cent on these various questions since 1967 and that 35 per cent felt that politics was more corrupt at the end of 1971 than it was ten years earlier, while only 8 per cent felt that it was less corrupt. The increasing proportion of independent voters among the nation's electorate suggests increasing alienation from the major political parties.

Third, elite domination becomes particularly salient because of the tremendous technological development in police and military equipment for surveillance and social control. Technological extensions of the eyes, ears, and long arm of law enforcers have surpassed the wildest dreams of science fiction writers, and the computer, though a boon to those involved in research and development, has become a bane to those concerned with protecting the privacy and civil liberties of individuals. Recent revelations that the U.S. Army had files or dossiers on 25 million Americans and that the Association of Credit Bureaus of America has compiled dossiers on 105 million Americans bear witness both to the computer's enormous capacity to store and retrieve information and to the *diminishing power* of the individual to be aware of, let alone to control, social forces affecting his existence.

Not only do very few determine the kind and level of technology produced in the United States, but the primary source of technological innovation has shifted since World War II from the economy to the military. This is the fourth major way in which the design of modern technology has increased the individual's sense of powerlessness. Gerth and Mills made this observation in 1953 and Seymour Melman (1972) has been carefully documenting and analyzing this crucial change since 1961. The nation's military defense budget has grown from under 80 million dollars in 1870 to 190 million in 1900, 794 million in 1930, 14 *billion* in 1950 and almost 85 *billion* today, an increase of a thousandfold in 100 years. It is no wonder then that the aerospace industry is the country's largest manufacturing employer, accounting for more than a million jobs. When the most sophisticated technological advances take the form of larger and more efficient instruments of destruction, does this not in its own way greatly increase the sense of powerlessness and insignificance of the common man? Shoben (pp. 423–24) states:

> For most of us, the impact of this phenomenal growth of science is felt far less through its intellectual processes and its basic concepts than through its manifestations in technology. The clearest of these technological derivatives of science, of course, is modern weaponry. Huge numbers of us live every day as literal targets for the nuclear warheads mounted on intercontinental missiles or carried in the bays of fast bombers, and the merciful fact that the missiles are not released or the planes sent on their destructive mission is not without its fateful consequences. While there is no doubt about our horror of nuclear war or the edgy guilt we feel over Hiroshima and Nagasaki, there is still evidence that we have grown calloused through familiarity with our atomic world. "Overkill" is the term in which we estimate our ultimate military capacity, and we debate in grim comfort the question of whether we would have the resources to rebuild our present culture if we were to sustain losses of over fifty million people in a nuclear "victory." In certain contexts, at

least, human life loses its individual distinctiveness and is conceived in a coldly statistical fashion, not as an end in itself but simply as instrumental in the reestablishing of a way of life risked in a holocaust. One need not make too much of either the odds or the attitude entailed by these considerations to find in the consequences of contemporary science a major revolution in man's concept of himself, in our way of thinking about ourselves and our fellows as human beings.

The consequences of living in this "nuclear age," according to Bernard, Ottenberg, and Redl (1970) could well be a form of "self-estrangement" they call "dehumanization." According to them, both self-directed dehumanization and object-directed dehumanization may be initially invoked as defense mechanisms, helping the individual to cope with the "painful and overwhelming emotions" aroused by his own sense of powerlessness to control the fateful decisions about nuclear war being weighed by his government's leaders and the "guilt and shame" he might otherwise feel over the use of such weapons against other people, as in Hiroshima and Nagasaki. On the other hand, they say (p. 21):

> this very essential of dehumanization, as with other defenses, makes for its greatest danger: that the constructive self-protection it achieves will cross the ever-shifting boundaries of adaptiveness and become destructive, to others as well as to the self. In combination with other social factors ... the perfection of modern techniques for automated killing on a global scale engenders a marked increase in the incidence of dehumanization.

The several aspects of "maladaptive dehumanization" which could then express themselves are: (1) increased emotional distance from other human beings; (2) diminished sense of personal responsibility for the consequences of one's action; (3) increasing involvement with procedural problems to the detriment of human needs; (4) inability to oppose dominant group attitudes or pressures; and (5) feelings of personal helplessness and estrangement.

One working assumption underlying the analysis of these authors is that the increased power of certain institutions over individuals could lead to the abdication of a sense of individual responsibility in interpersonal and intergroup relations as well as in relations to one's government. In a sense such a development would reflect some incorporation of the anonymity and impersonality of those powerful institutions into the individual's orientation toward the self and others; a form of identification with the oppressor which reduces human beings to robotlike automatons without purpose except to serve their technobureaucratic masters.

Some Important Qualifications

In a society as preoccupied with technology (both as a problem and as a solution to problems) as the United States, it is necessary to note some important qualifications. As Gerth and Mills make clear, there is no technological imperative in history. Between the third millennium B.C. and the eleventh century A.D., no important technological developments occurred in the West. To repeat an earlier theme, for technological innovations to take place, "institutions must raise effective demands for the incorporation of technical implements" (Gerth and Mills, p. 391).

Some social scientists have pointed out that industrialization and urbanization — the effects of technology — have not had the same impact on traditional values in non-Western countries that they allegedly have had in the West. Moreover, some changes that have taken place in the West and are taking place in developing areas of the world might be explained better by ideological rather than technological factors.

Furthermore, many aspects of contemporary American culture (such as the romantic love complex and democratic family pattern) which conventionally have been ascribed to the effects of modern technology have been demonstrated, in recent historical research, to have existed before the advent of the industrial revolution. In fact, many theorists indicate that the causal relationship may run the other way; that certain cultural patterns and social practices unique to Western society, America in particular, may have provided conditions especially favorable to the growth and spread of technological innovation.

One major implication of such research is that, in emphasizing the effects of technology on social personality in the United States, we risk ignoring the larger themes of cultural continuity which have not only provided a favorable climate for the growth of technology, but continue to exercise influence over its use. Certainly, rationalism, empiricism, mastery over nature, individualism, geographic and social mobility, preoccupation with self-improvement, and distrust of institutions are American cultural patterns that more closely reflect our Protestant and frontier heritage than the impact of technology. In fact, Merton (1957) argues that this "Protestant ethic" formed the value base for the origin and growth of modern Western science. The important distinction between genuine cultural change and simple variations within an established pattern is sometimes difficult to make in a society which presents almost every technical advance with the promise or warning that it will "revolutionize" whatever it touches.

Nevertheless, technology has provided men with the means to create marvels and monsters on a size and scale heretofore unimagined. The unique threat to survival, let alone human welfare, which it presents makes it absolutely imperative that we critically confront this new force while we can still choose.

References

Bernard, Viola W., Perry Ottenberg, and Fritz Redl
     1970   "Dehumanization: A Composite Psychological Defense in Relation to Modern War." Pp. 16–30 in Milton Schwebel (ed.), *Behavioral Science and Human Survival*. Palo Alto: Science and Behavior Books.
Erikson, Erik H.
     1963   *Childhood and Society*, 2d ed. New York: Norton.
Flacks, Richard
     1971   *Youth and Social Change*. Chicago: Markham.
Fromm, Erich
     1955   *The Sane Society*. Greenwich, Conn.: Fawcett.
Gerth, Hans, and C. Wright Mills
     1953   *Character and Social Structure: The Psychology of Social Institutions*. New York: Harcourt, Brace and World.

Habakkuk, H. J.
  1968 "Family Structure and Economic Change in Nineteenth Century Europe."
       Pp. 140–49 in Norman W. Bell and Ezra F. Vogel (eds.), *A Modern Intro-
       duction to the Family.* New York: The Free Press.
Keniston, Kenneth
  1967 *The Uncommitted: Alienated Youth in American Society.* New York: Dell.
Kolko, Gabriel
  1962 *Wealth and Power in America.* New York: Praeger.
Levine, Robert A., Nancy H. Klein, and Constance F. Owen
  1968 "Modernization and Father-Child Relationships in Urban Nigeria." Pp.
       558–74 in Bell and Vogel, *A Modern Introduction to the Family.*
Mead, Margaret
  1970 *Culture and Commitment: A Study of the Generation Gap.* Garden City,
       N.Y.: Doubleday.
Melman, Seymour
  1972 Address and remarks in "Symposium on Technology and Authority." Pp.
       49–76 in Charles A. Thrall and Jerold M. Starr (eds.), *Technology, Power,
       and Social Change.* Lexington, Mass.: Heath.
Merton, Robert
  1957 *Social Theory and Social Structure.* New York: The Free Press.
Mintz, Morton, and Jerry S. Cohen
  1971 *America, Inc.: Who Owns and Operates the United States?* New York:
       Dial.
Mumford, Lewis
  1934 *Technics and Civilization.* New York: Harcourt, Brace and World.
  1972 "Two Views on Technology and Man: Keynote Address." Pp. 1–16 in
       Charles A. Thrall and Jerold M. Starr (eds.), *Technology, Power, and Social
       Change.*
Ogburn, William F.
  1957 "Cultural Lag As Theory." *Sociology and Social Research* 41 (January-
       February):167–74.
Potter, David
  1954 *People of Plenty.* Chicago: Phoenix.
Riesman, David, with Nathan Glazer and Reuel Denney
  1953 *The Lonely Crowd: A Study of the Changing American Character.* Garden
       City, N. Y.: Doubleday-Anchor.
Roszak, Theodore
  1969 *The Making of a Counter-Culture: Reflections on the Technocratic Society
       and its Youthful Opposition.* Garden City, N. Y.: Doubleday-Anchor.
Seeman, Melvin
  1959 "On the Meaning of Alienation." *American Sociological Review* 24 (De-
       cember):783–91.
Shoben, Edward Joseph, Jr.
  1964–65 "Society, Love, and Worship." *Antioch Review* 24 (4):421–38.
Wheelis, Alan
  1958 *The Quest for Identity.* New York: Norton.
Wirth, Louis
  1938 "Urbanism as a Way of Life." *The American Journal of Sociology* 44 (July):
       1–24.

GEORGE FOSTER

The Traditional Rural Community

Despite the rapid urbanization of the twentieth century, more·than half of the world's population dwells in villages. Indian demographers estimate that in their country alone there are nearly 600,000 small rural communities. These communities — peasant villages, to use the historical term — have in recent years drawn the particular attention of specialists in public health, education, agriculture, and community development, because their inhabitants are less well situated to know about and participate in technological and social development than are their city cousins.

Peasant communities have also drawn the attention of anthropologists in recent years, both because the field methodologies of research first worked out in primitive tribes are applicable to such groups and because they afford important new knowledge about the total culture patterns of man. During recent years, and especially since World War II, a series of fine reports has appeared, so that we have a fairly good idea about peasant communities in most parts of the world. No two villages in different countries are the same. Matters of language, religion, political organization, and social structure determine the unique qualities of the communities of every major area. The technical specialist who familiarizes himself with the reports on the country in which he works is in a better position to work effectively than if he simply assumes that people are basically the same everywhere and what worked at home will work equally well here.

At the same time, it is abundantly clear that, although the content of peasant society — the cultural details — are infinite, the forms are astonishingly similar. Peasants in Mexico face economic problems very like those confronting the Hindu farmer; the Peruvian villager looks upon illness, and reacts to it, in a way that would be familiar to the Egyptian *fellāhīn;* the Chinese village family is rent by inheritance squabbles in the same fashion as its Italian counterpart.

The similarities in peasant life the world around are so marked that we are justified in sketching an "average" community to serve as a guide to what characteristics one may reasonably expect to find when attempting to introduce innovation. This is important, because even among people who have worked a good deal in such situations, there are often misconceptions about some very fundamental qualities of village life. For example, . . . it is often assumed that villagers, not too much influenced by the individualism of city life, are essentially cooperative in spirit. Action programs sometimes rest on this assumption. Yet in fact, and for reasons I will try to make clear, cooperation in peasant society occurs only in rather special situations, and it is usually not a sound basis on which to build new programs.

The "desirable" qualities in village life are often over-estimated by action workers; so are the "undesirable" qualities. We wonder why the peasant is skeptical of what we say, why he often doubts us. We marvel at his fatalism, while bemoaning its hold on him. We puzzle at his apparent reluctance to take advantage of new techniques, the advantages of which must be obvious to him. But whatever the nature of peasant society, and however it may affect us in our work, there is good reason underlying it. . . .

In analyzing the nature of a peasant community, the first thing to note is that it differs from an isolated Indian tribe, a band of Australian Bushmen, or the people of a Polynesian island before the arrival of the white man in that it is not a self-sufficient unit. Peasant communities exist in an intimate relationship with cities and towns. Peasants are primarily farmers, and sometimes artisans as well. They produce much of their food and are able to make many of the material items they need for life such as clothing and tools. But they depend on town markets to sell surplus produce and to buy items which they cannot make themselves. Kroeber aptly characterizes them as "part-societies" with "part-cultures," forming a class segment of a larger unit of civilization.[1]

The North American Indian, the Australian Bushman, and the Polynesian islander was self-sufficient with respect to his religion, his philosophy, and his government. But the peasant depends on the city for this kind of nourishment. His religion represents a simplified form of what Redfield has called the "Great Tradition" of his society; it comes to him from the outside and is not a product of his own creation. Many of his values likewise represent diffusion from urban centers. Politically, the peasant has little independence. Since time immemorial he has been governed from the city; his own community has but weakly developed leadership patterns.

Peasant communities represent the rural expression of large, class-structured, economically complex, preindustrial civilizations, in which trade and commerce and craft specialization are well developed, in which money is commonly used, and in which market disposition is the goal for a part of the producer's efforts. The city is the principal source of innovation for such communities, and it holds the political, religious, and economic reins.

Peasant communities should not be thought of as a "way station" midway between civilization and primitive tribal communities. They appeared with the first civilizations between five and six thousand years ago, and they have been an enduring way of life ever since, as essential to the city as the city is to them. Modern primitives who have found themselves in contact with an industrial world in this century will never be peasants — an industrial civilization requires adjustments that do not include a peasantry. Similarly, modern peasant communities represent a cultural lag from a preindustrial period, and ultimately they will disappear, simply because a peasant component is logically inconsistent with an industrial age. The fact that the peasant way of life ultimately will disappear, however, in no way lessens the present problems of such peoples.

Now let us look at the implications of the peasant communities' ties to urban centers. It is clear that *the basic decisions affecting such villages are made from the outside* and have always been so made. For generations the villager has been able to show initiative only in the most limited areas. Small wonder that he often has trouble in making up his mind about something new. Moreover, not only does the villager have little or no control over the basic decisions made from the outside, but *usually he doesn't even know how or why they are made.* The orders, the levys, the restrictions, the taxes that are imposed from the outside have for him the same quality of chance and capriciousness as do the visitations of the super- natural world. And the peasant feels much the same toward both the authorities of the city and the supernatural: he can plead, implore, propitiate, and hope for a miracle, but in neither case can he expect by his own action to have any effective control. A fatalistic attitude toward life? It is hard to imagine more favorable cir- cumstances in which it can develop, and hard to understand how it can be lessened until these circumstances are changed.

The villager has been victimized by persons more knowledgeable than he since the beginning of time. He knows he is a rustic, a country bumpkin who, in his necessary trips to town, will be taken advantage of by men without conscience. He needs the city, but he hates and fears it. He fumes at humiliation and imagines slights even when they are not intended. The Wisers, in the last chapter of their wonderful little book, *Behind Mud Walls*, sensitively put into words the Hindu villagers' feelings about their helplessness.

> In the cities they devise ways of exploiting us. . . . When we get our money and want to take home some cloth, the shopkeepers get out pieces which they have been unable to dispose of, and persuade us to buy them at exorbitant prices. We know that they are laughing at us. But we want cloth, and the next shopkeeper will cheat us as badly as the last. Wherever we go in the town, sharp eyes are watching to tempt our precious rupees from us. And there is no one to advise us honestly or to help us escape from fraudulent men.
>
> You cannot know unless you are a villager, how everyone threatens and takes from us. When you [the Wisers] go anywhere, or when a sophisticated town man goes anywhere, he demands service and gets it. We stand dumb and show our fear and they trample on us.[2]

In the mestizo village of Tzintzuntzan, Mexico, in which I have done research for many years, I know an intelligent and imaginative young man, a pottery mer- chant. He buys the lovely ware made by his fellow villagers and delivers it on commission to stores in Mexico City. At least once a month he climbs into the bus for the overnight run to the capital, his crates of pottery strapped to the roof. Upon his arrival he makes his deliveries, admires the city, and climbs on the bus for the return trip. The bus is like home; it is known, and safe. He has never spent a night in the big city, and he tells me he wouldn't know how to go about it.

Another villager in Tzintzuntzan, recognizing a need for better bus service to the nearby market town of Pátzcuaro, bought a second-hand bus from an official of a local line. He was delighted, and so were his neighbors. Now it would not be necessary to wait on the highway while bus after loaded bus passed without stop- ping; Tzintzuntzan would have its own service. Then our entrepreneur began learn- ing about the outside world. A franchise? Bus drivers unions? The official who sold the bus fought him on both scores, and won. Sadly he sold the bus back to the same man, at a fraction of its cost to him.

The peasant has learned that the outside world is fraught with dangers, that it is unpredictable and cannot be understood. Is it surprising that he has come to value his traditional ways and the predictable quality of life within this microcosmic world, his village?

With so much of the world not subject to control and not even understood, it is not surprising to find that the critical sense of the peasant operates within narrow limits. In my experience, and that of others, the peasant is able to believe the most improbable things. R. N. Adams found in Guatemala that blood withdrawn in health surveys was rumored to be a test to see if children were fat enough to be sent to the United States where children were delicacies for the tables of epicureans.[3]

Goswami and Roy found in India that an agricultural program in which land was being cleared and improved gave rise to the rumor that the local people would be cleared out after they had done the work and an American colony would move in.[4] Philips, describing the Rockefeller Foundation antihookworm campaign in Ceylon many years ago, tells how coolies distrusted medicine in capsule form: a highly successful whispering campaign warned that capsules were time bombs that would explode after months or even years.[5]

This lack of a critical sense, one of the most difficult things to deal with in working with villagers, is seen even in areas where it would appear that experience would have taught better. I have often listened to villagers in Tzintzuntzan tell stories of buried treasure. The fact that within living memory no one has ever found treasure in no way decreases the faith in its existence. One just needs luck, as in all other things.

With the outside world a constant threat, it might seem logical to expect a high degree of cooperation among villagers as a defense mechanism. Should not common adversity draw people together in the pursuit of common ends? Cannot a village find strength in unity? However natural this might seem, the evidence indicates that villagers frequently are suspicious of each other, filled with envy, ready to suspect the worst about their neighbors, distrustful in the extreme. The quality of interpersonal relations appears to be bad, and true cooperation is largely limited to certain traditional types of labor exchange in agriculture and house building.

Oscar Lewis' findings, in his classic account of the Mexican village of Tepoztlán,

> emphasize the underlying individualism of Tepoztecan institutions and character, the lack of cooperation, the tensions between villages within the municipio, the schisms within the village, and the pervading quality of fear, envy, and distrust in inter-personal relations.
>
> Gossip is unrelenting and harsh. . . . Facts about people are unconsciously or maliciously distorted. . . . Relatives and neighbors are quick to believe the worst, and motives are always under question. . . . Successful persons are popular targets of criticism, envy, and malicious gossip.[6]

The readers of accounts of Italian peasant life will not find this description surprising. Friedmann's superb analysis of the "world of *'La Miseria'*" in Calabria and Lucania dwells upon the peasants' "mentality of mutual distrust," their inability to work cooperatively and to collaborate for the common good; *La Miseria* is a "world in which to love one's neighbors, to let down one's guard in the face of the relentless struggle for existence, would simply mean to commit suicide." [7] Banfield found, in the south Italian village of Montegrano, that friends and neighbors are considered potentially dangerous. No family can stand to see another prosper without feeling envy and wishing the other harm; beyond the nuclear family, he finds, concerted action for the common good is impossible.[8]

The physician-psychiatrist Carstairs found a similar picture in a Rajasthan village in India. Villagers often made enthusiastic plans to work together for the mutual good, but these plans were rarely carried out. "Within an hour or two, one of the group would warn me that someone else was only in the scheme for his own advantage. . . . From the beginning to the end of my stay, my notebooks record instances of suspicion and mutual distrust." [9]

The list of illustrations could be extended, but the point should be clear: to a greater or lesser extent peasant life is characterized, within the village, by a bitter quality of mutual suspicion and distrust which makes it extremely difficult for people to cooperate for the common good. With this mentality, a new technical aid program which presupposes a high degree of village cooperation is obviously headed for trouble.

Why is the quality of village interpersonal relations often so poor? If we dig into the reasons, we find that quarrels about property, and particularly land ownership, are most frequently mentioned. For example, Simmons writes that in the Peruvian south coastal village of Lunahuaná the characteristic reaction to even those one knows well is suspicion and distrust; everyone is presumed to be out for himself and will use the most unscrupulous methods in pursuing his self-interest. "Sibling relations," he says, "after the abdication or death of parents, are characterized by disputes and feuds arising from conflicts over the division of land and the other goods of inheritance." [10] The Italian novelist Ignazio Silone describes village life in Fontamara in this fashion: "In bad weather months they arranged family affairs. That is, they quarreled about them. . . . Always the same squabbles, endless squabbles, passed down from generation to generation in endless lawsuits, in endless paying of fees, all to decide who owns some thornbush or other." [11] Adamic describes how the "seemingly perfect village life" of the Slovenes every once in a while is "shaken by fierce quarrels among peasants over the possession of a few feet of ground or a tool or a beast. . . ." [12] And in China, Smith tells how the division of land following the death of the owner almost always results in bitter feuds, even between brothers.[13]

If we look beneath these overt expressions of competition and bitterness, we see a second basic characteristic of peasant life (the first is impotence in the face of the outside world) which makes behavior more intelligible. This is, *peasant economy is essentially nonproductive;* peasants ordinarily are very poor people. Their resources, particularly land, usually are absolutely limited, and there is not enough to go around. Productive techniques, based on human and animal power and the simple tools first used before the time of Christ, are essentially static. Consequently, production is constant (except as affected by weather), and perhaps it declines over the centuries, as the result of erosion, deforestation, and other consequences of man's exploitive activities. That is, the total "productive pie" of the village does not greatly change, and moreover, *there is no way to increase it however hard the individual works,* unless new land and improved techniques become available.

In each village tradition has determined approximately what a family may expect as its share of this small productive pie. It can expect no more, and it zealously watches to make sure it receives no less. The consequences of this situation are apparent: *if someone is seen to get ahead, logically it can only be at the expense of others in the village.* The traditional division of the pie is being upset, and the rights of all are potentially threatened. Even if an individual cannot see that he is suffering as a consequence of another's progress, he knows that he must be; the logical premise on which his society is based tells him it *has* to be so.[14]

Looking at peasant economy in this fashion helps us to understand why the successful person invites the suspicion, the enmity, the gossip, the character assassination, and perhaps the witchcraft and physical attacks of his fellows. Any evidence of a change for the better in his situation is proof of guilt, all that is needed to show that, in some fashion, he has taken advantage of his neighbors. The villagers not unnaturally react in the most effective way known to them to discourage a neighbor from tampering with the traditional division of the pie. The force of public opinion in peasant society, through its very bitterness and mercilessness, is thus seen as a functional device whereby families protect themselves from economic loss through the real or imagined chicanery and dishonesty of their friends.

This economic focus also explains why peasant families usually attempt to conceal their economic improvements. Visible evidence of fortune will be interpreted as an open confession of guilt, and the lucky or hardworking family will be subject to slander and gossip and perhaps economic blackmail as a consequence. Again it is the Wisers who make so clear the villagers' attitude toward display of wealth.

> Our walls which conceal all that we treasure, are a necessary part of our defence. . . . they are needed against those ruthless ones who come to extort . . . our fathers built them strong enough to shut out the enemy, and made them of earth so that they might be inconspicuous. . . . But they are a better protection if instead of being kept strong they are allowed to become dilapidated. Dilapidation makes it harder for the covetous visitor to tell who is actually poor and who simulates poverty. When men become so strong that the agents of authority work with them for their mutual benefit, they dare to expose their prosperity in walls of better materials and workmanship. But if the ordinary man suddenly makes his wall conspicuous, the extortioner is on his trail. You remember what a short time it was after Puri put up his imposing new verandah with a good grass roof, that the police watchman threatened to bring a false charge against him. He paid well for his show of progress. Old walls tell no tales.[15]

In many peasant communities wealth can be displayed only in a ritual context — a church fiesta, for example — in which the pious individual may in fact go deeply into debt. So we have the striking contrast of poverty-stricken people spending enormous (for them) sums of money to maintain their standing in the community. And the individual who does not, at least once in his life, carry such a religious obligation, will be scorned by the traditionally minded. It is almost as if the society requires him to say, "Look, I have in no way consciously improved my position at your expense, and if I have had advantages about which I have not known, I want no part of them. To prove my sincerity, I am giving away most of what I have so that you can feast and enjoy yourselves, and we can worship our God. You will see that I do not even want to keep that which is rightfully mine."

Peasant culture places heavy burdens on those who wish to live by its rules. Yet it also provides the devices whereby, within the traditional framework, the individual is able to reach out and achieve some degree of security, however modest the level may be. Opposing the centrifugal forces which are constantly tearing at peasant societies are centripetal forces which hold it together. In some places — the Indian village is a good example — a strong feeling of unity marks the extended family and the caste, and mutual and reciprocal obligations mark the behavior of people bound together in such units. The Wisers, again paraphrasing the villagers, write,

> No villager thinks of himself apart from his family. He rises or falls with it. ... we need the strength of the family to support us. ... That man is to be pitied who must stand alone against the dangers, seen and unseen, which beset him. Our families are our insurance. When a man falls ill, he knows that his family will care for him and his children until he is able to earn again. And they will be cared for without a word of reproach. If a man dies, his widow and children are sure of the protection of a home.[16]

Sometimes the *ideal* of familial unity is extended to the village, even reaching across castes and in the face of real schisms and divisions that make village cooperation difficult. McCormack describes how in a Mysore village "The ideal of village unity emerges as an important element in the villagers' own interpretation of proposals for village improvement," and it is strongly felt that a unanimous vote is a precondition to going ahead.[17] In spite of the real picture, conflicts and notorious examples of lack of cooperation in families and within village groups are considered as "shameful," and an important task of hereditary leaders is the arbitration of disputes to restore what is imagined to be a normal village unity.

In other parts of the world — the Italian and Latin American data come to mind — the extended family is sometimes less strong, but its place it taken by a godparenthood system, tying individuals and families together with sacred sanctions which give them something of the group strength and social security afforded by an effective family unit. Formalized friendship, again, often functions to tie together the loose strands occasioned by the divisive forces extant in peasant society. In both formalized friendship patterns and the godparenthood system, we note the element of individual reciprocity based on a sense of *contract,* in contrast to the *ascriptional* basis of the kin-based group. The prevalence of these and other similar types of "fictive kinship" (the anthropological expression for godparent, blood brother, best friend, and similar kin-like relationships) in peasant society helps to explain one of the most important things an outsider must understand in working in such a community. A contract is a bargain between two or more people. It is *personal,* entered into freely by the participants. It implies both obligations and expectations. One must help a friend or a co-godparent (a *compadre,* to use the Spanish terminology) when such help is requested and to the best of one's ability. Conversely, aid and succor may be expected when needed. Relationships are *personalistic* in a society in which the individual contract is the only effective nonfamilial basis for social intercourse. One achieves through having the right friends with effective obligations toward one; conversely, one often does things for these friends, even if the reasons are not fully understood. Not infrequently community development workers have found that villagers have cooperated with them, not because they understood or desired the innovation, but because they felt they had established a friendship relation with the outsider which required that they do what the new friend asked, in return for previous or subsequent favors which he would bring.

It is for reasons like this that an effective worker must thoroughly understand the social structure of a community, the forces that divide people, and the forces that draw them together. The behavior of a peasant villager, however stubborn and unreasoned it may seem to an outsider, is the product of centuries of experience. It is an effective protective device in a relatively unchanging world. It is less effective in a rapidly industrializing world, and ultimately it becomes a serious hindrance. But the peasant is pragmatic; he is not going to discard the clothing that has served him well until he is convinced that he will profit by so doing. He sees that the future holds new things, but he remembers the past: "Our lives are oppressed by many fears. We fear the rent collector, we fear the police watchman, we fear everyone who looks as though he might claim some authority over us, we fear our creditors, we fear our patrons, we fear too much rain, we fear locusts, we fear thieves, we fear the evil spirits which threaten our children and our animals, and we fear the strength of our neighbour." [18]

Notes

1. A. L. Kroeber, *Anthropology*. New York: Harcourt, Brace and Co., 1948, p. 284.
2. Charlotte Viall Wiser and William H. Wiser, *Behind Mud Walls*. New York: Agricultural Missions, 1951, p. 167.
3. Richard N. Adams, "A Nutritional Research Program in Guatemala." In B. D. Paul (ed.) *Health, Culture and Community*. New York: Russell Sage Foundation, 1955, p. 448.
4. U. L. Goswami and S. C. Roy, "India." In Phillips Ruopp (ed.) *Approaches to Community Development*. The Hague, Bandung: W. Van Hoeve Ltd., 1953, p. 305.
5. Jane Philips, "The Hookworm Campaign in Ceylon." In Howard M. Teaf, Jr. and Peter G. Franck (eds.) *Hands Across Frontiers: Case Studies in Technical Cooperation*. Ithaca, New York: Cornell University Press, 1955, p. 287.
6. Oscar Lewis, *Life in a Mexican Village: Tepoztlan Restudied*. Urbana, Ill.: University of Illinois Press, 1951, pp. 429, 294.
7. F. G. Friedmann, "The World of 'La Miseria,'" *Community Development Review* 10, 1958, pp. 21, 24.
8. Edward C. Banfield, *The Moral Basis of a Backward Society*. Glencoe, Ill.: The Free Press, 1958, pp. 10, 121.
9. G. Morris Carstairs, *The Twice-born: A Study of a Community of High Caste Hindus*. Bloomington, Ind.: University of Indiana Press, 1958, p. 40.
10. Ozzie G. Simmons, "Drinking Patterns and Interpersonal Performance in a Peruvian Mestizo Community." *Quarterly Journal of Studies on Alcohol* 20, 1959, p. 104.
11. Ignazio Silone, *Fontamara*. Trans. by Michael Wharf. New York: Harrison Smith & Robert Haas, 1934, p. ix.
12. Luis Adamic. *The Native's Return*. New York: Harper & Brothers, 1934, p. 97.
13. Arthur H. Smith, *Village Life in China: A Study in Sociology*. New York: Fleming H. Revell Company, 1899, p. 328.
14. Banfield, *op. cit.*, pp. 115–116, noting the absence of a feeling of charity or even justice in the Italian village of Montegrano, comments that any advantage given to another is thought to be at the expense of one's family, and that all people outside the nuclear family are potential competitors, and hence potential enemies.

15. Wiser and Wiser, *op. cit.*, p. 157.
16. *Ibid.*, p. 160.
17. William C. McCormack, "Mysore Villagers' View of Change." *Economic Development and Cultural Change* 5, 1957, p. 257.
18. Wiser and Wiser, *op. cit.*, p. 160.

PHILIP E. SLATER

Kill Anything That Moves

Americans have always been a people with marked genocidal proclivities: our systematic extermination of the Indian, the casual killing of American blacks during and after slavery, and our indifference to dropping an atomic bomb on a large civilian populace — we are, after all, the *only* people ever to have used such a weapon — reflect this attitude. We have long had a disturbing tendency to see nonwhites — particularly Orientals — as nonhuman, and to act accordingly. In recent years this courtesy has been extended to the peoples of Communist nations generally, so that at present the majority of the earth's population are candidates for extermination on one count or the other. But white Communist countries usually enjoy the benefit of our fantasy that the people in those countries are ordinary humans enslaved by evil despots and awaiting liberation. When some event — such as the Bay of Pigs fiasco — disconfirms this fantasy, we are simply bewildered and turn our attention elsewhere. The same disconfirmation in a country like Vietnam tends to activate the genocidal assumptions that never lie far beneath the surface of our attitude toward nonwhite nations.

But if this is true — if Americans have always been genocidal, then the Vietnam conflict does not require any special explanation. Every society that has achieved a position of preeminence in the world has shown a remarkable capacity for brutality and violence — you don't get to be the bully of the block without using your fists. I am arguing that Vietnam is different only because it occurred in the face of a host of what might be expected to be inhibiting factors — practical as well as moral — that have arisen in the past few decades. We know from vast experience, for example, that military force is ineffectual in changing attitudes, that air power is cruel but ineffectual against civilian populations, that colonial expeditionary forces are ineffectual against organized indigenous popular movements of any size, and that military dictators will not and cannot broaden their own base of support. We watched carefully while France failed, and then repeated all her mistakes on a larger scale.[1] We helped to establish international principles in the U.N., at Geneva, and at Nuremberg, which we then violated or ignored. We live in a society in which the cruelties of war can be exposed in every living room through mass media. We discuss and debate constantly the appearance of any instance anywhere in the world of inhumane treatment of one person by another. We stress that every human life is a thing of value. We live, in short, in a modern, secure, civilized world, in which a single isolated act of violence is a calamity, an outrage. Yet we engage in the mass slaughter of innocent persons by the most barbarous means possible and show no qualms about it (resistance to the war has been largely in terms of expense and, secondarily, the loss of *American* lives). Since we are no longer crude frontiersmen or hillbillies what leads us to condone such savagery? When one observes that we devote the lion's share of our national budget to war and destruction, that capable scientists are tied up in biological and chemical warfare research that would make Frankenstein and his science-fiction colleagues look like Doctor Doolittle, we cannot avoid asking the question, do Americans hate life? Has there ever been a people who have destroyed so many living things?

The precipitating stimulus for these questions is Frank Harvey's *Air War — Vietnam,* supplemented by Robert Crichton's thoughtful review.[2] As Crichton points out, Harvey's book is particularly compelling because he was a military writer chosen by the Pentagon to publicize the air war, and was given access to information and experiences an unsympathetic reporter could never obtain. But although the Pentagon's efforts to censor Harvey's remarks were ultimately unsuccessful, the book has received surprisingly little attention.

Before describing the varieties of extermination practiced in Vietnam we should perhaps dispose at the outset of one objection that might be raised. For some people, the fact that an individual or group has been defined as an enemy and a combatant justifies whatever horror one wishes to inflict upon him, and nothing in what follows will be viewed by these readers as worthy of note. Unfortunately, however, in Vietnam it is difficult or impossible to determine who the enemy is. We have been repeatedly trapped in our own rhetoric on this matter — initially by portraying ourselves as aiding a friendly Vietnamese majority against a small, alien, and sinister minority. This created the expectation that villages "liberated" from the Viet Cong would welcome us with open arms, as Paris did in World War II. When it turned out that they were not pleased to be rescued from their husbands, brothers, sons, and fathers, we burned their villages and destroyed their crops, and began to give increased emphasis to the idea of outside agencies, particularly the North Vietnamese. To a considerable extent our attack on North Vietnam can be traced to our unwillingness to admit that we are fighting the people in South Vietnam.

Fortunately, the Air Force does not deceive itself when it comes to the welfare of its downed pilots, who are advised that when hit they should try to crash into the sea, since "everybody on the ground in South or North Vietnam (when you [float] down in a parachute, at least) must be considered an enemy." Pilots are also briefed never to say anything against Ho Chi Minh in South Vietnam since he is their national hero. Yet knowing this, knowing that "killing Viet Cong" may mean shooting up a Saigon suburb; knowing that Arvin troops regularly smuggle or abandon ammunition to the Viet Cong; knowing that north of Saigon there are almost no Arvin troops, and that those that do exist may at any time be suddenly recalled to quell a popular uprising, American troops seldom combine these data to draw the obvious conclusion — although they admire the Viet Cong, wonder why they keep fighting against such overwhelming technological superiority (especially when many are as young as 12 years old), and wish they were allies: "If we had them on our side, we'd wrap up this war in about a month." [3]

The examples that follow, then, do not concern merely an armed enemy force but an entire populace, whose relation to this force is highly ambiguous. Should a Vietnamese farmer shoot back when bombed and strafed, he is retroactively defined as "Viet Cong." He is certainly, by now, anti-American.

Pilots learn their trade in the Delta, where there are no trees for the peasants to hide under, and no anti-aircraft fire. It is so safe for Americans that one pilot described it as "a rabbit shoot." The young pilot "learns how it feels to drop bombs on human beings and watch huts go up in a boil of orange flame when his aluminum napalm tanks tumble into them. He gets hardened to pressing the firing button and cutting people down like little cloth dummies, as they sprint frantically under him." If he is shot down, there are so many planes in the area that his average time on the ground (or in the sea) is only eleven minutes. Thus it is a very one-sided war here — as Harvey says, the Vietnamese have about as much chance against American air power as we would have against spaceships with death rays.[4] This training prepares American pilots for the genocidal pattern of the overall war. It does not prepare them, however, for the slightly more equal contest of bombing North Vietnam in the face of anti-aircraft fire, where planes are lost in huge numbers and downed pilots are captured by the enemy. American pilots were most anxious to bomb North Vietnam until they had actually experienced the ground fire, at which point their motivation lessened markedly. It became difficult, in fact, to man these missions. According to Harvey, the Tactical Air Command in Vietnam loses a squadron of pilots a month for noncombat reasons. Killing in a dubious war is apparently much more palatable than getting killed, and Americans are not used to fighting with anything approaching equal odds (imagine our outrage if the North Vietnamese bombed us back). In the Delta, pilots seemed surprised and almost indignant when their massive weaponry is countered with small-arms fire. One pilot, asked if he had killed anyone on a mission, replied: "Yeah — thirty, maybe forty. . . . Those little mothers were shooting back today, though." We are reminded of the old French chestnut:

> Cet animal est très méchant,
> Quand on l'attaque, il se défend.

As Crichton points out, Americans have become so accustomed to what Harvey estimates as 1000 to 1 firepower odds that they come to feel it is their inherent right to kill people without retaliation.[5]

The administration of extermination in the Delta is highly decentralized. Decisions are made by forward air controllers (FACs) who fly about looking for signs of "guerilla activity" (which in most cases can be translated as "life"). They cruise around over the Delta like a vigilante posse, holding the power of life and death over the Vietnamese villagers living beneath." The weapons that they can call in have an unfortunate tendency to kill indiscriminately. There is napalm, which rolls and splatters about over a wide area burning everything burnable that it touches, suffocating those who try to escape by hiding in tunnels, pouring in and incinerating those who hide in family bomb shelters under their huts. Napalm is a favorite weapon, according to Harvey, and is routinely used on rows of houses, individual farms, and rice paddies. "Daisy cutters," or bombs which explode in the water, are also used against peasants hiding in rice paddies. White phosphorous bombs are another incendiary used, and Harvey saw a man in a civilian hospital with a piece of phosphorus in his flesh, still burning. Harvey considers the deadliest weapon to be cluster bomb units (CBUs), which contain tiny bomblets expelled over a wide area. With this device a pilot could "lawnmower for considerable distances, killing or maiming anybody on a path several hundred feet wide and many yards long." The CBUs are particularly indiscriminate since many have delayed action fuses, and go off when the "suspect," whose appearance provoked the FAC observer to trigger off this holocaust, is far away, and the victims being "lawnmowered" are children playing about in a presumably safe area or peasants going about their daily work. Victims who survive must sometimes undergo rather unusual surgery — if hit in the abdomen it must be slit from top to bottom and the intestine spilled out onto a table and fingered for fragments. With one type of CBU a plane can shred an area a mile long and a quarter of a mile wide with more than a million steel fragments. It is difficult to reconcile this kind of indiscriminate killing with speeches about "winning the hearts and minds of the Vietnamese people." [6]

The degree of initiative granted the FACs amounts to a mandate for genocide. If a FAC sees nothing suspicious below he is entitled to employ "Recon by smoke" or "Recon by fire." In the first case he drops a smoke grenade and if anybody runs from the explosion they are presumed guilty, and napalmed (if they run into their house) or machine-gunned (if they take to the rice paddies). "Recon by fire" is based on the same principle except that CBUs are used instead of smoke grenades, so that if the victims do *not* run they will be killed anyway. These techniques are a bit reminiscent of the ducking stool used in earlier centuries to test potential witches: if the woman was not a witch she drowned — if she did not drown this proved she was a witch and she was burned to death. As Harvey points out, American front-line volunteers enjoy shooting and killing, and do it more effectively than most people. It is the deadly efficiency of the slaughter that impresses us, and the at times bewildering overkill — dropping bombs on individuals or using multi-million-dollar planes to "barbecue" peasant huts. When a lone farmer standing in a field manages to hit one of these overarmed pilots with a rifle shot it is impossible to stifle a cheer. But the more usual result is for the upstart to be shredded by machine-gun bullets (fired at the rate of 100 rounds per *second*) and literally to disintegrate to a pile of bloody rags. This enthusiasm for killing was exhibited in an impersonal way by a pilot who suggested starting at the DMZ and killing every man, woman, and child in North Vietnam; and more personally by a "Huey" pilot who described killing a single man: "I ran that little mother all over the place hosing him with guns but somehow or other we just didn't hit him. Finally he turned on us and stood there facing us with his rifle. We really busted his ass then. Blew him up like a toy balloon" (the Huey gunship is a three-man helicopter equipped with six machine guns, rockets, and grenade-launchers).[7]

Harvey met a few FACs, at least, who did not enjoy killing civilians. One advertised his guilt feelings and was relieved of duty. Another, who apparently had learned the lesson of Nuremberg, questioned an order to shell a peaceful village filled with women and children. When the order was reaffirmed he directed the artillery fire into an empty rice paddy. For some pilots, however, their remoteness from their targets protects them from such awareness. B52 bombers, flying from Guam, over 2500 miles away, or from Thailand, dropping bombs from 40,000 feet so that they cannot be seen or heard from below, can wipe out an entire valley. In one of these "saturation" or "carpet" raids, fifty square miles of jungle can suddenly explode into flame without warning, from a rain of fire bombs. These raids are frequent, and in the areas they strike, nothing will live, animal or human, friend or enemy. It is almost as effective on plants and animals as defoliation, which kills three hundred acres in four minutes (the motto of the "Ranch Hands" is "Only You Can Prevent Forests"), probably not much more expensive (it costs almost two million dollars to keep a single plane defoliating for twenty-four hours), and a great deal more inclusive.[8]

Whenever American atrocities are discussed the answer is often given that the Viet Cong also commit atrocities, which is a little like saying that when an elephant steps on a mouse the mouse is equally aggressive when it bites the elephant's foot. A terrorist bomb is not equivalent to a B52 raid, nor the sadistic murder of a captured FAC (naturally the most hated of fliers) the equivalent of a CBU drop. With our overwhelming arsenal of grotesque weapons should go some minimal trace of responsibility. The Viet Cong are fighting for their existence while our pilots in the Delta are amusing themselves with impunity — their merry euphemisms, such as "hosing" and "barbecuing" express this freedom.

Implicit in the atrocity equation, of course, is the assumption that American lives are precious and other peoples' lives are of no more account than ants. The fantastic disproportion in firepower (". . . it is a little exaggerated. . . . We're applying an $18,000,000 solution to a $2 problem. But, still, one of the little mothers *was* firing at us") is justified in terms of saving American lives. At times Harvey seems to be describing some kind of aristocratic adventure: when Major Kasler was shot down over North Vietnam so many American planes were sent out to rescue him that they had difficulty avoiding collisions. But not all of the excess can be attributed to this concern: when a Huey gunship empties its ammunition into total darkness ("nobody will ever know if we hit anything but we certainly did a lot of shooting"), or a B52 rains bombs all over a forest in the hope that perhaps some Viet Cong are hiding in it, this can hardly be defined as saving American lives. It is simply gratuitous aggression, taking a form that owes much to the Toilet Assumption ["the notion that unwanted matter, unwanted difficulties, unwanted complexities, and obstacles will disappear if they are removed from our immediate field of vision," p. 15]. Furthermore, the excessive American firepower and its more grisly manifestations often backfire, and destroy those same expensive lives they are supposed to protect. Captured CBUs are made into booby traps and blow off American limbs. A large supply of our "Bouncing Betty" mines (so called because they are made to leap up and explode in the face), abandoned to the Viet Cong by the Arvins, have caused what Harvey calls "sickening" casualties to our own troops. Our planes collide because there are so many. Dragon ships are melted by their own flares. Fliers are endangered when the Navy and the Air Force try to "out-sortie" each other. Fliers sometimes napalm our own troops. After the *Forrestal* disaster a flier expressed momentary repugnance at having to drop bombs and napalm on North Vietnam after seeing what they had done to our own men.[9]

When all is said and done, American lives, while accorded an extraordinary value relative to those of Vietnamese civilians, still take a back seat relative to the death-dealing machinery they serve. Aircraft carriers, for example, are careless of human life even under the best of conditions, remote from the field of battle. Planes disappear under the sea with their pilots rather easily (the cost of planes lost through landing and takeoff accidents would have financed the poverty program), men are ignited by jet fuel, or devoured by jet engines, or run over by flight deck equipment, or blown into the sea by jet winds, or cut in half by arresting cables, or decapitated by helicopter blades. Even safety devices seem to be geared less to human needs than to the demands of the machinery: pilots ejected from F-4s regularly receive broken backs or other severe spinal injuries.[10] The arguments about Viet Cong atrocities and saving American lives become ludicrous in the face of the daily reality of America's life-destroying technology.

What enables civilized humans to become brutalized in this way? Why are not more of them sickened and disillusioned as men so often have been in the past when forced to engage in one-sided slaughter?

There are really two different types of human extermination involved in Vietnam, and they perhaps require two different kinds of explanation. First, there is extermination such as the Huey troops engage in — extermination at close range, in which the killer can see (and enjoy, apparently) the blood he sheds. Second, and far more common, there is extermination at a distance, in which the extent of the killing is so vast that the killer tends to think in terms of areas on a map rather than individuals. In neither case is the victim perceived as a person (such a perception would make modern war impossible), but in the first case the killer at least sees the immediate consequences of his act, whereas in the second case he does not. The "close-range" killers in Vietnam are confronting *something*, even if it has little to do with the root dissatisfactions in their lives (one of the Huey pilots in Harvey's book reenlisted because he could not tolerate the demands of civilian life).

But for the "long-range" killers — which in a sense includes all of us — do we need any explanation at all? Governments have always tried to keep their soldiers from thinking of "the enemy" as human, by portraying them as monsters and by preventing contact ("fraternization") with them, and modern weaponry makes it very easy for anyone to be a mass killer without much guilt or stress. Flying in a plane far above an impersonally defined target and pressing some buttons to turn fifty square miles into a sea of flame is less traumatic to the average middle-class American boy than inflicting a superficial bayonet wound on a single male soldier.[11] The flier cannot see the women and children being horribly burned to death — they have no meaning to him. Violence-at-a-distance, then, occurs simply because it is so easy — just another expression of the Toilet Assumption.

This is a necessary but not a sufficient condition for violence at a distance. Everyone who has a gun does not use it, and everyone who has an atom bomb does not drop it. Furthermore, one must explain why America has developed more elaborate, complex, and grotesque techniques for exterminating people at a distance than any nation in the history of the world. Our preference for slaughter from the air certainly has some practical basis in the need to insulate carefully reared soldiers from the horrors they cause, but practical considerations alone hardly account for the fiendishness of our weaponry. Can this all result from the miseries and frustrations of American life? Or the logical unfolding of institutional processes? Why does a peasant defending his home, his family, and his property arouse such massive retaliatory responses from American forces, and why are they equipped for genocide?

Other nations have weapons (perhaps less wildly elaborated than ours) capable of causing mass destruction at a distance, but they have not been utilized to any extent. There must therefore be some special factor to account for this uniquely American characteristic. Perhaps it is not an accident that Americans engage so intensively in killing from a distance — perhaps the distance itself carries special meaning. Perhaps Americans enjoy the mass impersonal killing of people who cannot fight back because they themselves suffer mass impersonal injuries from mechanical forces against which they, too, are powerless.

There are, indeed, two ways in which this occurs. The first arises from our tendency to handle interpersonal conflict by increasing individual autonomy, which, as we have seen, simply attenuates the directness of these conflicts. The clashes between people that are thereby avoided rebound upon us by a very circuitous route. We create elaborate mechanisms to avoid conflict with our neighbor and find as a result that we are beleaguered by some impersonal far-off agency. When we fight with our neighbor we can yell at each other and feel some relief, perhaps even make it up or find a solution. But there is little satisfaction in yelling at a traffic jam, or a faulty telephone connection, or an erroneous IBM card, or any of the thousand petty (and some not so petty) irritations to which Americans are daily subject. Most of these irritations are generated by vast impersonal institutions to which the specific individuals we encounter are only vaguely connected ("I only work here"). We not only feel helpless in relation to their size and complexity, but the difficulty of locating the source of responsibility for the problem is so overwhelming that attempts at redress are often abandoned even by middle-class persons, while the poor seldom even try. This is a situation that modern comedians have become adroit at satirizing, but aside from laughter and vague expressions of futile exasperation at "the system" we can do little to relieve our feelings. The energy required to avoid even the most obvious forms of exploitation by commercial enterprises in our society would not permit the individual to lead a normal active life. Like Looking-Glass Country, it takes all the running one can do to stay in the same place.

Powerlessness has always been the common lot of most of mankind, but in a preindustrial age one could at least locate the source of injury. If a nobleman beat you, robbed you, or raped your womenfolk you hated the nobleman. If a hospital removes a kidney instead of an appendix, or when there is only one kidney to remove (accidents that occur far more often than most people imagine, particularly to ward patients), whom do we hate? The orderly who brought the wrong record? The doctor who failed to notice discrepancies? The poor filing system?

The more we attempt to solve problems through increased autonomy the more we find ourselves at the mercy of these mysterious, impersonal, and remote mechanisms that we have ourselves created. Their indifference is a reflection of our own. Our preference for violence at a distance is thus both an expression of and a revenge against this process. We send bombers to destroy "Communism" in Vietnam instead of meeting our needs for collaboration and coordination at home. But part of the motivation for that particular kind of savagery comes from the very remoteness involved. Remote and unknown enemies have a special meaning to us — we associate them with the unknown forces that beset us. In other words, the very fact of Vietnam's remoteness and strangeness increases our hatred — our willingness to use sadistic and genocidal instruments. This becomes clear when we think of Vietnam in relation to Cuba: both are small countries involving no real threat to our power, but one is near and one is far, and we would hesitate using in Cuba the instruments of mass destruction that we employ in Vietnam.

The second process is closely tied to this one, and has to do with the way we arrange our opposing needs for stability and change. All societies, optimally, must allow for both change and stability, since: (a) effective adaptation to the environment requires both modification and consolidation of existing responses; (b) social integration depends both upon the preservation and upon the periodic dissolution of existing structural differentiation; and (c) personal happiness rests upon both familiarity and novelty in everyday life. Every society evolves patterns for attempting to realize these mutually incompatible needs.

Our society, as many have pointed out, has traditionally handled the problem by giving completely free rein to technological change and opposing the most formidable obstacles to social change. Since, however, technological change in fact forces social changes upon us, this has had the effect of abdicating all control over our social environment to a kind of whimsical deity. While we think of ourselves as a people of change and progress, masters of our environment and our fate, we are no more entitled to this designation than the most superstitious savage, for our relation to change is entirely passive. We poke our noses out the door each day and wonder breathlessly what new disruptions technology has in store for us. We talk of technology as the servant of man, but it is a servant that now dominates the household, too powerful to fire, upon whom everyone is helplessly dependent. We tiptoe about and speculate upon his mood. What will be the effects of such-and-such an invention? How will it change our daily lives? We never ask, do we *want* this, is it worth it? (We did not ask ourselves, for example, if the trivial conveniences offered by the automobile could really offset the calamitous disruption and depersonalization of our lives that it brought about.) We simply say "You can't stop progress" and shuffle back inside.

We pride ourselves on being a "democracy" but we are in fact slaves. We submit to an absolute ruler whose edicts and whims we never question. We watch him carefully, hang on his every word; for technology is a harsh and capricious king, demanding prompt and absolute obedience. We laugh at the Luddites (Nat Turners in the struggle for human parity with the machine) but they were the last human beings seriously to confront this issue. Since then we have passively surrendered to every degradation, every atrocity, every enslavement that our technological ingenuity has brought about. We laugh at the old lady who holds off the highway bulldozers with a shotgun, but we laugh because we are Uncle Toms. We try to outdo each other in singing the praises of the oppressor, although in fact the value of technology in terms of human satisfaction remains at best undemonstrated. For when evaluating its effects we always adopt the basic assumptions and perspective of technology itself, and never examine it in terms of the totality of human experience. We say this or that invention is valuable because it generates other inventions — because it is a means to some other means — not because it achieves an ultimate human end. We play down the "side effects" that so often become the main effects and completely negate any alleged benefits. The advantages of *all* technological "progress" will after all be totally outweighed the moment nuclear war breaks out (an event which, given the inadequacy of precautions and the number of fanatical fingers close to the trigger, is only a matter of time unless radical changes are made).

Let me make clear what I am *not* saying here. I do not believe in the noble savage and I am not advocating any brand of bucolic romanticism. I do not want to put an end to machines, I only want to remove them from their position of mastery, to restore human beings to a position of equality and initiative. As a human I must protest that being able to sing and eat watermelon all day is no compensation for being beaten, degraded, and slaughtered at random, and this is the nature of our current relationship to our technological order.

Nor am I attributing all these ills to capitalism. The Soviet Union and other planned economies are as enslaved as we. They may be allowed more freedom in working out the details of the commands given them, but they seem to have no more say in the basic policy-making. Technology makes core policy in every industrialized nation, and the humans adjust as best they can.

The much-vaunted "freedom" of American life is thus an illusion, one which underlies the sense of spuriousness so many Americans feel about their basic institutions. We are free to do only what we are told, and we are "told" not by a human master but by a mechanical construction.

But how can we be the slaves of technology — is not technology merely an extension of, a creation of, ourselves? This is only metaphorically true. The forces to which we submit so abjectly were not generated by ourselves but by our ancestors — what we create will in turn rule our progeny. It takes a certain amount of time for the social effects of technological change to make their appearance, by which time a generation has usually passed.

Science-fiction writers have long been fascinated with the notion of being able to create material objects just by imagining them, and have built novels, stories, and films around this idea. Actually, it is merely an exaggeration of what normally takes place. Technology is materialized fantasy. We are ruled today by the material manifestations of the fantasies of previous generations.

It is for this reason that the concept of the tyrannical father has never disappeared from American culture. Whereas in everyday family life the despotic patriarch is (and probably always has been, although each generation of Americans imagines the past to have been different)[12] a rare curiosity, it is an *idea* with which every American is on terms of intimate familiarity. If the personal authorities with whom Americans come into earliest and most intense contact are warm and benign, what is the basis of the other concept?

This question was raised two decades ago by Wolfenstein and Leites in their brilliant analysis of the cultural preoccupations revealed by American films.[13] They observed that in the typical popular film the hero's father was portrayed as a kindly, bumbling, ineffectual figure, but that the hero usually came into conflict with another male authority — a cattle baron, captain of industry, political leader, or racketeer — who was powerful, evil, despotic, iron-willed, and aggressive, quite unlike the kindly old father (who played the same inconsequential role he plays in TV situation comedies). Wolfenstein and Leites saw this discrepancy as revealing deeper and more primitive Oedipal fantasies, from the perspective of a child so small that any authority seems overpowering.

I would suggest, however, that this image derives some of its continuing force and appeal from the realities of everyday adult experience. We treat technology as if it were a fierce patriarch — we are deferential, submissive, and alert to its demands. We feel spasms of hatred toward it, and continually make fun of it, but do little to challenge its rule. Technology has inherited the fantasy of the authoritarian father. Furthermore, since the technological environment that rules, frustrates, and manipulates us is a materialization of the wishes of our forefathers, it is quite reasonable to say that technology *is* the authoritarian father in our society. The American father can be a good-natured slob in the home precisely because he is so ruthless toward the nonhuman environment, leveling, uprooting, filling in, building up, tearing down, blowing up, tunneling under. This ruthlessness affects his children only indirectly, as the deranged environment afflicts the eyes, ears, nose, and nervous system of the next generation. But it affects them nonetheless. Through this impersonal intermediary we inflict our will upon our children, and punish them for our generous indulgence — our child-oriented, self-sacrificing behavior. It is small wonder that the myth of the punitive patriarch stays alive.

From this viewpoint, then, delegating to technology the role of punitive patriarch is another example of the first process we described: the tendency to avoid interpersonal conflict by compartmentalization and a false illusion of autonomy — to place impersonal mechanisms between and around people and imagine that we have created a self-governing paradise. It is a kind of savage joke in its parental form. We say: "Look, I am an easy-going, good-natured, affectionate father. I behave in a democratic manner and treat you like a person, never pulling rank. As to all those roads and wires and machines and bombs and complex bureaucratic institutions out there, don't concern yourself about them — this is my department." But when the child grows up he discovers the fraud. He learns that he is a slave to his father's unconscious and unplanned whims — that the area of withheld power was crucial. He becomes angry and rebels, saying, "You were not what you pretended, and I cannot be what you encouraged me to be." He attacks "the system" and authority everywhere, trying to find the source of the deception, and using techniques that reflect his commitment to what his father deceived him into thinking he was — a person. But by this time he has also learned the system of avoiding conflict through impersonal mechanism and is ready to inflict the same deception on his own children.

Margaret Mead describes a mild, peaceful tribe — the Arapesh — that shares this device with us.[14] Whenever an Arapesh is angry at one of his compatriots he never attacks him directly. Instead he gets some of his "dirt" (body excretions, food leavings, etc.) and gives it to a sorcerer from the plains tribe nearby, who may or may not use it to destroy the victim through magic. If the man dies years later his death will be attributed to this sorcery, though the quarrel be long since forgotten. The Arapesh see themselves as incapable of killing each other — they do not even know any black magic. Death comes from the plains.

Our enlightened civilization proceeds on precisely the same model. We love and indulge our children, and would never dream of hurting them. If they are poisoned, bombed, gassed, burned, or whatever, it is surely not our fault, since we do not even know how to manipulate these objects. The danger comes from outside. Perhaps long ago we did something to deliver them into these impersonal hands, but we have forgotten, and in any case it is not our responsibility. Technology, in other words, is our plains sorcerer.

The joy in killing a far-off enemy, then, derives additional strength from this configuration. The "enemy" is distant and impersonal. Since injury comes to us from remote sources we must find a remote victim on which to wreak our vengeance.

Since the "real" enemy is our technologically strangled environment (ultimately of course ourselves and our ancestors) it may seem ironic that we avenge ourselves by killing an impoverished people who had not experienced this environment before we inflicted it upon them. We have utilized what oppresses us to oppress other human beings. But this has always been true of downtrodden classes — afraid to attack the oppressor they take out their rage on each other. Blacks have for centuries squandered their rebellion in fraternal slaughter, and other examples can be found in every period in history. Human beings as a whole, enslaved by their Frankenstein-monsters, behave no differently. And it is even less likely that the people of the United States and Vietnam will ever join together and consign the napalm, defoliants, Hueys, CBUs, and all other life-hating implements to oblivion. Misery loves company more than its own end. And Americans love machines more than life itself.

Notes

1. For some reason the escalation of failure has always been particularly popular with military lobbyists. When the war in the South failed they demanded to be allowed to bomb the North. When the bombing proved ineffectual they demanded that it be expanded. When poison gas proved ineffectual they demanded an increase in the amount and toxicity of gas used. The Pentagon here plays the part of the ne'er-do-well nephew who "borrows" our money, loses it at the racetrack, and when caught and confronted with his delinquency tries to brazen it out, saying: "Never mind how and why I got here, I've lost $500 of your money and you have to give me another $1000 so I can win it back."

   The escalation of failure has respectable but inauspicious precedents: Athens, unable to defeat Sparta, invaded Syracuse, and extinguished herself as a dominant political power.
2. Frank Harvey, *Air War — Vietnam* (New York: Bantam, 1967); Robert Crichton, "Our Air War," *New York Review of Books,* IX, January 4, 1968.
3. Harvey, pp. 15, 29–30, 67, 100, 104, 108–109, 115.
4. Harvey, pp. 2, 16, 55–56, 107, 116.
5. Harvey, pp. 108, 141, 146–147, 150, 154; Crichton, p. 3.
6. Harvey, pp. 54–57, 82 ff.; Crichton, pp. 3–4.
7. Harvey, pp. 57, 91–92, 102–104, 115, 174–175; Crichton, pp. 3–4.
8. Harvey, pp. 39–40, 62–63, 106–107, 126–127; Crichton, p. 4.
9. Harvey, pp. 65, 70, 72, 105, 109, 111, 112, 138, 150, 152; Crichton, p. 3–4.
10. Harvey, pp. 5–8, 11, 63, 115.
11. A wilderness-survival expert once pointed out to me that army training in hand-to-hand combat virtually ignores the body's own weaponry: ripping out the windpipe or jugular of one's opponent with one's teeth, for example, might be in many situations the most simple and expedient way of disabling him, but well-brought-up Americans shun such intimate contact with the victims of their mutilations.
12. W. G. Bennis and P. E. Slater, *The Temporary Society* (New York: Harper and Row, 1968), Chapter 2.
13. Martha Wolfenstein and Nathan Leites, *Movies: A Psychological Study* (Glencoe, Ill.: Free Press, 1950), pp. 106 ff., 149–174.
14. Margaret Mead, *Sex and Temperament in Three Primitive Societies* (New York: Mentor, 1950), p. 21.

6

STRATIFICATION: CASTE, CLASS, AND STATUS

Every society, regardless of its complexity, must solve the problem of dividing the necessary labor into specific tasks and recruiting people to perform those tasks. In sociological theory this process is usually called "social differentiation." As Aberle and others (1950, p. 105) explain:

> In any society there are activities which must be regularly performed if the society is to persist. If they are to be done dependably, these extensive and varied activities must be broken down and assigned to capable individuals trained and motivated to carry them out.

It is in the interest of the entire society that total human resources be utilized most efficiently; that the most able individuals are motivated to train for and assume the duties of those positions most crucial to the survival of the collectivity. Davis and Moore (1945) have hypothesized that this is accomplished by attaching differential rewards (such as power, wealth, and prestige) to various positions according to their relative importance. The abilities which are rewarded and the nature of the rewards must vary according to the economic organization of the society. Nevertheless, according to Davis and Moore, some level of institutionalized social inequality appears to be necessary for achieving the functional prerequisite of the society for adequate role differentiation and role assignment.

This proposition represents a vital contribution to solving the problem of the seeming universality and historical intransigence of at least some level of institutionalized social inequality. On the other hand, it tends to reify the concept of "functional prerequisite" or "societal demand" at the expense of recognizing that individuals with conflicting values, interests, and personal loyalties make the decisions and carry on the affairs of any society.

In varying degrees, people have always been torn between particularistic

169

norms (that is, one's primary obligation is to one's kin and personal associates) and universalistic norms (one's primary obligation is to the welfare of the entire society so that people and issues are evaluated by public rather than private criteria). As a consequence, all societies, to some extent, have experienced some rigidification of social inequality, resulting in the restriction of access to privileged positions to fewer and fewer elites. Access to such positions, then, becomes determined less by competence and more by connections; less by what you know than by who you know. This process results in what is called *social stratification*.

As distinguished from social differentiation, social stratification is the stable, hierarchical arrangement of groups of individuals between which social and material rewards are unequally distributed. To achieve stability, such systems of stratification must be legitimized or voluntarily accepted by most, especially the important, members of the society. Individuals in the same strata perform similar occupations, share similar life conditions, face a similar opportunity structure and, in time, come to further solidify their position through the development of kinship and friendship ties and identification with a similar set of beliefs and orientations.

Caste

The most rigid form of social stratification is by *caste* (a term derived from the Portuguese, meaning kin or breed). As implied, caste is ascribed on the basis of parents' position in the stratification hierachy rather than achieved by effort. Berreman (1960, p. 120) defines caste as "a hierarchy of endogamous divisions in which membership is hereditary and permanent." Although castes are economically interdependent, the relative distribution of wealth, power, prestige, and privilege differs enormously between them. Although there is some differentiation of rank within castes, the social barriers between them are absolute and of primary importance.

One's range of occupational choices is completely determined by caste membership and there is no opportunity to improve one's position — to become "vertically mobile" — in the social structure. Social interaction between members of different castes is severely circumscribed; some types of contacts are even considered contaminating by those of a higher caste. Members of different castes are residentially segregated and must worship at a separate place. As a result of these and other factors, they tend to develop different forms of subcultural behavior. India, medieval Europe, and medieval Japan are classic examples of caste-stratified societies.

Class

Stratification by caste is rarely found outside traditional preindustrial societies. In modern industrial societies stratification tends to take the form of class or status or both. Perhaps the earliest theoretical formulations of class are those of Marx (Feuer, 1959) and of Weber (Gerth and Mills, 1958). According to Marx, who did most of his writing in the mid- to late nineteenth century, distinct and antagonistic classes emerge in capitalist societies. Classes are defined by their function in the organization of production, including their relationship to the means of production. The production of goods in a capitalist economy requires four factors: land, labor, capital, and organization (the particular combination of the first three factors).

According to Marx the three basic classes are: (1) the old and fading class of landowners, (2) the capitalists, and (3) the workers. The capitalists provide the means of production; the money, physical plant, equipment, nonhuman power, and raw materials, and the workers provide the physical labor necessary to manufacture finished goods out of raw materials. Each class thus performs a different function in the productive process, and has a different relationship to the means of production. As a consequence, each class also derives its revenue from a different source. The landowner derives revenue from rent on the use of his property, the capitalist from profits and interest on his enterprises and investments, and the worker from salary or wages for his labor. Technically, then, a self-employed carpenter, although performing the same occupation for the same remuneration as a carpenter working for a large industrial firm, belongs to a different class. The former is a capitalist and the latter a worker.

Marx indicated that, although level of income, educational attainment, occupation, and consumption patterns may provide clues to an individual's class, these are better considered consequences of class position and are by no means identical to it. What is essential, in Marxist theory, is the ownership of the means of production, a factor which then determines who has power over others. Insofar as workers do not own the means of production, they are dependent upon capitalists for their life-sustaining revenue.

Marx predicted that monopoly capitalism, organized around an advancing technology, would eventually bankrupt small entrepreneurs (the *petit bourgeois*) and swell the ranks of the working class. In time, members of the working class, because of their similar economic interests and living conditions, would develop a class-consciousness which would motivate them to physically overthrow the oppressive capitalist class. They would then establish a transitional "dictatorship of the proletariat," which would evolve into a classless society in which the means of production were publicly owned. Finally, the institution of the state as an instrument for social control and the protection of private property would disappear.

Weber, who did most of his writing in the late nineteenth and early twentieth centuries, also saw property ownership, and the power which that implies, as the basic criteria of class membership. Both Marx and Weber, writing in a period of social upheaval before the significant spread of labor union movements to certain areas of production, saw the capitalists as being able to dictate work conditions and rewards because of their control over the means of production. Weber, however, did not postulate the historical inevitability of class conflict and revolution.

One key concept which has emerged from Weber's work is that of "life chances," or the relative opportunity to acquire different resources (wealth, power, prestige, safety, privilege, among others), given one's circumstances at birth. These circumstances, of course, are profoundly influenced by one's class position so that any opportunities an individual has to improve his circumstances in life are largely determined by the operation of competing economic interests in an open labor market. Weber's formulation provides some explanation for the stability or persistence of class boundaries, but his work did not consider the social psychological implications of this situation.

Status

Weber also discussed *status*, which is determined by one's membership in various groups or social circles of different standing in the community. Whereas class determines power, status determines prestige or what Weber calls "social honor." Whereas class is defined by one's relationship to the means of production, status is defined by one's patterns of consumption. Whereas class has direct implications for one's life chances, status has direct implications for one's life style. In sum, status is defined by one's membership in more or less bounded social circles with varying degrees of prestige, characterized by distinctive life styles.

Income level, rather than source, is more essential to maintaining or improving one's status. Property ownership does not determine status but is usually related to it. Class can serve as a condition for status (as a great deal of money and leisure time is required to maintain certain life styles), and status can serve as a condition for class (in cases where individuals in high-prestige status groups invest their revenue in financial enterprises), but the two are conceptually and empirically distinct.

Statuses may exist within classes. For example, membership in the upper upper class requires particularized training in certain leisure activities. This training only can come from the "right" family socialization ("breeding") and schooling. Access to this status may be barred even to the wealthiest of the capitalist class if they don't come from the right "stock," their money is too new (*nouveaux riches*), or their social credentials lacking in other respects. The primary function of restricting access to this elite core group, according to Hollingshead and Redlich (1958), is to limit access to informal sources of power and influence.

In the Soviet Union, where the major means of production are owned and controlled by the state, no social class distinctions are based on property. Nevertheless, as Inkeles (1950) and others have shown, differential rewards are given for various kinds of work. And status circles, which enjoy greater privileges and are able to provide their children with superior opportunities, have emerged.

Socioeconomic Status

Many attempts have been made since Marx and Weber to reformulate these concepts and to develop methods of "operationalizing" them (that is, specifying criteria and procedures for accurately measuring those characteristics which define class position). Various indices including measures of occupational prestige, level of family income, level of educational attainment, and degree of social participation have been used. Because 90 per cent of the American labor force works for a wage or salary, ownership of the means of production or source of revenue, although instructive for understanding the dynamics of power in the United States, are not useful criteria for evaluating relative opportunities. In contemporary studies the concepts of class and status have been combined into the concept of socioeconomic status (SES) to include all aspects of both.

Although SES is a somewhat cruder measure of life chances and life styles than the classical concepts of class and status, it can accurately differentiate strata within the general population and compares well to the implicit and explicit conceptions of class composition held by the people themselves. Over thirty years ago, Davis, Gardner, and Gardner (1941) showed that, although each class has a range and "modal average," some unity of class outlook is manifested in the expression of "resentment at exclusion from the class above and antagonism toward mobility from the class below" as well as in the maintenance of "a common set of beliefs, a common pattern of overt behavior, and other traits, which function as symbols of status." Hollingshead's classic community study of Elmstown's youth (1949) also provides data on the relationship between class membership, the treatment of the individual within certain institutional contexts (for example, the school), and the consequences this may have for the individual's personality development. In fact, some studies have even concluded that the effects of SES on some aspects of social personality appear to be so great as to outweigh ethnic and national differences.

Psathas (1957) discovered in his study of the relative effects of ethnicity and SES on adolescent independence from parental control that, when questionnaire responses were controlled for SES, all significant differences between the scores of Italian and Jewish youth on any dimension of independence were eliminated. In her study of the values and behavior patterns of adolescent boys in London, and Spokane, Washington, Himmelweit (1955) found that, in certain matters, differences in SES were more important than national differences.

And Pearlin and Kohn's cross-national study (1966, p. 478) of the relationships between SES, socialization practices, and personality concluded that

> the relationship of social class to parental values is much the same in both countries. In both Italy and the United States, middle-class parents put greater emphasis on the child's self-direction and working-class parents put greater emphasis on the child's conformity to external proscription. There is something intrinsic to social stratification that yields strikingly similar results in the two countries.

Most studies of the relationship between SES and personality have considered such problems as the differential effects of SES components (such as work conditions, level of formal education achieved, and family income), on social personality patterns such as sex role norms (especially role differentiation in the family); attitudes toward sex; extended family orientations; child-rearing values and practices; patterns of consumption; degree of participation in religious, political, and social groups and activities; ability to conceptualize abstractions; orientations toward authority; impulse control; self-esteem; feelings of alienation; attitudes toward racial and ethnic minorities; political ideology; types and levels of psychological pathology; levels of anxiety; aggression; achievement drives; and levels of educational and occupational aspiration.

The first selection by Keller and Zavalloni represents a decided advance in the conceptualization of a controversial problem area: the relationship between SES and achievement motivation. The authors manage to reconcile some of the apparently contradictory results reported in major studies by proposing that the separate factors of "relative distance" from goals, "relative value of goals," and "differential rewards" for the achievement of goals all be carefully assessed to understand the meaning and importance of ambition in the subcultures and social personalities of individuals from different social strata.

The article by Form and Huber (Rytina) investigates the relationship between SES and political ideology. Ideology is generally defined as any set of interrelated beliefs about society that characterize a particular group. Ideologies usually function to rationalize private interest in terms of public good. The authors not only examine the structure of various ideological orientations and how they vary between different strata, but they also discuss the functions of ideology for the personality system of the social actor.

In their concluding discussion they introduce the idea of "upper-class authoritarianism," in striking contradistinction to the increasingly discredited concept of "working-class authoritarianism" which has served as conventional wisdom in sociological literature for some time. This research by Form and Huber (Rytina) is particularly appropriate for studying the relationship between social structure and social personality. Inkeles (1953, p. 584) states that it is precisely these "conscious idea systems," enmeshed as they are in basic values and beliefs, which are rarely examined in traditional studies of culture and personality, but have "crucial relevance to the individual's social action and consequently for the social system."

References

Aberle, D. F., A. K. Cohen, A. K. Davis, M. J. Levy, Jr., and F. X. Sutton
    1950   "The Functional Prerequisites of a Society." *Ethics* 60 (January):100–11.
Berreman, Gerald D.
    1960   "Caste in India and the United States." *The American Journal of Sociology* 46 (September):120–7.
Bronfenbrenner, Urie
    1958   "Socialization and Social Class Through Time and Space." Pp. 400–425 in Eleanor E. Maccoby, Theodore M. Newcomb, and Eugene L. Hartley (eds.), *Readings in Social Psychology*, 3d ed. New York: Holt, Rinehart and Winston.
Cloward, Richard A.
    1959   "Illegitimate Means, Anomie, and Deviant Behavior." *American Sociological Review* 24 (April):164–76.
Davis, Allison, Burleigh B. Gardner, and Mary R. Gardner
    1941   *Deep South: A Social Anthropological Study of Caste and Class*. Chicago: University of Chicago Press.
Davis, Kingsley, and Wilbert E. Moore
    1945   "Some Principles of Stratification." *The American Sociological Review* 10(2):242–49.
Feuer, Lewis S. (ed.)
    1959   *Marx and Engels: Basic Writings on Politics and Philosophy*. Garden City, N. Y.: Doubleday.
Gerth, H. H., and C. Wright Mills (eds.)
    1958   *From Max Weber: Essays in Sociology*. New York: Oxford University Press.
Han, Wan Sang
    1969   "Two Conflicting Themes: Common Values Versus Class Differential Values." *American Sociological Review* 34 (October):679–90.

Harary, Frank
  1966   "Merton Revisited: A New Classification for Deviant Behavior." *American Sociological Review* 31 (October):693–737.
Himmelweit, Hilde T.
  1955   "Socio-Economic Background and Personality." *International Social Science Bulletin* 7(1):29–35.
Hollingshead, August B.
  1949   *Elmstown's Youth.* New York: Wiley.
Hollingshead, August B., and Frederick C. Redlich
  1958   *Social Class and Mental Illness.* New York: Wiley.
Howe, Louise Kapp (ed.)
  1970   *The White Majority: Between Poverty and Affluence.* New York: Vintage.
Inkeles, Alex
  1950   "Social Stratification and Mobility in the Soviet Union: 1940–1950." *American Sociological Review* 15 (August):465–79.
  1953   "Some Sociological Observations on Culture and Personality Studies." Pp. 577–92 in Clyde Kluckhohn and Henry A. Murray with David M. Schneider (eds.), *Personality: In Nature, Society, and Culture.* New York: Knopf.
Kohn, Melvin
  1959   "Social Class and Parental Values." *The American Journal of Sociology* 64 (January):337–51.
  1963   "Social Class and Parent-Child Relationships: An Interpretation." *American Journal of Sociology* 68 (January):471–80.
Kohn, Melvin L., and Carmi Schooler
  1969   "Class, Occupation and Orientation." *American Sociological Review* 34 (October):659–78.
Lipset, Seymour M.
  1960   *Political Man.* New York: Doubleday.
Pearlin, Leonard I., and Melvin L. Kohn
  1966   "Social Class, Occupation, and Parental Values: A Cross-National Study." *American Sociological Review* 31 (August):466–79.
Psathas, George
  1957   "Ethnicity, Social Class, and Adolescent Independence from Parental Control." *American Sociological Review* 22 (August):415–23.
Simmons, Roberta G., and Morris Rosenberg
  1971   "Functions of Children's Perceptions of the Stratification System." *American Sociological Review* 36 (April): 235–49.

SUZANNE KELLER
MARISA ZAVALLONI

Ambition and Social Class: A Respecification

The relationship between individual ambition and social opportunity has been a controversial topic in American sociology, particularly with reference to the influence of social class on the achievement of worldly success. Among two prominent recent views, one accounts for the lesser achievements of lower class individuals (as compared to the middle class) in terms of limited opportunities, the other, in terms of limited desires. The latter view may be gaining ground if its independent espousal by three influential social scientists may be so interpreted. Although their evidence varies, they agree in their conclusions: lower class individuals, in giving relatively low priority to a college education and to professional, or at least white collar work, are less ambitious than middle class individuals. This inference derives not from psychological information about the intensity of individual strivings but from sociological information about levels aspired to, a procedure posing logical as well as methodological problems. Nevertheless, this approach has the merit of challenging an earlier assumption, notably by Merton in his well-known paper on "Social Structure and Anomie," [1] that the motivation to succeed is shared by all classes. However, as we shall try to show, the later "correction" may err in the opposite direction. From the contention that the lower class not only has less but also wants less of what there is to be had, it is a small, though precarious, step to suggest that the lower class has less *because* it wants less.

The main line of the argument may be summarized as follows: In his original paper, Merton argued that the strain toward anomie in the lower class was a consequence of the desire for lofty goals combined with limited access to legitimate means. This is questioned by Hyman who found that the lower class does not set its sights quite so high as Merton had assumed and presumably then, its more limited means are quite consistent with its more modest ambitions. Although Hyman does not do so explicitly, one result of his reinterpretation would be to reject the hypothesis of a strain toward anomie, possibly to be replaced by a hypothesis more in line with the facts as he sees them, that is, of a strain towards security.

In a later article, Merton substantially accepts Hyman's reformulation and in-

Reprinted by permission of the publisher, the University of North Carolina Press, from Suzanne Keller and Marisa Zavalloni, "Ambition and Social Class: A Respecification," *Social Forces* 43:1 (1964). Sections of this paper were read at the annual meeting of the American Association for Public Opinion Research, May, 1962. Some footnotes omitted.

corporates it into his suggestions for further research, calling for data on the "extent to which Americans in different social strata have in fact assimilated the same culturally induced values." Specifically, information is needed on "socially patterned differentials" in:

(1) *exposure* to the cultural goal and norms regulating behavior oriented to that goal;

(2) *acceptance* of the goal and norms as moral mandates and internalized values.

In observing that lower class individuals do not typically entertain high hopes by pursuing lofty goals, Hyman has successfully challenged Merton's original conclusion. He did not, however, challenge the logic of his argument, principally, it would seem, because he was in implicit agreement with it. Both Hyman and Merton agree on one capital point: that the degree of personal ambition can be inferred from the cultural significance of the goal aspired to. If this goal ranks high, individual ambition must be great; if it ranks low, individual ambition must be small. By equating these two dimensions, Merton discovers structurally engendered frustrations; Hyman, structurally engendered submission, in the lower class. Their opposite conclusions rest on essentially the same premise. But to treat ambition and the rank of the success goal as interchangeable instead of interdependent may obscure the relationship between ambition and social class — a situation which this paper hopes to remedy.

The first clue as to the difficulties involved in this way of formulating the problem comes when one seeks to confront Merton's thesis with Hyman's evidence. It is then at once apparent that the degree of ambition can be equated with the rank of the desired goal only so long as this goal is left unspecified. As soon as this goal is specified, however, as Hyman does when he selects college and professional aspirations as possible yardsticks, the whole problem of differential class access to these goals-used-as-standards, and with it the necessity of devising class equivalents or substitute goals, comes to the fore.

Though Merton did consider the possibility of alternative goals, concentrating on monetary success only for the sake of simplicity, the alternatives he had in mind are all culturally rather than structurally defined. Instead of pecuniary success, for example, he suggests that intellectual or artistic success may be appropriate alternatives.[2] However, in both cases, the potential equivalents are goals to which the "cultural structure" attaches prestige and the social structure permits access.[3] In other words, ambition can be inferred only from goals with high general rank in the society at large. That this will undoubtedly "catch" some ambitious individuals but not all or even most of them, is evident once the overall success goal is specified not only in terms of culturally prestigeful alternatives, as Merton urges, but also in terms of socially structured ones. Class variations in the saliency of specific forms of success may thus reflect objective rather than subjective determinants of ambition.

The Concept of Relative Distance

We should thus be prepared to find class-determined variations in aspirations not because the individual class members are more or less ambitious but because the classes themselves are nearer to some goals than to others. The class-accessi-bility of a given goal will affect its saliency for that class independently from its saliency for the individuals within it. Social class alters the content of what is aspired to and thus constitutes an intervening variable between individual ambition and social achievement. Any given success-goal has both an absolute and a rela-tive value, the first referring to the general consensus regarding its over-all im-portance or desirability, the second, to its class accessibility. In order, therefore, to compare the extent of ambitiousness by social class, one needs to know not only the absolute rank-order of a given goal and group rates of endorsement of this goal — this would suffice were one dealing with a non-stratified society — but also the relative distance of each social class from it. Once stated it is of course self-evident that choosing to become a skilled craftsman may be a lofty ambition for the boy whose father never held a steady job but not for the boy whose father was a high-ranking business executive.

The concept of relative distance — all too self-evident, yet often ignored — en-ables us to respecify the relevant dimensions of ambition and opportunity by social class, by distinguishing the structural from the personal sources of ambition, and the absolute from the relative values of a success-goal.

Ambition Respecified

(1) A "structural" component of ambition — this refers to the amount of ambi-tion required to achieve a specific culturally ranked goal in the light of one's social class. It is determined by the relative distance of a social class from a success goal. The "structural" component of the ambition to attend college is lower for the mid-dle class than for the lower class because the middle class has more and better facilities for pursuing this goal.

(2) A "personality" component of ambition — this refers to the needs, capac-ities, and talents of individuals. Individuals whose relative distance to a goal is identical will nevertheless vary as regards their personal stakes in success, and some personal attributes will be more, some less, advantageous for achieving it.

Achievement Respecified

(1) A goal has an absolute value — as determined by the general consensus concerning its importance and desirability. Such a consensus exists even in highly heterogeneous and industrialized societies, as the N.O.R.C. and the Inkeles-Rossi findings have demonstrated.[4] Goals whose absolute values are high are those re-lating to professional and executive work.

(2) A goal has a relative value — as determined by the social class rating of its importance and desirability which in turn depends on a stratum's relative distance from it. As regards the individual, the relative worth of a goal will determine how much effort he will have to expend to pursue a goal irrespective of his personal drive and capacity. An example of a goal with a high relative value in the lower class but a low relative value in the middle class is skilled manual work.

General impressions notwithstanding, no reliable evidence on the extent of individual ambitiousness in the various social classes is as yet available. All so-called assessments of it are essentially assessments of the "structural" or the class-determined components. Moreover, the structural and the personality components of ambition are frequently confused, as when indicators such as college or specific occupational plans are used without reference to their accessibility by social class, thereby invalidating any comparisons of the "intensity of striving by social class." [5]

By distinguishing between the absolute and the relative values of success-goals and between personal and structural components of ambition, it is possible to reinterpret both Merton's and Hyman's conclusions. Along with Hyman one can expect the lower classes to pursue not the same but less important goals than the middle class, and along with Merton one can continue to expect lower class individuals to be no less ambitious than middle class individuals.

This leads to a reappraisal of a further hypothesis suggested in Merton's paper, that a lowering of levels of aspiration is a form of deviant behavior. Merton, with some reluctance to be sure, treats lower aspirations as deviant because of a presumed time sequence, implicit in his presentation, in which the individual starts out by having high hopes and then confronts the obstacles put in his path by his social class environment which prevent him from realizing them. In fact in his original articles, Merton considered the leveling of aspirations to be a form of ritualism, which "involves the abandoning or scaling down of lofty cultural goals of great pecuniary success and rapid social mobility to the point where one's aspirations can be satisfied." [6] This type of response, he predicted, would be found more frequently in the lower middle than in the lower class. However, if Hyman is right and lower goals are "normal" for the lower class, then lower class individuals can hardly be considered deviant in holding them. In this paper we will try to show that it is possible for lower class individuals to have lower goals and yet entertain great expectations about their own success, and that a class "leveling of aspirations" need be neither a form of deviant behavior nor a psychological mechanism for reducing status anxieties. [7]

Indicators of Ambition:
College and Professional Status

The concept of "relative distance" permits us to re-appraise the data regarding educational and occupational aspirations used by Hyman and others, and to reach quite opposite conclusions. For example, to use a few of Hyman's findings, the middle class is considered more ambitious than the lower class because more of them typically appreciate the importance of college: 91 percent of the prosperous but only 68 percent of the poor would like to see their children attend college; 58 percent of the wealthy males over forty but only 29 percent of the poor males are in favor of this; and 74 percent of the wealthy youths between 14 and 20 but only 42 percent of the poor youths value such an education. [8] Since it is obviously true that in each case more of the middle class endorse the value of college it might seem only natural to consider them more ambitious, except for one thing: college is far more accessible to the middle than to the lower class; in fact it has become a middle class norm. According to Lipset and Bendix, for example, "the great majority of university students regard their attendance at college as 'the thing to do' for the children of middle class families." [9] And Parsons observes: "Probably the best single index of the line between 'upper middle' class and the rest of the middle class is the *expectation* that children will have a college education, as a matter that is of status-right not of the exceptional ability of the individual." [10] College attendance is a middle class means of conserving or maintaining their social positions. Were most of them to choose not to go to college they would face the unpopular prospect of downward mobility. In fact, so far no index of middle class ambitiousness exists, for one can hardly, as most authors seem to do, use the desire for higher education *both* as a middle class norm and as a sign of middle class aspirations. To ascertain the ambitiousness of middle class youths, therefore, one would have to specify a "high-reaching" goal for them, something over and beyond college.

Occupational Aspirations

Another frequently used comparative index of ambition involves occupational aspiration, but the same argument applies here. Without taking into account the relative distance of middle and working class individuals from the professions, no adequate assessment of their ambitiousness is possible. In a sense, the middle class has no choice but to prefer professional work since skilled manual labor would mean a loss of social status for them. It is therefore significant to note that Hyman found from five to thirteen percent of the younger middle class men actually preferring skilled manual jobs, thereby choosing occupations that would downgrade their prestige in the eyes of their peers.

In sum, the concept of relative distance means that each and every concrete goal according to which class feelings might be compared must first be "adjusted or corrected" for this differential. The structural (in this case, social class) component of ambition is such a correction factor. This point was stressed by Kurt Lewin and his collaborators in a psychological context nearly two decades ago and it should now be applied to the sociological context in which ambition is generated and sustained.

The Meaning of College

College cannot be used as a yardstick of ambition even when relative distance has been controlled because its meaning varies from class to class. In general its significance is two-fold; as a gateway to generalized "prestige," and as a gateway to the higher-income professions. However, these two by no means always coincide for the graduate, especially when he happens to come from a lower class background. According to Lipset and Bendix, a college degree leads to but modest incomes "in the majority of cases," and skilled workers often earn higher incomes than men in positions requiring a college degree. Moreover, whatever the advantages of college, these can be realized only if the lower class boy actually sees it through the entire four years. "If they do not graduate, but only get some college, they are little better off than the sons of nonmanual workers who have not graduated from high school." [11] Not only does college typically not lead to wealth, but it cannot even match the economic rewards of certain occupations, such as county judge, labor leader, independent businessman, which do not require a college degree.

In addition, even when lower class boys complete college, their occupational destinations are less promising than those of middle class students. Students from working class backgrounds, the most extensive recent study has found, will enter the salaried, that is, the less lucrative professions such as teaching, social work, and engineering.[12] The middle class graduates, on the other hand, will enter the more lucrative independent professions, such as medicine, law, and architecture, the latter requiring expensive postgraduate training which sons of skilled workers can less readily afford. If lower class boys stand to gain in prestige but to lose in material benefits by attending college, they may well decide not to go. The "price" may be too great for those reared under the pressure of unsatisfied material needs, the personal and financial costs being incommensurate with the obtainable rewards. It would seem then, that far from expecting all or most lower class individuals to desire college, one should rather expect this group to be a minority, concentrated among those lower class families that enjoy a relative degree of economic security and are interested in raising their prestige, or those whose interest in prestige is such that it overrides all material considerations.[13]

The Rank Order of Goals: Relative Value

It goes without saying that once a minimum of economic security can be taken for granted, energetic and ambitious individuals will be eager to find jobs that will bring them prestige, self-fulfillment, and the promise of advancement. But when this economic minimum cannot be taken for granted, what then? Ideally a person will try to choose work that satisfies his desires for economic security and for prestige but since these two dimensions do not always coincide in the same position, some choice will usually have to be made, especially at the lower rungs of the class hierarchy. Whatever the variety of possible "things worth striving for" it is clear that in the modern world, income, prestige, and power are among them. Unfortunately, a specific goal may be promising with regard to one but not to all of these dimensions, so that again, a choice has to be made between them.[14] In fact, to advance our understanding of aspirations and ambition by social class, one of the problems calling for considerably more research than it has received to date is the degree to which each culturally high-ranking goal is seen to satisfy all three dimensions — money, prestige, and power — and thereby helps account for variations in group and class preferences.

Though little is known about the actual distribution of the desire for prestige, power, and money, whatever is known supports the notion that the desire for prestige will tend to be satisfied only after a given economic level has been reached. Accordingly, the lower classes ought to be more preoccupied with economic matters, the middle class with prestige. This may account for their different aspirations, and puts Hyman's observation that lower class respondents value economic benefits more than do middle class respondents in a new light — not as a sign of their lack of ambition but of the differential priority of success-goals. There is suggestive evidence that the lower classes are in fact more concerned about economic, material needs and desires than others. Several studies agree that income aspirations vary inversely with social class. A study of shipyard workers showed that they regarded wealth as the indispensable basis of privilege, had "an insatiable desire for it," and "were continually preoccupied with methods of obtaining it." [15] And Hollingshead vividly describes the role that money plays in the decisions of Elmstown's lower class youths to leave school in order to earn it.[16] Closely related to pecuniary ambitions is the desire for consumer goods whose importance to the lower class has likewise been noted by many observers.

Further support for the primacy of economic and material desirers among the lower class comes from their stress on "security." For those who cannot take security for granted it may not only loom as important but it may overshadow all other claims and ambitions. However, this striving for security in the lower class, is striving to attain something one does not have and is thus different in nature from the similar strivings among middle class individuals. Economic security (not wealth) is taken for granted in the middle class where everyone has a job, goes to work, can afford a car, a vacation, and adequate housing. In the lower class this much cannot be taken for granted — unemployment, being laid off from work, plant shut-downs, etc. are familiar and dreaded experiences. The drive for security is thus in a very real sense comparable to the middle class drive for respectability — it is something to be achieved and carefully guarded. Summarizing evidence for a number of countries on this matter, Inkeles reports that "workers, more often than the middle classes, will choose certainty of income, or security, over money with less security." [17] Although in recent years one hears much about the lack of adventurousness, the lack of risk-taking in the middle class as well, the emphasis on security is still a greater problem in the lower classes. Thus when Parsons observes that there has been a shift from "success goals to security goals" among the lower classes and relates this to their lesser motivation to succeed, he unwittingly implies that these two goals are mutually exclusive rather than differentially ranked in terms of priority.[18]

In order to compare levels of aspiration among different groups these must first be ranked according to (1) where they are in relation to the same goal, (2) which dimension of success this particular goal promises to gratify, and (3) to which of these dimensions and the subgoals associated with these they accord priority.

If economic problems have primacy in the life situations of the lower classes, it follows that before lower class individuals seriously pursue prestige or power goals in the society at large, they must first concentrate on getting and holding jobs; the most ambitious among them will go after skilled jobs. Survey findings as to their greater interest in these must be interpreted against the proper background. Moreover, because of the existence of differential priorities, we should expect to find that primarily those lower class individuals in relatively comfortable economic circumstances pursue higher education or white collar work. Existing evidence supports this.

The only group within the lower class for which security is more fact than wish — the stratum of skilled manual workers — is precisely the one, according to several recent studies, most anxious that its children obtain a college education.[19] And of those lower class individuals who do get into college, by far the largest portion comes from these "aristocrats of labor," the skilled workers: ". . . the greatest absolute increase . . . (in college attendance) . . . is for the sons of skilled workers . . . there is a very slight increase for the sons of unskilled workers." [20]

Thus neither college nor professional aspirations are satisfactory indicators of individual ambition, not only because they are not equally accessible to the members of the different classes, but also because they do not tap all types of ambitiousness. Since both the accessibility of goals and the priority accorded them vary from class to class, desire for them should likewise vary. The analytical distinction between the desire to succeed and the social evaluation placed on the success desired exposes the logical fallacy of inferring the intensity of ambition from the rank order of the goal toward which this ambition is directed. For while it is true that the ambitious middle class boy will direct his energies towards obtaining a more prestigeful job and the ambitious lower class boy towards a less prestigeful one, their hopes, their sacrifices, and the intensity of their strivings may be identical.

Differential Rewards

However, even if individual effort were maximized in each class, it follows from the ceiling on opportunities in a class-stratified society that rewards cannot be maximal for all. For those placed in different social classes from the start, equivalent strivings must yield unequal rewards. The ambitious lower class boy who succeeds in achieving any of the economic goals that have primacy in his environment must be satisfied with less than the middle class boy who has worked equally hard for a corresponding goal. The lower class boy, though he now has some measure of security, must still forego general prestige whereas the middle class boy has both. Individual exceptions notwithstanding, differential reward is a part of the collective destiny of the lower class, a structural constraint that operates independently of and in addition to the actual desires and endeavors of individuals. This is not to deny the significance of the latter, only to call for the proper appreciation of the former.

The concept of "differential rewards" may help account for a bewildering variety of contradictory findings regarding lower-class reactions to their life chances, such as: (1) the strain toward anomie, notably criminal and deviant behavior; (2) the prevalence of unhappiness and despair; (3) unrealistic high hopes; (4) abandonment of high hopes resulting in hedonism and a devil-may-care attitude; and (5) apathy and resignation.

In fact the lower class is in a peculiar position, caught between its knowledge of what forms of success are generally impressive and important, and what forms are possible within its class-bounded horizons. Whether or not this results in socially deviant or criminal behavior is still an open question in view of the findings that instead of resorting to illegitimate measures, lower class individuals may react to their class fate with unhappiness and despair. Even when they do pursue lower-ranking goals, moreover, it does not follow that they are content with their lot. Recent evidence suggests that unhappiness is endemic in lower class environments. Meier and Bell found that "hopelessness, discouragement, despair, and demoralization" are characteristic of the older men from the lower socioeconomic backgrounds.[21] And according to Inkeles, happiness and satisfaction with life are directly related to socioeconomic standing. Sadness and despair are far more characteristic of the "manual and depressed classes."[22] "Low income," concludes another study, "implies current unhappiness and worries, a lack of self-confidence in the future and the expression of anxiety through physical symptoms."[23]

Unhappiness and despair is one type of response, apathy and a "live for today" attitude may be another, both of these following, however, from the structural characteristics of lower class life rather than from hypothetical personality attributes of lower class individuals. A vivid illustration of the sociological mechanisms through which apathy or hedonism are engendered is provided in the following description of the current situation in the African nation of Nigeria:

> . . . the relationship between wages and prices is such that leisure seems a better buy than almost anything else. Where this relationship between income

and prices is more favorable, the preference for leisure is correspondingly weakened.... The problem of Africa... is that there is a discontinuity in the price range of things men want to buy. There is nothing between the shirt costing ten shillings and the bicycle costing fifteen pounds, and nothing between the bicycle and the motor car.... The range of things which men on low wages both want and can afford is therefore strictly limited.[24]

Of course in the contemporary United States, a society where the standard of living puts a motorcycle within reach of practically everyone, the "unreachable" goals will take another form but the attitudes engendered may be identical. If the maximum expenditure of effort typically does not lead to the maximum rewards promised by the culture, the response may well be that "you can't take it with you when you go," "I've got plenty of nothing," and "live for today." Such attitudes have carelessly been interpreted as "proving" that lower class individuals lack self-control, tend toward "impulse gratification," and unlike the middle class, are unable to "defer gratifications." [25] If by impulse gratification is meant a preoccupation with material comforts then there is no need to look for personality attributes: this response is entirely comprehensible from a knowledge of lower class experience with material scarcity and deprivation. The presumed capacity for self-discipline attributed to the middle class, on the other hand, may likewise be traced not to their personalities but to their social situations.

In sum, no clear-cut lower class personality type has as yet been isolated, nor, for that matter, any uniform reaction to the facts of lower class life. The strain toward anomie is but one among several consequences of differential rewards. Others are the prevalence of fantasy goals and a pervasive sense of malaise and despair.

The Achievement Motive

Two main difficulties confront the investigator who seeks to compare the extent of ambitiousness by social class. One concerns the problem, treated at length in this paper, that individual and class components of ambition have generally been used interchangeably. The other concerns the fact that most of the studies referred to thus far have tried to infer differential success motivations of the members of different classes from their values and aspirations rather than from some independent evidence of this motivation itself. Only one study, by Rosen,[26] has actually attempted to measure this motivation directly, that is, with reference to a social class context. Its results have been widely cited as demonstrating "through the use of a technical psychological measuring instrument, that lower class boys do *typically* have a lower intensity of the 'achievement motive' than middle class boys," [27] and of substantiating the "notion that the middle class is more oriented to achievement." [28] Rosen attempts to prove that differences in "achievement oriented motives and values" between different social strata tend to create "differential class rates of 'social mobility.' " Comparing the scores obtained from a Thematic Apperception Test type measure by students from various social classes in New Haven, Rosen claims to have found that lower class boys have a lower intensity of achievement motivation than middle class boys.[29] However, in order to prove, as the author intends, that "need achievement" has any bearing on the "differential levels of aspiration of social classes" he should be able to demonstrate the existence of some positive relationship between need achievement and the actual aspirations of individuals. That is, boys who score high on need achievement should exhibit high aspirations and vice versa. Failing this, the assumption that need achievement as measured by the McClelland test has a bearing on differential rates of mobility is unwarranted. But it is precisely on this crucial point that Rosen's findings are negative. No correlation was found between a high score on the achievement motive test and high aspirations. In actual fact the only positive relationship demonstrated by Rosen was that between need achievement scores and school grades, that is, those with high achievement scores have better grades. However, once grades are kept constant, social class makes no difference.[30] Thus, if the need achievement test is no better predictor of aspiration than school performance alone, it can hardly pretend to be an independent measure of ambition in the different social classes.[31] No more convincing is Rosen's attempt to discover the dynamic role of "value orientation" in social aspirations. For, the differences in educational aspirations between those boys who scored high on his "value orientation" index and those who scored low were minimal . . . .[32] For example, two-thirds of the lower class students who were classified as "overaspirers" scored low on the value orientation index. Until there is new and better evidence, we cannot accept Rosen's conclusion that since "achievement oriented motives and values are more characteristic of the middle than the lower strata, it is reasonable to suggest that these variables are, in part at least, factors which tend to create differential class rates of social mobility." [33] This conclusion is not supported by the data presented by Rosen.

Concluding Remarks

Not only has the claim that the middle class is more ambitious than the lower class not been substantiated, but this claim is actually contradicted by a set of findings that suggest intense success strivings among lower class individuals. Clearly some theoretical bridge is needed to reconcile these contradictory interpretations. The concepts of "relative distance," of "relative value of goals," and of "differential rewards" permit such a reconciliation, and they should be used as intervening variables between ambition and achievement. Since socially desirable success goals are not equally accessible to the different social classes, the motivation required to realize them cannot be treated as a constant.

In addition, because of the operation of these structural factors not only reactions to success but also reactions to failure might be expected to vary from class to class. And here it is that the middle class individuals, precisely because they are relatively closer to culturally important goals, may be expected to face greater psychological hardships. The reason for this has to be sought in the link between relative distance and relative deprivation.[34] For every culturally desirable goal, the middle class is absolutely less deprived than the lower class, being economically more secure, better educated, and occupied in cleaner and personally more rewarding work. However, for these very reasons, should middle class individuals fail to realize these things, they will suffer greater relative deprivation by comparison with their successful peers. Their failure to live up to expected achievements will tend to be interpreted in terms of personal shortcomings, in the feelings that they have been given a chance but failed to make proper use of it. The lower class on the other hand will have a ready excuse for failure by pointing to environmental barriers and impediments. Even when they might be held personally responsible for not having made full use of such opportunities as arose, they may tend to blame external factors such as bad luck or the ill will of others.

We might thus expect that whereas absolute deprivation varies directly with relative distance (as when fewer lower class youths are able to attend college), relative deprivation varies inversely with relative distance. Since college attendance is a middle class norm, the middle class boy who does not attend should feel more deprived than the lower class boy who does not attend.[35]

Furthermore, independently of their personality make-up, middle class individuals might be expected to perceive their personal inadequacies, lower class individuals, the outside world, as threatening.[36] Each social class situation thus has its built-in strains and difficulties. Anxiety over self-worth might be a familiar experience for middle class individuals; fantasy goals, anomie, and alienation, for lower class individuals.

Notes

1. Robert K. Merton, "Social Structure and Anomie," in *Social Theory and Social Structure,* rev. ed. (Glencoe, Ill.: The Free Press, 1957), p. 131–160.
2. Robert K. Merton, *Social Theory and Social Structure,* op. cit., p. 157.
3. Ibid., p. 183.
4. National Opinion Research Center, "Jobs and Occupations: a Popular Evaluation," *Opinion News* (September 1947), pp. 3–13, and A. Inkeles and P. H. Rossi, "National Comparisons of Occupational Prestige," *American Journal of Sociology,* 61, no. 4, pp. 329–39.
5. The same sorts of ambiguities are present when one tries, for example, to translate the second part of Merton's proposed scheme into empirical terms (see above). In trying to account for the sources of anomie, Merton observes that it "is the frequency of disjunction between the goal and the socially structured access to it which is of theoretical moment." But in order to measure the discrepancy between goals and opportunities, the influence of opportunities on the development of aspirations must first be included in the calculation. In point of fact, without considerably more evidence, it is not possible to decide whether lofty aspirations are consequences or precursors of anomie. Both are logically possible. Merton's formulation sees lofty aspirations as intervening variables between limited opportunities and anomie, but they may be *ex post facto* responses, that is fantasy adaptations to limited opportunities. The difference is not only a logical but also a psychological one, for lofty goals as intervening variables impel to action, whereas lofty goals as fantasy adaptations impede action. Lewin already suggested that the unsuccessful individual may set his goals very low or very high. Kurt Lewin, *Resolving Social Conflicts* (New York: Harper and Bros., 1948), p. 113.
   The former alternative corresponds to what has been called "leveling of aspirations." See also, Leonard Reissman, "Levels of Aspiration and Social Class," *American Sociological Review* (June, 1953), 18, no. 3, pp. 233–242. who found that among the young men in his study, the lower achievers had the higher aspirations.
6. Robert K. Merton, op. cit., p. 149.
7. Robert K. Merton, op. cit., p. 150.
8. Hyman, op. cit., pp. 431–432. The practice of combining the responses of the lowest levels of the lower class with the rest of that class has its drawbacks. This group, variously referred to as the "Lumpenproletariat" or the "Shack people," comprising as much as one-fifth of the lower class in most studies that care to isolate it has been shown to be so poor, disorganized, hopeless, and helpless that planning for anything but the immediate day

ahead appears to be out of the question. These people hold the least desirable and least well-paid jobs, are considered lazy and irresponsible by the communities in which they reside, and best exemplify Lazarsfeld's famous description of the bounded horizons of the underprivileged. Since they are in a sense beyond the pale they should not be included in studies of working-class aspirations since they undoubtedly bias the findings in the direction of reduced aspirations or of indecision.

9. Lipset and Bendix, *Social Mobility in Industrial Society*, op. cit., p. 100.
10. Talcott Parsons, "A Revised Analytical Approach to the Theory of Social Stratification," op. cit., p. 125.
11. Lipset and Bendix, *Social Mobility in Industrial Society*, op. cit., p. 101.
12. Morris Rosenberg, *Occupations and Values* (Glencoe, Ill.: The Free Press, 1957).
13. Confirmation that college may typically be seen as a gateway to prestige rather than to fortune or power comes from yet another quarter. Hyman presents but does not further analyze some puzzling findings that show women at all class and age levels to be more impressed with the value of a college education than men. Hyman, *op. cit.*, p. 431. This would seem to indicate, using Hyman's implicit criterion of ambition, that women are more ambitious than the men of their class or that men are less achievement motivated than women — an assertion not exactly implausible but as yet undemonstrated. However, if college is perceived as an avenue to prestige, then these findings make sense. Women are, after all, not expected to achieve economic success but to value respectability and a proper style of life which college may help them to realize. This same factor of prestige may explain the surprising findings, anticipated some thirty years ago by Lehman and Witty, that lower class Negro youths have higher educational and occupational aspirations than lower class white youths. H. C. Lehman and P. A. Witty, "A Study of Vocational Attitudes in Relation to Pubescence," *American Journal of Psychology* (1931), 43, 93–101. See also S. Gray, "The Vocational Preference of Negro School Children," *Journal of Genetic Psychology* (1944), 64, pp. 239–247. The usual interpretation of this has been that Negroes, because of discrimination and prejudice, can hope to improve their material lot primarily through higher education. This may well be the case but the intrinsic prestige value of college should not be overlooked. College is a symbol of respectability and thus may serve to enhance the thwarted self-esteem of a group hungry for prestige. For evidence relating to this point see: Aaron Antonovsky and Melvin J. Lerner, "Occupational Aspirations of Lower Class Negro and White Youth," *Social Problems*, 7, no. 2 (Fall 1959), pp. 132–138.
14. It is well known that a college professor is low on income but high on prestige, whereas a racing car driver is high on income but low on prestige. Max Weber called attention to the same phenomenon when he noted that the "typical American Boss, as well as the typical big speculator, deliberately relinquishes social honor." Max Weber, "Class, Status and Party," in H. H. Gerth and C. Wright Mills (eds.), *From Max Weber: Essays in Sociology* (New York: Oxford University Press, 1946), p. 180.
15. Katherine Archibald, "The Orientations of Shipyard Workers," in Bendix and Lipset (eds.), *Class, Status and Power*, op. cit., p. 400.
16. August B. Hollingshead, *Elmstown's Youth* (New York: John Wiley & Sons, 1950), p. 284.
17. Alex Inkeles, "Industrial Man: The Relation of Status to Experience, Perception, and Value," *American Journal of Sociology*, LXVI, no. 1 (July 1960), p. 10.
18. See: Talcott Parsons, op. cit., pp. 125. . . .
19. Vidich and Bensman, op. cit., p. 59.
20. David McClelland (ed.), *Talent and Society* (New York: Van Nostrand Company, 1958), p. 18. Hyman also provides corroborative evidence of this, op. cit., Table 1, p. 430.

21. Dorothy L. Meier and Wendell Bell, "Anomia and Differential Access to the Achievement of Life Goals," *American Sociological Review,* 24, no. 2 (April 1959), pp. 189–192.
22. Alex Inkeles, "Industrial Man: The Relation of Status to Experience, Perception and Value," *American Journal of Sociology,* LXVI, no. 1 (July 1960), pp. 1–31. . . .
23. G. Gurin, J. Veroff, S. Feld, *Americans View Their Mental Health* (New York: Basic Books, Inc., 1960), p. 281.
24. Quoted in Laurence Thompson, *The Challenge of Change* (London: Oxford University Press, 1956).
25. Louis Schneider and Sverre Lysgaard, "The Deferred Gratification Pattern: A Preliminary Study," *American Sociological Review,* 18, no. 2 (April 1953), pp. 142–149. . . .
26. Bernard C. Rosen, "The Achievement Syndrome," reprinted from *American Sociological Review,* in W. Atkinson, ed., *Motives in Fantasy, Action and Society* (New York: Van Nostrand Company, 1958), pp. 495–508.
27. Bernard Barber, *Social Stratification* (New York: Harcourt, Brace and Company, 1957), p. 314.
28. Lipset and Bendix, op. cit., p. 245.
29. Test developed by David McClelland et al., *The Achievement Motive* (New York: Appleton-Century, 1953).
30. In fact lower class respondents turn out to be slightly higher in need-achievement.
31. The criteria for scoring "achievement need" are (1) "evaluation of individual performance in relation to some standard of excellence, and (2) the linking of some negative or positive affect to the evaluated performance." This may account for the positive correlation between achievement need and school grades.
32. Although the author is careful to present "test of significance" for his first four tables, he omits specifying the lack of it in his fifth and makes no mention of this in his interpretation of the relationship between value orientation and educational aspiration.
33. Rosen, op. cit.
34. Relative deprivation was a term used by Stouffer and his associates to account for the varied reactions to the same objective situation — that is, to Army life — and to the same absolute deprivation by American soldiers during the last world war. Samuel Stouffer et al., *The American Soldier* (Princeton: Princeton University Press, 1949), Vol. I, p. 125. See also: James Davis, "A Formal Interpretation of the Theory of Relative Deprivation," *Sociometry,* 22 (1959), pp. 280–296.
35. This resembles the famous example of morale and promotion opportunities in the Army presented by Stouffer, where the units with the poorest record of promotion had the highest, the units with the best record, the lowest morale. Stouffer et al., op. cit., Vol. I, p. 252. Hyman makes a similar point when he notes that "for an oldster not to have gone to college is no great deprivation or stigma. By contrast, among the younger generation where higher education is commonplace, to be uneducated may really degrade the self, and to be educated may provide little or no distinction." Herbert H. Hyman, "Reflections on Reference Groups," *Public Opinion Quarterly,* 24, no. 3 (1960), pp. 383–396.
36. A recent study found that the better educated tended to account for their shortcomings in personal terms, whereas the lesser educated emphasized the characteristics of the environment. See Gurin, Veroff, Feld, op. cit., p. 80. The lower-class preoccupation with the limitations of their environment, moreover, may account for the general failure of psychotherapy with lower-class patients. See A. B. Hollingshead and F. C. Redlich, *Social Class and Mental Illness* (New York: John Wiley & Sons, 1958).

WILLIAM H. FORM
JOAN HUBER (RYTINA)

Ideological Beliefs on the Distribution of Power in the United States

Introduction

Stratification systems perpetuate inequalities which are maintained by a wide variety of mechanisms. Whatever mechanism is used, every system of stratification develops an ideology to legitimize or justify its presence and persistence. Ideologies presumaby describe the world as it is and as it ought to be. In stable societies, where there is little organized opposition to the system of inequalities, existential and normative statements in the ideology are similar and symmetrical, and one ideology predominates. That is, what ought to be, is, and what is, ought to be.

Obviously variations may exist in the symmetry between normative and existential beliefs about a stratification system. Members of some classes may insist that a high symmetry exists, while others may insist that asymmetry is typical. Such situations are potentially revolutionary because some classes may try to restore symmetry either by changing beliefs or conditions, so that existential and normative conceptions in the ideology will be more convergent. Longitudinal studies of ideologies may help us forecast changes which will occur in the stratification system. The present concerns with race and poverty in the United States suggest a situation where normative and existential beliefs of the ideology are in a state of asymmetry. This study explores possible asymmetry in a community situation.

Since an ideology explains and vindicates the unequal distribution of rewards in a society, it follows that those who are the most favored recipients of the rewards support the ideology most fervently and make strongest claims for the convergence of its normative and existential tenets. The "success" of an ideology is measured by the extent that the less favored, if they support the normative aspects, also agree on the convergence.

Rewards in a pecuniary-market society are best measured in monetary terms. In the long run, power and status are converted to income rewards.[1] Yet sociologists have shown little inclination to deal with this stratification variable, preferring less precise variables such as occupation, education, and prestige. It seems appropriate to use annual income as a chief indicator of position in a stratification system since it is the chief reward of that system in the American instance. The purpose of this study is to explore how rich, middle-income, and poor people in a Midwestern, middle-sized city appraise the power tenets of American ideology.

Reprinted by permission from *American Sociological Review* 34:1 (1969), pp. 19–31. The material in this project was prepared under a grant from the Office of Manpower Policy, Evaluation, and Research, U.S. Department of Labor, Grant No. 91–24–66–45.

The persistence of any particular allocation of rewards depends upon the distribution of power, or the political structure of the society. The power which maintains the system may be so legitimate, so authoritative, so ubiquitous, and so invisible that it may not be recognized as power. Sociologists are wont to call this type of power "social control." Such mechanisms predominate in a "traditional" stratification system. In a changing industrial society, the political mechanisms which sustain the economic and social structures of inequality become more visible. Politics becomes the means to maintain or change the allocative mechanisms of the society.

The Problem

Therefore what people believe about the political underpinnings of a stratification system is important especially in a relatively "open" society. The purpose of this study is to examine such beliefs from a stratification perspective. The choice of specific political beliefs for study was necessarily arbitrary. We selected beliefs related to democratic mechanisms of *political pluralism* as the major area for investigation. We define a political system as pluralistic when a variety of groups can influence policy in such a way that no single or no small number of groups can control it or, conversely, when all legitimate interest groups have an appreciable share of influence. We made three assumptions: First, people believe that political pluralism is the mechanism which *maintains* an open stratification system. Second, belief in the existence of political pluralism is essentially a belief in the viability of an open opportunity structure; and conversely, a denial of the existence of political pluralism as a system is a rejection of the belief that the ideology of an open stratification society is realized. Third, adherents of political pluralism should, logically, believe that political and governmental actions are necessary to redress any "temporary imbalances," injustices, or inequalities in the opportunity structure of the society.

Since an ideology legitimizes and vindicates a stratification system and therefore a power distribution in a given social order, we propose the following. First, since there are wide differences in distribution of rewards in American society, there will be no overriding consensus among different income strata in the belief that political pluralism accurately describes the distribution of power in the United States. Second, the higher their income, the greater the tendency for people to believe that the dominant ideology of political pluralism more or less accurately describes the way the system really works and, as a corollary, the lower their income, the less symmetry they see between normative and existential aspects of the ideology of political pluralism. Third, the lower their income, the greater the tendency for people to believe that political pluralism *should* be realized by the federal government, acting to restore inequalities produced by the system. Conversely, the higher their income the greater the insistence that government should not act to equalize opportunities. In terms of our frame of reference, higher income groups equate normative and existential statements about political pluralism, while lower income groups tend to deny their symmetry and thus support action to make them more credible. People in all income strata modify or adjust their beliefs about the operation of the political system in accord with their perceived interests.

Together, these hypotheses go beyond the observations commonly found in the literature stating that the poor, less educated and alienated masses reject democratic (pluralistic) philosophy because they do not understand it, feel politically ineffective,' and have authoritarian inclinations. (See Kornhauser, 1959; Lipset, 1960; Riesman, 1953; Scheler, 1961; and Milbrath, 1965.) The position taken in this research is that although the rich and better educated express more formal allegiance to the democratic creed of pluralism, like the poor, they do not understand it, nor do they apply it consistently. The authoritarianism of the poor is matched by an authoritarianism of the rich. Both rich and poor *selectively* respond to the ideology of pluralism and adhere to different elements which give support to their situation or aspirations.

The first part of this study focuses on beliefs concerning the actual operation of the political system, and the second part on beliefs about possible changes in the system.

Research Site

The site of the study was Muskegon, Michigan, an industrial community where the Standard Metropolitan Statistical Area (SMSA) population in 1960 was 149,943. Its economy is built principally around metals manufacturing, which is sensitive to fluctuations in economic conditions. According to the 1960 Census, about three-fifths of the labor force were manual workers and about half were employed in manufacturing. Median family income was $6,048, compared to $6,324 for metropolitan areas in the United States (U.S. Census: 1960). Approximately 10 per cent of the population were Negro.

The respondents interviewed in this research were heads of households or their spouses who lived in the area included in *Polk's City Directory*, 1965, roughly the Muskegon SMSA. For the larger study, of which this was a part, a systematic sample (N = 186) was drawn. Because such samples typically include few people at income extremes, we drew supplementary samples of rich and poor respondents. They were defined as "rich" if the annual family income was $25,000 or more, which, in the 1960 Census, was the top one percent of the income distribution. "Poor" was defined in terms of a scale adjusted for the number of dependents, ranging from less than $2,000 for any number of dependents to $6,000 for eleven or more persons.

The data reported here are based upon an analytic sample (N = 354; the systematic sample, plus the rich and poor samples) which included 37 poor Negroes, 70 poor whites, 48 middle-income Negroes, 152 middle-income whites, and 47 rich whites. The per capita income by households for these categories formed a "scale," the Negroes having lower incomes than the whites, for both poor and middle-income categories.[2] The sex distribution was approximately even in each of these categories. Education was associated with income: three-fifths of the respondents with 0–7 years of education were poor, and three-fifths of college graduates were rich. Although the primary independent variable of this study is income, the data will also be presented by race because recent events indicate that Negroes may have a singular view on political questions. Some responses are also shown in terms of highest grade of education completed. The research design did not justify the use of multivariate analysis; we did control for education but the small number of cases made interpretation risky.

Three Modes of Power Distribution

The main tenet of American political ideology examined here is the idea that power at the national level is distributed pluralistically. Some students of power have concluded that "the struggle for power is largely confined to struggles between the business and government sectors" (D'Antonio and Ehrlich, 1961:147). In this study, respondents were asked to consider only interest groups, not the governmental share in the distribution of power.[3]

The first research problem concerned the respondent's beliefs about the distribution of political power in the country. Two different types of questions were used because of the difficulty in survey research of framing questions that do not differentially elicit a particular response. One type of question suggested implicitly that the distribution of power was in accord with the dominant political ideology of political pluralism, and another suggested implicitly that it was not. At one point in the interview the respondent was read three statements, each purportedly describing a different model of distribution of power in this country, and asked to select what in his opinion was the most accurate description, thus suggesting that one of the descriptions was realistic. At another point in the interview the respondent was given a list of twelve interest groups and asked which one had the most influence over the way things were run in Washington, suggesting that one group was dominant. He was then asked which of these groups was least powerful, and last, which ought to be most powerful.

The three statements describing the distribution of power purportedly represent the positions of David Riesman (political pluralism), C. Wright Mills (the power elite), and the Marxists (big business control).[4] The order in which the three statements were read was rotated in each interview, and the respondent was not advised of their sources. The three statements were presented in this form:

(Riesman) No one group really runs the government in this country. Instead, important decisions about national policy are made by a lot of different groups such as labor, business, religious, and educational groups, and so on. These groups influence both political parties, but no single group can dictate to the others, and each group is strong enough to protect its own interests.

(Mills) A small group of men at the top really run the government in this country. These are the heads of the biggest business corporations, the highest officers in the Army, Navy, and Air Force, and a few important senators, congressmen and federal officials in Washington. These men dominate both the Republican and Democratic Parties.

(Marx) Big businessmen really run the government in this country. The heads of the large corporations dominate both the Republican and Democratic Parties. This means that things in Washington go pretty much the way big businessmen want them to.

Data in Table 1 reveal that three-fifths of the respondents selected Riesman's model of political pluralism; about one-fifth selected Marx; and one-fifth, Mills. Although pluralism is selected more frequently as the dominant model of political control, the percentage does not represent overwhelming consensus.[5]

TABLE 1
Selection of Societal Models of Power Distribution,
by Income and Race (Percentages)

		Models of power distribution			Total	
Income	*Race*	*Marx (economic dominance)*	*Mills (elitist)*	*Riesman (pluralistic)*	*%*	*(N)*
Poor	Negro	33	6	61	100	(36)
	White	23	22	55	100	(64)
Middle	Negro	40	16	44	100	(45)
	White	17	20	63	100	(143)
Rich	White	12	23	65	100	(43)
Total, analytic sample	%	22	19	59	100	(331)
	(N)	(74)	(62)	(195)		
Total, systematic sample [a]	%	18	19	63	100	(174)
	(N)	(32)	(33)	(109)		

[a] For poor vs. middle and rich, $\chi^2 = 1.80$, d.f. $= 2$, P $= <.50$. For Negro vs. white, $\chi^2 = 13.8$, d.f. $= 2$, P $= <.01$.

Differences in support of the pluralistic model by the income groups are relatively small, although they run in the predicted direction; i.e., the poor and Negroes see less existent pluralism. Although the Mills and the Marx descriptions were selected about equally, Negroes were much more likely to select the Marxian description, while whites were more likely to choose the Millsian position.

Perhaps beliefs about power distribution are more affected by years of education than by income. Data in Table 2 show that it does; clearly, in the analytic sample, the higher the education, the greater the belief in the existence of pluralist politics. Thus, almost three-quarters of the college graduates supported the Riesman statement and two-thirds of those having fewer than eight years of schooling rejected it. The Marxist description was more strongly supported than the Millsian among those with less than a high school education.

The data in Table 2 may be explained in at least two ways. First, that since schools teach a pluralistic ideology, the more educated, who also are richer, learn to prefer it. Second, that the pluralistic scheme is more difficult to understand, and that the less educated prefer the conceptually less difficult authoritarian Millsian or Marxist view of the world. Data presented later suggest that the second interpretation should be rejected.

Interest Group Power

For the second question on power, the respondent was given a list of twelve interest groups and asked to indicate which one(s) had most influence in Washington. The interest groups listed were: Protestants, Negroes, labor unions, Jews,

TABLE 2
Selection of Societal Models of Power Distribution,
by Years of Education (Percentages)

		Models of power distribution				
		Marx			*Total*	
Years of education		*(economic dominance)*	*Mills (elitist)*	*Riesman (pluralistic)*	%	*(N)*
0–7		40	26	33	99	(42)
8–11		28	16	57	101	(141)
12–15		14	19	67	100	(108)
16 or more		8	20	73	101	(40)
Total, analytic sample	%	22	19	59	100	
	(N)	(74)	(62)	(195)		(331)
Total, systematic sample [a]	%	18	19	63	100	
	(N)	(32)	(33)	(109)		(174)

[a] $\chi^2 = 11.46$, d.f. $= 6$, P $= .10$, when grades 12–15 and 16 years and above are combined.

farmers, Catholics, big businessmen, university professors, small businessmen, rich people, poor people, and military leaders. The intent was to include a variety of interest groups that might be considered influential in order to give the respondent a wide choice. No respondent in the 119 interviews completed by the chief interviewer questioned the assumption that some one group or groups must have most influence.

"Big businessmen" and "rich people" were presented separately although it is reasonable to suppose that all big businessmen are rich. We expected that, if respondents named one of these groups, those with higher incomes would tend to choose "big businessmen," and lower income respondents, "rich people." The choice of "rich people" is less in accord with the dominant political ideology than "big businessmen" because being rich does not imply that a man has engaged in a socially fruitful activity. The major differences among respondents occurred between whites and Negroes. Both middle-income and poor Negroes tended to choose "rich people" more often than "big businessmen." Among white respondents, the tendency to choose "big businessmen" more often than "rich people" increased with income.[6] In the subsequent analysis, these two categories are combined.

What is most striking about the response to this question is the high proportion who see "big businessmen and the rich" as most influential (see Table 3). About one-half of the respondents in both the analytic and systematic samples chose "big businessmen" or "rich people" as most influential and about 30 percent chose "labor unions." Less than one-tenth selected "military leaders," and the remaining eight interest groups were chosen by only ten percent of the respondents. Perhaps

TABLE 3

Interest Group Selected as Most Powerful,
by Income and Race (Percentages)

Income	Race	Unions	Big business and rich	Military	All others	Don't know	Total %	(N)
Poor	Negro	32	41	11	14	3	101	(37)
	White	14	46	10	17	12	99	(59)
Middle	Negro	17	54	13	8	8	100	(48)
	White	33	52	8	5	3	101	(150)
Rich	White	54	28	4	13	0	99	(46)
Total, analytic sample	%	30	47	9	10	5	101	
	(N)	(104)	(164)	(31)	(34)	(17)		(350)
Total, systematic sample [a]	%	26	52	6	10	6	100	
	(N)	(48)	(97)	(13)	(17)	(12)		(183)

[a] For unions vs. big business and rich vs. all others run against poor vs. middle and rich, $\chi^2 = 8.28$, d.f. $= 2$, $p = <.02$.

significant is the fact that all income strata in the analytic sample saw "the rich" and "big businessmen" as most powerful with the sole exception of the rich, who selected "labor unions" as most powerful. Equally important is the observation that there was more dispersion in the selections of the lower income groups, a situation which seems to refute the alleged categorical authoritarian thinking of the lower classes (Schatzman and Strauss, 1955:329–338). Although the greater dispersion in the lower income group could be interpreted as political fragmentation, it could also be interpreted as behaving according to the norms of political pluralism.

Again, education seems related to the choice of the most powerful group (see Table 4). While the relationship of income strata to perception of "big businessmen" and "the rich" as most powerful is curvilinear, the relationship of income strata to perception of "labor unions" as most powerful is linear. That is, a greater percentage of the middle educational strata see "big businessmen" and "the rich" as most powerful. The percentage seeing "labor unions" as most powerful increases with education to the point that a majority of college graduates take this view.

Comparing the results of Tables 1 and 3 may be fruitful. Thus, although data in Table 1 show that about 60 percent of the respondents believed that "all" interest groups share power, about 75 percent of them in Table 3 focused on just two of these interest groups. This finding does not necessarily indicate inconsistency, because respondents might have thought that "big businessmen" or "rich people" were just *slightly* more powerful than other groups, thus "big businessmen" might not necessarily be running everything. Still another interpretation might be that if the belief in political pluralism were strong enough, the question might have been rejected with such statements as "they are all the same," "it depends on the issue,"

TABLE 4
Interest Group Selected as Most Powerful,
by Years of Education (Percentages)

Years of education		Unions	Big business and rich	Military	All others	Don't know	Total %	Total (N)
0–7		14	38	14	20	14	100	(49)
8–11		27	46	10	11	6	100	(145)
12–15		33	52	6	6	2	99	(113)
16 or more		53	37	5	5	0	100	(43)
Total, analytical sample	%	30	47	9	10	5	101	
	(N)	(104)	(164)	(31)	(34)	(17)		(350)
Total, systematic sample [a]	%	26	52	6	10	6	100	
	(N)	(48)	(97)	(13)	(17)	(12)		(183)

[a] For unions vs. big business and rich vs. all others, $\chi^2 = 15.1$, d.f. $= 6$, P $= <.02$.

etc. Nevertheless, the results of the two responses indicate that the framing of a survey question makes considerable difference in possible interpretations of the results. Given a specific choice among interest groups, the respondents seem more likely to describe the distribution of political power in somewhat more neo-Marxist terms than in pluralist terms.

Respondents were also asked which group they thought was least powerful in Washington. The results in Table 5 show that there is less consensus on who does not have power than on who does. Interestingly enough, the rich seem to have least consensus on who has least amount of power.

In Table 5, "poor people" were identified as "least influential" oftener than any other group (36 percent). They were followed by "small businessmen" (15 percent), "farmers" (12 percent), and "Negroes" (11 percent). Poor Negroes were most likely to see "poor people" as least influential (46 percent),[7] and rich whites were most likely to choose "small businessmen" as least influential (26 percent); only twenty percent of rich whites chose "poor people" as least influential.

The last question on interest groups shifted to the normative area: which group *ought* to be most influential. Pre-test results had indicated that a number of persons thought that no one interest group should be dominant; so while this response was anticipated, the interviewers were instructed not to let such a response alter their presentation of the question. The responses to this question are presented in Table 6 for income and race, and Table 7 for education. The most striking finding from Table 6 is that 44 percent of the respondents refused to be bound by the question and volunteered the normative response that "all (groups) should be equal." The rich in the sample had highest agreement on who ought to have most power, with 30 percent in the analytic sample naming "big businessmen." The effect of education, seen in Table 7, is generally to reduce variations found by race and income.

TABLE 5
Interest Group Selected as Least Powerful, by Income and Race (Percentages)

Income	Race	Poor	Small business	Farmers	Negroes	Jews	University professors	All others	Don't know	Total %	Total (N)
Poor	Negro	46	11	11	19	8	0	3	3	101	(37)
	White	37	11	13	6	11	1	3	17	99	(70)
Middle	Negro	35	6	19	23	4	0	2	10	99	(48)
	White	35	17	12	9	4	6	7	10	100	(151)
Rich	White	20	26	7	9	4	11	24	0	101	(46)
Total, analytic sample	%	35	15	12	11	6	4	7	9	99	
	(N)	(122)	(53)	(42)	(39)	(22)	(15)	(25)	(33)		(352)
Total, systematic sample	%	36	14	15	7	4	5	6	13	100	
	(N)	(67)	(26)	(27)	(13)	(8)	(9)	(11)	(25)		(186)

TABLE 6
Interest Groups Which Ought to Be Most Powerful,
by Income and Race (Percentages)

Income	Race	All should be equal	Big busi- nessmen	Labor unions	All others	Don't know	Total %	(N)
Poor	Negro	64	0	14	8	14	100	(36)
	White	43	6	6	28	17	100	(65)
Middle	Negro	47	4	9	25	15	100	(47)
	White	40	9	13	29	9	100	(149)
Rich	White	39	30	0	27	4	100	(46)
Total, analytic sample	%	44	10	9	26	11	100	
	(N)	(150)	(34)	(32)	(88)	(39)		(343)
Total, systematic sample [a]	%	41	8	12	29	10	100	
	(N)	(76)	(15)	(22)	(55)	(18)		(186)

[a] For "all should be equal" vs. all others, and poor vs. middle and rich, $\chi^2 = 30.94$, d.f. $= 1$, P $= <.001$.

TABLE 7
Interest Groups Which Ought to Be Most Powerful,
by Years of Education (Percentages)

Years of education		All should be equal	Big busi- nessmen	Labor unions	All others	Don't know	Total %	(N)
0–7 years		52	2	4	23	19	100	(48)
8–11 years		48	4	13	22	13	100	(141)
12–15 years		38	19	10	25	8	100	(112)
16 years or more		38	14	0	41	7	100	(42)
Total, analytic sample	%	44	10	9	26	11	100	
	(N)	(150)	(34)	(32)	(88)	(39)		(343)
Total, systematic sample [a]	%	41	8	12	29	10	100	
	(N)	(76)	(15)	(22)	(55)	(18)		(186)

[a] For "all should be equal" vs. all others combined and 12–15 years and 16 years or more combined, $\chi^2 = 7.14$, d.f. $= 2$, P $= <.05$.

To conclude, respondents with highest income and education are most likely to think the Reisman description of the distribution of power best when they hear it, but they are least likely, left to their own devices, to think that this is the way things ought to be. Likewise, those who have the least income and education, and the least convenient skin color, are most likely to respond spontaneously that all interest groups should have equal power. This pattern contradicts some of the literature on political authoritarianism. Presumably, college graduates should be better equipped to think up a free response supporting political pluralism or democratic ideology than those with less than eight grades of education.[8]

Government and Opportunity Equalization

According to the dominant ideology, if a man works hard enough, he will get ahead. Getting ahead is defined as social and income mobility. To assure everyone equal opportunity to get ahead regardless of his condition at birth, free public education is provided. Other political action may be necessary (e.g., anti-trust legislation) to prevent *discrepancies* in the American creed (normative tenets) and American practice (existential tenets) from becoming fixed or structured. That is, the government must intervene when the free market and political pluralism have failed to live up to expectations.

Recent evidence suggests that there is some public recognition that the opportunity structure has not been operating according to the American Creed (see Miller and Rein, 1966). Specifically, poverty has become intergenerational, and this condition is more characteristic of Negroes than of whites. Therefore, federal intervention is needed. Three issues were selected which dealt with federal action to help the poor and Negroes: payment of regular wages to adult poor while they attend free schools to learn new skills at government expense, an evaluation of all current federal programs to help the poor, and an evaluation of federal roles in open occupancy.

The third hypothesis of this study was that, since an ideology is a vindication of a system of inequality which benefits those who receive most rewards of the system, there would be an inverse relationship between the amount of income of the respondent and his recognition that political intervention is necessary to help any particular stratum in the society achieve equality of opportunity. For the rich, the system is operating the way it "should," both in terms of distribution of rewards and in terms of its mechanisms (political pluralism). Thus, the political machine does not need repair unless it is operating against those who are receiving most rewards from the system.

Although both major political parties give verbal support to the aspirations of disadvantaged groups, the Democrats are generally thought to be more "liberal." Thus, findings on party preference may be of interest here. First, the analytic sample differed little from the systematic sample. Second, there were no poor Negro Republicans and no rich white Democrats in our samples. Among poor whites, Democrats out-numbered Republicans two to one, but among middle-income whites, the proportions were closer: 34 percent Republicans, 46 percent Democrats, five percent independents, and 16 percent no preference. Most of the middle-income Negroes were Democrats.

McClosky and co-workers (1960) offer some reason to doubt that among "ordinary voters" party affiliation is associated with sharp differences concerning government action in social welfare. Thus, in a national cross-section survey the views of the Republican rank and file were found to be much closer to those of Democratic than those of Republican leaders. Differences between Republican leaders and followers are largest "on those issues which have most sharply separated New

Deal–Fair Deal spokesmen from the hard core of Republican opposition — federal aid to education, redistribution of wealth through taxes on business, corporations, and the wealthy; public ownership of natural resources, public housing, regulation of business, Social Security, farm price supports, minimum wages, and trade union regulations" (McClosky et al., 1960:416).

Similar results can be inferred from a study of an affluent, lower middle class and working class community in the Boston area. Litt (1963) found that leaders in the higher income community showed more support than leaders in the other communities for pluralist beliefs, i.e., the democratic creed, politics as a process, and politics as harmonizing group conflicts. More importantly, the type of political training which high school students received corresponded with differences in support of the creed (ideology). In the poorest community the democratic creed was taught, but no stress was placed on the importance of political participation and political conflict to resolve intergroup differences. "Only in the affluent and politically vibrant community are insights into political processes and function of politics passed on to those . . . (who) will likely man those positions that involve them in influencing or making political decisions" (Litt, 1963:74).

When Muskegon respondents were asked whether the federal government should pay poor people to go to school and get appropriate job training, the proportion who thought that the government should not do so rose sharply with income and education (see Table 8). Such action was opposed by almost eight-tenths of the rich and three-tenths of Negro poor in the analytic sample.

When asked whether the federal government had not done enough or had done

TABLE 8
Opposition to Federal Help for Disadvantaged Strata (Percentages)

Income	Race	Government should not pay poor to go to school (a)	Government has done too much for poor (b)	Government should stay out of open occupancy (c)
Poor	Negro	30	8	8
	White	46	23	62
Middle	Negro	17	15	8
	White	64	32	73
Rich	White	78	72	96
Total, analytic sample	%	52	31	57
	(N)	(350)	(351)	(344)
Total, systematic sample [a]	%	63	29	64
	(N)	(118)	(54)	(119)

[a] χ^2's by income categories and (a), (b), and (c) and their residuals are not statistically significant. For race categories and column (a) and its residual, $\chi^2 = 9.06$, d.f. $= 1$, P $= <.01$. For race categories and column (b) and its residual, $\chi^2 = 4.14$, d.f. $= 1$, P $= <.05$. For race categories and column (c) and its residual, $\chi^2 = 6.67$, d.f. $= 1$, P $= <.01$.

too much for the poor, the proportion of respondents who thought that the government had done too much rose sharply with both income and education. Again, about seven-tenths of the rich and one-tenth of the Negro poor felt the federal government had done too much for the poor.

While open housing is not altogether an issue of economic mobility, it is an issue of racial stratification which has not been resolved by the politics of pluralism. On this issue, political intervention by the state is most highly rejected by rich whites, followed by middle-income whites. Almost all of the rich, 73 percent of the middle-income whites, and 62 percent of the poor whites reject federal intervention, while only eight percent of both Negro strata did so.

Discussion

Empirical research on the belief systems which comprise an ideology is sorely needed to understand the dynamics of political change. A stratification approach to the study of political ideology is especially fruitful because it reveals how different strata view the mechanisms for distributing rewards in a society. This study probed the verbal adherence of different income strata to the ideology of political pluralism, the mechanism which allegedly maintains an open stratification system in the United States. Although the results of the study are tenuous, certain conclusions are suggested. Perhaps the most important one is that the technique of inquiry clearly affects the observations made about ideological belief systems. Thus, when asked to select one of three general descriptive models of power distribution in the United States, respondents from different income and racial strata did not exhibit overriding consensus on political pluralism, for two-fifths of them accepted an elitist or Marxian view of the political order. Here the data tended to confirm the hypothesis that those who get most rewards from the system, namely those with higher incomes, tend more to see pluralist ideology as a good description of the way the system works.

However, a shift to other techniques of inquiry revealed a different pattern leading to the conclusion that, whatever the income or educational backgrounds of the respondents, few of them possessed a consistent or sophisticated political ideology.[9] Thus, when asked to select which interest group or groups were most powerful in the federal government, very few rejected the task on the grounds that it violated their pluralistic conception of politics. On the contrary, almost four-fifths of the respondents saw two coalitions, "the rich-big businessmen" and "labor unions," as the most powerful groups in federal politics, the poor and middle strata selecting "the rich-big businessmen," and the rich selecting the "labor unions." Some consistency was maintained in identifying the least powerful; a plurality of those at all income levels (the rich excluded) felt the poor were the least powerful.

Finally, the *ideal* of pluralism received least support from the most economically advantaged. In response to the question asking which group ought to be most powerful, the rich educated whites, less than any other category, spontaneously responded that "all interest groups should be equal." In fact, 30 percent felt that "the rich-big businessmen" ought to have most power. Their support of privileged position was maintained in exploring the question whether the federal government should take action to improve the position of the poor and of Negroes. The rich were much more likely than those in other categories to report that no action should be taken.

Although poorer income strata structured their beliefs in a somewhat different pattern, middle-income Negroes were least likely to see the model of political pluralism as an accurate description, and most likely to select the Marxian model, most likely to see the "rich-big businessmen" as most influential in politics, most likely to see Negroes as the least powerful interest group, and most highly supportive of federal action to equalize opportunities.[10] A speculative conclusion is that middle-income Negroes, with rising expectations, may become a new source of the kind of class conflict once associated with the American labor movement.

An overview of these findings suggests that the respondents whose political ideology is least consistent are those who receive most from the economic and political order. The richer and better educated more generally espouse political pluralism as a norm, but are more likely to see business dominance in politics as legitimate, and are least supportive of governmental action to equalize opportunity in the society. These observations support the growing evidence that the higher income groups clearly do not understand the principles of political pluralism, nor do they support them consistently (Prothro and Grigg, 1960:276–294). More than others, they have the most favorable attitude toward sources of power in the community; they have strongest feelings about their beliefs (Haer, 1956); they have the most outgroup antipathy; they are the most class conscious; and they are the most tightly organized to maintain privilege (Glantz, 1958:375–383). A case can be made that the syndrome amounts to an upper-class authoritarianism.

Unfortunately, the recent sociological literature dealing with stratification and politics has not considered ideology systematically. The findings suggest that the resentment of the poor, their feeling of political inefficacy, their low political participation, and their authoritarianism are due to their lack of knowledge and lack of faith in the democratic credo. Our data suggest that this oversimplification is perhaps due to an ideological bias on the part of the researchers and their failure to understand the functions of an ideology generally.

This research suggests that one function of a prevailing ideology, such as political pluralism, is to explain and vindicate the unequal distribution of rewards in a society for its dominant strata. These strata do not recognize conflicts or inconsistencies between their normative beliefs about the society and their view of how the society actually operates, i.e., their existential beliefs. Their collective ideas and sentiments about how power is distributed and *ought* to be distributed in a society are no more systematic, idealistic, or coherent than those of the lower income strata. Other strata, even when they support normative statements in the ideology, are quite knowledgeable about how the society operates when they do not concur with the existential beliefs of the privileged. Students of political movements of any type cannot long ignore the differential adherence of social strata to elements in the dominant ideology. A stratification approach to national studies of political ideologies is sorely needed.

Notes

1. As Max Weber remarked, "Money increasingly buys — at least on an intergenerational basis — *everything*" (Weber, 1956: 179).
2. The per capita income for the Negro poor was $671; for the white poor, $907; for middle income Negroes, $1,591; for middle income whites, $2,310; for rich whites, over $6,000.

3. Students of political power distinguish between "power" and "influence," but we did not expect the respondents to be aware of conceptual niceties, and, in this question, "power" and "influence" may be regarded as equivalent concepts.
4. Abstracted from Riesman (1953); Mills (1956); Feuer (1959). Descriptions of the employee (Peter Drucker) and the managerial (James Burnham) societies were included in the pre-testing, but were later dropped because very few respondents considered them meaningful.
5. We are not aware of national studies dealing with the degree of popular adherence to various models of power distribution. Community studies of power structure do investigate the views of special populations on elitist or pluralistic models of local decision making. See, for example, Form and Sauer, 1963; Haer, 1956; Horton and Thompson, 1962.
6. Nineteen percent of poor Negroes, 38 percent of poor whites, 21 percent of middle-income Negroes, 45 percent of middle-income whites, and 45 percent of rich whites chose "big businessmen." Twenty-two percent of poor Negroes, 9 percent of poor whites, 33 percent of middle-income Negroes, 7 percent of middle-income whites, and 4 percent of rich whites chose "the rich." Thirty-five percent of the total sample chose "big businessmen," and 12 percent chose "the rich."
7. Given the choice of indicating whether poor people or Negroes are least powerful, Negroes in the sample clearly saw poverty as being less powerfully represented than race in Washington.
8. Lipset has argued that the working class is more authoritarian than other classes (Lipset, 1960). Lipsitz says that when Lipset's data are controlled for education, the greater authoritarianism disappears (Lipsitz, 1965:103–109). Lipset himself has argued that "higher education often makes for greater tolerance, greater regard for due process, and increased tolerance for ambiguity" (Lipset, 1964:399). On the other hand, Key said that "the indoctrination of a high-status, high-income, literate class of persons, seems to be far more feasible than is the mobilization of lesser peoples who are supposedly easy to manipulate" (Key, 1964:125).
9. Campbell and co-workers found, in a national study, that few respondents employ ideological concepts in a sophisticated way (Campbell et al., 1964: 124–144).
10. See Goffman's study of the relation of status consistency to preference for change in power distribution (Goffman, 1957:275–281).

References

Campbell, Angus; P. E. Converse; W. E. Miller; D. E. Stokes, 1964. The American Voter, An Abridgement. New York: Wiley.

D'Antonio, William V. and H. J. Ehrlich (eds.). 1961. Power and Democracy in America. Notre Dame: University of Notre Dame Press.

Feuer, Lewis S. (ed.). 1959. Marx and Engels: Basic Writings. Garden City, N.Y.: Doubleday & Co. Pp. 9, 12, 18.

Form, William H. and Warren E. Sauer. 1963. "Labor and community influentials: a comparative study of participation and imagery." Industrial and Labor Relations Review 17 (October).

Glantz, Oscar. 1958. "Class consciousness and political solidarity." American Sociological Review 23 (August), 375–383.

Goffman, Irwin W. 1957. "Status consistency and preference for change in power distribution." American Sociological Review 22 (June), 275–281.

Haer, John L. 1956. "Social stratification in relation to attitude toward sources of power in the community." Social Forces 34 (December), 37–42.

Horton, John E. and Wayne E. Thompson. 1962. "Powerlessness and political negativism: a study of defeated local referendums." American Journal of Sociology 47 (March), 485–493.

Key, V. O., Jr. 1964. Politics, Parties and Pressure Groups. P. 125. New York: Crowell.

Kornhauser, William. 1959. Politics of Mass Society. Glencoe, Illinois: The Free Press.

Lipset, Seymour Martin. 1960. Political Man. Garden City: Doubleday. "Three decades of the radical right: Coughlinites, McCarthyites, and Birchers." 1964. P. 399 in Daniel Bell (ed.), The Radical Right. Garden City: Doubleday.

Lipsitz, Lewis. 1965. "Working class authoritarianism: a reevaluation." American Sociological Review 30 (February), 103–109.

Litt, Edgar. 1963. "Civic education, community norms and political indoctrination." American Sociological Review 28 (February), p. 74.

McClosky, Herbert; P. J. Hoffman; R. O'Hara. 1960. "Issue conflict and consensus among party leaders and followers." American Political Science Review 54 (June), 416.

Milbrath, Lester W. 1965. Political Participation. Chicago: Rand McNally.

Miller, S. M. and Martin Rein. 1966. "Poverty, inequality and policy." In Howard S. Becker (ed.), Social Problems. New York: Wiley.

Mills, C. Wright. 1956. The Power Elite. Pp. 269–297. New York: Oxford University Press.

Prothro, James W. and Charles M. Grigg. 1960. "Fundamental principles of democracy: Bases of agreement and disagreement." Journal of Politics 22 (May), 276–294.

Riesman, David. 1953. The Lonely Crowd. Pp. 242–258. Garden City: Doubleday.

Schatzman, Leonard and Anselm Strauss. 1955. "Social class and modes of communication." American Journal of Sociology 60 (January), 329–338.

Scheler, Max. 1961. Ressentiment. Lewis Coser (trans.). Glencoe, Illinois: The Free Press.

U.S. Census of Population. 1960. General Summary, Social and Economic Characteristics. Washington: U.S. Government Printing Office.

Weber, Max. 1956. Wirtschaft und Gesellschaft: Grundriss der Verstehenden Soziologie I. P. 179. Johannes Winckelman (ed.), Tübingen: J. C. B. Mohr.

7

STRATIFICATION: RACE

Racial stratification in any society means that one or more groups in the society constitute a *minority*. According to Robin Williams (1964, p. 304), minorities may be defined as

> any culturally or physically distinctive and self-conscious social aggregates with hereditary membership and a high degree of endogamy, which are subject to political, or economic, or social discrimination by a dominant segment of an environing political society.

Simpson and Yinger (1972, p. 12) indicate that, despite the basic similarity in their social position, minorities "differ in the symbols that set them apart, in the nature of their relationship to the dominant group, and in their reactions to their situation." However, other definitions of minority include behavior patterns which have been attributed to minority group members in different cultures and different historical periods as characteristic responses to their social position. For example, Shibutani and Kwan (1964, p. 35) state that members of a minority "come to regard themselves as objects of discrimination," "are often forced to assume roles that make it difficult for them to maintain their sense of self-respect," and "often develop a typical defensive mentality."

The effects of minority group membership on social personality are determined, first, by deciding whether and what differences exist between the dominant and minority groups, and, second, by parceling out the effects of variables other than racial stratification that might account for such differences. Ideally this problem would be resolved by instituting a variety of cross-cultural and historical comparisons of different minority groups. Unfortunately such a solution is often politically infeasible, very expensive, and complex. The result has generally been more detailed studies of the same minority. Blacks in the United States are a classic example because of the failure to resolve certain controversies despite the abundance of research on the subject. To draw any conclusions about the effects of institutionalized discrimination on the social personality of blacks, one would have to explore alternative biogenetic or cultural-historical explanations for any documented differences.

Proposed Explanations for Black-White Differences

Some postulate that the comparatively lower scores of blacks on standard intelligence tests, for example, are caused by the genetic inferiority of Afro-Americans (presumably as opposed to any and all Caucasian ethnic groups) for this particular trait. Jensen (1969) recently argued this position in analyzing previous research on the subject, although he acknowledged that more than three-fourths of all differences in the scores of test subjects were due to individual differences within racial aggregates rather than to differences between racial aggregates.

So far, those who have argued that black intelligence is genetically inferior to white intelligence have failed to convince most scholars. However, the issue has always been considered sufficiently topical to guarantee an audience for anyone willing to argue this position, even though many important unanswered criticisms have been raised about sampling procedures, conceptualization, and methods of measurement, among other aspects of such studies. For example, many social scientists have objected to the instruments used to measure intelligence in such research, charging that the many forms and expressions of intelligence that might legitimately be considered are not included in such tests, and that the test questions are too closely bound to white middle-class experiences and learned skills. Moreover, the major tests used (e.g., Stanford-Binet) have been found to predict school performance accurately for only the top 10 to 12 per cent of the test population and are not generalizable beyond that elite group.

Blacks and whites in the United States do not constitute separate and distinct anthropological types for accurate sampling procedures. In fact, pure races (or subspecies in plants and other animals) exist only in asexual organisms and are unknown in human beings, among whom cross-breeding has occurred for thousands of years. Careful estimates suggest that 20 per cent of all people classified as white in the United States have some African ancestry. The proportion of blacks with Caucasian parentage has been put as high as 75 per cent. In fact, an estimated one-third of the total gene pool of all persons currently classified as "Negro" in the United States is believed to be Caucasian, European in origin.

Obviously, if there were any genetically related differences in social personality between blacks and whites (in this particular case, in intelligence), we would need fairly precise information either on the genotypes or the genealogies of those included in the study sample. Scientists have not yet been able to determine which genes are related to intelligence. Controlling for genealogies is also difficult because of the scarcity of accurate multiple-generation biographical information for many blacks. Consequently, generalizations about racial hereditary traits of any kind must be regarded with the greatest skepticism. In fact, such psychologists as Jane Mercer (1971) and George Mayeske (1971) have shown that differences in IQ and achievement tests between white and minority students disappear when the data are controlled for social and environmental factors. Insofar as the opposite case (there are no social personality traits which are not genetically based, if not determined) has not been positively demonstrated, we cannot completely foreclose on this possibility. However, given the present social inequalities, the burden of proof is clearly on those who postulate genetic differences.

Others have argued that certain patterns of behavior seemingly characteristic of black subcultures and social personality have their origins in African culture and, therefore, are not attributable to the social position of blacks in the United States. However, little evidence has been offered in support. The only major research postulating the retention of African cultural traits among blacks (despite the deliberate, systematic attempt by slave owners to eradicate all forms of African culture) is contained in Melville Herskovits's *The Myth of the Negro Past* (1958). Yet Herskovits has been criticized seriously by other anthropologists because he is able to document effectively relatively few Africanisms among American blacks, principally in the areas of music, folklore, and religion.

Many others propose that most blacks in the United States manifest distinctive social personality traits as a result of their historical experience of enslavement, followed by institutionalized discrimination and physical segregation. However, this group of social scientists (Daniel Moynihan, perhaps, is their most vocal advocate) claim that these personality differences, to the extent that they can be determined, are not caused by strategic adjustments to prevailing socioeconomic conditions, but rather to the formation and maintenance of a distinctive "culture of poverty" in which successive generations of black children are socialized. Although they don't usually make all their theoretical assumptions explicit, this school takes a very orthodox psychoanalytic position on the determination of personality. As a result, they tend to overemphasize the influence of the family, as opposed to the school, peer group, and mass media, in personality formation. They also tend to exaggerate the importance of infancy and early childhood at the expense of later developmental stages.

Differential Effects of SES

Probably the most common error committed in research seeking to establish general propositions about black subculture and social personality — regardless of whether such differences are attributed to differences in genetic heredity, cultural history, or minority group position — has been the failure to adequately control for the differential effects of socioeconomic status upon both blacks and whites: a critical deficiency insofar as about four times as many blacks (almost two in five) as whites live in families with incomes below the poverty line.

Some more well-known examples of such research perpetuate such stereotyped beliefs as that blacks do not have a stable family life and value one less than whites; that black families are characterized by a maternal rather than a paternal or democratic pattern of control; that blacks want and have more children than they can afford; and that blacks are unable to defer gratification, spending a large portion of their meager income on luxuries. For example, a 1970 federal report disclosed that almost 30 per cent of black families are headed by women, as compared to slightly less than 10 per cent of white families. Also, almost 20 per cent of black children up to fourteen years of age are raised by mothers only, as compared to slightly less than 6 per cent of white children, and some 11 per cent of black children are orphaned, as compared to only about 2 per cent of white children.

Such comparisons are often made to support the contention that stable family life is less valued among blacks than among whites, a situation many claim breeds various forms of pathology ranging from homosexuality to juvenile delinquency and including those traits characteristic of the culture of poverty. A favorite explanation for this alleged lack of a stable family tradition among blacks in America is that it is caused by the residual effects of the disruption of black families during slavery when the black male was not permitted to assume a proper paternal role.

Such analyses obviously ignore the over 70 per cent of black families headed by both parents and the 60 to 65 per cent of black children who grow up with both parents in the home (in most cases without interruption throughout childhood and adolescence). Even more important, such analyses ignore the crucial effects of SES on family stability.

A comparison of the proportion of only middle-class black and white families shows them to be equal in the proportion of both-parent households, about 90 per cent. Using 1960 census data, Rainwater (1967) demonstrates that the proportion of broken homes among black and white families differs sharply when the data are controlled for income level and rural vs. urban residence. The proportion of female-headed families in rural areas is 14 per cent for blacks and 4 per cent for whites, whereas in urban areas it is 23 per cent for blacks and 7 per cent for whites.

Moreover, comparing only urban families with an income of $3,000 or more, the proportion of female-headed homes is only 8 per cent for blacks and 4 per cent for whites. Below $3,000 the proportions jump to 47 per cent and 38 per cent, respectively. If one were to make more precise distinctions within the income categories and factor in the higher living costs for blacks these differences probably would completely disappear. (Numerous studies have conclusively demonstrated that blacks pay more for poorer quality produce at supermarkets and higher prices or more rent for poorer quality housing.) Thus, high family instability rates appear to be primarily an urban lower-class phenomenon for both blacks and whites. The most critical factor in determining family stability appears to be the capacity of the husband and father to provide sufficient income to support his family.

Because supporting data are appallingly inadequate, it is shocking that such indiscriminate generalizations about black family structure have been raised to the level of subcultural stereotypes of the black family being matriarchal and the white family patriarchal, with all that this is supposed to imply about the self-esteem and occupational aspirations of males raised in such families. Here again, recent research has failed to confirm the stereotype. Geismar and Gerhart's investigation (1968) of the social functioning of urban black, white, and Puerto Rican families concludes that SES is more important than ethnicity in determining the nature of family functioning.

Middleton and Putney's study (1960) of blacks and whites of both high and low SES found that the equalitarian pattern of family decision-making appears to predominate in all cases. A similar study by Ten Houten (1970) concluded that black husbands appear to be powerful influences in their families. Moreover, though lower-class white husbands tend to be highly dominant in the conjugal role, they are less dominant in child socialization — a finding consistent with previously cited research on the relationship between SES and role differentiation within the family.

Popular notions about black fertility patterns are subject to the same empirical deficiencies. Campbell (1965, p. 209) asserts that, when SES is held constant, "by the time non-white couples are one generation or more removed from the rural South, their fertility is very much like that of the white population." Moreover, a 1960 *Growth of American Families* study revealed that nonwhite wives actually want fewer children than white wives. The bulk of the white-black fertility differential can be attributed to the higher proportion of very large families among blacks — concentrated almost exclusively among very poor blacks. Orshanksy (1965) has calculated that "the poverty rate for all families with 5 or 6 children is three and a half times as high as for families with 1 or 2 children."

In many cases, the simple availability of birth control information and devices could sharply reduce the fertility rate. In his research on unwed black mothers, Furstenberg (1970) states that over 90 per cent of those in his sample thought they did not know enough about how to use birth control and two-thirds said that, if possible, they would want to use birth control every time they had sexual relations. More than 95 per cent of their mothers were "very sure" that they would like their daughters to be in a medical program which would provide different methods of birth control.

Although birth control clinics have proven to be both popular and effective in poor black communities (for example, nonwhite births in Chicago dropped 22 per cent between 1960 and 1965 as a result of such a program), a recent nationwide survey revealed that only one of five medically indigent women of childbearing age were receiving family planning services. Nevertheless, sufficient progress has been made in this area so that *The New York Times* was able to report in 1972 that poor black women had 49 fewer babies per thousand in the second half of the 1960's than in the first half. Among poor families in general the reduction was 32 babies per thousand; among affluent families it was 17.

Controlling for the differential effects of SES, as Simon and Simon (1968) have demonstrated, also helps to destroy the myth about black consumption patterns. Previous comparisons had used gross statistical measures like the absolute or relative amount of the total income saved by the average black and white wage earners, despite the fact that the median black income is only about 60 per cent that of the median white income. Simon and Simon found that, when you control the analysis for income level, blacks actually save a larger proportion of their income than do whites; behavior which makes sense among people who are usually the last hired and first fired. Yet such spurious correlations as that between race and life style, which fail to control for SES, have often been cited as evidence supporting the contention that black poverty can be explained by blacks' relative inability to defer gratification, a pattern supposedly consistent with an "expressive" (as opposed to "instrumental") attitude toward life.

Certainly, the higher proportion of poor people among blacks is a direct result of their minority group position. However, middle-class blacks are also part of this minority — also the object of institutionalized discrimination — but do not

seem to manifest the principal behavior patterns often cited as being characteristic of blacks in the United States.

Effects of Minority Group Membership
on Black Social Personality

What, then, are the direct effects of minority group membership on black
social personality? Probably the most widely reported and consistently documented personality trait attributed to the minority position of blacks is low self-
esteem, in extreme cases self-hatred, resulting from internalizing the negative
evaluations of themselves imposed upon them by members of the dominant
group and closely related to skin-color perception. Yet recent research by Yancy,
Rigsby, and McCarthy (1972) and Heiss and Owens (1972) fails to confirm this
contention — a variety of other factors are shown to affect the extent to which
such a response to minority group status might take place.

Furthermore, some research on the effects of desegregation (for example, Yarrow, Campbell, and Yarrow, 1958; Works, 1962; and Bullough, 1967) suggests
that feelings of powerlessness and alienation decrease and self-esteem increases
among blacks as a result of residential integration or even a two-week shared
summer camp experience in which black children relate to white children on an
equal status. Such research questions the profundity and permanence of personality patterns resulting from minority group status and suggests the possible
importance of the prevailing situational context on self-esteem.

Also historically important social and economic changes in the United States
have had significant influence on the structure of race relations and, by implication, the social personality of blacks. In the past sixty years, the growth of industry and mechanization of agriculture have led to the enormous migration of blacks
from rural areas in the South to Northern and Western urban areas. Although
such migration resulted in a generally increased level of education and living
standard for blacks, its total effects can be interpreted as forming the conditions
for both the organized social protest and ghetto riots that occurred throughout
the middle and late 1960's.

Direct economic dependence on particular individuals in the white community was greatly reduced as a result of the migration. Blacks raised in large
uban centers in the North and West, though still a minority, did not grow up
under the close white supervision and control that characterized social life in
the rural South. By the 1960's expectations for social and economic achievement
began to exceed actual improvements for most blacks, giving rise to a heightened sense of relative deprivation. Research on ghetto rioters (for example, Sears
and McConahay, 1970, and Caplan and Page, 1968) revealed them to be younger,
more educated, more likely Northern-born and more sensitive to white racism
than nonparticipants.

Moreover, rapid generational changes in social personality were facilitated by
the greater influence of peer, as opposed to family, socialization in the city.
Families, organized around the intergenerational transmission of attitudes and
information, are inherently conservative institutions. Peer groups are more egalitarian and present-oriented. To belong, you have to get "with it" where it's
"happening." All these factors have meant the emergence, especially over the

past three decades, of a changing black social personality — more militant and aggressive about social change and more self-consciously proud of black culture and tradition. Several historical triumphs in the movement of blacks toward greater equality have both benefited from and contributed to this change as they influenced the consciousness of blacks everywhere. It is a long way from Stepin Fetchit to Superfly, but the black man in America has traveled this road over the past forty years.

Varieties of Black Subculture

The present variety of life styles and modes of adjustment to minority group status among blacks make any single characterization of black subculture and social personality very problematic. The authors of *The Eighth Generation Grows Up* (1960), a follow-up study to *Children of Bondage* (1940), conclude that the impact of "class" and "caste" on black children growing up in New Orleans is differential. According to them, the "self-identity" and "basic social attitudes" of black children are influenced more profoundly by the more immediate and distinctive "social world" in which the child is socialized. Social worlds identified by the authors include the middle class, the matriarchy, the nuclear family, and the gang with a uniquely marginal position characterizing the many unable to identify with any of these groups.

In their research on the "culture of poverty," Parker and Kleiner (1970) compared a low-income mentally ill black population to a low-income black community group in Philadelphia. The authors considered "goal striving" (by income level and occupational prestige), perception of barriers to achievement, perception of personal success, and level of self-esteem. They concluded that a modal set of attitudes can be labeled a subculture of poverty and characterizes the attitudes of blacks living in poverty. However, these attitudes represent only a part of the total range of attitudes and values in the poverty setting. Parker and Kleiner infer that these modal attitudes have an adjustive function for persons living in poverty, that they help them to preserve their sanity by maintaining a "painful compromise" between their ideal aspirations and the "realistic constraints" of their social situation.

Black anthropologist Johnetta B. Cole (1970) has listed four different life styles that broadly describe the variety of black life in America: the "street life style," which is the "cool world centering around hustling"; "the down home life style," the basically rural and southern traditional way of "black folks"; the "militant life style," "the political world, centered on today's college campus, in high school Black Student Unions and in the urban ghettos"; and the "upward bound life style," best portrayed by E. Franklin Frazier in *Black Bourgeoisie* (1965).

In theorizing about black subculture, Cole suggests that, in addition to many components drawn from mainstream American culture, blacks manifest traits characteristic of "oppressed peoples" (that is, minority groups) in different societies throughout history. As examples of the latter, she cites the "minority sense," a reaction of minority group members to "sense out where there is severe hostility and bigotry" in the interest of self-protection, and the "denial urge," which is the "condemnation of one's status and by extension of one's self." The denial urge often causes many minority group members to alter their appearance and behavior in a pathetic attempt to be more like the dominant group. Cole's "minority sense" can be compared to Shibutani and Kwan's conception of a "defensive mentality" and her "denial urge" to their conception of impaired self-esteem caused by the effects of being compelled to play inferior social roles.

Cole also cites two themes in black American life which she considers distinctive: "soul" and "style." According to her, soul is the particular kind and expression of long suffering by blacks, a capacity for deep emotion in all acts of life, and the feeling of togetherness with all black people as a result of their shared experiences. Style is "the combination of ease and class, among black folks it is the ability to look rich when you are poor, the ability to appear loose when you're uncomfortable or tense: the ability to appear distinctive among many" (p. 42).

In her effort to describe the parameters of black subculture and social personality, Cole does not make any claims for their uniqueness. Rather, she examines the "combination of traits," "subtleties associated with universal attributes," and "emphasis on certain themes" that distinguish black people. In fact, upon further analysis, "soul," like low-down blues, appears to reflect the deep suffering of common oppression among black Americans, and "style," like hot jazz, the exuberant, brassy denial of such oppression. Cole doesn't claim that her discussion is either precise or inclusive. In fact, she concludes her article by calling for an anthropology of black subculture presumably to determine which, if any, social personality characteristics can differentiate black from white Americans and to what factors (for example, minority group position, cultural history, biogenetic differences) they can be attributed. Unsupported ideological assertions, ranging from the white racist position of irreconcilable, genetically determined differences to the traditional, liberal position of everyone being the same under the skin, simply will not do in attempting to resolve a question of such political and intellectual importance. The traditional liberal position makes the mistake of confusing sameness with equality and begs the question of whether ethnic cultural pluralism is compatible with the structural assimilation of minorities into mainstream American life.

Most of such an anthropology of black subculture as Cole suggests would have to be done by blacks themselves — blacks who can use social science to organize and interpret the intimate experiences of their own lives and those around them. In today's social climate, such a project would have significant political as well as intellectual consequences. I think it is particularly appropriate that the selections on racial stratification and social personality in this book are not only reflections on black personality by two black scholars, Robert Staples and Clemont Vontress, but also their debate about the intellectual and ideological issues each has raised.

References

Bullough, Bonnie
   1967   "Alienation in the Ghetto." *American Journal of Sociology* 72(5):469–78.

Campbell, A. A.
 1965 "Fertility and Family Planning among Nonwhite Married Couples in the United States." *Eugenics Quarterly* 12 (3).

Caplan, Nathan S., and J. M. Page
 1968 "Study of Ghetto Rioters." *Scientific American* 219 (August):15–21.

Cole, Johnetta B.
 1970 "Culture: Negro, Black and Nigger." *The Black Scholar* (June):40–4.

Coles, Robert
 1965 "Serpents and Doves: Non-Violent Youth in the South." Pp. 223–59 in Erik H. Erikson (ed.), *The Challenge of Youth*. Garden City, New York: Doubleday-Anchor.

Dai, Bingham
 1967 "Some Problems of Personality Development Among Negro Children." Pp. 545–66 in Kluckhohn, Clyde, and Henry A. Murray with David M. Schneider (eds.). *Personality in Nature, Society and Culture*. New York: Knopf.

Davis, Allison
 1941 "American Status Systems and the Socialization of the Child." *American Sociological Review* 6:345–54.
 1946 "Social Class and Color Differences in Child-Rearing." *American Journal of Sociology* 51:305–13.

Davis, Allison and John Dollard
 1940 *Children of Bondage: The Personality Development of Negro Youth in the Urban South*. New York: Harper and Row.

Fishman, Jacob and Fred Solomon
 1963 "Youth and Social Action: I. Perspectives on the Student Sit-in Movement." *American Journal of Orthopsychiatry* 33(5):872–82.

Frazier, E. Franklin
 1965 *Black Bourgeoisie: The Rise of a New Middle Class in the United States*. New York: Collier.

Furstenberg, Frank F., Jr.
 1970 "Premarital Pregnancy Among Black Teen-agers." *Transaction* (May):52–55.

Geisman, Ludwig L., and Ursula C. Gerhart
 1968 "Social Class, Ethnicity, and Family Functioning: Exploring Some Issues Raised by the Moynihan Report." *Journal of Marriage and the Family* 30(3):480–87.

Heiss, Jerold, and Susan Owens
 1972 "Self-Evaluations of Blacks and Whites." *American Journal of Sociology* 78 (September):360–70.

Hill, Adelaide Cromwell, and Frederick S. Jaffe
 1967 "Negro Fertility and Family Size Preferences: Implications for Programming of Health and Social Services." Pp. 205–24 in Talcott Parsons, and Kenneth B. Clark (eds.), *The Negro American*. Boston: Beacon.

Herskovits, Melville J.
 1958 *The Myth of the Negro Past*. Boston: Beacon.

Jensen, Arthur R.
 1969 "How Much Can We Boost IQ and Scholastic Achievement?" *Harvard Educational Review* 39 (Winter):1–123.

Liebow, Elliot
 1967 *Tally's Corner*. Boston: Little, Brown.

Mayeske, George
 1971 Report on race and IQ for U.S. Office of Education.

Mercer, Jane R., and Joyce M. Smith
 1971 "Subtest estimates of the WISC full scale IQ's for Children." Rockville, Md.: National Center for Health Statistics. Can be obtained from Superintendent of Documents, U.S. Government Printing Office.

Middleton, Russell, and Snell Putney
  1960 "Dominance in Decisions in the Family: Race and Class Differences."
        American Journal of Sociology 65:605–9.
Office of Policy Planning and Research, U.S. Dept. of Labor
  1965 *The Negro Family: The Case for National Action.* (March).
Orshansky, Mollie
  1965 "Who's Who Among the Poor: A Demographic View of Poverty." *Social
        Security Bulletin* (July).
Parker, Seymour, and Robert J. Kleiner
  1970 "The Culture of Poverty: An Adjustive Dimension." *American Anthropolo-
        gist* 72–73:516–27.
Pouissant, Alvin
  1967 "A Negro Psychiatrist Explains the Negro Psyche." *New York Times Maga-
        zine,* August 29.
Powdermaker, Hortense
  1943 "The Channeling of Negro Aggressions by the Cultural Process. *American
        Journal of Sociology* 48:750–58.
Rainwater, Lee
  1967 "Crucible of Identity: The Negro Lower-Class Family." Pp. 160–204 in
        Parsons and Clark, *The Negro American.*
Rohrer, John H., and Monro S. Edmonson (eds.), Harold Lief, Daniel Thompson and
        William Thompson (co-authors)
  1960 *The Eighth Generation Grows Up: Cultures and Personalities of New
        Orleans Negroes.* New York: Harper and Row.
Sears, David O., and John B. McConahay
  1970 "Racial Socialization, Comparison Levels, and the Watts Riot." *Journal of
        Social Issues* 26(1):121–40.
Shibutani, Tamotsu, and Kian M. Kwan with contributions by Robert H. Billigmeier
  1964 *Ethnic Stratification: A Comparative Approach.* New York: Macmillan.
Simon, Julian L., and Rita James Simon
  1968 "Class, Status, and Savings of Negroes." *The American Sociologist* 3
        (August):218–19.
Simpson, George Eaton, and J. Milton Yinger
  1972 *Racial and Cultural Minorities: An Analysis of Prejudice and Discrimina-
        tion,* 4th ed. New York: Harper and Row.
Ten Houten, Warren D.
  1970 "The Black Family: Myth and Reality." *Psychiatry* 33 (May):145–73.
Valentine, Charles A.
  1968 *Culture and Poverty.* Chicago: University of Chicago Press.
Whelpton, P. K., and A. A. Campbell, and J. Patterson
  1966 *Fertility and Family Planning in the United States.* Princeton, N.J.: Prince-
        ton University Press.
Williams, Robin M., Jr.
  1964 *Strangers Next Door.* Englewood Cliffs, N.J.: Prentice-Hall.
Works, Ernest
  1962 "Residence in Integrated and Segregated Housing and Improvement in
        Self-Concepts of Negroes." *Sociology and Social Research* 46(3):294–301.
Yancey, William, Leo Rigsby, and John D. McCarthy
  1972 "Social Position and Self-Evaluation: The Relative Importance of Race."
        American Journal of Sociology 78 (September):338–59.
Yarrow, Marian Radke, John D. Campbell, and Leon J. Yarrow
  1958 "Acquisition of New Norms: A Study of Racial Desegregation." *Journal of
        Social Issues* 14(1):8–28.

ROBERT STAPLES

The Myth of the Impotent Black Male

In white America there is a cultural belief that the Black community is dominated by its female members, its men having been emasculated by the historical vicissitudes of slavery and contemporary economic forces. This cultural belief contains a duality of meaning: that black men have been deprived of their masculinity and that black women participated in the emasculinization process. The myth of the black matriarchy has been exploded elsewhere.[1] Black female dominance is a cultural illusion that disguises the triple oppression of black women in this society. They are discriminated against on the basis of their sex role affiliation, their race and their location in the working class strata of this upper-class dominated country.

The assumption that black men have been socially castrated has yet to be challenged. Before examining the fallacies of black male castration, it is important to understand the function of these cultural images of black men and women for maintaining the status quo level of black deprivation and white privilege. Most of these theories of black life come from the field of social science, a discipline, ostensibly dedicated to the pursuit of truth. It would be more realistic to view social science research as a form of ideology, a propaganda apparatus which serves to justify racist institutions and practices. Social science as ideology is a means of social control exercised by white America to retain its privileges in a society partially sustained by this ideology. As one observer noted:

> Social scientists and journalists in America generally operate under an ideology-laden code of professional conduct that requires objectivity. . . . But this objectivity is in effect a commitment to the ruling class.[2]

Stereotypes of the black male as psychologically impotent and castrated have been perpetuated not only by social scientists but through the mass media and accepted by both blacks and whites alike. This assault on black masculinity is made *precisely because black males are men;* not because they are impotent and that is an important distinction to make. As one sociologist candidly admits, "Negro men have been more feared, sexually and occupationally, than Negro women."[3] She further admits that the Negro man had to be destroyed as a man to "protect" the white world.[4] It should be added that the attempt to destroy him failed but the myth of his demasculinization lingers on. One can see in this myth an unmitigated fear of black male power, an unrelenting determination on the part of white America to create in fiction what it has been unable to accomplish in the empirical world.

Reprinted by permission from *The Black Scholar* 2:10 (1971), pp. 2–9.

From a historical perspective, the black male's role has changed as he has traversed from the African continent to the shores of North America. This span of time has introduced the forces of slavery, racism and wage exploitation in the determination of his masculine expressions. In Africa, he resided in a male-dominated society. Although women had an important place in African society, most important decisions were made by male members of the community.[5]

Taken forcibly from his African roots, the black man experienced radical changes in his status. In the beginning of the period of slavery, black men greatly outnumbered black women. It was not until 1840 that there was an equal sex ratio among blacks.[6] As a result of this low sex ratio, there were numerous cases of sex relations between black slaves and indentured white women. The intermarriage rate between black men and white women increased to the extent that interracial marriages were prohibited. Previously, black men were encouraged to marry white women in order to augment the human capital of the slave-owning class.[7]

After black women were brought over to the New World, they served as breeders of children, who were treated as property, and as the gratifiers of the carnal desires of white plantation owners. More importantly, they became the central figure in black family life. The black man's only crucial function within the family was that of siring the children. The mother's role was far more important than the father's. She cleaned the house, prepared the food, made clothes and raised the children. The husband was at most his wife's assistant, her companion and her sex partner. He was often thought of as her possession, as was the cabin in which they lived. It was common for a mother and her children to be considered a family without reference to the father.[8]

Under slavery the role of father was, in essence, institutionally obliterated. Not only was the slave father deprived of his sociological and economic functions in the family but the very etiquette of plantation life eliminated even the honorific attributes of fatherhood from the black male, who was addressed as boy — until, when the vigorous years of his prime were past, he was permitted to assume the title of uncle. If he lived with a woman, "married," he was known as her husband (e.g., Sally's John), again denying him a position as head of the household.[9]

That black men were reduced to a subordinate status in the family is quite true. That they abdicated their responsibility to their families probably highlights the unusual — not the prosaic behavior of black men. Although somewhat unusual, for example, there was the case of a black slave who, when his wife complained of the beating she had taken from the overseer, took her to a cave away from harm. He fixed it up for her to live in, he brought her food; he protected her. Three children were born in the cave and only with emancipation did the family come out to join him.[10]

There are those who say that slavery prevented black men from coming to emotional maturity, that they were childlike, docile creatures who were viewed not as objects of fear or hatred but as a source of amusement.[11] In conflict with this view is the observation that:

> In spite of all attempts to crush it, the slave had a will of his own, which was actively, as well as passively, opposed to the master's. And it is this stubborn and rebellious will — tragic, heroic, defeated or triumphant — that, more than all else . . . haunted the master, frustrating his designs by a ceaseless though perhaps invisible countermining. . . . The slave expresses his

hatred of enslavement and his contempt for his enslaver in less subtle and more open ways, such as taking what belonged to him, escaping or assisting others to escape, secretly learning or teaching others to read and write, secret meetings, suicide, infanticide, homicide, and the like.[12]

In addition to this covert resistance the so-called "docile" slave put together a number of elaborate conspiracies and insurrections. According to Aptheker, over 250 slave revolts were planned.[13] After slavery, however, the black male continued to encounter assaults on his manhood. In every aspect of his life, white America has tried to subjugate him. The historical literature, for instance, suggests that Jim Crow was directed more at the black male than the black female.[14] Black women, in a very limited way, were allowed more freedom, suffered less discrimination and provided more opportunities than black men.

The structural barriers to black manhood were great. In a capitalistic society, being able to provide basic life satisfactions is inextricably interwoven with manhood. It is the opportunity to provide for his family, both individually and collectively, which has been denied the black man. After emancipation, the economic role of the black woman was strengthened as blacks left the rural areas and migrated to the cities where it was difficult for black men to obtain employment. Although they had previously held jobs as skilled craftsmen, carpenters, etc., they were forced out of these occupations by a coalition of white workers and capitalists. In some instances they found employment only as strikebreakers.[15]

Through this systematic denial of an opportunity to work for black men, white America thrust the black woman into the role of family provider. This pattern of female headed families was reinforced by the marginal economic position of the black male. The jobs available to him lacked the security and level of income necessary to maintain a household and in some cases were simply not available. Additionally, certain jobs performed by black men (e.g. waiter, cook, dishwasher, teacher, social worker etc.) often carry a connotation in American society as being woman's work.[16]

Economically destitute black families may be forced into a welfare system where it makes "sense" in terms of daily economic security for black men to leave their families. An example is this black woman who refused to permit her husband back into the family after he got a job. She said:

> Not me! With him away I've got security. I know when my welfare check is coming and I know I can take him to court if he doesn't pay me child support. But as soon as he comes back in, then I don't know if he's going to keep his job; or if he's going to start acting up and staying out drinking and spending his pay away from home. This way I might be poor, but at least I know how much I got.[17]

White society has placed the black man in a tenuous position where manhood has been difficult to achieve. Black men have been lynched and brutalized in their attempts to retain their manhood. They have suffered from the cruelest assault on mankind that the world has ever known. For black men in this society it is not so much a matter of acquiring manhood as a struggle to feel it their own. As a pair of black psychiatrists comment:

> Whereas the white man regards his manhood as an ordained right, the Black man is engaged in a never ending battle for its possession. For the Black

man, attaining any portion of manhood is an active process. He must penetrate barriers and overcome opposition in order to assume a masculine posture. For the inner psychological obstacles to manhood are never so formidable as the impediments woven into American society.[18]

After placing these obstacles to manhood in the black man's way, white America then has its ideological bearers, the social scientists, falsely indict him for his lack of manhood. There are various sociological and psychological studies which purport to show how black males are de-masculinized, in fact may be latent homosexuals. The reason they cite is that black males reared in female-centered households are more likely to acquire feminine characteristics because there is no consistent adult male model or image to shape their personalities.[19] One sociologist stated that since black males are unable to enact the masculine role, they tend to cultivate their personalities. In this respect they resemble women who use their personalities to compensate for their inferior status in relation to men.[20]

If the above reasoning seems weak and unsubstantiated, the other studies of black emasculation are equally feeble. Much of this supposition of the effeminate character of black men is based on their scores on the Minnesota Multiphasic Inventory Test (MMPI), a psychological instrument that asks the subject the applicability to himself of over five hundred simple statements. Black males score higher than white males on a measure of femininity. As an indicator of their femininity, the researchers cite the fact that black men more often agreed with such feminine choices as "I would like to be a singer" and "I think I feel more intensely than most people do." [21]

This is the kind of evidence that white society has marshalled to prove the feminization of the black male. The only thing this demonstrates is that white standards can not always be used in evaluating black behavior. Black people live in another environment, with different ways of thinking, acting and believing than in the white, middle-class world. Singers such as James Brown and others represent successful role models in the black community. Black male youth aspire to be singers because this appears to be an observable means for obtaining success in this country — not because they are more feminine than white males. Additionally, music is an integral part of black culture.

One can easily challenge the theory that black males can not learn the masculine role in father-absent homes. Black people are aware — if whites are not — that in female-headed households in the black community, there is seldom one where adult males are totally absent. A man of some kind is usually around. He may be a boyfriend, an uncle or just the neighborhood bookie. Even if these men do not assume a central family role, the black child may use them as source material for the identification of masculine behavior.[22]

Furthermore, men are not the only ones who teach boys about masculinity. Sex roles can also be learned by internalizing the culturally determined expectations of these roles. Consequently, black mothers can spell out the role requirements for their fatherless sons. She can symbolically communicate to him the way that men act. He will be showed the way men cross their legs, how they carry their books, the way they walk, etc. Through the culture's highly developed system of rewards for typical male behavior and punishment for signs of femininity, the black male child learns to identify with the culturally defined, stereotyped role of male.[23]

Black males are put in the psychological trick-bag of being "damned if they do, damned if they don't." If they acted effeminate they would be considered effeminate. Because they act like real men, they are charged with an exaggeration of normal masculine behavior to compensate for, or disguise, their femininity. The psychologists ignore one of their own tenets in this case: if men define situations as real, then they are real in their consequences.[24] If men define their behavior as masculine, for all practical purposes it becomes masculine to them. For black men, masculinity is the way they act. White America's definition of masculinity is of little importance, or validity, to them.

The myth of the black matriarchy is accompanied by the falsehood that the model black father has abdicated his paternal responsibilities. That this is untrue is confirmed in a study by Schulz which found that most black men assume a very responsible quasi-father role vis-à-vis their women and her children. Black men, however, have to spend a large part of their lives bargaining for a familial relationship, the major impediment being a limited income that cannot equal the combined resources of their present job plus their woman's welfare check. These men, who are not officially father or husband, play a more supportive role than is generally acknowledged.[25]

While some black men, obviously, relinquish their paternal role functions, most black men perform ably in that role considering the circumstances under which black families must live. Typical of the black father's concern for his children is this man's statement:

> My youngest boy is seven. All my kids are in school. I try to instill in their minds that the only sound way to succeed is by laying a good foundation of learning and then to get actual experience. I hope to be able to see them all through college. I own property where I live and have a few dollars in the bank. I own a car, too. My greatest ambition is to see my children come along and keep this cleaning and pressing business of mine going, or else get into something they like better.[26]

That many black fathers never realize their aspirations for their children can be attributed to America's racist social structure. Instead, black women are charged with complicity with white men to subordinate the black male to his lowly position. Contrary to this assumption, one finds that when the Afro-American male was subjected to such abject oppression, the black woman was left without protection and was used — and is still being used — as a scapegoat for all the oppression that the system of white racism has perpetrated on black men. The system found it functional to enslave and exploit them and did so without the consent, tacit or otherwise, of black women. Moreover, while black men may be subjected to all sorts of dehumanizing practices, they still have someone who is below them — black women.[27]

Nevertheless, black women have had a variety of responses to the plight of black men. Some black women accepted the prevailing image of manhood and womanhood that depicted black men as shiftless and lazy if they did not secure employment and support their families as they ought to. There are reported instances of the black male ceasing to provide any economic support for the family and having his wife withdraw her commitment from him and from the marriage.[28] Other black women have ambivalent feelings about black men and remember painful experiences with them. They believe that black men do not fully appreciate the role of black women in the survival of the black race. Some even internalize white society's low regard for black men but are bothered by their appraisals.[29]

These attitudes on the part of black women are understandable. There are many black male-female conflicts which are a result of the psychological problems generated by their oppressed condition. Under a system of domestic colonialism, the oppressed peoples turn their frustrations, their wrath, toward each other rather than their oppressor.[30] Being constantly confronted with problems of survival, blacks become more psychologically abusive toward their spouses than perhaps they would under other circumstances.

On the other hand some black women are very supportive of their men. As Hare notes, black women realize that they must encourage the black man and lay as much groundwork for black liberation as he will let her. She realizes that it is necessary to be patient with black men whenever they engage in symbolic assertions of manliness. Her role is to assist strongly but not dominate.[31] Black women, however, may not realize the contradiction between their desire for a comfortable standard of living and wanting the black man to exercise his masculinity. The expression of black masculinity can frequently be met with the harshest punishment white society can muster. Physical punishment, and economic deprivation, are frequently the white response to expressions of black manliness.

Whatever the role of the black woman, she realizes that the mythical castrated black male can rarely be dominated. In the dating situation, he has the upper hand because of the shortage of black men in the society. Black women, if they want a black man, frequently have to accept the relationship on male terms. If she does not give in to his demands, there are always other women who will. The henpecked black husband is usually a mythical figure. The fact that black wives carry a slightly larger share of the housework than white wives[32] — while not a particularly desirable situation — effectively dispels any notion of the black husband in the role of a domestic servant.

It was mentioned earlier that the attempt to emasculate the black male was motivated by the fear of his sexual power. As Bernard has stated, "the white world's insistence on keeping Negro men walled up in the 'concentration camp' was motivated in large part by its fear of their sexuality." [33] One needs a deep understanding of the importance of sex in the United States in order to see the interrelationship of sex and racism in American society. In a society where white sexuality has been repressed, the imagined sexual power of the black male poses a serious threat. According to Hernton:

> There is in the psyche of the racist an inordinate disposition for sexual atrocity. He sees in the Negro the essence of his own sexuality, that is, those qualities that he wishes for but fears he does not possess. Symbolically, the Negro at once affirms and negates the white man's sense of sexual security. . . . Contrary to what is claimed, it is not the white woman who is

dear to the racist. It is not even the black woman toward whom his real sexual rage is directed. It is the black man who is sacred to the racist. And this is why he must castrate him.[34]

Whether the white woman is dear to the racist is debatable. It certainly appears that he is concerned about preserving the purity of white womanhood. Since 1698 social censure and severe penalties were reserved for the association of black men and white women.[35] The evidence for these suppositions is voluminous, ranging from the accusations by lynch mobs that the black man raped or threatened to rape the white woman, the white South's obsession with the purity of white womanhood, the literal castration of black men for centuries, and in the death of an Emmet Till, who was killed for looking at a white woman. As Fanon comments, the white man fears that the black man will "introduce his daughter into a sexual universe for which the father does not have the key, the weapons, or the attributes." [36]

The question might be posed: what is the empirical basis of black male sexual superiority? Contrary to prevailing folklore, it is not the size of his genitalia. According to the Kinsey Institute, the majority of both white and black penises measured in their sample were less than or equal to four and a half inches in the flaccid state and less than or equal to seven inches in their erect state.[37] However, three times as many black males had penises larger than seven inches in length. The Masters and Johnson Report indicates no particular relationship between penis size and sexual satisfaction except that induced by the psychological state of the female.[38]

What, then, can be said about the sexual abilities of white men and black men? First, it must be acknowledged that sexual attitudes and behavior are cultancularly determined — not inherent traits of a particular group. But — sex relations have a different nature and meaning to black people. Their sexual expression derives from the emphasis in the black culture on feeling, of releasing the natural functions of the body without artificiality or mechanical movements. In some circles this is called "soul" and may be found among peoples of African descent throughout the world.

In a concrete sense, this means that black men do not moderate their enthusiasm for sex relations as white men do. They do not have a history of suppressing the sexual expression of the majority of their women while singling out a segment of the female population for premarital and extramarital adventures. This lack of a double standard of sexual conduct has also unleashed the sexual expression of black women. Those black women who have sexual hangups acquired them by their acculturation of the puritanical moral values of white society.

The difference between black men and white men in sexual responses may be explained by realizing that for white men sex has to be fitted into time not devoted to building the technological society, whereas for black men it is a natural function, a way of life. An example of this is that white men when confronted with their woman's state of sexual readiness may say business first, pleasure later. The black man when shown the black woman's state of sexual excitation manages to take care of both the business and pleasure task. If one task is left unfinished, is is unlikely that the black woman is left wanting.

It is this trait of the black male that white society would prefer to label sexual immorality. The historical evidence reveals, however, that the white man's moral code has seldom been consistent with his actual behavior. The real issue here is one of power. In a society where women are regarded as a kind of sexual property, the white male tries to insure that he will not have to compete with black men on an equal basis for any woman. Not only may the white male experience guilt over his possession of black womanhood but he fears that as the black man attains a bedroom equality he will gain a political and economic equality as well.

Sexual fears, however, do not totally explain the attempted castration of black men. White society realizes quite well that it is the men of an oppressed group that form the vanguard, the bulwark, of any liberation struggle. By perpetrating the myth of the impotent black male on the consciousness of black and white people, they are engaging in wishful thinking. It is patently clear that men such as Nat Turner, Denmark Vesey, Frederick Douglass and Malcolm X were not impotent eunuchs. The task of black liberation has been carried out by black men from time immemorial. While black women have been magnificently supportive, it is black men who have joined the battle.

White America will continue to perpetuate the myth of the impotent black male as long as it serves their purpose. Meanwhile, the task of black liberation is at hand. It will continue to be in the hands of black men. While racists fantasize about the impotency of the black man, his childlike status, the liberation struggle will proceed, with one uncompromising goal: total freedom for all black people, men and women alike.

Notes

1. Robert Staples, "The Myth of the Black Matriarchy," *The Black Scholar,* February, 1970, pp. 9–16.
2. William Ellis, *White Ethics and Black Power,* Chicago: Aldine Publishing Company, 1969, p. xiii.
3. Jessie Bernard, *Marriage and Family Among Negroes,* Englewood Cliffs, New Jersey: Prentice-Hall, Inc., 1966, p. 69.
4. Ibid. p. 73.
5. John Hope Franklin, *From Slavery to Freedom,* New York: Random House, 1947.
6. Ibid.
7. E. Franklin Frazier, *The Negro Family in the United States,* Chicago: University of Chicago Press, 1939.
8. Maurice Davie, *Negroes in American Society,* New York: McGraw-Hill, 1949, p. 207.
9. Stanley M. Elkins, *Slavery: A Problem in American Institutional and Intellectual Life,* Chicago: University of Chicago Press, 1968, p. 130.
10. B. A. Botkin, *Lay My Burden Down,* Chicago: The University of Chicago Press, 1945, pp. 179–80.
11. Elkins, op. cit., p. 128.
12. Botkin, op. cit., pp. 137–38.
13. Herbert Aptheker, *American Negro Slave Revolts,* New York: International Publishers, 1963.
14. C. Vann Woodward, *The Strange Career of Jim Crow,* New York: Oxford University Press, 1966.
15. C. F. Pierre Van Der Berghe, *Race and Racism,* New York: John Wiley, 1967.

16. Harold Proshansky and Peggy Newton, "The Nature and Meaning of Negro Self-Identity," in *Social Class, Race and Psychological Development,* Martin Deutsch, et al., eds., New York: Holt, Rinehart and Winston, 1968.

17. William Yancey, Vanderbilt University, personal communication 1971.

18. William H. Grier and Price M. Cobbs, *Black Rage,* New York: Basic Books, 1968, p. 49.

19. Thomas Pettigrew, *A Profile of the Negro American,* Princeton, New Jersey: D. Van Nostrand Company, 1964, pp. 17–22.

20. E. Franklin Frazier, *Black Bourgeoisie,* New York: Crowell-Collier Publishing Co., 1962, p. 182.

21. J. E. Hollanson and G. Calder, "Negro-White Differences on the MMPI," *Journal of Chemical Psychology,* 1960, pp. 32–33.

22. Ulf Hannerz, "The Roots of Black Manhood," *Transaction,* October, 1969, p. 16.

23. David Lynn, "The Process of Learning Parental and Sex Role Identification," *Marriage and Family Living,* 28, November, 1966, pp. 466–570.

24. C. F. W. I. Thomas and Florence Znaniecki, *The Polish Peasant in Europe and America,* New York: Alfred A. Knopf, 1927.

25. David Schulz, "The Role of the Boyfriend in Lower Class Negro Life," *The Family Life of Black People,* Charles V. Willie, ed., Columbus, Ohio: Charles E. Merrill, 1970, pp. 231–246.

26. St. Clair Drake and Horace Cayton, *Black Metropolis,* Chicago: University of Chicago Press, 1945, p. 665.

27. Frances Beal, "Double Jeopardy: To Be Black and Female," *New Generation.* 51, Fall 1969, pp. 23–28.

28. Lee Rainwater, "Crucible of Identity: The Negro Lower Class Family," *Daedulus,* 95, Winter 1966, pp. 251–255.

29. Nathan and Julia Hare, "Black Women 1970," *Transaction,* 8, November, 1970, pp. 66–67.

30. C. F. Frantz Fanon, *The Wretched of the Earth,* New York: Grove Press, 1966.

31. Hare, loc. cit.

32. Robert O. Blood, Jr. and Donald M. Wofe, "Negro-White Difference in Blue Collar Marriages in a Northern Metropolis," *Social Forces,* 48, September, 1969, pp. 59–63.

33. Bernard, op. cit., p. 75.

34. Calvin Hernton, *Sex and Racism in America,* Garden City, New York: Doubleday, 1965, pp. 111–112.

35. Frazier, *The Negro Family in the United States,* op. cit., pp. 50–51.

36. Frantz Fanon, *Black Skin, White Masks,* New York: Grove Press, 1967, p. 163.

37. Allan Bell, *Black Sexuality, Fact and Fancy,* a paper, Black America Series, Indiana University, Bloomington, Indiana, 1968.

38. William Masters and Virginia Johnson, *Human Sexual Response,* Boston: Little, Brown and Co., 1966.

CLEMMONT E. VONTRESS

The Black Male Personality

Among many psychiatrists the term personality is used almost in its literal sense; i.e., reference to the mask worn on stage by actors in ancient Rome. Personality is like a mask in that it is made up of patterns of behavior through which the individual expresses his uniqueness. It develops as a result of actual contacts with the world and the organization of experiences gained from these contacts into an integrated whole.[1] An individual learns to behave in a particular way as a result of interactions with people, not because he possesses innate imperatives for certain kinds of behavior. The individual's most distinctive and fundamental human qualities are products of his experiences with other human beings. He "learns" his personality as a result of the events in his personal history. That is to say, personality development is largely a function of social conditions under which one grows up.

Personality attributes are first acquired through the child's imitation of parental behavior, which is usually transmitted unconsciously in the context of love and care.[2] The family constitutes the primary agent for interpreting the world to the child.[3] It emphasizes certain modes of behavior and de-emphasizes others. Parents and older siblings provide the models which the child imitates in the acquisition of his social behavior. As he matures, significant others contribute to the socialization process. In this way, society determines the way individuals react to people, places, and things. It tinges perceptions, sharpens or dulls feelings, and stunts or promotes growth, both intellectual and physical. Culture, in both its technological and socially regulatory aspects, is what our forebears have been taught and have confirmed or modified on the basis of their own experiences, which they then pass on to their offspring and to those for whom they have the responsibility of socializing.[4] According to Ruth Benedict,[5] nearly all individuals who are born into any given society always assume the behavior dictated by that society, including the idiosyncrasies of its institutions.

If this definition of personality can be accepted, then it seems logical to apply it in an analysis of the black personality in America. Whenever groups of people are separated one from the other for whatever reason, each develops unique behavior patterns. Each group approaches nature and man in terms of its own heritage, experiences, and traditions. So long as the group shares an impressive sameness of experiences, members of that group tend to perceive, behave, and think alike.[6]

Black people in this country have all been subjected to the agony and night-

Reprinted by permission from *The Black Scholar* 2:10 (1971), pp. 10–16.

mare of racism. Since our abduction to this continent, we have been set apart and reacted to uniquely by the dominant group. We were so abhorrent to our slavemasters that legal barriers were instituted to prevent the natural process of assimilation, which historically has almost always taken place in other societies inhabited by the conquerer and the conquered or the superior and the inferior.

Historically, it is inaccurate to compare the black experience with that of other racial or ethnic groups who have come to this country.[7] The black man was brought to this land forcibly and was completely cut off from his past. He was robbed of language and culture. He was forbidden to be an African and never allowed to be an American. After the first generation and with each new group of slaves, the black man had only his American experience on which to draw. Unlike other people who came to those shores, he was debated over as to whether he had a soul, whether he could learn, whether he should become a citizen, whether he should be slave or free, and indeed whether he was human.

Today, the black man is at one end of a psychological continuum which goes back to slavocracy.[8] He is still victimized by a racist society which reacts to him as a phobogenic object. Indeed, the black experience is a unique experience in this country. During their stay in America, blacks have begged and pleaded to become a part of the total community and to be accepted as equals; and during their stay, they have continuously been denied this status, simply because of their color. There thus is a rationale for conceptualizing the black personality.

Components of the Black Personality

Although personality theorists concede the unity of personality, they perforce parcel out dimensions, variables, factors, or components. American blacks have never been a cohesive group. Some were never enslaved; some passed over into the white group; some lost themselves in religion or other forms of escapism; and some just stopped living. Even though outwardly blacks as individuals have reacted differently to their horrific experiences in this country, they all share common damages from them.

Self-hatred

In examining collectively the black personality, there is one component which stands out above all others: self-hatred. When one is a member of an ostracized, excluded, or outside group, he tends not only to despise his group, but also to hate himself for being a member of that group. In this country, black people in general have unconsciously identified with their oppressors, and, consequently, we have developed contempt and hatred of ourselves. As products of a racist society, we have acquired the same cultural attributes as have whites. Included among these are anti-black sentiments. This helps to account for the desperate attempt to approximate the looks and behavior of whites. The destructive infighting among blacks can also be explained in terms of self-rejection. Hatred of oneself is inseparable from hatred of others, even though on the surface the opposite may appear.[9]

Since black self-hatred is simply a reflection of hatred which whites have for blacks, it seems imperative to examine the genesis of the root hatred. Historically, blacks have not always been phobogenic objects to whites. Setting foot on the shores of West Africa in 1550, the Englishman was struck by the African's religion, which he called paganism; his behavior, which he labeled savage; his color, which some of his kind thought was a severe sunburn; and his "Propagator," which he perceived monstrous. In 1623, Richard Jobson wrote that Mandingo men were "furnisht with such members as after a sort burthensome unto them." [10] In other words, whites perceived blacks to be inferior to them in every way except one — their sexual endowments.

In this country, the white man has been obsessed with black sex. He has possessed black women, because he perceived them to be more libidinous than his own; and because he felt this way, he, as an aging slavemaster, was invigorated to perform other impossible lusty feats. At the same time, he showed an almost unnatural interest in black males. This interest is indicated by the slave buyer's ritualistic examination of the genitals of bucks, before deciding to make a purchase. Unusual also was the bizarre punishment of castrating or otherwise mutilating the genitals of slaves accused of sexual aggression in the 17th and 18th centuries.[11]

Although one might be quick to suggest that white men were simply treating their human property as they would their bulls, it seems obvious that this punishment was an expression of the white man's deep and agonizing sexual insecurity vis-à-vis the black male. Having created the myth about the black man's sexual greatness, he then proceeded to punish him for his own figment of the imagination. Thus, it seems clear that the white man's sexual jealousy of the black man is at the heart of the race problem in this country. Since the fear operates on the unconscious level, it is all the more difficult to deal with, and certainly not to be acknowledged.

There is reason to believe that the white man's sexual jealousy is on the upswing. To whites, the black man represents the biological, the savage instinct in man, the Id, if you will. He symbolizes the animal (Id) which must be kept encaged, except under certain conditions. Today, young blacks with their wooly hair, loud colors, and peacock stances project and incite more dramatically than ever the animal image of them which lurks in whites. White women who must pass through the ghetto at night declare their fear and rejection of blacks. In this connection, J. A. Rogers,[12] in analyzing the meaning of such an attitude, states that although a white woman may violently reject blacks as a group, from time to time she meets one who excites her physically; thus, she is angry with herself and black men as well.

To be sure, the American society is shot through with pernicious racism and hatred of blacks. The hate is character-conditioned, as opposed to reactive hatred. That is to say, the white hate for blacks is a continuous readiness to hate as opposed to hatred resulting from a particular incident or situation. Since white hatred for black people, especially black men, is sexually-based, and usually unconscious, it is apt to remain intact and become more intense, especially now when black men are moving about in the open with white women hanging onto their arms. An understanding of the genesis of white hatred should in due time help blacks to "get themselves together" quicker.

Erratic Behavior

According to Shaffer and Shoben,[13] the most obvious and important effect of frustration is that it ordinarily leads to varied behavior. In this country, blacks have tried a variety of ways to escape their oppression. Those who could have denied their racial membership and "passed." Others have left the country entirely. Some have become passive, avowing that things are not all that bad and have communicated this attitude to the delight of their oppressors. In many cases, blacks who could not pass for white have identified with the dominant group by assuming their life-style. Others have become aggressive toward their oppressors, running the risk of being decimated. Many middle-class blacks have blamed their own kind for their situation and have therefore striven to become what whites say they must be in order to be accepted. Still others have tried to endure their victimization status by narcotizing the psychological effects of it.

Tendencies to escape from pain and its consequences by habitual use of alcohol and drugs, or the anodyne of excessive preoccupation with the hereafter, may be related to the general health situation within the lower-class black community, Drake[14] has indicated. In general, it seems safe to say that until the black man finds a solution to his terrible situation in this country, he will continue to explore new avenues to freedom. This is in the nature of the frustrated animal, human or sub-human.

Black Compulsiveness

Here, "compulsiveness" is used to refer to an individual's tendency to be perfect, constricted, and "up tight." Living within the white ideal was at one time a common mode of adjustment for black people. Today, most blacks have learned that no matter how exemplary their behavior is, they still are considered "just niggers" by the majority of whites in this country. A minority, however, still cling to the idea that if you act right, "they will accept you." In the main, there are some twenty percent who can be roughly classified as middle-class and a handful of "colored" who are still trying to please their masters, hoping that by so doing, their oppressors will show them some degree of favoritism.

Middle-class blacks find themselves in a cultural limbo, so to speak. They identify with whites, who will not completely accept them, and reject blacks, whom they consider beneath themselves. Living in a manner which they think would be approved by their "white friends," they have nobody but themselves. Even so, they continue to pattern their behavior after that of middle-class whites.[15] Their mode of adjustment consists of moving to suburbia, albeit black; joining churches other than Baptist or Methodist (usually Catholic); participating in the right uplift activities; declaring that they, unlike whites, will not discriminate (often employing white secretaries and maids); and of expressing disdain for "black racists." Although they behave in a manner superior to those whom they try to ape, they are still not a part of the white community, of which they want so desperately to be a member.

In their child-rearing practices, they are insistent that their boys and girls will not talk like those "kids from the ghetto;" that they (the children) will restrain their movements on the dance floor; that their offspring will go to a private school and not to one of those inner-city "stunting factories;" that the children will then go on to the "right college;" and finally, that the youngsters will marry into the right family, albeit a black one.

Many "colored" people, although not on par with the black bourgeoisie, also live and behave in a manner which they perceive to be acceptable to whites. They suppress their hostility and learn to say the right thing at the right place. The effect of all these security operations is insidious and terribly damaging to their self-esteem, spontaneity, freedom of expression, and creativity.[16] Constricting their lives so, they are by middle-age seriously damaged personalities. Resigned and apathetic, colored people live lives which are stereotyped, ritualistic, and minimally expressive of their genuine feelings.

Masculine Protest

One who feels insecure about some aspect of himself may assume the opposite outward behavior of what he actually feels inside. In psychoanalytic terms, the adoption of an attitude opposite to that which produces anxiety is called reaction formation. A classic example of the behavior is the little boy who whistles as he passes the graveyard at night. Another might be a man who, although happily married, must pursue every "skirt" obtainable. Psychoanalytically, the individual feels insecure about his masculinity and therefore must forever prove his manhood to himself.

As has already been suggested, the black man in America has been denied his manhood. Being a man means more than being a male, biologically speaking. It means being able to take care of one's family, being looked up to as a man among men, and being respected by one's children and spouse, because he is head of the household. Few black men, because of their economic disfranchisement in this country, have been able to assume this kind of masculine role. This fact helps to explain why so many black men exaggerate the most obvious, external signs of masculinity.

In the male child, the sense of maleness is permanently fixed before he reaches the classic phallic stage.[17] His sexual identity comes about as a result of a process by which he comes to perceive and respond to himself as he is first perceived and responded to by the significant figures in his early life.[18] The child may acquire the proper sexual identity in the absence of one parent, or he may acquire the wrong identity in the presence of both, depending on the psychological atmosphere and interactive behavior patterns of the home.

Consider the black mother whose husband was killed in Vietnam, about six months after the birth of their son. The mother, filled with love and respect for her deceased husband, was forever talking to her son about what a great, strong, and proud man his father was. She had come from a patriarchal home and knew and respected the male role; she communicated this to her son, who grew up with a secure male identity, even though he came from a one parent home.

Although boys who closely identify with their fathers tend to have more characteristically masculine attitudes than their peers who do not,[19] the mere presence of a father does not insure son-father identification. One of the most crucial determinants of the development of masculinity in young boys is the nature of the father-son relationship.[20] If the father is nurturant, affectionate, and consistent in his attitude toward the son, a strong masculine identification usually takes place. In general, boys are more likely to identify with fathers whom they perceive as rewarding, gratifying, understanding, and warm, than with fathers who are not perceived in these ways.[21]

There are other factors which impinge on the identification process. The frequent absence of the father or fear of him often results in passivity in boys and a tendency on their part to imitate the attitudes, interests, and manners of the mother.[22] It is not uncommon for sons of military men who are away from home a great deal to develop an unusual and often unhealthy identification with their mothers. Masculine identification also depends on the strength of the mother. The more masculine the mother, the less strongly the boy tends to identify with his father. Furthermore, since the masculine woman tends to dominate the home environment, she is also the primary source of gratification and reward for her son.[23]

Perhaps the most significant determinant of son-father identification is the attitude the mother has toward the father, as already pointed out. If the mother sees her husband as the ideal model for the son, she rewards the child for behaving like her spouse.[24] If she wants him to be different from her husband, she does not reward him for being like her husband, whether he is present or not. When the mother points out negatives about the father to the child, the child responds in kind. This helps to explain why some boys may be heard to say "I'd do anything for my mother, but I won't do a thing for my no-good daddy!"

Today, almost one-quarter of all black families in this country are headed by women, a rate which continues to rise. In some sections of major cities, the rate is almost one-half. Black men without jobs are forced from the home by welfare workers. Unable to stay in the family to provide the role model for their sons, they are forced to adjust to their emasculated status the best way they know how. They are denied the primary signs of manhood in the American society: making money and supporting their families. Unable to assume this role because of a society that discriminates against them, they resort to emphasizing secondary aspects of masculinity. These include having good clothes on your back, money in your pockets, a woman from whom you can get whatever you need, and not working or having to work.

This, then, becomes the role model for young boys in the ghetto. These are the men they come to know, either in their homes or in the streets. Indeed, there is no lack of adult men to show a boy what men are like.[25] Although socialization is informal, it does take place in the ghetto as in other places in society. The boy develops a basic mode of operating sexually. Attitudes toward sexual relations are generally extremely competitive among one's own sex peers, and highly exploitative toward the opposite sex.[26] Emphasis is always placed on being "a man" in a society that suppresses black manhood.

Although the black woman, tired, desperate, and alone with a brood to look after, often declares black men no-good, she finds one thing far worse; and that is a sissy. A boy who is weak is often reprimanded by all the women in the household as well as his peers on the street.[27] If there is anything the ghetto culture demands it is obvious, clearly visible manhood. The boy must look, talk and act like a man, even though he may not feel like one — and usually he does not. How can he be in a society that denies black manhood?

Although black women who maintain households in which developing boys mature have little respect for weak men, they unwittingly succeed in molding generation after generation of men who are insecure about their manhood. The mere woman-dominated environment and the succession of "no-good" men drive the boy into the street where he can prove to his peers that even though he lives among women he is indeed a "real man."

Among adolescent and pre-adolescent black males, "playing the dozens" is a significant aspect of masculine protest. It is an informal game in which they make insulting remarks about each other's mothers and/or other females in the family (and sometimes about the father as well, if he happens to be a weakling). The remarks usually pertain to the sexual aspects of life. The boy who cannot retaliate with an equally derogatory and pornographic remark or who resorts to fighting loses the game. The game is also played by street corner adults and those in prisons and the military, although, perhaps, to a lesser degree. Psychologists generally view playing the dozens as an attempt to declare one's masculinity and emancipation from female domination.[28]

Conclusions

Although four personality components have been singled out for discussion, it seems quite clear that the basic and most debilitating variable of the black personality is self-hatred. It also seems obvious that self-hatred in black people is but the other side of the coin of racism in white people; and that creates the dilemma inherent in any attempt to rid blacks of their self-rejection. Basic to creating positive self-perceptions in black people is the elimination of racism in the American society. The prognosis for this is not good, for it, being based to a great degree on the white man's sexual jealousy of the black man, is not easy to get at, except through massive therapy for a whole nation of white people. Racism is thoroughly transmitted through all the institutions in society: the school, the church, government agencies, and the homes. So transmitted, it is a powerful, continuous force, constantly reinforced and passed on from one generation to another.

In order to excise self-hatred from black people, an effort more potent than the racist forces must be launched. Any such plan to inculcate racial pride must be systematically designed to neutralize and nullify the racist influences, which have had four hundred years of lead time. Although black rhetoric and racially chauvinistic dress and hair styles are signs in the right direction, these are but feeble attempts to do the massive job required. Young black children must be taught directly that they are black and proud; they must be taught the horrible aspects of their history. In so doing, it is necessary to teach them at the same time the injustices inflicted upon their forebears by whites. This may mean that some students so taught will come to hate whites more than they already do, at least initially; but this is the risk that must be taken, if blacks are to stop hating themselves, because of their color.

Further, it is not enough to teach the lesson once. It must be constantly reinforced. Black parents must come to know themselves; they must become proud of their heritage and communicate that pride to their children. Black men and women must be re-educated to help them understand what racism has done to their families. A massive program similar to that launched by the Muslims is needed in order to help black men and women to respect their roles as fathers and mothers, and as husbands and wives. Until such massive efforts are attempted and made to work, the present problems of the black personality in America will remain realities.

Notes

1. Clemmont E. Vontress, "The Negro Personality Reconsidered," *Journal of Negro Education* 35:210–217, Summer, 1966.
2. Albert Bandura, "Role of Imitation in Personality Development," *Journal of Nursing Education* 18:207–215, April, 1963.
3. Robert H. Dalton, *Personality and Social Interaction,* Boston: D.C. Heath and Co., 1961, p. 332.
4. O. Hobart Mowrer, "The Psychologist Looks at Language," *American Psychologist* 9:660–694, November, 1954.
5. Ruth Benedict, *Patterns of Culture,* New York: New American Library, 1934, p. 253.
6. Lawrence K. Frank, *Personality and Culture,* New York: Hinds, Hayden Eldredge, Inc., 1948, p. 4.
7. William H. Grier, and Price M. Cobbs, *Black Rage,* New York: Basic Books, Inc., 1968, pp. 27–28.
8. Ibid., p. 24.
9. Erich Fromm, "Selfishness and Self-Love," *Psychiatry* 2: 507–523, 1939.
10. Winthrop D. Jordan, *White Over Black,* Baltimore: Penguin Books, Inc., 1968, ch. 1.
11. Ibid., p. 155.
12. J. A. Rogers, *Sex and Race,* Vol. III, Helga M. Rogers, New York, 1944, p. 82.
13. Laurence F. Shaffer and Edward J. Shoben, Jr., *The Psychology of Adjustment,* 2nd ed., Houghton Mifflin Co., Boston, 1956, pp. 99–100.
14. St. Clair Drake, "The Social and Economic Status of the Negro in the United States," *Daedalus,* 94:771–814, Fall, 1965.
15. Clemmont E. Vontress, "The Negro Suburban Retreat and Its Implications," *The Chicago Jewish Forum,* 25:18–22, Fall, 1966.
16. Harold I. Lief, "An Atypical Stereotype of the Negroes' Social Worlds," *American Journal of Orthopsychiatry,* 32:86–88, January, 1962.
17. Robert J. Stoller, "The Sense of Maleness," *The Psychoanalytic Quarterly,* 34:207–218, April 1965.
18. Thomas Colley, "The Nature and Origins of Psychological Sexual Identity," *Psychological Review,* 66:165–177, May, 1959.
19. D. E. Payne and P. H. Mussen, "Parent-Child Relations and Father Identification Around Adolescent Boys," *Journal of Abnormal and Social Psychology,* 52:358–362, May, 1956.
20. Paul Mussen and Eldred Rutherford, "Parent-Relations and Parental Personality in Relation to Young Children's Sex-Role Preferences," *Child Development,* 34:598–607, September, 1963.
21. Payne and Mussen, op. cit.
22. Georgene H. Seward, *Sex and the Social Order,* New York: McGraw-Hill, 1946, pp. 153–154.

23. Payne and Mussen, op. cit.
24. Donn Byrne, *An Introduction to Personality,* New Jersey: Prentice-Hall, Inc., Englewood Cliffs, 1966, p. 449.
25. Ulf Hannerz, "Roots of Black Manhood," *Trans-action,* 6:13–21, October, 1969.
26. Lee Rainwater, "Some Aspects of Lower Class Sexual Behavior," *Journal of Social Issues,* 22:96–108, April, 1966.
27. Hannerz, op. cit.
28. Clemmont E. Vontress, "The Negro Speech Pattern: Index of Assimilation," *The Chicago Jewish Forum,* 25:267–270, Summer, 1967.

ROBERT STAPLES
CLEMMONT E. VONTRESS

A Black Scholar Debate

A Response to Clemmont Vontress

The June, 1971 issue of *The Black Scholar* carried a number of excellent articles on the black male, a subject greatly in need of the black perspective. Among those articles was one by Clemmont E. Vontress entitled "The Black Male Personality." Upon first reading it, I was impressed with how he attacked white racism and the white man's sexual hangups for making black men insecure about their masculinity, creating self-hatred in them, and generating all sort of erratic and compulsive elements in their behavioral patterns. With a second reading and more profound contemplation, I suddenly realized that here was the Moynihan report reincarnated: another scholar, this time a black one, had introduced a brief indictment of slavery and racism to justify his subsequent slander of the black population.

While I usually refrain from open disagreement with a fellow black scholar, the issues raised by Vontress are too important to ignore. I, of course, have been on the receiving end of such criticism as the May, 1970 issue of *The Black Scholar* which contained the article "Black Women and Women's Liberation" by Linda La Rue. In her article, Miss La Rue falsely labeled me as America's number one black male chauvinist for the views I expressed in my article, "The Myth of the Black Matriarchy" which appeared in the February, 1970 issue of *The Black Scholar.* The La Rue–Staples controversy reached across the continent and I received numerous letters from black male chauvinists encouraging me to stand my ground. One interesting aspect of this controversy is that I wrote a letter to *The Black Scholar* (June 1970) denying the charges she had made against me.

Reprinted by permission from *The Black Scholar* 3:3 (1971), pp. 42–49.

Instead of responding to my denial, she subsequently reprinted the article in a white magazine which repeated the same allegations.

In light of this experience, I wish to make quite clear my objections to the Vontress article. They are both methodological and ideological. The methodological objections refer to the broad statements he made about the pathological black male personality without adequate validation. Ideologically, I fail to see how delineating the host of behavioral anomalies black people supposedly suffer from will achieve our liberation. Additionally, I dislike his apolitical analysis of our problems and even more his grotesque solution to those problems.

Examining the Vontress study, we find that he begins with the psychological view of the human personality. Already, it is clear that white referents will be used to explain black personalities. Vontress trots out the normative social science models to explain the black psyche. In my article which preceded his, I had elaborated on how social science research is a form of ideology, a propaganda device which functions to rationalize racist institutions and practices. This was particularly true, I said, of the stereotype of black males as psychologically impotent and castrated. Ergo, nine pages later we catch Brother Vontress in the act of resurrecting these theories to show how psychologically deranged we are. If it was not bad enough that white behavioral scientists have labeled us psychological misfits, we now have to suffer the additional burden of reading it in black journals. To illustrate, let us examine, with care, exactly how Brother Vontress arrived at his conclusions.

He begins by outlining the four components of the black male personality. Curiously enough, none of them relates to the strengths of black men that have allowed them to withstand the virulent racism and exploitation they have encountered for four hundred years. Instead, he describes self-hatred as the most basic variable of the black personality. He states: "Black people in general, have unconsciously identified with their oppressors, and consequently, we have developed contempt and hatred of ourselves. As products of a racist society, we have acquired the same cultural attributes as have whites. Included among these are anti-black sentiments."

Indeed! And what evidence does Brother Vontress have for this assertion? Paradoxically, despite the plethora of weak and unsubstantiated research showing blacks full of self-hatred, Vontress cites none of it. The logic of his position can be summed up as: if white hate us, we must hate ourselves. All this, of course, occurs on the unconscious level and is difficult to empirically validate.

One can reject this assumption for two reasons. First, it is common logic that people collectively, do not hate themselves, consciously or unconsciously. Inevitably, cultural formations emerge to give people a sense of worthiness. Obviously, blacks realize that they occupy a lower caste position in this white-dominated society. But, it does not follow that they will supinely accept this subordinate position as indicative of their self-worth. If so, why all the black protests against their condition since they arrived on these shores? If they accepted their oppressors' valuations of their worth, acquiescence to their low status should ensue.

Secondly, if one accepts the axiom that we tend to see ourselves as others see us, there is no definitive evidence that blacks use whites as significant others to pro-

duce what Charles Horton Cooley called the "looking glass self." Instead of directing hatred inward, blacks become part of a solidarity group which helps them to
cope with the views and actions of the fascist society. The black male can rely upon
a group which possesses a well-articulated ideology which explains his subordinate
position in the society. Or, in other words, there are positive elements in the black
community to counteract the negative views of the oppressive majority.

An article by McCarthy and Yancey, "Uncle Tom and Mr. Charlie: A Review
of the Negro-American's Self-Esteem" (*American Journal of Sociology*, November,
1970) found that the evidence supporting the theory of black self-hatred was unanimous in its ambiguity and is generally of less than desirable quality. A common
technique used in psychological studies of blacks is to compare their indices of
self-hatred with an ideal personality state. That is, the Afro-American's self-esteem
is measured by what it should be, not by the prevailing psychological state of
other groups.

The second component of Vontress' black male personality is composed of erratic behavior. Here, he refers to the black male's use of alcohol and drugs to
narcotize the psychological effects of his victimization. This is especially true, he
says, of the lower class black community. Referring to the McCarthy and Yancey
study again, we find that with controlled comparisons of suicide, mental health
and alcohol rates, in each case the black rate is lower than the white rate. The
differences are especially great at the lower status levels, while among the middle-
class groups the racial difference is relatively small.

Going on to the third component of Vontress' black male personality, we encounter black compulsiveness. This refers to an individual's tendency to be perfect,
constricted and uptight. As an example of this, he alludes to middle-class blacks
who identify with whites and reject blacks. This is an area on which we can agree,
since E. Franklin Frazier and Nathan Hare earlier demonstrated the validity of
this thesis. It is probably not as true today as in past years.

But, Vontress is not satisfied with approximating some aspect of the black reality. He then proceeds to include all black folks in on this variable. He states, many
"colored" people also live and behave in a manner which they perceive to be acceptable to whites. As a result, they experience terrible damage to their self-esteem,
freedom of expression and creativity. According to him, blacks are resigned and
apathetic, living lives which are stereotyped, ritualistic, and minimally expressive
of their genuine feelings.

One can only wonder where Vontress got this idea from. What group in this
country has produced all the freedom of expression and creativity this society has
ever known? Where does he think the word "soul" came from? Furthermore, what
group is he comparing us with? Or, are we being compared again with some ideal
state of affairs? Vontress would even find it difficult to marshal white support for
this notion.

Nonetheless, let us look at Vontress' fourth component of the black male personality. Perhaps he plans to redeem us at the end. It appears not. Vontress has
dredged up the familiar spectre of the black man's masculinity. According to him,
black men exaggerate the most obvious, external signs of masculinity because this
society has not allowed them to assume the "normal" masculine role.

Not surprisingly, he cites all the decadent literature purporting to show that in every black man there is a woman trying to get out. He notes the prevalence of the female-headed household among blacks and concludes that they unwittingly succeed in molding generation after generation of men who are insecure about their manhood. Since I have already stated that white models of manhood cannot be used to evaluate black masculinity, I will not pursue this matter much further. Suffice it to say that Vontress' evidence is no more convincing than his white predecessors.

For instance, he cites some unnamed psychologist's views that playing the dozens is an attempt to declare one's masculinity and emancipation from female domination. Or, in other words, one man's dozen player is another man's latent homosexual. As with most psychological theory, it is an interpretation of unconscious motives. Since it deals with unconscious drives, it cannot be empirically certified. Therefore, we have to take the psychologist's word for it.

Also cited in this determination of the black male's personality traits is the emphasis on sexual relations to prove black manhood. Hence, Vontress begins to make moral judgments. Are we to assume that a man should only have so much sex, and all after that is an attempt to prove his masculinity? If so, how much sex is enough? Or, if not the quantity of sex relations, is it the number of sexual partners? If monogamy is an index of normal manhood and polygamy an example of exaggerated masculinity, what does this say about the seventy per cent of the world's societies which permit polygamy? What does it say about the monarchs in the Middle East with their harems? In a sexually healthy society, people just might realize that men have pre-marital, marital and extra-marital sex relations simply because they enjoy it. Only the sexually frustrated need look for other reasons.

Reviewing the Vontress article, one can perceive the subtle danger of his kind of reasoning. In what may be a sincere attempt to show the negative consequences of racist victimization, he has, in his description of the Afro-American's psychological and social adaptations to his oppressed position, provided scientific credibility for many of the prevailing white views of black people. His views may be very compatible with the political strategy that seeks a solution to the problems black people face by changing individuals rather than oppressive institutions.

It has been acceptable to denigrate poor blacks as pathological adapters to socio-economic circumstances if the burden is initially placed upon the savagery and oppression against them that happened one hundred years ago. This allows white America to escape trial for its crimes of today. Their theme is: blacks were not initially born inferior, they have been made inferior by generations of harsh treatment. While the theory may be different, the results are the same: although piously claiming all men to be equal, the society still regards blacks as inferior.

Whereas the destructive psychological effects of colonialism and oppression have been pointed out by Fanon and others, they at least advocated a political solution to these problems. Throughout his analysis, Vontress eschews a political analysis of the debilitating effects of racism on the black male personality. Instead he speaks of sexual jealousy of the white man as the basic reason for racism in American society; a problem which requires massive therapy for a whole nation of white people.

Considering this solution somewhat impractical, he suggests a program similar to the Muslims to aid black men and women· to respect their roles as fathers and mothers, and as husbands and wives. Or, in other words, the same old refrain: the way to liberate black men is by subjugating black women. It is quite clear that Vontress has accepted the fallacy of the black matriarchy and emasculated black male theory. His acceptance of these myths and stereotypes have shaped the solution he advocates for the problem he defines.

If we put black women in their "proper" role, we will still have capitalism and racism with us. What we will not have is that sector of our population, that has been so instrumental in our survival, fighting alongside us. Fighting oppression with oppression seems to be a foolhardy thing to do.

If we are lucky, the defection of Brother Vontress from the ranks of the revolutionary black scholars may be only temporary. As Fanon once observed, the intellectual does eventually return home to the masses. We cannot continue to depend on and imitate white ideologists when we need a revolutionary black ideology for the liberation of our people. My critique of the Vontress article is made in the spirit of helping us achieve this goal.

Won't you come home, Brother Vontress, and assist us in this task?

A Response to Robert Staples

Before responding to specific points on which Staples says he disagrees with me, I would like to make some general comments about his reactions to my article. First of all, he apologizes for his "open disagreement with a fellow black scholar." This he need not do, for differing with one's academic peers is in the nature of scholarship, which may be defined as a bold search for truth. Thus, hopefully the scholar, whatever color he happens to be, pursues truth not propaganda, no matter what topic is being analyzed. Each scholar must or should be true to himself. If he is an opportunist, jumping on whatever bandwagon happens to be passing, he will be found out for what he really is — an academic quack or charlatan.

Staples also states that he does not like my "apolitical analysis of our problems." What he means by "apolitical" is not clear. However, I assume that he is suggesting that I did not take sides, racio-politically speaking, and that I tended to be objective in my discussion and allowed the chips to fall where they may. If that is what he means, then I stand guilty. There is no place in scholarship for propaganda, no matter how just or important selective causes may be.

Brother Staples further indicates that I have defected from the "ranks of the revolutionary black scholars." It may be of some interest to him to know that I have never declared myself to be in the ranks in the first place. I have resisted the temptation to position myself on the black ideological continuum, after having discovered that many self-appointed black revolutionaries are phonies. I have always felt that one's deeds speak louder than his words. I, for one, have never gone in for the "I am blacker than you are black" rhetoric. All too often the black dude who goes about screaming about how black and proud and beautiful he is has a white wife or girlfriend. In essence, his deeds contradict his words. In a nutshell, deliver me from phonies, whoever they are.

I would like to react now to specific points on which Staples declares that he disagrees with me. First, he finds a psychological view of human personality objectionable. There's nothing wrong with that, since there are several theories to explain human behavior. Hall and Lindzey[1] discuss over twelve theories of personality in their classic work. Although one may reject a "pure" psychological theory, one is obliged to accept at least a socio-psychological explanation of personality development. Individuals react to their social setting, and their reactions involve perception, a psychological phenomenon.

If Staples finds unacceptable a psychological discussion of the black male personality, why doesn't he formulate a counter theory? This, he fails to do. He rejects my theoretical formulations, but fails to erect his own.

Staples agonizes because I indicated that blacks identify with their oppressors and therefore hate themselves. He wants to know what evidence I have to support my assertion. I would call his attention to Gordon W. Allport's *The Nature of Prejudice*,[2] a classic work, which indicates that oppressed people, wherever they may be, react in predictable fashion. One may cite Jews in Hitler's Germany who pretended that they were not Jewish and therefore treated their fellow Jews more harshly than did the gentiles; one may cite also inmates in penal institutions, many of whom assume the airs of the "screws," especially when they consider that by so doing, their lot will be made easier. In other words, the phenomenon of the oppressed identifying with the oppressors is hardly new. I am surprised that Brother Staples has never heard of it.

Staples declares that "it is common logic that people collectively do not hate themselves, consciously or unconsciously." He feels that cultural heritage ("formations") give people a sense of worth. That people reject themselves as a group is fairly well supported by research and observation. Perhaps the most extensive and sophisticated support has been collected by Safilios-Rothschild[3] and Wright[4] who analyze how the physically and psychologically disabled react to their stigma status. Additional light is shed on the phenomenon by *Perspectives on Human Deprivations*.[5]

To be sure, some minority groups are able to endure their stigma status more than others. In the American society, it appears that their threshold of endurance of stigma status is related to several exclusion variables. Color, curl of the hair, and previous servitude (slave heritage) are primary ones; low socio-economic status, inferior education, unique language patterns, and ethnic personality characteristics may be categorized as secondary exclusion variables. Groups feel stigmatized to the extent that these selective variables operate singly or interactively against them, causing them to be rejected by the dominant group.

Minority groups which have kept their heritage (language, religion, customs, etc.) intact are more able to withstand exclusion in a hostile environment than those who have been stripped of everything which causes a people to be proud of itself. Such, unfortunately, was exactly what happened to Africans who were abducted to the Americas. On the other hand, American Jews, armed with a religion, a language of their own, and customs which antedate Christ, have been able to surmount their self-rejection, except during times of great persecution.

The basic fallacy of Staples' argument against self-rejection in the black personality is his failure to examine the phenomenon globally. That is, he should consider self-hatred as a human phenomenon first and secondarily as a black experience. However, in order to do this, it is imperative to accept the fact that blacks are human beings first and individuals of African descent secondly.

Staples takes some exception to the second component of the black male personality which I discussed: erratic behavior. Here his disagreement is less intense, probably because he realizes he is on very weak grounds. It is a well established psychological principle that when the human organism is frustrated, it resorts to varied responses, in order to relieve the annoying stimuli. Blacks employ a variety of mechanisms to endure their minority status in the American society. Alcoholism, drug abuse, physical attack on one's fellows, sexual promiscuity, suicide, conspicuous consumption, rapping to the delight of whites — these are but a few of the defense mechanisms used by Americans of African descent to endure their exclusion status in the United States.

Citing only one study, McCarthy and Yancey's, to support the contention that blacks experience fewer psychological problems than whites is sophomoric. It is almost impossible to ascertain the rate of psychological morbidity among blacks, because they are less apt to come to the attention of authorities. Whites expect blacks to act "strange," whereas Caucasians are called in for observation when they manifest deviant behavior. Blindness to psychologically erratic behavior among blacks helps to explain why an inordinate percentage of blacks are in penal institutions today. They are more apt to be placed in penitentiaries when they are accused of crimes, while whites are committed to facilities for the psychologically disabled.

Alas, Staples agrees with me on one point: that a basic component of the black male personality is compulsiveness. Even so, he appears to do so reluctantly, calling attention to the fact that E. Franklin Frazier and Nathan Hare have already cited the phenomenon. For Frazier and Hare, I am indeed grateful. Otherwise, I would have been taken to task on this point, too.

To be sure, there is little indication that compulsivity in Americans of African descent has lessened in recent years. Blacks still ape a white image in their dress, their behavior, and in their general life style. There is at the same time pervasive in the American society what has been characterized as a "do-your-own-thing" syndrome. On the surface, the manifested behavior appears to be a flaunting defiance of the middle-class establishment life style. If one examines the manifestation more carefully, it becomes obvious that much of the display is reaction formation and attention-getting behavior. In the case of whites, it is the establishment's attention they seek; with blacks, it is the attention of whites in general they so desperately want.

In general, however, reaction formation and attention seeking behavior are defensive mechanisms employed by only a minority of Americans of African descent. The majority of blacks still live and behave in such a way as to gain the respect and trust of those in control — whites. This is especially true of those who want to get ahead in the system — and that includes a majority, in spite of the rhetoric of the vocal minority.

I often use the umbrella concept, *American of African descent*, in order to isolate psychologically at least three groups of people who used to be lumped together and labelled "Negroes." Blacks are those who declare they have gotten themselves together; that they know not only who they are now but who their enemy is as well. About ten per cent of the African descent group in this country are potentially bright, urban rather than rural, more apt to be male than female, and are found on predominantly white campuses (usually in black cocoons) rather than on black ones.

Negroes, the silent majority of people of African descent, are individuals who try to "make it" within the system. They are generally fairly well educated, hard working, and usually do not dress and behave in such a way as to upset the white establishment on whom they depend for their livelihood. Although some blacks are quick to label Negroes as Uncle Toms, the fact is that most blacks, especially young college students, depend on Negroes in the person of their parents for much of their support.

Colored people are individuals for whom the so-called Civil Rights Movement has meant absolutely nothing. Often living and working in close proximity with whites on whom they must depend for a living, they dare not admit to themselves the deep hatred they have for those who determine the depth and breadth of their very existence.

Although these three groups exist in the same physical environment, their perception of it differs, mainly because of differences in age, geography, sex, education, and general life style. Thus, it is difficult to analyze in the space allocated here, the overall reactions of Americans of African descent to their existence in a frustrating environment. I am sure that Brother Staples must realize this.

Staples' refutation is somewhat tenable up to the point where he explodes over my discussion of the fourth component of the black male personality: masculine protest. Here, he loses his cool when he declares that I cite "all the decadent literature purporting to show that in every black man there is a woman trying to get out." Nowhere in the article did I refer to authorities who describe the black male thus. In fact, I tried to make clear that I was using the concept *masculinity* with its broadest connotation to refer to man's social role, not to the restricted biological one which Staples immediately misinterpreted and seized upon. In the American society, a man, no matter what color he happens to be, is expected by the dictates of societal norms to fulfill certain masculine roles. Some of these are basic to being a man and some are only peripheral to his masculine identity. A man's basic roles include providing for and protecting his family. The black male has never been able to fulfill these and other vital masculine demands, because white men as potent controllers of white society, primarily through economic disenfranchisement, deny him his manhood, while simultaneously catering to his women, not only through physical gestures, but also by allowing them economic and social advantage over black males.

The black male finds himself in a situation where he must prove himself not only to white society, but to his black women as well. Stripped of his economic and social leverage, he is left with nothing but his body, his biological manhood, if you will. This, he uses to prove himself to his women; but without social manhood to accompany his biological efforts, he is left high and dry.

In sum, Staples goes off on an emotional binge and reads too much into my discussion of masculine protest. Since he got carried away so, I am prepared to say that, although there is little empirical evidence directly related to black males, it seems tenable, in light of general psychological insight, to conclude that social and economic impotence leads to a host of psychological problems. I would not go so far as to say that homosexuality, overt or covert, is one of them, although it seems logical to accept such a possibility, on the basis of the limited understanding which psychologists have of its etiology. Also, Staples goes too far when he suggests that I maintain that playing the dozens has some direct relationship with sexual perversion. To cite it as an example of masculine protest does not imply *ipso facto* that it masks latent sexual confusion, although often it does.

In general, it appears that Brother Staples read my article with a psychological set which prevented him from receiving the message intended. I therefore invite him to read it again with a more open mind.

Finally, it seems crucial that people of African descent stop lying to themselves. Severe problems face us in our struggle for freedom and justice; but we can never begin to attain our goal, until we start seeing straight. We have got to call a spade a spade, no matter how much it may hurt. We cannot begin to solve our problems until we know what they are. It seems to me that the role of the black scholar is to set an example in terms of seeing straight. If we lie to ourselves, then we lie to others. This we cannot afford to do, especially to white Americans who in fact, because of their reactions to us, have created the black personality in the first place.

Right on, Brother Staples! You rap beautifully.

Notes

1. Calvin S. Hall and Gardner Lindzey, *Theories of Personality,* John Wiley & Sons, Inc., New York: 1957.
2. Gordon W. Allport, *The Nature of Prejudice,* Addison-Wesley, Cambridge, Massachusetts: 1954.
3. Constantina Safilios-Rothschild, *The Sociology and Social Psychology of Disability and Rehabilitation,* Random House, New York: 1970.
4. Beatrice A. Wright, *Physical Disability — A Psychological Approach,* Harper & Brothers, New York: 1960.
5. U.S. Department of Health, Education and Welfare, *Perspectives on Human Deprivations Biological, Psychological, and Sociological.* U.S. Government Printing Office, Washington, D.C.: 1970.

8

WORK

To assess the consequences of various kinds of work on the social personalities of the employees, some criteria and method must be developed to distinguish between the individual's personality before taking a particular job and the subsequent impact of the occupational role.

For example, psychologist Robert Mills's personality profile of the typical policeman, based on the clinical analysis of psychological tests, includes such trait descriptions as exhibitionistic, authoritarian, extrapunitive, nonintrospective, energetic, enterprising, and gregarious. To what extent does this reflect the characteristics of those most attracted to police work? To what extent does it reflect the selective recruitment and training of the police, the definition of their role by authorities in the institution, or the effects of the general conditions and peculiar experiences of the job?

To make any precise determination of the specific effects of the occupational role on the social personality of the employee, we would have to parcel out the relative effects of all these other relevant factors. Certainly, today's employers are concerned with the practical implications of this issue as they strive to develop measures that will help them find the best fit between the demands of the role and the personal resources of applicants for the job. Organizations have to protect themselves from the consequences not only of placing too much responsibility in the hands of less competent employees, but also of "underutilizing" other employees. Resentment bred from the frustration of feeling one's talents are being ignored is the principal explanation offered for the several billion dollars in employee theft recorded each year.

The whole burden of recruitment, evaluation, and assignment does not fall exclusively on the organization, however. To some extent, knowledge of selection criteria, work conditions, and rewards enter into the candidate's original decision to apply for a particular position. According to Blau and others (1956, p. 542), "The social structure affects occupational choice in two analytically distinct respects, as the matrix of social experiences which channel the personality development of potential workers, and as the conditions of occupational opportunity which limit the realization of their choices." The occupational choice an individual makes will depend on the information he has about the technical (achieved) or social (ascribed) qualifications required by occupational alternatives and his evaluation of the rewards offered. The information held by the individual is especially important as the demand for specific skills can change rapidly.

Occupational choice, then, represents "a compromise between preferences for and expectations of being able to get into various occupations" (p. 542). Evaluation and compromise goes on throughout life and influences future occupational decision making just as previous occupational commitments affect the range of alternatives later available. The entire process is conditioned by generational changes in the rewards of particular occupations, in the cultural values by which such rewards are assessed, and in the structure of the economy.

The structure of the economy is important not only because of the changing demand for skills, but because of the relative distribution of opportunities across social strata. An individual's race or SES will greatly influence his opportunity to acquire certain technical qualifications requiring formalized training. It will also determine whether he satisfies the nonfunctional social role requirements (for example, racial, ethnic, and class background, appearance, and "social" behavior). Therefore, we must assess the nature of the compromise each individual makes and its consequences for him.

The same occupational role (with the same work conditions and rewards) should have different effects on different people, depending on their knowledge, preferences, expectations, intelligence, need for achievement, and other relevant factors. Examinations of the differential effects of the same occupational roles on different people are practically nonexistent, however. Most research in this field studies the comparative effects on the personality patterns (such as attitudes, beliefs, and ideology) of categories of people performing a few selected occupational roles.

Changes in the Structure of Occupational Roles

To appreciate how and why the nature and conditions of work might affect the social personality of the individual, one must first recognize how dramatically the division of labor in the United States has been altered by the modern revolution in technology. While the proportion of the total labor force engaged in skilled labor (approximately 11–13 per cent) and service work (approximately 10–12 per cent) has remained relatively unaffected, this has not been true for other occupations. The proportion engaged in unskilled labor declined from about 12 per cent to below 6 per cent between 1870 and 1970, while the demand for operatives doubled from 9 per cent to 18 per cent. The biggest changes have occurred in the farm and non-manual categories. The proportion of farmers in the nation's work force has fallen dramatically from about 50 per cent in 1870 to 22 per cent in 1930 to less than 5 per cent in 1970. On the other hand, the proportion of professional, technical, and managerial employees has increased from 4 per cent in 1870 to 14 per cent in 1930 to 25 per cent in 1970. The proportion of white collar and sales personnel has increased from 4 per cent in 1870 to 14 per cent in 1930 to 25 per cent in 1970. Over the years, then, the place of work for most Americans has increasingly shifted from the family farm, shop, or store to the corporate office or factory.

According to Mills (1951), the loss of skill due to the technologizing and rationalizing of work has affected men at all levels — from laborers and operatives to white collar workers. He states (p. 220):

> Craftsmanship as a fully idealized model of work gratification involves six major features: There is no ulterior motive in work other than the product being made and the processes of its creation. The details of daily work are meaningful because they are not detached in the worker's mind from the product of the work. The worker is free to control his own working action. The craftsman is thus able to learn from his work; and to use and develop his capacities and skills in its prosecution. There is no split of work and play, or work and culture. The craftsman's way of livelihood determines and infuses his entire mode of living.

In the West, the Renaissance view of work as intrinsically meaningful, creative activity gave way to the Protestant view of work as a means to religious salvation. Under bureaucratically administered capitalist enterprise, neither conception of work has prevailed. The mechanization of labor at the blue-collar level and bureaucratization at the white-collar level have substantially reduced the opportunities for developing and exercising skill as well as for understanding and meaningfully participating in the whole productive process. Worse yet, it has leveled men into faceless, interchangeable automatons, whose very personalities have become commodities to be bought, sold, manipulated, and exploited by scientific managers.

As a consequence, work and the rest of man's cultural life, particularly play, have become sharply split. Work has become an unsatisfactory means to make the money with which to acquire the necessities of life and, perhaps, also enjoy mass leisure. According to Mills, the mass leisure that characterizes American social life astonishes, excites, and distracts but does not enlarge reason or feeling or allow spontaneous dispositions to unfold creatively. Unlike work it is glossy, colorful, and fantastic. Like work, it is remote, superficial, and uninvolving.

Alienated Labor

Karl Marx was, perhaps, the first major social theorist to express deep concern about the personal consequences of the "dehumanization" of work through the reduction of labor to a commodity under large-scale capitalist enterprise. Marx (1962 edition) analyzed the character and consequences of what he called "alienated labor," starting with the premise upon which capitalism rests — private ownership of the means of production. He asserted that labor in such a political economy alienates man from the product of his labor and from nature, mankind, and himself. He is alienated from the product of his labor because an increasingly fragmented division of labor substantially reduces each individual's role in the whole productive process. Furthermore, the product which results, in part, from his labor doesn't belong to him and even becomes an antagonistic force by increasing the property and power of the capitalists who have control over him.

Man becomes alienated from nature insofar as he ceases to relate to it as a world of sensuous experience and a vital source of the means for man's physical subsistence; rather, he learns to regard it as simply raw material to be transformed into commodities. He becomes alienated from mankind as a species in that alienated labor "makes some cold and abstract notion of individual life and toil into the goal of the entire species." Labor becomes a mere "means of satisfying his drive for physical existence" rather than the essence of life itself — the free, conscious re-creation of the objective world in accordance with the laws of beauty.

Man becomes alienated from himself in much the same way. Basically, the work he performs is not personal and does not allow for the free development and expression of his physical and mental capacities. Instead, it is physically exhausting and mentally debasing. This poignantly critical theme of Marx has been more recently expressed in the perceptive fulminations of Harvey Swados (1962, p. 111):

> The plain truth is that factory work is degrading. It is degrading to any man who ever dreams of doing something worthwhile with his life; and it is about time we faced the fact. The more a man is exposed to middle class values, the more sophisticated he becomes and the more production-line work is degrading to him. The immigrant who slaved in the poorly lighted, foul, vermin-ridden sweatshop found his work less degrading than the native-born high school graduate who reads . . . the funnies and works in a fluorescent factory with ticker-tape production-control machines. For the immigrant laborer, even the one who did not dream of socialism, his long hours were going to buy him freedom. For the factory worker of the fifties, his long hours are going to buy him commodities . . . and maybe reduce a few of his debts.
>
> Almost without exception, the men with whom I worked on the assembly line last year felt like trapped animals. . . . They were sick of being pushed around by harried foremen (themselves more pitied than hated), sick of working like blinkered donkeys, sick of being dependent for their livelihood on a maniacal production-merchandising setup, sick of working in a place where there was no spot to relax during the twelve-minute rest period.

One need not concede the existence of biological human needs to worry legitimately about the effects of various kinds of work on man's psychological well-being. Such worry may be about the fit between an individual's earlier socialization experiences and later occupational demands or about the potential psychological growth which might occur under more ideal work conditions.

Though Swados's observations reveal insights, the first two selections in this chapter, by Lewis Lipsitz and William Sexton, are more systematic efforts to measure the satisfactions and complaints of different grades of industrial laborers about the conditions of their work, as well as to determine how such conditions affect the social personalities of the workers.

In the first article, Lipsitz explores the relationship between type of work and social and political attitudes. He compares three grades of industrial workers and uncovers systematic differences between the men at each job level in their satisfactions, complaints, and general attitudes. He also finds that most members of all three groups share several basic orientations toward big business, human nature, and political participation. The potential effects of very low level labor is a paramount problem:

> Men in a work environment they cannot control may be to some unknown degree damaged in their sense of mastery, and this damage may render them less capable of coping with and altering an environment they find unsatisfactory. To the extent that such damage occurs, men become victims rather than creators. To the extent that work life contributes to such incapacities, it needs improvement in modern societies. Industrial democracy may yet prove to be a prerequisite to political and social democracy.

William Sexton examines this relationship — between degree of job structure and degree of individual need satisfaction — as well as the relationship of these two variables with the degree of individual effectiveness at work and comes up with some surprising conclusions. Sexton finds no significant negative correlation between job structure and need satisfaction; no significant positive correlation between job structure and individual effectiveness; and no significant negative correlation between individual effectiveness and need satisfaction. The concept of tight organizational controls resulting in increased worker effectiveness at the cost of personal need fulfillment is refuted.

Sexton concludes that, given the "dramatic" differences in intelligence, educational level, and cultural background, it seems "presumptuous for the academician" to "stand back and tell the line worker that his job is boring and monotonous." Sexton conjectures that line workers may have a "need for highly predictable patterns of interaction, a stable work environment, and freedom from the personal challenge of the unusual or unfamiliar," which is satisfied in their present work situation. Furthermore, precisely because the work demands so little attention, the individual is "largely free to socialize with fellow workers and to initiate his own activities autonomously."

Sexton notes that other researchers also have failed to find any relationship between organizational constraints and individual need satisfaction. But other studies have produced quite different results. For example, in his study of industrial workers, Vroom (1962) found that persons ego-involved in their jobs are given higher job performance ratings than those less involved. Moreover, within this group of ego-involved workers, job satisfaction and satisfaction with self are positively related to the amount of opportunity for self-expression in their jobs.

Baumgartel and Goldstein's panel study of airline mechanics (1961) before and after moving to a new plant shows similar results. Despite the improved working conditions of the new plant (such as "air conditioning, more work space, less physical strain, and a greatly improved aesthetic appearance"), there was a marked breakdown in interpersonal relationships" and "consistently increased dissatisfaction with, and lower evaluations of the skills and abilities of foremen and general foremen" (p. 37).

The authors attribute these outcomes to a "loss of status" experienced by the workers as a result of the move. The employees were permitted no real participation in the decision to relocate, yet had to make basic adjustments (such as traveling farther to work or, in some cases, changing residences). The new jobs were more restricted and the production process was more controlled, which meant less variety and skill in their work and more formality in their supervisory relations, a situation apparently conducive to their low morale and angry feelings toward supervisors.

Social Psychological Reactions to Work in Bureaucracies

Shifting our analysis from working-class labor to middle-class occupations, Merton (1957), like Mills, has also identified bureaucratization as the process which has led to the control of man by his social relations to the instruments of production. As Merton explains (p. 197),

> More and more people discover that to work, they must be employed. For to work, one must have tools and equipment. And the tools and equipment are increasingly available only in bureaucracies, private or public. Consequently, one must be employed by the bureaucracies in order to have access to tools in order to work in order to live.

Merton's essay, "Bureaucratic Structure and Personality," does not include the effects of working in a bureaucracy on the personality of the worker. Rather, Merton describes how the bureaucracy's formalized norms of impersonality become internalized by functionaries in their role performance and how such indiscriminate conformity to categorical rules acquires a value of its own which can lead to inefficient misapplications. In short, means become transformed into ends, leading to a rigid formalism in the behavior of the bureaucrat that sometimes conflicts with the goals of the organization and often gets mistaken for arrogance by clients pleading special problems.

It must be conceded that, at least in more differentiated clerical, managerial, and professional jobs, the demands and obligations of the occupational role may be interpreted differently by different individuals. As Levinson (1959) indicates, each case has varying degrees of fit between the diverse demands placed upon the individual, the resources made available to him for meeting these demands, and the personal way in which the individual himself defines his commitments and priorities. Levinson explains (p. 177):

> Role-definition may be seen from one perspective as an aspect of personality. It represents the individual's attempt to structure his social reality, to define his place within it, and to guide his search for meaning and gratification. Role-definition is, in this sense, an ego achievement — a reflection of the person's capacity to resolve conflicting demands, to utilize existing opportunities and create new ones, to find some balance between stability and change, conformity and autonomy, the ideal and the feasible in a complex environment.

Levinson argues (p. 177) that most organizational settings have several modal patterns of role performance, rather than a single dominant type because, except in highly structured occupational roles with very coherent requirements, "role-performance will reflect the individual's attempts at choice and compromise among diverse external and internal forces."

These qualifications notwithstanding, Bensman and Rosenberg (1960) have carried Merton's analysis a step farther by outlining some consequences the "negative tendencies" in bureaucracy might have for some workers. To play his role effectively, a bureaucrat must pay a "heavy social and psychological price," avoiding conflict at all costs. Bensman and Rosenberg state (p. 182): "Up and down the line, large-scale organization puts a high premium on muted discord and surface harmony, as it does on everyone's being likeable and pleasant."

Much more than this is required, however, if one is ambitious for success. In this case, the up-and-coming young bureaucrat must undergo thorough "self-rationalization." As the authors explain (p. 183), "Self-rationalization appears when the official begins to view himself as a merchandisable product which he must market and package like any other merchandisable product. . . . The bureaucratic personality is molded out of available raw materials, shaped to meet the fluctuating demands of the market." The individual thus organizes his presentation of self (such as grooming, dress, and manner) as well as his private life (friends and associates, social activities, and family life) around the demands of the bureaucratic marketplace. This analysis, of course, would apply much more to middle- and upper middle-class professionals, managers, and technocrats pursuing personal careers than to lower level clerks in large public or private bureaucracies.

Nevertheless, all who work in bureaucracies, according to the authors, experience various pressures and tensions. Some personal pathologies often resulting from these pressures are a reduced capacity for spontaneous and genuine emotion in the interest of preserving a bureaucratic mask of controlled civility; a deep feeling of loneliness and isolation stemming from the awareness that the institutional emphasis on togetherness, other-directedness, teamwork, and cooperation makes it difficult for members to relate to associates in anything other than a deceptively shallow way; the loss of personal identity through overidentification with the organization and its rules; and acute feelings of powerlessness caused either by low rank or by the fragmentation of work roles so that "no one person can envisage the total task" (p. 191) and his role in its accomplishment.

One potential reaction to this feeling of powerlessness is resentment, which Bensman and Rosenberg define (p. 191) as "that peculiar emotion which begins with striving and is heightened by impotence." According to them, it leads to "disidentification" from the bureaucracy, which in its more advanced stage may be expressed in the form of sabotaging one's superiors or the task at hand. Another response to powerlessness is to become a submissive "yes" man who, for all intents and purposes, fails to provide his superior with the information he needs to make and revise important decisions. Still another is to become a ruthless seeker after higher position in the authoritarian hierarchy.

The general depersonalization caused by the demands of bureaucracy has been cited frequently in literature critical of modern American life. Whyte (1956), Riesman (1953), and others have waxed profusely on the dilemma of contemporary man: dehumanized, other-directed, enslaved by the organization, and manipulated by the mass media. Yet, as Harold Rosenberg (1959) argues, such broad invectives often smack more of sermonizing for their particular milieu of "organized" professional intellectuals about abandoning the Protestant ethic and rugged individualism, rather than social analysis valid for all classes of people in the United States. Gathering hard evidence to support such a thesis is still required.

The selection by Aiken and Hage represents such an attempt. They compare sixteen welfare organizations to analyze the relationship between two types of alienation (from work and from expressive relationships) and two structural properties of organizations (centralization and formalization). Aiken and Hage discover that alienation from work and from expressive relationships, in fact, is more prevalent in highly centralized and highly formalized organizations. More specifically, participation in decision making, job codification, and rule observation are the variables most closely correlated with work alienation, whereas rule observation is the single best predictor of alienation from expressive relations.

Generalized Consequences of Work Role

Even if the relationship between occupational role and personal satisfaction could be conclusively determined, however, the larger question of the generalized consequences of satisfaction or frustration at work would still remain. Melvin Seeman attempts to measure the social consequences (that is, political hostilities, frenetic leisure, social movements, race cleavages, and the like) of alienated labor using a sample of several hundred male workers in Sweden.

Seeman concludes that, although some work was clearly more alienated (that is, "unrewarding in its own right") than other work, little evidence indicates that alienated work has the generalized consequences often imputed to it. According to the author, "the alienated worker is not more hostile to ethnic minorities, less knowledgeable and engaged in political matters, less sanguine about or interested in the possibility of exercising control over socio-political events, more status minded, or more anomic." Thus, Seeman finds no real evidence to document Lipsitz's worry that lack of mastery at work may lead to a similar orientation in private and political life.

Seeman doesn't claim that his research explores all facets and implications of the personal consequences of alienated work. Nor does he claim that his research addresses itself to "the case against an industrial system that breeds alienated work." Rather, he is led to the simple conclusion that

> work is nothing else than what it is known to be — often not very rewarding in itself, and always necessary. And the big task for the worker is not to convert it into a major source of intrinsic satisfaction, but to manage it so that it can be an acceptable life of the moment by creating occasions, however small, for humor, sociality, decision-making, competition, argument, etc., that are at once trivial and remarkable.

Other studies contradict Seeman's conclusions. For example, Maurice Zeitlin (1966a, 1966b) proposes a positive relationship between work history and attitudes toward the revolution among Cuban workers. Zeitlin's data indicate that those who had the highest prerevolutionary unemployment were most likely to support the revolution and, among whites but not among blacks, to be procommunist before the revolution.

Moreover, satisfaction or discontent with work before and after the nationalization of industry, especially prerevolutionary "estrangement" from work (that is, sense of exploitation in the Marxist sense), determined the degree of support for the revolution. Thus the individual's perceptions of and feelings about his work, according to Zeitlin, can influence his political ideology.

So the evidence is mixed. One thing is certain: millions of Americans spend roughly half of almost every waking day for most of their lives in some kind of structured work activity. We also know that the degree of consensus is high with respect to the relative prestige of different occupational roles, and that in modern achievement-oriented societies like the United States, occupational role is a primary means of identification and source of identity for people. Occupations also tend to vary greatly in extrinsic rewards and opportunities for the gratification of inner needs. Specifying the most appropriate criteria and methods for measuring occupational differences as well as determining the *particular* needs gratified or frustrated in the work setting remains a theoretical and empirical problem. The many questions we have been asking have much more to do with precisely how, rather than whether, work affects the social personality of the individual.

References

Baumgartel, Howard, and Gerald Goldstein
   1961   "Some Human Consequences of Technical Change." *Personnel Administration* 24(4):32–40.
Bensman, Joseph, and Bernard Rosenberg
   1960   "The Meaning of Work in Bureaucratic Society." Pp. 181–98 in Maurice Stein, Arthur J. Vidich, and David Manning White (eds.), *Identity and Anxiety: Survival of the Person in Mass Society.* New York: The Free Press.
Blau, Peter, John W. Gustad, Richard Jessor, Herbert S. Parnes, and Richard C. Wilcock
   1956   "Occupational Choice: A Conceptual Framework." *Industrial and Labor Relations Review* 9:531–43.
Levinson, Daniel J.
   1959   "Role, Personality, and Social Structure in the Organizational Setting." *Journal of Abnormal and Social Psychology* 58:170–80.
Marx, Karl
   1962   "Alienated Labor." Trans. Eric and Mary Redmer Josephson. Pp. 93–105 in Eric and Mary Josephson (eds.), *Man Alone: Alienation in Modern Society.* New York: Dell.
Merton, Robert
   1957   "Bureaucratic Structure and Personality." Pp. 195–206 in Robert Merton, *Social Theory and Social Structure.* Glencoe, Ill.: The Free Press of Glencoe.
Mills, C. Wright
   1951   *White Collar: The American Middle Classes.* New York: Oxford University Press.
Riesman, David with Nathan Glazer and Reuel Denney
   1953   *The Lonely Crowd: A Study of the Changing American Character.* Garden City, N.Y.: Doubleday-Anchor.
Rosenberg, Harold
   1959   *The Tradition of the New.* New York: Horizon.
Swados, Harvey
   1962   "The Myth of the Happy Worker." Pp. 106–13 in Eric and Mary Josephson, *Man Alone.*
Vroom, Victor H.
   1962   "Ego-involvement, Job Satisfaction, and Job Performance." *Personnel Psychology* 14(2):159–77.

Whyte, William H., Jr.
   1956 *The Organization Man.* Garden City, N.Y.: Doubleday-Anchor.
Zeitlin, Maurice
   1966a "Alienation and Revolution." *Social Forces* 45(2):224–36.
   1966b "Economic Insecurity and the Political Attitudes of Cuban Workers."
   American Sociological Review 31 (February):35–51.

LEWIS LIPSITZ

Work Life and Political Attitudes: A Study of Manual Workers

For centuries men have speculated about the human consequences of work. Slowly, a considerable body of information has begun to accumulate concerning the relationships between people's jobs and other aspects of their lives. Investigators have pointed out the connections between certain types of jobs and certain personality disorders, job satisfaction, productivity, attitudes toward union and management, social relations on the job, leisure activities, and other things.[1] Extending such findings, this study concludes that a particular job situation can have important effects on a man's political outlook.

Political studies have long classified individuals according to occupation, yet there have been extremely few efforts to penetrate within specific occupational categories to discover the causal triggers of occupational attitude differences. Political scientists have, on the whole, been content to work with relatively large groupings such as "semi-skilled" manual workers, "unskilled" manual workers, etc. Several efforts have been made, however, in the direction this study takes; exploring specific job characteristics and their effects on political attitudes. Seymour Lipset cites a work that established a relation between size of factory and voting Communist or Nazi in pre-Hitler Germany. William Kornhauser observes the connection between the rate of expansion of a particular industry in the early stages of industrialization and the political ideology of the emerging labor movement.[2] In such findings, we move somewhat closer to establishing a causal relationship between something about a particular work situation and certain attitudes or behavior of the job holders.

But more specifically, concerning the problem of job satisfaction, Lipset, writing in 1960 observed that it was yet to be shown that "job satisfaction and creativity contribute independently to political behavior over and beyond differences in status and economic conditions. . . ."[3] The present study indicates that a particular work situation, that of the automobile assembly-line, affects the political and social at-

Reprinted by permission from *American Political Science Review* 52 (1964), pp. 951–962. Some footnotes omitted.

titudes of the automobile workers involved. The ways in which the cor
situation affects the worker's political attitudes are determined by the
and social setting of the job itself. Specifically, assembly-line workers a
be more fatalistic, more punitive, and more politically radical than otl
of comparable salary and education who work in the same plant.

I

Before proceeding to the findings themselves, it may be helpful first to consider briefly the nature of assembly-line work, in comparison with other occupational types.

The social and psychological consequences of work have been much debated.
The factory is a symbol of modern life, and the assembly-line in particular has
often been thought to embody in extreme form the worst tendencies of industrial
work. Other analysts have argued, to the contrary, that modern industrial societies
offer more individuals more chances for genuine work satisfaction than any previous societies.[4] It would serve little purpose here to get involved in this controversy,
for even if the issues raised remain unresolved, certain facts about modern worklife relevant to our inquiry are quite clear. First, manual workers generally indicate
lower work satisfaction than non-manual workers. Second, within the manual
group, satisfaction varies with skill: the higher the skill, other things being equal,
the greater the satisfaction. The table below provides some frame of reference for
dealing with the question of job satisfaction in manual and non-manual jobs.

Beyond the question of how workers respond when asked if they are satisfied

TABLE 1

Proportion in Various Occupations Who Would Choose Same Kind
of Work If Beginning Career Again [a]

Professional occupations	%	Working class occupations	%
Mathematicians	91	Skilled printers	52
Physicists	89	Paper workers	52
Biologists	89	Skilled automobile workers	41
Chemists	86	Skilled steelworkers	41
Lawyers	83	Textile workers	31
Journalists	82	Unskilled steelworkers	21
		Unskilled automobile workers	16

Source: Robert Blauner, "Work Satisfaction and Industrial Trends in Modern
Society," *Labor and Trade Unionism: An Interdisciplinary Reader,* ed. Walter
Galenson and Seymour Martin Lipset (New York, 1960), p. 343.

[a] The extent of satisfaction expressed is clearly in part a function of the particular question asked. For example, a group of American unskilled workers asked
"Are you satisfied or dissatisfied with your present job?" showed 72% indicating
they were satisfied. Exactly what satisfaction means in such a case is not at all
clear. See Alex Inkeles, "Industrial Man: The Relation of Status to Experience,
Perception and Value," *American Journal of Sociology,* Vol. 66 (July, 1960), p. 6.

with their jobs, a more important question concerns the *effects* of work; what impact the job has on a man's life outside of the factory. Many writers and analysts have speculated about this. Much of the analysis of industrial work emphasizes its destructive or negative aspects and focuses attention on the elimination of skill and the increase of simple, repetitive, assembly-line style work. Yet, there have been only a few studies of assembly-line jobs.

The development of the assembly-line was part of what one observer has called the "second industrial revolution." Although overhead conveyors were employed from the 1870s on in the American packinghouse industry, they were not introduced on a large scale until 1914, when Ford's Highland Park, Michigan plant became conveyor equipped. After 1920, assembly-lines were rapidly adopted in many areas of heavy industry.

Charles Walker and Robert Guest, who made probably the most thorough study of assembly-line work, characterized the "pure" assembly-line job as involving the following six elements.[5]

1. Mechanical pacing of work
2. Repetitiveness
3. Minimum skill requirement
4. No choice in the use of tools or techniques
5. Minute subdivision of the product worked on
6. The need for constant surface attention.

The expectation that men would dislike assembly-line work is borne out by current research. Consistently, investigators have found that conveyor-paced jobs in mass production industries show lower levels of satisfaction than other manual and non-manual jobs. Blauner concludes that assembly-line work is more disliked than any other major type of work.[6] Within the automobile industry, which is the setting of this study, the position of the semi-skilled line worker is difficult. Possibilities of advancement within the ranks are extremely slim. Wage differentials between the highest and lowest paid production jobs are small.[7]

Automobile assembly-line workers have little control over the pacing of work. The average worker on the line performs no more than five operations, remains at his station at all times, and repeats the same operations about 40 times an hour. For most workers, the work cycle is between one and two minutes, regulated by the conveyor speed.

Characteristically, the assembly-line worker is alone on his job. The technology of the line increases the worker's sense of impersonality and presents barriers to group cohesiveness. Moreover, there appears to be no adjustment to the assembly-line as time passes. The longer a man has held an assembly-line job, the more likely he is to have an unfavorable attitude toward all aspects of work experience.[8]

What do we know about the effects of assemby-line work? Compared to other groups of manual workers, assembly-line workers show few grievances, little use of pressure tactics, and much internal disunity and evidence of suppressed discontent. They permit leadership to gravitate to aggressive individuals with a strong need to dominate. They accept certain elements of their work life as inevitable, and they lack self-confidence.[9]

When Walker and Guest compared workers holding "pure" assembly-line jobs with another group of workers whose jobs were more skilled, varied and autonomous, they found that absenteeism was much higher on repetitive, conveyor-paced jobs; repetitiveness was negatively correlated with interest in work; limitations on talking were a source of frustration to line workers; mass production methods tend to increase the worker's sense of anonymity.[10] My study indicates that the differences Sayles and Walker and Guest find between different groups of semi-skilled factory workers carry over into the area of political attitudes.

II

Three samples of workers were used here as the basis for comparisons:

1. assembly-line workers, or men with jobs approximating those of the assembly-line
2. repair, relief, and utility workers
3. skilled maintenance workers.

Repair, relief and utility workers were chosen as the semi-skilled group for purposes of comparison because their jobs provided them with greater autonomy and variety than the line workers had. Repair jobs, for example, could not be time-studied and were not completely repetitive. Individual judgment and some choice of tools were required. Relief and utility workers both performed as stand-ins for men along the assembly-line, but were competent to handle many kinds of line jobs within a given department of the shop. Their work was more varied and likely to lead to a stronger sense of pride and a deeper interest in the task.

The repair, relief and utility workers, like the assembly-line operatives, would normally be classified as semi-skilled in a social class or occupational breakdown. Skilled workers were also included since they would furnish an important comparison with both semi-skilled groups and might exhibit in greater detail or more extensive development tendencies found in the other groups.

Names were selected at random from the files of the local union. Men willing to participate were interviewed in their homes. The interview questions were almost entirely open-ended. In addition to the interviews, each man completed a questionnaire which incorporated various attitude scales and other questions. All of the men interviewed were married, native-born, and white. The three groups were closely comparable in many respects. Educationally, all three groups averaged between nine and ten years of education completed. A majority of each group was Catholic. The mean age of each sample was between 40 and 50. Assembly-line workers interviewed had been on their present jobs an average of six years; repair workers, twelve years; and skilled workers, thirteen years. Pay rates in the two semi-skilled groups varied between $2.40 and $2.74 an hour, while in the skilled group the rates ranged from $2.96 to $3.39.

The assembly plant in which these men worked was located in Linden, New Jersey. At the time of these interviews, between 2900 and 3000 men were employed at the plant. The general effort was to study intensively the political orientations of a relatively small group of men, to gain some insights of general applicability that could then be tested on a larger sample, more systematically.

III

The three work groups showed attitude differences in five areas: the job; the union; a fatalistic view of social life; the extent of preoccupations with economic problems; and the extent of sympathy and tolerance.

The Job

Assembly-line workers view their jobs with a mixture of anger and resignation. Almost all of them complain bitterly of overwork, physical strain, and monotony. They feel subjected to undue pressures because of the excessive speed of the line, but they feel powerless to control this speed. Relationships with supervisors are marked by inequality and anxiety. These men feel expendable. They know there is nothing unique about their performances at work.

All the repair, relief and utility workers have ambivalent attitudes toward their jobs. Many complain of pressure and overwork, of physical and emotional strain. Yet they also note compensating factors: variety, skill, and the very important fact that the men on the assembly-line have much more unpleasant jobs than theirs.

The fifteen skilled workers present a picture of their jobs in extremely vivid contrast to those offered by the other two groups. Not a single man dislikes his job, and the degree of satisfaction is high in most cases. By and large, these men note as important the fact that they set their own pace of work; they are not closely supervised. They speak of pleasure in the creative use of their skills. They feel themselves in a position to perform useful and appreciated services for others. They have relatively good relations with supervisors. They show no sense of resignation to the inevitable; they know they can leave the corporation since they possess skills needed elsewhere. They have a certain self-confidence built on the knowledge that they have something valuable to sell.

The following tables [see Tables 2, 3, 4] will convey some notion of the differences in job attitudes among the three groups.

The Union

The twelve line workers show slightly favorable attitudes toward unions. Only four are altogether favorable. Five others are ambivalent, citing both good and bad features of unionism. Finally, three men are largely hostile toward unions.

TABLE 2
Major Complaints about Job

| | Per cent citing | | | | | |
Occupation	Pressure or overwork	Physical or mental strain	No skill or monotony	Bad supervision	Exploita- tion	N
Line	75	50	75	58	50	12
Repair	50	43	7	36	43	14
Skilled	13	13	0	20	7	15

TABLE 3
Major Sources of Job Satisfaction

			Per cent citing			
Occupation	Variety or skill	Good supervision	Autonomy on Job	Better than line	Any kind of satisfaction	N
Line	0	0	0	0	42	12
Repair	78	28	0	57	78	14
Skilled	80	67	27	67	100	15

TABLE 4
Attitude toward Leaving Present Job

Occupation	% Who would leave if possible	% Who feel stuck	N
Line	91	75	12
Repair	71	64	14
Skilled	27	13	15

Those with anything good to say about unions note "protection" as the most important union function; indeed, it is the one positive union function the line workers cite. They see the union as the only force that blunts the exploiting bent of the company. Several of the men mention seniority as an especially important kind of protection. Those who criticize the union concentrate their attention on the idea that unions are not controlled by the workers but rather by a clique which serves its own interests. They assert unions are corrupt and uninterested in the rank-and-file. As a group, these men are not closely attached to their union. They give no indication of a sense of participation or solidarity.

The views of the repair, relief and utility workers resemble those of the line workers in several respects, but differ in several others. These workers show more favorable feelings toward unions generally and also toward their own union. Eight of the fourteen men have pro-union attitudes, while six are ambivalent. None is completely anti-union. Like the line workers, they stress the importance of "protection" as a union function, but four of the men also note union benefits such as vacations, company paid insurance, etc. Within the repair group, only one man accuses unions of being oligarchical. Criticisms move in other directions and seem to be less intensely felt than among the line workers.

Much as might be expected, the skilled maintenance men also show relatively favorable attitudes toward unions. Seven are wholly pro-union, while the eight others are ambivalent. This group, too, emphasizes the "protection" the union offers, but stresses union benefits even more than the other groups. None of these skilled workers show the sense of abandonment found in the line sample. And none of them criticize unions as oligarchies.

Attitudes toward Walter Reuther, President of the United Auto Workers, are

TABLE 5
Overall Attitude toward Unions

	% Generally favorable	% Pro-UAW critical of others	% Ambivalent	% Generally unfavorable	N
Line	33	0	42	25	12
Repair	28.5	28.5	43	0	14
Skilled	46	0	54	0	15

TABLE 6
Attitudes toward Walter Reuther

	% Favorable or ambivalent	% Unfavorable	N
Line	25	75	12
Repair	36	64	14
Skilled	86	14	15

quite revealing. Both the line and repair workers are sharply critical of their union head. A majority in both groups condemns Reuther as a man out for himself, personally ambitious, and uninterested in the fate of the ordinary worker. Even men who praise the UAW as a whole, and unions generally, are wholly negative where Reuther is concerned. The skilled workers, by contrast, are overwhelmingly favorable toward Reuther; praise his skill and intelligence, as well as his honesty and dedication. In all, attitudes toward Reuther are more extreme (both positive and negative) than attitudes toward unions generally, or the UAW in particular. The line workers, who are most unhappy at work, are least happy with unions and with Reuther. The skilled workers, who are most satisfied on the job, are largely pleased with unions and with Reuther. The repair group occupies a middle position in both areas.

Fatalistic Attitudes

It is sometimes argued that fatalistic attitudes do not characterize industrial man. Fatalism, it is held, is characteristic of the peasantry, lending support to rigid class distinctions and to the idea that the political order is not to be tampered with.[11]

No doubt citizens of industrial societies are not as fatalistic as their ancestors. Yet it is also clear that the social and technical structures of industrial societies themselves produce certain fatalistic orientations, and that these are related to the specific kinds of work men are engaged in. Those workers who are conscious of having the least control over their own lives at work show the most pronounced tendency to view the social and political worlds as unalterable.

To say the very least, it is difficult to determine the degree of fatalism comprised in an individual's outlook. In an effort to find an approximate means of measurement, individuals were scored on a fatalism scale composed of four open-ended interview questions. The table below indicates the results of this scoring.

TABLE 7
Fatalism Scores by Job Groups[a]

Occupation	Number of fatalistic answers					Mean score
	None	*One*	*Two*	*Three*	*Four*	
Line	0	2	3	5	2	2.58
Repair	3	2	5	2	2	1.86
Skilled	3	6	3	3	0	1.40

[a] The four questions that made up the scale were:
1. Will men and nations always fight wars with one another?
2. Will there always be poverty in the world?
3. Do you think the ordinary man is helpless to change some aspect of government he doesn't like, or is there something he can do about it?
4. Some people say they can plan ahead for long-range goals and then carry out their plans. Others say, "Whatever's going to be is going to be and there's no sense planning." How do you feel about it?

The four questions form a Guttmann-type scale with a reproducibility coefficient of .91, and a minimal marginal reproducibility of .671.
Analysis of Variance significant at .05; t Test for Line and Repair significant at .15; t Test for Line and Skilled significant at .01.

There are clear differences among the three work groups and these differences are in the expected direction. The assembly-line workers are the most strongly fatalistic. Though there is not space here to explore the types and nuances of fatalistic attitudes, a few important points need to be made. First, as a group, these men are most strongly fatalistic about the problem of war. The idea of the inevitability of aggression fits well with the picture these men have of human nature. Second, fatalistic attitudes are weakest in the area of the political potency of the ordinary citizen. These men retain the notion that a letter to one's congressman will change things. They hold to this idea despite the fact that on other questions they indicate their belief that public officials don't really care about the common person.

The non-fatalistic workers in the sample stand out most strongly from their fatalistic fellows in two respects. First, they are indignant rather than merely sullen and resigned about conditions they find unacceptable. Second, the non-fatalists tend to blame themselves as well as others for social failures. They emphasize the possible triumph of justice, even if only in the distant future, and the possibility of humane and rational behavior, even though many of them consider such behavior unlikely.

Economic Preoccupations and Political Radicalism

The assembly-line group is more politically radical than the other two samples of workers. This manifests itself in favorable attitudes toward governmental economic controls and antagonisms toward private ownership and the privileged

orders; it is closely related to a strong tendency among the line workers to emphasize economic problems and interpretations.

The distribution of attitudes along the liberal-conservative continuum is in the
expected direction. The assembly-line workers are the most radical, the skilled
workers the least. The patterns for the three groups bears a close resemblance to
the scores for skilled, semi-skilled manual workers which Centers found in a nationwide sample in the late 1940's.

TABLE 8
Work Group Scores on Liberalism-Conservatism Scale[a]

	% Ultracon-servative	% Con-servative	% Indeter-minate	% Radical	% Ultra-radical	N
Line	0	8	33	42	17	12
Repair	8	15	54	23	0	13
Skilled	13	33	27	20	7	15

$X^2 - .10$

[a] The Liberalism-Conservatism Scale is taken from Richard Centers' book *The Psychology of Social Classes* (Princeton, Princeton University Press, 1949). The scale was
part of the questionnaire administered with each interview. One man in the repair category never completed this questionnaire and so only 13, instead of 14 men are scored
above. The Centers scale basically compares 19th century liberalism (conservative) with
20th century liberalism (radical — welfare state). The questions explore management
versus labor identification; belief in the possibilities of economic opportunity; attitude
toward government ownership and social insurance.

Symptomatic of their economic preoccupations, two contrasts emerge among the
work groups in which the line workers attach a greater emphasis to economic considerations. First, they tend more strongly to view economic problems as the most
important ones confronting America today. Fifty-eight percent of the line group
ranks economic problems most important as compared with 36 per cent of the
repair group and 33 per cent of the skilled workers.

The kinds of economic problems mentioned by the different groups were also
quite distinct. All of the men in the assembly-line group who mentioned economic
problems at all concerned themselves either with unemployment or poor working
conditions; both problems very close to home. In contrast, men in the other two
groups raised questions about high taxes, foreign aid, welfare excesses, salary differentials, and the demise of free enterprise.

Second, the concern with economic difficulties shows itself in responses to a
question that asks about the nature of the "chains" men feel. The question was
phrased, "A man once said: 'Man is born free, but everywhere he is in chains.'
Does this mean anything to you?" Table 9 arranges the responses according to
whether the individual saw Rousseau's "chains" in economic terms.

Table 9 is significant not only because the line and repair workers tend to perceive "chains" in economic terms, but also because they tend to see these "chains"
as oppressive. Remisik, a repairman, typifies much of the commentary: ". . . has to
earn his bread. He's chained to a job of some sort, regardless of whether it's here
or any other concern. . . ." The "chains" these men see range over bills, the regi-

TABLE 9
Responses to Rousseau

	% Offering economic interpretation	% Offering non-economic interpretation	N [a]
Line	86	14	7
Repair	77	23	13
Skilled	27	73	11

$X^2 - .02$

[a] Percentages are based only on those who offered some interpretation and therefore exclude the "don't knows."

mentation of factory life, and the income tax. On the other hand, most of those who offer non-economic interpretations think of "chains" without the element of oppression. Harris, a maintenance painter, serves as a good example: "Yeah, every-body is born free, true — but then we acquire chains. It has to be. There's law, regulations that we have to abide by. . . . We're always in chains, but chains can get awfully heavy in some of these countries."

Sympathy and Tolerance

None of the questions in the interview schedule was designed directly to ex-plore dimensions of sympathy or tolerance. Yet, several of the questions seemed to elicit punitive responses from some of the men but not from others. All of these questions touched on attitudes toward "out-groups." The four questions were:

1. Why are people poor?
2. What should our policy be toward Russia?
3. Do you think it was a good idea to drop atomic bombs on Japan in World War II?
4. How do you feel about capital punishment?

Though the evidence is very skimpy and impressionistic, it appears that the as-sembly-line group is less sympathetic and tolerant than the others. In all of the four cases, the line workers are slightly more punitive as a group. They tend more strongly to blame the poor themselves for poverty. They were more likely to ap-prove the bombing of Japan without showing any sympathy for the Japanese, and to recommend a policy of toughness toward Russia. Finally, they were somewhat more likely to favor the death penalty.

These findings are worth noting largely because they tend to confirm previous conclusions about authoritarianism and social class. Within this group of workers, punitive attitudes are associated with work frustration and lack of control over worklife. These facts point up the possible significance of everyday frustrations in conditioning attitudes toward out-groups.[12] The possibility that such frustrations might play an important role in shaping attitudes is one that psychoanalytic re-search has left open for the moment.[13]

IV

In two important areas the three groups show attitudes that are much alike but are important to describe nonetheless in order to give greater definition to the picture of working class views drawn thus far. First, a majority of the men in all three groups emphasize the manipulative nature of much of social life. They express concern about the exploiting and unfair practices of their corporation and of big business generally. Moreover, approximately half the men express concern about two-faced, deliberately deceptive tactics of the government and mass media which they see as closely related. Table 10 shows the distribution of such attitudes in the three work groups.

TABLE 10
Per Cent Perceiving Manipulative Practices
by Big Business or Corporation X,
and by Government or Mass Media[a]

	See manip. by Corp. X or big business	See manip. by govt. or mass media	N
	(%)	(%)	
Line	92	50	12
Repair	79	43 ·	14
Skilled	60	47	15

[a] The specific questions asked were:
  1. How do you feel about big business?
  2. How do you feel about Corporation X?
  3. Do you feel there's much corruption in politics? Why?

Where big business is concerned, these workers see manipulative practices everywhere. A few believe big business or the rich run the United States. Others are not quite so explicit, but believe that big business is free of the restraints that bind ordinary mortals: businesses can initiate wars, bribe judges and representatives and manage to get the government to follow their dictates. In some of these men, hostile attitudes toward big business and especially toward their own corporation, attain a frenzied pitch and a deep bitterness.

Most of the men feel that the corporation acts as it does because its primary concern is profit-making. Some see businesses caught in a competitive rat-race in which it is do or die. The methods of the rich, as these workers describe them, are not subtle. These men simply affirm the idea that "money talks." Very few of them have any praise for big business. Most simply accept it as a fact of life, unable, like the line worker Tencio, to visualize a world without it: "Well, without big business, what could the working man do? He gotta work for big business."

It is not particularly surprising to learn that many of these working class men are critical of big business. But it is very much another thing to find that almost half of the 41 men are critical of manipulative and deceptive aspects of American government and the mass media. The chief theme of the critics is that the government is immune to popular pressures. The general picture is of a group of men who arrange to keep themselves in power and who don't care about the requests of the common people. The means of governmental manipulation are varied: nepotism, misleading propaganda, suppression of information, bribery, silencing of dissent. The credibility of the media is to some degree tied up with the credibility of the government. Several of the men feel that the radio, papers, television only convey what they are told to. They are tools, willing or unwilling, of the politicians. Five men criticize the media as manipulative in their own right. All who discuss the media do so in terms of their deceptive political content.

Some of the workers who are concerned about manipulations tend in the direction of a conspiracy theory of social control. Yet few of them actually express anything resembling a theory of a hidden oligarchy or oligarchies. At most, seven men give any clear indications of holding to such a picture of American society. In all seven cases, it is the "rich," or "big business" which is said to be the ruling elite.

The remaining two-thirds of the men who criticize various manipulative practices give no indication of adhering to a power-elite theory. They criticize business, government and media for attempting to manipulate the common man, but their criticism is specific and piecemeal. They do not have any clearly formulated picture of social life, nor any precise notions about who is to blame for the seamy side of things. They are critical of the excessive power of big business and yet do not believe that big business runs the country. They can believe that people in the government attempt to mislead the public without going sour on government as a whole.

Yet, behind their vagueness and their sense of their own ignorance, most of these men actually have developed an explanation for the practices they criticize. First, they see a society directed toward profit-making. Second, they are aware of wide disparities of power. Out of these elements, these men have constructed a suspicion of human nature. It is human nature and nothing less, they say, which leads to the malpractices of business and government. Thus, it is not a particular group of evil men who are to blame, but rather the selfishness supposedly inherent in almost all of us.

These workers generally accept the profit-motive as a satisfactory explanation of business behavior. But this does not account for governmental behavior. Why these failures, large and small, in the democratic system?

A substantial majority of the men believe that politics, like most other aspects of our society, is basically a business. Three-quarters of the line workers, 57 per cent of the repair sample, and 60 per cent of the maintenance men see politicians as predominantly self-seeking. They see elections and platforms designed to fool the public; politicians seeking to perpetuate their own domination; stealing, nepotism, the wasting of public funds, etc. A government composed of such individuals could not possibly be very attentive to the kinds of problems these workers are concerned about. It is not surprising then that they see failures in the political system. The selfish nature of politicians springs from their unfortunate and seemingly indelible humanity.

The second important area of similarity among the three groups is political participation. Unexpectedly, all three groups were strikingly alike in regard to voting, discussions of politics, and interest in political affairs. A majority of the men in all three groups reported talking politics at least sometimes. Only one man indicated he was not interested in presidential elections. Only a handful felt that the outcome of the 1960 presidential election made no difference. All of the men said they had voted in 1960.

Only in two areas did any tentative difference appear among the three work groups. First, the skilled workers were more likely than the other groups to participate in political activities beyond voting. Two-thirds of the skilled group had contributed money, gone to party meetings or actively campaigned in recent years. In the repair group, the figure was 43 per cent, and in the line group, 36 per cent.

Second, the quality of partisan commitment varies considerably among these groups. Very crudely, there are two sorts of commitment: positive and negative — being in favor of, or being against. Most notably, the line workers phrase their political commitments in terms of their aversion for the Republican Party as well as their preference for the Democrats. Five of the twelve line workers speak of their ill-feeling toward the GOP. This ill-feeling runs the gamut from quiet discontent to raw bitterness. Dolski, a line worker, speaks with particular resentment on the subject of poverty: "Why do we have poor people in this state? I'll tell you: Republicans got in there. They kept everything for themselves. Now we got the poor in. . . ."

V

Much of the evidence set out in the preceding sections is impressionistic and statistically insignificant. Yet the weight of the evidence points in a single direction.

It is clear that the two groups of semi-skilled auto workers hold different views in various areas of life. First, the men who work on repetitive, assembly-line jobs dislike their work more and are more hostile toward and alienated from the union. Second, the assembly-line workers are more fatalistic, less sympathetic with and tolerant of others. The line workers are also more radical in their political views.

Recent investigations of Arthur Kornhauser tend to confirm these findings. In an as yet unpublished work and in a recent article, Kornhauser explores the relationships between skill level and various psychological and attitude variables. He finds that skill level in manual jobs is clearly related to mental health and also to certain political and social attitudes. He concludes that the higher the skill level of the job, the more likely that men will show high mental health, while mental health is lowest among workers with repetitive conveyor-paced jobs.[14]

Kornhauser's measures of mental health coincide, in part, with dimensions of attitudes also examined in this study. His indices include measures of: anxiety and tension; hostility *versus* trust in people; self-esteem *versus* negative self-feelings; sociability *versus* withdrawal; personal morale *versus* anomie or social alienation. He also found, consistent with the findings here, that workers in lower skill jobs were higher on economic "liberalism," but lower in liberal attitudes on race relations and international affairs. Kornhauser concludes that the workers at various skill levels differ most sharply in feelings of defeat, pessimism, personal inadequacy, futility, and distrust of others.[15]

Assembly-line workers, as we have seen, do not find their work interesting. They complain bitterly and consistently about monotony. In many respects, automobile assembly-line work reflects the most unhealthy characteristics of industrial work. Line workers have a sense of futility. They are frustrated and at the same time are seeking to undo their sense of inadequacy. Their frustrations are clearly reflected in their alienation, *i.e.,* their feelings of powerlessness, and its attendant consequences. Their feelings of helplessness are reflected in their fatalistic acceptance of their lot and of the agonies of the great world. Their efforts to restore their self-esteem are reflected in their desires for economic improvement.

What are the implications of these findings for our understanding of political life?

First, it seems reasonable to suppose that assembly-line workers and others whose jobs deprive them of control over their physical movements are more likely to sympathize with radical and mass agitations. Assembly-line workers are more isolated and more likely to feel disenfranchised than other industrial workers. Their feelings about politics are likely to be influenced by desires for relatively radical change, even if these feelings are partly suppressed.

Second, it seems clear that the job structure of industry is one factor that needs to be understood in grasping the impact of industrialization. Kornhauser has pointed out that it is not industrialization per se, but rather "discontinuities" in industrial development that have been the basis for antidemocratic movements.[16] Among these discontinuities are excessive rapidity of industrialization or the acute break-down of the economy. Perhaps along with these factors we should also turn our attention to the job structure of emerging industries, focusing on the proportion of assembly-line type jobs.

Third, specific job groups may show a clearer relationship to political party allegiance in countries with multi-party systems than they seem to in America. The great majority of workers in all of the sample groups examined here were Democrats, yet the groups differed in the extent to which they favored liberal economic measures, and in the intensity of their antagonism to the Republicans. In a country where a greater variety of political choices is offered, such differences within the strata of manual workers may show up more sharply in party allegiances. And conversely if most of the men in most circumstances vote Democratic anyway, regardless of differences in their feelings, party organizers here may well be content to get them to the polls and ignore their feelings.

Finally, how widely can these findings be generalized? If recent work in industrial psychology is any indication, a large percentage of manual and white collar workers are not interested in their work. It seems as yet an open question whether interest in work and control over work will increase or decrease with the spread of various forms of automation. At any rate, millions, if not tens of millions of Americans in the foreseeable future are likely to be working at uninteresting, repetitive jobs. Perhaps such workers, even if they are not manual workers, will internalize the tensions and dissatisfactions of their work.

I am not attempting to argue that a bored clerk in a department store, a dish-washer in a restaurant, an auto assembly worker, and an IBM card puncher are likely to respond to their jobs in the same manner. Their political and social at-titudes are conditioned by the content and status of their jobs, as well as the circumstances and expectations they bring with them, and other factors. Yet it seems possible that at each status level, those with the most repetitive, least interesting or controllable jobs will be the most dissatisfied, alienated, and politically "radical."

VI

Various political analysts have argued that there is a causal connection between industrialization and democracy. Among the most prominent of these probably is Lipset, who has shown correlations between stable democratic systems and various indices which provide a way of measuring the relative modernity of nations.[17] In his view, contradicting Marx, industrialization tends to produce the preconditions for political democracy because the class struggle is shaped in moderate directions. Relative wealth and increased education tend to preclude extremism in the lower classes. The absence of deep and stable class differences also makes it possible for the rich and privileged to acknowledge the poor as members of the same species.

Robert Lane has recently buttressed Lipset's argument from another direction. His research, in depth interviews, of the attitudes of a sample of "common men" in an Eastern city reveals that the work situation in which these men find themselves is conducive to the formation of democratic norms. Most of his sample have substantial independence at work, find satisfaction in their jobs, exercise some skill, are in a position to assert their competence and to exchange views with co-workers and superiors. Lane's findings also move in the direction of substantiating Blauner's hypothesis that modern industrial work provides wider opportunities for the exercise of skill than work in previous societies. Lane concludes that the data on industrial work substantiate Lipset's correlation between democracy and advanced industrial development.[18]

The findings reported here, as well as those of Kornhauser noted above, are not nearly so optimistic as Lane's or Blauner's. It seems that at some lower skill levels work alienation is considerable, and has serious psychological and political consequences, some of which are not very healthy for a democratic polity. On the basis of the very incomplete knowledge we have about the effects of different types of work, skepticism about the overall consequences of industrial work is still in order.

The manual workers examined in this study are not extremists in the sense of favoring truly radical change, revolution, violence, or of lending support to undemocratic political movements. But it is not their jobs, at least in the case of the two groups of semi-skilled workers, that have made them supporters of the status quo, nor taught them very much about the nature of democratic social relationships. If these men are defenders of the political status quo it seems to be largely because of their status as consumers, not because of their work lives. If they have very much sense of personal adequacy, it is because of the control and judgment they are able to exercise outside their jobs. Though industrial work, for many reasons, may be more conducive to the development of democratic sentiments than the life of the peasant, it is quite another thing to argue that industrial work, at least of the repetitive variety, is generally healthy or enhances an individual's sense of worth.

Lipset's argument concerning the relationship between industrialization and democracy seems to run counter to the analyses of writers such as C. Wright Mills and Erich Fromm. Fromm and Mills emphasize the alienation and apathy characteristic of bureaucratized industrial societies.[19] They argue that democracy is far from being a reality in today's world. As they picture it, many ordinary citizens have become passive and alienated, feel unable to control their fates, and have lost sight of the significant issues of political life. Both Mills and Fromm relate these characteristics of industrial societies to the structure of work. Both argue that alienation and passivity at work breed alienation and passivity elsewhere. If they are right and industrialization creates many kinds of work situations which are not conducive to the development of democratic attitudes, then how can industrialization and democracy be related?

A great part of the difficulty in resolving this antithesis may lie in definitions and points of view. Lipset's definition of democracy is an arbitrary, operational one. He speaks of two characteristics: competitive parties and the absence of strong anti-democratic political groups.[20] It is a "democracy" fitting this definition which Lipset finds related to his indices of modernity. Both Fromm and Mills speak of democracy and democratic attitudes in a different sense. Both bring normative judgments to bear on present reality. So, it is possible to agree that Lipset's correlation is correct and important, and yet to agree with Mills and Fromm that present-day democracies are not as democratic as they might be.

Robert Lane has argued that ego strength is a crucial psychological correlate of democracy. Without having experienced an inner sense of mastery as well as a sense of mastery over the environment, men do not develop the requisite ego strength to pursue a consistent, long-term course, or to effect much social change. One of the most important, if unproven, implications of this study is that the work men do can have important consequences for their ego strength. Here the concerns of Fromm and Mills are significant. Men in a work environment they cannot control may be to some unknown degree damaged in their sense of mastery, and this damage may render them less capable of coping with and altering an environment they find unsatisfactory. To the extent that such damage occurs, men become victims rather than creators. To the extent that work life contributes to such incapacities, it needs improvement in modern societies. Industrial democracy may yet prove to be a prerequisite to political and social democracy.

A few final caveats: first, the severe dissatisfactions found among automobile assembly-line workers are probably not typical of the attitudes of most modern industrial workers. The nature of the assembly-line itself intensifies the problems of a mechanized job. These findings therefore represent only one segment of the working class. Their relevance to men in other types of jobs which are less intensely disliked remains to be seen.[21] Second, the findings presented in the tables above are for the most part based on a rather crude dichotomizing of attitudes as these attitudes appeared in the setting of open-ended interviews. Such findings, especially in view of the small size of the sample, are at best suggestive and exploratory. Most important, the question of the intensity with which various attitudes are held must remain moot in many of the areas this article has explored. For example, though many of the men criticize what they consider to be manipulative practices by political figures, most of them are not "alienated" from the political system. How deep their cynicism may go on occasion, is a question this study has not touched.[22]

Notes

1. See in particular Georges Friedmann, *Industrial Society: The Emergence of the Human Problems of Automation,* trans. Harold L. Sheppard (Glencoe, 1955), p. 276; Robert Blauner, "Work Satisfaction and Industrial Trends in Modern Society," *Labor and Trade Unionism: an Interdisciplinary Reader,* ed. Walter Galenson and Seymour Martin Lipset (New York, 1960), pp. 339–360; E. L. Trist and K. W. Bamforth, "Some Social and Psychological Consequences of the Longwall Method of Coal-getting," *Human Relations,* Vol. 4 (1951), pp. 3–38; Charles R. Walker and Robert Guest, *The Man on*

the Assembly Line (Cambridge, Harvard University Press, 1952); Frank J. Jasinski, "Technological Delimitation of Reciprocal Relationships: A Study of Interaction Patterns in Industry," *Human Organization*, Vol. 15 (1956), pp. 24–28; David Armstrong, "Meaning in Work," *New Left Review*, No. 10 (July-August, 1961), pp. 16–23; and Georges Friedmann, *The Anatomy of Work — Labor, Leisure and the Implications of Automation*, trans. Wyatt Rawson (New York, 1961), p. 107.

2. Lipset, "The Psychology of Voting," *Handbook of Social Psychology*, ed. Gardner Lindzey (Cambridge, Addison-Wesley, 1954), II, 1139; Kornhauser, *The Politics of Mass Society* (Glencoe, 1959), p. 154.

3. *Political Man* (Garden City, N. Y., 1960), p. 237.

4. Blauner, loc. cit.

5. Walker and Guest, loc. cit., p. 19.

6. Blauner, loc. cit., pp. 346–347.

7. Arthur N. Turner, "Impersonality and Group Membership: A Case Study of an Automobile Assembly Line" (unpublished Ph.D. dissertation, Cornell University, 1958), pp. 13–16.

8. Ibid., p. 26.

9. Leonard Sayles, *Behavior of Industrial Work Groups: Prediction and Control* (New York, 1958).

10. Walker and Guest, loc. cit.

11. See Daniel Lerner, *The Passing of Traditional Society: Modernizing the Middle East* (Glencoe, 1958); and David Riesman, Nathan Glazer, and Reuel Denny, *The Lonely Crowd: A Study of the Changing American Character* (New Haven, Yale University Press, 1950).

12. Lipset points out that the unemployed, feeling resentful and alienated, are less tolerant of minority groups than are employed workers, a finding that seems related to the conclusions here about the assembly-line group. See S. M. Lipset, *Political Man: The Social Bases of Politics* (Garden City, 1960), p. 114. For a discussion of the importance of attitudes toward out-groups, see T. W. Adorno and associates, *The Authoritarian Personality* (New York, 1950), chs. 2–4.

13. See Bjorn Christiansen, *Attitudes Towards Foreign Affairs as a Function of Personality* (Oslo, Norway, Oslo University Press, 1959), p. 59.

14. Arthur Kornhauser, "The Mental Health of the Industrial Worker — A Detroit Study" (preliminary draft, August, 1962); "Mental Health of Factory Workers: A Detroit Study," *Human Organization*, Vol. 21 (1962), pp. 43–46. The following table, ibid., p. 45, will indicate his findings. These relationships held when the author controlled for education.

Mental Health of Factory Workers		
Men in 40s (age)	% With good mental health scores	N
Skilled	56	45
High semi-skilled	41	98
Ordinary SS	38	82
Repetitive SS	26	73
Repetitive machine-paced only (subdivision of preceding category)	16	32

15. Though I have spoken of a causal relationship between jobs and attitudes, I have not really "proven" such a relationship exists. The crucial problem is

one of pre-selection. Perhaps men on assembly-line jobs differ
semi-skilled workers because they were different before they ever
jobs, rather than because they have been changed by their emplo
haps it is only men with a low sense of self-esteem and strong
tendencies who stay on the assembly-line. Kornhauser tries to handle this
problem by exploring the life of his interviewees before they took their
present jobs. He concludes that there is demonstrable evidence that jobs
change attitudes, regardless of what those attitudes were before the job was
taken. If so, then personality differences that exist before taking the job do
not explain occupational group differences in mental health. See "Mental
Health of Factory Workers," loc. cit., p. 46.

16. Kornhauser, *The Politics of Mass Society,* op. cit.
17. "Some Social Requisites of Democracy," *American Political Science Review,*
    Vol. 53 (March 1959), pp. 69–105; see also his *Political Man,* op. cit., ch. 2.
18. *Political Ideology,* ch. 15.
19. Mills' point of view is set out in *White Collar, The American Middle Classes*
    (New York, Oxford Univ. Press, 1951); *The Power Elite* (New York, Ox-
    ford Univ. Press, 1959), and *The Causes of World War III* (New York,
    1960). Fromm's views can be found, in part, in *The Sane Society* (New
    York, 1955).
20. *Political Man,* p. 48.
21. For a comparison of "alienation" in several quite different industrial settings,
    see Robert Blauner, *Alienation and Freedom* (Chicago, 1964).
22. Allen Schick provides a perceptive discussion of the need to deal realistically
    with the presence of ambivalent political attitudes in his paper, "Alienation
    and Politics," delivered at the 1964 American Political Science Association
    convention.

WILLIAM P. SEXTON

Organizational and Individual Needs: A Conflict?

   Each man performs the same task over and over: tightens identical nuts,
lifts identical parts off of a rack, and applies each one of them precisely to a
something that is exactly like its predecessor to the thousandth of an inch.
This accurate monotonous toil goes on swiftly, amid hissing air-valves and
paint-streams, roar of drying ovens, clatter of tools, thunder of trucks arriving
and departing. As evidence of the organizing faculty in master minds, as a
study in unity and synchronized power over diverse beings and things, the
action is impressive, in totality almost beautiful; but for its individual contribution it leaves something to be desired as an expression of the art of
life. Not altogether for this, surely, is man made.[1]

Reprinted by permission from *Personnel Journal* 46:6 (June 1967), pp. 337–343.

Pound's account of work with mechanized equipment is possibly an exaggeration or, at best, only applicable to a small portion of jobs in industry today. Nevertheless, his observation introduces a common thesis fostered by several contemporary organization theorists. That is, there is a basic conflict between the individual's satisfaction of his egoistic needs and the demands placed upon him by the implementation of the organization and control principles of present-day management.

Theoretical Framework

The sheer pressure of consumer demand, together with the consequently heightened complexities of large-scale industrial organization, have forced modern management to adopt certain organization and control techniques for the sake of efficiency. The operational economy contributed by the specialization of labor, methods, standardization, organization structure, policies, and procedures certainly need not be argued. However, one could view each of these techniques in terms of the boundaries it places on the behavior of the individual in his work environment. Specifically, at the lower levels of the organization, much of the work is highly structured and may call for nothing more than a preoccupation with the performance of a highly synchronized set of physical motions in the assembly or checking of a continual stream of identical parts. The emphasis is clearly on structure. It is the uniformity and consistency afforded by the certainty of proceduralized duties performed repetitiously that is necessary for the efficiency of the large-scale industrial enterprise. In this study, the term "structure" refers to the degree to which the individual's range of behavior as an organization member is restricted, confined, or reduced by virtue of organizing and control techniques, e.g., the specialization of labor, methods, mechanical pacing, procedures, and rules.

It is with this structuring of behavior that certain organization theorists are gravely concerned. The resultant work environment has been characterized by Argyris as "making demands on relatively healthy individuals that are incongruent with their needs!" [2] Argyris contends that the worker is placed in an environment where (1) he is provided minimal control over his work-a-day world (2) he is expected to be passive, dependent, and subordinate, (3) he is expected to have a short-time perspective, and (4) he is induced to perfect and value the frequent use of a few superficial abilities.[3] Argyris argues that, in contrast to these conditions, the individual is activated by the following needs: the need to define for himself the ratio of activity to passivity (autonomy); the need to feel that he has the respect of his fellow workers (recognition); the need to express feelings of interdependence in relation to the other people in the organization (affiliation); and the need to obtain from his job a degree of creature sufficiency (self-actualization).[4]

These needs make up the higher-level needs of the "need hierarchy" which is the foundation of Maslow's theory of motivation.[5] The need hierarchy is an ordered arrangement of man's needs based on their motivational capacity and strength. Physiological needs and security needs are the lower-level needs. These are essentially the needs for subsistence and for protection against danger, threat, and arbitrary deprivation. The basic tenets of the theory are that man is a wanting animal and that as soon as a need is satisfied it is no longer motivating, but another need takes its place in motivating behavior. The order of this succession is governed by the hierarchy. For example, the need for air would likely be the strongest motivator of behavior were one deprived of it as in the case of the asthmatic patient. With the exception of such unusual circumstances, few are so motivated due to the fact that they already enjoy a reasonable satisfaction of such needs. It follows that when his lower-level needs are satisfied, the individual is then freed to pursue the satisfaction of higher-level needs, e.g., belonging, achievement, recognition, self-fulfillment.

Drawing on Maslow's premise that a satisfied need is no longer motivating, McGregor[6] argues that present day management's efforts to motivate the behavior of workers will be necessarily abortive due to its allegedly obstinate emphasis on tangible, economic needs. He suggests that, by virtue of incentive programs, assorted insurance programs, and the existence of unions, the physiological and security needs are, in large measure, satisfied and, therefore, no longer motivators of behavior. He contends that the higher-level needs have taken the place of these satisfied needs and are now motivating the behavior of the average industrial worker. Such needs are those for fellowship, for the feeling of doing something worthwhile, for receiving acknowledgement for achievement, and for a sense of creativity or craftsmanship.

In consonance with Argyris' proposition, McGregor has concluded:

> The typical industrial organization offers only limited opportunities for the satisfaction of egoistic needs to people at lower levels in the hierarchy. The conventional methods of organizing work particularly in mass production industries give little heed to these aspects of human motivation. If the practices of 'scientific management' were deliberately calculated to thwart these needs — which, of course, they are not — they could hardly accomplish this purpose better than they do.[7]

The Nature of the Study

It is with the objective of testing the theoretical conclusions regarding the alleged conflict between the structure producing demands of the organization and individual needs that an empirical study was undertaken at a midwest manufacturing plant of a large scale producer of electronic equipment. In an effort to test the thesis, the following hypotheses were formulated.

1. It is hypothesized that the degree of individual need satisfaction will correlate negatively with the degree to which the individual's range of behavior as an organization member is restricted, confined, or reduced by virtue of organization and control techniques.

2. It is hypothesized that individual effectiveness, i.e., the degree to which the individual meets formal performance standards, will correlate positively with the behavioral restriction occasioned by the imposition of these organization and control techniques.

3. It is hypothesized that individual effectiveness will correlate negatively with the degree of individual need satisfaction.

The Study Setting and the Sample

The setting of the study was a large manufacturing plant, with modern physical facilities which display the results of the company's concern for the problems of plant layout and work flow. The process is one of continuous manufacturing, with a number of production and assembly lines serving as the bases for the intermediate stages of the product's manufacture. In association with these conditions, a high degree of specialization is readily observable and a wide range of skills is required. Of the 8,000 employees, approximately 85% are hourly-paid and involved in tasks contributing directly to the production process.

Participants in the study were all hourly-paid line workers. With the use of a "random numbers" table, 170 subjects were selected from the company's personnel rolls. While the employees were selected at random, the selection procedure was continued until 17 subjects were obtained from each of ten job classifications. The job classes were: (1) bench hand, (2) process checker, (3) tester, (4) wireman, (5) machinist, (6) toolmaker, (7) technician, (8) layout operator, (9) inspector, and (10) electrician.

These jobs were selected on the basis of the job structure scores which they were assigned by immediate supervision and the industrial engineering department. That is, first level supervisors and industrial engineering personnel were asked to score the job categories in the production organization as to the degree of structure involved. Since the phenomenon of structure as typically employed, has a perceptive connotation, a "perceived job structure" score was obtained for each respondent by a questionnaire. The rank-order correlation coefficient between the structure scores obtained by the questionnaire and those obtained from supervision and engineering was found to be .922. In other words, the worker himself tends to agree with managers and technicians relative to the degree to which his job is structured.

A sample size of 83 was obtained from the original 170 subjects to whom questionnaires were sent. There were no more than nine nor fewer than six subjects in each of the ten job categories from which the original number were selected. Twenty-eight percent of those who returned the questionnaire were female, which was identical to that proportion of females employed by the company. The average age of those responding was 34 years, with a range from 22 years to 51 years. The shortest company service was 10 months and the longest, 8 years, with an average of 4 years, 1 month. These statistics are virtually identical with those of the original sample and of the 8,000 employees of the company.

Method of Measurement

In order to test the hypotheses, a Likert type questionnaire was developed to quantify perceived structure and the satisfaction of each of five higher-level needs. Definitely, these are:

1. *Achievement need.* A need to feel that one is accomplishing something of value or importance.
2. *Affiliation need.* A need to be related to people; to have friends; to have the feeling of belonging; to be accepted by one's fellows.

3. *Autonomy need.* A need to feel that one has power over one's actions; is independent; has freedom to make decisions and initiate effective action.

4. *Recognition need.* A need to feel that one is valued by others; that one's achievements are acknowledged; that one's achievements are communicated to others.

5. *Self-actualization need.* A need to realize the extent of one's potential; to feel that one's activities contribute to continual self-development and self-fulfillment.

The questionnaire presented the subjects with a number of items which were to be assessed on the basis of (1) their importance to the individual in any job he might undertake, and (2) the accuracy of their description of the individual's present job. The items were one-word descriptive adjectives referring to the individual's job, to his performance of his job, or to the conditions surrounding his job. Forty-eight such items were included in the final questionnaire, eight items measuring each of the five higher-level needs and eight items measuring the structure variable.

In order to obtain scores for both the intensity and the satisfaction of the needs, the same sets of items were used in each case. That is, in Section I, the respondent was asked to rate the importance of each item to him as a quality of *any* job, his performance of *any* job, or the conditions surrounding *any* job which he might undertake. His response was by way of a check on a scale graduated from "No Importance" to "Extreme Importance." Responses were then scored from 0 to 8, 0 representing "No Importance," 4 representing "Undecided," and 8, "Extreme Importance." (See example below.) In Section II, the respondent was asked

An Example of Item Scoring

Section I:
Independent

No Importance — Little Importance — Undecided — Important — Extreme Importance

(In this instance, the response would receive a score of 5 on the scale measuring the satisfaction of the subject's autonomy need.)

Section II:
Independent

Not at all — Somewhat — Undecided — Quite — Very much

(In this instance, the response would receive a score of 3, on the scale measuring the satisfaction of the subject's autonomy need.)

to rate the same items as to the accuracy of their description of his *present* job, his performance of his *present* job, or the conditions surrounding his *present* job. He was asked to check a point on a scale graduated from "Not at All" to "Very Much." Responses were again scored in the same fashion from 0 to 8. (See example.)

Likert's system of scoring calls for totaling the scores on the individual items to obtain a measure of the subject's attitude. In this way, the questionnaire provided a measure of the intensity and the satisfaction of each of the five higher-level needs and the "perceived structure" variable on scales ranging from 0 to 64.

The extent of a respondent's need satisfaction was measured in two ways. A score for "need satisfaction," per se, was obtained by merely totaling the responses in Section II as to the extent to which the various eight item sets describe the individual's *present* job. To supplement this measure, a satisfaction discrepancy score was calculated by taking the difference between the satisfaction and the intensity scores for a particular need.

Results

In order to evaluate the relationships between these variables, product-moment correlation coefficients were calculated. Table 1 displays the correlations between the job structure scores and the satisfaction and satisfaction discrepancy score for each need. As will be readily apparent, with the exception of the self-actualization need, significant positive correlations exist between need satisfactions and job structure. In the instance of the satisfaction discrepancy scores, again with the exception of the self-actualization need, all correlations are negative. There was a significant negative correlation between job structure and the satisfaction discrepancy of the affiliation need.

TABLE 1
Correlation Coefficients between Job Structure and Need Satisfactions

Needs	Satisfaction	p	Satisfaction discrepancy	p
Achievement	.309	.01	−.169	ns
Affiliation	.412	.001	−.286	.01
Autonomy	.280	.01	−.070	ns
Recognition	.385	.001	−.153	ns
Self-actualization	.156	ns	.151	ns

Finally, multiple correlation coefficients of .539 and .436 were found between job structure and need satisfactions and satisfaction discrepancies respectively. (These are both significant at the .025 level.) In the latter case, all beta coefficients were, of course, negative. Based on these findings, it is clear that hypothesis 1 must be rejected. That is, it does not seem likely that job structure has the devastating effect on the worker's satisfaction of his egoistic needs as Argyris and McGregor contend.

In addition to the above measures, an effectiveness rating was completed by the immediate and second level supervisors for each subject. Product-moment correlations between this variable and (1) need intensity, (2) need satisfaction, and (3) satisfaction discrepancy were calculated. As Table 2 shows, with the exception of the autonomy need, all correlations between effectiveness and need satisfaction are negative. Likewise, with this exception, all correlations between effectiveness and need intensities are positive. A correlation coefficient of −176 (p = .1) was found between effectiveness and the satisfaction discrepancy of the autonomy need. These findings do not support hypothesis 3.

TABLE 2

Correlation Coefficients between Effectiveness and
Need Satisfaction, Need Intensity,
and Satisfaction Discrepancy

Needs	Satisfaction	Intensity	Satisfaction discrepancy
Achievement	−.017	.009	−.028
Affiliation	−.036	.059	−.030
Autonomy	.096	−.115	−.176
Recognition	−.072	.070	.004
Self-actualization	−.059	.040	.004

In the case of the relationship between job structure and effectiveness (hypothesis 2), no significant correlation was found. The hypothesis that individual effectiveness would correlate positively with job structure was not, therefore, supported.

Implications

On the basis of the findings of this study, the popular notion that the imposition of procedure, methods, standardization, etc., has an inhibiting or restrictive effect on the worker's satisfaction of his egoistic needs is rejected. While the theoretical conclusions of certain contemporary writers commend themselves from the humanistic point of view, there would appear to be mounting evidence that they are not supported by empirical testing. It is noted that the findings of Stogdill [8] in a recent study of a wide variety of business organizations indicate the same conclusions. In a related study of a large insurance organization, Beer's findings lend further support.[9]

There would appear to be several alternative explanations for a direct correlation between the satisfaction of higher-level needs and job structure. While many factors may serve to condition the degree to which a worker may satisfy his higher-level needs, among these would be included: (1) his expectations, (2) the satisfaction of his need for security, and (3) the extent to which his mental processes are freed by the nature of his job. There should be no question that a worker's expectations of future outcomes, and his perception of the probability and desirability of these events would be more highly crystallized with the certainty occasioned by job structure. There is little ambiguity surrounding the line worker's job.

In most jobs, the realization of goals and the consequent fulfillment of a need such as recognition will probably require a good deal of time. While this is also true of the line worker's job, by virtue of the certainty of job structure, he has the ability to predict these events. Unlike his counterpart, the staff assistant, the line worker has formalized promotion channels, bonus and incentive systems, and the elaborate communication circuitry of the informal organization on which to base his expectations. It seems clear, then, that the expectations themselves could in a real sense act as an initial stage of goal accomplishment and need-fulfillment. Therefore, of the line worker, expectation as well as a typical consummatory response could be a satisfaction producing variable.

It seems unrealistic for academicians to suggest that this sort of need satisfaction would be diminished by virtue of its being obtained through the performance of an allegedly menial task. It seems presumptuous for the academician who has a radically divergent set of values to stand back and tell the line worker that his job is boring or monotonous. Menial is surely a relative term and perhaps it is also true of work that "one man's meat is another man's poison."

According to Maslow's theory of motivation, prior to a satisfaction of the higher-level needs, the need for security must first be fulfilled. Once again, it may be that those who contend that the average worker is adequately provided with the means for satisfying his security needs are attempting to evaluate the matter with a hastily conceived set of values. The emphasis is placed on security as a tangible value. In order to prove the alleged fulfillment of the security need in modern industrial work, attention has been drawn by certain writers to incentive systems, fringe benefits, economic security, and the power of the unions for personal security against arbitrary treatment. Security could well mean much more to the line worker. It might include the need for highly predictable patterns of interaction, a stable work environment and freedom from the personal challenge of the unusual or unfamiliar. It is granted that this sort of certainty might well displease the scientist or the engineer. However, it is pointed out that the study was performed with line workers. While there is yet no substantiating data, the possession of certain personal characteristics could be the factor which may lead to such a desire for certainty and uniformity. Such characteristics would include intelligence, sex, marital status, cultural background, and educational level. Once again, if this were the case, it would account for the possibility of some theoretical discrepancies. It is clear that those who have characterized present-day industrial operative work as monotonous and boring are actually speaking for themselves. Their allegations probably apply also to scientists, engineers, and most managerial personnel. Certainly a dramatic differential exists between this latter group and the line worker so far as intelligence, educational level, and cultural background are concerned. The point to be made is that the relatively unstructured jobs of the electrician, the toolmaker, or the machinist whose backgrounds are compatible with those of the line worker may not provide an acceptable level of such security. If this need is prepotent as McGregor argues, then this could account for there being less higher-level need satisfaction in such unstructured work.

From a purely pragmatic point of view, perhaps it is the line worker rather than the staff assistant who has variety in his job. Usually, the staff assistant must direct his unwavering attention to his work. This is contrasted with the line worker whose work may demand little concentration and, as a result, may provide him with a sense of "freedom." The problem here is the confusion between monotony and habit. The Gilbreths were likely the first to point out the fundamental question.[10] Monotony and habit are in many ways related. For example, the everyday acts of dressing, of eating, and of walking are performed virtually the same way each time. Certainly, they are not monotonous but, rather, habitual. The reason lies in the fact that, while both habit and monotony involve the repetition of a routine undemanding task, the task is not monotonous unless the individual is forced to concentrate on it. It follows, then, that the individual whose work demands little attenion may perform his job habitually. By virtue of his habits of work, he may direct his mental processes to whatever he desires. Certainly he is largely free to socialize with fellow workers and to initiate his own activities autonomously.

Summary

In this study of line workers at the midwest plant of a large manufacturer of electronic equipment, there were significant correlations found between the degree of job structure and the satisfaction of higher level needs. These findings are contrary to the popular theses which were hypothesized. In addition, effectiveness was not correlated significantly with need satisfaction or with job structure. On the basis of these findings and in light of current studies, the popular thesis that the imposition of job structure thwarts the industrial worker's satisfaction of his higher level needs is rejected. Regarding the absence of a significant correlation between effectiveness and need satisfaction, it seems clear that the interaction of these variables is certainly complex and not to be explained by oversimplified theses.

Notes

1. Arthur Pound. *The Iron Man of Industry*. Boston: The Atlantic Monthly Press, 1922.
2. Chris Argyris, *Personality and Organization*. New York: Harper & Row, 1957.
3. Ibid., p. 66.
4. Chris Argyris, "Organizational Leadership and Participative Management," *The Journal of Business*, Vol. 27, No. 1, Jan. 1955, p. 4.
5. Abraham Maslow, *Motivation and Personality*. New York: McGraw-Hill Book Company, 1954.
6. Douglas McGregor, *The Human Side of Enterprise*. New York: McGraw-Hill Book Company, Inc., 1960.
7. Ibid., pp. 38–39.
8. Ralph M. Stogdill, *Managers, Employees, Organizations*. Columbus: Bureau of Business Research, Ohio State University, Monograph 125, 1965.
9. Michael Beer, *Leadership, Employee Needs, and Motivation*. Columbus: Bureau of Business Research, Ohio State University, Monograph No. 129, 1966.
10. Frank B. and Lilian M. Gilbreth, *Applied Motion Study*. New York: Sturgis & Walton Company, 1917.

MICHAEL AIKEN
JERALD HAGE

Organizational Alienation:
A Comparative Analysis

A persistent theme both in contemporary novels and in commentaries about modern life is the alienation of modern man. Social scientists have also become enamored, and perhaps inebriated, with the idea of alienation in modern society and have attempted to forge indices of man's sense of malaise. One major fault of most of these discussions is that alienation has been defined, measured, and discussed as if it represented some "free floating" human condition irrespective of specific social contexts which produce such mental states.

Our concern in this paper is to examine the relationship between two dimensions of organization — centralization and formalization — and two types of alienation — alienation from work and alienation from expressive relations. For this purpose sixteen welfare organizations, staffed largely by professional workers, were compared on these dimensions.

Alienation from work reflects a feeling of disappointment with career and professional development, as well as disappointment over the inability to fulfill professional norms. Alienation from expressive relations reflects dissatisfaction in social relations with supervisors and fellow workers. These two types of alienation can be compared with two of those discussed by Marx, namely, alienation from the process of production and alienation from fellow workers.[1]

By *centralization* we mean the degree to which members participate in decision-making. Our concept of centralization is similar in part to that of Pugh and his associates. They define centralization as ". . . the locus of authority to make decisions affecting the organization." [2] But there are two important aspects of centralization. First, organizations vary in the extent to which members are assigned tasks and then provided with the freedom to implement them without interruption from superiors; we call this the degree of hierarchy of authority.[3] A second, and equally important, aspect of the distribution of power is the degree to which staff members participate in setting the goals and policies of the entire organization; we call this the degree of participation in decision-making.

The findings of a number of studies suggest that highly centralized organizations — those with little autonomy over individually assigned tasks and little

Reprinted by permission from *American Sociological Review* 31:4 (1966), pp. 497–507. This investigation was supported in part by a research grant from the Vocational Rehabilitation Administration, Department of Health, Education, and Welfare. Some footnotes omitted.

participation in agency-wide decisions — are likely to have high rat
alienation. Blauner argues that workers have strong feelings of powe
industries such as textiles and automobiles in which the workers have l
over the conditions of employment (with respect to both company-w
and the individual worker's immediate process).[4] Pearlin noted greate
among nurses if the authority structure was too rigid and impersonal.[5] Still other
studies suggest that organizations characterized by a rigid hierarchy of authority
have little cohesion among workers.[6] This lack of cohesion should be reflected
in a high degree of alienation from fellow workers.

The potential for both types of alienation in organizations with an unequal
distribution of power should be even greater in those that have a professional
staff than in those that lack such a staff. Professionals have advanced training and
normally adopt codes of professional behavior that foster norms of autonomy
and expectations of involvement in shaping the goals of the organization.[7] If they
are denied access to the seat of power, they are likely to become dissatisfied with
their jobs. Job alienation may spill over into other aspects of organizational life.
Thus organizations in which expectations of decision-making are violated may also
have less communication among staff members, and alienation from fellow workers may increase.

Another tradition of research in industrial relations has been concerned with
the correlates of worker morale. In a review of the literature, Herzberg et al.
summarized studies which demonstrate that quality of supervision is highly related to worker morale.[8] This tradition of research is obviously tapping some of
the same dimensions or organizational life that we have attempted to capture.
However we have chosen to conceive of dissatisfaction with work situation in
terms of alienation. Few of the studies reported by Herzberg looked at organizational characteristics as they relate to morale; most were psychologically oriented.

This discussion leads us to hypothesize that both alienation from the job and
alienation from fellow workers will be greater in highly centralized organizations
than in decentralized ones.

By *formalization* we mean the degree of work standardization and the amount
of deviation that is allowed from standards. Blau and Scott have described bureaucratic formalization as:

> ... official procedures ... which prescribe the appropriate reactions to recur-
> rent situations and furnish established guides for decision-making.[9]

A high degree of formalization implies not only a preponderance of rules defining
jobs and specifying what is to be done, but also the enforcement of those rules.
The two French public agencies described by Crozier had an almost obsessive
reliance on routines and procedures, and these organizations were characterized
not only by workers' dissatisfaction with the conditions of employment, but also
by little worker solidarity.[10] In a study of an air force tracking station Gross
noted that the great emphasis on rules in the organization resulted in workers
feeling that the work was meaningless.[11] Worthy found that an increase in supervisory pressures brought about a decline in worker morale.[12] Such findings would
lead us to expect alienation from work and from expressive relations to be greater
in organizations which place too much reliance on codification of tasks and observa-

tion of rules. The nature of professional social welfare work simply does not lend itself to easy codification of jobs or reliance on rules without numerous exceptions. We therefore hypothesize that the degree of alienation from work and from fellow workers will vary concomitantly with the degree of formalization of an organization.

Study Design and Methodology

The data upon which this study is based were gathered in 16 social welfare agencies located in a large midwest metropolis in 1964. Ten agencies are private; six are either public or branches of public agencies. These agencies are all of the larger welfare organizations that provide rehabilitation and psychiatric services or services for the mentally retarded as defined by the directory of the Community Chest. The agencies vary in size from 12 to several hundred. Interviews were conducted with 314 staff members of these 16 organizations. Respondents within each organization were selected by the following criteria:

a. All executive directors and department heads;
b. In departments of less than ten members one half of the staff selected randomly;
c. In departments of more than ten members, one-third of the staff selected randomly.

Nonsupervisory administrative and maintenance personnel were not interviewed.

This sampling procedure divides the organization into levels and departments. Job occupants in the upper levels are selected because they are most likely to be key decision-makers and determine organizational policy; job occupants in the lower levels are selected randomly. The different ratios within departments ensure that smaller departments are adequately represented. Professionals, such as psychiatrists, social workers, and rehabilitation counselors, are included because they are intimately involved in the achievement of organizational goals and are likely to have organizational power. Non-professionals, such as attendants, janitors and secretaries, are excluded because they are not directly involved in the achievement of organizational goals and have little or no power. The numbers of interviews varied from 7 in the smallest to 41 in one of the larger agencies.

The units of analysis in this study are organizations and not individuals in the organizations. Information obtained from respondents is pooled to reflect properties of the 16 organizations. These properties are then related to one another. Aggregating individual data in this way presents methodological problems for which there are as yet no satisfactory solutions. For example, if all respondents are equally weighted, undue weight is given to respondents lower in the hierarchy. Yet those higher in the chain of command — not those lower in the chain of command — are most likely to make the decisions which give an agency its ethos.

We attempted to compensate for this by computing an organizational score from the means of social position within the agency.[13] A social position is defined by the level or stratum in the organization and the type of professional activity. For example, if an agency's professional staff consists of psychiatrists and social workers, each divided into two hierarchical levels, the agency has four social positions: supervisory psychiatrists, psychiatrists, supervisory social workers and social workers. A mean is then computed for each social position in the agency. The organizational score for a given variable is determined by computing the average of all social position means in the agency.

Computation of means for each social position has the advantage of avoiding the potential problem created by the use of two sampling ratios. In effect, responses are standardized by organizational location — level and occupation — and then combined into the organizational score. Computation of means of social position also has the major theoretical advantage of focusing on the sociological perspective of organizational reality. An organization is a collection of social positions rather than an aggregate of individuals; sociological properties are more than a summation of psychological properties.

The two types of alienation discussed in this paper were measured with an index of work alienation and an index of alienation from expressive relations. Alienation from work was computed on the basis of responses to the following six questions:

1. How satisfied are you that you have been given enough authority by your board of directors to do your job well?

2. How satisfied are you with your present job when you compare it to similar positions in the state?

3. How satisfied are you with the progress you are making towards the goals which you set for yourself in your present position?

4. On the whole, how satisfied are you that (your superior) accepts you as a professional expert to the degree to which you are entitled by reason of position, training and experience?

5. On the whole, how satisfied are you with your present job when you consider the expectations you had when you took the job?

6. How satisfied are you with your present job in light of career expectations?

Alienation from expressive relations was computed on the basis of responses to the following two questions:

1. How satisfied are you with your supervisor?

2. How satisfied are you with your fellow workers? [14]

There was a strong relationship between these two indices of alienation ($r = 0.75$).

The two aspects of centralization were measured by an index of hierarchy of authority and an index of participation in decision-making. The index of hierarchy of authority was computed by first averaging the replies of individual respondents to each of the following five statements:

1. There can be little action taken here until a supervisor approves a decision.

2. A person who wants to make his own decisions would be quickly discouraged here.

3. Even small matters have to be referred to someone higher up for a final answer.

4. I have to ask my boss before I do almost anything.

5. Any decision I make has to have my boss' approval.

Responses could vary from 1 (definitely false) to 4 (definitely true). The individual scores were then combined into an organizational score as described above.[15]

The index of participation in decision-making was based on the following four questions:

1. How frequently do you usually participate in the decision to hire new staff?

2. How frequently do you usually participate in decisions on the promotion of any of the professional staff?

3. How frequently do you participate in decisions on the adoption of new policies?

4. How frequently do you participate in the decisions on the adoption of new programs?

Respondents were assigned numerical scores from 1 to 5 depending on whether they answered "never," "seldom," "sometimes," "often," or "always," respectively, to these questions. An average score on these questions was computed for each respondent, and then the data were aggregated into organizational scores as described above.

The index of hierarchy of authority shows the extent of reliance upon supervisors in making decisions about individually assigned tasks. The index of participation in decision-making reflects the relative degree of participation in decisions affecting the entire organization, such as those involving the adoption of new programs, new policies, and the hiring and promotion of personnel. There is a strong inverse relationship between these two measures of centralization, as shown in Table 1.

TABLE 1

Product-Moment Correlations between Measures of Centralization
and Formalization, for Sixteen Welfare Organizations

Measures of centralization and formalization	Centralization		Formalization	
	Hierarchy of authority	Participation in decision-making	Job codification	Rule observation
Centralization				
Hierarchy of authority		−.55	.14	.43
Participation in decisions			−.12	−.26
Formalization				
Job codification				−.03
Rule observation				

Note: The units of analysis are the 16 organizations in our study, not the 314 individual respondents. With so few cases, product-moment correlation coefficients are highly sensitive to even slight modifications of numerical scores. Since these 16 organizations constitute a universe of organizations, tests of statistical significance are inappropriate.

The two aspects of formalization were measured with two scales: the index of job codification and the index of rule observation. The index of job codification was based on the following five questions:

1. I feel that I am my own boss in most matters.

2. A person can make his own decisions without checking with anybody else.

3. How things are done here is left up to the person doing the work.

4. People here are allowed to do almost as they please.

5. Most people here make their own rules on the job.

Replies to these questions were scored from 1 (definitely true) to 4 (definitely false), and then each respondent's answers were averaged. Organizational scores were then aggregated as described previously.

The index of rule observation was computed by averaging, as described previously, responses to the following two statements:

1. The employees are constantly being checked on for rule violations.

2. People here feel as though they are constantly being watched, to see that they obey all the rules.

The index of job codification reflects the degree to which job incumbents must consult rules in fulfilling professional responsibilities; the index of rule observation reflects the degree to which employees are observed for rule violations. These measures are not related. (See Table 1.)

Findings

Centralization and Alienation

These professionalized and semi-professionalized social welfare organizations in our study have little hierarchy of authority, although there is considerable variation in the index of participation in decision-making. The organizational scores on the index of hierarchy of authority vary from 1.50 to 2.10 (where the possible scores range from a low of 1.00 to a high of 4.00). In a possible range of scores on the index of participation in decision-making from 1.00 (low participation) to 5.00 (high participation), these agencies had scores of 1.68 to 3.69.

Litwak has suggested that organizations performing primarily non-uniform tasks are more likely to be decentralized.[16] All of our organizations, because they provide physical and social rehabilitation services, perform relatively non-uniform tasks. The 16 organizations are skewed in the direction of decentralization (as measured by the index of hierarchy of authority), although they tend to be more centralized on the index of participation in decision-making. There is still considerable variation among these agencies in their degree of centralization, however, and such variations have important implications for the degree of alienation.

There is a correlation of 0.49 between the degree of hierarchy and alienation from work as shown in panel A of Table 2. The relationship between degree of hierarchy and alienation from expressive relations is approximately the same (0.45). Organizations that rely heavily on hierarchical arrangements are likely to be characterized by both work alienation and alienation from expressive relations. These more centralized authority structures also have less cohesion among staff members. One way to explain these results is that a strict hierarchy of job authority reduces the opportunities for communication among the members of the organization; the consequence of reduced communication is alienation from fellow workers.

The lack of participation in agency decision-making is strongly related to

alienation from work (r = −0.59), as shown in panel A of Table 2. Thus alienation is higher in those organizations in which staff members have a small voice
in agency-wide decisions. Limited participation in decision-making has less of an
effect on alienation from expressive relationships (r = −0.17).[17]

These results are broadly consistent with the generalizations derived from the
Human Relations school of organizational behavior. A high degree of centralization as measured by participation in organization-wide decisions and degree of
control over assigned tasks is related to the presence of work alienation and dis-
enchantment with expressive relations, especially with superordinates.

TABLE 2

Product-Moment Correlations between Measures of
Alienation and Measures of Centralization and
Formalization, for Sixteen Welfare Organizations

	Measures of alienation	
Measures of centralization and formalization	*Alienation from work*	*Alienation from expressive relations*
A. Centralization		
Hierarchy of authority	.49	.45
Participation in decisions	−.59	−.17
B. Formalization		
Job codification	.51	.23
Rule observation	.55	.65

Formalization and Alienation

The agencies in our study were found to have relatively little formalization.
On the index of job codification, which may range from 1.00 (low formalization)
to 4.00 (high formalization), the scores of our agencies were between 2.22 and
2.70. On the index of rule observation, the second indicator of formalization, our
16 organizations had organizational scores of 1.11 to 1.90 on a scale which may
range from 1.00 (low rule observation) to 4.00 (high rule observation).

As shown in panel B of Table 2, there is a direct relationship between the degree
of job codification and both alienation from work (r = 0.51) and alienation from
expressive relations (r = 0.23). The former relationship is much stronger than the
latter. This means that there is great dissatisfaction with work in those organizations in which jobs are rigidly structured; rigidity may lead to strong feelings of
work dissatisfaction but does not appear to have such a deleterious impact on
social relations in the organization.

There is a strong direct relationship between the index of rule observation and
both alienation from work (r = 0.55) and alienation from expressive relations
(r = 0.65). Organizations in which rules are strictly enforced have high degrees
of both work alienation and alienation from expressive relations. The relationship
between rule observation and the latter type of alienation is slightly greater than
with alienation from work, suggesting that disruptions in social relations may be

more likely to occur under conditions of strict enforcement of rules while work alienation may be more likely to occur under conditions of highly structured jobs.[18]

Multivariate Analysis of Centralization, Formalization, and Alienation

One of the problems confronting the social scientist is determining the effect of a variable independently of all others. The relationship between variables such as hierarchy of authority and work alienation may be merely the accidental consequence of their relationships with a third variable, such as participation in decision-making. In an attempt to determine the net effect of independent variables we employed partial and multiple regression analyses.

The first question concerns the two measures of centralization — hierarchy of authority and participation in decision-making — and their relationships with alienation from work and alienation from expressive relations. Panel A of Table 3 shows that participation in decision-making is more closely associated with work alienation than hierarchy of authority when the effect of each is controlled. While the partial correlation coefficients of each with work alienation is less than the zero-order correlation, the partial correlation of participation in decisions ($r_{Y2 \cdot 1} = -0.45$) is greater than that of hierarchy of authority ($r_{Y1 \cdot 2} = 0.24$). The beta weights show a similar relationship. On the other hand, hierarchy of authority is more strongly related to alienation from expressive relations than participation in decision-making when the effect of the latter is controlled. The partial correlation of hierarchy of authority with alienation from expressive relations, controlling for participation in decisions, is essentially the same as the zero-order relationship ($r_{Z1 \cdot 2} = 0.43$). The relationship between participation in decisions and alienation from expressive relations is still weak, and reversed, ($r_{Z2 \cdot 1} = 0.10$) when the effect of hierarchy is controlled. Again, the beta weights show similar results. It seems that work alienation depends more on the degree to which staff members participate in agency-wide decision-making, while alienation from fellow workers depends more on the degree to which supervisors must be consulted in fulfilling individually assigned tasks. Thus disruptions in social relations seem to emerge from the closeness of interaction implicit in little autonomy in decisions about individual tasks. Decisions about the allocation of agency resources should — and do — have little effect on the nature of social relations.

Both rule observation and job codification, our two measures of formalization, have strong and independent relationships with work alienation as shown in panel B of Table 3. The partial correlation coefficients of each with alienation from work, controlling for the influence of the other, are 0.66 and 0.63 respectively. In each case the partial correlation is slightly greater than the zero-order correlation. The presence of either or both of these aspects of formalization in an organization appears to be associated with a high degree of work alienation. This is not the case with respect to alienation from expressive relations, however. The degree of rule observation has a much stronger relationship with alienation from expressive relations than the degree of job codification as shown in Panel B of Table 3. The relationship between job codification and alienation from expressive relations is slightly increased when the influence of rule observation is removed, however.

Having considered the relative influence of the indicators of centralization and

TABLE 3

Coefficients of Partial Correlation and Beta Weights Indicating
Relative Importance of Measures of Centralization and Formalization
in Affecting Alienation, for Sixteen Welfare Organizations

| | Measures of alienation | | | |
| | Alienation from work (Y) | | Alienation from expressive relations (Z) | |
Measures of centralization and formalization	Coefficients of partial correlation	Beta weights[a]	Coefficients of partial correlation	Beta weights[a]
A. Centralization				
1. Hierarchy of authority	.24	.234	.43	.511
2. Participation in decisions	−.45	−.465	.10	.107
Multiple correlation	.63		.46	
B. Formalization				
3. Job codification	.63	.522	.32	.244
4. Rule observation	.66	.569	.68	.660
Multiple correlation	.76		.70	

[a] Regression coefficients in standard measure.

formalization separately, we now ask which of these organizational properties is most importantly associated with our two types of alienation. As shown in Table 4, the degree of participation in decision-making ($r_{Y2 \cdot 134} = -0.57$), the degree of rule observation ($r_{Y4 \cdot 123} = .63$), and the degree of job codification ($r_{Y3 \cdot 124} = 0.67$) have strong and independent effects on alienation from work. In fact, each of the two indicators of formalization has a slightly higher relationship with work alienation than participation in decision-making when the effect of the other variables is removed, but the differences are small. Thus, we could infer that the presence of a high degree of either aspect of formalization or a low degree of participation in organizational decisions is likely to induce work alienation. Among the four structural properties examined in this analysis, rule observation still has the strongest relationship with alienation from expressive relations when the effect of other variables is controlled ($r_{Z4 \cdot 123} = 0.61$). Both hierarchy of authority and job codification have some independent and adverse effect on social relationships in these organizations, but the degree of rule observation is much more strongly related to alienation from expressive relations than either of these two factors.

Participation in decisions that shape the organization's direction, relatively unstructured jobs, and freedom from the restraints of enforced rules are important conditions for a climate of high work morale. Professionals in welfare organizations, by virtue of their advanced training, can make legitimate claims to involvement in policy formulation as well as demands for freedom from excessive constraints of rules; it is in those organizations where professionals are denied access to power or denied such freedom, or both, that work alienation is greatest. It is

TABLE 4

Coefficients of Partial Correlation and Beta Weights Indicating
Relative Importance of Measures of Centralization and Formalization
in Affecting Alienation, for Sixteen Welfare Organizations

| | Measures of alienation | | | |
| | Alienation from work (Y) | | Alienation from expressive relations (Z) | |
Measures of centralization and formalization	Coefficients of partial correlation	Beta weights[a]	Coefficients of partial correlation	Beta weights[a]
Centralization				
1. Hierarchy of authority	−.01	−.005	.27	.245
2. Participation in decisions	−.57	−.421	.17	.141
Formalization				
3. Job codification	.67	.470	.30	.225
4. Rule observation	.63	.460	.61	.591
Multiple correlation	.86		.72	

[a] Regression coefficients in standard measure.

rule observation — a dimension of formalization — that is most highly associated with alienation from expressive relations. Rule observation is more highly related to this form of alienation than is either job codification or the two measures of centralization. As suggested earlier, rule observation implies close supervision by superiors which leads to disruptions in supervisor-staff member relations; this disruption in social ties evidently spills over into social relations with fellow workers.

Summary and Conclusions

In this study, we used the organization as the unit of analysis relating variation in several dimensions of agency structure to two kinds of alienation. This conceptualization is in the tradition of Marx's attempt to relate conditions of work to feelings of alienation. While Marx was primarily interested in the economic organization of total societies and its relationship with alienation, this study indicates that the problem of alienation also occurs in welfare agencies, schools and hospitals, both private and public.

We have shown that highly centralized and highly formalized organizational structures are characterized by greater work alienation and greater alienation from expressive relations. Specifically, these two types of alienation are related to the absence of staff opportunities to participate in decisions concerning organizational policies and individually assigned tasks, and they are manifested where there are strict rules governing jobs and where rules are rigidly enforced. These findings confirm the position that it is indeed important — as Marx suggested more than a century ago — to consider different types of alienation. It is also important to consider the different aspects of organizational structure which give rise to distinctive forms of alienation. We have found that participation in decision-making — an aspect of centralization — as well as a high degree of both job codification and rule observation — aspects of formalization — have strong and independent effects on the degree of work alienation, while the degree of rule observation — an aspect of formalization — is the single best predictor of alienation from expressive relations. Excessive supervision was found to be associated with both types of alienation, but other structural properties were also associated with alienation from work. Future research should attempt to locate those structural properties that are associated with other types of alienation.

While a few previous research studies have explored the relationship between organizational structure and alienation, most prior organizational studies have not. Those which have were either: (1) case studies of single organizations which permitted only limited comparisons; or (2) studies which used the individual as the unit of analysis, relating individual perceptions of organizational structure to other individual reactions.

This research was done in social welfare organizations in which most staff members had some type of professional training. An organizational structure which restricts work-place freedom and participation in setting the goals of the organization was found to be associated with feelings of work alienation even among the members of professions — those individuals who have relatively high pay and prestige in our society.[19]

Variations in other aspects of organizational structure such as the degree of stratification, the relative emphasis on quality or quantity of client services, or the number and types of effective channels of communication may induce different types of alienation in an organization — perhaps types of alienation other than those discussed in this report. These results clearly indicate the importance of comparative organizational analysis.

Notes

1. See *Karl Marx: Early Writings*, T. B. Bottomore (ed.), New York: McGraw-Hill, 1963, pp. 120–134. For a discussion of the pre-Marxian uses of the concept of alienation, see Nathan Rotenstreich, "On the Ecstatic Sources of the Concept of Alienation," *Review of Metaphysics*, 16 (March, 1963), pp. 550–555.
2. D. S. Pugh, D. J. Hickson, C. R. Hinings, K. M. Macdonald, C. Turner and T. Lupton, "A Conceptual Scheme for Organizational Analysis," *Administrative Science Quarterly*, 8 (December, 1963), pp. 289–315. . . .
3. What we have called hierarchy of authority has been referred to by some researchers as "closeness" or "tightness" of supervision. See, for example, Peter M. Blau and W. Richard Scott, *Formal Organizations*, San Francisco: Chandler Publishing Company, 1962, pp. 140–164.
4. Robert Blauner, *Alienation and Freedom*, Chicago: University of Chicago Press, 1964.
5. Leonard Pearlin, "Alienation from Work: A Study of Nursing Personnel," *American Sociological Review*, 27 (June, 1962), pp. 314–326.
6. Blauner, op. cit.; Arthur J. Kover, "Reorganization in an Advertising Agency," *Human Organization*, 22 (Winter, 1963–64), pp. 252–259; Michel Crozier, *The Bureaucratic Phenomenon*, Stanford: Stanford University Press, 1963; Tom Burns and G. M. Stalker, *The Management of Innovation*, London: Travistock Publications, 1961. . . .
7. See Mary E. W. Goss, "Physicians in Bureaucracy: A Case Study of Pro-

fessional Pressure on Organizational Roles," (unpublished doctoral dissertation) Columbia University, 1959, chapter 1, a discussion of the various pressures against the exertion of control over professionals. For a review of the conflicts between professionals and managers see William Kornhauser, *Scientists in Industry,* Berkeley: University of California Press, 1962, chapter 1; and Peter Blau and W. Richard Scott, *Formal Organizations,* op. cit., pp. 60–74.

8. Frederick Herzberg et al., *Job Attitudes: Review of Research and Opinion,* Pittsburgh: Psychological Service of Pittsburgh, 1957, pp. 37–93.

9. Blau and Scott, op. cit., p. 240.

10. Crozier, op. cit.

11. Edward Gross, "Some Functional Consequences of Primary Controls in Formal Work Organizations," *American Sociological Review,* 18 (August, 1953), pp. 368–373.

12. James C. Worthy, "Organizational Structure and Employee Morale," *American Sociological Review,* 15 (April, 1950), pp. 169–179.

13. The two procedures produce very similar results. Product-moment correlation coefficients between them are as follows:

Hierarchy of authority	.70
Rule observation	.88
Actual participation in decisions	.90
Job codification	.68
Alienation from work	.89
Alienation from expressive relations	.88

14. The items in these indices were selected on the basis of a principal components solution factor analysis of 13 items concerning the degree of satisfaction with various aspects of the respondents' work situation. The original battery of 13 items was taken from Neal Gross, Ward Mason and Alexander McEachern *Explorations in Role Analysis,* New York: John Wiley, 1958, Appendix B. In their research they used a split-half reliability test while we used a factor analysis to determine unidimensionality. Etzioni called this latter concept "cohesion." See Amitai Etzioni, *A Comparative Analysis of Complex Organizations,* New York: The Free Press, 1961, pp. 196–198.

15. The items in this index were selected on the basis of a principal components solution factor analysis of 21 items in a "hierarchy of authority" battery and a "rules" battery, as reported by Richard H. Hall in "An Empirical Study of Bureaucratic Dimensions and Their Relation to Other Organizational Characteristics," unpublished Ph.D. dissertation, Ohio State University, 1961. See also Richard H. Hall, "The Concept of Bureaucracy: An Empirical Assessment," *American Journal of Sociology,* 69 (July, 1963), pp. 32–40. Our factor analysis indicated that there were several discrete dimensions among Hall's hierarchy of authority and rules batteries, including the index of job codification and the index of rule observation — indicators of formalization that are discussed below. We chose to base our analysis on the factor analytic structure of these items, to assure us of discrete measures, rather than to retain Hall's scales for sake of comparability.

16. Eugene Litwak, "Models of Bureaucracy Which Permit Conflict," *American Journal of Sociology,* 67 (September, 1961), pp. 177–184.

17. One could argue that a low degree of participation in decision-making may have a different impact on satisfaction with relations with supervisors than with fellow workers. When we separated these two components, we found that there was a moderately strong inverse relationship between participation in decisions and alienation from supervisors ($r = 0.40$) but a direct relationship between participation and alienation from fellow workers ($r = +0.23$). This finding suggests that greater paticipation in organizational decisions is associated with positive affect towards supervisors but with negative affect

towards fellow workers. Other relationships discussed in this paper were unaffected by analyzing the two components of this index separately.

18. Some might argue that such relationships as these might simply be a function of various environmental factors such as age of the organization, auspices (whether private or public), size of the organization, and major function (limited commitment to clients — as in social casework agencies, or high commitment to clients — as in sheltered workshops and psychiatric hospitals). This will be the subject of a forthcoming paper; preliminary analysis suggests that the relationships discussed in this paper remain essentially unchanged when these factors are controlled.

19. Such findings are consistent with others which stress the importance of the content of the job in leading to work satisfaction. See, for example, Nancy C. Morse and Robert S. Weiss, "The Function and Meaning of Work and the Job," *American Sociological Review,* 20 (April, 1955), pp. 191–198.

MELVIN SEEMAN

On the Personal Consequences of Alienation in Work

The radical criticism of industrial society, from Marx to the moderns, has centered its attack on alienation in work. The concern for alienated labor is perhaps the central theme in the literature on the mass society, a literature in which the craftsman's control over the work process and his personal engagement in it, are contrasted with the modern worker's routinization and management.

The criticism embodies two quite distinct propositions: (1) alienated work (i.e., work which is not intrinsically satisfying) is typical of modern society, and this fact *in its own right* constitutes an indictment of the industrial order. In so important an experience as one's work life, alienation represents an immoral denial of man's potential. (2) *Alienated work has consequences,* since extended participation in unfulfilling work cannot help but have serious social effects. Thus, the price we pay for alienated labor is not simply the denial of personal fulfillment, but the further trouble it generates in social life — i.e., political hostilities, frenetic leisure, social movements, race cleavages, and the like.

This paper is concerned with the second of these propositions, while in no way implying that the first proposition is unimportant. Mass society and neo-Marxian theory typically invoke both of them, for they often incorporate both an ideology and a set of predictions. It is to the latter that this work is addressed. Though these predictions are quite varied (and frequently implicit), it is possible to derive a set of reasonably coherent expectations.

Reprinted by permission from *American Sociological Review* 32:2 (1967), pp. 273–285. Some footnotes omitted.

1. People whose work provides little opportunity for decision (see their world as being more generally unmanageable. They will selves as being relatively powerless to affect a wide range of soci; outcomes.

2. Where work is relatively meaningless in itself, people will finc substitute extrinsic ends as important goals. Thus, when work is fractionatea, spe-cialized, and typically performed under conditions of high mobility, one may expect heightened attention to the status-conferring features surrounding work life (and, indeed, if Mills is correct in his analysis of the "status panic," [1] to the status-conferring features of leisure as well).

3. With long hours given over to unrewarding tasks, alienated workers build up a reservoir of frustration and disaffection. Minority groups are likely targets for this hostility, hence alienation in work and prejudiced attitudes should tend to co-exist.

4. Work which provides little opportunity for individual commitment in an orderly career should encourage a relatively anomic view of life. Thus, where work does not bind the individual meaningfully, the social order should generally be viewed as being less supportive and trustworthy.

5. Alienated work does not reward motivational investment in the work process. It is *par excellence* an occasion for withdrawal, and it teaches the lesson of withdrawal — a lesson which the alienated worker carries over into political life by his avoidance of political activity and ignorance of political affairs.

This is certainly only a partial list of the relevant propositions, but a general theme can easily be identified with the help of this list, namely, the theme of "generalization." Alienated work is troublesome because its effects generalize out of the work sphere into other areas of social life: the lack of control in work leads to a sense of low control in political and social affairs; the hostility bred in the work situation overflows into intergroup antagonism; the disengagement at work encourages loose commitment to the normative order in general.

Though little has been done to test directly such negative consequences of alienated work, we know enough already to be cautious about a monolithic image of work experience. We know, for example, that despite wide variations in work conditions and despite the extent of routinization in work, there is a remarkably widespread tendency for people to say that they are satisfied with their work; and we also know that, by some standards at least, the level of alienation in work is surprisingly low.[2]

The study reported here represents an effort to test the generalization theme, seeking to establish the limits of its applicability and the conditions which mute or exaggerate its operation. The effort is part of a series of papers devoted to a clarification of the alienation problem as it is reflected chiefly in the mass society literature. Though mass theory is certainly not essential to the study of alienation, one can find in this theory the beginnings of an orderly theoretical ground for the predictions described above. The theory sets out, in effect, a tripartite scheme: social structural conditions (e.g., the decline of kinship, the emergence of rationalized work procedures) are presumed to have alienative effects (in any one of various alienative modes — e.g., isolation, powerlessness, self-estrangement), and this in turn leads to determinate consequences in attitude and behavior (e.g., polit-

.al withdrawal or mass movements). The present work focuses on the "alienation has consequences" feature of this mass society model: it asks whether work which is self-estranged, in the sense that it provides little intrinsic satisfaction, has the attitude and behavior correlates that the generalization theme would predict.

Method

The data are based upon interviews carried out among a sample of the male work force in Malmö, Sweden. This is the third largest city in Sweden, with a population of roughly 240,000 and a concentration in commercial and seaport occupations. A random sample of males between the ages of twenty and seventy-nine years was drawn from the official population register, a total of 558 workers being finally interviewed (in Swedish). An additional 115 interviews were unobtainable — of which only 37 were refusals, the remainder being persons who were seriously ill, had moved to an unknown address, or the like. The effective sample in the analysis below is substantially less than 558, since the retired workers (N = 54) and those who failed to complete relevant portions of the interview were excluded.

The primary problem was the development of an index of work alienation. To that end, the interview included fifteen questions (taken largely from Blauner's recent volume on the industrial worker)[3] dealing with work experience. Blauner has shown that these questions discriminate among historically different work situations — e.g., skill industries (printing) vs. machine industries (textiles) vs. assembly-line (automobile) and automated work (chemicals). The replies were then subjected to factor analysis, with not only work responses but other attitude and behavior items (e.g., the powerlessness questions described below) being included in the analysis. A clear cluster of work responses emerged from the factoring, a cluster which is referred to here as the index of "work alienation." The seven items comprising this scale (listed below) all ask essentially whether the respondent finds his work engaging and rewarding in itself:

1. Is your job too simple to bring out your best abilities or not?
2. Can you do the work on the job and keep your mind on other things most of the time, or not?
3. Which one of the following statements comes closest to describing how you feel about your present job? (Four statements, from "Interesting nearly all the time" to "Completely dull and monotonous")
4. Does your job make you work too fast most of the time, or not?
5. Does your job really give you a chance to try out ideas of your own or not?
6. If you had the opportunity to retire right now, would you prefer to do that or would you prefer to go on working at your present job?
7. On an ordinary workday, do you have the opportunity to make independent decisions when you are carrying out your tasks, or is it rather routine work?

With respect to our dependent variables, it is plain that we must deal here with the *correlates* of work alienation, rather than with *consequences* in any literal sense, though the implication is that alienation in work leads to the troubles we sought to examine in the interview. The five propositions described above served as a guide to the measures required as outcomes of work alienation.

1. *Generalized powerlessness.* The individual's expectancies for control were measured by means of a forced-choice scale which has been used in a number of American studies and whose characteristics have been reported elsewhere.[4] The fifteen items used in the present study were very similar to those employed by Neal and Seeman, offering the respondent a choice between an expression of mastery and of powerlessness. Two examples follow:

> a. — Many times I feel that I have little influence over the things that happen to me.
> — I do not believe that chance and luck are very important in my life.
> b. — Becoming a success is a matter of hard work; luck has little or nothing to do with it.
> — Getting a job depends mainly on being in the right place at the right time.

2. *Intergroup hostility.* A Bogardus-type social-distance test was developed, offering a standard set of nearness alternatives (from marriage to citizenship) and employing five groups relevant to the Swedish situation: Negroes, Americans, Estonians, Jews, and Gypsies. The Kuder-Richardson reliability coefficient for this prejudice score was 0.91.

3. *Political awareness.* A sixteen-item information test was prepared and pretested, dealing with both Swedish politics and international affairs (e.g., "Sweden's foreign minister at the present time is Östen Unden"; "Switzerland is a member of the European Economic Community"). The respondent was instructed not to guess, and three answer alternatives were provided: True; False; Don't know. The individual's score was the number of correct answers. The reliability estimate was 0.73 for this knowledge test.

4. *Status-mindedness.* A Swedish translation was prepared of the "mobility orientation" scale used in several U.S. studies. In the present case, the scale consisted of fourteen items (all presented in the usual Likert format) intended to measure the degree to which the respondent placed the value of occupational mobility above other values in his hierarchy of goals. Two examples will suffice to illustrate the meaning of a high (status-oriented) score:

> a. I'd probably turn down a substantial advancement if it involved being away from the family a good deal. (Agree = low score)
> b. I wouldn't let my friendship ties in a community stand in the way of moving on to a better job. (Agree = high score)

5. *Normlessness.* A Swedish version of Srole's anomia scale was administered in the interview. This five-item Likert-type scale has been widely used and is intended as a measure of the individual's sense for a dependable social order characterized by interpersonal trust and clarity of normative demands, the obverse of which is "self-to-other alienation."[5]

6. *Expert orientation.* Since we were mainly concerned with various forms of withdrawal, putatively occasioned by work experience that is characterized by low control and low engagement, an attitude item especially designed for the Swedish

situation was included. Sweden, on the whole, makes heavy use of experts in the conduct of government (e.g., considerable weight is assigned to expert-based committee reports on social policy). We were interested in a rough assessment of the connection between work experience and the respondent's willingness to turn matters over to the specialists' control. Thus, the respondents were asked whether they agreed or disagreed (on a five-point scale) with the statement: "Actually, the basic decisions on political and social questions should be made by the specialists and experts." Respondents who opt for specialist control (a "high" score meaning agreement with the item) are relatively disengaged from political affairs, though clearly this one expression of a "let-the-experts-do-it" attitude has both methodological and philosophical difficulties. For example, its reliability is unknown (but a recent study using the same item in the U. S. produced radically lower expert acceptance, as one might expect), and the counter-argument that there are long-range democratic controls over the experts remains unanswered. Nonetheless, we present the evidence on the specialist question here for what it may provisionally tell about the "retreat" into expertise.

Results

The Correlates of Work Alienation

We have three major tasks in the analysis of these data: (1) to examine the correlations obtained for the work alienation index; (2) to establish the appropriate controls showing that the associations are not spurious; and (3) to determine whether the relationships are affected by social factors that are commonly employed in mass theory as important conditioners of the hypothesized outcomes (chiefly, membership in mediating organizations and participation in an occupational community).

Table 1 presents (in its first line) the correlations required to test the notion that work alienation has negative outcomes. The full set of intercorrelations among the dependent variables is also given in Table 1, for these r's reflect upon the quality and reasonability of the outcome measures, and they are of interest in their own right.

The most striking feature of Table 1 is the contrast it shows: work alienation is not consistently and significantly related to the postulated outcomes, yet the outcome measures themselves are patterned in significant and predictable ways. For example, the powerlessness measure (column 5 in Table 1) is unrelated to work alienation, for both the manuals and non-manuals; but high powerlessness clearly goes, as it should, with high anomia, high expert orientation, high prejudice, and low political knowledge.

These are not likely to be instrument-generated correlations (i.e., correlating attitudes that may be quite similar but have been named differently), though this may partially be the case for anomia and powerlessness. The political knowledge correlations (-0.21 and -0.17 in the last row of Table 1), for example, involve the subject's responses to a factual test of *information* about world affairs, and this test score correlates with a measure of the person's *expectancies* for control of a wide variety of socio-economic matters (war, inflation, occupational success, national prestige, and governmental policy). The important fact in Table 1 can be

TABLE 1
Intercorrelation of Work Alienation and Outcome Indices, for Manual and Non-Manual Workers in Sweden

| | Manual workers (N = 282) | | | | | | Non-manual workers (N = 171) | | | | | |
Outcome measure	(1) Anomia	(2) Expert orientation	(3) Mobility attitude	(4) Prejudice	(5) Powerlessness	(6) Political knowledge	(1) Anomia	(2) Expert orientation	(3) Mobility attitude	(4) Prejudice	(5) Powerlessness	(6) Political knowledge
Work alienation	.15ᵃ	.14ᵃ	−.14ᵃ	.05	.05	.04	.06	.05	−.05	.02	.09	−.13
1. Anomia		.24ᵇ	.12	.18ᵇ	.37ᵇ	−.19ᵇ		.32ᵇ	.08	.38ᵇ	.39ᵇ	−.33ᵇ
2. Experts			.08	.11	.13ᵃ	−.03			.17ᵃ	.22ᵇ	.29ᵇ	−.28ᵇ
3. Mobility attitude				.07	.15ᵃ	−.18ᵇ				.17ᵃ	.14	−.07
4. Prejudice					.24ᵇ	−.11					.29ᵇ	−.21ᵇ
5. Powerlessness						−.21ᵇ						−.17ᵃ

Note: The work alienation score ranges from 7 to 16 for the manuals (mean = 10.02; S.D. = 1.72); and from 6 to 14 for the non-manuals (mean = 9.25; S.D. = 1.49). The mean difference is significant (see footnote 10). A table similar to the one presented here, but for the sample as a whole, shows no important change in the pattern above, hence the breakdown of the two major occupational groups is retained here.

ᵃ P < .05.
ᵇ P < .01.

put as follows: three quite different measures — namely, a prejudice score (obtained via a social-distance scale), a powerlessness score (obtained by a forced-choice procedure), and a political knowledge score (obtained through a true-false information test) — show no correlation with work alienation. However, they show consistent relationships among themselves and with other outcome variables.

Thus, these unimpressive *r*'s between work alienation and its presumed consequences raise serious questions about the validity of the generalization thesis, and they do so in a context of other associations which suggest that our respondents are making meaningful discriminations in their interview replies. It seems unlikely that the answers to the work questions alone can be suspected on technical grounds, particularly in view of Blauner's evidence showing that these items discriminate well among different work situations. Blauner reports, for example, (1) that the percentage of male workers who "can think of other things while working" (see question 2 in the work alienation measure) varies from 19 percent in the paper industry to 46 percent in the highly-routinized textile industry; and (2) that the percent who find their job "dull and monotonous" (see question 3) varies from 4 percent in a craft industry (printing) to 34 percent who complain of monotony in the assembly-line automobile industry.[6]

Still, it is true that the total scores on work alienation are narrowly distributed, with a relatively heavy concentration in the middle range. It seemed wise, therefore, to look more closely at the extremes — i.e., to trichotomize the distribution and compare the "high" and "low" alienation groups to determine whether differences in these extreme groups were being obscured by the moderates. Among the manuals, for example, these extreme categories involved, respectively, 41 and 47 cases (with 162 being "moderates"). There is no need to present the results of this analysis in its entirety. The gist of it is given in Table 2 where the extreme groups on work alienation are compared using two of the outcome variables (the two selected for presentation representing the range, in a sense, of the dependent variables: the expert question, a single item attitude measure; and the political knowledge test, a "hard" criterion true-false information score).

The data of Table 2 (including the data similar to it from the other outcome variables, not presented here) support two conclusions: (1) as in Table 1, but here using only the extremes in work alienation, the basic finding for both manuals and non-manuals is one of low and non-significant association; and (2) the trends, such as they are, typically go in the direction that the generalization thesis would predict (e.g., those high in work alienation tend to be somewhat more expert-oriented). But these are slim trends, indeed, and the main drift of the analysis for the extreme groups is that again we fail to find evidence for the generalization process.

The question, naturally, arises as to whether the usual background variables may be masking or suppressing the expected relationships. It would be more likely that education, occupational prestige and the like, would produce spuriously *high* associations between work alienation and the outcome indices, but a test of the possibility that appropriate controls would produce more convincing evidence of generalization seemed in order. Accordingly, controls were established for each of the following variables: age, education, income, occupational prestige level, number of years on the present job, and size of present workplace.

The general findings of this analysis are illustrated in Table 3, where the control

TABLE 2
Percent (and Frequencies) High and Low on Two Outcome Measures for Workers High and Low in Alienation

Outcome measure		Manual workers				Non-manual workers			
		Low work alienation (N = 47)		High work alienation (N = 41)		Low work alienation (N = 59)		High work alienation (N = 34)	
		%	N	%	N	%	N	%	N
Expert orientation	High	47	(22)	66	(27)	46	(27)	62	(21)
	Low	53	(25)	34	(14)	54	(32)	38	(13)
		100%		100%		100%		100%	
Political knowledge	High	49	(23)	54	(22)	86	(51)	74	(25)
	Low	51	(24)	46	(19)	14	(8)	26	(9)
		100%		100%		100%		100%	

Note: The "middle" group in the trichotomized distribution for work alienation (low-middle-high) is omitted.

TABLE 3
Percent High on Various Outcome Indices, Controlling for Education,
among Non-Manual Workers Differing in Degree of Work Alienation

Outcome measure	Low education		High education	
	Low alienation (N = 56)	High alienation (N = 43)	Low alienation (N = 44)	High alienation (N = 26)
Anomia	40	37	18	17
Expert orientation	57	72	46	54
Mobility attitude	26	19	27	42
Prejudice	41	37	11	19
Powerlessness	41	44	18	23
Political knowledge	71	67	98	92

Note: None of the chi-squares for these fourteen distributions (using the full range of the breakdown, not simply a comparison of percentages scoring high on the outcome variable) reaches a statistically significant level.

for education among the non-manual workers is displayed. Education is presumably a crucial variable (and especially so among the non-manuals, where the variance on education is appreciable), since we are dealing with outcome variables that are known to be heavily influenced by education — e.g., anomia, prejudice, and political knowledge. Table 3 is quite typical of the product yielded by the other control variables, and it shows that, with the control applied, work alienation has very little indeed to do with the outcomes measured here.

The import of these results (and of the parallel results for the other controls, not presented here) is that the appropriate controls do not make the generalization phenomenon more evident; if anything, these controls make the three barely significant r's in Table 1 (between work alienation and the outcome measures) more suspect as indicators of generalization in any meaningful sense. These remarks apply to income as well as education: one might suppose that the poorly paid worker engaged in unsatisfying work would show the negative outcomes most clearly, but the correlations for the low-income group are not distinctively higher. There is no way of knowing, without comparative data, whether the socialized Swedish economy, with its orderliness and wage stability, constitutes a rather special and more favorable case either for the low income worker in particular, or for all workers.

Control over the Work Process

For Marx, as for more recent critics of industrial society, a key feature of work alienation is found in the worker's lack of control over his work life. As Blauner has noted, this lack of control can be manifested in ways that need to be distinguished; but surely one of the most fundamental of these is the lack of control over the immediate work process. As Blauner comments: "Reacting to the rhythms of technology rather than acting in some independent or autonomous manner, (the worker) approaches most completely the condition of *thingness*, which is the essence of alienation." [7]

The measure of work alienation discussed above has some bearing upon work autonomy, but a more direct treatment of control over the work process is possible. We included a question which asked directly, "How much control do you have over the work pace in your job?" — the respondent then choosing an answer from among three statements saying, essentially, that he had a great deal of control, some control, or very little control. The score for this (perforce narrowly distributed) item correlates in the expected fashion with work alienation: e.g., among the manuals, with education controlled $(N = 213)$, $r = -0.21$ (high alienation goes with low control).

The control item, however, does not correlate with the outcome indices; it yields, that is, the same minimal associations that the work alienation measure revealed. Table 4 shows these results for both the manual and non-manual workers. None of the differences in that table is significant or appreciable, yet the control item works as one might anticipate with respect to the manual versus non-manual distinction: the non-manuals are significantly higher in their sensed control over the work process (see footnote to Table 4).[8]

TABLE 4

Percent High on Various Outcome Indices among Workers High and Low in Control of the Work Process

	Manual		Non-manual	
Outcome measure	*Low control* $(N = 118)$	*High control* $(N = 132)$	*Low control* $(N = 51)$	*High control* $(N = 120)$
Anomia	31	27	31	30
Expert orientation	53	55	57	58
Mobility attitude	36	30	26	27
Prejudice	31	30	31	28
Powerlessness	42	41	34	33
Political knowledge	46	52	80	80

Note: The only significant difference in this table is found in the manual vs. non-manual *frequency distribution*, with the non-manuals being more heavily concentrated in the "high control" category ($\chi^2 = 12.759$; df $= 1$; P $< .001$).

Social Bonds and Work Alienation

Some would suggest that our search for outcomes is unduly individualistic, pointing to the likelihood that social features connected with work are important mediators of alienation and its effects. There is, for example, the familiar argument that membership in a work organization can serve both to moderate the worker's alienation and to mute its negative effect by providing an instrument of control that the worker sees as representing his work-relevant interests. Similarly, work-related affective bonds (e.g., a sense of occupational community) may operate in the same meliorative way. Indeed, Pearlin has provided some evidence along these lines in his study of alienation among nurses. He writes: "Thus, alienation occurs less among those who have established extra-work friendship relations with fellow workers and this was found to be especially true when the friends are part of the same face-to-face work group."[9]

The question at stake is a dual one: do such social bonds moderate the sense of alienation in work; and, whatever the answer to that question, do these bonds bear upon the generalization of alienated work into the negative outcomes with which we are here concerned — i.e., do such bonds mute or accentuate the tie between alienated work and its postulated outcomes?

These questions required two indices of social bonds (organization and community); and a word is in order about how these were derived. The idea of organizational ties can refer both to membership itself or to engagement in the life of the organization. For the manual workers in Sweden, the latter is a necessary measure since nearly all of the manuals have formal membership (only 25 out of 282 report no membership). Hence, a series of questions were asked dealing with the worker's attitude toward and participation in the organization, and from these an index of organizational involvement was derived. These questions concerned (1) attendance at organization meetings; (2) importance of the organization to the worker; (3) perceived influence of the worker in organizational affairs; and (4) participation as an officer of the organization.

The measure of occupational community was borrowed from the well-known study of the printers' union by Lipset, et al.,[10] and was based upon three factors: (1) having close friends in the same occupation; (2) having close friends in the same workplace; and (3) seeing these friends frequently outside the work sphere.

Table 5 presents the correlations between work alienation and its presumed outcomes for those who were high and low in organizational involvement and in occupational community (for manual workers only, in the interest of clarity and space; the non-manual data require no alteration of the conclusions). The table

TABLE 5
Correlations between Work Alienation and Various Outcomes for Manual Workers Differing in Their Organizational Involvement and Occupational Community

	Organizational involvement		Occupational community	
Measure	*Low* (N = 147)	*High* (N = 103)	*Low* (N = 124)	*High* (N = 126)
Anomia	.17[a]	.13	.18[a]	.13
Expert orientation	.16	.10	.17	.10
Mobility attitude	−.32[b]	.04	−.08	−.23[b]
Prejudice	.10	−.04	.06	.03
Powerlessness	.05	.05	.14	−.03
Political knowledge	.08	−.03	.00	.06
Mean work alienation	9.9	10.1	9.9	10.1
International interest	.07	−.11	.01	−.02
Discuss my work	−.17[a]	−.11	−.25[b]	−.04

Note: The organizational involvement score excludes workers who were not members of a work organization (see text discussion).
[a] P < .05.
[b] P < .01.

includes the mean work alienation scores for these subgroups. The last two lines of Table 5 require comment. The interview began with four questions concerning the degree of interest respondents had in various activities (intended chiefly as an easy introduction to the interview process). Two of these interests are relevant to the meaningfulness of the measures under discussion here, namely, the respondent's interest in "international affairs" and in "discussing my work." These are quite different interests, and they ought to show a differential relation to the work alienation measure. Unless there is a rather high degree of generalization, work alienation should be unrelated to interest in international affairs, but one might expect alienation to be associated with the interest in discussing one's work. Thus, these two interests provide a point of discrimination about the work alienation index. Again, the question is: does this measure work as it logically should, and is there evidence for a high degree of generalization?

The main conclusion derivable from Table 5 is that the effects of involvement and community are not substantial:

1. The workers who are engaged in the life of the organization, or in an occupational community, are not different in the mean level of work alienation they express.

2. The degree of correlation between alienation and its outcomes is not materially affected by the differences in social bonds. Though the *r*'s are increased in some instances (most consistently showing that high work alienation goes with low occupational striving), the basic pattern of minimal association is maintained.

3. So far as the differentiation of worker's interests is concerned, these data show the expected pattern: those high in work alienation have significantly less interest in discussing their work with others, especially where the worker is not in an occupational community or organizationally involved; but work alienation is unrelated to interest in international affairs.[11]

Intrinsic Orientation toward Work

The kind of work a person has may be far less important than what he is *oriented to* in that work — i.e., the rewards he finds most satisfying in the job. Here the same distinction between intrinsic and extrinsic activity applies, and it seems wise to examine the relevance of an alienated orientation for the problem of generalization.

We offered the respondents a fairly standard set of job values, asking them to select "the feature of your present job that you like the most." The following eight alternatives were supplied: (1) it's interesting work; (2) has high prestige; (3) good working conditions; (4) it's educational work; (5) a secure job; (6) pays good wages; (7) uses my skill; and (8) good chances for promotion. Choices 1, 4 and 7 were considered "intrinsic" since they focus upon the nature of the work itself, whereas the "extrinsic" items describe the job's consequences (wages, promotion, prestige) or the conditions under which it is performed. Only four of these alternatives drew a substantial number of first choices among both manual and non-manual workers, and, as it happens, two of these were intrinsic values and two extrinsic: interesting work and uses my skill. vs. working conditions and security (see Table 6 for the respective N's). As might be expected, and as other

TABLE 6

Mean Outcome Scores for Manual Workers Oriented to Intrinsic and
Extrinsic Job Values with Education Controlled

Measure	Intrinsic choice		Extrinsic choice	
	Interest-ing work (N = 94)	Uses my skill (N = 30)	Working conditions (N = 41)	Security (N = 54)
Anomia	11.4	11.4	12.2	11.7
Expert orientation	3.6	3.2	3.5	3.6
Mobility attitude	38.9	41.6	38.9	39.2
Prejudice	3.6	2.9	4.8	4.5
Powerlessness	5.0	4.2	5.2	5.4
Political knowledge	6.7	6.7	6.0	6.5
Work alienation	9.6	9.7	10.4	10.6[a]
International interest	2.8	2.9	2.8	2.6
Discuss my work	3.3	3.5	2.9	2.7[a]

Note: The control for education excludes 39 manual workers who offered one of these
four values as their choice. Among non-manual workers the respective N's for the four
choices were: Interesting work, 91; Uses my skill, 40; Working conditions, 14; and Security, 11.

[a] Differences among the four choice groups significant at the .01 level in a one-way
analysis of variance.

studies have shown, the extrinsic values of security and working conditions are
more heavily chosen among the manual workers.

There are grounds for supposing that these differences in work orientation might
be related to the variables that are here treated as outcomes. Rosenberg, for example, presents evidence showing that college students who make an extrinsic
choice among occupational values (those who rank "a chance to earn a good deal
of money" as a first choice) score significantly lower on a generalized "faith in
people" scale.[12] This is, of course, simply a relationship among expressed attitudes,
since none of these students was actually engaged in an occupation. The question
is, does an unalienated orientation toward one's actual work (a focus upon intrinsic
values in the work itself) relate to the variables under discussion? It is more difficult, of course, to speak here of "outcomes." Though being engaged in alienated
work may easily be thought of as producing (let us say) ethnic hostility, it is more
reasonable to think of an intrinsic orientation as part of a syndrome of attitudes
— a syndrome that may or may not include such variables as hostility, powerlessness, knowledge, and the like.

Table 6 presents the data bearing upon the existence of such a syndrome.
Though Table 6 presents the data for manual workers only, the same pattern is
found among the non-manuals (these data not being presented because the control
for education sharply reduces the available cases per cell). The results presented
here are coordinate with what has gone before: (1) the analysis of variance for
the six "outcome" variables shows that none of these is significantly bound up with

an intrinsic orientation toward work (though the prejudice scores vary considerably and in the direction one would predict); (2) as in the earlier material, the interest scores show the expected differentiation, with those who are intrinsically oriented showing greater interest in discussing their work (but no difference in international interest); and (3) the work alienation scores vary as one would expect: those who emphasize intrinsic values are actually engaged in less alienative work.[13]

Summary and Conclusions

We have found little evidence that alienated work, in the sense of work which is unrewarding in its own right, has the generalized consequences often imputed to it. The alienated worker is not more hostile to ethnic minorities, less knowledgeable and engaged in political matters, less sanguine about or interested in the possibility of exercising control over socio-political events, more status minded, or more anomic. With respect to the latter two variables, there are small signs (particularly among the manual workers) that the extreme groups in work alienation do generalize their work attitude to include a rather diffuse disaffection (anomia) and a retreat from mobility striving (status mindedness). To the extent that there is evidence of generalization, it is chiefly found in attitudes that are more or less work related, but the generalization does not go very far (nor appear very consistently among both manual and non-manual workers).

This failure to demonstrate the generalization phenomenon occurs in a context of other meaningful associations which makes it highly unlikely that the failure can be dismissed on methodological grounds. We find, for example, that these supposed outcomes are meaningfully related to one another in predictable ways: high powerlessness and low political knowledge go together, for both manual and non-manual workers, and powerlessness likewise correlates positively with ethnic prejudice. Furthermore, the measure of work alienation relates, as it should, to various characteristics of the Swedish workers who were interviewed. For example, it is higher among the manuals than the non-manuals, lower among those with higher income, lower among those who stress the intrinsic features of their job, and lower among those who express little interest in discussing their work with others. But work alienation is not consistently or strongly related to outcomes which range from a single agree-disagree attitude scale that basically taps one's personal disaffection with the world (the Srole anomia scale) to an objective test of knowledge about world affairs (the true-false political knowledge test).

How can one interpret these basically negative results? In the first place, cross-cultural validation of these findings is essential, since it is entirely possible that the effects of work alienation are tempered by the surrounding social system — in the present case, by the highly-organized, relatively stable, fundamentally democratic and economically advanced social order that modern Sweden represents. It is possible that alienated work, especially at the lower income levels, is something else again in the U.S. or in France.

Certainly, too, the case against an industrial system that breeds alienated work, whatever the surrounding economic setting, cannot rest upon the existence of the consequences with which we have been concerned. For one thing, work life absorbs a major portion of the day, and an ethical stance concerning it must come to terms with that fact, regardless of any further consequences of such labor. For another, it is reasonable to argue either that the outcomes we have treated constitute an insufficient list (the data say little about the quality of family life, for example), or that the consequences will reveal themselves in a longer-term, cumulative way — for example, in revolutions or in the irregular outbursts of a wildcat strike.

Nevertheless, the outcomes reviewed here cover a rather broad spectrum, and they are varied enough to embody the several "dynamics" or motivational principles involved in the propositions about work that are derived from Marxian and mass society theory. These propositions, like the five presented at the outset of this paper, typically depend upon one (or a combination) of the following:

1. The principle of *frustration-aggression;* e.g., alienated work builds frustrations which find release in ethnic hostility.

2. The principle of *substitution;* e.g., since alienated work fails to provide requisite intrinsic satisfactions, workers are driven to seek substitute, and generally shallow, satisfactions (status, power, display, etc.).

3. The principle of *social learning;* e.g., through alienated work, people learn that they are objects of control by others, and this learning is applied to a wider range of socio-political affairs in which a sense of powerlessness is displayed.

It is through the operation of these dynamics that generalization is said to take place. Despite the eminent reasonability of these mechanisms of generalization, the present data raise doubts about their validity as descriptions of what is, in fact, going on in the world of work. One is forced to entertain alternative images of that world. One such alternative would suggest that workers simply come to terms, more easily than our theories imply, with the only work life they know and can reasonably expect for themselves. There is, in this view, no constant comparison with some ideal standard or with someone else's work. Work is nothing else than what it is known to be — often not very rewarding in itself, and always necessary. And the big task for the worker is not to convert it into a major source of intrinsic satisfaction, but to manage it so that it can be an acceptable life of the moment by creating occasions, however small, for humor, sociality, decision-making, competition, argument, etc., that are at once trivial and remarkable.

That this kind of "coming to terms" does take place was the burden of the well-known study by Morse and Weiss on the meaning of work, and of Chinoy's study among automobile workers which documented the ways in which workers develop defenses allowing them to come to terms with their low position in a society that stresses advancement.[14] At one point, Chinoy comments:

> . . . men cannot spend eight hours per day, forty hours each week, in activity which lacks all but instrumental meaning. They therefore try to find some significance in the work they must do. Workers may take pride, for example, in executing skillfully even the routine tasks to which they are assigned. . . . They may derive a moral satisfaction from doing "an honest day's work." . . . They may try to squeeze out some sense of personal significance by identifying themselves with the product, standardized though it may be, and with the impersonal corporation in which they are anonymous, replaceable entities.[15]

It is impossible to say whether such "makeshift substitutes for full-bodied emotional satisfaction on the job" can be thoroughly effective in the sense that they not only get the worker through the day but also maintain a reasonably unimpaired self-regard. It seems likely that this could be so, especially in the more extreme cases of routinization of labor where, as Swados suggests, workers are more likely to be "either resigned to their fate, furiously angry at *themselves* for what they are doing, or desperately hunting other work. . . ." [16]

The present data do not focus directly on such personal matters of self-image, or on the documentation of whether the worker furiously dislikes his work, blames himself as a failure for being in it, or is hopelessly resigned to it. The question has been, in effect, whether that potential fury, blame and resignation find relatively immediate expression beyond the limited work sphere. The data suggest that people can work out fairly effective adjustments to varied kinds of work, *if* by "effective" we simply mean leading a work life that has little generalized effect upon the standard forms of hating, striving, withdrawing and complaining reviewed here.

One way to summarize the matter is to suggest that although these data tell nothing about what work could or should be in ideal circumstances, they may tell a good deal about our theories of work in the present circumstances. They tell us that the free use of the generalization model is probably unwarranted, and, by the same token, that the theories we now employ are probably premature. Mass society theory and neo-Marxian theory, at any rate, appear to underestimate by far the social-psychological subtleties of the work process. Perhaps what is needed now is a closer look at that process as it is lived by the worker, a detailed description of work experience that will tell us just how the worker manages to "call it a day." The ultimate aim, of course, goes well beyond the description itself, for this kind of knowledge ought to be a vehicle for improving our very conception (theoretically most unsatisfying at present) of self-estrangement, of what it really means to talk about intrinsically rewarding activity, at work or elsewhere.

Notes

1. C. Wright Mills, *White Collar*, New York: Oxford University Press, 1951, Chapter 11.
2. See, for example, Robert Blauner, "Work Satisfaction and Industrial Trends in Modern Society," in W. Galenson and S. M. Lipset, editors, *Labor and Trade Unionism*, New York: John Wiley and Sons, 1960, pp. 339–360; and Harold Wilensky, "Varieties of Work Experience," in H. Borow, editor, *Man in a World of Work*, New York: Houghton, Mifflin, 1964, pp. 125–154. . . .
3. Robert Blauner, *Alienation and Freedom*, Chicago: University of Chicago Press, 1964.
4. In addition to the work cited in note 5 above, see Julian B. Rotter, "Generalized Expectancies for Internal Versus External Control of Reinforcement," *Psychological Monographs*, 80, No. 1 (Whole #609, 1966), pp. 1–28.
5. Leo Srole, "Social Integration and Certain Corollaries: An Exploratory Study," *American Sociological Review*, 21 (December, 1956), pp. 709–716. The scale apparently has a heavy component of generalized negativism or discouragement. For evidence on this, see (among others) Edward L. McDill, "Anomie, Authoritarianism, Prejudice and Socio-Economic Status: An Attempt at Clarification," *Social Forces*, 39 (March, 1961), pp. 239–245.
6. Blauner, op. cit. (1964), p. 175. Within the present data there are similar signs that a purely measurement argument against the work alienation index is a dubious one. For example, among the non-manuals, the correlation between income and work alienation is -0.31 (P $<$ 0.01); and those who are in non-manual occupations of relatively higher prestige show significantly

low alienation as one would expect ($\chi^2 = 8.781$; df $= 1$; P < 0.01). As expected, too, the manual workers are higher in work alienation than the non-manuals (the mean scores are 10.02 and 9.25, respectively; t $= 6.154$; P $<$ 0.001, with N $= 453$.).

7. Ibid., p. 20. For a discussion of loss of control over the work process, see William A. Faunce, "Automation and the Automobile Worker," *Social Problems,* 6 (Summer, 1958), pp. 68–78.

8. Each item of the work alienation measure was also treated separately, on the possibility that the total score was masking consequences relating to particular features of the person's work experience. Though there are occasional significant chi-squares in this extended analysis (a chi-square for each of seven items against each of six outcomes, for both manual and non-manual workers), the weight of the evidence is consistent with the analysis already presented.

It may be suggested that these work alienation items are simply an index of work satisfaction. The notion of alienation employed here refers to *intrinsic reward* in work, an idea that is not equivalent to satisfaction with the job, even though the two may be correlated. Unfortunately, the Swedish interview did not include a question on general job satisfaction, but the preliminary results of a later American study are instructive. In a sample of 172 Negro manual workers (all males), an r of —0.02 was obtained between the work alienation index (using the same items as in the Swedish case) and a question on work satisfaction. As Berger remarks, ". . . job satisfaction does not necessarily tell us much about alienation . . . one can be quite alienated from work but quite satisfied with one's job" (op. cit., p. 42).

9. Leonard I. Pearlin, "Alienation from Work: A Study of Nursing Personnel," *American Sociological Review,* 27 (June, 1962), pp. 314–326; p. 325. Pearlin's work alienation refers to "subjectively experienced powerlessness to control" one's work, a definition which is narrower than that employed here.

10. Seymour M. Lipset, Martin A. Trow and James S. Coleman, *Union Democracy,* Glencoe: The Free Press, 1956.

11. Of the 16 comparisons possible in Table 5 between r's obtained for the "high" and "low" groups (12 for the outcome measures, and 4 for the interest scores), only one attains statistical significance (the —0.32 vs. 0.04 for mobility attitude).

12. Morris Rosenberg, *Occupations and Values,* Glencoe: The Free Press, 1957; especially Chapter III.

13. Though alienated work *circumstances* and alienated work *orientations* are related in Table 6, they are hardly the same. Among those who report their work to be unalienated, there are those who emphasize extrinsic rather than intrinsic values in the job. A control for actual work circumstances was carried out, but this control produced no substantial change in the pattern shown in Table 6. Thus, the absence of significant correlations between alienated work and the various outcomes cannot be attributed to the fact that it is the individual's orientation in his work that counts.

14. Nancy C. Morse and R. S. Weiss, "The Function and Meaning of Work and the Job," *American Sociological Review,* 20 (April, 1955), pp. 191–198; and Ely Chinoy, *Auomobile Workers and the American Dream,* Garden City, New York: Doubleday and Co., 1955.

15. Chinoy, op. cit., pp. 130–131.

16. Harvey Swados, "The Myth of the Happy Worker," in Eric and Mary Josephson, editors, *Man Alone: Alienation in Modern Society,* New York: Dell, 1962, p. 111.

IV
Agents of Socialization

9

FAMILY

The nuclear family (that is, parents and children only) is one of the oldest and most universal institutions known to man. Indeed, a major sociological controversy is whether the nuclear family has existed in every known culture. After analyzing 250 societies, Murdock (1949) concluded that the nuclear family is a "universal human social grouping," which performs at least four basic functions for the larger society: regulation of the gratification of the sexual drive; economic cooperation based on the sexual division of labor; reproduction of the species; and socialization of new generations. Because each function is prerequisite for the maintenance of society, Murdock concluded that the nuclear family itself is a structural prerequisite of human society.

Among the 250 societies studied by Murdock, the Nayars of the Malabar coast of precolonial India have been found to be an exception, however. Research by Gough (1968), among others, has established that the social organization of the Nayar did not include what one could justifiably call a nuclear family. Children of the Nayar were raised within a matrilineage in the context of a caste-stratified society. It was necessary for the mother to be ritually married to a man of appropriate caste, with the paternity of the child vouched for by at least one man of appropriate caste, for the child to enter the caste lineage of the mother. Once this was done, however, the child was raised by the mother with the help of her matrilineage. Thereafter the father, who was usually away fighting, had no rights to his wife or children.

The mother could obtain male assistance in rearing her child from one of her brothers or from one of a succession of "lovers" from linked kinship lineages. Both parents and their children never lived together as a legal residential or economic unit and children born to any union were not recognized as the legitimate offspring of both parents. Although a child born to a woman under culturally approved circumstances was accorded full citizenship rights in the society, the nuclear family as an institution did not exist. Ira Riess (1965) points out that Harold Driver's study of North American Indians and Judith Blake's study of the Caribbean also fail to find evidence for nuclear family units containing a husband and father role.

Melford Spiro (1954) offers another exception to Murdock's thesis in his analysis of the structure of the family in the Israeli kibbutz. Spiro notes that adult members of the kibbutz are "expected to form a more-or-less permanent bisexual union," which includes a common domicile, high rate of interaction and emotional intimacy, an exclusive sexual relationship, and the right to have children. Obviously, this constitutes a structurally and psychologically unique relationship within the kibbutz. Furthermore, children of this union know who their parents are, are permitted to visit with them at appointed times, and learn to identify with them as important role models. Nevertheless, the children are reared in a communal children's dormitory and the bulk of their socialization is delegated to specially designated nurses and teachers. Moreover, the production and distribution of goods and services is carried out in and for the kibbutz society as a whole. Thus, economic cooperation is also not a function performed by the bisexual union. Strictly speaking, the nuclear family is also absent in the kibbutz society.

Marion Levy (1968) has noted that although various circumstances have tended to increase the actual incidence of the small family unit in society, the significant culturally ideal family for a great many societies has been the extended family. Traditional agricultural societies with their low level of technological development provide natural settings for the extended family. The notion of scarcity or limited goods in such societies leads to complex variations of reciprocity relationships designed to safeguard the welfare of all members of the mutual obligation network and regulate quarrels about property. Reciprocity networks provide for the redistribution of goods and services from those with abundance to those in need as well as protecting members' property from nonmembers, cementing and ritualizing social bonds, and delineating the particularistic rights, duties, and privileges of members toward each other.

In such societies, the extended family tends to constitute the basic social unit around which economic production takes place and within which the individual's core social identity is formed. Kinship extends horizontally and vertically; dependence on the group, as opposed to individualism, is a primary cultural value. Individuals are severely censured for failure to honor their reciprocity obligations, for this threatens the legitimacy of the only system which provides social security for its members. Members tend to live physically close to each other, often sharing the same domicile, and are in frequent interaction. In Southeast Asia the extended family pattern is prevalent even among the prosperous, urban, more Western-oriented members of the society.

Industrialization and the Nuclear Family

The reciprocity pattern and its concomitant emphasis on the extended family tends to break down, however, with the introduction of industrialization. Workers engaged in industry are paid on a contract basis with no other obligations implied in the employer-employee relationship. Workers must protect their material resources to finance other operations or meet such social obligations as taxes. Efficiency rather than personal ties is more rewarded and the living circumstances of the worker usually does not permit the accommodation of other relatives for long periods. In discussing modernization in the Philippines, for example, Carroll (1968, p. 12) observes that urbanization appears to have the following effects on traditional family patterns:

> [there is] less widespread interaction on a day-to-day basis among members of the extended kin group; more limited and narrowly defined obligations among members; greater freedom in the choice of allies both inside and outside the group; less control by the extended kin group over the nuclear family; greater responsibility on the part of the latter for its own economic welfare and for meeting the emotional needs of its members.

As industrialization spreads, it requires the migration of greater numbers of workers to urban areas with factories, financial institutions, transportation junctions, supply depots, and market outlets. This geographic mobility reduces contacts between the constituent nuclear units of the extended family. The differential success of families in the new stratified, cash economy has the effect of further reducing the strength of extended family ties; the basis of personal relationships increasingly becomes common social, intellectual, occupational, and economic interests.

Fifty years ago, approximately half of all American homes included at least one other adult (usually a relative) besides the parents. Today this is true of less than 5 per cent of American homes. For many of the preceding reasons, the nuclear family model tends to be much more prevalent in the middle classes than in the upper and lower classes. Shares in the family estate and more rigidly defined status norms tend to hold many upper-class extended families together, whereas scarce resources and mutual dependence bind together many lower-class extended families. However, although improved mass transportation and communication facilities in the more advanced stages of industrialization have permitted more frequent contact between members of the modern extended family, it only remotely approaches the former intimacy of the traditional extended family.

Furthermore, the functions which the family unit performs for its members are increasingly limited in industrial society. The family ceases to be the basic unit of economic production and is reduced to consumption, property ownership, and the socialization of children. Modern institutions emerge which assume functions formerly performed by the extended family. The police, court, and prison system now provides protection against outsiders. Banks, insurance companies, pension plans, public charities, state welfare, government taxation, and other institutions and programs redistribute resources and provide relief from present need and protection against future want. And ritualized gift and card exchange ceremonies (at birthdays and Christmas, for example) maintain and symbolize social bonds and furnish psychological security for the individual.

As the society becomes increasingly sophisticated, new institutions of socialization and social control, like the school, peer group, and mass media even encroach on the socialization function of the family. The father's work takes him outside of the family for long periods, while the children spend more and more time in the company of peers and under the supervision of outside authorities.

This description of the process and effects of industrialization is most appropriate to European and American society. It has yet to be demonstrated that this model is appropriate for understanding industrialization in countries with different cultures and institutional arrangements. In fact, many values and institutional practices which characterize Western industrial countries (especially the United States) seem to have been in existence before the advent of industrialization. For example, Furstenberg's analysis (1966) of the accounts of foreign travelers to colonial America documents the preindustrial existence of the democratic (as opposed to patriarchal) family pattern with its high degree of permissiveness in child-rearing. Lantz, Snyder, Britton, and Schmidt (1968) have shown, similarly, that the romantic love complex with its emphasis on "personal happiness" in mate selection (as opposed to the pattern of parental control) appears to be indigenous to Western culture and not a result of the impact of industrialization on courtship patterns.

In a cross-cultural analysis Greenfield (1961) concludes that urbanization and industrialization may exist without the small nuclear family and, conversely, that the small nuclear family may exist without industrialization and urbanization. He observes that this family type existed in Europe and the United States before the industrial revolution. And Goode (1968) goes even farther in stating that "family variables are themselves independent and have an impact on the total social structure"; in the American case probably facilitating the acceptance of industrialization. He further contends that the nuclear family is a less common social form than the "conjugal" family which includes one or more extended kinship ties in addition to the immediate family. Moreover, according to Goode, the change from the extended to the conjugal family cannot be explained by the degree of industrialization alone, but must also be accounted for by the ideological appeal of a family form which grants greater autonomy to the disadvantaged, the young, women, and the educated. He concludes (p. 120) that: "Machines do not make social structures; people with specific social patterns make machines."

Controversy over the Modern Family

Whatever its origins, the modern, nuclear family has come under severe ideological attack in the United States. Barrington Moore (1960) has argued that the family itself is incompatible with a modern, high technology society. He states that child-rearing restricts opportunities for the self-development of parents, particularly mothers, whose own career aspirations may be frustrated by this special burden. Moreover, parents have yielded to the mass media and peer group in providing role models for their children. Furthermore, according to Moore, many children would probably be better off cared for and socialized by professionals within a specially designed institutional environment than by frustrated, hostile, or inadequate parents. He contends that only our middle-class sentimentality sustains support for an institution which compels often unwarranted affection, fails to provide adequate guidelines and standards for many children, and causes widespread discontent.

On the other hand, many have defended the family as an institution; they consider it to be positively functional for the health of the individual and the society. Parsons (1954), has argued that the development of need systems which motivate the growing child to develop the appropriate attitudes and goal-striving is most effectively achieved in the family. Riess (1965) contends that the only universal definition of the family institution consistent with available empirical evidence is that of "a small kinship structured group with the key function of nurturent socialization of the newborn," and, furthermore, that the family is the institution best suited to perform this vital function. Pollak (1971) has suggested that the family may be the only institution in bureaucratic society in which the need to express hostility may be gratified without irreparable consequences, members may experience genuine intimacy (in the sense of entering the fears of the partner), and individuals can gain understanding and support for their confrontations with the outside world.

Lidz (1963) has also emphasized the protective function of the family "providing the emotional security of acceptance because of affectional ties rather than because of achievement." He also says that the nuclear family, rather than being incompatible with the demands of modern civilization, "contains the potential advantage of being suited for raising children trained for adaptability to rapidly changing circumstances." At the same time it "creates a network of kinship systems that help stabilize even an industrial society"; regulating the sexual and companionship needs of the parents; socializing the children; and providing status, incentives, and roles for its members within the larger society. In his view, families fail in these functions primarily when parents fail to integrate their properly complementary roles.

Parsons (1965) has pointed out that although one of four marriages in the United States ends in divorce, most divorces are concentrated in the early periods of marriage and in childless couples. He further states that despite what he perceives to be greater economic opportunity for women, the proportion of the population married and living with their spouses is extraordinarily high and the "family home" has increasingly become the preferred residential pattern. In fact, Philippe Ariès (1962) has shown that the very notion of childhood as a distinct period of education for adulthood, along with the organization of the family around the achievement of this goal, did not emerge in the West until the seventeenth century and has become increasingly pervasive since then. Others further contend that the failure of many modern marriages, in great part, can be explained by the increasing standards of individuals for sexual, intellectual, and emotional fulfillment in the marital relationship.

On the other hand, Herbert Otto (1970) has reported that some marriage specialists estimate that anywhere from 40 to 60 per cent of all marriages are at any given time "subclinical" (that is, the couples could benefit substantially from the aid of a marriage counselor, but never reach the clinic). And serial monogamy is becoming so widespread that, according to one analyst, we are approaching the day when 85 per cent of all men and women reaching the age of 65 will have been remarried at least once. Furthermore, according to John T. Wheeler (1973, p. 66), "many experts believe at least 65,000 children are seriously abused each year by adult attacks. About 25 per cent are said to be seriously, sometimes permanently, injured. Perhaps 6,000 are killed." Obviously not all parents who bear children are prepared to cope with them.

The advance of technology and the emergence of the counterculture have opened numerous alternatives to the conventional nuclear family pattern: childless marriages with children being raised by "professional" families or nurseries, government sponsored nurseries, homosexual family units, polygamy (it is estimated that there are some 30,000 such underground family units among the Mormons of Utah), and communal child-rearing, to name just a few. Though hostile neighbors and restrictive housing regulations make determining the number of people currently living in communal arrangements exceedingly difficult, modest estimates run as high as 120,000.

Communes are not without their own strains — principally conflicts over the division of labor, disciplining of children, and sexual jealousies. For many, the savings in time, space, and money in addition to the interpersonal gratifications and periodic relief from child-rearing more than compensate for the difficulties. Opposition to such alternatives is not based on just emotional or moral grounds, however. Changes in the basic character of the family would have important political and economic consequences.

As mentioned, the family (in capitalist countries and to a lesser extent in socialist countries) is the basic unit of property ownership and the transmission of social advantage and disadvantage. In the introduction to Chapter 6, "Stratification," it is pointed out that the individual's opportunities in life are mostly determined by the position of his family in the social structure. In caste-stratified societies, the individual's life chances are completely determined by the rank of his kin. In class-stratified societies, access to the resources and opportunities necessary to success are significantly influenced by his family's social position.

One implication of this thesis would be that all attempts at what we might term social reform represent, in essence, attempts by various means (for example, inheritance tax, civil service, mass public education, and civil rights legislation) to weaken this link between the family and the economy. This, as a consequence, tends to weaken the link between the individual and his family — for the individual may now claim opportunities and aspirations independent of his family's status and values. Indeed, he increasingly demands recognition as an individual and not as a member of his family (unlike the situation throughout most of the preindustrial world). How much the state can, should, or is at all willing to support this kind of individualism is highly problematic.

Changes which threaten to eliminate or even significantly reduce the family's role in the socialization of the child also have other significant political repercussions. The family is an inherently conservative institution; it is organized, primarily, around the transmission of values, norms, and interpersonal orientations from the older generation to the younger. Therefore, its utility tends to vary according to the rate of change in the culture.

H. Kent Geiger (1968) has written a fascinating essay on the efforts of the Bolshevik regime in the early years of the Soviet Union to abolish the "bourgeois" institution of the family to more effectively socialize children into the new society and to achieve purer socialism. The policy was later discarded and the family retained for a variety of reasons (for example, the burden of divorced women on the state, public attitudes toward the exploitation of women, the desire to maintain the birth rate for national strength, and the desire to strengthen the social order). As Geiger states (p. 61), "the proposition that human society can do without the family was never seriously tested in Soviet Russia." Nevertheless,

Geiger also points out how the state was able to use the school, mass media, and youth organizations to undermine the influence of parents hostile to the new government. And Inkeles (1955) has shown how the values emphasized by Russian parents in child-rearing changed over generations in response to changes in social conditions instituted by the new Soviet government.

Role in Socialization

Regardless of its universality, strengths, weaknesses, or political and economic role, the nuclear family remains a powerful agent of primary socialization in the Western world. Freud held that the individual's basic personality is structured in the first six years of childhood. Indeed, three of his six stages of growth (the oral, anal, and genital) occur in this period. Although he gives a great deal of attention to identity formation in adolescence and young adulthood, Erikson's theory of personality development proposes that three of man's eight stages of growth (each of which describes a different psychosocial crisis) are confronted in the context of the family before the child attends school or begins to relate meaningfully with peers.

More sociologically oriented behavioral scientists have abandoned the Freudian attempt to establish direct causal linkage between the timing and nature of specific child-rearing practices and adult personality traits. After a thorough review of the relevant literature, Sewell (1961, p. 350) has concluded,

> empirical studies of the consequences of child training have given a great deal of attention to such aspects of infant discipline as manner of nursing, weaning, scheduling, bowel and bladder training, but have found very little or no relationship between these experiences and childhood personality traits and adjustment patterns.

More contemporary personality theorists are likely to concentrate, instead, on the general quality of the parent-child relation. They are also more likely to talk about the *interaction* of parents and children, allowing that children may have different physiologically determined temperaments that may affect the parent's behavior in turn. Lansky (1963) has gone so far as to attempt to prove that the sex of the children influences the sex-role identification of the parents which, in turn, affects the child's learned sex-role identification.

More scientists are disposed to regard the family as less important an agent of socialization in modern society because of the emergence of other socializing institutions and changes in the organization of the individual life cycle. This position would stipulate that although early learning experiences do condition the choice, perception, retention, and general effects of later experiences, later experiences have their own independent effect on the individual's personality. As Inkeles has pointed out, a great deal of social role-learning can only take place later in the life cycle when the individual has achieved the necessary physical, emotional, and social maturity.

More scientists are likely to point out the importance of chance factors and accidents in the development of the individual personality, acknowledging the limits to which any society can "program" the experiences of its members. Finally, many scientists are likely to recognize the effects of the social and economic conditions which impinge on the parents' relations with the child and on the extent to which ideologically preferred courses of socialization may be followed. Minturn and Lambert (1964, p. 291) state:

> It now appears that the pressures impinging upon the growing child are much more in the nature of by-products of the horde of apparently irrelevant considerations that impinge upon the parents. These considerations of household composition, size of family, work load, and the like, determine the time and energy that mothers have available to care for children. They determine the range and content of mother-child relations and the context in which the relations take place. The coerciveness of these forces becomes apparent in the broad spectrum of cross-cultural comparison. . . . Each [mother] must solve the problems of these worlds and pass on to her children, both the problems and the solutions. We think that the message that each passes to her children is more a function of the problems than of a theory of child rearing.

All social scientists would agree, however, that these early years within the family are most influential in the child's development. It is in the family where the child develops the capacity to communicate symbolically, to develop empathy, and to achieve consciousness of self. Here the child first learns the basic concept of a relationship — with all the constraints, accommodations, compromises, and gratifications that it entails. Indeed, it is in the family that he first becomes a person. He learns to interpret and express his needs and adjust to those of others. He learns basic interpersonal orientations and situational responses which tend to color all subsequent experiences. In sum, he acquires the basic rudiments of culture, which means he learns how to use his senses to recognize social cues and respond in terms that others can understand.

As would be expected, the volume and range of research on the family and personality is enormous. Any pretense to a general review of the research would be more misleading than instructive. Extensive research examines the relationship between aspects of family structure (such as presence or absence of either parent, birth order position of child, and number, gender, and proximity in age of siblings); parental role behavior (the division of labor in the family, the distribution and locus of power); parental treatment of the child (permissive vs. strict, tolerant vs. intolerant, warm vs. cold); and other such factors on measured individual personality traits (social and political attitudes, deviant vs. conforming behavior, impulsivity, extraversion vs. introversion, dependence, aggressiveness, achievement motivation, self-concept and level of self-esteem, and sex-role identification).

The two articles selected for this section represent well-conceived, systematic attempts to measure the effect of some aspect of the family on some aspect of the individual's personality. The Brim essay, organized around analysis of previous research by Helen Koch and others on family structure and sex-role learning, is ingenious and concerned with a subject of tremendous current interest. Perhaps its most noteworthy feature is that it considers the consequences of sibling rather than parent-child interaction, a much neglected aspect of research on the family and personality.

The essay by Rosenberg on parental interest (vs. indifference) and the child's self-esteem is also outstanding. Most important, it parcels out the subtle dimension of the level of parent-child interaction, examining its effect on the child's self-esteem, both independent of and in interaction with the content of that interaction. The findings are very suggestive and direct attention to a relatively unresearched facet of family functioning with important social consequences.

In today's changing world we cannot afford anything less than a thorough, critical examination of the nature and consequences of our basic institutions, particularly those charged with the responsibility of preparing children for the world they will inhabit as adults. As the oldest and most pervasive agent of socialization known to man, the family is certainly an appropriate place to begin this inquiry.

References

Ariès, Philippe
  1962   *Centuries of Childhood: A Social History of Family Life.* New York: Knopf.
Carroll, John H.
  1968   "The Family in a Time of Change." *Solidaridad* 3 (January):11–18.
Furstenberg, Frank F., Jr.
  1966   "Industrialization and the American Family: A Look Backward." *American Sociological Review* 31 (June):326–37.
Geiger, H. Kent
  1968   "The Fate of the Family in Soviet Russia: 1917–1944." Pp. 48–67 in Norman W. Bell and Ezra F. Vogel (eds.), *A Modern Introduction to the Family.* New York: The Free Press.
Goode, William I.
  1968   "Industrialization and the Family." Pp. 113–20 in Bell and Vogel, *A Modern Introduction to the Family.*
Gough, E. Kathleen
  1968   "Is the Family Universal? — The Nayar Case." Pp. 80–96 in Bell and Vogel, *A Modern Introduction to the Family.*
Greenfield, Sidney M.
  1961   "Industrialization and the Family in Sociological Theory." *American Journal of Sociology* 67 (November):312–22.
Inkeles, Alex
  1955   "Social Change and Social Character: The Role of Parental Mediation." *Journal of Social Issues* 11:12–23.
Lansky, Leonard M.
  1963   "The Family Structure Also Affects the Model: Sex Role Identification in Parents of Preschool Children." *Merrill-Palmer Quarterly* 10 (January): 39–50.
Lantz, Herman R., Eloise C. Snyder, Margaret Britton, and Raymond Schmitt
  1968   "Pre-Industrial Patterns in the Colonial Family in America: A Content Analysis of Colonial Magazines." *American Sociological Review* 33 (June): 413–26.
Leventhal, Gerald
  1970   "Influence of Brothers and Sisters on Sex-Role Behavior." *Journal of Personality and Social Psychology* 16(3):452–65.
Levy, Marion J., Jr.
  1968   "The Predominance of the Small Family Unit." Pp. 102–110 in Bell and Vogel, *A Modern Introduction to the Family.*
Lidz, Theodore
  1963   *The Family and Human Adaptation.* New York: International Universities Press.

Litwak, Eugene
    1960 "Geographic Mobility and Extended Family Cohesion." *American Sociological Review* 25 (June):385–94.

Lynn, David
    1966 "The Process of Learning Parental and Sex-Role Identification." *Journal of Marriage and the Family* 28(4):466–70.

Minturn, Leigh, and William Lambert
    1964 *Mothers of Six Cultures: Antecedents of Child-Rearing.* New York: Wiley.

Moore, Barrington, Jr.
    1960 "Thoughts on the Future of the Family." Pp. 391–401 in Maurice Stein, Arthur J. Vidich, and David Manning White (eds.), *Identity and Anxiety: Survival of the Person in Mass Society.* New York: The Free Press.

Murdock, George Peter
    1949 *Social Structure.* New York: Macmillan.

Otto, Herbert A.
    1970 "Has Monogamy Failed?" *Saturday Review* (April 25):23–25, 62.

Parsons, Talcott
    1954 "The Incest Taboo in Relation to Social Structure." *The British Journal of Sociology* V:101–17.
    1965 "Youth in the Context of American Society." Pp. 110–41 in Erik H. Erikson (ed.), *The Challenge of Youth.* Garden City, N.Y.: Doubleday-Anchor.

Pollak, Otto
    1971 "The Family of the Future." *Wharton Quarterly* (Spring):25–29.

Riess, Ira L.
    1965 "The Universality of the Family: A Conceptual Analysis." *Journal of Marriage and the Family.* Pp. 113–20 in Bell and Vogel, *A Modern Introduction to the Family.*

Sewell, William
    1961 "Social Class and Childhood Personality." *Sociometry* 24(4):340–56.

Slater, Philip
    1962 "Parental Behavior and the Personality of the Child." *The Journal of Genetic Psychology* 101:53–68.

Spiro, Melford E.
    1954 "Is the Family Universal?" *American Anthropologist* 56 (October):839–46.

Wheeler, John T.
    1973 "Some Parents Abuse Children Physically, Emotionally, Sexually." *Philadelphia Inquirer,* March 25, 1973:66.

ORVILLE G. BRIM, JR.

Family Structure and Sex-Role Learning by Children: A Further Analysis of Helen Koch's Data

The structure of a social group, delineated by variables such as size, age, sex, power, and prestige differences, is held to be a primary influence upon the patterns of interaction within the group, determining in major part the degree to which any two group members interact. It is held, second, that social roles are learned through interaction with others, such interaction providing one with the opportunity to practice his own role as well as to take the role of the other. On this basis one may hypothesize that group structure, by influencing the degree of interaction between group members, would be related to the types of roles learned in the group: one would learn most completely those roles which he himself plays, as well as the roles of the others with whom he most frequently interacts. This argument is applied in this paper specifically to the relation between family structure, described in terms of age, sex, and ordinality of children, and the sex role learning by the children.

The process of role learning through interaction, which has been described in detail by Mead (15), Cottrell (2), and others, can be sketched as follows. One learns the behavior appropriate to his position in a group through interaction with others who hold normative beliefs about what his role should be and who are able to reward and punish him for correct and incorrect actions. As part of the same learning process, one acquires expectations of how others in the group will behave. The latter knowledge is indispensable to the actor, in that he must be able to predict what others expect of him, and how they will react to him, in order to guide his own role performance successfully. Accurate or erroneous understanding and prediction are respectively rewarding and punishing to the actor, and learning proceeds systematically through the elimination of incorrect responses and the strengthening of correct ones.

It has been the distinctive contribution of sociology to demonstrate that learning the role of others occurs through the actor's taking the role of the other, i.e., trying to act as the other would act. While this role-taking of the other can be overt, as with children who actively and dramatically play the role of the parent, it is commonly covert in adults, as with the husband who anticipates what his wife will say when he returns home late, or the employee who tries to foresee his employer's reaction when he asks for a raise.

It follows that, whether taking the role of others is overt or covert, certain re-

Reprinted by permission from *Sociometry* 21 (March 1958), pp. 1–16. Footnotes omitted.

sponses (belonging to the role of the other) are in fact made, run through, completed, and rewarded if successful, i.e., accurate, and that this process adds to the repertoire of possible actions of a person those actions taken by others in their own roles. Such actions, as part of one's repertoire or pool of learned responses, are available for performance by an actor, not now simply in taking the role of the other, but as resources which he can use as part of his *own* role performances.

The critical fact is that the actor not only can, but *does,* make use of responses learned in role-taking in his own role performances. There are two senses in which this happens. The first, which does not concern us in this paper, involves the direct transfer of the role of the other to a new and parallel status of one's own, where there is a straightforward adoption of the other's role. Such transfer may be appropriate and rewarded, as where the oldest child performs the role of the parent to his sibs, or simply interesting and tolerated, as where the new assistant professor plays the department chairman to the graduate students.

The second sense, which is our major concern here, involves a more complex process of convergence between one's own role and that of the other which he takes, where there is a spill-over of elements belonging to another's role into one's own performance when it is not necessarily appropriate. Our basic hypothesis, set forth by Cottrell (2) and others, is that interaction between two persons leads to assimilation of roles, to the incorporation of elements of the role of the other into the actor's role. Thus, one says, husbands and wives grow more alike through time, and long-time collaborators in research begin to think alike.

While not pretending to a full analysis of the process underlying assimilation, several causes can be described. First, the actor may note that the other is successful to a high degree in some of his behavior and consciously transfer to his own role such behavioral elements for trial. To the extent that they prove successful for him, in his performance, and are not eliminated through punishment from others for being inappropriate, he will adopt them. Second, faced with novel situations where his "own" behavior fails, the elements of others' roles are already learned and available for trial and hence would tend to be tried prior to the development of totally new responses; again, if successful, they tend to be assimilated to the role. Third, the actions learned by taking the role of others are ordinarily performed implicitly and under limited conditions, e.g., in interaction with the other. However, the cues which guide and elicit one's own role performance may be difficult to differentiate from cues eliciting taking the role of the other. It would appear that for the young child this is especially difficult, and data indeed show that the child has difficulty discriminating between reality and fantasy, between what his role is or even what his self is, and what belongs in the category of the "other." In this way, behavior learned through role-taking and appropriate to the other is confused with and undifferentiated from behavior learned as part of one's own role. The latter becomes tinged or diluted with characteristics belonging to someone else's role.

Among the hypotheses which are derivative of the general hypothesis of assimilation through interaction, two are pertinent here. First, the process of discrimination between what belongs to oneself and what belongs to the other is aided by the guidance of other persons. Thus, the parent helps the son differentiate between what belongs to him and what belongs to his sister; the fledgling nurse is assisted in a proper demeanor and in separating her duties from those of the physician. Rewards and punishments administered by others govern the discrimination process. Where the process of assimilation comes primarily from inability to discriminate between roles, it follows that where greater attention is paid to helping the learner discriminate, the process of assimilation is to a greater degree arrested.

Second, given two other persons with whom one interacts and who differ in power over the actor, i.e., differ in the degree to which they control rewards and punishments for the actor, one would predict that the actor would adopt more of the characteristics of the powerful, as contrasted to the less powerful, other person. This follows from the fact that it is more important to the actor to predict the behavior of the powerful figure, that he is motivated more strongly to take his role, that the rewards and punishments are more impressive and the learning consequently better. Interaction between two figures of unequal power should give a parallel result, namely, there would be a greater assimilation of the role of the other into the actor's role for the less powerful figure, for the same reasons as above. Thus the employee gravitates toward the boss more than the reverse, and the child becomes more like the parent than the other way round. However, this is not to imply that the more powerful figure need not take the role of the other, nor that he does not assimilate (to a lesser degree) elements from the other's role. The weaker figure always has some control over rewards and punishments, requiring therefore that his reaction be considered. The displeased employee can wound his boss through expressions of dislike, and the angry child can hurt his parents in a variety of ways, from refusing to eat to threatening to leave home.

Turning now to a consideration of sex-role learning specifically, pertinent reviews (1, 17) of the data show that sex-role prescriptions and actual performance begin early. The accepted position is that children in a family learn their appropriate sex roles primarily from their parents. There is remarkably little data, other than clinical materials, on this topic, perhaps because of its obviousness. What systematic data there is, is not inconsistent with the role learning propositions set forth above. Sears, Pintler, and Sears (14) have shown that in families where the father is absent the male child is slower to develop male sex-role traits than in families where the father is present, a finding predictable from the fact that there is no father whose role the child needs to take. Both Sears (13) and Payne and Mussen (12) have shown that father role-playing, identification with the father, and masculinity of attitudes are positively related to the father's being warm, affectionate, and rewarding. This strikes one as the same type of finding as the first, but at the other end of the interaction range; insofar as warm, affectionate, and rewarding fathers interact more with their sons, or are perceived as such because they interact more, it follows that the sons have more experience in taking their role.

In regard to the effects of sibling characteristics upon sex-role learning, there is again almost no information. Fauls and Smith (3) report that only children choose sex-appropriate activities more often than do children with older same-sex siblings, a finding which seems to fit none of our role-learning propositions. While one might hold that the only child has more interaction, because of sibling absence, with his same-sex parent, hence learns his sex role better, one might equally say, especially for the young boys, that it is the cross-sex parent with whom the child interacts and hence the only child should not learn his sex role well. In any case, the finding serves to stress the limitations of the data we are to report, namely, that they pertain to variations within two-child families, and that generalization to families of varying sizes is unwarranted. We return to this point later.

Even with respect to theory concerning the effects of siblings on sex-role learning, we have not noted any systematic predictions in the literature. It seems to us implicit in Parsons' recent analysis (11) of sex-role learning in the nuclear family that when the child begins his differentiation between the father and mother sex roles he would be helped in making the differentiation if he had a cross-sex sibling; this is not formally stated, however, and we may be guilty of misinterpretation.

It is against this background of comparative absence of research and theory on the effects of siblings on sex-role learning that our own report must be viewed. The very valuable data on personality traits of children presented in recent publications by Helen Koch (4, 5, 6, 7, 8, 9, 10) provide the opportunity to apply several of the general hypotheses set forth above to the substantive area of sibling effects on sex-role learning. The specific application of these hypotheses can be summarized as follows:

First, one would predict that cross-sex, as compared with same-sex, siblings would possess more traits appropriate to the cross-sex role. When taking the role of the other in interaction, cross-sex siblings must take the role of the opposite sex, and the assimilation of roles as delineated above should take place.

Second, one would predict that this effect would be more noticeable for the younger, as compared with the older, sibling in that the latter is more powerful and is more able to differentiate his own from his sibling's role.

Third, on the assumption that siblings close in age interact more than those not close in age, one would predict that this effect would be more noticeable for the siblings who are closest together in age. This is in essence an extension of the first hypothesis to deal with variations in interaction within the cross-sex sibling groups.

Procedures

Our description of procedures must of necessity be broken into two parts. The first consists of a brief description of the procedures in Helen Koch's original study; complete details are available in the publications cited previously. The second consists of our mode of further analysis of the reported data.

In her series of papers Helen Koch has reported results from a major research project concerned with the relation between structural characteristics of the family, namely, sex of child, sex of sibling, ordinal position of child, and age difference between siblings, and the child's ratings on more than fifty personality traits. In her study, all subjects were obtained from the Chicago public schools and one large private school. The characteristics of the children used as subjects can be summarized as follows. All children were from unbroken, native-born, white, urban, two-child families. The children were five- and six-year-olds, free of any gross physical or mental defect. In most cases only one sibling in a family was a subject in the study.

The subjects numbered 384. "The experimental design included three sibspacing levels, two ordinal positions, subjects of two sexes and siblings of two sexes. There were 48 children in each of the following categories — male with a male sib older, male with a male sib younger, male with a female sib older, male with a female sib younger, female with a male sib older, female with a male sib younger, female with a female sib older, and female with a female sib younger. Each of these groups of 48 children was composed of three subgroups of 16 children, representing the following three sibling-age-difference levels: siblings differed in age by under two years, by two to four years, and four to six years, respectively. Hence our basic subgroups of 16 numbered 24" (7, p. 289). The groups were matched, approximately, on an individual subject basis with respect to age of child and father's occupational status.

Teachers' ratings were made for each child on 58 traits. The teachers, all of whom were women, were trained in a conference or two to make the ratings. No teacher rated a child with whom contact had been less than three months, and in most cases the contact ranged from six to nine months. The 58 traits included 24 of the Fels Child Behavior Scales, and 34 items from the California Behavior Inventory for Nursery School Children. All ratings were made on line scales, converted later to 9-point scales. Ratings on each trait were subsequently normalized, prior to analysis of the data.

The relation between personality trait ratings and the structure of the family from which the children came was assessed by analysis of variance for each of the 58 traits. Helen Koch presents in her publications the findings from the variance analyses. It is this data on which we made our further study.

The procedures for the further analysis involved several steps. First, the writer, with the assistance of three professional persons as additional judges, judged each of the 58 traits in terms of its pertinence to either a masculine or feminine role. Our conception of the characteristics of the two sex roles was based on recent empirical studies describing sex-role differences in small problem-solving groups (16) and in the nuclear family (18), and on the major theoretical treatment of such differences by Talcott Parsons (11). In these studies the now-familiar distinction between the instrumental or task role and the expressive or social-emotional role in a social group is shown to be related to sex-role differentiation, particularly in the family, with the male customarily taking the instrumental role and the female the expressive role. Hence in the judging process our decision as to whether a trait was masculine or feminine was essentially dependent on whether we believed the trait to belong to the instrumental or expressive role respectively.

Substantial descriptive data are available on sex-role differences in children for some of the traits which we judged. These findings, summarized by Terman and Tyler (17), were consulted after the judging was completed and strongly corroborate our assignment of traits: e.g., male children are judged higher on traits we believed instrumental, such as dominance and aggression, and lower on traits we judged to pertain to the expressive role, such as affection and absence of negativism.

In judging the traits it was recognized that many of them would be part of the role requirements for both roles. However, it was clear that there exists for each of the roles what is essentially a rank order of characteristics in terms of their importance for the role. Hence the basis for our judgments was whether the trait appeared to be higher in the rank order of requirements for the instrumental or the expressive role. Traits which seemed pertinent to neither, e.g., stammering, or for which no judgment of greater importance could be made, e.g., curiosity, were not ascribed to either role and were omitted from subsequent steps in the analysis. It was possible to assign 31 of the 58 traits to either the instrumental or expressive role. Twenty of the 31 traits pertain to the expressive role, the children evidently having been rated on a predominantly female cluster of traits.

Some of the traits were stated in a negative way which made them, while pertinent to the role, incongruent with the role conception. Thus, "uncooperativeness with group" seemed clearly to be relevant to the expressive role but as an incongruent trait. In like manner, both affectionateness and jealousy seemed most important as aspects of the expressive role, the former being congruent with the role conception, the latter incongruent. It therefore was necessary to make a second judgment regarding each trait, namely, whether it was a congruent or incongruent aspect of the role to which it pertained.

Table 1 lists the 31 traits, the role to which they seemed most pertinent, and the indication of whether the trait was a congruent or incongruent characteristic of the role.

With the judging of the traits completed, the next step was a careful reading of Helen Koch's findings. A tabulation was made of all differences on the 31 traits between the 16 basic subgroups reported by her as significant (close to or at the .05 level, based on the separate analyses of variance). Such differences involved single structural characteristics, e.g., first-born versus second-born; single interactions of characteristics, e.g., girls with brothers versus girls with sisters; and multiple interactions, e.g., first-born boys with sisters versus first-born boys with brothers. These significant differences in traits were then entered in some preliminary forms of Tables 2 and 3. The procedure for entering differences was somewhat complicated and is described as follows:

First, with respect to a trait judged pertinent to the male or instrumental role, and considered a *congruent* aspect of that role: when any subgroup or groups were rated significantly higher than others on that trait, the number of the trait was entered in the high masculinity column for such a group; the subgroups or groups they were higher than, i.e., the low groups, had the number of the trait entered in the low masculinity column. Second, with respect to a male trait considered an *incongruent* aspect of the role: when any subgroup was rated higher than another on such a trait, the trait number was entered in the low masculinity column for such a group; for the group it was higher than, i.e., the low group, the trait number was entered in the high masculinity column. The procedure for the female or expressive traits was identical, except the female columns were used.

This procedure means that for any subgroup, entries in the high masculinity column consist of congruent male traits on which the group is high, and incongruent male traits on which it is low; entries in the low masculinity column consist of incongruent male traits on which the group is high, and congruent male traits on which it is low. Female column entries are read the same way. An example may be helpful at this point. Consider in Table 3 the subgroup "Younger Boy with Older Brother" at the four- to six-year age difference. In the high masculinity column the entry of trait number 2 means that the group was rated significantly *high* on aggressiveness; the entry of trait number 10 means that the group was rated significantly *low* on wavering in decision. In the low masculinity column, trait number 6 indicates a *high* rating on dawdling and procrastinating, while trait number 7 indicates a *low* rating on responsibleness.

The preliminary forms of Tables 2 and 3 were complicated and two further steps toward simplification were taken before reaching the present form. The

TABLE 1

Traits Assignable to Male (Instrumental) or Female (Expressive) Roles

Trait name	Pertains primarily to instrumental (I) or expressive (E) role	Trait is congruent (+) or incongruent (−) characteristic of role
1. Tenacity	I	+
2. Aggressiveness	I	+
3. Curiosity	I	+
4. Ambition	I	+
5. Planfulness	I	+
6. Dawdling and procrastinating	I	−
7. Responsibleness	I	+
8. Originality	I	+
9. Competitiveness	I	+
10. Wavering in decision	I	−
11. Self-confidence	I	+
12. Anger	E	−
13. Quarrelsomeness	E	−
14. Revengefulness	E	−
15. Teasing	E	−
16. Extrapunitiveness	E	−
17. Insistence on rights	E	−
18. Exhibitionism	E	−
19. Uncooperativeness with group	E	−
20. Affectionateness	E	+
21. Obedience	E	+
22. Upset by defeat	E	−
23. Responds to sympathy and approval from adults	E	+
24. Jealousy	E	−
25. Speedy recovery from emotional disturbance	E	+
26. Cheerfulness	E	+
27. Kindness	E	+
28. Friendliness to adults	E	+
29. Friendliness to children	E	+
30. Negativism	E	−
31. Tattling	E	−

initial tables were marred by the occurrence of duplicate trait-number entries in the cells, arising primarily from the multiple reporting of the original data and the multiple differences emerging between the various subgroups. Hence, where duplicate trait-entries occurred, only one entry was kept. The result is to make each entry read that that subgroup is significantly higher (or lower) than some other group *or groups* on that particular trait. Second, the tables were complicated by the fact that for all subgroups there were at least some trait numbers which appeared in *both* the high and low subdivisions of either the male or female col-

TABLE 2

Instrumental and Expressive Traits for Five- and Six-Year-Old Girls

Subjects	Sib age difference	Male (or instrumental) traits		Female (or expressive) traits	
		High masculinity ratings	Low masculinity ratings	High femininity ratings	Low femininity ratings
Older girl with younger sister	0–2 years	2,5,7	4,6,9,10	13,14,15,16, 17,18,19,20, 21,24,30	22,23,25, 26,27
	2–4 years	7	2,4,9,10, 11	13,14,15,16, 17,18,19,20, 21,24,30	22,23,26, 27,28
	4–6 years	7	2,4,6,9, 10,11	13,14,15,16, 17,18,19,20, 21,24,30	22,23,25, 26,27,28
Older girl with younger brother	0–2 years	1,2,3,4,5, 9,10	6	13,14,15,16, 19,20,21,25, 26,27,30	22,24
	2–4 years	1,2,3,4, 9,10	6	13,14,15,16, 19,20,25,26, 27,30,31	22,24
	4–6 years	1,2,3,4,7, 9,10	6	13,14,15,19, 20,21,25,26, 27,28,30	22,24,31
Younger girl with older sister	0–2 years	2,5,6,7,8	3,4,9,10, 11	12,13,14,15, 16,18,19,20, 21,22,23,30	17,25,26, 27
	2–4 years		3,4,5,8,9, 10,11	12,13,14,15, 16,18,19,20, 21,22,23,30	17,25,26, 27,28
	4–6 years	6,7	2,3,4,9, 10,11	12,13,14,15, 16,18,19,20, 21,22,23,30	17,25,26, 27,28
Younger girl with older brother	0–2 years	1,2,4,6,7,8, 9,10,11		12,13,14,15, 16,18,19,20, 21,22,23,25, 26,27,28,30	
	2–4 years	1,4,6,7, 10,11		12,13,14,15, 16,18,19,20, 21,22,23,25, 26,27,28,30	
	4–6 years	2,4,5,10,11		12,13,14,15, 16,18,19,20, 21,22,23,25, 26,27,28,30	

Note: Trait numbers refer to listing in Table 1. Traits entered in high masculinity rating column are male-congruent traits with high ratings, male-incongruent traits with low ratings. The reverse is true for low masculinity rating column. Female trait entries are made in the same manner.

TABLE 3
Instrumental and Expressive Traits for Five- and Six-Year-Old Boys

Subjects	Sib age difference	Male (or instrumental) traits		Female (or expressive) traits	
		High masculinity ratings	Low masculinity ratings	High femininity ratings	Low femininity ratings
Older boy with younger brother	0–2 years	9,10	1,2,7,11		12,13,14,15, 16,19,22,23, 25,26,27,30
	2–4 years	4,9,10	1,2,5,7,11		12,13,14,15, 16,19,20,21, 22,23,25,26, 27,28,30
	4–6 years	2,4,9,10	1,7,11		12,13,14,15, 16,19,20,22, 23,25,26,27, 30,31
Older boy with younger sister	0–2 years	11	2,4,7,9,10	25,26,27,31	12,13,14,15, 16,17,18,19, 20,21,22,23, 24,30
	2–4 years	2,3,5,11	4,7,9,10	25,26,27,28	12,13,14,15, 16,17,18,19, 20,21,22,23, 24,30
	4–6 years	3	2,4,7,9,10	25,26,27,28	12,13,14,15, 16,17,18,19, 20,21,22,23, 24,30
Younger boy with older brother	0–2 years	4,9,10	1,2,3,5,6, 7,8	22,23,24	13,16,18,19, 20,21,25,26, 27,28,30
	2–4 years	4,9,10	1,3,6,7	22,23,24	13,16,18,19, 20,21,25,26, 27,28,30
	4–6 years	2,4,5,8, 9,10	6,7	22,23,24,29	13,16,18,19, 20,21,25,26, 27,28,30
Younger boy with older sister	0–2 years		2,4,5,6,7, 8,9,10	17,22,23,24, 25,26,27	13,19,30
	2–4 years		2,4,6,9,10	17,22,23,24, 25,26,27,28	13,16,19,20, 21,30
	4–6 years		2,4,6,7, 9,10	17,22,23,24, 25,26,27,28	13,16,19,20, 21,30

Note: See note to Table 2.

umn. This indicated, of course, that a subgroup was higher (or lower) than some other group on that trait, but also lower (or higher) than still another group; i.e., on the ranking of mean ratings on the trait, the subgroup would have differed significantly from both the top and bottom ranks. To clarify the tables, and also substantially to increase the reliability of the subgroup differences reported here, all traits on which a subgroup had both high and low entries were dropped for that subgroup. In summary, the result of this step, combined with the one above, is to make *each entry in the final tables read that that subgroup is significantly higher (or lower) than one or more groups on that trait, and is significantly lower (or higher) than none.*

Results and Discussion

The data presented in Tables 2 and 3 can be brought to bear upon our hypotheses by considering the distribution by subgroups of the traits indicating high or low masculinity or femininity. Our concern is with the frequency of trait entries of the four types, rather than with the descriptive content of any particular trait. Essentially we give each separate trait an equal weight, then summarize in terms of masculinity (many high rating, few low rating entries) and of femininity, associated with each subgroup.

With respect to our first hypothesis, that through interaction and taking the role of the other the cross-sex sibs would have more traits of the opposite sex than would same-sex sibs, an examination of the distribution in Table 2 shows that this is clearly the case. Controlling for ordinality, the older girl with a younger brother has more high masculinity traits and fewer low masculinity traits, than does her counterpart, the older girl with a younger sister. This distribution of traits is even more pronounced for the girls in the second ordinal position, the younger girl with older brother being substantially higher on masculinity than her counterpart with an older sister. One will note that the acquisition of male traits does not seem to reduce the number of feminine traits of the girls with brothers. The more accurate interpretation is that acquisition of such traits adds to their behavioral repertoire, probably with a resultant dilution of their feminity in behavior, but not a displacement.

Examination of Table 3 with respect to this first hypothesis indicates that it holds for boys also. While not pronounced for the boys in the eldest child position, the boy with the sister is feminine to a greater degree than the boy with the brother. For the boys who are second-born, the difference is clear: the boy with the elder sister is substantially more feminine than his counterpart with an older brother. For the boy with the older sister the acquisition of feminine traits would seem to have displaced, rather than simply diluted, his masculinity and he thus contrasts with the girls for whom this did not occur. We can offer no explanation for this, but it may provide a lead for further study in this area.

In connection with this result, the role of the parent requires attention. While all would agree that parents actively assist cross-sex sibs in separating their sex roles, the data show they are unsuccessful in completely arresting the process of assimilation. Perhaps in earlier times, when children's sex roles were stressed more strongly, and perhaps today for some parents making an extreme effort, the effects of interaction would be reduced. However, it certainly appears that the average parent today cannot completely avoid the effects of such sib interaction. Even were more attention given by parents to cross-sex as opposed to same-sex sibs in this matter, we believe that the tremendously greater cross-sex interaction of the former would leave its mark.

With respect to our second hypothesis, that because of differences in control of rewards and punishments and in ability to discriminate between self and other roles the effects of role-taking would be more pronounced for the younger child, an examination of Tables 2 and 3 again seems to support the hypothesis. While the younger, as contrasted with the older, girl with a brother manifests only a slightly greater degree of masculinity, this difference for boys is quite striking: the younger, as contrasted with the older, boy with a sister is substantially more feminine.

With respect to our third hypothesis, that on the assumption of interaction varying inversely with age-gap and greater interaction producing greater role-taking, the effects of role-taking would be largest for the sibs closest in age, the results in both tables are negligible. One might discern some such relationship for the boy with an older sister, and the girl with an older brother, but even here it is tenuous. Because the assumption that interaction varies with sib age differences may in fact be untenable, we cannot in this instance say we have made a direct test of the hypothesis that more frequent interaction produces more role assimilation. Since the first hypothesis, which in essence states the same point, was so strongly confirmed, our inclination is to reject our assumption that interaction varies with age difference, at least to a degree sufficient to produce differences in role-taking.

There are two further aspects of Tables 2 and 3 which are quite noticeable and which need comment. We refer first to the fact that girls with brothers appear to be masculine to a greater degree than do any of the males themselves. The simplest and most likely explanation, hence the one which we favor, is that this result occurs because of certain biases in the teachers' ratings. We submit that teachers implicitly rated boys and girls on different scales, i.e., girls were implicitly rated on a girls' scale, boys on a boys' scale. The girl with an extreme masculine trait — extreme, that is, for a girl — receives a very high rating; a boy with the same absolute degree of such a trait, or even more of it, would on the boys' scale not be extreme and his rating consequently would be reduced. In the subsequent analysis of variance, where the male and female ratings are treated as if on the same absolute scale, certain girls extremely high for girls would score significantly higher than even certain boys high on the trait. To some extent we see the same effect in reverse for the younger boys with an older sister; while not being more feminine than girls, they almost tie certain girls, e.g., older girls with younger sisters. The probable use of different implicit rating scales, the implausibility of any group of girls being more masculine than all boys, and the important fact that when girls and boys are assuredly rated on the same absolute scale (e.g., 3, 17) boys regularly outscore girls on masculine traits, all tend to support this interpretation.

The second additional aspect of the tables which merits discussion is that all girls seem to be more feminine than the boys are masculine; indeed, the major characteristic of the boys is to be antifeminine, not masculine. In part this is explained by the assumed bias in the ratings mentioned above; boys are outscored on their own traits by some girls. In part also this is explained by the preponderance of feminine traits used in the ratings, so that boys could only express their masculinity, as it were, by being rated low on such traits. In part, and an intriguing part indeed, it may be explained by certain developmental processes commonly assumed in clinical theory and recently put in a role theory context by Parsons (11, pp. 95–101). Parsons points out that both boy and girl first identify with the mother and tend to play an expressive role. In development the boy must break away and establish a new identification with the father, which is difficult and involves much new learning, in the role-taking sense. At the same time, the boy must "push far and hard to renounce dependency." Girls, continuing identification with the mother and the expressive role, face neither of these problems. It may be, then, that the girls' femininity and the boys' antifemininity and yet lack of masculinity which shows itself in Tables 2 and 3 arises in part because the children have been caught by the raters at an age where the boy is trying to shift his identification from mother to father.

To conclude, our analysis of Helen Koch's data indicates that cross-sex siblings tend to assimilate traits of the opposite sex, and that this effect is most pronounced in the younger of the two siblings. These findings support the role-learning theory presented here, and also stand as a substantive contribution to the area of sex-role learning. We wish now to stress two points mentioned earlier.

First, these findings must be subject to strict limitations to two-child families. Not only does the Fauls and Smith study demonstrate this limitation with regard to only-child families, but observation suggests that in larger families other variables come into play; e.g., in the four-child family with a three and one sex split, parents may actively help the solitary child in differentiating sex roles; or in the four-child family with a two and two split, siblings may pair off by sex and the cross-sex role-taking effect is minimized.

Second, with respect to the substantive value of these results, we would point out that even though parents must remain as the major source of sex-role learning, almost every child has a mother and father to learn from. Hence the *variations* in type and amount of sex-role learning occur on top of this base, so to speak, and in this variability the effect of a same or a cross-sex sib may play as large or larger a role than variations in parental behavior, mixed versus single-sexed schooling, sex of neighborhood playmates, and the like. Speculations on the durable and considerable effects of sex of sib on sex-role learning thus seem warranted and lead one to consider problems such as the effect of sex of sibling on one's later role in the marital relation, on career choices, and on other correlates of the adult sex role.

Summary

This paper reports some relations between ordinal position, sex of sibling, and sex-role learning by children in two-child families. The findings are based on a further analysis of Helen Koch's data relating personality traits of children to their sex, sex of sibling, ordinal position, and age difference from sibling. In this analysis the personality traits were classified as pertaining either to the instrumental (masculine) role or the expressive (feminine) role. The distribution of such traits in children as a correlate of family structure was then assessed.

General propositions describing role learning in terms of interaction with others, including taking the role of the other, leads to hypotheses that cross-sex siblings will have more traits of the opposite sex than will same-sex siblings, and that this effect will be greater for the younger, as contrasted with the older, sibling. Both hypotheses are confirmed by the data presented.

References

1. Brim, O. G., Jr., "The Parent-Child Relation as a Social System: I. Parent and Child Roles," *Child Development,* 1957, 28, 344–364.
2. Cottrell, L. S., Jr., "The Analysis of Situational Fields in Social Psychology," *American Sociological Review,* 1942, 7, 370–382.
3. Fauls, L. B., and W. D. Smith, "Sex Role Learning of Five-Year-Olds," *Journal of Genetic Psychology,* 1956, 89, 105–117.
4. Koch, H. L., "The Relation of 'Primary Mental Abilities' in Five- and Six-Year-Olds to Sex of Child and Characteristics of His Sibling," *Child Development,* 1954, 25, 210–223.
5. Koch, H. L., "Some Personality Correlates of Sex, Sibling Position, and Sex of Sibling Among Five- and Six-Year-Old Children," *Genetic Psychology Monographs,* 1955, 52, 3–50.
6. Koch, H. L., "The Relation of Certain Family Constellation Characteristics and the Attitudes of Children Toward Adults," *Child Development,* 1955, 26, 13–40.
7. Koch, H. L., "Attitudes of Children Toward their Peers as Related to Certain Characteristics of Their Sibling," *Psychological Monographs,* 1956, 70, No. 19, (whole No. 426).
8. Koch, H. L., "Children's Work Attitudes and Sibling Characteristics," *Child Development,* 1956, 27, 289–310.
9. Koch, H. L., "Sibling Influence on Children's Speech," *Journal of Speech and Hearing Disorders,* 1956, 21, 322–328.
10. Koch, H. L., "Sissiness and Tomboyishness in Relation to Sibling Characteristics," *Journal of Genetic Psychology,* 1956, 88, 231–244.
11. Parsons, T., "Family Structure and the Socialization of the Child," in T. Parsons and R. F. Bales, *Family, Socialization and Interaction Process,* Glencoe, Illinois: Free Press, 1955.
12. Payne, D. E., and P. H. Mussen, "Parent-Child Relations and Father Identification Among Adolescent Boys," *Journal of Abnormal and Social Psychology,* 1956, 52, 359–362.
13. Sears, P. S., "Child-Rearing Factors Related to Playing of Sex-Typed Roles," *American Psychologist,* 1953, 8, 431 (abstract).
14. Sears, R. R., M. H. Pintler, and P. S. Sears, "Effect of Father Separation on Preschool Children's Doll Play Aggression," *Child Development,* 1946, 17, 219–243.
15. Strauss, A., *The Social Psychology of George Herbert Mead,* Chicago: Phoenix Books, University of Chicago Press, 1956.
16. Strodtbeck, F. L., and R. D. Mann, "Sex Role Differentiation in Jury Deliberations," *Sociometry,* 1956, 19, 3–11.
17. Terman, L. M., and L. E. Tyler, "Psychological Sex Differences," in L. Carmichael (ed.), *Manual of Child Psychology,* (2d ed.), New York: Wiley, 1954.
18. Zelditch, M., Jr., "Role Differentiation in the Nuclear Family: A Comparative Study," in T. Parsons and R. F. Bales, *Family, Socialization and Interaction Process,* Glencoe, Illinois: Free Press, 1955.

MORRIS ROSENBERG

Parental Interest
and Children's Self-conceptions

In dealing with the types of parental behavior which might be considered relevant for child development, research studies have run the gamut from such specific child-rearing practices as breast-feeding or bottle-feeding, time of bladder and bowel-training, time of weaning, etc.,[1] to such broad categories of parental behavior as emotional support, overprotection, hostility, autonomy, punitiveness, etc.[2] One point which has been relatively neglected, however, is the simple question: How *interested* is the parent in the child? Is the child an object of importance to the psychic and emotional life of the parent? Beyond this, what is the relationship between such parental interest or indifference and the child's feeling of self-worth, his level of self-esteem? In terms of one's level of self-acceptance, is it more deleterious to have parents who are indifferent but nonpunitive or parents who are interested in the child but hostile toward him? These are some of the questions to which the present study is directed.

Sample and Method

The relationship of parental interest to the child's self-esteem[3] was investigated in a study of high school juniors and seniors selected from a stratified random sample of ten high schools in New York State. Three separate but overlapping questionnaires were administered alternately to the respondents; each student completed one questionnaire. The questionnaire form which contained items dealing with parental interest was thus completed by one-third of the sample, i.e., 1684 respondents.[4]

Indicators of Parental Interest

Two conspicuous methodological difficulties stand out in attempting to obtain a measure of parental interest in the child: (1) since the possibilities of expressing such interest exist in an almost infinite number of parent-child interactions through the years, it is difficult to select a sample of such expressions of interest which will satisfactorily reflect the whole; and (2) since the questionnaires are directed toward the children, we face the problem of inferring the parental attitudes and behavior from the child's reports.

In light of these problems, our procedure in constructing the questionnaires was to index parental interest *indirectly* by selecting three *recurrent* but *diverse* areas of life which represented fairly specific points of contact between parent and

Reprinted by permission from *Sociometry* 26:1 (1963), pp. 35–49.

child. We selected *recurrent* situations in order to obtain a wider sampling of interaction than reports of single specific events, e.g., age of toilet-training. We selected *diverse* situations on the assumption that idiosyncratic factors might determine behavior in any specific situation but that this danger would be reduced if several diverse situations were considered. We approached the matter *indirectly* by asking about objective behavior in order to reduce bias; in each case an effort was made to give the questions a relatively "neutral" or "objective" slant. Finally, we used three diverse situations in order to observe whether the use of different indicators of the same concept ("interest in the child") would yield essentially the same results. If so, it would reduce the danger that the result was merely an artifact of the particular measure used. It is the *consistency* of the data in these three areas, then, rather than the adequacy of any particular measure, upon which the brunt of the present argument rests.

The three areas of life selected for examination were: (1) relationships with friends; (2) reactions to the child's academic performance; and (3) responsiveness to the child at the dinner table. Since the types of inferences to be drawn vary with each of these three areas of parent-child interaction, we will deal with each separately.

Parents' Knowledge of the Child's Friends

During the period of middle childhood, a child's emotions tend to be deeply involved in his friends; indeed, friends may be the child's main ego-extensions. The parents' reactions to the child's friends may thus be an indirect indicator of their interest in the child.

In order to examine this question, we attempted to rivet the student's attention to a recurrent situation and to hold the image of what went on in these situations in the forefront of his attention. "We would like you to think back to a specific period of your childhood, namely, when you were in the 5th and 6th grades. For most children this would be about the age of 10 or 11. Try to keep this period generally in mind when answering the following questions. Although your feelings and experiences may have varied, try to answer the questions in terms of your *average* or *typical* experiences at this time."

After asking whether the child had many friends, whether he visited them in their homes and whether they visited him in his home, we asked: "During this period, did your mother know who most of your friends were?"

Table 1 indicates that there is little difference in the self-esteem of those who said their mothers knew "all" or "most" of their friends, but that the self-esteem of these respondents is substantially higher than those who said their mothers knew "some" or "none" of their friends.[5] It should be noted, however, that only 8 per cent said their mothers knew "some" or "none" of their friends. These responses thus appear to indicate an *extreme* lack of interest. It is among this exceptional group that low self-esteem is particularly likely to appear.

The question is, however: Is the student's report of his mother's knowledge of friends fairly realistic or is it entirely determined by the student's bias? It is possible that students feel that their mothers *should* have known the child's friends — that this would be the "good," "right," "proper" thing to do. It may thus be that students who hold negative attitudes toward their mothers will report that their

TABLE 1
Reports of Mother's Knowledge of Child's Friends and Subject's Self-esteem

| | *"During this period (age 10 or 11) did your mother know who most of your friends were?"* | | | | |
Respondent's self-esteem	*All of them*	*Most of them*	*Some of them*	*None, or almost none*	*Don't know or can't remember*
High	47%	45%	33%	30%	27%
Medium	23	24	27	15	38
Low	30	31	41	55	35
Total per cent	100	100	101	100	100
Number	848	559	113	20	26

$\chi^2 = 19.0$; d.f. $= 8$; P $< .02$.

mothers knew few of their friends. In this case, the relationship cited above might simply reflect an association between unfavorable attitudes toward one's mother and one's self-esteem.

In order to check on this possibility, we have selected two questions which may reflect the student's attitude toward, or closeness to, his mother. The first question, dealing with the *past,* is: "When you were about 10 or 11 years old, to whom were you *most* likely to talk about personal things?" The second question, dealing with the *present,* is: "When your parents disagree, whose side are you usually on — your mother's or your father's?" Table 2 shows that those respondents who said their mothers knew most of their friends had higher self-esteem than those who said she knew few, *irrespective of whether they confided in their mothers, in someone else, or in no one in childhood.*[6] Similarly, Table 3 indicates that the same relationship is maintained irrespective of whether the respondent currently sides with his mother, his father, or both equally in parental disagreements. The

TABLE 2
Reports of Mother's Knowledge of Child's Friends and Subject's Self-esteem, by Tendency to Confide in Others

	Most likely to talk about personal things to . . .					
	Mother		*Other person*		*No one or can't remember*	
			Mother knew friends . . .			
Respondent's self-esteem	*All or most*	*Some or none*	*All or most*	*Some or none*	*All or most*	*Some or none*
High	51%	39%	41%	35%	46%	29%
Medium	23	32	26	20	21	30
Low	26	29	33	45	34	41
Total per cent	100	100	100	100	101	100
Number	540	41	537	55	195	27

TABLE 3

Reports of Mother's Knowledge of Child's Friends and Subject's Self-esteem by Identification with Parents

	Student currently identifies chiefly with ...					
	Mother		*Father*		*Both equally*	
			Mother knew friends ...			
Respondent's self-esteem	*All or most*	*Some or none*	*All or most*	*Some or none*	*All or most*	*Some or none*
High	43%	32%	39%	27%	52%	39%
Medium	23	22	29	33	22	29
Low	34	45	32	40	27	32
Total per cent	100	99	100	100	101	100
Number	381	40	185	15	407	31

results, then, do not appear to be attributable to the student's past recollections of, or present attitudes toward, his mother.

Another possibility must, however, be considered, viz., that it may not be the child's attitude toward his mother in general, but his recollection of how she behaved toward his *friends* in particular, that colors his recollection of whether she knew his friends. We thus asked those students who said their mothers knew any of their friends: "How did she usually act toward them?" Table 4 shows that *irrespective of whether the students said their mothers were friendly or not friendly*, those who said their mothers knew all of their friends had higher self-esteem than those who said their mothers knew few of their friends. Their recollection of whether their mothers knew their friends is, then, not simply a reflection of their favorable or unfavorable memories of their mothers' behavior toward their friends.

TABLE 4

Reports of Mother's Knowledge of Child's Friends and Subject's Self-esteem by Mother's Behavior toward Friends

	How mother acted toward child's friends					
	Very friendly		*Fairly friendly*		*Not friendly*	
			Mother knew child's friends			
Respondent's self-esteem	*All or most*	*Some or none*	*All or most*	*Some or none*	*All or most*	*Some or none*
High	**48%**	34%	45%	33%	32%	21%
Medium	23	24	26	27	29	26
Low	29	41	29	39	40	53
Total per cent	100	99	100	99	101	100
Number	1091	58	259	51	38	19

We thus see that irrespective of whether the child says he did or did not chiefly confide in his mother, irrespective of whether he identifies with her, with his father, or with both equally, and irrespective of whether he says she was friendly or unfriendly to his mates, the student who reports that his mother knew most of his friends tends to have higher self-esteem than the one who does not. It is likely, then, that the reported differential knowledge of friends does not simply reflect the student's biased perception of, or attitudes toward, his mother. Such differential knowledge probably represents a reflection of the mother's interest in the child and in his ego-extensions.

It should be mentioned that those students who said their mothers knew few of their friends but were courteous toward them were actually slightly *less* likely to have high self-esteem than those who said their mothers knew most of their friends but were discourteous (41 per cent to 34 per cent). This difference is not statistically significant, but it does suggest the possibility that simple interest (as reflected in knowledge of friends) may be even more important than parental pleasantness or unpleasantness (as reflected in parental courtesy). While this finding is at best suggestive, it is relevant in the light of other findings to be presented later.

Now let us consider the father's knowledge of the child's friends. Once again we find that parental interest is not strongly associated with self-esteem except for the extreme group who said their fathers knew "none, or almost none" of their friends. This small group — 8 per cent of the respondents — were clearly more likely to have low self-esteem than those who reported that their fathers knew some, most, or all of their friends (Table 5). This difference obtains even when mother's knowledge of friends is held constant. Both exceptional maternal indifference and exceptional paternal indifference thus appear to be associated with low self-esteem in the child.

TABLE 5
Reports of Father's Knowledge of Child's Friends and Subject's Self-esteem

	"During this period (age 10 or 11) did your father know who most of your friends were?"				
Respondent's self-esteem	*All of them*	*Most of them*	*Some of them*	*None or almost none*	*Don't know or can't remember*
High	49%	46%	41%	35%	34%
Medium	22	25	26	20	32
Low	28	29	33	46	34
Total per cent	99	100	100	101	100
Number	366	534	431	123	41

$\chi^2 = 20.7$; df $= 8$; P $< .01$.

Academic Performance

We now turn to a second recurrent but fairly specific point of contact between parent and child which may serve as an indicator of parental interest in the child, viz., the parents' response to the child's performance in school. While it is possible for the parent to be generally oblivious to what happens to the child in school, at one point the totality of performance is tightly summarized for him on a single sheet — the report card. His response to the report card, then, may importantly epitomize his attitude toward the child's achievements and qualities.

In order to learn something about the parents' typical reactions, we asked our respondents: "When you were in the 5th and 6th grades in school, what did your *mother* usually do when you brought home a report card with high grades? (Check as many as apply)." [7] We then asked: "How about when you brought home a report card from the 5th or 6th grades which contained low marks? What did your mother *usually* do then? (Check as many as apply.)" [8] The same questions were asked about the father's reactions.

Let us consider first the parents' reactions to *poor* grades, since the issue is more sharply highlighted in this regard. The parental response to poor grades may roughly be divided into three types: (1) The punitive reactions — scolding the child, criticizing him, depriving him of something he wants; (2) the supportive reactions — praising him for the subjects in which he did do well, trying to help him in subjects in which he was doing poorly, or discussing the reasons for his poor performance; and (3) the indifferent reactions — paying no attention to grades, simply taking the poor report cards for granted, or not even looking at the report card.

In terms of Mead's[9] principle of reflected appraisals, our expectations would be obvious: those students whose parents were critical or punitive would have the lowest self-esteem; those whose parents were supportive and helpful would have the highest self-esteem; and those whose parents were indifferent would be in-between. The results, however, do not bear out these expectations. Table 6 indicates that it is not the punitive responses which are most closely related to low self-esteem, but the *indifferent* ones. Once again, we find, the proportion who give the indifferent responses is very small. We may thus assume that such responses represent rather extreme indifference. Those who do report such indifference, however, not only have lower self-esteem than those who report supportive responses, but are also somewhat lower than those who report *punitive* responses.

It is interesting to note that those students who report only supportive responses do not differ from those who report *both* supportive and punitive responses. Both groups, however, have higher self-esteem than those who report only punitive responses; those who report indifferent responses, as noted, are lowest in self-esteem.

Another possible indication of parental indifference is the following: We asked our respondents whether their marks in the 5th and 6th grades were above or below average, and then inquired: "(If your marks were average or below average) Was your mother satisfied with your grades in school?" As we would expect, those students who said that their mothers were satisfied even when their grades were average or below average had higher self-esteem than those who reported that their mothers were dissatisfied. More interesting, however, is the fact that the lowest self-esteem appears not among those who report that their mothers were dissatisfied but among those who said, "She seldom commented on my marks." It should be pointed out that less than four per cent gave this last response. Among this small group, however, fully 54 per cent had low self-esteem, compared with 39 per cent of those who said their mothers were dissatisfied, 31 per cent of those who said their mothers were fairly satisfied, and 25 per cent of those who said their mothers were very satisfied. Once again we see that *maternal indifference is more highly predictive of low self-esteem than overt dissatisfaction.*

TABLE 6
Report of Parental Reaction to Low Marks and Subject's Self-esteem[a]

Respondent's self-esteem	Mother's reaction			
	Supportive and punitive	*Supportive only*	*Punitive only*	*Indifferent*
High	49%	44%	34%	26%
Medium	25	25	25	13
Low	26	30	41	61
Total per cent	100	99	100	100
Number	178	533	228	23

$\chi^2 = 22.2$; d.f. $= 6$; P $< .01$.
Indifferent vs. all others: $\chi^2 = 8.4$; d.f. $= 2$; P $< .02$.

Respondent's self-esteem	Father's reaction			
	Supportive and punitive	*Supportive only*	*Punitive only*	*Indifferent*
High	47%	46%	36%	34%
Medium	28	25	24	19
Low	25	30	40	47
Total per cent	100	101	100	100
Number	139	413	241	85

$\chi^2 = 19.8$; d.f. $= 6$; P $< .01$.
Indifferent vs. all others: $\chi^2 = 8.0$; d.f. $= 2$; P $< .02$.

[a] In this table both boys and girls who report indifferent responses are more likely than those who report punitive or supportive responses to have low self-esteem. The boys who report indifferent responses, however, are less likely than other boys to have medium self-esteem and slightly more likely to have high self-esteem. Since the boys' responses are based upon only 10 cases (mother's reaction) and 41 cases (father's reaction), it is uncertain whether this is a meaningful difference or a matter of chance fluctuation.

When we turn to parents' reactions to high grades, our analysis is restricted for the following reason: we cannot compare punitive responses with indifferent ones because a parent will rarely chastise or punish his child for doing well in school. We can, then, only classify the parental responses as supportive (praised you, gave you something you wanted) or indifferent (paid no attention to it, did not see report cards). As we would expect, those students who reported that their mothers and fathers gave supportive responses had higher self-esteem than those who reported indifferent responses.

While many people are inclined to treat the report card as a trivial part of life, it holds a special and almost unique significance in the development of the self-concept. Among the myriad criteria upon which an individual's worth may be judged, the report card is almost the only objective, unequivocal measure of a certain aspect of the individual's worth. Whether a person is kind, courageous, principled, likeable, etc., may be matters of opinion, with much variation, sub-

TABLE 7

Mother's Satisfaction with Child's Grades and Subject's Self-esteem

	"(If your marks were average or below average) was your mother satisfied with your grades in school?"				
Respondent's self-esteem	Yes, very satisfied	Yes, fairly satisfied	No, not satisfied	She seldom commented on my marks	Don't know
High	48%	45%	38%	28%	35%
Medium	27	24	24	20	25
Low	24	30	38	53	40
Total per cent	99	99	100	101	100
Number	221	438	372	40	40

$\chi^2 = 22.1$; d.f. $= 8$; P $< .01$.

jective interpretation, or distortion of facts; but a report card is a black-and-white, strictly measurable and comparable, characterization of the individual. With due recognition of the different degrees of importance attached to it, we would argue that total indifference to the report card is very difficult, and, as our respondents indicate, it is actually very rare.

It may thus be that most parents who are totally uninterested in the child's school performance are likely to be uninterested in the child. The parent may be punitive — may scold the child, deprive him of something, etc. — if he does poorly in school, but at least he is interested, concerned, involved with the child. Apparently more than depreciation and chastisement, and certainly more than praise or support, such indifference is associated with lower self-esteem in the child.

Participation in Mealtime Conversations

The discussion of knowledge of friends and reactions to report cards referred to recurrent situations in the past. We now turn to an everyday recurrent situation in the present which may reflect parental interest in the child, viz., family interaction at the evening meal. The responses to these items are somewhat more subjective in nature, although, as above, we have tried to make the question fairly neutral and indirect. Although in this area the questions are probably more "contaminated" than in the "friends" and "report card" situations, they are so close to our central theme that they may merit presentation.

The importance of the evening meal lies in the fact that it is a constant, persistent, frequent point of contact between parents and children. What goes on at the dinner table not only represents a great multitude of interactions, but may well epitomize the total range of parent-child interactions which occurs in other areas of life.

In order to learn something about what goes on at the dinner table, we asked our respondents:

1. Do all the members of your family eat the evening meal together?

2. (If your family usually or always eats together) How often do you participate actively in the mealtime conversation?

3. As far as you can tell, how interested are the other family members in what you have to say on such occasions?

Fewer than 6 per cent of the respondents said that they "rarely or never" participated in the mealtime conversation and an equally small proportion of those who did participate felt that others were "not interested" in what they had to say. Tables 8 and 9 indicate that these respondents were considerably more likely than others to have low self-esteem.

The student's belief that others are interested in him is thus closely related to his self-conception. His self-conception, of course, undoubtedly contributes to his belief that others are interested. The child who thinks little of himself is automatically inclined to assume that others are uninterested in his opinions and activities. At the same time it is likely that something in the actual attitudes and behavior of others toward him contributes to his belief that they are or are not interested in what he has to say. The student has, after all, interacted with his

TABLE 8
Frequency of Respondent's Participation in Mealtime Conversation, and Self-esteem

Respondent's self-esteem	"(If your family usually or always eats together) how often do you participate actively in the mealtime conversation?"			
	Always	Usually	Sometimes	Rarely or never
High	52%	45%	33%	33%
Medium	23	27	25	16
Low	25	28	42	52
Total per cent	100	100	100	101
Number	698	446	173	89

$\chi^2 = 48.2$; d.f. $= 6$; P $< .001$.

TABLE 9
Subject's Estimate of Family's Interest in His Opinions, and Self-esteem

Respondent's self-esteem	"As far as you can tell, how interested are the other family members in what you have to say on such occasions?"			
	Very interested	Fairly interested	Not interested	Don't know
High	56%	43%	19%	37%
Medium	23	26	20	17
Low	21	30	61	46
Total per cent	100	99	100	100
Number	432	833	80	108

$\chi^2 = 77.7$; d.f. $= 6$; P $< .001$.

family tens of thousands of times. He has thus been exposed to almost innumerable signs as to whether others are interested in what he has to say: the stifled or open yawn when he speaks, the interruption or changing of the subject, the look of distractedness when he expresses an opinion; or, on the other hand, the light of interest when he presents his views, the responses appropriate to his comment, the encouragement to continue, the request for his opinion on a subject which others have initiated — all these are clear and unmistakable signs of whether others are interested in what the individual has to say. Thus, while the individual's self-conception undoubtedly influences his belief that others are interested in his views, it seems unlikely that something in their actual attitudes and behavior has not contributed at least in some measure to his appraisal of their level of interest.

Summary Measure of Interest in the Child

In order to learn something about parental interest in the child, we have focused upon three recurrent sets of life experiences — friends, report cards, dinner conversations. While no one of these areas of interaction may in itself be an adequate reflector of parental interest in the child, the consistency of the results in all three areas suggests that there may be a real relationship between parental indifference and low self-esteem in the child.

It should be noted that reports of parental indifference are clearly the exception; very few students indicate that their parents gave the "uninterested" or "indifferent" response to any of these items, let alone most of them. In order to provide the most liberal interpretation of parental indifference, we have combined all those who reported *any* lack of interest on the part of their parents. Twenty per cent of the sample did report such indifference. This is an exceptional, but not an insignificant, group; it is also large enough to enable us to introduce certain controls. Table 10 indicates that 45 per cent of these students had low self-esteem, compared with 26 per cent of the others.

It may be noted that this association between parental indifference and children's self-esteem is not an artifact of associated status or role characteristics. In other words, whether one belongs to the upper, upper middle, lower middle, or lower social classes;[10] whether one is a Protestant, Catholic, or Jew; whether one is

TABLE 10
"Parental Interest" Index and Subject's Self-esteem

	Parental interest	
Respondent's self-esteem	No evidence of lack of interest	Some evidence of lack of interest
High	49%	29%
Medium	25	26
Low	26	44
Total per cent	100	99
Number	945	241

$\chi^2 = 39.2$; d.f. $= 2$; P $< .001$.

male or female; whether one lives in a large city, a medium-sized community, or a small town — whichever of these conditions obtain, the result is essentially the same: if the parents manifest indifference to the child, that child is less likely to have a high level of self-regard.

Similarly, we find that it is not simply a question of whether parents were strict or lenient with the child or whether the respondent feels that the punishment he received as a child was generally deserved or undeserved. Whether the student says that his parents were stricter or less strict than others or whether he says that the punishment he received was generally deserved, partly deserved and partly undeserved, or generally undeserved, the result is the same: students who report a lack of parental interest have lower self-esteem than others. In fact, students who reported a lack of parental interest but who felt that the punishment in childhood was deserved had somewhat lower self-esteem than those who indicated that their parents were interested but who felt their punishment in childhood was generally undeserved.

Summary and Discussion

It has been our aim in this discussion to select three diverse but recurrent life situations which involve parent-child relationships and to infer something about the parent's level of interest in the child. In all three areas, the evidence is consistent in suggesting that parental indifference is associated with lower self-esteem in the child. It should be emphasized that reports of parental indifference are clearly the exception; very few students indicate that their parents give the "uninterested" or "indifferent" response to any of these items. In several cases we find that whether the parents appear to be very interested or only fairly interested in the child makes little difference for his self-esteem level. It is only when the response indicates a clear and rather extreme lack of interest in the child — as reflected in the small proportion of students who check this answer — that clear and conspicuous differences in self-esteem appear. It would thus appear that rather extreme indifference is associated with low self-esteem, but whether the interest in the child is strong or mild often appears to make less difference.

The second point is the following: students who report only punitive responses tend to have lower self-esteem than those who report only supportive responses, but students who report indifferent responses have lower self-esteem than either of these groups. The differences between the indifferent responses and the punitive responses are not significant, but they are consistent. For example, children whose mothers were interested in them but acted discourteously toward their friends had somewhat higher self-esteem than those whose mothers were uninterested in them but acted courteously toward their friends. Similarly, among the students who received poor report cards, those who said their parents scolded or criticized them had higher self-esteem than those who said their parents paid no attention. Again, those who said their mothers were dissatisfied with their poor marks had either self-esteem than those who said their mothers seldom commented on their marks. These results suggest the possibility that even if the mother is only sufficiently interested in the child to chastise or berate him, even if she is discourteous enough to be unpleasant to his friends, this level of interest is associated with higher self-esteem than is maternal indifference.

Of course, it is probably not simply interest *per se* which accounts for the observed relationships. Very likely such lack of interest in the child goes along with lack of love, a failure to treat the child with respect, a failure to give him encouragement, a tendency to consider the child something of a nuisance and to treat him with irritation, impatience, and anger. But whatever other kinds of parental behavior may be reflected in these indicators, they probably at least reflect the idea that the child is *important* to someone else, that others consider him of worth, of value, of concern. The feeling that one is important to a significant other is probably essential to the development of a feeling of self-worth.

Notes

1. Allison Davis and Robert J. Havighurst, "Social Class and Color Differences in Child-Rearing," in Guy E. Swanson, Theodore M. Newcomb, and Eugene L. Hartley, *Readings in Social Psychology*, rev. edit., New York: Holt, 1952, pp. 539–550.
2. Earl S. Schaefer, "A Circumplex Model for Maternal Behavior," *Journal of Abnormal and Social Psychology*, 59 (September, 1959), pp. 226–235.
3. Self-esteem was measured by means of a ten-item Guttman scale which had a satisfactory level of reproducibility and scalability. The respondents were asked to strongly agree, agree, disagree, or strongly disagree with the following items: (1) On the whole, I am satisfied with myself. (2) At times I think I am no good at all. (3) I feel that I have a number of good qualities. (4) I am able to do things as well as most other people. (5) I feel I do not have much to be proud of. (6) I certainly feel useless at times. (7) I feel that I'm a person of worth, at least on an equal plane with others. (8) I wish I could have more respect for myself. (9) All in all, I am inclined to to feel that I am a failure. (10) I take a positive attitude toward myself.

   The reproducibility of this scale is 93 per cent and its scalability is 72 per cent. All items have been dichotomized; strongly agree and agree have been combined, and strongly disagree and disagree have been combined. Since three "contrived items" were utilized in the development of the scale, the 11-point scale has been condensed into a 7-point scale. The first contrived item is based on questions 3, 7, and 9. The "positive" response is indicated if the respondent gave the low self-esteem answer to two or more of these questions. The second contrived item is based on questions 4 and 5. The "positive" response is indicated if the respondent gave the low self-esteem answer to either of these questions; the same is true of the third contrived item, which is based on questions 2 and 6. In this paper, "high" self-esteem signifies a score of 0 or 1 on this scale; "medium" self-esteem signifies a score of 2; and "low" self-esteem signifies a score of from 3 to 6.

   The logic of the Guttman scale appears in Samuel A. Stouffer, *et al., Measurement and Prediction,* Princeton: Princeton University Press, 1950, Chapter 3. The scalability measure is discussed in Hebert Menzel, "A New Coefficient for Scalogram Analysis," *Public Opinion Quarterly,* 17, (Summer, 1953), pp. 268–280. The method of "contrived items" is presented in Samuel A. Stouffer, Edgar A. Borgatta, David G. Hays, and Andrew F. Henry, "A Technique for Improving Cumulative Scales," *Public Quarterly,* 16 (Summer, 1953), pp. 273–291.

   A discussion of the relationship of self-esteem to psychosomatic symptoms and depressive affect is presented in Morris Rosenberg, "The Association Between Self-Esteem and Anxiety," *Journal of Psychiatric Research,* 1 (1962), pp. 135–152. There are some data to suggest that this scale is moderately reliable. Among 50 students who filled out these scales 9 months apart, 80 per cent either had identical scores or were within one step of their original scores on this 7-point scale.
4. The questionnaires were administered during a single class period to all juniors and seniors present on the day of administration. Since a number of the

students did not answer some of the questions (chiefly because they did not complete the questionnaire in the allotted time period), there is some variation in totals from table to table, and all totals are less than the complete sample.

5. Except as noted, all the relationships presented in this paper for which tests of statistical significance are reported are maintained for boys and girls separately. Due to the small number of indifferent responses in some social classes, it has not been possible to control on social class for each table. However, in the final summary table (Table 10), in which the various indifferent responses are combined to provide a larger number of cases, social class (and various other factors to be mentioned) does not account for the relationship between reported parental indifference and self-esteem.

6. Table 2 indicates that within each sub-classification (or partial association) created by the introduction of the test factor, the direction, and generally the size, of the relationship between maternal interest and self-esteem is maintained. Within each partial association, however, the differences are no longer statistically significant because of the reduction in the number of cases. This statement also applies to Tables 3 and 4.

7. The alternatives offered were: did not receive any report cards with high grades; praised you; gave you something you wanted; paid no attention to it; told you that you should be able to do even better; took good report cards for granted; did not see your report cards; other (What?); can't remember.

8. The alternatives presented were: did not receive any report cards with low grades; scolded you; criticized you; deprived you of something you wanted; praised you for subjects in which you were doing well; paid no attention to it; took bad report cards for granted; tried to help you in subjects in which you were doing poorly; discussed with you the reasons for poor performance; didn't see your report cards; other (What?); can't remember.

9. George Herbert Mead, *Mind, Self and Society,* Chicago: University of Chicago Press, 1934, especially Part II.

10. The number of indifferent responses in the upper class is, however, very small, and the difference in this sub-group therefore cannot be considered reliable.

10

CHURCH

Organized religious activity is one of the oldest institutions. As a dominant institutional influence on personality development, it is also one of the five agents of socialization analyzed in this section. I will not attempt to evaluate the relative effects of organized religion on social personality in different societies where the church as an institution may vary considerably in its relation to the polity and the economy. Our inquiry is still circumscribed by the scope and subject of social scientific research, and our principal intent continues to be with the impact of specific institutions on individuals in modern industrial societies — particularly the United States. In such societies, as the introduction to Chapter 5 indicates, the church seems to be losing its influence on social personality to other agencies such as the school, peer group, and mass media.

Decline of the Church in America

The 1960's featured a major assault on the authority of organized religion throughout the United States and elsewhere. According to the Gallup poll, the proportion of the general public attending church slid from 49 per cent in 1958 to 40 per cent in 1971. By 1969, 70 per cent of all adults surveyed thought that "religion is losing its hold on life in this country," as opposed to only 14 per cent who believed that religion "is increasing its influence" — an almost precise reversal of the findings of a similar poll conducted in 1957. The fragile theological empire of Roman Catholicism came under severe attack from a number of quarters. More than once, Pope Paul VI tried to still the rising chorus of criticism. In 1968 Murphy reported:

> From Pope Paul's public talks over the past year, it is obvious that the Holy Father is disturbed by the call for violence in the settlement of social, racial and political problems in various parts of the world. At Bogota in August, he ruled out theological justification for violence as a means of achieving economic and social justice. . . .

343

Complaining of radical attacks from within the church on the truths of the faith, Pope Paul admonished Catholic thinkers against contributing to the breakdown of moral values. He blamed extremists for innovations in the celebration of Mass and other liturgical rites not authorized by Roman authority, and he cautioned theologians against watering down doctrines dealing with the Scriptures and with truths that do not please the modern mentality, such as the virgin birth of Christ, a literal understanding of Christ's resurrection from the dead, original sin and the Pope's own reiteration of the ban on artificial methods of birth control.

In 1967, the year prior to the Pope's call to order, the number of ordained priests in the American Catholic Church declined for the first time in many years. Agitation on a number of issues continued. A study of 5,000 active priests, 800 priests who had left the active ministry, and 250 bishops released by the National Opinion Research Center in 1971 revealed that a sizeable majority (from 56 per cent to 60 per cent) felt that priests should be free to marry, disagreed with the Church's teachings against artificial birth control, and disagreed with the Church's position that divorce is "unacceptable under all circumstances." Almost two-thirds of those surveyed felt that the Pope misused his authority in issuing his 1967 encyclical against artificial birth control. Although almost three-fourths of the bishops surveyed considered the encyclical "competent and appropriate," this was true for only 42 per cent of the major superiors of religious orders.

Among Catholics generally dissent was even more in evidence. Fully 75 per cent of those surveyed by Louis Harris and Associates in 1967 opposed their church's ban on birth control and 38 per cent ignored it. Among those under thirty-five years of age, 60 per cent used birth control pills or other contraceptives. Also, 50 per cent opposed the church's proscription on divorce and 65 per cent wanted annulments allowing re-marriage for "the innocent party to a divorce." Almost half felt that priests should be allowed to marry.

Ecumenism was the movement among liberal Protestant denominations in the 60's, but the mergers and liaisons created appeared as much motivated by an effort to consolidate the church's position in the face of rising challenges and declining attendance as by a desire to articulate a new role for the church in this secular, scientific age. Glock and Stark (1968) reported on the basis of their research that a "demythologized modernism is overwhelming the traditional Christ-centered mystical faith."

The radical manifesto of this new modernism was Baptist minister Harvey Cox's *The Secular City*, which argued that life in the "technopolis" of modern man posed a whole set of pragmatic and profane problems to which the language and concepts of the church did not address themselves. Cox suggested the church might have to declare a moratorium on talk about "God" until a more adequate and powerful expression of the word was discovered. Debate raged in many circles over whether God was dead and, if so, whether and how He should or could be resurrected.

The response among youth to the decline of organized religion was manifold. Many continued to relate to the church in a way indistinguishable from their elders; many others pressed for reform within the church. Particular concern was expressed for making the language and structure of religious services more contemporary (including increased participation on the part of the congregation) and for applying the church's moral authority and material resources to contemporary social problems such as war, racism, and poverty. A 1968 Gallup poll showed that more young people (49 per cent among those 21 to 29) felt the clergy should "express their views on day-to-day social and political questions" than did those 30 to 40 (42 per cent) and those 50 and over (35 per cent). Still others dropped out of organized religion and plunged deeply into total commitment to any of a number of new religious sects which emerged in the middle to late '60's. Hare Krishna, the Jesus Movement, and the Guru Maharaj Ji are the most well known of these sectarian movements, although there are a great many others. From all appearances they share a rejection of the materialistic life style of middle America and the preoccupation with drugs of many alienated youth; they seek happiness, fulfillment, knowledge, or revelation through prayer, study, or meditation. Conversion to the group appears to be sudden, total, and restricted to teenagers and young adults desperately in search of spiritual direction in an age of disbelief.. Whether this presently limited phenomenon will attain the status of a movement remains to be seen.

A great many youths simply disaffiliated themselves from religion. Although church attendance dropped 6 per cent between 1958 and 1968 among the total adult population, the decrease was 14 per cent for those 21 to 29 years of age, bringing attendance among this age group down to 28 per cent. Between 1966 and 1972 the proportion of incoming university freshmen who claimed they had no religious preference more than doubled, from 8 per cent to 18 per cent.

The church probably never occupied that central a role in the socialization of the young in the United States. It is, after all, a country founded in large part by people seeking to escape the religious persecution of their homelands and to enjoy the benefits of religious liberalism in the New World. In a predominantly Protestant country with a formal separation of church and state and a frontier heritage, there has never been much deference to institutionalized religious authority. All one needed was the "good book" and a proper belief in God to dwell among the faithful. In a society becoming increasingly disenchanted and demythologized by science and technology and acquiring an increased awareness of the relativity of cultural beliefs as well as an increased emphasis on material life style, holy reverence and disciplined sacrifice seem incomprehensible demands.

Nevertheless, something quite basic in the religious experience may explain its tenacious hold on the minds and hearts of many. Long ago, Durkheim (1961 edition) suggested that "the idea of society is the soul of religion"; that it is through common worship that the collectivity is able to achieve clear consciousness of itself, allowing individuals both the exultation of being able to transcend their separateness and to experience the moral force of the collective conscience.

Freud (1961 edition) suggested that the psychological source for the "oceanic" feeling of "eternity" that religion inspires in many can be traced to early infancy before the demands of a society hostile to direct instinctual gratification encroach upon the pure, boundless, pleasure-seeking activity of the primitive ego. He also suggested that religion essentially reduces people to "psychical infantilism," drawing them into a "mass delusion" that depresses the value of life and offers the consolation of an afterlife free from the limitations, but also the pleasures, of the body. And, of course, many also have a deeply infantile longing for an omnipotent father figure to answer their prayers and acknowledge their remorse with forgiveness.

Other analyses of the religious experience are more approving in tone and content, but it is not necessary to explore this issue here. We will simply note that what are often described as religious feelings and experiences are not the same as identification with or participation in organized religious activities. We must recognize that religious principles and ideas can become secularized (that is, divested of their specifically religious character and generalized to the entire culture) thus continuing to affect social life and social personality in a less direct and specific, but more pervasive way. In this section we will not attempt to deal with that, however. Instead, we will concentrate specifically on the measured effects on social personality of formal religious affiliation and religiosity; of the impact of the church as an agent of socialization on the individual.

Allowing for such qualifications does not eliminate all our problems, however. As Glock (1959) has suggested, it is important to recognize that religiosity is a complex phenomenon and involves at least four dimensions — the experiential, ideological, ritualistic, and consequential. Each individual may rank the relative importance of these dimensions differently and the larger social changes taking place may affect each dimension differently.

Furthermore, Fichter (1956) notes that "the religious role of the modal Catholic is not a total and integrated social role conforming to the value-norms of the Church, nor is the religious role the only, or the most important component of his social personality." According to Fichter, although we cannot yet evaluate the influence of the Catholic's religious role over his many other social roles, it appears that his religious role is not his key social role and "cannot and will not become the integrator and elevator of his total social personality."

Moreover, as Abramson and Noll (1966) have demonstrated, SES has as important an effect on attitudes toward religion as toward other matters. Even with SES held constant, the diversity of opinion related to ethnic differences among Catholics, as with denominational differences among Protestants, is still very great.

Influence of Religious Affiliation on Achievement Motivation

Despite all these additional qualifications, an abundance of research has established systematic differences in social personality correlates between people of different religions and different degrees of religiosity. The correlates most often examined include: achievement motivation, delinquency, sense of meaninglessness, intellectuality, authoritarianism, anxiety, and ethnic prejudice.

Certainly one of the most controversial issues in this area is the relative effect of different religious affiliations on achievement motivation. The theoretical premise for such research is derived from Max Weber's classic thesis, *The Protestant Ethic and the Spirit of Capitalism* (1930). Weber looked at the conditions of production in India, China, and Western Europe and observed that, although the material conditions were essentially the same, large-scale formally rational capitalistic enterprises emerged only in Western Europe and America. He discovered the crucial variable to be the countries' different religious systems and theorized that only in parts of Western Europe and in America where ascetic, rationalized Puritanism was the dominant religion, calling for *self-control, action, and salvation in this world,* did the spiritual precondition for capitalism exist. The other-worldly, mystical system of India and the contemplative harmony-with-man-and-nature system of China conflicted with the inner dynamic of a capitalist economy. As Weber states (p. 171):

> The religious valuation of restless, continuous, systematic work in a worldly calling as the highest means to asceticism, and at the same time the surest and most evident proof of rebirth and genuine faith, must have been the most powerful conceivable lever for the expansion of that attitude toward life which we have here called the spirit of capitalism.

Ironically, however, the very success of the devout led many to a preoccupation with materialism and a turning away from the church. According to Weber, religious charisma became routinized in the form of bureaucratic administration, and entrepreneurial activity became stripped of any of its religious and ethical meaning. "The Puritan wanted to *work in a calling;* we are forced to do so," he says caustically. "For of the last stage of this cultural development," Weber gloomily observes (p. 182), "it might well be truly said: 'Specialists without spirit, sensualists without heart; this nullity imagines that it has attained a level of civilization never before achieved.' "

Some time passed before sociologists systematically tested Weber's proposition that differences in religious values lead to differences in economic behavior, accounting for the early structural development of capitalism only in Protestant countries. The first major study of this kind was done by Lenski (1963) whose famous book, *The Religious Factor,* contains numerous significant differences between Protestant and Catholic politics, family life, and other areas as well as economics. Lenski did not control for ethnic differences within his religious groupings, but, in general, his study received high praise for its methodological sophistication. Lenski reported that both occupational self-employment and disapproval of installment buying (as an indirect measure of the value of thrift) is greater among actively involved Protestants than among Catholics and less actively involved Protestants. He also found that both membership and interest in unions is least among active Protestant churchgoers and, most importantly, that Protestants take a more positive attitude toward more demanding and rewarding positions than do Catholics.

Jackson, Fox, and Crockett (1970) provided some support for Lenski's thesis in their analysis of 1957 national sample data. Even when results were controlled for ethnicity, region of origin, age, generation, and size of community of origin, they found (p. 60): "moderate religious differences in occupational achievement: (1) Protestants are more likely than Catholics of the same occupation origin to enter professional and business occupations; (2) Catholics are more likely than Protestants of the same origin to enter (more secure) white collar occupations; and (3) Protestants are more often sharply upwardly mobile; Catholics are more often sharply downwardly mobile."

On the other hand, a careful replication of Lenski's study by Schuman (1971) eight years later failed to confirm any of the original findings, with one exception. A slightly larger proportion of Protestants than Catholics (6 per cent in 1958 and 5 per cent in 1966) still felt that the principle "work is important and gives a feeling of accomplishment" was a more important criterion for choosing a job than such reasons as "high income," "no danger of being fired," "working hours short, lots of free time," and "chances for advancement." Schuman presents many complicated reasons for the numerous discrepancies between his and Lenski's results, and his work has compelled a more careful specification of the precise effects of the religious factor.

Moreover, Glenn and Hyland (1967) have used survey data from the mid-1940's and mid-1960's to show that, though Protestants outranked Catholics in income, occupation, and education in 1943, Catholics had moved ahead of Protestants in all aspects of status except college experience by the mid-1960's, and even this difference had disappeared among younger adults. These authors concluded that the effects of any Protestant-Catholic differences in influence on worldly success are small in relation to the effects of other factors, such as region and size of community of residence, that favor Catholics.

Featherman's study (1971) of the socioeconomic achievement of white religious and ethnic subgroups shows that the achievement-related work values and motivations of adults "proved insufficient to explain away the gross occupational and economic variation for the subgroups studied" (pp. 220–21). Accordingly, factors other than religious affiliation must be taken into consideration in understanding the relation between social background and achieved socioeconomic success. As is apparent, the research on religion and achievement motivation remains highly inconclusive. The same can be said for the research on religion and juvenile delinquency.

Other Effects of Religious Affiliation and Orthodoxy

Contrary to common belief, most research on religiosity and delinquency has failed to find any consistent relationship between them. For example, Allen and Sandhu (1967) found no relationship between church attendance and delinquency, a conclusion also supported by Hirshi and Stark (1969), who reveal that children who attend church are no more likely than nonattenders to accept ethical principles and only slightly more likely to respect conventional authority.

The classical conception of the church as an effective agent of moral constraint and, thus, social control does not seem to find any support in research on juvenile delinquency in contemporary America. However, this by no means implies that religious activity has no meaning for those who participate.

On the contrary, Benson (1966) has found that, although the effects tend to vary according to parents' education, year in college, and religion, students active in religious organizations and students who attend religious services are likely to manifest less of a sense of meaninglessness than those who do not. Also, some religious affiliations (for example, Catholics and Church of Christ members) tend to have lower meaninglessness scores than others (such as Presbyterians, Disciples of Christ, Baptists, Jews, Lutherans, and Unitarians).

It can also be argued, consistent with our earlier discussion of the relative decline of religiosity in America, that this sense of meaning which participation in organized religion can provide is antithetical to the greater sophistication, rationality, and personal autonomy that life in a highly technological urban society tends to promote. For example, Campbell and Magill (1968) cite numerous studies that indicate that persons high in religiosity, particularly Catholics, lack intellectual disposition and have a more authoritarian and dogmatic orientation toward life. In their own study of college students, these authors found a consistent negative relationship between extreme levels of religiosity and intellectuality. Although these effects are much clearer for Protestants than Catholics, the authors are still able to show that as the intensity of religious involvement decreases, the percentage of students with an "open mind," those committed to intellectual values, and those who value a cognitive, theoretical orientation increases. In his study, Lenski also finds a marked inverse correlation between doctrinal orthodoxy and intellectual autonomy among Protestants, although not among Catholics.

Greeley (1963) and Rhodes and Nam (1970) have also investigated the relationship between religious affiliation and intellectual values. Contrary to some previous studies, Greeley finds that Catholics are as likely to go to graduate school, choose an academic career, specialize in the physical sciences, and plan a life of research as Protestants, even under SES and other demographic controls. Rhodes and Nam find (p. 253) that:

> teenagers with Jewish mothers are most likely to plan to attend colleges; those connected with the largest Protestant denominations (except Baptists) and the Roman Catholic Church are next most likely to plan for college; while teenagers whose mothers identify with many of the smaller Protestant denominations are least likely to plan for college. ... the results of this study are consistent with a theory that the values imparted by some religious denominations are more supportive of high levels of educational aspiration than those imparted by other denominations.

Spilka (1958) has drawn on Allport's distinction between interiorized religious belief (that is, higher value systems or ethics which are embraced as a way of life for the individual) and institutionalized belief (lower value systems which involve only a recognition of formal church structure and its systems of rites and beliefs) in his research on the relationship between religious orientation and personality. His study of college students establishes that the religious-ethnocentric group (characterized by institutionalized belief) possesses significantly more manifest anxiety, rigidity, and self concept instability than the religious nonethnocentric (interiorized belief) group.

His explanation for those findings rests on associations established in previous research studies between rigid modes of problem-solving behavior with anxiety, and with adherence to such conforming and conventional systems as organized religion. He also points out that the church can function as an authoritarian, stabilizing influence by performing as a father surrogate, which might have a special appeal to persons who are insecure, anxious, and who possess unstable and inadequate self-images. In this research, Spilka only discusses the different personality characteristics of people with divergent orientations toward religion. The limitations of his data do not allow him to ask whether involvement in the Church tends to cause personalities to develop in any particular direction, independent of or in interaction with other factors.

Religious ethnocentrics, as defined by Spilka, have also been shown to evince greater prejudice toward racial and ethnic minorities than nonethnocentrics. In his research on Catholic college students, O'Reilly (1954) found that "there was a very significant tendency . . . for those scoring high on the religion scale to be less favorable toward Jews and Negroes and to favor segregation of Negroes in their own parishes, while those who scored low on the religion scale were significantly less prejudiced and were opposed to segregation." Similarly, Blum and Mann (1960) demonstrate, among other things, that students belonging to religious clubs are more anti-Semitic than students who do not belong to such clubs.

Burnham, Connors, and Leonard (1968) find large differences in levels of racial prejudice between different religious affiliations. Catholics were found to be less tolerant than Protestants (a large proportion of which were Quakers in this study), Jews, or those claiming no religion. Those claiming no religion were the most tolerant, followed by both Jews and Protestants. More germane to our previous discussion, the authors find a curvilinear relationship among Catholics between church attendance and racial prejudice. Nonattenders had the lowest proportion of less prejudiced respondents, those who went more than regularly the next lowest, and regular attenders (weekly and the major feasts) the highest proportion. Although this curvilinear relationship did not turn up among Protestants and Jews, it is consistent with other research and the article by Allport and Ross in this section.

Allport and Ross also examine the relationship between religiosity and ethnic prejudice. Their article is especially useful because they elaborate the various arguments regarding the logically expected relationships between religiosity and ethnic prejudice. Allport and Ross distinguish between persons with an extrinsic religious motivation, who use their religion to achieve other ends such as "security, solace, sociability and distraction, status and self-justification"; and those with an intrinsic motivation, who internalize and live their religion so that "all needs are subject to an overarching religious commitment." The authors note that previous research supports the following generalizations: (1) On the average, churchgoers are more prejudiced than non-churchgoers; (2) the relationship is curvilinear; and (3) people with an extrinsic religious orientation are significantly more prejudiced than people with an intrinsic religious motivation.

The Allport-Ross study confirms these propositions and suggests the need for still another one. They define a fourth type: persons who are indiscriminately proreligious (answering affirmatively to questions on both the intrinsic and extrinsic religiosity scales). According to their findings, persons of this type "are more prejudiced than the consistently extrinsic, and very much more prejudiced than the consistently intrinsic types."

Also in this section Putney and Middleton explore a wide variety of relationships between different dimensions of religiosity; such personality characteristics as authoritarianism, status concern, anomie, and political conservatism; and such independent demographic variables as sex, region of college attendance, year in college, religion, SES, and size of community. They sampled twelve hundred students taking social science courses at thirteen colleges in the Northeast and Southeast. The authors devote much more space to describing their methodology and reciting their results than to interpreting their data, which means the reader should carefully analyze the content and implications of each finding.

Although the research on the church and social personality is quite varied and much of it is inconclusive, some characteristic effects have been demonstrated. The two articles in this section are better examples of such research.

References

Abramson, Harold J., and C. Edward Noll
  1966 "Religion, Ethnicity and Social Change." *The Review of Religious Research* 8(1):11–26.
Allen, Donald E., and Harsit S. Sandhu
  1967 "A Comparative Study of Delinquents and Non-Delinquents: Family Affect, Religion, and Personal Income." *Social Forces* 46(2):263–268.
Benson, J. Kenneth
  1966 "Meaninglessness and Religious Involvement: An Explanatory Study." *Procedures of the Southwest Sociological Association* 16:76–94.
Blum, Barbara Sandra, and John H. Mann
  1960 "The Effect of Religious Membership on Religious Prejudice." *Journal of Social Psychology* 52:97–101.
Burnham, Kenneth E., John F. Connors III, and Richard C. Leonard
  1969 "Religious Affiliation, Church Attendance, Religious Education and Student Attitudes Toward Race." *Sociological Analysis* 30 (Winter):235–44.
Campbell, Douglas F., and Dennis W. Magill
  1968 "Religious Involvement and Intellectuality Among University Students." *Sociological Analysis* 29 (Summer):79–93.
Durkheim, Emile
  1961 *The Elementary Forms of Religious Life.* Trans. Joseph Ward Swain. New York: Collier.
Featherman, David L.
  1971 "The Socioeconomic Achievement of White Religio-Ethnic Subgroups: Social and Psychological Explanations." *American Sociological Review* 36 (April):207–222.
Fichter, Joseph H.
  1956 "Religious Values and the Social Personality." *American Catholic Sociological Review* 17 (June):109–116.
Freud, Sigmund
  1961 *Civilization and Its Discontents.* New York: W. W. Norton.
Glenn, Norval D., and Ruth Hyland
  1967 "Religious Preference and Worldly Success: Some Evidence from National Surveys." *American Sociological Review* 32 (February):73–85.
Glock, Charles Y.
  1959 "Differential Commitment to Religion: Some Sources and Consequences." Paper presented at the Annual Meeting of the American Sociological Association, Chicago, September.
Glock, Charles Y., and Rodney Stark
  1965 "Is There an American Protestantism?" *Trans-Action* 3 (November-December):8–13.
  1968 "Will Ethics Be the Death of Christianity?" *Trans-Action* 5 (June):7–14.
Greeley, Andrew M.
  1963 "Influence of the 'Religious Factor' on Career Plans and Occupational Values of College Graduates." *American Journal of Sociology* 68 (May):658–71.
Hirshi, Travis, and Rodney Stark
  1969 "Hellfire and Delinquency." *Social Problems* 17(2):202–13.
Jackson, Elton F., William S. Fox, and Harry J. Crockett, Jr.
  1970 "Religion and Occupational Achievement." *American Sociological Review* 35 (February):48–63.

Lenski, Gerhard
    1963 *The Religious Factor.* New York: Doubleday-Anchor.
Murphy, Rev. Francis
    1968 "Change Rocking Foundations of Papal Authority." *Boston Sunday Globe*
        (November 17):86.
O'Reilly, Charles T.
    1954 "Religious Beliefs of Catholic College Students and their Attitudes Toward
        Minorities." *Journal of Abnormal and Social Psychology* 49:378–80.
Rhodes, A. Lewis, and Charles B. Nam
    1970 "The Religious Context of Educational Expectations." *American Sociological Review* 35 (April):253–67.
Schuman, Howard
    1971 "The Religious Factor in Detroit: Review, Replication, and Reanalysis."
        American Sociological Review 36 (February):30–48.
Spilka, Bernard
    1958 "Some Personality Correlates of Interiorized and Institutionalized Religious Belief." *Psychological Newsletter* 9:103–107.
Weber, Max
    1930 *The Protestant Ethic and the Spirit of Capitalism.* Trans. Talcott Parsons.
        New York: Scribner's.

GORDON W. ALLPORT
J. MICHAEL ROSS

Personal Religious Orientation and Prejudice

Previous psychological and survey research has established three important facts regarding the relationship between prejudiced attitudes and the personal practice of religion.

1. On the average, church attenders are more prejudiced than nonattenders.

2. This overall finding, if taken only by itself, obscures a curvilinear relationship. While it is true that most attenders are *more* prejudiced than nonattenders, a significant minority of them are *less* prejudiced.

3. It is the casual, irregular fringe members who are high in prejudice; their religious motivation is of the extrinsic order. It is the constant, devout, internalized members who are low in prejudice; their religious motivation is of the *intrinsic* order.

The present paper will establish a fourth important finding — although it may properly be regarded as an amplification of the third. *The finding is that a cer-*

From Gordon Allport and Michael Ross, "Personal Religious Orientation and Prejudice," *Journal of Personality and Social Psychology* 5:4 (1967), pp. 432–443. Copyright 1967 by the American Psychological Association. Reprinted by permission.

tain cognitive style permeates the thinking of many people in such
are indiscriminately proreligious and, at the same time, highly preji

But first let us make clear the types of evidence upon whi(
propositions are based and examine their theoretical significance

Churchgoers Are More Prejudiced

Beginning the long parade of findings demonstrating that churchgoers are more intolerant of ethnic minorities than nonattenders is a study by Allport and Kramer (1946). These authors discovered that students who claimed no religious affiliation were less likely to be anti-Negro than those who declared themselves to be Protestant or Catholic. Furthermore, students reporting a strong religious influence at home were higher in ethnic prejudice than students reporting only slight or no religious influence. Rosenblith (1949) discovered the same trend among students in South Dakota. *The Authoritarian Personality* (Adorno, Frenkel-Brunswik, Levinson, and Sanford, 1950, p. 212) stated that scores on ethnocentricism (as well as on authoritarianism) are significantly higher among church attenders than among nonattenders. Gough's (1951) findings were similar. Kirkpatrick (1949) found religious people in general to be slightly less humanitarian than nonreligious people. For example, they had more punitive attitudes toward criminals, delinquents, prostitutes, homosexuals, and those in need of psychiatric treatment. Working with a student population Rokeach (1960) discovered nonbelievers to be consistently less dogmatic, less authoritarian, and less ethnocentric than believers. Public-opinion polls (as summarized by Stember, 1961) revealed confirmatory evidence across the board.

Going beyond ethnic prejudice, Stouffer (1955) demonstrated that among a representative sample of American church members those who had attended church within the past month were more intolerant of non-conformists (such as socialists, atheists, or communists) than those who had not attended. It seems that on the average religious people show more intolerance in general — not only toward ethnic but also toward ideological groups.

Is this persistent relationship in any way spurious? Can it be due, for example, to the factor of educational level? Many studies show that people with high education tend to be appreciably less prejudiced than people with low education. Perhaps it is the former group that less often goes to church. The reasoning is false. Sociological evidence has shown conclusively that frequent church attendance is associated with high socioeconomic status and with college education (Demerath, 1965). Furthermore, Stouffer's study found that the intolerant tendency among churchgoers existed only when educational level was held constant. Struening (1963), using as subjects only faculty members of a large state university (all highly educated), discovered that nonattenders were on the average less prejudiced than attenders. These studies assure us that the association between churchgoing and prejudice is not merely a spurious product of low education.

Turning to the theoretical implications of these findings, shall we say that religion in and of itself makes for prejudice and intolerance? There are some arguments in favor of such a conclusion, especially when we recall that certain powerful *theological* positions — those emphasizing revelation, election (chosen people), and theocracy (Allport, 1959, 1966) — have throughout history turned one ιgion against another. And among *sociological* factors in religion we find many that make for bigotry. One thinks of the narrow composition of many religious groups in terms of ethnic and class membership, of their pressure toward conformity, and of the competition between them (see Demerath, 1965; Lenski, 1961). It does seem that religion as such makes for prejudice.

And yet it is here that we encounter the grand paradox. One may not overlook the teachings of equality and brotherhood, of compassion and humanheartedness, that mark all the great world religions. Nor may one overlook the precept and example of great figures whose labors in behalf of tolerance were and are religiously motivated — such as Christ himself, Tertullian, Pope Gelasius I, St. Ambrose, Cardinal Cusa, Sebastian Castellio, Schwenckfeld, Roger Williams, Mahatma Gandhi, Martin Luther King, and many others, including the recently martyred clergy in our own South. These lives, along with the work of many religious bodies, councils, and service organizations would seem to indicate that religion as such *unmakes prejudice.* A paradox indeed.

The Curvilinear Relationship

If religion as such made *only* for prejudice, we would expect that churchgoers who expose themselves most constantly to its influence would, as a result, be more prejudiced than those who seldom attend. Such is not the case.

Many studies show that frequent attenders are less prejudiced than infrequent attenders and often less prejudiced even than nonattenders. Let us cite one illustrative study by Struening (1963). The curvilinear trend is immediately apparent in Table 1. In this particular study nonattenders had lower prejudice scores than any group, save only those devotees who managed to attend 11 or more times a month. Without employing such fine time intervals other studies have shown the same curvilinear trend. Thus, in *The Authoritarian Personality* (p. 212) we learned that in 12 out of 15 groups "regular" attenders (like nonattenders) were less prejudiced than "seldom" or "often" attenders. Employing a 26-item Desegregation Scale in three separate studies, Holtzman (1956) found the same trend as shown

TABLE 1
Church Attendance and Prejudice among
Faculty Members of a Midwestern
University

Frequency of attendance (times per mo.)	N	Prejudice score
0	261	14.7
1	143	25.0
2	103	26.0
3	84	23.8
4	157	22.0
5–7	94	19.9
8–10	26	16.3
11 or more	21	11.7

Note: From Struening (1957).

in Table 2. If more evidence for the curvilinear relationship is needed, it will be found in community studies made in New Jersey (Friedrichs, 1959), North Carolina (Tumin, 1958), New England (Pettigrew, 1959), and Ohio and California (Pinkney, 1961). One could almost say there is a unanimity of findings on this matter. The trend holds regardless of religion, denomination, or target of prejudice (although the case seems less clear for anti-Semitism than for prejudice against other ethnic groups).

TABLE 2
Church Attendance and Prejudice among Students in the
Border States

	1956 study % intolerant	Mean score on D scale	
		1958 study	1960 study
Nonattenders	37	41.3	38.1
Once a mo.	66	48.5	51.4
Twice a mo.	67	50.6	48.4
Once a wk. or oftener	49	44.5	44.3

Note: Adapted from Holtzman (1956), Kelley, Ferson, and Holtzman (1958), Young, Benson, and Holtzman (1960).

What are the theoretical implications? To find that prejudice is related to frequency of church attendance is scarcely explanatory, since it may reflect only formal behavior, not involvement or commitment to religious values. And yet it seems obvious that the regular attenders who go to church once a week or oftener (and several studies indicate that oftener than once a week is especially significant) are people who receive something of special ideological and experiential meaning. Irregular, casual fringe members, on the other hand, regard their religious contacts as less binding, less absorbing, less integral with their personal lives.

At this point, therefore, we must pass from external behavioral evidence into the realm of experience and motivation. Unless we do so we cannot hope to understand the curvilinear relationship that has been so clearly established.

Extrinsic versus Intrinsic Motivation

Perhaps the briefest way to characterize the two poles of subjective religion is to say that the extrinsically motivated person *uses* his religion, whereas the intrinsically motivated *lives* his religion. As we shall see later, most people, if they profess religion at all, fall upon a continuum between these two poles. Seldom, if ever, does one encounter a "pure" case. And yet to clarify the dimension it is helpful to characterize it in terms of the two ideal types.

Extrinsic Orientation

Persons with this orientation are disposed to use religion for their own ends. The term is borrowed from axiology, to designate an interest that is held because it serves other, more ultimate interests. Extrinsic values are always instrumental and utilitarian. Persons with this orientation may find religion useful in a variety of ways — to provide security and solace, sociability and distraction, status and self-justification. The embraced creed is lightly held or else selectively shaped to fit more primary needs. In theological terms the extrinsic type turns to God, but without turning away from self.

Intrinsic Orientation

Persons with this orientation find their master motive in religion. Other needs, strong as they may be, are regarded as of less ultimate significance, and they are, so far as possible, brought into harmony with the religious beliefs and prescriptions. Having embraced a creed the individual endeavors to internalize it and follow it fully. It is in this sense that he *lives* his religion.

A clergyman was making the same distinction when he said,

> Some people come to church to thank God, to acknowledge His glory, and to ask His guidance. . . . Others come for what they can get. Their interest in the church is to run it or exploit it rather than to serve it.

Approximate parallels to these psychological types have been proposed by the sociologists Fichter (1954) and Lenski (1961). The former, in studying Catholic parishioners, classified them into four groups: the dormant, the marginal, the modal, and the nuclear. Omitting the dormant, Fichter estimated in terms of numbers that 20% are marginal, 70% modal, and less than 10% nuclear. It is, of course, the latter group that would most closely correspond to our conception of the "intrinsic." Lenski distinguished between church members whose involvement is "communal" (for the purpose of sociability and status) and those who are "associational" (seeking the deeper values of their faith).

These authors see the significance of their classifications for the study of prejudice. Fichter has found less prejudice among devout (nuclear) Catholics than among others (see Allport, 1954, p. 421). Lenski (1961, p. 173) reported that among Detroit Catholics 59% of those with a predominantly "communal" involvement favored segregated schools, whereas among those with predominantly an "associational" involvement only 27% favored segregation. The same trend held for Detroit Protestants.

The first published study relating the extrinsic-intrinsic dimension directly to ethnic prejudice was that of Wilson (1960). Limiting himself to a 15-item scale measuring an extrinsic (utilitarian-institutional) orientation, Wilson found in 10 religious groups a median correlation of .65 between his scale and anti-Semitism. In general these correlations were higher than he obtained between anti-Semitism and the Religious-Conventionalism Scale (Levinson, 1954). From this finding Wilson concluded that orthodoxy or fundamentalism is a less important factor than extrinsicness of orientation.

Certain weaknesses may be pointed out in this pioneer study. Wilson did not attempt to measure intrinsicness of orientation, but assumed without warrant that it was equivalent to a low score on the extrinsic measures. Further, since the items were worded in a unidirectional way there may be an error of response set. Again,

Wilson dealt only with Jews as a target of prejudice, and so the generality of his finding is not known.

Finally, the factor of educational level plays a part. Wilson used the California Anti-Semitism scale, and we know that high scores on this scale go with low education (Christie, 1954; Pettigrew, 1959; Titus & Hollander, 1957; Williams, 1964). Further, in our own study the extrinsic subscale is negatively correlated with degree of education $(r = -32)$. To an appreciable extent, therefore, Wilson's high correlations may be "ascribed" to educational level.

At this point, however, an important theoretical observation must be made. Low education may indeed predispose a person toward an exclusionist, self-centered, extrinsic, religious orientation and may dispose him to a stereotyped, fearful image of Jews. This fact does not in the least affect the functional relationship between the religious and the prejudiced outlooks. It is a common error for investigators to "control for" demographic factors without considering the danger involved in doing so. In so doing they are often obscuring and not illuminating the functional (i.e., psychological) relationships that obtain (see Allport, 1950).

Following Wilson the task of direct measurement was taken up by Feagin (1964) who used a more developed scale — one designed to measure not only extrinsic orientation but also the intrinsic. His scales are essentially the same as those discussed in a later section of this paper. In his study of Southern Baptists Feagin reached four conclusions: (a) Contrary to expectation, extrinsic and intrinsic items did not fall on a unidimensional scale but represented two independent dimensions; (b) only the extrinsic orientation was related to intolerance toward Negroes; (c) orthodoxy as such was not related to the extrinsic or intrinsic orientation; (d) greater orthodoxy (fundamentalism of belief) did, however, relate positively to prejudice.

Taking all these studies together we are justified in assuming that the inner experience of religion (what it means to the individual) is an important causal factor in developing a tolerant or a prejudiced outlook on life.

Yet, additional evidence is always in place, and new insights can be gained by a closer inspection of the rather coarse relationships that have been established up to now.

The Present Study

We wished to employ an improved and broader measure of prejudice than had previously been used. And since direct measures of prejudice (naming the target groups) have become too sensitive for wide use, we wished to try some abbreviated indirect measures. Further, we wished to make use of an improved Extrinsic-Intrinsic scale, one that would give reliable measures of both extrinsic and intrinsic tendencies in a person's religious life. For these reasons the following instruments were adopted.

Social Problems Questionnaire

This scale, devised by Harding and Schuman (unpublished [1]; see also Schuman and Harding, 1963, 1964), is a subtly worded instrument containing 12 anti-Negro, 11 anti-Jewish, and 10 anti-other items (pertaining to Orientals, Mexicans, and Puerto Ricans). The wording is varied so as to avoid an agreement response set.

Indirect Prejudice Measures

Six items were taken from Gilbert and Levinson's (1956) Custodial Mental Illness Ideology Scale (CMI). Example: "We should be sympathetic with mental patients, but we cannot expect to understand their odd behavior. a) I definitely disagree. b) I tend to disagree. c) I tend to agree. d) I definitely agree."

Four items are related to a "jungle" philosophy of life, suggesting a generalized suspiciousness and distrust. Example: "The world is a hazardous place in which men are basically evil and dangerous. a) I definitely disagree. b) I tend to disagree. c) I tend to agree. d) I definitely agree."

In all cases the most prejudiced response receives a score of 5 and the least prejudiced response, 1. No response was scored 3.

From Table 3 we see that while the indirect measures have a positive correlation with each other and with direct measures the relationship is scarcely high enough to warrant the substitution of the indirect for the direct. The high correlations between prejudice for the three ethnic target groups once again illustrate the well-established fact that ethnic prejudice tends to be a broadly generalized disposition in personality.

TABLE 3
Intercorrelations between Five Measures of Prejudice

	Anti-Jewish	Anti-Other	Jungle	CMI
Anti-Negro	.63	.70	.20	.25
Anti-Jewish		.67	.24	.31
Anti-Other			.33	.36
Jungle				.43

Note: N = 309.

Religious Orientation Measure

The full scale, entitled "Religious Orientation," is available from ADI.[2] It separates the intrinsically worded items from the extrinsic, gives score values for each item, and reports on item reliabilities. In all cases a score of 1 indicates the most intrinsic response, a score of 5, the most extrinsic. While it is possible to use all 20 items as one continuous scale, it will soon become apparent that it is often wise to treat the two subscales separately. A sample item from the extrinsic subscale follows: "What religion offers me most is comfort when sorrows and misfortune strike. a) I definitely disagree, 1. b) I tend to disagree, 2. c) I tend to agree, 4. d) I definitely agree, 5." A sample item from the intrinsic subscale: "My religious beliefs are what really lie behind my whole approach to life. a) this is definitely not so, 5. b) probably not so, 4. c) probably so, 2. d) definitely so, 1.

Sample

While our sample of six groups of churchgoers shows some diversity of denomination and region, it is in no sense representative. Graduate-student members of a seminar collected the 309 cases from the following church groups: Group A, 94 Roman Catholic (Massachusetts); Group B, 55 Lutheran (New York State); Group C, 44 Nazarene (South Carolina); Group D, 53 Presbyterian (Pennsylvania); Group E, 35 Methodist (Tennessee); Group F, 28 Baptist (Massachusetts).

We labeled the groups alphabetically since such small subsamples could not possibly lead to valid generalizations concerning denominations as a whole. All subjects knew that they were invited to participate as members of a religious group, and this fact may well have introduced a "proreligious" bias.

Gross Results

If we pool all our cases for the purpose of correlating religious orientation with prejudice, we discover that while the findings are in the expected direction they are much less impressive than those of previous studies, especially Wilson's.

Correlations with Extrinsic Subscale

Since Wilson employed an extrinsic scale similar to ours, we first present in Table 4 our findings using this subscale and the various measures of prejudice. Whereas Wilson found a correlation of .65 between his extrinsic and anti-Semitic measures, our correlation falls to .21. In part the reason no doubt lies in certain features of Wilson's method which we have criticized.

TABLE 4
Correlations between Extrinsic Subscale
and Prejudice

Anti-Negro	.26
Anti-Jewish	.21
Anti-Other	.32
Jungle	.29
CMI	.44

Note: N = 309.

Correlations with Combined Extrinsic-Intrinsic Scale

From the outset it was our intention to broaden Wilson's unidirectional (extrinsic) measure to see whether our hypothesis might hold for the total scale (combined scores for the 11 extrinsic and 9 intrinsic items). As Table 5 shows, matters do not improve but seem to worsen. The logic of combining the two subscales is of course to augment the continuum in length and presumably enhance the reliability of the total measure. It soon became apparent, however, that subjects who endorse extrinsically worded items do not necessarily reject those

TABLE 5
Correlations between Total Extrinsic-
Intrinsic Scale and Prejudice

Anti-Negro	.26
Anti-Jewish	.18
Anti-Other	.18
Jungle	.21
CMI	.17

Note: N = 309.

worded intrinsically, or vice versa. It turns out that there is only a very low correlation in the expected direction between the two subscales ($r = .21$). Obviously at this point some reformulation is badly needed.

Reformulation of the Approach

Examination of the data reveals that some subjects are indeed "consistently intrinsic," having a strong tendency to endorse intrinsically worded items and to reject the extrinsically worded. Correspondingly others are "consistently extrinsic." Yet, unfortunately for our neat typology, many subjects are provokingly inconsistent. They persist in endorsing any or all items that to them seem favorable to religion in any sense. Their responses, therefore, are "indiscriminately pro-religious."

The problem is essentially the same as that encountered by the many investigators who have attempted to reverse the wording of items comprising the F scale, in order to escape an unwanted response-set bias. Uniformly the effort has proved to be frustrating, since so many subjects subscribe to both the positive and negative wording of the same question (see Bass, 1955; Chapman and Bock, 1958; Chapman and Campbell, 1959; Christie, 1954; Jackson and Messick, 1957).

An example from our own subscales would be: "My religious beliefs are what really lie behind my whole approach to life" (intrinsic). "Though I believe in my religion, I feel there are many important things in my life" (extrinsic).

The approach used by Peabody (1961) offers us a model for analyzing our data in a meaningful way. Peabody administered both positive and negative F-scale items to subjects at two different testing sessions. By comparing each individual's responses to the same question stated positively at one time and in reverse at another he was able to separate out those who were consistently pro or anti toward the content of authoritarian items. But he found many who expressed double agreement (or disagreement) with both versions of the same question. Table 6 applies Peabody's paradigm to our data.

In assigning our 309 cases to these categories we employed the following criteria.

Intrinsic type includes individuals who agree with intrinsically worded items on the intrinsic subscale, and who disagree with extrinsically stated items on the extrinsic subscale. By the scoring method employed these individuals fall below the median scores on both subscales.

Extrinsic type includes individuals who agree with extrinsically stated items on

TABLE 6

Four Patterns of Religious Orientation

	Agrees with intrinsic choice	*Disagrees with intrinsic choice*
Agrees with extrinsic choice	Indiscriminately proreligious	Consistently extrinsic in type
Disagrees with extrinsic choice	Consistently intrinsic in type	Indiscriminately antireligious or nonreligious [a]

[a] Not found in present sample.

the extrinsic subscale, and who disagree with items on the intrinsic subscale. By our scoring method these individuals all fall above the median scores on both subscales.

Indiscriminately proreligious includes those who on the intrinsic subscale score at least 12 points less than on the extrinsic subscale. (This figure reflects the fact that a subject gives approximately 50% more intrinsic responses on the intrinsic subscale than we should expect from his extrinsic responses to the extrinsic subscale.)

Indiscriminately antireligious or nonreligious includes those who would show a strong tendency to disagree with items on both subscales. Since nonchurchgoers are excluded from our samples, such cases are not found. (Some pilot work with markedly liberal groups indicates that this type does exist, however, even among members of "religious" organizations.)

Table 7 gives the percentage of the three types.

TABLE 7

Percentage of Each Religious Type in Each Subsample

Religious group	N	*Consistently intrinsic*	*Consistently extrinsic*	*Indiscriminately proreligious*
A	(94)	36	34	30
B	(55)	35	36	29
C	(44)	36	39	25
D	(53)	32	30	38
E	(35)	31	29	40
F	(28)	39	39	22

Results of the Reformulation

The five measures of prejudice were analyzed by a 6 (Groups) $\times$ 3 (Religious Types) analysis of variance. Table 8 presents the overall effects for religious types for each of the five measures of prejudice. The multivariate analysis of variance indicates that there is both a significant difference between the three types of religious orientation and between the six subsamples in the level of prejudice.[3] Examination of the means shows two trends: (a) The extrinsic type

TABLE 8
Prejudice and Religious Orientation

	Mean prejudice score			
Target of prejudice	Intrinsic type N = 108	Extrinsic type N = 106	Inconsistent type N = 95	F ratio
Anti-Negro	28.7	33.0	36.0	8.6[b]
Anti-Jewish	22.6	24.6	28.9	11.1[b]
Anti-Other	20.4	23.3	26.1	10.9[b]
Jungle	7.9	8.7	9.6	8.4[b]
CMI	10.2	11.8	13.4	20.4[b]

Multivariate analysis of variance		
Source of variation	F ratio	df
Religious type (A)	5.96[c]	10,574
Sample groups (B)	3.19[c]	25,668
A × B	1.11[a]	50,1312

[a] $p > .25$.
[b] $p > .001$.
[c] $p > .0005$.

is more prejudiced than the intrinsic type for both direct and indirect measures; (b) the indiscriminate type of religious orientation is more prejudiced than either of the two consistent types. Statistically all these trends are highly significant.

We note especially that the scores of the indiscriminate type are markedly higher on all measures than the scores of the intrinsic type. Corresponding *F* ratios for paired comparisons range from 8.4 for the jungle scale to 20.4 for the CMI scale. The differences between the indiscriminate and extrinsic types are smaller. For the anti-Jewish and CMI scales these differences are, however, beyond the .005 level; for the anti-other and jungle scales, at the .05 level. For the anti-Negro the difference falls below significance.

The relationship between the indiscriminately proreligious orientation and prejudice receives support (see Table 9) when we compare subjects who are *moderately*

TABLE 9
Degrees of Indiscriminateness and Average Prejudice Scores

Target of prejudice	Moderately indiscriminate N = 56	Extremely indiscriminate N = 39	F ratio
Anti-Negro	35.4	37.9	.97
Anti-Jewish	28.0	30.1	.90
Anti-Other	24.9	28.2	3.25[a]
Jungle	9.5	10.2	1.11
CMI	10.2	14.6	3.99[a]

[a] $p > .05$.

indiscriminate with those who are *extremely* indiscriminate. (In the first group the scores on the intrinsic subscale average 16 points lower than on the extrinsic subscale, whereas the extreme cases average 23 points less on the intrinsic than on the extrinsic subscale.)

The discovery that the degree of indiscriminateness tends to relate directly to the degree of prejudice is an important finding. It can only mean that some functional relationship obtains between religious muddleheadedness (for that is what indiscriminate scores imply) and antagonism toward ethnic groups. We shall return to this interpretation in the concluding section of this paper.

Results for Subsamples

It would not be correct to assume that the variance is distributed equally over all the subsamples, for it turns out that the denominational groups differ appreciably in prejudice scores and in religious type, as Tables 10 and 11 indicate.

TABLE 10
Anti-Negro Prejudice: Mean Scores on Social Problems Scale

Religious group	*Intrinsic type*	*Extrinsic type*	*Indiscriminate type*	*Group* M
A	27.4 (34)	34.8 (32)	32.2 (28)	31.4 (94)
B	27.2 (19)	32.3 (20)	31.9 (16)	30.4 (55)
C	22.4 (16)	36.2 (17)	35.0 (11)	30.9 (44)
D	35.5 (17)	28.7 (16)	42.5 (20)	36.1 (53)
E	40.5 (11)	35.5 (10)	43.0 (14)	40.1 (35)
F	22.6 (11)	27.9 (11)	28.7 (6)	26.0 (28)
Type *M*	28.7 (108)	33.0 (106)	36.0 (95)	32.5 (309)

Analysis of variance			
Source of variation	df	MS	F *ratio*
Religious type (A)	2	1077.8	8.6[b]
Religious group (B)	5	952.2	7.6[b]
A × B	10	251.1	2.0[a]
Error (w)	291	125.6	

[a] $p > .10$.
[b] $p > .001$.

It is true that when we combine subsamples all the trends are in the expected direction, but troublesome exceptions occur for single groups as indicated by the nearly significant interaction effects. The most troublesome contradictions appear in relation to the anti-Negro measures based on the Harding-Schuman scale. Table 10 discloses certain sore points, even though the average trend over all the subsamples is in the predicted direction.

For Groups A, B, and C we note that the indiscriminate type is slightly less prejudiced than the extrinsic type, and for Groups D and E the extrinsic type seems actually less prejudiced than the intrinsic. (Groups D and E are consistently more troublesome than other subsamples, perhaps because of some salient racial issue in the local community. It will be noted that both these groups are considerably more anti-Negro than the other subsamples.)

By way of contrast we present in Table 11 the results for the short (five-item) CMI scale. With the exception of the indiscriminate type in Group F, the progression of scores is precisely as expected. Each subsample shows that the intrinsic type is less prejudiced toward the mentally ill than the extrinsic type, and the extrinsic type is less prejudiced than the indiscriminately proreligious.[4]

TABLE 11
Indirect (CMI) Measure of Prejudice

Religious group	Intrinsic type	Extrinsic type	Indiscriminate type	Group M
A	11.2 (34)	12.4 (32)	13.6 (28)	12.3 (94)
B	10.1 (19)	10.8 (20)	13.4 (16)	11.3 (55)
C	9.5 (16)	12.2 (17)	12.6 (11)	11.3 (44)
D	10.6 (17)	11.4 (16)	14.8 (20)	12.4 (53)
E	8.6 (11)	12.9 (10)	13.6 (14)	11.8 (35)
F	9.2 (11)	10.7 (11)	9.2 (6)	9.8 (28)
Type *M*	10.2 (108)	11.8 (106)	13.4 (95)	11.9 (309)

Analysis of variance

Source of variation	df	MS	F ratio
Religious type (A)	2	255.0	20.4[b]
Religious group (B)	5	36.5	2.9[a]
A × B	10	15.3	1.2
Error (w)	291	12.5	

[a] $p > .05$.
[b] $p > .001$.

Returning in a different way to the original question of whether consistent extrinsic and intrinsic orientations make for prejudice and for tolerance, respectively, we shall now examine this matter in each subsample separately. Inspection of the mean scores and variance for the total scale indicates that we are dealing with a relatively narrow range of variation. To minimize the effect of a narrow range of scores and skewed distributions, we used Kendal's (1955) tau as a measure of degree of relationship between prejudice and consistent religious orientation. The results are given in Table 12. While the correlations are not high (14 are significant in the expected direction), only one (in the troublesome Group E) is significant in the reverse direction.

Educational Differences

Computing the actual years of schooling for all groups we find that the indiscriminate type has significantly less formal education than the intrinsic cases

TABLE 12

Correlations between Combined Extrinsic-Intrinsic Religious Scores (for Consistent Subjects) and Prejudice (Kendal's Tau)

Religious group	Anti-Negro	Anti-Jewish	Anti-Other	Jungle	CMI
A	.31[c]	.26[c]	.24[c]	.14[a]	.19[c]
B	.19[a]	.13	.15	−.05	.03
C	.32[c]	.17[a]	.35[c]	.14[a]	.28[c]
D	−.12	.05	−.09	.03	.11
E	−.24[a]	−.11	−.13	.26[a]	.46[c]
F	.39[c]	.13	.25[a]	−.01	.24[a]

[a] $p > .10$.
[b] $p > .05$.
[c] $p > .01$.

($p > .005$, $F = 18.29$), and somewhat less than the extrinsic type ($p > .10$, $F = 2.89$). Comparing extrinsic with intrinsic types we find that the former has finished fewer years of schooling ($p > .10$, $F = 3.45$). (Oddly enough the groups with highest average education are D and E, which also displayed the highest anti-Negro and anti-Semitic prejudice — perhaps because of particular local conditions.)

In our survey of earlier studies we saw that educational level is often a factor in the various relationships discovered between religion and prejudice. We have also argued that demographic factors of this sort should not be allowed to obscure the functional (psychological) analysis that the data call for. Granted that low education makes for indiscriminate thinking, the mental confusion that results from low education may have its own peculiar effects on religious and ethnic attitudes.

Summary and Interpretations

At the outset we stated three propositions that seem to be firmly established: (a) Churchgoers on the broad average harbor more ethnic prejudice than non-churchgoers; (b) in spite of this broad tendency a curvilinear relationship in fact exists; (c) the intrinsically motivated churchgoers are significantly less prejudiced than the extrinsically motivated. Our present research supplies additional strong support for the second and third of these propositions.

To these propositions we add a fourth: *churchgoers who are indiscriminately proreligious are more prejudiced than the consistently extrinsic, and very much more prejudiced than the consistently intrinsic types.*

The psychological tie between the intrinsic orientation and tolerance, and between the extrinsic orientation and prejudice, has been discussed in a series of papers by Allport (1959, 1963, 1966). In brief the argument holds that a person with an extrinsic religious orientation is using his religious views to provide security, comfort, status, or social support for himself — religion is not a value in its own right, it serves other needs, and it is a purely utilitarian formation. Now prejudice too is a "useful" formation: it too provides security, comfort, status, and social support. A life that is dependent on the supports of extrinsic religion is likely to be dependent on the supports of prejudice, hence our positive correlations between the extrinsic orientation and intolerance. Contrariwise, the intrinsic religious orientation is not an instrumental device. It is not a mere mode of conformity, nor a crutch, nor a tranquilizer, nor a bid for status. All needs are subordinated to an overarching religious commitment. In internalizing the total creed of his religion the individual necessarily internalizes its values of humility, compassion, and love of neighbor. In such a life (where religion is an intrinsic and dominant value) there is no place for rejection, contempt, or condescension toward one's fellow man. Such is our explanation for the relationship between extrinsic religion and prejudice, and between intrinsic religion and tolerance.

Our present task is to discover, if we can, some similar functional tie between prejudice (as measured both directly and indirectly) and the indiscriminately proreligious orientation. The common factor seems to be a certain cognitive style. Technically it might be called "undifferentiated thinking," or excessive "category width," as defined by Pettigrew (1958). Rokeach (1960) notes the inability of the "dogmatic" mind to perceive differences; thus, whereas some people distinguish in their thinking and feeling between Communists and Nazis, the undifferentiated dogmatist has a global reaction (cognitive and emotional) toward "Communazis."

We have no right, of course, to expect all our subjects to make discriminations exactly corresponding to our own logic. Nor should we expect them to read and respond to every item on the Extrinsic-Intrinsic scale according to its full meaning as intended by the investigators. Perhaps we should be gratified that two-thirds of our cases can be safely classified as "consistent" (i.e., having about the same strength of disposition toward an extrinsic or intrinsic orientation across most of the items). These consistent cases, as we have seen, support the hypothesis with which we started. It is the remaining (indiscriminate) one-third of the cases which obscure the trend (or diminish its statistical significance).

In responding to the religious items these individuals seem to take a superficial or "hit and run" approach. Their mental set seems to be "all religion is good." "My religious beliefs are what really lie behind my whole life" — Yes! "Although I believe in my religion, I feel there are many more important things in my life" — Yes! "Religion is especially important to me because it answers many questions about the meaning of life" — Yes! "The church is most important as a place to formulate good social relationships" — Yes!

There seems to be one wide category — "religion is OK." From the way in which the scale is constructed this undifferentiated endorsement can be the product of an agreement response set. Our inconsistently proreligious may be "yeasayers" (Couch and Keniston, 1960). But if so, we are still dealing with an undifferentiated cognitive disposition. We recall likewise that the inconsistent cases have a lower level of formal education than the consistent cases. This factor also is relevant to the formation and holding of overwide categories.

But why should such a disposition, whatever its source, be so strongly related to prejudice, in such a way that the *more* undifferentiated, the *more* prejudiced — as Table 9 shows?

The answer is that prejudice itself is a matter of stereotyped overgeneralization, a failure to distinguish members of a minority group as individuals (Allport, 1954,

Chaps. 2, 10). It goes without saying that if categories are overwide the accompanying feeling tone will be undifferentiated. Thus, religion as a whole is good; a minority group as a whole is bad.

It seems probable that people with undifferentiated styles of thinking (and feeling) are not entirely secure in a world that for the most part demands fine and accurate distinctions. The resulting diffuse anxiety may well dispose them to grapple onto religion and to distrust strange ethnic groups. The positive correlation between the jungle items and other prejudice scales (Table 3) is evidence for this interpretation.

Our line of reasoning, readers will recognize, is compatible with various previous contributions to the theory of prejudice. One thinks here of Rokeach's concept of dogmatism; of Schuman and Harding's (1964) discovery of a "confused" type in their study of the relation between rational consistency and prejudice; of the same authors' work on sympathetic identification (1963); of studies on the dynamics of scapegoating, the role in insecurity, of authoritarian submission, of intolerance for ambiguity, and of related concepts.

All in all we conclude that prejudice, like tolerance, is often embedded deeply in personality structure and is reflected in a consistent cognitive style. Both states of mind are enmeshed with the individual's religious orientation. One definable style marks the individual who is bigoted in ethnic matters and extrinsic in his religious orientation. Equally apparent is the style of those who are bigoted and at the same time indiscriminately proreligious. A relatively small number of people show an equally consistent cognitive style in their simultaneous commitment to religion as a dominant, intrinsic value and to ethnic tolerance.

One final word: our research argues strongly that social scientists who employ the variable "religion" or "religiosity" in the future will do well to keep in mind the crucial distinction between religious attitudes that are *intrinsic, extrinsic,* and *indiscriminately pro.* To know that a person is in some sense "religious" is not as important as to know the role religion plays in the economy of his life. (The categories of *nonreligious* and *indiscriminately antireligious* will also for some purposes be of central significance, although the present research, confined as it is to churchgoers, does not employ them.)

Notes

1. J. Harding and H. Schuman, "Social Problems Questionnaire," Cornell University.
2. The full Religious Orientation scale has been deposited with the American Documentation Institute. Order Document No. 9268 from ADI Auxiliary Publications Project, Photoduplication Service, Library of Congress, Washington, D. C. 20540. Remit in advance $1.25 for microfilm or $1.25 for photocopies and make checks payable to: Chief, Photoduplication Service, Library of Congress.
3. The multivariate F reported here is Wilk's lambda (Anderson, 1958). Statistical computations are summarized by Bock (1963) and programmed for the IBM 7090 by Hall and Cramer (1962). The univariate tests to be reported are adjusted for unequal Ns to obtain orthogonal estimates according to mathematical procedures described in Hall and Cramer.
4. If we apply a more severe test, asking whether *all* differences between groups are significant, we find the following results. In four of the six groups (in both Tables 10 and 11) the extrinsic type is significantly more prejudiced than the

intrinsic. Likewise in four out of six groups (Table 10) and five out of six (Table 11), the indiscriminate type is significantly more prejudiced than the intrinsic. However, in only two of the six groups (in both Tables 10 and 11) is the indiscriminate type significantly more prejudiced than the extrinsic.

References

Adorno, T. W., Frenkel-Brunswik, E., Levinson, D. J., and Sanford, R. N. *The authoritarian personality*. New York: Harper, 1950.

Allport, G. W. Review of S. A. Stouffer, E. A. Schuman, L. C. De Vinney, S. A. Star, and R. W. Williams, Jr., *The American soldier*. Vol. 1. *Adjustment during Army life. Journal of Abnormal and Social Psychology*, 1950, 45, 168–173.

Allport, G. W. *The nature of prejudice*. Reading, Mass.: Addison-Wesley, 1954.

Allport, G. W. Religion and prejudice. *The Crane Review*, 1959, 2, 1–10.

Allport, G. W. Behavorial science, religion, and mental health. *Journal of Religion and Health*, 1963, 2, 187–197.

Allport, G. W. Religious context of prejudice. *Journal for the Scientific Study of Religion*, 1966, 5, 447–457.

Allport, G. W., and Kramer, B. M. Some roots of prejudice. *Journal of Psychology*, 1946, 22, 9–39.

Anderson, T. W. *An introduction to multivariate statistical analysis*. New York: Wiley, 1958.

Bass, B. M. Authoritarianism or acquiescence. *Journal of Abnormal and Social Psychology*, 1955, 56, 616–623.

Bock, R. D. Programming univariate and multivariate analysis of variance. *Technometrics*, 1963, 5, 95–117.

Chapman, L. J., and Bock, R. D. Components of variance due to acquiescence and content in the F-scale measure of authoritarianism. *Psychological Bulletin*, 1958, 55, 328–333.

Chapman, L. J., and Campbell, D. T. The effect of acquiescence response-set upon relationships among the F-scale, ethnocentrism, and intelligence. *Sociometry*, 1959, 22, 153–161.

Christie, R. C. Authoritarianism re-examined. In R. C. Christie and M. Jahoda (Eds.), *Studies in the scope and method of the authoritarian personality*. New York: Free Press of Glencoe, 1954. Pp. 123–196.

Couch, A., and Keniston, K. Yeasayers and naysayers: Agreeing response set as a personality variable. *Journal of Abnormal and Social Psychology*, 1960, 60, 151–174.

Demerath, N. J., III. *Social class in American Protestantism*. Chicago: Rand McNally, 1965.

Feagin, J. R. Prejudice and religious types: A focused study of southern fundamentalists. *Journal for the Scientific Study of Religion*, 1964, 4, 3–13.

Fichter, J. H. *Social relations in the urban parish*. Chicago: University of Chicago Press, 1954.

Friedrichs, R. W. Christians and residential exclusion: An empirical study of a northern dilemma. *Journal of Social Issues*, 1959, 15, 14–23.

Gilbert, D. C., and Levinson, D. J. Ideology, personality, and institutional policy in the mental hospital. *Journal of Abnormal and Social Psychology*, 1956, 53, 263–271.

Gough, H. G. Studies in social intolerance: IV. *Journal of Social Psychology*, 1951, 33, 263–269.

Hall, C. E., and Cramer, E. *General purpose program to compute multivariate analysis of variance on an IBM 7090*. Washington, D. C.: George Washington University Biometric Laboratory, 1962.

Holtzman, W. H. Attitudes of college men toward non-segregation in Texas schools. *Public Opinion Quarterly*, 1956, 20, 559–569.

Jackson, D. H., and Messick, S. J. A note on ethnocentrism and acquiescence response sets. *Journal of Abnormal and Social Psychology*, 1957, 54, 132–134.

Kelly, J. G., Ferson, J. E., and Holtzman, W. H. The measurement of attitudes toward the Negro in the South. *Journal of Social Psychology,* 1958, 48, 305–317.

Kendal, M. G. *Rank correlation methods.* (2nd ed.) London: Griffin, 1955.

Kirkpatrick, C. Religion and humanitarianism: A study of institutional implications. *Psychological Monographs,* 1949, 63 (9, Whole No. 304).

Lenski, G. *The religious factor.* Garden City, N. Y.: Doubleday, 1961.

Levinson, D. J. The inter-group workshop: Its psychological aims and effects. *Journal of Psychology,* 1954, 38, 103–126.

Peabody, D. Attitude content and agreement set in scales of authoritarianism, dogmatism, antiSemitism, and economic conservatism. *Journal of Abnormal and Social Psychology,* 1961, 63, 1–11.

Pettigrew, T. F. The measurement and correlates of category width as a cognitive variable. *Journal of Personality,* 1958, 26, 532–544.

Pettigrew, T. F. Regional differences in anti-Negro prejudice. *Journal of Abnormal and Social Psychology,* 1959, 49, 28–36.

Pinkney, A. The anatomy of prejudice: Majority group attitudes toward minorities in selected American cities. Unpublished doctoral dissertation, Cornell University, 1961.

Rokeach, M. *The open and closed mind: Investigations into the nature of belief systems and personality systems.* New York: Basic Books, 1960.

Rosenblith, J. F. A replication of "Some roots of prejudice." *Journal of Abnormal and Social Psychology,* 1949, 44, 470–489.

Schuman, H., and Harding, J. Sympathetic identification with the underdog. *Public Opinion Quarterly,* 1963, 27, 230–241.

Schuman, H., and Harding, J. Prejudice and the norm of rationality. *Sociometry,* 1964, 27, 353–371.

Stember, H. C. *Education and attitude change.* New York: Institute of Human Relations Press, 1961.

Stouffer, S. A. *Communism, civil liberties, and conformity.* Garden City, N. Y.: Doubleday, 1955.

Struening, E. L. Antidemocratic attitudes in a Midwest university. In H. H. Remmers (Ed.), *Anti-democratic attitudes in American schools.* Evanston: Northwestern University Press, 1963. Ch. 9.

Titus, H. E., and Hollander, E. P. The California F scale in psychological research: 1950–1955. *Psychological Bulletin,* 1957, 54, 47–64.

Tumin, M. *Desegregation: Resistance and readiness.* Princeton: Princeton University Press, 1958.

Williams, R. M. *Strangers next door: Ethnic relations in American communities.* Englewood Cliffs, N. J.: Prentice-Hall, 1964.

Wilson, W. C. Extrinsic religious values and prejudice. *Journal of Abnormal and Social Psychology,* 1960, 60, 286–288.

Young, R. K., Benson, W. M., and Holtzman, W. H. Changes in attitudes toward the Negro in a southern university. *Journal of Abnormal and Social Psychology,* 1960, 60, 131–133.

SNELL PUTNEY
RUSSELL MIDDLETON

Dimensions and Correlates
of Religious Ideologies

   Religious attitudes are generally acknowledged to be important elements in the social-psychological make-up of the individual. Despite the proliferation of empirical studies of religiosity and its correlates, the findings remain cloudy and curiously inconclusive. Religiosity is a complex phenomenon, and Charles Glock[1] has suggested that it involves four dimensions — the experiential, ideological, ritualistic, and consequential. Much confusion has resulted in the past from the failure to differentiate these dimensions.
   Only one of the dimensions of religiosity — the ideological — relates to religious beliefs as such. However, there are also several dimensions of religious ideology, and they too have often been confused or mixed indiscriminately. Most of the studies have measured religious ideology by means of single *ad hoc* questions, Thurstone scales, or Likert, Guttman, or other types of scales. The questions are usually focused on measuring the commitment to orthodox Christian dogma, but questions are often included on other aspects as well, especially the importance to the individual of his beliefs. Thus an atheist whose convictions were important to his self-conception might receive a spuriously high score if the scale were re-garded as a measure of orthodoxy, and a spuriously low score if the scale were regarded as a measure of the subjective importance of his belief. Studies correlating scores on such scales to other characteristics are limited by the confusion in the scales. On the other hand, studies using scales which have been shown to be unidimensional are usually restricted in scope, concentrating upon only one dimen-sion of religious ideology.
   The relation of an individual to any ideological system admits of at least four dimensions or types of variation: his acceptance or rejection of the tenets of the system, his orientation toward other persons with respect to his beliefs, the sig-nificance of his beliefs to his self-conception, and the degree to which he recog-nizes ambivalence in his beliefs. The present study is intended first to investigate the interrelations of these four dimensions as applied to religious ideology, and then to ascertain the relation of each of these dimensions to other social and attitudinal characteristics.
   As applied specifically to religious ideology, the four dimensions may be de-noted as follows: *orthodoxy* (what might be termed, among Protestants at least,

Reprinted by permission of the publisher, the University of North Carolina Press, from Snell Putney and Russell Middleton, "Dimensions and Correlates of Religious Ideolo-gies," *Social Forces* 39:4 (1961). Financial support for this study was furnished by the Florida State University Research Council. This is a revised and expanded version of a paper read at the twenty-third annual meeting of the Southern Sociological Society, April 9, 1960. Some footnotes omitted.

the degree of "fundamentalism"), *fanaticism* (the degree of "missionary zeal" to spread a particular belief as a panacea for social and personal ills), *importance* (the degree to which convictions about religion are felt to be a central and essential element of the self), and *ambivalence* (the degree to which the individual is conscious of having contradictory attitudes relating to religion).

Each of these dimensions could be largely independent of the others. Thus an individual inclining toward fanaticism could be either fundamentalist or atheist in the orthodoxy of his belief. An individual who rated his beliefs very important to his self-conception would not necessarily be fanatic about spreading these beliefs to others. Someone who was highly orthodox might, or might not, be conscious of ambivalence.

To differentiate orthodoxy, fanaticism, and importance, Likert-type scales were constructed on conceptual grounds in each area and then pretested for internal consistency. Items of lower discriminatory power were discarded [2] until three scales of six questions each were established.[3] The fourth dimension, ambivalence, was deemed capable of measurement by a single question calling for a Likert-type rating of the statement "Although one is stronger than the other, there is part of me which believes in religion and part of me which does not." A check list of statements was also used which permitted subjects to be classified as "skeptics" who do not believe in a personal god, "modernists" who believe in a personal god but do not interpret the Bible literally, and "conservatives" who believe that every word of the Bible is literally true.

Other personality characteristics which might be related to the four dimensions were measured by appropriate scales: authoritarianism,[4] status concern,[5] anomia,[6] and conservatism.[7] Social characteristics such as education, sex, region of residence, church affiliation, and size of community of residence were determined by direct questions, and socio-economic status was estimated by the Vaughan scale.[8]

The data were gathered by means of a questionnaire administered to approximately 1200 students enrolled in social science courses at 13 colleges and universities located in the following states: New York, New Jersey, Pennsylvania, Florida, Georgia, and Alabama. Approximately half of the students were attending institutions in the northeastern states and half in the southeastern states. Although college students cannot be considered representative of the general population, such a sample facilitated comparisons between different religious persuasions, since it provided an adequate number of skeptics within a smaller sample than would have been possible among the general population. Since the focus of this study is Christian religious ideology, students of the Jewish and other non-Christian faiths were excluded from the sample, leaving a total of 1,126 subjects.

For purposes of statistical analysis, all of the attitude scales were dichotomized at the center point. For example, on the orthodoxy scale, which ranges from a minimum of 6 to a maximum of 42, the cut-point was set at 24. Chi square values were computed from two-by-two or two-by-three tables to determine the level of significance of the findings, and the degree of association between variables was measured by calculation of Yule's Q and the contingency coefficient.[9]

Findings

Table 1 shows the distributions of the scores on the four dimensions compared to the responses to the check list of religious positions. It is evident that

TABLE 1

Ideological Categories and Dimensions of Religious Beliefs

Ideological categories	N	Percent high in orthodoxy	Percent high in fanaticism	Percent high in importance	Percent high in ambivalence
Skeptics	130	7.7	12.3	55.4	64.6
Modernists	632	62.0	47.2	81.6	47.2
Conservatives	359	91.9	72.1	97.2	23.2
Contingency coefficient		.46[a]	.34[a]	.32[a]	.27[a]

[a] Chi square value significant at the .001 level.

there is a very close correspondence between the check list responses and the orthodoxy scale, thus lending validity to the latter. Only 7.7 percent of the skeptics as compared with 91.9 percent of the conservatives scored relatively high on the orthodoxy scale.

It had been hypothesized that those who took extreme positions on the check list — the skeptics and the conservatives — would tend to have the highest scores on fanaticism and importance and the lowest scores on acknowledgment of ambivalence. In other words, it was expected that a "U" curve would be observed in the distribution of these variables with the "extremists" at either end similar to each other and different from the "middle-of-the-roaders." This proved not to be the case. All of these dimensions showed a simple linear relationship to the classification derived from the check list. Skeptics were by far the lowest on both fanaticism and subjective importance of beliefs, the modernists were intermediate, and the conservatives highest. Conversely, the skeptics acknowledged the greatest ambivalence, the moderates were again intermediate, and the conservatives acknowledged the least. All of these relationships were significant at the .001 level.

The implication of these results would seem to be that adherents of the atheistic or agnostic positions on religious issues find their viewpoints less essential to their self-conception, are more conscious of ambivalence concerning them, and feel less interest in converting others than those who subscribe to orthodox religious doctrines. There is no reason why an individual could not be an ardent atheist, feel his atheism essential to his self-conception, deny any ambivalence concerning it, and devote himself to trying to convert others to his viewpoint. But such individuals seem to be in the minority among the skeptics observed.

Table 2 presents the relations of the four dimensions of religious ideology to each other. Orthodoxy, fanaticism, and importance are directly related to one another, and admission of ambivalence is inversely related to each of them. All of the relationships are significant at the .001 level. The relations of orthodoxy to importance, of importance to fanaticism, and of fanaticism to orthodoxy are the strongest. The relations between ambivalence and the other dimensions are weaker, but still highly significant statistically. These findings are presumably related to the findings discussed above. The orthodox individual on the scale is very likely to be the conservative individual on the check list. Thus it would be expected that either would show the same fanaticism and high subjective importance of conviction.

TABLE 2

Interrelations of Dimensions of Religious Beliefs[a]

	Orthodoxy	Fanaticism	Importance
Fanaticism	+.74[b]		
Importance	+.82[b]	+.81[b]	
Ambivalence	−.47[b]	−.46[b]	−.51[b]

[a] The measure of association is Yule's Q. There are approximately 1,126 cases for the calculation of each Q.
[b] Chi square significant at the .001 level.

The fact that the dimensions are significantly correlated with each other could be interpreted as indicating that it is of less practical significance to distinguish between them than might be supposed on *a priori* grounds. And certainly there is less need to differentiate them than there would be, for example, if fanaticism were found to be unrelated (or related in an inverse or nonlinear way) to orthodoxy. Nevertheless, the correlations, especially for ambivalence, are far from perfect. The divergence of the dimensions may have as much theoretical import as their associations with each other.

This assumption tends to be confirmed by Table 3 which shows considerable variation in the degree to which the dimensions are associated with other social

TABLE 3

Relations of Dimensions and Correlates of Religious Beliefs[a]

Correlates	Dimensions			
	Orthodoxy	Fanaticism	Importance	Ambivalence
Personality characteristics				
Authoritarianism	+.43[b]	+.30[b]	+.41[b]	−.18[b]
Status concern	+.20[b]	+.20[b]	+.21[b]	+.05
Anomia	+.04	+.13	.00	.00
Conservatism	+.26[b]	+.27[b]	+.30[b]	−.21[b]
Social characteristics				
Socio-economic status	−.13	−.02	+.02	−.07
Year in college	−.24[b]	−.25[b]	−.17[b]	+.02
Sex (male)	−.23[b]	−.09	−.45[b]	+.30[b]
Residence in the South or outside the South (southern)	+.39[b]	+.31[b]	+.28[b]	−.17[b]
Protestant-Catholic affiliation (Protestant)	−.49[b]	−.13	−.12	+.15[b]
Size of community of residence	−.06	−.14[b]	+.02	−.01

[a] The measure of association is Yule's Q. In the case of normal categories the sign indicates relationship to the characteristic in parentheses. There are between 1,059 and 1,126 cases for the calculation of each Q.
[b] Chi square value significant at the .05 level.

and psychological characteristics of the subjects. These relations may be summarized briefly as follows:

 1. The person who is highly orthodox in religious beliefs tends to be authoritarian, highly concerned about his social status, and conservative in political and economic questions. Such an individual is more likely than the person low in orthodoxy to be a lower classman, to be a female, to have lived mostly in the South, and to be a Catholic rather than a Protestant. The orthodox may or may not be anomic, may or may not be middle class, and may come from either a small or a large metropolitan city.

 2. The person who scores relatively high on fanaticism (or missionary zeal) shows the same general characteristics as the highly orthodox individual. However, two of the correlates significantly associated with orthodoxy — sex and church affiliation — are not significantly associated with fanaticism. On the other hand, size of community of residence, which was not significantly related to orthodoxy, is inversely associated with fanaticism.

 The fanatic, then, resembles the orthodox individual, especially in his tendency toward authoritarianism, high concern over social status, conservatism, freshman status and southern residence.

 3. The persons who rate their beliefs most important to their self-conceptions share with the orthodox and the fanatic the tendency to be authoritarian, concerned over social status, conservative, freshmen and southern. They are also far more likely to be female than male as was the case with the orthodox but not with the fanatic. Importance is not significantly associated with either religious affiliation (as was orthodoxy) or with size of community (as was fanaticism).

 4. Those who do not acknowledge feelings of ambivalence concerning whether or not they believe in religion are likely to be authoritarian, conservative, male, southern, and Catholic. Unlike orthodoxy, fanaticism, and importance, ambivalence is not significantly associated with status concern or year in school. Unlike fanaticism it is not significantly associated with size of community.

 These specific relationships between the dimensions and the correlates may be less important, however, than the simple fact that the four dimensions relate in different ways to the correlates. Orthodoxy is significantly associated with seven correlates, importance and fanaticism with six, and ambivalence with five. Or, approaching it in terms of the correlates, only three (authoritarianism, conservatism, and region of residence) relate significantly to all four dimensions, three (status concern, year in college, and sex) relate significantly to three dimensions, one (Protestant-Catholic affiliation) relates significantly to two dimensions, and one (size of community) relates significantly to only one dimension. Socioeconomic status and anomia are not significantly related to any of the dimensions, although there is some tendency for the more anomic to be more fanatic and for those of higher socio-economic status to be less orthodox.[10]

 In the case of problems involving the relation of religion to these correlates, the distinctions between the dimensions of religious ideology could well determine whether or not a relationship would be found. Further research into the problem of differentiating dimensions of religious ideology would seem definitely warranted.

A final observation might be made about the degree of association observed between the dimensions and the correlates. Most of the relationships observed seem relatively low. Clearly religious ideology is neither a major determinant nor a simple resultant of personality characteristics, such as authoritarianism, conservatism, or anomia, or social factors such as place of residence, year in college, or even church affiliation.

Notes

1. Charles Y. Glock, Differential Commitment to Religion: Some sources and Consequences. Paper presented at the annual meeting of the American Sociological Association in Chicago, Illinois, September 1959.
2. For a discussion of the Likert discriminatory power technique see T. W. Adorno, et al., *The Authoritarian Personality* (New York: Harper and Brothers, 1950).
3. Each question was scored according to the following response scale: 7, strong agreement; 6, moderate agreement; 5, slight agreement; 4, no answer or don't know; 3, slight disagreement; 2, moderate disagreement; 1, strong disagreement. Reverse scoring items are indicated by an asterisk.

Orthodoxy Scale

    1. I believe that there is a physical Hell where men are punished after death for the sins of their lives.
    2. I believe there is a supernatural being, the Devil, who continually tries to lead men into sin.
    3. To me the most important work of the church is the saving of souls.
    4. I believe that there is a life after death.
    5. I believe there is a Divine plan and purpose for every living person and thing.
    *6. The only benefit one receives from prayer is psychological.

Fanaticism Scale

    1. I have a duty to help those who are confused about religion.
    2. Even though it may create some unpleasant situations, it is important to help people become enlightened about religion.
    *3. There is no point in arguing about religion, because there is little chance of changing other people's minds.
    *4. It doesn't really matter what an individual believes about religion as long as he is happy with it.
    5. I believe the world would really be a better place if more people held the views about religion which I hold.
    6. I believe the world's problems are seriously aggravated by the fact that so many people are misguided about religion.

Importance Scale

    1. My ideas about religion are one of the most important parts of my philosophy of life.
    2. I find that my ideas on religion have a considerable influence on my views in other areas.
    3. Believing as I do about religion is very important to being the kind of person I want to be.
    4. If my ideas about religion were different, I believe that my way of life would be very different.
    *5. Religion is a subject in which I am not particularly interested.
    6. I very often think about matters relating to religion.

4. The five-item version of the F-scale developed by the Department of Scientific Research of the American Jewish Committee was utilized. Leo Srole, "Social Integration and Certain Corollaries: An Exploratory Study," *American Sociological Review*, 21 (December 1956), pp. 709–716.

5. Walter C. Kaufman, "Status, Authoritarianism, and Anti-Semitism," *American Journal of Sociology*, 62 (January 1957), pp. 379–382.

6. Dorothy L. Meier and Wendel Bell, "Anomia and Differential Access to the Achievement of Life Goals," *American Sociological Review*, 24 (April 1959), pp. 189–202.

7. Herbert McClosky, "Conservatism and Personality," *American Political Science Review*, 52 (March 1958), pp. 27–45.

8. Charles L. Vaughan, "A Scale for Assessing Socio-Economic Status in Survey Research," *Public Opinion Quarterly*, 22 (Spring 1958), pp. 19–34.

9. Parametric measures of association were not appropriate because attitude scales of this type yield only ordinal data. Since rank order correlations are not well adapted to large samples with many cases of ties, a somewhat cruder measure of association was utilized in this study. Moreover, it was considered desirable to use the same measure of association for the attitudinal variables as for the purely nominal categories, such as sex or Protestant-Catholic affiliation, which cannot be subjected to rank correlation analysis.

10. The failure to obtain statistically significant relations with socio-economic status may be due to the overconcentration of subjects in the middle class level and to the tendency for the Vaughan scale to differentiate more adequately from the middle class downward than from the middle class upward. When father's occupation and father's education were used alone as indices of social class position, however, the findings were not essentially different from those based upon the Vaughan scale.

11

SCHOOL

In the broadest sense, education is the structured preparation of the young to assume adult roles in the society. This includes transmitting cultural values and norms in addition to providing knowledge and training in specific skills. In primitive societies, most education takes place within the family, is limited to very small children, and is mostly imitation by doing.

In addition, some primitive communities may also include religious and sex-role instruction in secret societies. The individual is usually separated from his family for a period of time (varying cross-culturally from a few months to a few years) and grouped with others of the same sex and similar age. Education in the secret society constitutes a complex rite of passage from childhood to adulthood, with graduation usually taking place with the achievement of puberty.

In the West, Ong (1963) has suggested that Latin language study for male youths during the Renaissance served the same functions as a puberty rite or rite of passage into the adult world. It meant the learning of secret meanings, was restricted to males, was supposed to "toughen" the mind and character, was taught under the threat of a frequent flogging, and meant a radical break with the past.

The first European universities were established at Bologna and Paris in the eleventh and twelfth centuries. According to Haskins (1965), the rise of these and other medieval universities was caused by the discovery of manuscripts and artifacts from previous eras and the increasing contact between different civilizations as a result of improved navigation leading to expanded exploration and commercial trade. Such universities, according to Halsey (1961), consisted of scholastic training for a few elite and monastic training for the priesthood. They were an organic part of religious rather than economic life, and genuine innovation was violently opposed by the powerful institutions in the society.

Most inventions during this era consisted of weapons of war and instruments of torture to be used by political and military elites. The spirit of modern science, promoting free inquiry into the nature of the world and leading to the establish-ment of the modern secularized university, did not emerge until the late seven-teenth and early eighteenth centuries in Germany and England. Even then, uni-versity enrollment remained restricted to an elite. The education of the common man was confined to the family or to special craft guilds in which he could ap-prentice in a trade. Mass public education and the availability of higher educa-tion to larger segments of the population did not become institutionalized in the West until the late nineteenth and twentieth centuries.

Since then, the growth of the educational establishment in America has been tremendous. The proportion of youth aged 14–17 enrolled in high school has increased from about 2 per cent in 1870, to 11 per cent in 1900, 51 per cent in 1930, 86 per cent in 1960, and 95 per cent in 1970. The proportion of 17-year-olds graduating from high school has increased from 2 per cent in 1870, to 6 per cent in 1900, 29 per cent in 1930, 65 per cent in 1960, to almost 80 per cent in 1970. The proportion of youth aged 18–21 enrolled in college has increased from around 2 per cent in 1870, to 4 per cent in 1900, 12 per cent in 1930, 34 per cent in 1960, to about 50 per cent in 1970.

By the end of 1971, over 60 million students were enrolled in more than 113,000 schools in the United States, including about 8.4 million college students enrolled in about 2,500 institutions of higher learning (including four-year col-leges and universities, two-year junior colleges, and nondegree programs). Over 85 billion dollars were required to maintain these institutions, staffed by almost 3 million teachers and 225 thousand administrators and supervised by 138 thou-sand school board members. From 1960 to 1970, the numbers increased by 13 million more students, 1 million more teachers, and 80 thousand more admin-istrators at a cost increase of 160 per cent, from 27 to 70 billion dollars. About 30 per cent of the total American population currently studies or works in a school of some kind. What economist Fritz Machlup calls the "knowledge in-dustry," of which the university is the center, has grown to account for almost 30 per cent of the gross national product.

Explanations for the Growth of Mass Public Education

How can we account for this revolutionary increase in the demand for education? Three different theoretical explanations have been proposed. The structural functional explanation postulates modernization as the primary cause. According to this theory, technological change directly affects the skill require-ments of jobs in industrial society. As a result, many jobs are upgraded in skill requirements and the proportion of high-skill to low-skill jobs increases. As a final consequence, more formal education is instituted to provide the general and specific training necessary to satisfy the skill requirements of the more spe-cialized occupational roles.

In contradistinction to this proposition, a 1972 Department of Labor report indicates that 80 per cent of all jobs don't even require a bachelor's degree as eligibility criteria. Furthermore, according to a 1971 Department of Labor study of education and employment, "In eight of ten occupations, there was no rela-tionship between the workers' educational attainment and their degree of job success." In fact, a study by the Survey Research Center at the University of

Michigan reveals that high school dropouts actually earn slightly more than high school graduates even after taking their greater job seniority into account. A thorough evaluation of other data necessary to document this theory also fails to provide adequate confirmation. As Randall Collins (1971, p. 1007) explains:

> Economic evidence indicates no clear contributions of education to economic development, beyond the provisions of mass literacy. Shifts in the proportion of more skilled and less skilled jobs do not account for the observed increase in education of the American labor force. Education is often irrelevant to on-the-job productivity and is sometimes counterproductive; specifically vocational training seems to be derived more from work experience than from formal school training. The quality of schools themselves, and nature of dominant student cultures suggest that schooling is very inefficient as a means of training for work skills.

A second explanation for the educational revolution derives from the conflict theory of educational stratification. According to this theory, the kind and level of education received by an individual is primarily a function of membership in a particular status group. Increasing levels of education for certain groups in the society results from their increasing power to demand more education for their children, especially when such demands converge with elite concerns for maintaining social control by hiring only respectable, properly socialized employees for middle level positions. Collins states (p. 1015), "Led by the biggest and most prestigious organizations, employers have raised their educational requirements to maintain both the relative prestige of their managerial ranks and the relative respectability of middle ranks." He explains (pp. 1010–11):

> The main activity of schools is to teach particular status cultures, both in and outside the classroom. In this light, any failure of schools to impart technical knowledge (although it may also be successful in this) is not important; schools primarily teach vocabulary and inflections, styles of dress, aesthetic tastes, values and manners. The emphasis on sociability and athletics in many schools is not extraneous but may be at the core of the status culture propagated by the schools. Where schools have a more academic or vocational emphasis, this emphasis may itself be the content of a particular status culture, providing sets of values, materials for consumption, and shared activities for an associational group making claims to a particular basis for status.
>
> Insofar as a particular status group controls education, it may use it to foster control within group organizations. Educational requirements for employment can serve both to select new members for elite positions who share the elite culture and, at a lower level of education, to hire lower and middle employees who have acquired a general respect for these elite values and styles.

Evidence for this theory may be obtained from historical and descriptive studies of schools which support the generalization that they are places where particular status cultures are acquired and studies establishing that education has been used as a means of cultural selection by employers. Collins cites many such studies, supporting the proposition that educational attainment still tends to be primarily symbolic of status (albeit in many cases, necessary to solidify ascribed status) rather than functional for the achievement of higher status.

Numerous studies not cited by Collins (see, for example, Spaeth, 1968; Eckland, 1970; Kahl, 1953; Sewell and Shah, 1968; and Sewell, 1971) all provide convincing evidence that parental socioeconomic status has significantly more influence on educational opportunities, aspirations, and achievement than any other variable including measured intellectual ability. According to a 1971 *The New York Times* report, under 20 per cent of youth from families with an income of $3,000 or less go on to college, as compared to about 35 per cent from families with an income of $4,000–$6,000, over 50 per cent from families making $7,500–$10,000, and 85 per cent from families earning $15,000 or more. Given the great importance of SES, it should be no surprise that the Department of Education reports that some 50 per cent of the top 5 per cent and 57 per cent of the top 20 per cent of all high school graduates do not graduate from college in the United States. Among those who do attend college, important status discrepancies are still maintained. For example, over half the sons of families listed in the Social Register attend Harvard, Princeton, or Yale. Most of the others attend other Ivy League or fringe Ivy League schools with their sisters attending such "sister colleges" as Radcliffe, Vassar, or Smith.

According to Becker (1964), what a student really learns in college is independence from his family, how to handle himself in social situations, and a more generalized work skill which includes the ability to set long range goals, to budget time and effort efficiently, and to achieve long range goals despite institutional obstacles. The product of such an education is an organizationally committed middle-class employee.

According to a third explanation for the expansion of formal education in the United States, governments in new nation states (wishing to increase and consolidate their power in a heterogeneous and fragmented society) may expand the educational system to use schools to inculcate political knowledge and a commitment to the national government which, in part, transcends loyalties to local membership groups. Many examples of such use of schools abound in the literature on modern nation building in the developing world.

Evidence also suggests that the desire by American elites to socialize European immigrants into the dominant culture was mainly responsible for the rapid expansion of primary education and compulsory schooling in the United States. Citing the works of Cremin (1961) and Curti (1935), Collins states (p. 1011), "the public school system in the U.S. was founded mainly under the impetus of WASP elites with the purpose of teaching respect for Protestant and middle class standards of cultural and religious propriety, especially in the face of Catholic, working class immigration from Europe."

The debates over immigration quotas through the years certainly reflect concern over the political impact of this large immigration of foreign working-class peoples. And certainly the content of American public school education has always been centered on WASP culture, in ways ranging from the obvious (for example, explicit training in the rights and duties of citizenship, including pledging allegiance to and singing the praises of the state, learning the proper care and display of the flag, and participating in mock elections) to the more covert (teaching a very selective "presidents, generals, and folklore" version of American history, civics, and economics as well as other fields). In fact, the concept of education for citizenship dates back at least to Jefferson.

Related to public education for citizenship is the use of compulsory education to manage the relation between labor supply and demand. According to Greer (1969), the extension of compulsory schooling from 12 years of age to 14 in 1917 and then 16 in 1925 was caused by the shrinking unskilled job market. Students who could prove they had a job to go to could be excused from the requirement. This makes the school, in part, a bureaucratic babysitter, alleviating strain on the job market while keeping the kids off the streets and out of mom's way. Conversely, government policies regarding the school have also been changed to increase the production of manpower trained for more specialized sectors of the labor market. After the embarrassing success of the Soviet space program in launching an earth satellite, billions of dollars were poured into colleges and universities to encourage program development and student enrollment in science and technology.

Between 1957 and 1965 the percentage of government expenditures for scientific research and development out of the total federal budget more than doubled, from 5.8 per cent to 12.6 per cent. Most of this money was channeled into the major universities in the form of student scholarships and faculty research grants, further exacerbating the discrepancy in operating capital between the rich and poor schools. Kolko (1962) observed that in 1959 one-fifth of the colleges in the United States accounted for nearly two-thirds of the scholarship funds awarded. By 1970, research subsidies, 85 per cent of which were provided by the federal government, constituted about 21 per cent of the total operating revenue of the major universities.

By the late 1960's, widespread student criticism of university ties to the government, particularly to defense-related research, influenced the administrations of some universities to phase out classified research and to reevaluate the relationship between the university and the military. At the same time, as a result of campus disruptions, fiscal demands from other areas, and the general hostility of the Nixon administration toward the liberal intellectual establishment, the federal government substantially cut aid to higher education. Antagonism toward campus unrest and the deteriorating economic situation also reduced private gifts and grants to universities. By late 1970, about half the smaller liberal arts colleges in the nation were defined as marginal financial operations. Rogers A. Freedman, special assistant to President Nixon, announced that "If present trends continue, most of the 1,500 private colleges — about two-thirds of all institutions of higher learning in the country — may within the next two decades have to close their doors to the public."

School as an Agent of Social Control

These relatively recent historical developments underline Brim's statement (1958, p. 15) that "the educational institution possesses legitimate power to pursue its aims only to the extent that they are in fact those which society considers desirable." Though citizens have some degree of direct or indirect control over local public school matters, most educational policy is determined by political and economic elites. Economic elites can always influence the course of higher education, either directly by threatening to withhold private contributions or indirectly by devaluing degrees as a requirement for employment.

The formal heads of university government, the trustees, are thoroughly "establishment" in background and policy orientation. According to a 1969 Educational Testing Service study, the average trustee is white, Protestant, and in his 50's (more than a third are over 60). He is also well educated and wealthy (more than half report incomes exceeding $30,000, including a sixth earning more than $100,000 per year).

Some 60 per cent of the trustees vote Republican and 35 per cent Democratic. The majority describe themselves as politically moderate, 22 per cent conservative, and only 16 per cent liberal. Relatively few read any books or journals on higher education and most believe that almost all policy decisions should be made by them and the college administrators alone. Half the business executives who sit on the boards expressed the opinion that "running a college is like running a business." The evidence so far causes radical critics of higher education to agree. Many claim that the elementary and secondary schools and most universities today (particularly the huge multiversities) are analogous to nineteenth-century factories, processing human commodities for the technobureaucratic society.

Probably the most characteristic value of American public schools is "discipline." A 1972 Gallup poll of public attitudes toward school revealed that "lack of discipline" was ranked as the first problem, ahead of "lack of proper financial support," "problems of integration," "lack of parental interest in their children's education," "use of dope, drugs," among others. Professional educators considered finance and integration more important than discipline, which ranked third ahead of lack of parental interest. Some 41 per cent of those surveyed thought that students had too many rights and privileges as opposed to only 11 per cent who thought students should have more rights.

Perhaps most important, the study also found that the main reasons parents want children to get a good education are nonintellectual. The three leading reasons are: "to get better jobs," "to get along better with people at all levels of society" and "to make more money — achieve financial success." It would seem reasonable to infer from these responses that the public tends to see proper schooling primarily as the way to assimilate the status culture necessary to material success. In essence, then, any attempt to utilize the school as a vehicle for upward mobility must entail an acceptance of the school as an instrument of socialization and social control.

Beginning at the elementary level, students are evaluated on culturally appropriate behavior as well as academic performance. Grades are issued for "self-control," "courtesy," and "citizenship," and teachers, counselors, and administrators encourage the student to display the right attitude toward authority, homework, exams, and other institutional demands. Continued controversy over prayer in the school, sex education, and other issues reveals the extent to which many adults see the school as the appropriate institution (along with the family and church) for the moral training of the child.

In lower-class schools, both teachers and children tend to sense the meaninglessness and irrelevance of the experience and are more openly antagonistic toward each other. In middle-class schools, however, the children tend to approach the situation with more gravity; they are anxious to excel to achieve the approval of their parents through achieving the approval of their teacher. As Jules Henry (1957, 1959) shows, it is easy for a teacher anxious about student criticism and hungry for attention to inadvertently promote an atmosphere conducive to destructive intragroup aggression. The "witch-hunt syndrome" can take the form of anything from providing frequent opportunities for students to carpingly criticize each other's performance, to organizing "vigilance clubs" in which the students not only publicly confess "evil" deeds, but inform on each other. This creates or reinforces docility, feelings of vulnerability, fear of internal aggression, and boredom. Even "permissive" classrooms may have nefarious effects if the teacher overpersonalizes her relationship with the students to be able to induce guilt in the child when he fails to conform to her expectations.

The first selection by Henry is a brilliant radical criticism of contemporary education, illustrated by careful observations of actual classroom situations. Henry argues that "the function of education has never been to free the mind and the spirit of man, but to bind them; and to the end that the mind and the spirit of his children should never escape *Homo sapiens* has employed praise, ridicule, admonition, mutilation, and even torture to chain them to the cultural pattern." Henry's premise is that "school is an institution for drilling children in cultural orientations" and, as such, it teaches children to be stupid.

Public school teachers, drawn disproportionately from upwardly striving members of the lower middle class, tend to emphasize inculcating respectability and social acceptance at the expense of intellectual curiosity and self-expression. This orientation is reinforced by the whole system of inspections and grading to which the teachers themselves are subjected. According to Spindler (1955), an analysis of teachers' ratings yielded the following composite of the ideal American boy: sociable, popular, well-rounded, athletic (but not a star), healthy, ambitious, considerate of others, patriotic, clean-cut, Christian, of average academic ability and average intellectual capacity. Coleman's research on the adolescent subculture of the high school (cited in the introduction to Chapter 12) fails to consider whether teachers might also share, if not encourage, such nonintellectual values of the student subculture. C. Wayne Gordon, in *The Social System of the High School* (1957), suggests that many teachers unconsciously tend to reward students on the basis of their popularity with other students. Some evidence for this may be found in a 1968 study by Schafer and Armer which concluded that athletes got better grades than nonathletes in high school, even when matched against students who obtained the same scores in intelligence tests and had the same motivation.

In most cases, school officials can enforce their demands by using corporal punishment. According to a national survey of elementary school teachers by *Grade Teacher* magazine in 1968, nearly half the nation's elementary teachers admit they struck children at least once during the school year, and one out of ten hit pupils more than five times. About three out of four schools surveyed permitted physical punishment (almost all of them with limitations about who may administer the punishment or the use of witnesses). Only one in four specifically prohibited it.

However, the primary sanction that schools use to maintain discipline over their students is the grading system. In 1967, the Yearbook Committee of the Association for Supervision and Curriculum Development said that, although it had not yet developed a satisfactory alternative, the present grading system is so bad that it has to be eliminated. Yet by 1972, the only significant progress in this direction had been made on the elementary level where many schools had replaced report cards with written teacher evaluations and teacher-parent conferences. Only 2 per cent of all institutions of higher learning had implemented a totally nontraditional grading system. High schools had a larger but still very small proportion. Some three out of five colleges and universities had incorporated nontraditional methods of student evaluation into their grading systems, but only on a very modest scale; for example, in many cases, the student is allowed to take one course per semester (providing it's not in his major field of study) on a pass/fail basis.

General resistance to radical change in the traditional grading system seems to be shared by school board members, administrators, parents, and students alike. A 1967 Gallup poll revealed 78 per cent of school board members rejecting a proposition to "eliminate competition by issuing only 'pass/fail marks' " along with 83 percent of the parents. Moreover, a Princeton University study found that even the students believed "they learn more, work closer to their capacity, are more motivated to learn and more actively participate in numerically graded courses than ones marked pass/fail."

Kitsuse and Cicourel (1968, p. 48) point out that the high school also "serves as a 'clearing house' which receives and releases information concerning adolescents from and to other agencies including college admissions offices and prospective employers." Moreover, "the school is confronted with the task not only of identifying and developing the talent, but also of motivating it" (p. 50). Thus, any discrepancy between the student's measured ability and his classroom achievement becomes defined as "an academic problem" (either an "overachiever" or an "underachiever"), to promote the adjustment of the adolescent into the adult world. And so the unsolicited psychological observations of well-intentioned counselors is added to the oppressive reality of an accumulating biography of graded performance. As the time for application to college draws near, the awesome burden of this life "record" begins to exact its toll. And for those accepted to college, the pressure continues. According to the American Council on Education, over one-fifth of all incoming college freshmen admit to cheating.

It is little wonder that in 1970, 1,500 adolescent runaways were reported every day and, as Harvard psychiatrist Mathew Ross reports (1969), suicide is the second most frequent cause of death among college students and third most frequent among high school youth. In 1966 nearly one hundred thousand college students threatened suicide, one in ten actually tried, and one thousand succeeded. This rate is 50 per cent higher than for the American population as a whole. Among all youths 15–24 years old suicide was the fourth most frequent cause of death. The most universal reason, according to Ross, is the pressure to achieve high grades. If many, if not most, youth are trained to measure their self-worth by their graded achievement in school, and if they really expect that opportunities to acquire the "good things" in life are circumscribed closely by school performance (the grades-job-money-happiness syndrome), then it can be understood how some could contemplate and even commit suicide when confronted with the prospect of failure and social ridicule.

Despite these problems, an abundance of research (see, for example, Dynes, 1967; Sanford, 1963; Lehman and Payne, 1963; Edelstein, 1962; Lane, 1968; and Feldman and Newcomb, 1969) suggests that at least the college experience has positive effects for the growth and differentiation of the self. Despite many complex methodological deficiencies most research indicates that the general effect of the college experience for many students is to make them more politically informed and active; more liberal toward social, political, and economic matters (such as religion, war, racial minorities, government intervention in the economy, and party affiliation); less authoritarian, dogmatic, ethnocentric, and prejudiced; and freer to express impulses, but also *more critical about extreme statements of any kind.*

This last effect could account, in large part, for all the others. The traditional mark of a properly educated person has been moderation of opinion, categorically eschewing extremes. Insofar as the validity of most surveys measuring personality change in students ultimately is based on the student's willingness to agree or disagree with propositions, decreases in dogmatism, ethnocentrism, and the like might reflect socialization to a moderate response orientation appropriate to the student's status. This is only speculation, however. Certainly much of the college experience could operate to produce a genuine broadening and liberalization of the student's personality.

The second selection, by Christenson and Capretta, represents some of the better research in this field. Its authors are aware of important previous research findings and sensitive to the methodological problems in this area of research.

References

Becker, Howard
    1964   "What Do They Really Learn in College?" *Trans-Action* (May):14–17.
Brim, Orville
    1958   *Sociology and the Field of Education.* New York: Russell Sage.
Coleman, James
    1961   *The Adolescent Society.* Glencoe, Ill.: The Free Press.
Collins, Randall
    1971   "Functional and Conflict Theories of Educational Stratification." *American Sociological Review* 36 (December):1002–19.
Cremin, Lawrence A.
    1961   *The Transformation of the School.* New York: Knopf.
Curti, Merle
    1935   *The Social Ideas of American Educators.* New York: Scribner's.
Dynes, Wallace
    1967   "Education and Tolerance: An Analysis of Intervening Factors." *Social Forces* 46 (September):22–33.
Eckland, Bruce
    1970   "Social Class and College Graduation." *American Journal of Sociology* 70:36–50.
Edelstein, Alex A.
    1962   "Since Bennington: Evidence of Change in Student Political Behavior." *Public Opinion Quarterly* 26(4):564–77.

Feldman, Kenneth, and Theodore Newcomb
  1969   *The Impact of College on Students*. San Francisco: Jossey-Bass.
Gordon, C. Wayne
  1957   *The Social System of the High School*. Glencoe, Ill.: The Free Press.
Greer, Colin
  1969   "Public Schools: The Myth of the Melting Pot." *Saturday Review* (November 15):84–86, 102.
Halsey, A. A., Jean Floud, and C. Arnold Anderson (eds.)
  1961   *Education, Economy, and Society*. New York: The Free Press.
Haskins, Charles Homer
  1965   *The Rise of the Universities*. Ithaca, N.Y.: Cornell University Press.
Hawes, Gene R.
  1967   "The Colleges of America's Upper Class." Pp. 73–80 in Esther Lloyd-Jones and Herman A. Estrin (eds.), *The American Student and His College*. Boston, Mass.: Houghton Mifflin.
Henry, Jules
  1955   "Docility or Giving the Teacher What She Wants." *The Journal of Social Issues* 2:33–41.
  1957   "Attitude Organization in Elementary School Classrooms." *The American Journal of Orthopsychiatry* 27 (January):117–33.
  1959   "Spontaneity, Initiative, and Creativity in Suburban Classrooms." *The American Journal of Orthopsychiatry* 29 (April):266–79.
Kahl, Joseph A.
  1953   "Educational and Occupational Aspirations of 'Common-Man' Boys." *Harvard Educational Review* 23(3).
Kitsuse, John I., and Aaron V. Cicourel
  1968   "The High Schools' Role in Adolescent Status Transition." Pp. 44–52 in Robert R. Bell and Holger R. Stub (eds.), *The Sociology of Education: A Sourcebook*, rev. ed. Homewood, Ill.: Dorsey.
Kolko, Gabriel
  1962   *Wealth and Power in America: An Analysis of Social Class and Income Distribution*. New York: Praeger.
Lane, Robert E.
  1968   "Political Education in the Midst of Life's Struggles." *Harvard Educational Review* 38(3):468–94.
Lehman, Irwin J., and Isabelle K. Payne
  1963   "An Exploration of Attitude and Value Changes of College Freshmen." *Personnel Guidance Journal* 41 (January):403–408.
Ong, Walter J., S.J.
  1963   "Latin Language Study as a Renaissance Puberty Rite." Pp. 444–66 in George D. Spindler (ed.), *Education and Culture — Anthropological Approaches*. New York: Holt, Rinehart and Winston.
Ross, Mathew
  1969   "Suicides Rise among Students," *Boston Globe* (April 25):1.
Sanford, Nevitt
  1963   "The Freeing and Acting Out of Impulse in Late Adolescence: Evidence From Two Cases." Pp. 4–39 in Robert H. White (ed.), *The Study of Lives, Essays on Personality in Honor of Henry A. Murray*. New York: Atherton.
Schafer, Walter W., and J. Michael Armer
  1968   *Trans-action* (November).
Sewell, William H.
  1971   "Inequality of Opportunity for Higher Education." *American Sociological Review* 36 (October):793–809.
Sewell, William H. and Vimal Shah
  1968   "Parents' Education and Children's Educational Aspirations and Achievements." *American Sociological Review* 33 (April):191–209.
Spaeth, Joe L.
  1968   "Occupational Prestige Expectations Among Male College Graduates." *American Journal of Sociology* 73:548–58.

Spindler, George
   1955   "Education in a Transforming American Culture." *The Harvard Educational Review* 25:145–56.

JULES HENRY

Golden Rule Days: American Schoolrooms

Introduction

School is an institution for drilling children in cultural orientations. Educationists have attempted to free the school from drill, but have failed because they have gotten lost among a multitude of phantasms — always choosing the most obvious "enemy" to attack. Furthermore, with every enemy destroyed, new ones are installed among the old fortifications — the enduring contradictory maze of the culture. Educators think that when they have made arithmetic or spelling into a game; made it unnecessary for children to "sit up straight"; defined the relation between teacher and children as democratic; and introduced plants, fish, and hamsters into schoolrooms, they have settled the problem of drill. They are mistaken.

Education and the Human Condition

Learning to Learn

The paradox of the human condition is expressed more in education than elsewhere in human culture, because learning to learn has been and continues to be *Homo sapiens'* most formidable evolutionary task. Although it is true that mammals, as compared to birds and fishes, have to learn so much that it is difficult to say by the time we get to chimpanzees what behavior is inborn and what is learned, the learning task has become so enormous for man that today learning — education — along with survival, constitutes a major preoccupation. In all the fighting over education we are simply saying that we are not yet satisfied — after about a million years of struggling to become human — that we have mastered the fundamental human task, learning. It must also be clear that we will never quite learn how to learn, for since *Homo sapiens* is self-changing, and since the *more* culture changes the *faster* it changes, man's methods and rate of learning will never quite keep pace with his need to learn. This is the heart of the problem of "cultural lag," for each fundamental scientific discovery presents man with an incalculable number of problems which he cannot foresee. Who, for example, would have anticipated that the discoveries of Einstein would have presented us with the social problems of the nuclear age, or that information theory would have produced unemployment and displacement in world markets?

Fettering and Freeing

Another learning problem inherent in the human condition is the fact that we must conserve culture while changing it; that we must always be *more* sure of surviving than of adapting — *as we see it.* Whenever a new idea appears our first concern as *animals* must be that it does not kill us; then, and only then, can we look at it from other points of view. While it is true that we are often mistaken, either because we become enchanted with certain modes or thought or because we cannot anticipate their consequences, this tendency to look first at survival has resulted in fettering the capacity to learn new things. In general, primitive people solved this problem simply by walling their children off from new possibilities by educational methods that, largely through fear (including ridicule, beating, and mutilation) so narrowed the perceptual sphere that other than traditional ways of viewing the world became unthinkable. Thus throughout history the cultural pattern has been a device for binding the intellect. Today, when we think we wish to free the mind so it will soar, we are still, nevertheless, bound by the ancient paradox, for we must hold our culture together through clinging to old ideas lest, in adopting new ones, we literally cease to exist.

In searching the literature on the educational practices of other civilizations I have found nothing that better expresses the need to teach and to fetter than the following, from an account by a traveler along the Niger River in Africa in the fourteenth century:

> ... their zeal for learning the Koran by heart [is so great that] they put their children in chains if they show any backwardness in memorizing it, and they are not set free until they have it by heart. I visited the *qadi* in his house on the day of the festival. His children were chained up, so I said to him, "Will you not let them loose?" He replied, "I shall not do so until they learn the Koran by heart." [1]

Perhaps the closest material parallel we have to this from our own cultural tradition is the stocks in which ordinary English upper-class children were forced to stand in the eighteenth century while they pored over their lessons at home. The fettering of the mind while we "set the spirit free" or the fettering of the spirit as we free the mind is an abiding paradox of "civilization" in its more refined dimensions. It is obvious that chimpanzees are incapable of this paradox. It is this capacity to pass from the jungles of the animal world into the jungle of paradox of the human condition that, more than anything else, marks off human from animal learning. It is this jungle that confronts the child in his early days at school, and that seals his destiny — if it has not previously been determined by poverty — as an eager mind or as a faceless learner.

Since education is always against some things and for others, it bears the burden of the cultural obsessions. While the Old Testament extols without cease the glory of the One God, it speaks with equal emphasis against the gods of the Philistines; while the children of the Dakota Indians learned loyalty to their own tribe, they learned to hate the Crow; and while our children are taught to love our American democracy, they are taught contempt for totalitarian regimes. It thus comes about that most educational systems are imbued with anxiety and hostility, that they are against as many things as they are for. Because, therefore, so much anxiety inheres in any human educational system — anxiety that it may free when it should fetter; anxiety that it may fetter when it should free; anxiety that it may teach sympathy when it should teach anger; anxiety that it may disarm where it should arm — our contemporary education system is constantly under attack. When, in anxiety about the present state of our world, we turn upon the schools with even more venom than we turn on our government, we are "right" in the sense that it is in the schools that the basic binding and freeing processes that will "save" us will be established. But being "right" derives not so much from the faults of our schools but from the fact that the schools are the central conserving force of the culture. The Great Fear thus turns our hostility unerringly in the direction of the focus of survival and change, in the direction of education.

Creativity and Absurdity

The function of education has never been to free the mind and the spirit of man, but to bind them; and to the end that the mind and spirit of his children should never escape *Homo sapiens* has employed praise, ridicule, admonition, accusation, mutilation, and even torture to chain them to the culture pattern. Throughout most of his historic course *Homo sapiens* has wanted from his children acquiescence, not originality. It is natural that this should be so, for where every man is unique there is no society, and where there is no society there can be no man. Contemporary American educators think they want creative children, yet it is an open question as to what they expect these children to create. And certainly the classrooms — from kindergarten to graduate school — in which they expect it to happen are not crucibles of creative activity and thought. It stands to reason that were young people truly creative the culture would fall apart for originality, by definition, is different from what is given, and what is given is the culture itself. From the endless, pathetic, "creative hours" of kindergarten to the most abstruse problems in sociology and anthropology, the function of education is to prevent the truly creative intellect from getting out of hand. Only in the exact and the biological sciences do we permit unlimited freedom, for we have (but only since the Renaissance, since Galileo and Bruno underwent the Inquisition) found a way — or *thought* we had found a way — to bind the explosive powers of science in the containing vessel of the social system.

American classrooms, like educational institutions anywhere, express the values, preoccupations, and fears found in the culture as a whole. School has no choice; it must train the children to fit the culture as it is. School can give training in skills; it cannot teach creativity. All the American school can conceivably do is nurture creativity when it appears. And who has the eyes to see it? Since the creativity that is conserved and encouraged will always be that which seems to do the most for the culture, which seems at the moment to do the most for the obsessions and the brutal preoccupations and anxieties from which we all suffer, schools nowadays encourage the child with gifts in mathematics and the exact sciences. But the child who has the intellectual strength to see through social shams is of no consequence to the educational system.

Creative intellect is mysterious, devious, and irritating. An intellectually creative child may fail, for example, in social studies, simply because he cannot understand the stupidities he is taught to believe as "fact." He may even end up agreeing with his teachers that he is "stupid" in social studies. Learning social studies is, to no small extent, whether in elementary school or the university, learning to be stupid. Most of us accomplish this task before we enter high school. But the child with a socially creative imagination will not be encouraged to play among new social systems, values, and relationships; nor is there much likelihood of it, if for no other reason than that the social studies teachers will perceive such a child as a poor student. Furthermore, such a child will simply be unable to fathom the absurdities that seem transparent *truth* to the teacher. What idiot believes in the "law of supply and demand," for example? But the children who do tend to *become* idiots, and learning to be an idiot is part of growing up! Or, as Camus put it, learning to be *absurd*. Thus the child who finds it impossible to learn to think the absurd the truth, who finds it difficult to accept absurdity as a way of life, the intellectually creative child whose mind makes him flounder like a poor fish in the net of absurdities flung around him in school, usually comes to think himself stupid.

The schools have therefore never been places for the stimulation of young minds. If all through school the young were provoked to question the Ten Commandments, the sanctity of revealed religion, the foundations of patriotism, the profit motive, the two-party system, monogamy, the laws of incest, and so on, we would have more creativity than we could handle. In teaching our children to accept fundamentals of social relationships and religious beliefs without question we follow the ancient highways of the human race, which extend backward into the dawn of the species, and indefinitely into the future. There must therefore be more of the caveman than of the spaceman about our teachers.

Up to this point I have argued that learning to learn is man's foremost evolutionary task, that the primary aim of education has been to fetter the mind and the spirit of man rather than to free them, and that nowadays we confront this problem in our effort to stimulate thought while preventing the mind of the child from going too far. I have also urged that since education, as the central institution for the training of the young in the ways of the culture, is thus burdened with its obsessive fears and hates, contemporary attacks upon our schools are the reflection of a nervousness inherent in the school as a part of the central obsession. Finally, I argued that creativity is the last thing wanted in any culture because of its potentialities for disruptive thinking; that the primordial dilemma of all education derives from the necessity of training the mighty brain of *Homo sapiens* to be stupid; and that creativity, when it is encouraged (as in science in our culture), occurs only after the creative thrust of an idea has been tamed and directed toward socially approved ends. In this sense, then, creativity can become the most obvious conformity. In this sense we can expect scientists — our cultural maximizers — to be socially no *more* creative than the most humble elementary school teacher, and probably less creative socially than a bright second-grader.

Communication

Much of what I have to say in the following pages pivots on the inordinate capacity of a human being to learn more than one thing at a time. Although it is true that all the higher orders of animals can learn several things at a time, this capacity for polyphasic learning reaches unparalleled development in man. A child writing the word "August" on the board, for example, is not only learning the word "August" but also how to hold the chalk without making it squeak, how to write clearly, how to keep going even though the class is tittering at his slowness, how to appraise the glances of the children in order to know whether he is doing it right or wrong, et cetera. If the spelling, arithmetic, or music lesson were only what it appeared to be, the education of the American child would be much simpler; but it is all the things the child learns *along with* his subject matter that really constitute the drag on the educational process as it applies to the curriculum.

A classroom can be compared to a communications system, for certainly there is a flow of messages between teacher (transmitter) and pupils (receivers) and among the pupils; contacts are made and broken, messages can be sent at a certain rate of speed only, and so on. But there is also another interesting characteristic of communications systems that is applicable to classrooms, and that is their inherent tendency to generate *noise*. *Noise,* in communications theory, applies to all those random fluctuations of the system that cannot be controlled. They are the sounds that are not part of the message: the peculiar quality communicated to the voice by the composition of the telephone circuit, the static on the radio, and so forth. In a classroom lesson on arithmetic, for example, such *noise* would range all the way from the competitiveness of the students, the quality of the teacher's voice ("I remember exactly how she sounded when she told me to sit down"), to the shuffling of the children's feet. The striking thing about the child is that along with his arithmetic — his "messages about arithmetic" — he learns all the noise in the system also. It is this inability to avoid *learning the noise with the subject matter* that constitutes one of the greatest hazards for an organism so prone to polyphasic learning as man. It is this that brings it about that an objective observer cannot tell which is being learned in any lesson, the *noise* or the formal subject matter. But — and mark this well — it is *not* primarily the message (let us say, the arithmetic or the spelling) that constitutes the most important subject matter to be earned, but the noise! The most significant cultural learnings — primarily the cultural drives — are communicated as *noise*.

Let us take up these points by studying selected incidents in some of the suburban classrooms my students and I studied over a period of six years.

The Realm of Song

It is March 17 and the children are singing songs from Ireland and her neighbors. The teacher plays on the piano, while the children sing. While some children sing, a number of them hunt in the index, find a song belonging to one of Ireland's neighbors, and raise their hands in order that they may be called on to name the next song. The singing is of that pitchless quality always heard in elementary school classrooms. The teacher sometimes sings through a song first, in her off-key, weakishly husky voice.

The usual reason for having this kind of a song period is that the children are broadened, while they learn something about music and singing.

It is true that the children learn something about singing, but what they learn is to sing like everybody else, in the standard, elementary school pitchlessness of the English-speaking world — a phenomenon impressive enough for D. H. Lawrence to have mentioned it in *Lady Chatterley's Lover.* The difficulty in achieving true pitch is so pervasive among us that missionaries carry it with them to distant jungles, teaching the natives to sing hymns off key. Hence on Sundays we would hear our Pilagá Indian friends, all of them excellent musicians in the Pilagá scale, carefully copy the missionaries by singing Anglican hymns, translated into Pilagá, off key exactly as sharp or as flat as the missionaries sang. Thus one of the first things a child with a good ear learns in elementary school is to be musically stupid; he learns to doubt or to scorn his innate musical capacities.

But possibly more important than this is the use to which teacher and pupils put the lesson in ways not related at all to singing or to Ireland and her neighbors. To the teacher this was an opportunity to let the children somehow share the social aspects of the lesson with her, to democratically participate in the selection of the songs. The consequence was distraction from singing as the children hunted in the index and raised their hands to have their song chosen. The net result was to activate the competitive, achievement, and dominance drives of the children, as they strove with one another for the teacher's attention, and through her, to get the class to do what they wanted it to do. In this way the song period on Ireland and her neighbors was scarcely a lesson in singing but rather one in exhorting the maximal benefit for the Self from *any situation.* The first lesson a child has to learn when he comes to school is that lessons are not what they seem. He must then forget this and act as if they were. This is the first step toward "school mental health"; it is also the first step in becoming absurd. In the first and second grades teachers constantly scold children because they do not raise their hands enough — the prime symbol of having learned what school is all about. After that, it is no longer necessary; the kids have "tumbled" to the idea.

The second lesson is to put the teachers' and students' criteria in place of his own. He must learn that the proper way to sing is tunelessly and not the way *he* hears the music; that the proper way to paint is the way the teacher says, not the way he sees it; that the proper attitude is not pleasure but competitive horror at the success of his classmates, and so on. And these lessons must be so internalized that he will fight his parents if they object. The early schooling process is not successful unless it has accomplished in the child an acquiescence in its criteria, unless the child *wants* to think the way school has taught him to think. He must have accepted alienation as a rule of life. What we see in the kindergarten and the early years of school is the pathetic surrender of babies. How could it be otherwise?

Now, if children are taught to adopt alienation as a way of life, it follows that they must have feelings of inadequacy, for nothing so saps self-confidence as alienation from the Self. It would follow that school, the chief agent in the process, must try to provide the children with "ego support," for culture tries to remedy the ills it creates.

Hence the effort to give recognition; and hence the conversion of the songfest into an exercise in Self-realization. That anything essential was nurtured in this way is an open question, for the kind of individuality that was recognized as the children picked titles out of the index was mechanical, without a creative dimension, and under the strict control of the teacher. Let us conclude this discussion by saying that *school metamorphoses the child, giving it the kind of Self the school can manage, and then proceeds to minister to the Self it has made.*

Perhaps I have put the matter grossly, appearing to credit the school with too much formative power. So let us say this: let us grant that American children, being American, come to school on the first day with certain potentialities for experiencing success and failure, for enjoying the success of their mates or taking pleasure in their failure, for competitiveness, for cooperation, for driving to achieve or for coasting along, et cetera. But school cannot handle variety, for as an institution dealing with masses of children it can manage only on the assumption of a homogeneous mass. Homogeneity is therefore accomplished by defining the children in a certain way and by handling all situations uniformly. In this way no child is directly coerced. It is simply that the child must react in terms of the institutional definitions or he fails. The first two years of school are spent not so much in learning the rudiments of the three Rs, as in learning definitions.

It would be foolish to imagine that school, as a chief molder of character, could do much more than homogenize the children, but it does do more — it sharpens to a cutting edge the drives the culture needs.

If you bind or prune an organism so it can move only in limited ways, it will move rather excessively in that way. If you lace a man into a strait jacket so he can only wiggle his toes, he will wiggle them *hard.* Since in school children are necessarily constrained to limited human expression, under the direction of the teacher, they will have a natural tendency to do with exaggerated enthusiasm what they are permitted to do. They are like the man in the strait jacket. In class children are usually not permitted to talk much, to walk around much, to put their arms around each other during lessons, to whistle or sing. But they are permitted to raise their hands and go to the pencil sharpener almost at will. Thus hand-raising, going to the pencil sharpener, or hunting in the back of a song book for a song for the class to sing are not so much activities stemming from the requirements of an immediate situation as expressions of the intensified need of the organism for relief from the five-hour-a-day pruning and confining process. This goes under the pedagogical title of "release of tension"; but in our view the issue is that what the children are at length permitted — and invited — to do, and what they therefore often throw themselves into with the enthusiasm of multiple pent-up feelings, are cultural drive-activities narrowly construed by the school. In that context the next example is not only an expression by the children of a wish to be polite, but an inflated outpouring of contained human capacities, released enthusiastically into an available — because approved — cultural channel.

On Hanging Up a Coat

The observer is just entering her fifth-grade classroom for the observation period. The teacher says, "Which one of you nice, polite boys would like to take [the observer's] coat and hang it up?" From the waving hands, it would seem that all would like to claim the title. The teacher chooses one child, who takes the observer's coat. The teacher says, "Now children, who will tell [the observer] what we have been doing?"

The usual forest of hands appears, and a girl is chosen to tell. . . . The

teacher conducted the arithmetic lessons mostly by asking, "Who would like
to tell the answer to the next problem?" This question was usually followed
by the appearance of a large and agitated forest of hands, with apparently
much competition to answer.

What strikes us here are the precision with which the teacher was able to mobilize the potentialities in the boys for proper social behavior, and the speed with
which they responded. One is impressed also with the fact that although the teacher
could have said, "Johnny, will you please hang up [the observer's] coat?" she chose
rather to activate all the boys, and thus give *them* an opportunity to activate their
Selves, in accordance with the alienated Selfhood objectives of the culture. The
children were thus given an opportunity to exhibit a frantic willingness to perform
an act of uninvolved solicitude for the visitor; in this way each was given also a
chance to communicate to the teacher his eagerness to please her "in front of
company."

The mere appearance of the observer in the doorway sets afoot a kind of classroom destiny of self-validation and actualization of pupil-teacher communion, and
of activation of the cultural drives. In the observer's simple act of entrance the
teacher perceives instantly the possibility of exhibiting her children and herself,
and of proving to the visitor, and once again to herself, that the pupils are docile
creatures, eager to hurl their "company" Selves into this suburban American tragi-
comedy of welcome. From behind this scenery of mechanical values, meanwhile,
the most self-centered boy might emerge a *papier maché* Galahad, for what he
does is not for the benefit of the visitor but for the gratification of the teacher and
of his own culturally molded Self. The large number of waving hands proves that
most of the boys have already become absurd; but they have no choice. Suppose
they sat there frozen?

From this question we move to the inference that the skilled teacher sets up
many situations in such a way that *a negative attitude can be construed only as
treason*. The function of questions like, "Which one of you nice polite boys would
like to take [the observer's] coat and hang it up?" is to bind the children into
absurdity — to compel them to acknowledge that absurdity is existence, to acknowledge that it is better to exist absurd than not to exist at all.

It is only natural, then, that when the teacher next asks, "Now who will tell
what we have been doing?" and "Who would like to tell the answer to the next
problem?" there should appear "a large and agitated forest of hands," for failure
to raise the hand could be interpreted only as an act of aggression. The "arithmetic" lesson, transformed by the teacher, had become an affirmation of her matriarchal charisma as symbol of the system.

The reader will have observed that the question is not put, "Who *has* the answer
to the next problem?" but "Who *would like to tell*" it? Thus, what at one time in
our culture was phrased as a challenge to skill in arithmetic, becomes here an invitation to group participation. What is sought is a sense of "groupiness" rather
than a distinguishing of individuals. Thus, as in the singing lesson an attempt was
made to deny that it was a group activity, in the arithmetic lesson the teacher
attempts to deny that it is an individual one. The essential issue is that *nothing* is
but what it is made to be by the alchemy of the system.

In a society where competition for the basic cultural goods is a pivot of action, people cannot be taught to love one another, for those who do cannot compete with one another, except in play. It thus becomes necessary for the school, without appearing to do so, to teach children how to hate, without appearing to do so, for our culture cannot tolerate the idea that babies should hate each other. How does the school accomplish this ambiguity? Obviously through competition itself, for what has greater potential for creating hostility than competition? One might say that this is one of the most "creative" features of school. Let us consider an incident from a fifth-grade arithmetic lesson.

At the Blackboard

Boris had trouble reducing "12/16" to the lowest terms, and could only get as far as "6/8". The teacher asked him quietly if that was as far as he could reduce it. She suggested he "think." Much heaving up and down and waving of hands by the other children, all frantic to correct him. Boris pretty unhappy, probably mentally paralyzed. The teacher, quiet, patient, ignores the others and concentrates with look and voice on Boris. She says, "Is there a bigger number than two you can divide into the two parts of the fraction?" After a minute or two, she becomes more urgent, but there is no response from Boris. She then turns to the class and says, "Well, who can tell Boris what the number is?" A forest of hands appears, and the teacher calls Peggy. Peggy says that four may be divided into the numerator and the denominator.

Thus Boris' failure has made it possible for Peggy to succeed; his depression is the price of her exhilaration; his misery the occasion for her rejoicing. This is the standard condition of the American elementary school, and is why so many of us feel a contraction of the heart even if someone we never knew succeeds merely at garnering plankton in the Thames: because so often somebody's success has been bought at the cost of our failure. To a Zuñi, Hopi, or Dakota Indian, Peggy's performance would seem cruel beyond belief, for competition, the wringing of success from somebody's failure, is a form of torture foreign to those noncompetitive redskins. Yet Peggy's action seems natural to us; and so it is. How else would you run our world? And since all but the brightest children have the constant experience that others succeed at their expense they cannot but develop an inherent tendency to hate — to hate the success of others, to hate others who are successful, and to be determined to prevent it. Along with this, naturally, goes the hope that others will fail. This hatred masquerades under the euphemistic name of "envy."

Looked at from Boris' point of view, the nightmare at the blackboard was, perhaps, a lesson in controlling himself so that he would not fly shrieking from the room under the enormous public pressure. Such experiences imprint on the mind of every man in our culture the *Dream of Failure,* so that over and over again, night in, night out, even at the pinnacle of success, a man will dream not of success, but of failure. *The external nightmare is internalized for life.* It is this dream that, above all other things, provides the fierce human energy required by technological drivenness. It was not so much that Boris was learning arithmetic, but that he was learning the *essential nightmare. To be successful in our culture one must learn to dream of failure.*

From the point of view of the other children, of course, they were learning to yap at the heels of a failure. And why not? Have they not dreamed the dream of flight themselves? If the culture does not teach us to fly from failure or to rush in, hungry for success where others have failed, who will try again where others have gone broke? Nowadays, as misguided teachers try to soften the blow of classroom failure, they inadvertently sap the energies of success. The result will be a nation of chickens unwilling to take a chance.

When we say that "culture teaches drives and values" we do not state the case quite precisely. One should say, rather, that culture (and especially the school) provides the occasions in which drives and values are *experienced in events* that strike us with *overwhelming and constant force*. To say that culture "teaches" puts the matter too mildly. Actually culture invades and infests the mind as an obsession. If it does not, culture will not "work," for only an obsession has the power to withstand the impact of critical differences; to fly in the face of contradiction; to engulf the mind so that it will see the world only as the culture decrees that it shall be seen; to compel a person to be absurd. The central emotion in obsession is fear, and the central obsession in education is fear of failure. In order not to fail most students are willing to believe anything and to care not whether what they are told is true or false. Thus one becomes absurd through being afraid; but paradoxically, *only by remaining absurd can one feel free from fear.* Hence the immovableness of the absurd.

Notes

1. Ibn Battuta, *Travels in Asia and Africa,* London: Broadway House, Carter Lane, 1957, p. 330. (Translated and selected by H. A. R. Gibb, from the original written in 1325–54.)

REO M. CHRISTENSON
PATRICK J. CAPRETTA

The Impact of College on Political Attitudes: A Research Note

Research concerning the impact of college on political attitudes has contributed both to our fund of knowledge and to our confusion. Studies may be found supporting conclusions that a college education produces: (1) no appreciable effect upon political attitudes,[1] (2) a liberalizing of political attitudes,[2] and (3) more conservative political (or economic) attitudes.[3]

Reprinted with permission from *Social Science Quarterly* 49 (September 1968), pp. 315–320.

The present study was undertaken to further explore the political effects of college on students from varying social backgrounds, having different majors, or pursuing different occupational objectives.

Research Methods

A questionnaire consisting of 22 public policy questions covered those areas in which liberal-conservative differences have been most pronounced and most clearly differentiated in recent years. Eight of these questions involved civil liberties and civil rights (censorship, loyalty oaths, House Committee on Un-American Activities, the Fifth Amendment, rights of communists, mass demonstrations, open housing, fair employment legislation); six were concerned with domestic economic policies (democracy and capitalism, deficit spending, federal tax policy, state and local tax policy, labor union power, the union shop); four covered other domestic policy issues (the welfare state, centralization of power in Washington, "socialized medicine," federal aid to public schools), and four involved international policy attitudes (negotiations with communist countries, foreign economic aid, disarmament, world government).[4]

Respondents were asked to select one of three to five position alternatives offered for each of the issues. The number of alternatives varied, because in some policy areas tested only three readily distinguishable positions had significant numbers of supporters; in others, there were four or five such positions. Care was also taken to avoid constructing alternatives so finely differentiated that the politically unsophisticated would fail to discern the differences; on the other hand, an attempt was made to construct the responses so that reasonably modest attitude changes — rather than only major changes — would be measured. Finally, the responses were presented in a scrambled order so that students would not so readily detect and avoid polar positions.

Alternatives were assigned values ranging from 1 to 5, with Number 1 representing the most liberal position and Number 5 the most conservative position.[5]

A tabulation was made of the weights assigned to the answers chosen by respondents, and a mean index of political attitudes was obtained for each respondent. The most liberal possible score was 1.56 and the most conservative, 4.39.

The questionnaire was administered to two groups of students at Miami University (Oxford, Ohio) during 1965.[6] Some 668 seniors responded anonymously to the questionnaires in the spring of 1965; this represented approximately 73 percent of those to whom the questionnaires were sent. (Names were chosen by consecutive selection from the senior class roll.) In the fall of the same year, 427 freshmen, newly enrolled in the introductory government course, were also tested. (Comparisons of ACT scores indicated that freshmen enrolled in this course did not differ significantly from the other freshmen. Furthermore, since freshmen and seniors were compared by social characteristics, such as sex, major and family income, the importance of these differences between samples was minimized.)[7]

While it might seem desirable to follow a specific group of students from their freshman year through their senior year, this procedure would have been defective in one important respect. During 1961–1965, a rather marked general liberalizing trend took place; national attitudes on civil rights, deficit spending, tax reduction, and disarmament, for example, probably changed sufficiently so that a questionnaire confined to college students (without a control group of non-college persons) might well be attributing attitude changes to college training which more accurately reflect shifting attitudes in the population at large. By allowing a time lapse of no more than four months (from spring seniors in 1965 to fall freshmen in 1965), the distortion factor of changes in national opinion was minimized.

Findings

Table 1 shows a statistically significant increase in liberalism with education for the males but not for the females; between the freshmen (who expressed an interest in a particular major, though not actively pursuing it at the time) and seniors in education, government and sociology; and between freshmen and seniors coming from families having incomes between $5,000 and $15,000.

TABLE 1
Political Attitudes of Freshmen and Seniors, by Sex, Major, and Family Income

	Freshmen		*Seniors*		
	N	*Index score*	*N*	*Index score*	*P* [a]
Sex					
Males	283	2.91	327	2.62	<.01
Females	144	2.87	343	2.68	NS
Both	427	2.90	670	2.65	<.01
Major					
Business	64	2.94	105	2.83	NS
Economics	10	2.82	22	2.59	NS
Education	69	3.00	218	2.76	<.05
English	30	2.77	53	2.66	NS
Government	183	2.89	89	2.43	<.01
Psychology	15	2.82	30	2.57	NS
Sociology	11	2.82	34	2.53	<.05
Family Income					
Under $5,000	11	2.97	27	2.72	NS
5,000–7,499	69	2.90	70	2.60	<.01
7,500–9,999	118	2.94	145	2.70	<.05
10,000–15,000	133	2.89	197	2.60	<.01
Over 15,000	89	2.82	208	2.71	NS

[a] These probabilities are based on a one-tail t test of differences between mean index scores.

While comparative mean indices between *identical* groups of freshmen and seniors for individual questions were not calculated, breakdown by question categories are presented in Table 2. Differences between the two groups were significant in all categories. Although not presented in tabular form, highly significant differences toward greater liberalization among seniors were found for questions involving the political rights of communists (freshmen-senior differences = .74), foreign economic aid (.58), deficit spending (.46), House Un-American Activities Committee (.42), the welfare state (.39), and national health insurance (.38). On only

TABLE 2

Political Attitudes of Freshmen and Seniors by Question Category

Category	Freshmen (N = 427) index score	Seniors (N = 668) index score	P
National, non-economic	2.70	2.50	<.01
National, economic	3.02	2.82	<.01
International policies	2.76	2.60	<.05
Civil liberties, civil rights	2.95	2.71	<.01

two questions did the students register a slightly more (but non-significant conservative attitude as seniors than as freshmen — fair housing laws (−.11) and limited world government (−.07).

Finally, Table 3 offers comparison of freshmen and seniors concerning their own and their parental political party affiliations. Significant differences were found on four of the eleven political groupings.

It will be observed that, in comparison with their perception of parental partisanship, a substantially smaller percentage of seniors (19 percent) identified with the Republican party, while of those who remained, almost twice as many considered themselves "liberal" Republicans. Most of those departing from the Republican ranks did not join the Democrats, however, but swelled the ranks of the independents to 40 percent.

The trend away from the Republicans, toward the "independents" and/or toward a more liberal position within their party, had already begun among the freshmen, but was not nearly so pronounced. About 31 percent of the freshmen considered themselves more liberal members of their parents' party than they perceived their parents to be, or had moved away from the Republican party; 60 percent of the

TABLE 3

Political Attitudes of Freshmen and Seniors by Party Self-Identification and Parental Party-Identification

Party-ideology identification	Freshmen		Seniors			Seniors' parents[a]
	N	Index score	N	Index score	P	N
Conservative Republican	44	3.30	60	2.92	<.01	134
Middle-of-the-road Republican	73	2.94	86	2.91	NS	161
Liberal Republican	52	2.84	85	2.65	<.05	45
Conservative Democrat	22	2.83	28	2.66	NS	47
Middle-of-the-road Democrat	61	2.79	77	2.54	<.05	75
Liberal Democrat	18	2.68	65	2.10	<.01	48
Independents	26	2.76	63	2.63	NS	19
Independents leaning Republican	28	2.99	92	2.85	NS	45
Independents leaning Democrat	35	2.67	110	2.54	NS	50

[a] Parents of freshmen and seniors were found to have approximately the same partisan preferences.

seniors considered themselves more liberal members of their parents' party than they perceived their parents to be, or had moved away from the Republican party.

Conclusions

The trend toward political liberalism manifested itself in *every* student group tested and was borne out with almost equal consistency for each student group in each of the four policy categories tested.

Yet, although the liberalizing movement was uniform, it is significant that the index variations between polar groups tended to widen between the freshman and senior years. Thus, while college experience at Miami may produce more liberalism, it also produces a wider range of opinion concerning controversial public issues. More diversity, rather than more uniformity, developed.[8]

The accuracy with which both freshmen and seniors placed themselves in partisan categories and sub-categories coinciding with their expected positions on a liberal-conservative continuum was also striking. Students manifest more political sophistication in accepting a differentiated partisan label than some might have expected.

The most liberal indices were recorded by the student categories which are presumably the most academically proficient. Thus, honors students and those intending to teach on the college level registered the most liberal attitudes; conversely, students enrolled in those schools which are regarded as the least academically demanding (business and education) were the most conservative.

Without exception, students majoring in the social sciences were more liberal upon entering college than their class average, and were also more liberal upon departure. Similarly, students planning to teach social studies were more liberal than other students in the School of Education.

Whether or not most college graduates are more conservative on economic questions than high school graduates,[9] the index scores of economics majors (compared to other students enrolled in the School of Business) and the consistent movement toward liberalization within every student group on the economic category questions (although upper-income students changed only slightly) clearly indicated that a college experience at Miami does produce increasing economic liberalism.

The data on seniors should bear the usual caveats. The 27 percent who declined to return questionnaires were probably the most politically indifferent, and their attitudes and attitude changes might well have been different from those of seniors who co-operated in the study. The findings, moreover, were based on students at one midwestern university, which may, of course, differ from other colleges and universities.

Why did Miami students become more liberal and less pro-Republican? It is reasonable to assume that the Kennedy era, followed by the Goldwater capture of the GOP, the disastrous defeat which ensued and the high public esteem in which President Lyndon B. Johnson was initially held, probably had much to do with the partisan shifts which occurred. To a much lesser degree, these developments may also have had some relationship to the acceptance of more liberal political attitudes toward controversial public policies.

Faculty members in the departments of government, economics, sociology and psychology were considerably more liberal than either freshmen or seniors;[10] their attitudes as well as the reading materials which they assigned their students doubtless had a liberalizing impact on their students. Social experiences with students of different racial and national backgrounds could be expected to produce certain liberalizing effects, as would the studies of foreign cultures and languages. It would be rather remarkable if a college experience in a public institution at which 43 percent of the students were enrolled in the liberal arts college did not produce some liberalizing effects. It is altogether probable, however, that the temper of the times has an important effect upon the *degree* of liberalization which takes place.[11] When a liberal tide is running, this will probably accelerate the normal liberalizing effect of liberal arts colleges; when a more conservative atmosphere appears, the liberalizing effect will be reduced.

Notes

1. See, for example, Philip E. Jacob, *Changing Values in College: An Exploratory Study of the Impact of College Teaching* (New York: Harper & Brothers, 1957), p. 50; Charles G. McClintock and Henry A. Turner, "The Impact of College upon Political Knowledge, Participation, and Values," *Human Relations*, 15 (May, 1962), p. 175; Bernard R. Berelson, Paul F. Lazarsfeld and William N. McPhee, *Voting: A Study of Opinion Formation in a Presidential Campaign* (Chicago: University of Chicago Press, 1954), p. 334 (the authors find no relationship between education and voting patterns if socioeconomic status is controlled); and Walter T. Plant, "Longitudinal Changes in Intolerance and Authoritarianism for Subjects Differing in Amount of College Education over Four Years," *Genetic Psychological Monographs*, 72 (Nov., 1965), pp. 277–278, 281–282 (the author finds little difference in attitudes toward authoritarianism and toleration between students who go to college and those who aspire to go but do not attend).
2. See, for example, Harold Webster, Mervin Freedman, and Paul Heist, "Personality Changes in College Students," in Nevitt Sanford (ed.), *The American College: A Psychological and Social Interpretation of the Higher Learning* (New York: John Wiley & Sons, Inc., 1962), pp. 827–828; Philip Nogee and Murray B. Levin, "Some Determinants of Political Attitudes among College Voters," *Public Opinion Quarterly*, 22 (Winter, 1958), p. 462; Eleanor E. Maccoby, Richard E. Matthews and Anton S. Morton, "Youth and Political Change," *Public Opinion Quarterly*, 18 (Spring, 1954), pp. 37–39; Arthur W. Kornhauser, "Changes in the Information and Attitudes of Students in an Economics Course," *Journal of Educational Research*, 22 (June-Dec., 1930), pp. 296–298; Alex S. Edelstein, "Since Bennington: Evidence of Change in Student Political Behavior," *Public Opinion Quarterly*, 26 (Winter, 1962), pp. 564–565, 571; Robert E. Lane and David O. Sears, *Public Opinion* (Englewood Cliffs, N.J.: Prentice-Hall Inc., 1964), p. 26; and Russell Middleton and Snell Putney, "Student Rebellion against Parental Political Beliefs," *Social Forces*, 41 (May, 1963), p. 383.
3. See, for example, Richard W. Dodge and Eugene S. Uyeki, "Political Affiliation and Imagery across Two Related Generations," *Midwest Journal of Political Science*, 6 (Aug., 1962), pp. 275–276; and V. O. Key, Jr., *Public Opinion and American Democracy* (New York: Alfred A. Knopf, 1961) pp. 338–340. The latter asserts that "College experience in some institutions may impart a liberal cast of mind; in others the effect may be the opposite; and still other colleges may succeed magnificently in affecting the attitude of their students not at all. Yet college-trained persons generally manifest more conservative attitudes on economic issues than do persons of lesser education."
4. Copies of the questionnaire are available upon request.

5. The weightings depended upon our estimate of the point on a five-point liberal-conservative continuum at which an answer would properly fall. For some questions, no answer commanding significant numbers of supporters seemed to properly carry a weight of either 1 or 5, while other questions bore answers representing opinion more commonly regarded as "extreme."

6. Miami University is primarily an undergraduate state institution, with over 10,000 students. About 80 percent of the students are Ohio residents. The undergraduates come from a rather homogeneous middle-class background and are largely drawn from the upper 20 percent of their high school classes.

7. Freshmen were questioned both in the introductory government courses and by the same alphabetical sampling procedure employed for seniors. Since only about 30 percent of the freshmen sample returned questionnaires, it was decided to use the returns gathered from students enrolled in the government course.

8. This finding of increased diversity is supported by Harold Webster, "Changes in Attitudes During College," *Journal of Educational Psychology,* 49 (June, 1958), p. 116.

9. See Key, *Public Opinion,* pp. 338–340.

10. The same questionnaire was given to faculty members of various departments at Miami University in the spring of 1965. Of six departmental faculties tested, government ($N = 13$) scored the lowest at 1.93; followed by economics ($N = 10$), 2.09; sociology ($N = 8$), 2.11; psychology ($N = 9$), 2.30; zoology ($N = 7$), 2.67; and chemistry ($N = 6$), 3.01.

11. Both Maccoby, Matthews and Morton, *op. cit.,* p. 38, and Lane and Sears, *Public Opinion,* p. 25 n., also refer to this possibility.

12

PEER GROUP

The peer group, an increasingly important agent of socialization in modern society, is any group in which all members are of roughly the same age and social status. Thus, anyone may have several peer group affiliations throughout his life. However, the peer group exerts its greatest influence on personality development during childhood and adolescence. Consequently, youth groups have received the greatest amount of attention in the social science literature.

As Eisenstadt (1965) points out, youth groups tend to emerge in societies where the family plays a relatively diminished role; where the major political, economic, social, and religious functions are performed by groups outside the family; and, consequently, where socialization within the family is not adequate to prepare individuals to assume full adult status. According to Eisenstadt, the peer group is a transitional primary group which helps the individual achieve the necessary change in role orientation from the particularistic and collectivistic values of the family to the universalistic, achievement-oriented, and individualistic values of modern industrial society.

Youth groups have existed in many types of societies. However, though youth groups in primitive and traditional societies are usually part of a wider organization of age groups that cover a very long period of life, from childhood to late adulthood and even old age, the youth group stands alone in modern societies. The activities of youth peer groups concentrate on the problems of that particular developmental stage in the life cycle of its members: from childhood through early and late adolescence, and into young adulthood. Peer groups evolve their own values and norms, introduced and reinforced in the group through information exchange, role-modeling, and interpersonal controls.

The peer group performs various functions necessary to the personality development of its members. For example, it expands the social horizons of the individual, making him into a more complex person. The peer group teaches "taboo" subjects (like sex or drugs) which are not part of the individual's institutionalized socialization, and it disseminates information about current fashions and trends which may be outside the experience of adult authorities.

Most important, the peer group provides the individual with experience in egalitarian relationships and with sources of emotional gratification and models of identification which permit him to achieve an increasingly greater degree of independence from his family. As mentioned, the family is an inherently conservative institution, whereby knowledge and values are transmitted from the older generation to the younger. Although Margaret Mead (1970) has contended that adults may also learn from children in modern society, the lines of generational authority are still clearly drawn. Although peer groups may have an informal authority structure, based on prestige and popularity, they are essentially egalitarian and present-oriented. If you want to know "what's happening," you have to "get with it" and be "where the action is." A high value is placed on things which are contemporary or "now." Because of this, the peer group is a vitally important agent of socialization in societies where knowledge and customs are constantly changing.

Three Types of Peer Groups: Cliques, Crowds, and Gangs

Three kinds of peer groups quite familiar to Americans and all other modern societies are *cliques, crowds,* and *gangs.* One of the finest ethnographies of adolescent peer groups was conducted by Dexter Dunphy (1963) in Sydney, Australia. For two years, Dunphy studied about three hundred predominantly middle-class adolescent males and females between 13 and 21 years of age. He observed that socialization within the peer group is, in many important respects, a similarly patterned continuation of socialization within the family.

The early adolescent peer group is a unisexual clique, which represents the continuation of the preadolescent "gang." This clique is roughly the size of the family (average size six members) and requires a high degree of conformity from group members, which is achieved primarily through identification with the clique leader who embodies many of the social skills admired in the group. The clique becomes a subsystem of the crowd (average size twenty members) and the crowd a subsystem of a hierarchy of crowds.

The unisexual cliques primarily prepare for and evaluate the larger and more organized social functions, like parties and dances, which serve as the central activities of the heterosexual crowds. By middle adolescence the cliques themselves become heterosexual — first leaders and then all members establish significant relationships with members of the opposite sex. Dunphy concludes (p. 246):

> The crowd persists long enough to ensure that the basic role characteristics underlying this relationship are thoroughly acquired. It then breaks up into cliques of loosely associated couples as members move toward marriage. The social structure of urban adolescent peer groups has the effect of maintaining a high level of achievement which ensures that most adolescents progressively acquire an increasingly mature heterosexual role.

Any of you who reflect back on your own heterosexual development and peer relations from junior high through high school into college may find Dunphy's analysis surprisingly accurate. Of the numerous studies of adolescent peer groups in the United States, James Coleman's *The Adolescent Society* (1961) is perhaps the most well known. Coleman was primarily interested in the relationship between peer group subcultures and the process of education in American high schools. He surveyed almost nine thousand students from ten different high schools (five rural, two suburban, and three city) as well as all their teachers and parents.

Coleman contends that the extended formal education which is related to increasing industrialization has created such settings as the school in which children and adolescents are "cut off" from the rest of society and forced to involve themselves deeply in the "small society" of their peers. Although they still remain oriented toward parental expectations, they learn to strive for peer approval as well. In Coleman's study, those who cited parental disapproval as the "hardest thing" for them to take (approximately 53 percent) exceeded those who named "breaking with a friend" (approximately 43 percent) by only a slight margin.

The peer group subculture tends to stress values that run counter to the goals of the institution. Scholastic achievement ranks well below achieving popularity through projecting a pleasing personality in the peer group subculture. Boys strive to become a member of the "leading crowd" mainly through athletics and cars, whereas girls emphasize good looks and nice clothes. Involvement in extracurricular activities is also a route to the top, but not without other crucial attributes like coming from the right family. C. Wayne Gordon (1957) discovered similarities in his study of high school students. He found that the "dominant motivation" for most students was "to meet the expectations of the informal [student] culture" rather than to gain status within the organization of the whole school (pp. 1–2). Alexander and Campbell (1964), among others, have shown that peer-group affiliation within the social system of the high school even has a strong influence on whether or not a student aspires to attend college and whether he is likely to actually attend.

Coleman says that once the individual is immersed in his peer group, its expectations and demands begin to conflict with those of parents, teachers, and other significant adult authorities. However, adolescents and young adults may vary in their peer vs. parent orientation, with varying consequences for their behavior and development. A study by Reckless, Dinitz, and Murray (1956) of "good" boys in high delinquency areas pointed to the strong influence of the family in promoting a self-concept "insulated" against delinquency. Parental supervision and interest was conspicuous in the home and the boys viewed their home life as pleasant and their parents as understanding. The most important difference between the good boys and the delinquency-prone boys was that the mothers of the good boys "thought their sons to be more active, punishment to be less frequent and severe, and parental tranquility to be more pervasive" than did the mothers of the delinquents.

A basic distinction must be made between corner-boy gangs, which are loosely organized groups of working-class boys who hang out together, and delinquent gangs. There have been many theoretical explanations of the dynamics of delinquent gangs. Thrasher (1927) stressed the utilitarian function of gangs which, through organized collective activity, are able to steal goods which their members would be unable to obtain otherwise.

Cloward and Ohlin (1960) have distinguished between three types of gangs on the basis of their dominant activity and orientation. According to them, all gangs value toughness and excitement, but some stress violent confrontations with rival gangs, others stress getting off on drugs and stealing to support their habit, and others stress well-organized criminal activity.

According to Matza and Sykes (1961), delinquent gangs have simply chosen more covert values in the mainstream culture: "the search for kicks, disdain for work, desire for the 'big score,' and acceptance of aggressive toughness as proof of masculinity."

Cohen's theory of delinquent behavior (1955) emphasizes the negativistic, destructive, nonutilitarian nature of much gang activity. He proposes that this represents a deliberate inversion of middle-class values by the delinquent gang member to strike back at the authorities who have frustrated him in school and thereby seriously threatened his self-esteem.

Because they are a "social problem" in the eyes of adult authorities, much research has been done on the backgrounds, motivations, and activities of working- and lower-class delinquents, especially males. However, as Stephen Buff illustrates in the first article, there are at least three distinctive types of working-class youth as seen by the youth themselves. His essay on "greasers," "dupers," and "hippies" is an excellent example of careful participant observation reporting that provides descriptive detail and social perspective which could not be achieved by any other method.

Effects of Reference Groups

The second article, by Alberta and Sidney Siegel, is an examination of the relative influence of reference and membership groups on attitude change. In *reference groups,* the individual "aspires to attain or maintain membership," but he does not necessarily belong. If it is a true reference group for the individual he will be aware of and apply its standards of judgment to his own behavior. An abundance of literature documents the role of reference-group identification in attitude maintenance and change. Homans' exchange theory (1958) is based on the premise that personal integrity and group attractiveness are the critical variables in questions of attitude change. Shils and Janowitz (1948) in studying POW camp behavior showed that the effect of Nazi propaganda on the attitudes of the prisoners was considerably weakened when confronted with high primary group solidarity and increased in inverse proportion to it. In this case, the mutual exchange of approval among members as a reward for retaining group attitudes outweighed the physical reward for conversion held out by a hostile authority.

A landmark study of the relationship between reference groups and individual attitudes was conducted by Theodore Newcomb (1958) at Bennington College in the 1930's. In his analysis of the adjustment patterns of the female students to the college environment, Newcomb concluded (p. 275), "In a community characterized by certain approved attitudes, the individual's attitude development is a function of the way in which he relates himself both to the total membership group [the college community] and to one or more reference groups [family and friendship cliques]." Newcomb discovered that students confronted with a conflict between their family attitudes and their college community's attitudes could use the total membership group as either a positive or negative reference. Most everyone identified with the college community to some extent as evidenced by the greater tolerance and flexibility scores on psychological tests as well as the more liberal political attitudes of the seniors as compared to the freshmen. Personal popularity, other things being equal, was mainly a function of how much one identified with the liberal college community.

Pearlin's study of college women (1954) indicated that the process of changing to more positive attitudes toward blacks involved changing from reference groups holding negative attitudes toward blacks to new groups favorable to blacks. Fendrich (1967) found that "positive reference group support influences both favorable attitudes and actions toward the attitude object" and that "perceived reference group support determines both racial attitudes and overt behavior" even though racial attitudes are still a partially independent determinant of overt behavior. And Steiner (1954, p. 270) has found that "perceived primary group pressures can have considerable effect on attitudes even when there is reason to doubt that group norms and sanctions are operating."

I do not wish to overstate the case for individual conformity to group norms in personality formation and behavior. To a great extent people can choose their friends. Hartley (1960) has pointed out that individuals are more likely to accept a new reference group when compatibility is greater between the values of the individual and the perceived values of the group. Any individual may have a variety of reference groups whose standards may conflict with each other in any given situation. Finally, complete conformity is only one of many modes of adjustment to group pressures. Gorden (1952) suggests that the "typical pattern is for the individual to compromise between his private opinion and his conception of the group opinion when expressing his public opinion." Nevertheless, there are obviously a variety of social and economic constraints on our freedom of association and families, schools, and other institutions typically impose even greater restrictions on our range of relationships. And, because groups are obviously more than simply the sum of their members and do have an independent reality of their own, it then becomes necessary to understand the dynamic relationship between peer groups and their members in the development of the individual's personality.

References

Alexander, C. Norman, Jr., and Ernest Q. Campbell
    1964   "Peer Influences on Adolescent Educational Aspirations and Attainment."
          American Sociological Review 29 (August):568–75.
Cloward, Richard A., and Lloyd E. Ohlin
    1960   *Delinquency and Opportunity*. Glencoe, Ill.: The Free Press.
Cohen, Albert K.
    1955   *Delinquent Boys*. Glencoe, Ill.: The Free Press.
Coleman, James S.
    1961   *The Adolescent Society*. Glencoe, Ill.: The Free Press.
Dunphy, Dexter
    1963   "The Social Structure of Urban Adolescent Peer Groups." *Sociometry* 26:230–46.
Eisenstadt, S. N.
    1965   "Archetypal Patterns of Youth." Pp. 29–50 in Erik H. Erikson (ed.), *The Challenge of Youth*. Garden City, N.Y.: Doubleday-Anchor.

Fendrich, James M.
   1967   "Perceived Reference Group Support: Racial Attitudes and Overt Be-
          havior." *American Sociological Review* 32 (December):960–970.
Gorden, Raymond L.
   1952   "Attitude and the Definition of the Situation." *American Sociological Re-
          view* 17:50–58.
Gordon, C. Wayne
   1957   *The Social System of the High School.* Glencoe, Ill.: The Free Press.
Hartley, Ruth E.
   1960   "Relationships Between Perceived Values and Acceptance of a New Refer-
          ence Group." *Journal of Social Psychology* 51 (February):181–90.
Haskell, Martin Roy
   1960–61   "Toward a Reference Group Theory of Juvenile Delinquency." *Social
          Problems* 8(3):219–30.
Homans, George
   1958   "Social Behavior as Exchange." *American Journal of Sociology* 63 (May):
          597–606.
Matza, David, and Gresham M. Sykes
   1961   "Juvenile Delinquency and Subterranean Values." *American Sociological
          Review* 26 (October):712–20.
Mead, Margaret
   1970   *Culture and Commitment: A Study of the Generation Gap.* Garden City,
          N.Y.: Doubleday.
Newcomb, Theodore M.
   1958   "Attitude Development as a Function of Reference Groups: The Benning-
          ton Study." Pp. 265–75 in Eleanor Maccoby, Theodore M. Newcomb, and
          Eugene L. Hartley (eds.), *Readings in Social Psychology.* New York: Holt,
          Rinehart and Winston.
Pearlin, Leonard I.
   1954   "Shifting Group Attachment and Attitudes Toward Negroes." *Social Forces*
          33:47–50.
Polsky, Howard W., Irving Karp, and Irwin Berman
   1962   "The Triple Bind: Toward a Unified Theory of Individual and Social Devi-
          ance." *Journal of Human Relations* 11(1):68–69.
Reckless, Walter C., Simon Dinitz, and Ellen Murray
   1956   "Self Concept as an Insulator against Delinquency." *American Sociological
          Review* (December):744–46.
Shils, Edward, and Morris Janowitz
   1948   "Cohesion and Disintegration in the Wermacht in World War II." *The
          Public Opinion Quarterly* 12:280–315.
Steiner, Ivan D.
   1954   "Primary Group Influences on Public Opinion." *American Sociological Re-
          view* 19 (June):260–67.
Thrasher, Frederic
   1927   *The Gang.* Chicago, Ill.: University of Chicago Press.

STEPHEN A. BUFF

Greasers, Dupers, and Hippies: Three Responses to the Adult World

This essay is about the working-class youth of a place we shall call Grey Park, a community area, on the southwest side of Freight City, a sprawling, industrial, Midwestern metropolis. The neighborhood area is about two miles square, nearer to the city limits than to the central business district. Factories, warehouses, and city facilities are spread throughout the area, making Grey Park a mixed residential and light-industry neighborhood, intersected by two major highways and two railway systems.

Streets are laid out, for the most part, along a monotonously flat terrain, broken only by the raised superhighways. Every half-dozen blocks or so, one comes to a long commercial thoroughfare, treeless, arched by electric cables for the buses, lined with stores, restaurants, and neighborhood taverns, advertised by neon signs. Large late-model cars (few of them more than three or four years old) dominate the scene — parked bumper to bumper at night on the side streets or filling the back-alley garages — while the main streets are filled with bright dealers' showrooms, gas stations, and crowded used-car lots. One cannot tell when the storefronts were built, and the only structures which give an impression of a particular era are the garish drive-ins and carry-out restaurants of the sixties — all surrounded by ample parking areas — that serve *Kentucky Fried Chicken, Burger-King, Tastee-Freeze.*

The dwellings vary from rows of bungalows to rectangular three-story apartment buildings of darkened brick to large two-family houses sided with wooden clapboard or shingles, whose paint jobs haven't stood up well against the smog, harsh winters, and blistering summers. On some residential streets there are few trees and narrow front lawns, while on others there is more space between houses and lovely old trees which make the houses shady and pleasant in summer and hide their imperfections in winter.

Nothing in Grey Park rises much over two stories and those few structures that do are massive and uninviting — a beige concrete Sears department store and a thick-walled public high school with steep garrets reminiscent of some Victorian institution. There are many churches in the area — large Catholic churches of sculptured, light-gray stone, and modest Methodist and Baptist churches of red brick, fitting into the neighborhood unobtrusively. Residential areas are dotted with

Reprinted by permission of the author. Originally published by Random House in *The White Majority: Between Poverty and Affluence* edited by Louise Kapp Howe. This research was supported by a General Research Support Grant, FR-05666-02 from the General Research Support Branch, National Institute of Mental Health, and a Public Service Grant, HD-02257.

small parks taking up one or two blocks with grass or concrete, filled with small shrubbery, a red brick field house, swings, benches and playing fields of grass or a basketball court of concrete.

The people who live in Grey Park are white, working-class and lower-middle-class, and predominantly Catholic. The ethnicity is heterogeneous, with most people claiming Irish, Polish, Eastern European or Italian ancestry. Sections of Grey Park were once predominantly Jewish, but now only elderly Jews remain and their children have moved to the suburbs. Appalachian whites, Puerto Ricans, and some blacks are moving closer to the area as they move out from the central city, but few have moved into Grey Park.

Throughout the vast white working-class neighborhoods of northwest Freight City, people of high school and college age (fourteen to twenty-four) congregate in parks, on street corners, and at small restaurants and drive-ins — at whatever central locations adults and police allow or tolerate their presence.

For my own work, I have "hung" with various groups of kids, participating in their recreational activities in the evening and night (e.g., going to parties with them, taking their side in any confrontation with adults, going to the police station with them when they were called in, leaving street corners with them when the police chased them away). A recurrent and fascinating theme that struck me from the outset of my observations was the existence of different categories that young people would use to describe themselves, one another, and outside groups. Three major types emerged: greasers, hippies and dupers. When inquiring how they differed, these three would be identified, first of all, in terms of dress.

Greasers are boys accurately identified as those wearing "black leathers" — not the motorcycle jackets of the fifties, but hip-length jackets with patch pockets of a fairly soft leather or simulated leather. They often wear work clothes — gray denim shirts and gray or green work trousers (baggies) — black laced shoes, sometimes pointed in the European style, or high black combat boots. In the summer they usually wear sleeveless undershirts (dago-tees) but may go bare-chested, and even in the winter they frequently keep their jackets and shirts unbuttoned. Their pants are generally black and tight and they wear Ban-lon sweaters of a dark shade. Depending on the style of the particular group, they may wear floppy British style working-class caps with a brim, or berets. Hair is worn fairly long, about collar-length, combed back from the forehead in a pompadour, unparted, and always aided by some hair cream or oil.

Duper boys are characterized by bright shirts, penny loafers or sneakers, and wheat jeans. Their dress is patterned in some way after the "collegiate" style of the early sixties. Trousers usually have cuffs and are narrow (but not pegged like those of some greasers), or they may be cut like jeans in any number of colors or fabrics. They wear wool sweaters and woodsman-style wool jackets and, later in the year, ski jackets or wool winter coats. They usually have shorter hair than greasers, parted, with their forelocks combed diagonally over part of their foreheads — "pulled all over to one side," as a greaser has described it.

Hippies (or long-hairs) costume themselves with jeans, usually with flared cuffs (bellbottoms), sneakers (or they go barefoot), floppy-brimmed hats, blue cotton work shirts, army-surplus jackets, beads and other decorations, such as painted tee-shirts or the peace symbol, on the back of their jackets. But the most notable features, according to nonhippies, are beads and long hair, which is worn over the ears, sometimes shoulder-length, often parted in the center and tied with a head-band.

The most pronounced differences and the items of dress are summarized in the table which follows.

The males show greater differentiation in their apparel than the females. Greaser girls used to be easily identified — and can still be to some extent — by their ratted hair, black leather jackets and heavy make-up. But they now seem to be tending more and more toward a common middle-class style. Bouffant hairdos are declining, and straight hair with less teasing is in vogue. When youths describe differences in dress among greasers, dupers, and hippies, they mention male dress primarily, because, given the similar "natural" hair styles, bellbottoms, and suede jackets that are increasingly common to all groups of girls, it is often difficult to identify girls in one of these three modalities if they aren't accompanied by boys.

TABLE 1
Distinctive Types of Clothing Worn by Males
in Greaser, Duper, and Hippie Groups

Type of clothing	Greaser	Duper	Hippie
Jackets			
Black leather jacket (hip-length)	Common	Very rare	Rare
Quilted nylon jacket	Common	Occasional	Rare
Team jackets and sweaters with school emblem	Never	Common	Never
Army jackets	Common	Common	Common
Shirts			
Dark-colored "knits" (Ban-lons)	Common	Rare	Rare
Work shirts	Common	Never	Common
Brightly colored or plaid sport shirts	Never	Common	Never
Trousers			
"Baggies" (work pants)	Common	Never	Occasional
Black pegged pants	Common	Rare	Occasional
Wheat jeans	Never	Common	Rare
Bellbottoms	Very rare	Rare	Common
Shoes			
Heavy work shoes or combat boots	Common	Never	Very rare
Penny loafers	Never	Common	Never
Pointed black shoes (European style)	Common	Rare	Rare
Tennis sneakers	Never	Common	Occasional
Other			
Outlandish costume	Never	Never	Common
Beads	Never	Never	Common
Grooming			
Shoulder-length hair	Never	Never	Occasional
Clean-cut	Very rare	Common	Never
Pompadour and slicked-back hair	Common	Very rare	Very rare

Greasers

Differences among greasers, hippies, and dupers begin but certainly do not end with dress. As one hippie said, "The dress goes along with it [the behavior]. If you dress like a greaser, of course you're going to act like a shit-stud dude [a tough guy]." Hippie or long-hair kids refer to the greaser kids as tough, ready for a street battle, thinking it cool to fight and push guys around. The hippie girls described what greaser girls are like in these two comments:

> It's ninety degrees out and their hair's all ratted up and they wear black sweaters and it's ninety degrees out and they stand there sweating and try to get picked up.

> A whole bunch of make-up and ratted hair and black leather and black sweaters and they like to beat up other girls.

Seen from the hippie's point of view, then, a dominant trait of greaser boys and girls is their "toughness." More generally, they seem to conform to the middle-class stereotype of working-class, street-corner gang kids (although the groups observed thus far are gangs only in the sense in which sociologist Walter B. Miller uses the term — loose aggregates who "hang together" with a very limited sense of territoriality and without any necessary formalization of leadership roles).

The greaser groups that I have been most involved with are fairly stable in terms of the ages of the members. Members of each age-graded group know members in the older and younger grades, know where they hang out, and expect to hang out in the older spot when their grade moves up.

Many of the interests and activities of greasers are not out of the ordinary: they play the traditional sports, especially baseball and football, and are avidly interested in repairing old autos and "souping up" the newer ones, and many of them are caught up in the drag-racing scene. But their relationship to the adult world, especially The Law, is problematic. School appears to be a punishing and/or boring experience for the boys, though not necessarily for the girls. There is a high drop-out rate (perhaps over 50 percent after age sixteen); however, many boys do get their diplomas eventually at night school or in the armed forces.

The attitude of greasers to police is complex and ambiguous. Police, more than any other group, set close limits around their freedom. Aside from fighting, petty thievery, car thefts, or other more spectacular delinquent acts, the greasers, and other groups for that matter, are very often in a position to be harassed for some minor delinquent act or annoyance: being out late after the ten-thirty weekday curfew, possessing grass or any other drug, drinking beer out of doors, being too noisy on a street corner so that neighbors complain, or becoming too numerous in a business establishment, so that the manager complains. Cops, in turn, are to be outwitted, to be beaten at their own game, to be provoked and confronted and put on.

On the other hand, these kids might secretly dig cops — they have the fast cars, the authority, and the legitimate opportunity for violence — but this is pure speculation at this point. There is further ambivalence because, after all, this is the population from which many cops are recruited. The cop-hating kid, when confronted with an occupational choice, may well choose police work. The more knowledge of the street the kid has, the better neighborhood cop he will eventually make and the tougher he will probably make it in turn for street kids because he knows how "bad" they are and how to catch them at their own game. The system of passage from oppressed to oppressor, then, seems to resemble a fraternity hazing system in which those who have been "hassled" the most are the most oppressive in hazing the next incoming cohort. The major difference is that freshmen join a fraternity while greasers or street kids seem to back into police work.

An early identification with the world of work is evident among greasers. There is a great deal of shopping around by trial and error for a job that isn't too boring, routine or dead-end. A job in "the trades" is highly preferred but police work also pays well. The service is often seen as an avenue for job advancement, offering a second chance to receive a high school diploma and the best possible chance to receive vocational, highly technical or college-level training. If one adopts an instrumental approach the years of military service can fit in with one's career plan; it serves as the IBM, the paternalistic corporation, for much of this population (see Paul Goodman, *Growing Up Absurd*). Those not planning to use the military in this way experience the expectation of the draft as two or more years of discontinuity with any of their life plans. The draft may function to postpone any serious decisions or a realistic future orientation. Since the draft will certainly disrupt one's future plans, why make any?

Greaser kids take pride in their mechanical and vocational skills. Pride and investment in work is often dependent on getting into the trades or going to vocational school. If their horizons are not broadened, if they are not allowed to exercise a body of skills, as in a trade, they may stay in their jobs out of inertia, or just for the money. Kids are often tied to their jobs because of (1) the pressure to contribute to family income and (2) the financial drain that comes from owning and caring for cars.

The recreational life of the group involves the camaraderie of hanging together, cars, sports, "boozing, balling and blowing pot," parties, and music. Boys and girls meet at the park and may pair off later, but much of their time together is spent with the entire group. I'm not sure if a double standard exists in terms of a value being placed on virginity. Girls who make themselves available are "sluts," but any girl will make love, according to some boys, if she is going with a guy for more than four to six months. According to the social workers, however, the girls are "prick teasers" and not as available as they may appear to be.

Taking drugs (virtually any "soft" drug) and drinking are the main pastimes. All greasers that I have met drink, and many also take drugs. Drinking starts in early adolescence as does glue-sniffing. Most kids have tried marijuana before they have tried LSD, psilocybin, amphetamines, mescaline, or any other "soft" drug. The main impediment to the use of hard drugs is the fear of addiction and the fear of "needles." Anything that can be swallowed, however, is acceptable and is experimented with in many combinations. "Uppers" and "downers," wine, and beer may be taken within a short time span. They may "trip" one evening and get drunk the next, or they may take alcohol and drugs almost simultaneously. The greasers who don't take drugs have tried them but they don't "do anything for them." (They may partake of a culture in which drug use is valued, but they may not value the use of that drug themselves.) Drug use is seen as cool, fun, enjoyable, and is a valued experience among "heads" (those greasers who take drugs), but its use has not brought other notable changes in behavior along with it as it has among the hippies. Although the use and abuse of drugs has become a major pastime, it seems to be incremental and adaptive to the other concerns of the greasers rather than a main element. The vocabulary of motives for the use of drugs is far slimmer among greasers than among hippies. No outstanding change in life style or world view seems to accompany or to be induced by the use of drugs.

Hippies

"Grease" is the most widespread cultural mode of dress and behavior. Most hippies are "greaser converts," although some were formerly dupers. Grease may be an irresistible form of posturing for young adolescents (twelve to fourteen) who wish to express their toughness. But the newest subcultural style of working-class youth is the hippie style.

Only greasers, hostile to the adult world, and dupers, tractable to the adult world, existed in the area beforehand. The long-hair, among youth in this area, is relatively new. The diffusion of the hippie life style into the working class is interesting in itself and may point more to general processes altering the consciousness of this population.

Hippie culture was originally a middle- and upper-middle-class movement, with its images coming from the mass media, from acid or hard-rock groups, the large psychedelic dance halls and, to a much lesser extent, from the underground press. But to point out these sources is not saying anything, necessarily, about the process of becoming a working-class hippie. I have not, as yet, been able to locate all the contingencies in this process. One important element in understanding the change from a grease to a hip style of life is to learn what differences hippies see in themselves since the conversion.

Firstly, hippies realize that "it isn't cool to beat up on other people" or to push them around as greaser boys and girls are reputed to enjoy doing. Hippies have stopped fighting. If they are insulted by greasers, they ignore it rather than fight. They look down on greasers as kids who have not matured past a certain hostile stage of development, who aren't with it and who cannot see the foolishness of their own ways.

Secondly, drugs are believed by the hippies to have brought about this conversion to peacefulness. Either marijuana or LSD is purported to bring about a nonbelligerent attitude toward life — "Acid and fighting just don't mix." Drugs, in addition to being peace-instilling, exciting, and a groove, help a person with his life: acid opens up one's world; speed makes one able to live faster, to attain one's goals more quickly because everything is speeded up; grass makes one mellow and peaceful and helps one to think things through. In the weekly bull sessions (or "drug sessions") of the local youth with social workers, the hippies' ideological justifications for drug use are better developed, better integrated, and more subtle than the "straight" arguments for non-use put forward by the youth workers.

Thirdly, the hippies see themselves "hassled" by a square adult world which has nothing to offer them except condemnation, discrimination by storekeepers and neighbors, police repression, deadly boring jobs, "bullshit rules" of dress and conduct in schools which teach them nothing. Much of this seems to be objectively true: the pizzeria owner on the corner won't let them in because he is afraid they're "holding" drugs. Neighbors complain, and cops chase them off corners, perhaps with more vehemence than they would with the other groups of kids.

Unlike the greasers, who admit the existence of a generation gap but avoid an up-front conflict with adults, the hippies enjoy actively "putting on" adults. They sometimes like to "freak them out" by bizarre dress or actions — panhandling, exploring the drainage sewers, drinking on the rooftop of a factory. Their hijinks are put-ons intended to "blow the minds" of the adult world, a flaunting of the world taken for granted, while a similar infraction by a greaser would be a testing of the authority or coercive power of the adult world and the indication of one's own "badness," or manliness. A greaser, insofar as he acts against the adult world, tries to *outwit* the authorities; a hippie tries to blow their minds while blowing his own mind in the process.

The hip flaunting of the conservative adult-dominated world may have far more harsh consequences in a working-class milieu than in some sectors of the more permissive upper-middle-class milieu — whose members not only tolerate but attempt to coopt and derive vicarious satisfaction from the iconoclastic cultural forms of youth. One indication of this is the very high drop-out rate among local hippies over the age of sixteen. Only one boy in the area has graduated from high school and only one other that I know of is still in school. The hippies' rejection of ordinary career goals, and their refusal to comply with the strict standards of dress (short hair and conventional clothing) and conduct imposed by the school administration, probably contribute to this rate, but it also appears to be an effort of the administration at the high school to get rid of people they consider to be undesirable and potentially or actually disruptive. Career planning, if it exists at all, is vague, and the boys are usually not engaged in, or they put off, the steps that *they* see as necessary to their plans — "I'll start going back to night school. I'd like to get my diploma." But the *time* of that start remains undefined. With little or no orientation toward the future and vague or unrealistic career plans, the kids concentrate on and seem fully immersed in (the enjoyment of) the present.

Jobs are regarded as a source of sustenance ("bread") rather than a vehicle for self-advancement. The youth switch from one dead-end job to another, not working unless they have to. One boy has refused to engage in any more repetitive "robot-like" work and has taken up dealing in drugs as a source of income. Hippies may hold jobs for an even shorter length of time than the greasers, but most of the members of both groups show irregular and unstable job trajectories. I have yet to sort out how much of the hippies' tenuous situation is due to a self-fulfilling prophecy, how much is a consequence of their choice to drop out, and how much is due to actual discrimination and repression by school authorities, police, courts, and employers which make their situation more difficult than that of other youths.

The hippies are interested in music, and those at the center of the group (those who are most "hip") are more experimental in their listening tastes. The hippies of long standing have catholic tastes in music — any acid or hard-rock variations or most forms of jazz are popular, but soul music is frowned upon, while it is popular with greasers and with the recent greaser converts to a hip style — those who have been dropping acid for a few months to a year. The greaser converts are therefore considered to be a few months or even a few years behind in their musical tastes. While greaser kids and greaser converts listen to music avidly and know the lyrics, the old-time hippies are not only just as familiar with the music but they also own instruments and have their own jam sessions.

Hippies tend to be somewhat apolitical, discounting much of what they read and hear as "bullshit." But they are strongly against the war, and when one recent greaser convert backslid to join the Air Force, the rest of the group derided him behind his back. Another boy had clear-cut plans for becoming a jet-maintenance expert, but when he was rejected for physical reasons he was pleased with his non-draftable status. I said, "I hear you had problems with the military." He said, "They rejected me; that's a problem?" None of them ever plan to go into police work or into a military career, and many of them devise elaborate plans (even going so far as to assume a new identity) to evade or avoid the draft. They are unimpressed by national achievements such as the exploration of the moon, which they described jokingly as "no more significant than our own explorations of the neighborhood sewers." Some of the hippies participated in the protests surrounding the 1968 Democratic National Convention and were gassed. But this event was not seen entirely as a highly political act but as an exciting and dangerous kind of "high." This is not to say that they learned no political lessons from the confrontation.

As hippies, kids have picked up other parcels of cultural baggage. They dig the underground newspaper and they like science fiction and fantasy. They are more knowledgeable about drugs than the greasers, and insist that they know how to "pace" their drug intake so they will not abuse themselves.

Dupers

The word "duper" or "dooper" comes from the acronym of "Dear Old Upton Parker." Upton Park is an old, slightly declining, respectable middle-class suburb, so a duper is one who affects middle-class dress, behavior, or life style. Dupers do not hang on street corners like other groups. According to one hippie in the area, they hang in back alleys near the garages of residential homes or flats so they will not have to confront hostile greasers or be tempted by hippies.

Greasers view dupers as "sissified," and they probably have a lot more to say about them, while hippies consider the duper kids to be conceited snobs, who put on a real "clean-cut front" and act as if they are better than everybody else. Here are some hippie opinions about dupers:

They're snots, real snots.

The guys, their whole life ambition is to be insurance salesmen and the girls want to be housewives and Marlo Thomases. . . .

They like to look rich, even if they're from the slums they walk around. . . .

They look on the hippies and greasers as if they're mud. If you're not a duper, you're shit to them.

They hate us. We are everything they want to be and can't be. They just listen to their parents and follow them, even though they may not know what's going on either. We're doing what we want to do and that's something they just can't do.

Dupers seem to be close, then, to all adult socialization institutions, especially their families, their schools and, to a lesser extent, the church. One greaser male told me, "The greasers hang out in the stores and commercial places. . . . The dupers hang in the school or schoolyards." But their involvement in school is not merely limited to "hanging." Not only do they tend to stay in school but they seem to be well integrated into the student culture of the school and are the mainstay of extracurricular activities, especially sports. This is what gives dupers the reputation for being "jocks." Sports and school life seem to be a central theme for dupers, just as cars and booze are central for greasers, and music and drugs are central for hippies.

Dupers are rarely labeled or defined as "bad kids" by the police and the courts; they do not pose a "problem" for adults. Social workers of a local youth agency provide guidance and sponsorship for some of their activities, such as chaperoning dances, but they do not regard dupers as alienated youth, while greasers and hippies often fall in this category.

Youth Cultures

Peer groups and the cultures that are generated and adopted by them are quite pervasive, so much so that Herbert Gans, in *The Urban Villagers,* has typified his entire working-class population as a "peer-group society" because most of their relationships are with peers of the same age, sex, and life-cycle status. The types of working-class youth cultures attached to these peer groups are quite widespread and show remarkable similarity to the ones we have described (see James Q. Wilson's "The Young People of North Long Beach," in *Harper's,* December 1969, and Jeremy Bugler's article on "skinheads" — Great Britain's version of greasers — in *New Society,* November 13, 1969). Let us inquire, all too briefly, into some of the sociological reasons for the prevalence and pervasiveness of these youth cultures.

Peer-group cultures can be seen as a collective response to the problems that youths find in their life situations, particularly to the demands that adult authorities make upon them. The peer-group cultures that we have described contain many elements, but the most outstanding ones are, first, *the nature of the response to adult authority,* and second, *the nature of the generalized stance toward the adult world and the amount of preparation for that world.* Members of duper cultures seem to respect adult authorities, accept the adult world and prepare for membership in that world (preferably in the more middle-class segments of that world). Greasers participate in a culture that stresses rejection of adult authorities (especially law-enforcement officials and, to a lesser extent, teachers) but emphasizes a positive relationship to the adult world and preparation for adult (mostly blue-collar) occupations. Those socialized to hippie culture, however, reject the legitimacy of the adult world and also seem to avoid serious planning or preparation for future adult status.

These various cultures associated with peer groups serve as the normative screens and the arbiters of reality through which many of the demands and pleas of the adult world are perceived, accepted, acted upon, or rejected. Whether one should stay in school or drop out, get a job, or become a "bum," enlist in the military or steer clear of it, get married or remain single, etc., are often discussed, interpreted and decided upon within the framework of common perspectives arrived at by the peer group. Participation in the peer group not only influences attitudes but also leads to concrete behavior that may alter one's path or paths in and out of schools, jobs, the military, reformatories, or jails. The thrusts and emphases of greaser, duper, and hippie cultures may act as significant links in the youthful careers of individuals as they move or are impeded in their paths toward adulthood, and thereby may significantly enter into the process of personal and social change.

ALBERTA ENGVALL SIEGEL
SIDNEY SIEGEL

Reference Groups, Membership Groups, and Attitude Change

In social psychological theory, it has long been recognized that an individual's *membership groups* have an important influence on the values and attitudes he holds. More recently, attention has also been given to the influence of his *reference groups:* the groups in which he aspires to attain or maintain membership. In a given area, membership groups and reference groups may or may not be identical. They are identical when the person aspires to *maintain* membership in the group of which he is a part; they are disparate when the group in which the individual aspires to *attain* membership is one in which he is not a member. It has been widely asserted that both membership and reference groups affect the attitudes held by the individual (4).

The present study is an examination of the attitude changes which occur over time when reference groups and membership groups are identical and when they are disparate. The study takes advantage of a field experiment which occurred in the social context of the lives of the subjects, concerning events considered vital by them. The subjects were not aware that their membership and reference groups were of research interest; in fact, they did not know that the relevant information about these was available to the investigators.

The field experiment permitted a test of the general hypothesis that both the amount and the direction of a person's attitude change over time depends on the attitude norms of his membership group (whether or not that group is chosen by him) and on the attitude norms of his reference group.

This hypothesis is tested with subjects who shared a common reference group at

From Alberta Engvall Siegel and Sidne⟨ Siegel, "Reference Groups, Membership Groups, and Attitude Change," *Journal of Abnormal and Social Psychology* 55 (1957), pp. 360–364. Copyright © 1957 by the American Psychological Association. Reprinted by permission. This study was supported by grants from the Committee for the Study of Values at Stanford University and from the Stanford Value Theory Project.

the time of the initial assessment of attitudes. They were then randomly alternative membership groups, some being assigned to the chosen others to a nonchosen group. Attitudes were reassessed after a year of in these alternative membership groups with divergent attitude norms. course of the year, some subjects came to take the imposed (initially nonpreferred) membership group as their reference group. Attitude change after the year was examined in terms of the membership group and reference group identifications of the subjects at that time.

The Field Experiment

The *S*s of this study were women students at a large private coeducational university. The study was initiated shortly before the end of their freshman year, when they all lived in the same large freshman dormitory to which they had been assigned upon entering the university. At this university, all women move to new housing for their sophomore year. Several types of housing are available to them: a large dormitory, a medium-sized dormitory, several very small houses which share common dining facilities, and a number of former sorority houses which have been operated by the university since sororities were banished from the campus. These latter are located among the fraternity houses on Fraternity Row, and are therefore known as "Row houses." Although the Row houses are lower in physical comfort than most of the other residences for women, students consider them higher in social status. This observation was confirmed by a poll of students (5, p. 205), in which over 90 per cent of the respondents stated that Row houses for women were higher in social status than non-Row houses, the remaining few disclaiming any information concerning status differences among women's residences.

In the Spring of each year, a "drawing" is held for housing for the subsequent year. All freshmen must participate in this drawing, and any other student who wishes to change her residence may participate. It is conducted by the office of the Dean of Women, in cooperation with woman student leaders. Any participant's ballot is understood to be secret. The woman uses the ballot to rank the houses in the order of her preference. After submitting this ballot, she draws a number from the hopper. The rank of that number determines the likelihood that her preference will be satisfied.

In research reported earlier (5), a random sample was drawn from the population of freshman women at this university, several tests were administered to the *S*s in that sample, and (unknown to the *S*s) their housing preferences for the forthcoming sophomore year were observed by the investigator. The *S*s were characterized as "high status oriented" if they listed a Row house as their first choice, and were characterized as "low status oriented" if they listed a non-Row house as their first choice. The hypothesis under test, drawn from reference group theory and from theoretical formulations concerning authoritarianism, was that high status orientation is a correlate of authoritarianism. The hypothesis was confirmed: freshman women who listed a Row house as their first choice for residence scored significantly higher on the average in authoritarianism, as measured by the E-F scale (1, 2) than did women who listed a non-Row house as their first choice. The present study is a continuation of the one described, and uses as its *S*s only those members of the original sample who were "high status oriented," i.e., preferred to live in a Row house for the sophomore year. In the initial study (5), of the 95 Ss whose housing choices were listed, 39 were "high status oriented," i.e., demonstrated that the Row was their reference group by giving a Row house as their first choice in the drawing. Of this group, 28 were available to serve as Ss for the follow-up or "change" study which is the topic of the present paper. These women form a homogeneous subsample in that at the conclusion of their freshman year they shared a common membership group (the freshman dormitory) and a common reference group (the Row). These Ss, however, had divergent experiences during their sophomore year: nine were Row residents during that year (having drawn sufficiently small numbers in the housing drawing to enable them to be assigned to the group of their choice) and the other 19 lived in non-Row houses during that year (having drawn numbers too large to enable them to be assigned to the housing group of their choice).

E-F scores were obtained from each of the 28 Ss in the course of a large-scale testing program administered to most of the women students at the university. Anonymity was guaranteed to the Ss, but a coding procedure permitted the investigators to identify each respondent and thereby to isolate the Ss and compare each S's second E-F score with her first.

To prevent the Ss from knowing that they were participating in a follow-up study, several procedures were utilized: (a) many persons who had not served in the earlier study were included in the second sample, (b) the testing was introduced as being part of a nation-wide study to establish norms, (c) the test administrators were different persons from those who had administered the initial tests, (d) Ss who informed the test administrator that they had already taken the "Public Opinion Questionnaire" (E-F scale) were casually told that this did not disqualify them from participating in the current study.

The Ss had no hint that the research was in any way related to their housing arrangements. Testing was conducted in classrooms as well as in residences, and all procedures and instructions were specifically designed to avoid any arousal of the salience of the housing groups in the frame of reference of the research.

The annual housing drawing was conducted three weeks after the sophomore-year testing, and, as usual, each woman's housing ballot was understood to be secret. In this drawing, each S had the opportunity to change her membership group, although a residence move is not required at the end of the sophomore year as it is at the end of the freshman year. If an S participated in this drawing, the house which she listed as her first choice on the ballot was identified by the investigators as her reference group. If she did not, it was evident that the house in which she was currently a member was the one in which she chose to continue to live, i.e., was her reference group. With the information on each S's residence choice at the end of her freshman year, her assigned residence for her sophomore year, and her residence choice at the end of her sophomore year, it was possible to classify the subjects in three categories:

A. Women ($n = 9$) who had gained assignment to live on the Row during their sophomore year and who did not attempt to draw out of the Row at the end of that year;

B. Women ($n = 11$) who had not gained assignment to a Row house for the sophomore year and who drew for a Row house again after living in a non-Row house during the sophomore year; and

C. Women ($n = 8$) who had not gained assignment to a Row house for the sophomore year, and who chose to remain in a non-Row house after living in one during the sophomore year.

For all three groups of Ss, as we have pointed out, membership group (freshman dormitory) and reference group (Row house) were common at the end of the freshman year. For Group A, membership and reference groups were identical throughout the sophomore year. For Group B, membership and reference groups were disparate throughout the sophomore year. For Group C, membership and reference groups were initially disparate during the sophomore year but became identical because of a change in reference groups.

As will be demonstrated, the Row and the non-Row social groups differ in attitude norms, with Row residents being generally more authoritarian than non-Row residents. From social psychological theory concerning the influence of group norms on individuals' attitudes, it would be predicted that the different group identifications during the sophomore year of the three groups of Ss would result in differential attitude change. Those who gained admittance to a Row house for the sophomore year (Group A) would be expected to show the least change in authoritarianism, for they spent that year in a social context which reinforced their initial attitudes. Group C Ss would be expected to show the greatest change in authoritarianism, a change associated not only with their membership in a group (the non-Row group) which is typically low in authoritarianism, but also with their shift in reference groups, from Row to non-Row, i.e., from a group normatively higher in authoritarianism to a group normatively lower. The extent of attitude change in the Ss in Group B would be expected to be intermediate, due to the conflicting influences of the imposed membership group (non-Row) and of the unchanged reference group (Row). The research hypothesis, then, is that between the time of the freshman-year testing and the sophomore-year testing, the extent of change in authoritarianism will be least in Group A, greater in Group B, and greatest in Group C. That is, in extent of attitude change, Group A < Group B < Group C.

Results

Group Norms

From the data collected in the large-scale testing program, it was possible to determine the group norms for authoritarian attitudes among the Row and the non-Row women at the university. The E-F scale was administered to all available Row residents ($n = 303$) and to a random sample of residents of non-Row houses ($n = 101$). These Ss were sophomores, juniors, and seniors. The mean E-F score of the Row women was 90, while the mean E-F score of the non-Row women was 81. The E-F scores of the two groups were demonstrated to differ at the $p < .001$ level ($\chi^2 = 11.1$) by the median test (6, pp. 111–116), a non-parametric test, the data for which are shown in Table 1.

TABLE 1
Frequencies of E-F Scores above and below
Common Median for Row and Non-Row Residents

	Residents of non-row houses	Residents of row houses	Total
Above median	36	166	202
Below median	65	137	202
Total	101	303	404

Attitude Change

The central hypothesis of this study is that attitude change will occur differentially in Groups A, B, and C, and that it will occur in the direction which would be predicted from knowledge of the group norms among Row and non-Row residents in general. The 28 Ss of this study had a mean E-F score of 102 at the end of their freshman year. The data reported above concerning authoritarianism norms for all women residing on campus would lead to the prediction that in general the Ss would show a reduction in authoritarianism during the sophomore year but that this reduction would be differential in the three groups; from the knowledge that Row residents generally are higher in authoritarianism than non-Row residents, the prediction based on social group theory would be that Group A would show the smallest reduction in authoritarianism scores, Group B would show a larger reduction, and Group C would show the largest reduction. The data which permit a test of this hypothesis are given in Table 2. The Jonckheere test (3), a nonparametric k-sample test which tests the null hypothesis that the three groups are from the same population against the alternative hypothesis that they are from different populations which are ordered in a specified way, was used with these data. By that test, the hypothesis is confirmed at the $p < .025$ level.

Discussion

Substantively, the present study provides experimental verification of certain assertions in social group theory, demonstrating that attitude change over time is related to the group identification of the person — both his membership group identification and his reference group identification. The hypothesis that extent of attitude change would be different in the three subgroups of Ss, depending on their respective membership group and reference group identifications, is confirmed at the $p < .025$ level; in extent of change in authoritarianism, Group A < Group B < Group C, as predicted.

Another way of looking at the data may serve to highlight the influence of membership groups and reference groups. At the end of the freshman year, the Ss in Groups A, B, and C shared the same membership group and the same reference group. During the sophomore year, the Ss in Group A shared one membership group while those in Groups B and C together shared another. From membership group theory, it would be predicted that the extent of attitude change would be

TABLE 2

Freshman-Year and Sophomore-Year E-F Scores of Subjects

Group	End of freshman year	End of sophomore year	Difference
	E-F score		
A	108	125	−17
	70	78	−8
	106	107	−1
	92	92	0
	80	78	2
	104	102	2
	143	138	5
	110	92	18
	114	80	34
B	76	117	−41
	105	107	−2
	88	82	6
	109	97	12
	98	83	15
	112	94	18
	101	82	19
	114	93	21
	104	81	23
	116	91	25
	101	74	27
C	121	126	−5
	87	79	8
	105	95	10
	97	81	16
	96	78	18
	108	73	35
	114	77	37
	88	49	39

greater among the latter Ss. This hypothesis is supported by the data (in Table 2): by the Mann-Whitney test (6, pp. 116–127), the change scores of these two sets of Ss (Group A versus Groups B and C together) differ in the predicted direction at the $p < .025$ level. This finding illustrates the influence of *membership* groups on attitude change. On the other hand, at the conclusion of the sophomore year, the Ss in Groups A and B shared a common reference group while those in Group C had come to share another. From reference group theory, it would be predicted that attitude change would be more extensive among the subjects who had changed reference groups (Group C) than among those who had not. This hypothesis is also supported by the data (in Table 2): by the Mann-Whitney test, the change scores of those two sets of Ss (Groups A and B together versus Group C) differ in the predicted direction at the $p < .05$ level. This finding illustrates the influence of *reference* groups on attitude change. Any inference from this mode of analysis (as contrasted with the main analysis of the data, by the Jonckheere test) must be qualified because of the nonindependence of the data on which the two Mann-Whitney tests are made, but it is mentioned here to clarify the role which membership and reference groups play in influencing attitude change.

The findings may also contribute to our understanding of processes affecting attitude change. The imposition of a membership group does have some effect on an individual's attitudes, even when the imposed group is not accepted by the individual as his reference group. This relationship is shown in the case of Group B. If the person comes to accept the imposed group as his reference group, as was the case with the Ss in Group C, then the change in his attitudes toward the level of the group norm is even more pronounced.

Methodologically, the study has certain features which may deserve brief mention. First, the study demonstrates that it is possible operationally to define the concept of reference group. The act of voting by secret ballot for the group in which one would like to live constitutes clear behavioral specification of one's reference group, and it is an act whose conceptual meaning can be so directly inferred that there is no problem of reliability of judgment in its categorization by the investigator. Second, the study demonstrates that a field study can be conducted which contains the critical feature of an experiment that is usually lacking in naturalistic situations: randomization. The determination of whether or not a woman student would be assigned to the living group of her choice was based on a random event: the size of the number she drew from the hopper. This fact satisfied the requirement that the treatment condition be randomized, and permitted sharper inferences than can usually be drawn from field studies. Third, the test behavior on which the conclusions of this study were based occurred in a context in which the salience of membership and reference groups was *not* aroused and in which no external sanctions from the relevant groups were operative. This feature of the design permitted the interpretation that the E-F scores represents the Ss' internalized attitudes (4, p. 218). Finally, the use of a paper-and-pencil measure of attitude and thus of attitude change, rather than the use of some more behavioral measure, is a deficiency of the present study. Moreover, the measure which was used suffers from a well-known circularity, based on the occurrence of pseudo-low scores (1, p. 771; 5, pp. 221–222).

Summary

In the social context of the lives of the subjects, and in a natural social experiment which provided randomization of the relevant condition effects, the influence of both membership and reference groups on attitude change was assessed. All subjects shared a common reference group at the start of the period of the study. When divergent membership groups with disparate attitude norms were socially imposed on the basis of a random event, attitude change in the subjects over time was a function of the normative attitudes of both imposed membership groups and the individuals' reference groups. The greatest attitude change occurred in subjects who came to take the imposed, initially nonpreferred, membership group as their reference group.

References

1. Adorno, T. W., Frenkel-Brunswik, Else, Levinson, D. J., and Sanford, R. N. *The authoritarian personality*. New York: Harper, 1950.
2. Gough, H. G. Studies of social intolerance: I. Some psychological and socio-logical correlates of anti-Semitism. *J. soc. Psychol.*, 1951, 33, 237–246.
3. Jonckheere, A. R. A distribution-free k-sample test against ordered alternatives. *Biometrika*, 1954, 41, 133–145.
4. Sherif, M., and Sherif, Carolyn W. *Groups in harmony and tension*. New York: Harper, 1953.
5. Siegel, S. Certain determinants and correlates of authoritarianism. *Genet. Psychol. Monogr.*, 1954, 49, 187–229.
6. Siegel, S. *Nonparametric statistics: For the behavioral sciences*. New York: McGraw-Hill, 1956.

13

MASS MEDIA

The mass media of communication are agents of socialization unique to modern society. Newspapers and magazines didn't achieve wide public circulation until the late 1800's; records, film, radio, and television didn't appear until the twentieth century. Despite this recent emergence, however, the degree of public exposure which the media have achieved is phenomenal. Currently 1,750 newspapers are published in the United States with a readership of over 100 million adults a day. The number of paperback book titles increased from 15,000 to 80,000 in the last decade alone. In 1960, it was reported that almost 40 million Americans read a magazine every day. Roughly 200 thousand comic books were sold in 1972, a sharp decrease from their 1960 average of about a million.

The average American sees seven films per year at one of the almost 15,000 movie theaters in the United States. At least 75 million Americans listen to the radio every day. But the primary medium in the United States is television, where almost 90 million sets, representing more than a third of the world total of 225 million, are currently in operation. More than 95 per cent of all American homes are equipped with television, and about one-fourth have two sets. Some 75 million people watch television nightly and the average family has its set on about six and a half hours a day. In fact, it is estimated that, between the ages of 2 and 65, the average American spends 3,000 entire days (almost nine years of his life) watching television.

The vast potential for social influence which the media seem to embody has caused considerable public concern. The introduction of each new medium has provoked alarm in some segments of the society, particularly those committed to the more traditional agents of socialization like the family, church, and school. Actually measuring and documenting the individual or social effects of any of the mass media is a complex and difficult problem, however. Let us take television, the newest and most popular medium as an example.

Effects of Television

One initial worry expressed about television was that it would interfere with the child's homework and adversely affect his education. However, most research has found that although the time children with television spend in outdoor and indoor play and helping with household chores may be somewhat reduced (perhaps up to an hour and a half a day) according to Maccoby (1963), the major impact made is on other media activity. Children with television are likely to spend less time reading comic books, watching movies, or listening to the radio. Television ownership does not appear to affect the time children spend on their homework or reading books.

On the positive side, in some cases a child's interest in classical music or literature has been sparked by television exposure, and the vocabulary of preschool children with television tends to be larger than those without it. For the most part, however, children are far more interested in programs which merely entertain rather than educate. Children seriously interested in acquiring information about a subject seek it from books, magazines, and newspapers. And though middle-class parents demand higher programming standards for their children than working-class parents, both seem quite willing to use television as a pacifier or babysitter for their children.

The typical research designed to measure the effects of television on personality either compares children growing up without television to a similar sample of children of the same generation growing up with television, or compares the knowledge, attitudes, or behavior of a sample of children before and after exposure to one or more media presentations. The former kind of research, of course, is much less possible in the United States today than it was in the early days of television.

At least two basic questions have been asked about the effects of television. First, will children or adults using television primarily for escape become addicted to the manufactured excitement of televised fantasy and correspondingly less able either to find satisfaction in their everyday experiences or to develop insight into the nature and source of their frustrations? The function of escape in this context refers to dependence on television for wish fulfillment or substitute gratification for frustrated goals or impulses, rather than to occasional vicarious enjoyment or merely distraction from routine. Second, despite their intentions, are people socialized by television; in fact, do they learn attitudes and modes of behavior which may or may not be good for them or society?

To answer the first question, research indicates that television is used heavily as a substitute gratification for frustrated individuals. Schramm, Lyle, and Parker (1961) conclude that children who read little and watch a great deal of television disproportionately tend to be of lesser intelligence and lower socioeconomic status (SES). This "high TV/low print" group tends to be much less in favor of statements espousing the virtue of deferred, as opposed to immediate, gratification. Adolescents who are higher users of both print *and* television (i.e., "high TV/high print"), though evenly distributed on the SES scale, tend to be below average in intelligence, but with high job and educational aspirations; in short, another group likely to experience higher levels of frustration and to use the media as a form of escape.

In a study of over 600 elementary school children, Lotte Bailyn (1959) observed that "the need for escape and ego protection through passive release of aggression is particularly great in boys of the Catholic religion where fathers are workers in service jobs." William Hazard (1967) has found that the audience for fantasy-oriented television programs is primarily people who are high in manifest anxiety and low in cultural participation or of low SES or both.

Even conceding that much of the correlation between TV use and SES may be due to the inability of lower SES persons to afford other entertainment, other researchers, for example Leonard Pearlin (1957), find strong tendencies toward using television as escape among those with severely frustrated occupational aspirations who are confused and uncertain about the structure of power and opportunity in the social system. As television viewing under these circumstances diverts the individual from his tensions, thus deferring any constructive response to his problem, Pearlin feels it does more harm than good.

Douglas Waples (1942) has stated that exposure to escapist media has the psychological effect of distracting the individual from his "somewhat habitual anxieties," and the sociological effect of reducing "the violence of assaults upon the existing social structure by cooling the discontent of underprivileged groups" (p. 14). Certainly this "cooling out" function of the "boob tube" or "idiot box" would be quite consistent with the nature of program content and the class interests of those who control the television industry. However, it just might be that television is simply the most modern form of the mass media — performing a needed escapist tension-reduction function for its audience on demand. Essentially, it has replaced radio, as radio managed to successfully adopt many popular themes of silent movies which, themselves, drew on penny-back thrillers and stories of romance based on classic stories from literature and religion. For example, in commenting on the role of a once popular radio soap opera in the psychological adjustment of working-class women to their demanding and unexciting lives, Warner and Henry (1953, p. 434) said:

> The Big Sister program acts constructively in the lives of the women and functions for them very much as did the morality plays of former times. The dramatis personae, in act and symbol, express the conflicting forces of good and evil. The audience happily identifies with the Devil as well as God's Angels but forever demands the Devil be punished for what he does. Thus emotions are rebased adaptively, beliefs are socially oriented, and the values of the group are reaffirmed in their experiences of the audience.

Similarly, studies of confession magazine readers have shown them to be predominantly working-class housewives who seek both emotional titillation and moral reinforcement. Interestingly, readers of such magazines tend to be much less frequent churchgoers than nonreader counterparts and to claim to use the articles as a source of moral advice. Katz and Foulkes in the first article in this section, seek to clarify the concept of escape and to place the issue in a more sophisticated social psychological perspective than is usually done.

It is extremely difficult to establish that media presentations have any direct effect on the viewer. The old Payne Fund investigations of the effects of motion pictures on children, like the one by Peterson and Thurstone (1933), for example, were quite bold in their assertions. These researchers claimed to have established that "the attitude of children toward a social value can be measurably changed by one exposure to a picture," that "the effect of pictures upon attitudes is cumulative," and that the shifts created by exposure to a film have "substantial permanence." However, the greatest effect in this study, which examined attitudes toward minority groups, was observed among children who had little previous experience with members of the group in question.

Most studies which have followed have been far more modest in their conclusions. Himmelweit, Oppenheim, and Vince (1958) in a large-scale study of the effect of television on English children indicated that television has considerable influence on job attitudes, career ideas, and some life styles. However, in general, effects on children's leisure, interests, knowledge, outlook, and values were found to be quite minimal. Moreover, they found that television has the least effect in areas of life with which the child is most familiar (such as family and peer relations).

Melvin and Louis De Fleur (1967) suggest that much incidental learning about the nature of adult occupations is gained from television, but that the character of the children's knowledge of the world of work reflects the stereotypic, superficial, and misleading way in which occupational roles are portrayed.

Limitations on Media's Impact

Thus far, no study has been able to establish with any certainty that television has caused anyone to change his basic values or behavior in any way. The old paradigm of powerful mass media acting directly on impressionable, atomized individuals has been discarded in favor of a much more complex model that includes the numerous factors which tend to limit the impact of television or any other medium.

First, learning from television or any medium represents "incidental socialization." Unlike the situation in the family, church, school, or peer group, no rewards or punishments are issued for proper behavior. Thus, strictly speaking, there is no extrinsic motivation to learn (other than the peer recognition which some opinion leaders may derive from sharing certain information gained from the media). Moreover, television viewing or listening to the radio often tends to be simply an accompaniment to other activities in the home, and the intensity and duration of attention is usually quite uneven and often minimal.

Second, individuals tend to self-select exposure to various communications based on existing predispositions and avoid communications with a different point of view. The individual's social background and personality also influence him to selectively perceive and retain material that supports his own views and to ignore and forget material which does not.

Third, primary group influences tend to modify responses to the media. For example, Brouwer (1964), studying the immediate and long-term effects of contrasting film presentations to Indian students from several schools, suggests that the opportunity for discussion between members of the two experimental groups that had viewed contrasting film presentations may have cancelled out the effects of the original film on individual student attitudes in over half the schools in the test. Certainly, individuals can collaboratively reinterpret communications material to reduce, if not eliminate, threatening inconsistencies. This group influence is particularly important because much media content is acquired from opinion leaders in the context of peer groups rather than directly from the media themselves.

Fourth, the individual's position in the social structure and his total social milieu greatly influence his selection, perception, retention, and use of media content. For example, Gerson (1966) and Greenberg and Dominick (1969) indicate that lower-class adolescents, particularly blacks, watch more television, are more likely to believe that television accurately depicts real life, and most often use television to learn to behave in a socially acceptable way (that is, like middle-class whites), especially in their dating behavior. Here again the media have the most credibility with those who have the least familiarity with the subject matter.

Also, any discussion of psychological disturbance or behavior modification as a result of media exposure must consider the individual's existing personality needs, conflicts, and predispositions. All the leading researchers — Schramm (1961), Himmelweit (1958), Maccoby (1954), Coffin (1955), and others — concur that socially integrated children without serious psychological problems are not likely to watch an inordinate amount of television, be unusually attracted to programs of crime and violence, or be harmed by anything they see.

The sum of all this, according to Joseph Klapper (1963), Director of Social Research for CBS, is that the mass media are much more likely to act as an agent of reinforcement, rather than change, for the individual. It may also be concluded tentatively that television is unlikely to trigger antisocial behavior among any but already disturbed children who might derive inspiration or direction for their behavior from other sources anyway.

Television Violence

This worry — that television may encourage children's antisocial behavior — is paramount among many parents, educators, religious leaders, and legislators. To be sure, television programs portray an inordinate amount of violence. In fact, Erik Barnow, a former chairman of the Writer's Guild of America, has said that writers are often told that their drama scripts must follow a formula laid down by sponsors who insist on crime and violence to attract audiences. In 1960, producer Worthington Minor (Frankenheimer, 1960) said the situation was so bad that the "sponsors often insist on contracts specifying a minimum number of killings or shootings per program."

Despite periodic outcries, the flow of violence on television continues unabated. A study of television violence by George Gerbner (1973) discovered violence in 80 per cent of the shows observed. Moreover, children's programs featured six times as many violent episodes as adult-oriented programs. Half of all leading characters committed some violence, one in ten turned killer, and one in twenty was killed.

The possible effects on the viewer of all this mayhem is quite another question, however. Insofar as surveys establishing a correlation between more aggressive children and higher levels of exposure to violent programs are incapable of specifying cause and effect, the controlled laboratory experiment tends to be the research method most often used to investigate this phenomenon. As mentioned, many researchers are quite skeptical about the possibility of observed media violence being translated into real-life aggression except possibly for already psychologically disturbed children.

Apologists for the networks take the position that watching so much televised violence actually reduces the probability that a child will commit an aggressive act in real life. According to them, the child is able to achieve emotional catharsis through identification with television characters, sublimating unconscious aggressive impulses. However, in an exhaustive review of the relevant research, Richard Goranson (1969) reports only one study that supports the catharsis hypothesis and, even there, the findings were subject to another interpretation.

Critics of television violence claim that it does stimulate aggressive behavior in viewers. For example, Hanratty and others (1969) found that viewing ten minutes of filmed aggression was sufficient to provoke higher levels of aggression in play among 4- and 5-year-old children. Berkowitz and Rawlings (1963) found that students who were deliberately angered by an experimenter and who then watched a violent film in which the aggression was labeled as justified were even angrier after viewing the film.

Other researchers (see, for example, Walters and Thomas, 1962; Lefcourt and others, 1966; Rosekrans and Hartup, 1967; Garry, 1967; Berkowitz and Geen, 1966; and Bandura, Ross, and Ross, 1963) have specified that viewing aggression might lead to aggressive behavior, but only under some circumstances. Important factors include whether the media aggression is consistently rewarded, inconsistently rewarded, or consistently punished; whether it is presented in a fantasy or realistic context; whether the viewer is emotionally aroused before exposure to the media aggression; whether the opportunity for aggression later becomes available to the viewer; and the personal attributes of the individual himself.

Many of these experiments measure aggression against objects rather than people, or in play rather than serious situations and, thus, might not be generalizable to real-life violence against other human beings. Still, exposure to so much media violence may have other more subtle effects. According to Lovibond (1967), children highly exposed to crime comics and films may not commit any delinquent acts unless (1) opposing moral influences are weak, (2) the appropriate opportunity presents itself, and (3) the possibilities of punishment are considered reasonably low. However, high levels of exposure to media violence are more likely to result in (1) decreased readiness to oppose delinquent behavior and the associated system of ideas, and (2) a decreased readiness to take humanitarian action when the situation so demands. Maccoby (1963, p. 125) explains:

> Children who see an unusually large number of crime programs do not continue indefinitely to become aroused to an intense emotional state with each program; the process would be emotionally too exhausting. They therefore repress their emotional reactions, with the result that they tend to be somewhat depressed and apathetic after viewing such programs, and seem to be less capable of sympathetic reaction toward people who are in trouble than are children who do not see a great many crime programs.

Moreover, William Catton (1969) has stated that television, in effect, "advertises" violence much like the sponsors' products. According to him, it is difficult to assess the cumulative, long-term, and large-scale effects of such pervasive violent stimuli — especially in an increasingly unstable, change-oriented society. He even asks whether the violent frontier heritage of American society might not have been abandoned were it not for television. The second article in this section, by Otto Larsen, is an entertaining and informative discussion of the pertinent issues and major positions in the media violence controversy.

Media Censorship

Our examination of the mass media and social personality is still incomplete, however. The medium of television, to extend our previous discussion, has an enormous potential to provide information and modes of community participation otherwise unavailable to people in a mass society. In fact, many social scientists feel that what effects television *doesn't* have on people is at least as important as the effects it does have. But the principal problem here is that the media, particularly television, are giant industries guided mainly by commercial values, rather than art forms guided by esthetic or critical values.

Newspapers have become such big business that there are now one-third fewer papers in the country than in 1910 when the population was less than half what it is today. Currently, more than 95 per cent of all daily newspapers in the United States have no local print competition and depend primarily on two international newsgathering services for much of what they publish.

Television advertising at prime viewing time sells for between $40,000 and $50,000 per minute on the three major networks. Even candidates for public office must pay through the nose. A half-hour now costs a national candidate more than $100,000 and a local politician has to pay as much as $8,000 for a 1-minute spot. In 1970, the TV industry grossed $2.8 billion, half of which went to the networks and the stations they owned. Such artists as John Frankenheimer (1961), a director from the "golden age" of television, have stated caustically:

> The way television is set up in this country right now, it can in no way be called an art form, because basically what you're doing, when it all comes right down to it . . . is selling a product. Now, whether you're doing it by means of a soap opera, an old movie, or a television dramatic show, the result that really is counted by the network officials and by the sponsor is how many tubes of toothpaste you've sold. And I don't think that in these terms television can be called an art form anymore.

According to Stan Opotowsky, author of *TV — The Big Picture* (1962), television's greatest problem is how it is financed. It is a slave to the advertiser who, in turn, must be a slave to the bland formulas that assure him the largest possible audience at the least possible cost. This alleged concern for not offending any potential consumers of the sponsor's product has led to what Rod Serling has called an "objectionable censorship of ideas," which, in turn has fostered an "inability to even find a point of view."

Television has been notoriously guilty of the widespread censorship of anything that smacks of controversy (such as sex, religion, or politics). Recently, for example, several network and Public Broadcasting System station affiliates around the country blacked out programs dealing with homosexuality, abortion, and venereal disease — simply because of the subject matter itself, not the treatment which was marked by the rather bland sense of "balance" which has come to be defined as "objectivity" by network spokesmen.

The 1969 cancellation of the Smothers Brothers Comedy Hour for its mildly irreverent political and religious satire made many people aware of the extent to which even the old justification about marketplace considerations ruling out controversial material was only half the truth. For the show itself was relatively popular, as judged by the official ratings services. Despite its innocent pose, television has consistently exercised stringent political censorship over its program content because it is controlled by political and economic elites which strive to support the status quo by manipulating as much as reflecting public opinion.

Because of the dependence of local stations on network programming (nine of ten prime-time shows are produced by networks for local stations) and the dependence of the networks on the large corporations for advertising revenue, political censorship is institutionalized in the television industry. A 1972 poll of members of the Writer's Guild of America revealed that 86 per cent have found, from personal experence, that censorship exists in television. Some 81 per cent of the writers believe that television is "presenting a distorted picture of what is happening in the country today — politically, economically and racially" and only 8 per cent believe that current television programming is "in the public interest, convenience, and necessity," as required by the 1939 Federal Communications Commission Act. In testimony before Senator Sam Ervin's Subcommittee on Constitutional Rights, David Rintels (1972, p. 17), a television writer and Chairman of the Committee on Censorship of the Writer's Guild of America, West, reported:

> Writers by the dozens report that they have written characters who are black and have seen them changed to white; they have proposed shows about South African apartheid, Vietnam, old folks, mental disease, politics, business, labor, students, and minorities; and they have been chased out of the studios.

Widespread censorship was not the only fact documented at the Committee on Censorship hearings, however. It became clear that television has engaged in deliberate propaganda. For example, ABC and the FBI used to claim at the beginning of each show of "The FBI" that its programs were based on real FBI cases, when they frequently were not, and still claim that its programs are "inspired" by real FBI cases when they frequently are not. Many stories on the show, according to the testimony of many writers, are invented solely by the writer or producer. In eight years, not one single episode has ever been written about the violation of the civil rights of a minority, the violation of antitrust laws, or anything which the "establishment" considers controversial. Nor has any agent on the show ever bugged a house, tapped a phone, hired a paid informant, or done anything that is done in real investigatory work but might reflect badly on the bureau's image.

Neither, does it appear, is the industry even willing to sell air time to legitimate organizations with a political message "offensive" to their interests. The Business Executives Move for Vietnam Peace was refused the opportunity to buy air time from the *Washington Post–Newsweek* station WTOP in Washington to present recorded 1-minute ads in opposition to the Vietnam war. The Democratic party, which complained of general difficulty in buying air time, joined them in a suit against the broadcasting interests, charging violation of the "fairness doctrine." The plaintiffs won the case at the circuit court level, which the broadcasting interests and the FCC appealed to the Supreme Court (claiming that, unlike the telephone company, broadcasters are not common carriers and do not have to make facilities available to everyone).

Even more alarming is the admission by FCC chairman Dean Burch in a congressional investigation that he had wiretapped the office phones of some of the commission's employees during five weeks of 1970 in an effort to stop a "suspected leak of information." Moreover, Burch, the general counsel of the FCC, and two former general counsels defended this activity as reasonable and legal. Burch did not reverse his position until the Justice Department advised the subcommittee that it did not agree with the FCC's legal position.

Theoretically noncommercial public television, subsidized by the government and by concerned private citizens, is supposed to offer an alternative to network television. In practice, however, National Educational Television and the Public Broadcasting Service must cope with pressure from political elites which is too intimidating to ignore. A notorious example was the late 1972 cancellation of a "Special Report" from "The Great American Dream Machine" program in which three former FBI informants claimed they carried out instructions to infiltrate New Left groups to trigger violent incidents that would give law officials an excuse to take action against them. Continued pressure from the Nixon administration culminated in a decision by the Corporation for Public Broadcasting to compel PBS to discontinue all national broadcasts of a political nature in 1973. Shows like "Black Journal," "Washington's Week in Review," William F. Buckley's "The Firing Line," and Bill Moyer's "Journal" were all cancelled. The only option remaining for PBS has been to explore ways of operating on a regional basis with private funding.

Newspapers, the other major source of information for the public, are also heavily conservative. About two of three newspapers have pro-Republican editorial policies; and four of five endorsed Nixon against McGovern in 1972. The capacity of newsmen to investigate controversial stories, like corruption in high places or radical dissent, has been threatened by the determination of powerful conservatives to plug news leaks in the government bureaucracies and deprive social critics of any public platform by issuing subpoenas and contempt-of-court citations against newsmen unless they reveal the sources of their information even when confidentiality has been promised. Some reporters have complied with the government; others have gone to jail in defiance of this dangerous assault on the newsgathering capacity of a free press. Many newsmen publicly admit that the effect of such government intimidation has been to even further increase the self-censorship exercised by the media themselves.

Despite public support for the newsmen (by a margin of 57 per cent to 34 per cent, according to a Gallup poll in December 1972), by February 1973, the

Reporters Committee for Freedom of the Press had compiled a list of thirty cases in which reporters were hit with subpoenas, court orders, or police action to disclose information.

Role of Media in Social Change and Social Control

All of this raises an important question about the effects of the mass media on social personality. First, although research on the impact of the media on basic values and patterns of behavior is highly inconclusive, this does not preclude important effects on the shape of public opinion. Joseph Klapper is one scholar who is openly skeptical about the personality effects of the mass media, yet even he admits (1963, p. 76) that "the media are quite effective in changing attitudes to which audience members are not particularly committed."

Because political conflict centers primarily on programs and policies rather than basic values, the media, in fact, have great power to influence public opinion, either by creating opinions about "new" issues or by selectively ignoring programs and policies with important implications and, thus, failing to provide the conditions under which public opinion can form, let alone be mobilized. Gerbner (1960, p. 6) points out that "between existence and our consciousness of existence stands the symbolic representation and imaginative re-creation of existence we call culture." In a mass society, people must be increasingly dependent upon the mass media of communications for their knowledge of events which affect their existence.

Thus, it is a case, as Lazarsfeld and Merton (1957) put it, of the media failing "to raise essential questions about the structure of society" and, as a consequence, indirectly but effectively restraining "the cogent development of a genuinely critical outlook" (p. 11). Moreover, it is also a case, as Gerbner (1963) says, of the media "cultivating common assumptions of what is, what is important, and what is right." The media can "structure the issues," "set the stage, arrange the climate, and shape the collective outlook in which most private and public decision-making goes on" (p. 10).

Historically, the mass media have been used by nations to both promote or prevent social change. In new nations, desirous of increasing socal cohesion and centralized political control, the media can be used, like the schools, to forge a common national identity transcending traditional regional and status boundaries. Nations wishing to prevent the emergence of a common national identity must either have a monopoly over the communications media or severely limit their impact. In wealthy South Africa, for example, the government has banned television, despite a rising popular demand, because it knows that South African television would be almost wholly dependent on canned English-language film. The government has expressed the fear that this would result in a growing "Anglicization" of South African life (including the "liberalistic" political and racial ideas originating from Britain and the United States) and a consequent undermining of "Afrikanerdom" and its apartheid system.

The American media, particularly television, have also been used as agents of social control. In so doing, the media may not only be failing to provide the conditions by which American society can change, grow, and adapt, but they may be actively undermining forces for constructive change, growth, and adaptation.

Of course, the same principle applies to the individual personality. Klapper points out that, although the media usually act as agents of reinforcement for the individual, they can act as agents of change by providing new information and experiences to persons who, for one reason or another, become "predisposed to change." However, change can only occur if the desired or required information and experience are available to the individual. As mentioned in the introduction to this book, genetically based abilities require certain forms of environmental stimulation before they can be actualized.

As we also have established, culture can be seen as both potentiating and constraining. It can mobilize human energies and shape human perception in ways which allow human beings to experience and become things otherwise beyond them. On the other hand, it can impede or even prevent people from experiencing or becoming things which, in terms of some scheme of higher values or human needs, may be good for them or for society. As an agent of socialization and, thus, a transmitter of culture, the mass media can provide the conditions for both greater potentiation (that is, self-actualization), or greater constraint (or self-suppression). Their position in the structure of the society, to a significant extent, will determine their use. In the last analysis, we must look at who controls the media and for what purpose to understand the effects they do or do not or are likely or unlikely to have on the social personalities of members of the society.

References

Bailyn, Lotte
   1959 "Mass Media and Children: A Study of Exposure Habits and Cognitive Effects." *Psychological Monographs* 73(1):1–48.
Bandura, Albert, Dorothea Ross, and Sheila A. Ross
   1963 "Vicarious Reinforcement and Initiative Learning." *Journal of Abnormal and Social Psychology* 67(6):601–607.
Berkowitz, Leonard, and Edna Rawlings
   1963 "Effects of Film Violence on Inhibitions Against Subsequent Aggression." *Journal of Abnormal and Social Psychology* 66(5):405–12.
Berkowitz, Leonard, and Russell G. Geen
   1966 "Film Violence and the Cue Properties of Available Targets." *Journal of Personality and Social Psychology* 3(5):525–30.
Brouwer, Martin
   1964 "Mass Communication and the Social Sciences: Some Neglected Areas." Pp. 547–67 in Lewis Dexter and David White (eds.), *People, Society, and Mass Communications*. New York: The Free Press.
Catton, William
   1969 "Mass Media as Producers of Effects: An Overview of Research Trends." Pp. 247–59 in Robert K. Baker and Sandra J. Ball (eds.), *Violence and the Media: a Staff Report to the National Commission on the Causes and Prevention of Violence*. Washington, D.C.: Government Printing Office.
Coffin, Thomas E.
   1955 "Television's Impact on Society." *American Psychologist* 10(10):630–41.
DeFleur, Melvin, and Louis DeFleur
   1967 "The Relative Contribution of Television as a Learning Source for Children's Occupational Knowledge." *American Sociological Review* 32:777–89.
Elkin, Frederick
   1952 "God, Radio, and the Movies. *Hollywood Quarterly* 5:108–11.

Frankenheimer, John
  1960 "Playboy Panel: TV Problems and Prospects." *Playboy Magazine,* 12(11).
Garry, Ralph
  1967 "Television's Impact on the Child." Pp. 7–13 in *Children and TV; Television's Impact on the Child.* Washington, D.C.: Association for Childhood Education International, Bulletin 21-A.
Gerbner, George
  1960 "The Individual in a Mass Culture." University of Illinois: Institute of Communications Research. (Published with minor changes in *The Saturday Review,* June 18, 1960.)
  1963 "Mass Communication and the Humanization of Homo Sapiens." *AAUW Journal* (March).
  1973 "Violence in Television Drama: Trends and Symbolic Function." Pp. 28–187 in George A. Comstock and Eli A. Rubenstein (eds.), *Television and Social Behavior: Media Content and Control,* Vol. I. Washington, D.C.: U.S. Government Printing Office.
Gerson, Walter
  1966 "Mass Media Socialization Behavior: Negro-White Differences." *Social Forces* 45:40–50.
Goranson, Richard E.
  1969 "The Catharsis Effect: Two Opposing Views." Pp. 453–59 in Baker and Ball, *Violence and the Media.*
Greenberg, Bradley, and Joseph Dominick
  1969 "Racial and Class Differences in Teen-agers' Use of Television." *Journal of Broadcasting* 13:3331–3344.
Hanratty, M. A., R. M. Liebert, L. W. Morris, and L. E. Fernandez
  1969 "Imitation of Film-Mediated Aggression Against Live and Inanimate Victims." Proceedings of the 77th Annual Convention of the American Psychological Association, pp. 457–58.
Hazard, William
  1967 "Anxiety and Preference for Television Fantasy." *Journalism Quarterly* 44:461–69.
Himmelweit, Hilde, A. N. Oppenheim, and Pamela Vince
  1958 *Television and the Child: An Empirical Study of the Effect of Television on the Young.* London: Oxford University Press.
Klapper, Joseph T.
  1963 "The Social Effects of Mass Communication." Pp. 65–76 in Wilbur Schramm (ed.), *The Science of Human Communication.* New York: Basic Books.
Lazarsfeld, Paul F., and Robert K. Merton
  1957 "Mass Communication, Popular Taste and Organized Social Action." Pp. 457–73 in Bernard Rosenberg and David Manning White (eds.), *Mass Culture: The Popular Arts in America.* New York: The Free Press.
Lovibond, S. H.
  1967 "The Effect of Media Stressing Crime and Violence Upon Children's Attitudes." *Social Problems* 15:91–100.
Lefcourt, Herbert M., Keith Barnes, Ross Park, and Fred Schwartz
  1966 "Anticipated Social Censure and Aggression-Conflict as Mediators of Response to Aggression Induction." *Journal of Social Psychology* 70:251–63.
Maccoby, Eleanor E.
  1951 "Television: Its Impact on School Children." *Public Opinion Quarterly* 15 (Fall):421–44.
  1954 "Why Do Children Watch Television?" *Public Opinion Quarterly* 18:239–244.
  1963 "The Effects of Television on Children." Pp. 116–27 in Schramm, *The Science of Human Communication.*
Meyersohn, Rolf B.
  1957 "Social Research in Television." Pp. 345–57 in Rosenberg and White, *Mass Culture.*

Opotowsky, Stan
  1962   *TV — The Big Picture.* New York: Collier.
Pearlin, Leonard I.
  1957   *The Social and Psychological Setting of Communications Behavior.* Colum-
         bia University: Unpublished Ph.D. thesis.
  1959   "Social and Personal Stress and Escape Television Viewing." *Public Opinion
         Quarterly* 23:255–59.
Peterson, Ruth C., and L. L. Thurstone
  1933   *Motion Pictures and the Social Attitudes of Children.* New York: Macmil-
         lan.
Rintels, David W.
  1972   "How Much Truth Does 'The FBI' Tell About the FBI?" *The New York
         Sunday Times,* March 5, pp. 1, 17.
Rosekrans, Mary A., and William W. Hartup
  1967   "Imitative Influence of Consistent and Inconsistent Response Conse-
         quences to a Model on Aggressive Behavior in Children." *Journal of Social
         Psychology* 70:251–63.
Schramm, Wilbur, Jack Lyle, and Edwin Parker
  1961   *Television in the Lives of Our Children.* Stanford: Stanford University Press.
Walters, Richard H., and Edward L. Thomas
  1963   "Enhancement of Punitiveness by Visual and Audiovisual Displays." *Ca-
         nadian Journal of Psychology* 17:244–55.
Waples, Douglas
  1942   *Print, Radio and Film in a Democracy.* Chicago: University of Chicago
         Press. Quoted in Joseph T. Klapper, *The Effects of the Mass Media.* New
         York: Columbia University, Bureau of Applied Social Research, 1949.
Warner, W. Lloyd, and William E. Henry
  1953   "The Radio Day-Time Serial: A Symbolic Analysis." In Bernard Berelson
         and Morris Janowitz (eds.), *Public Opinion and Communication.* Glencoe,
         Ill.: The Free Press.
Van Den Haag, Ernest
  1957   "Of Happiness and Despair We Have No Measure." Pp. 504–36 in Rosen-
         berg and White, *Mass Culture: The Popular Arts in America.* New York:
         The Free Press.
Young, Ruth
  1969–70   "Television in the Lives of Our Parents." *Journal of Broadcasting* 14(1):
            37–46.

ELIHU KATZ
DAVID FOULKES

On the Use of the Mass Media as "Escape": Clarification of a Concept

Berelson's recent requiem for communication research[1] is probably appropriate to the main, but very narrow, tradition of communication research known as the study of "campaigns" or, in other words, the ability of the mass media to effect dramatic changes in opinions, attitudes, and actions. It is all too clear that mass media "campaigns" do not have the power to brainwash or to induce radical changes. What we have learned from these years of research is how complex the process of mass persuasion really is.

Two viable programs seem open to communication research — viable in the sense that, first of all, they derive from what has been accomplished so far and, second, that the necessary research tools are available to carry them forward.

One of these programs is research on the diffusion of new ideas, products, and practices. This is a direct continuation of the study of mass media "campaigns," with the addition of a more sophisticated frame of reference. The emphasis now is on following the itinerary of social and technical change through a variety of media as well as the formal and informal networks of social relations rather than focusing narrowly on the effects of mass media per se. This approach has been discussed elsewhere at some length.[2]

The second of the two programs is the study of the "uses and gratifications" of mass communications. This approach proceeds from the assumption that the social and psychological attributes of individuals and groups shape their use of the mass media rather than vice versa. This is the approach that asks the question, *not* "What do the media do to people?" but, rather, "What do people do with the media?"

On Uses and Gratifications

Such research has a respectable history, of course. Indeed, some of the earliest media studies focused on problems of uses and gratifications: why women listen to soap operas, the gratifications provided by quiz programs, the functions of newspaper reading, the motives for getting interested in serious music on the radio, are famous examples.[3] And, rather recently, there has been a new crop of studies concerned with the uses children make of television and of its char-

Reprinted by permission from *The Public Opinion Quarterly* 26:3 (1962), pp. 377–388. This article is a revision of a paper presented to the American Association for Public Opinion Research at its annual conference in May 1961.

acteristic content: adventure stories and aggressive heroes.[4] But, in between these two periods and in general, such studies have been far outnumbered by the study of "campaigns." It is a most intriguing fact in the intellectual history of social research that the choice was made to study the mass media as agents of persuasion rather than as agents of entertainment.

There is an important difference between the two phases of "use" studies, however. In the forties, a "use" study typically was reported in terms of a list of functions served by a given type of communications content. Thus, soap operas were alleged to be sources of advice, targets of vicarious identification, sources of reassurance that the listener was not alone in her troubles, etc., and newspapers were found to provide ritualistic activity, orientation to everyday living (and dying), conversation starters, and the like. Studies in the fifties, however, proceeded somewhat differently. Typically, they began with a classification of individuals in terms of some psychological or social attribute — social integration and isolation, for example, or the extent of worrying — and then examined the patterns of mass media behavior of the individuals so classified.

In addition to the obvious fruitlessness of this approach (judging from research so far), the study of uses and gratifications represents a bridge to two major sources of ideas that have remained largely untapped in empirical mass media research. One of these, obviously, is functional theory. Klapper and Wright have illustrated the applicability of Merton's functional paradigm to mass media behavior, and there is little doubt that it will easily overtake the behavioristically oriented, stimulus-response type of theory which has been prevalent heretofore.[5] Second, however, the uses and gratifications approach represents a bridge to the theorists of popular culture — the group of humanists, psychoanalysts, reformers, etc., who have been speculatively analyzing the mass media and mass society. Until very recently, they have been paid no heed by the empirically oriented mass media researcher and have returned the compliment. One reason for the gulf, it may be suggested, is that while the mass media researcher was asking, "What do the media do to people?" the theorist of popular culture — while no less interested in the impact of the media — was asking, among other things, "What do people do with the media?" If empirical mass media research now turns to this latter question, there is some reason to believe that it can draw profitably on the reservoir of hypotheses proposed by the theorists of popular culture.[6]

On the Use of Mass Media as Escape

The favorite answer of the popular-culture writers to this question, "What do people do with the media?" is that they use it for escape. People are deprived and alienated, it is suggested, and so they turn to the dreamlike world of the mass media for substitute gratifications, the conseqence of which is still further withdrawal from the arena of social and political action. This answer appears to suggest that everyday roles in modern society give rise to tensions or *drives* (stemming from alienation or felt deprivation) which lead one to *high exposure* to mass media with its characteristic *context* (e.g., the movie palace) and its characteristic *content* (e.g., fantasy) from which, via *psychological processes* such as identification, one can obtain compensatory gratification and, perhaps as an unanticipated *consequence,* "narcotization" of other role obligations. Such use of the mass media, in other words, would have negative feedback to one's everyday roles.

While it is probable that most critics, both humanist and social-scientific, of popular culture, have something like this process in mind, their discussions most often focus upon one or another isolated element in the process. Thus the drives which lead one to mass media exposure, or high exposure itself, or the social context of exposure, or the content of the media, or the psychological process involved in mass media consumption are singled out and labeled "escapist."

This paper will examine these limited applications of the concept of escape, based, as they are, on the often unwarranted assumption that there is a necessary association between the various elements (drive, high exposure, social context of exposure, content, psychological process) and certain dysfunctional consequences. It will be argued that the ultimate referent of the term "escape" should have to do with the consequences of media usage, consequences which cannot be inferred automatically from other elements in the above model of the escape process. The evidence of the necessity for adopting such a position will indicate the usefulness of functional analysis in the study of media behavior. In fact, the entire discussion is an attempt to illustrate the fruitfulness of approaching media behavior via "uses and gratifications."

Drives: Deprivation, Alienation, Etc.

The starting point for any study of the uses of the mass media is some particular social or psychological attribute in terms of which a population can be stratified. The theorists of escape suggest alienation. Alienation may mean the feeling of powerlessness or meaninglessness, or the feeling of ideological or social isolation.[7] Alienation produces the desire to escape, a desire which the mass media are presumed to be instrumental in satisfying.

As Klapper has pointed out, there are now a number of studies that support the hypothesis that alienation or deprivation do, indeed, appear to lead to increased exposure to the mass media.[8] One set of data, for example, shows that women who worry more or who report themselves as more anxious than others are more frequent consumers of confessional magazine fiction and of radio soap operas and the like.[9] The Rileys found that children who were relatively isolated from peers were slightly more exposed to adventure stories.[10] Maccoby found that middle-class children who experience difficulty in the parent-child relationship spend more time with TV than other middle-class children,[11] and Pearlin explicitly related high stress and liking for "programs that help us forget our personal problems." [12] More recently, by means of a demographic analysis, Olsen has tried to demonstrate that the extent of in-migration and intra-city mobility in a community is predictive of the extent of movie going.[13] Finally, two very recent studies have major contributions to make in this area. Schramm *et al.* find that disparities between a child's own aspirations for himself and the perceived aspirations of his peers or parents are related to high use of "fantasy-oriented" media and low use of "reality-oriented" media.[14] The greater the degree of parent-child conflict (where parents' aspirations are higher than the child's), the higher the consumption of television, radio, and movies and the lower the use of magazines and books. Johnstone studied adolescents' use of the media and found, for example, that the lower one's self-esteem the more time one spends with TV; the less one has of whatever it is that one's schoolmates happen to value (grades, athletic prowess, money), the more heavily one is exposed to the media; the more one feels "out in the cold," the more one is likely to be a rock-'n'-roll fan, and so on.[15]

Considered together, these studies present impressive evidence that alienation or deprivation are associated with increased exposure to particular media or particular kinds of media content. However, even if it is true that alienation or deprivation tend to drive people to seek refuge in the mass media, it is not at all self-evident what they find when they get there. If mass media exposure is sought for relief from, or compensation for, inadequacies in certain of an individual's social roles, that does not mean, necessarily, that positive feedback is impossible for the roles in question. It certainly does not mean that such feedback is impossible for *other* of the individual's roles. A drive, in other words, may well be "escapist," but its fulfillment may or may not be. Escape may or may not be the *result* of the operation of such a drive.

High Exposure

The foregoing evidence suggests that increased media exposure may be sought as a means of escape from everyday role situations. This has led some critics to equate high media exposure itself with escape. Yet it seems quite clear that the media may also be sought for purposes of strengthening one's position in his immediate network of social relations. Eliot Freidson has suggested that children who are attached to their parents use TV to draw themselves more closely to the bosom of the family, while children who are closer to their peers reject TV in favor of movies, the medium of the peer group.[16] Johnstone supports Freidson's hypothesis with much more adequate data and finds, particularly, that sociometric status and feelings of attraction to the peer group are highly predictive of mass media behavior: group listening to popular music, for example, serves the socially integrated adolescent as much as listening alone to popular music, or watching TV, appeases the isolate.[17]

These studies suggest that the media may be both sought and used not only to compensate for abortive or ineffective social relations but also to maintain extant and presumably effective ones. It may also be — although this goes beyond the data reported — that the mass media behavior of the alienated and deprived also contains an element of striving to reestablish effective interpersonal contacts.

Escapist Content

"Escapist content," that much-heard epithet, is the next issue to consider. Escapist worlds, for most critics, are made up of unreal or improbable people who are very good or very bad (or very good-bad) and whose successes and failures conveniently cater to the supposed wishes of the audience. Vicarious participation in the lives and adventures of such fictional characters is considered escapism. Others have been concerned not so much with the unreality of this world as with its unrepresentativeness. Working class people are underrepresented, ethnic types are cast in the role of villain, and so on. It is somehow considered escapist for members of the working class to people their fictional world with upper-middle-class characters. Still other critics have focused on the danger of trying to apply the pat wisdom obtained from participation in the mass media world to real life. Taking advice from a soap opera is the classic example.

Content analyses assume the risk of inferring uses or effects from mere examination of content. It is true, of course, that what little we know does give some support to the hypothesis that so-called escapist content is employed wishfully and vicariously. For example, the Rileys demonstrate that children isolated from their peers use adventure stories as a basis for fantasizing.[18] Another illustration of this hypothesis is the worship of movie stars, although this is something we know very little about.[19]

But to emphasize that media content is "escapist" when it is used for vicariousness and make-believe is to avoid serious consideration of the function of fantasy and ignore other probable uses of this very same content. Surely, respite may be obtained, at least in the short run, and this is by no means irrelevant to the performance of one's roles. And who is to say that what goes on inside the spectator's head when exposed to fantasy materials does not feed back, indirectly, to his other roles? Indeed, it has been argued repeatedly (to choose a far-out example) that the old-fashioned black-and-white Western contributes to the resolution of the Oedipus complex, and that it is precisely the ostensible unreality of the story (the apparently "escapist content") that enables one to circumvent one's own inner defenses and to identify.[20] Again, the Rileys have shown that the "escapist" story may be used by socially integrated children in quite unsuspected ways — as a basis for the assignment of roles in group games, for example,[21] and Bogart reports that comic strip characters are used in working class groups as a topic for conversation and as a typology by means of which personalities may be classified.[22]

It is clear that content usually classified as "escapist" may be put to uses that are not at all implied by that label. If one takes advice from a soap opera, however unreal, or uses an adventure story as a basis for group games, or resolves one's Oedipus complex, there is feedback to one's real-life social roles. Moreover, content that generally is not described as "escapist" may serve functionally to promote escape. If one feels alienated from one's role as citizen — if politics is remote and the feeling of personal effectiveness is low — the latest news from Luang Prabang or Ruandi-Urundi may provide as much escape as does a frontier town of the Old West. And, altogether, it is very difficult to infer uses, or effects, from content.

The Social Context of Media Exposure

Rather than the specific content of the media, however, there might be some reason to believe that it is the situation in which media exposure occurs which, per se, provides much of the opportunity to escape. It seems plausible to assume that certain types of content do serve some purposes better than others, but at least as important may be the fact that *all* content is characteristically received in certain socially defined contexts.

The viewing situation — or, more generally, the situation of attending to the media — is one which society affords a certain amount of protection. "Shh, Daddy is reading the newspaper," or "Can't you see we're trying to watch this program?" imply that exposure to the media is sufficient to justify a degree of insulation or immunity from other pressures. One would be less likely to hear, "Be quiet, Daddy is *thinking*." One may legitimately hide from one's wife behind the newspaper at the breakfast table, or cut oneself off in this way from fellow subway and bus passengers (including female standees). Going to the movies or to the theater absolves one of certain responsibilities: one is permitted by society, to cut oneself off from other roles.

But if the situation of attending to the mass media may serve as a façade for individual retreat, it may also serve to promote certain kinds of social activities which are less easily, or subtly, accomplished under other circumstances. Freidson shows that the media may be used to keep oneself close to desired others, and it is obvious that the movies are used in this way.[23]

It is very difficult to dismiss these latter functions with the epithet "escape." Moreover, the application of the term seems equally questionable in cases where attending to the mass media seems only to serve the function of social retreat. That the media transport one to the world outside of one's immediate environment is the very essence of their function. The better question to ask would seem to be whether these excursions feed back to one's real-life concerns, personal or social. The use of the newspaper as a shield to protect one from the immediate demands of other roles does not mean that reading the newspaper is therefore merely "escape." The media, of course, may also bring one closer to society and, perhaps, to one's more immediate social environment.

The Psychological Process

A question that has peered out at several points in the discussion so far has to do with the psychological dimension in the process of escape. Escape, viewed psychologically, appears to imply a kind of checking of one's social roles at the movie-house door. Escape, for most theorists who have thought in these terms, seems to mean identifying with a star or hero to the point that one loses oneself in a dream which cannot possibly have any feedback to real life.

But the fact is that identification with the hero is by no means the only psychological process at work in the mass media exposure situation. Indeed, radio and television do not so much have stars with whom one identifies as stars whom one plays opposite. Horton and Wohl have given the label "para-social interaction" to the kind of program aimed, they say, at lonely and alienated viewers and offering companionship and inviting "interaction." [24] Such programs, it is suggested, *bolster* the real-life ego rather than overwhelm it. Surely these programs also offer possibilities for escape, but exposure to them involves something quite different from the process of identification or identity loss. It is too facile to pronounce the psychological process involved in attending to media content as "escape," and, furthermore, it tends to obscure the variety of possible consequences that may follow.

Consequences

Ultimately, those concerned with the process of escape are concerned with consequences. They fear the "narcotizing dysfunction" of exposure to the media.[25] In the simplest sense, it is certainly true that the media must affect the performance of one's social roles by virtue of the mere number of hours invested in mass media exposure. But the more subtle problem is to specify exactly the way in which particular patterns of exposure feed back to particular social roles, whether the feedback is functional or not, and whether it is a consequence of exposure per se or exposure to particular content.

Clearly, this is the realm of functional analysis. Much of the discussion, to this point, has focused on the manifest gratifications of the media, but the concern, now, is also with the latent, or unanticipated, consequences of exposure.[26] Some examples of possible dysfunctions at several levels, as a consequence of either specific content or mere exposure, are given in the accompanying table. But it should be clear that an individual operates at many levels and that a given pattern of exposure can contribute functionally at one level and dysfunctionally at another. The same behavior that causes an individual to withdraw from social and political participation may contribute to the success of his performance at work the next day. And what is true within the same individual is also true among individuals: the same usage may have different consequences for different individuals. Thus, Schramm, Lyle, and Parker say that children's use of the mass media for fan-

Some Domains of Escape: Selected Illustrations

Level where dysfunction is noted	Origin of dysfunction	
	Symbolic dimension (media content)	*Spatial-temporal dimension (media exposure or context)*
1. Social, political affairs	A housewife is assured in a soap opera that there is perfect justice in the world and, as a result, is socially unconcerned and politically apathetic.	A man watches TV continually in his spare time and, simply as a result of the time he spends in this behavior, has no time for social causes or political participation.
2. Interpersonal relations (in the family)	A daytime TV "persona" becomes a husband substitute on account of his greater thoughtfulness than the real husband, and there is a consequent impairment in husband-wife relations.	An adolescent goes to the movies, whatever is playing, to get away from his parents, and there is a resulting strain in the child-parent relationship.
3. Intrapsychic	Through identification with a drama character, a person's own impulses are negated or denied, impairing personality integration.	A person carries a transistor radio with him all the time, playing it continually whatever program is on, since its constant distraction means he does not have to think about his inner impulses and thoughts.

tasizing may "*either* (a) drain off some of the discontent resulting from the hard blows of socialization; (b) provide insights and analogies that may help an alert viewer see himself better; *or* (c) lead a child into withdrawal from the real world, encourage the confusion of real situations with fantasy, and thereby cause him more trouble than he should have in learning the rules of the real world; (d) build up aggression, rather than draining it off, so that socially acceptable adjustment becomes more difficult." [27]

Conclusions

It is probably true that the concept of escape blurs too many distinctions to be genuinely serviceable. Still, given the current shift of research interest from the study of "campaigns" to the study of the functions and effects of "entertainment," the concept is likely to be invoked more and more. Hence this attempt to take seriously some of the loose talk about escape, in order, at least, to clarify the issues involved.

We found that social scientists and students of popular culture have, at one time or another, applied the notion of "escape" to every step in the social-psychological process of attending to the mass media. And the label "escapist" has been used to characterize the psychological drives that motivate exposure, the extent of exposure itself, the contexts in which exposure takes place, the content of the media, the psychological processes involved in attending, and the consequences of all these things.

So long as the exact referent of the terms "escape" or "escapist" is clear, no harm is done, of course; indeed, the concepts may even be useful. There is little doubt that some people *do* go to the movies, for example, "to forget about their troubles" or "to lose themselves." To call this an "escapist" drive is to be faithful to common-sense usage. The label is similarly appropriate for various of the other aspects of the process of mass media exposure.

Our objections are rather different. We object, basically, to the assumption, usually implicit and often unwarranted, that "escapist" drives or "escapist" content or "escapist" patterns of involvement with the media are invariably dysfunctional for the individual and society. Clearly it is an empirical question whether one's escape was actually "successful" or not, or whether escaping from one role or one level of functioning does not lead to active and positive involvement in another role or level. A recent discussion of "regression in the service of the ego," in which it is argued that psychoanalytically derived mechanisms of what might be called "escape" may even have functional consequences, seems to parallel our argument here.[28]

By the same token, we object not only to the assumption of an invariant connection between one or another of these forms of "escapism" and ultimate consequences but to the assumption of an invariant relationship among the elements themselves. Thus "escapist drives" do not invariably lead to "escapist exposure patterns"; indeed, there are routes of escape available in addition to the mass media. Nor does "escapist content" function as escape for all who are exposed; indeed, "nonescapist" content may function for some as escape. And so on. The evidence available to date suggests that these linkages cannot be taken for granted.

Other Routes of Escape: An Exploratory Note

It has just been noted that routes of escape other than exposure to the mass media are available in modern society, and it is curious that discussions of the mass media — even functionally oriented ones — so rarely take these into account. Deprivation, alienation, loneliness — the very same drives which are supposed to lead to escape via the mass media — are motives which have been traditionally associated with suicide, alcoholism, drug addiction, spiritualism, etc. It is clear that a theory of the relationship between deprivation and the use of the mass media must inquire into the conditions under which individuals choose one route rather than another.

The discussion can only be opened up in this paper. The most obvious difference between the mass media and these other escape routes is the comparative risk involved. Compared with the mass media, one of the major hazards of these other routes is that they not only transport one from the cares of everyday reality but that they often fail to bring one back. The narcotizing dysfunctions are so great, that is, that one is often prevented from performing any of one's roles at all.

Still, the parallel between the uses of the mass media and the uses of alcohol is instructive. Like the mass media, alcohol may be "used" quite differently by different sorts of people: it may be used to withdraw from society, or it may be used to come closer to society. And what shall we say about the musician who performs better under the influence of drugs? Functional feedback to a basic social role surely is not escape.

But because of the lesser hazard involved and perhaps because of some of their manifestly positive functions, the mass media constitute a more legitimate escape route. "Don't disturb Daddy, he's drinking," clearly has a lower priority.

But rather than consider alcohol or drugs or spiritualism or any of the other possible routes of escape in greater detail, it may be worth concluding by turning to the most pervasive route of all — more widespread than the mass media — sleep. In a suggestive analysis, Auber and White catalogue the social and psychological attributes and functions of sleep.[29] Of all types of withdrawal from society, sleep is the most protected: "Be quiet, Daddy is sleeping," has the very highest priority. Sleep time, say Auber and White, is a legitimate façade for a variety of hidden activities, such as deviance, or creativity, or even marital sex relations. The sleeper is not held responsible for his daytime roles; indeed, it is legitimate for him to lose his very identity — not to know who he is — in the course of the night. Dreams in some societies have meaning for the real world: they may be signs, for example, and there are dream books to interpret their meaning. In our society, however, dreams are essentially invalid and unreal as portents for society (though they may be diagnostic of the individual's own inner workings), and, perhaps, suggest Auber and White, this is why the content of dreams in our society is so irrelevant. It is a sobering idea, considering the state of the mass media, to suggest, as do Auber and White, that if we thought that dreams were more meaningful we might have better ones.

Notes

1. Bernard Berelson, "The State of Communication Research," *Public Opinion Quarterly,* Vol. 23, 1959, pp. 1–6.

2. See Elihu Katz, "Communication Research and the Image of Society: Convergence of Two Traditions," *American Journal of Sociology,* Vol. 65, 1960, pp. 435–440, and "The Social Itinerary of Technical Change: Two Studies in the Diffusion of Innovation," *Human Organization,* Vol. 20, Summer 1961, pp. 70–82.

3. The series edited by Paul F. Lazarsfeld and Frank Stanton contained many of the best of these studies. See *Radio Research 1941* and *Radio Research 1942–43,* New York, Duell, Sloan & Pearce, 1941 and 1944; and *Communication Research 1948–49,* New York, Harper, 1949.

4. For a general statement in this area, one which clearly parallels the emphasis of the present paper, see Wilbur Schramm, Jack Lyle, and Edwin B. Parker, *Television in the Lives of Our Children,* Stanford, Calif., Stanford University Press, 1961. Specifically on aggressive content, see R. S. Albert, "The Role of Mass Media and the Effect of Aggressive Film Content upon Children's Aggressive Responses and Identification Choices," *Genetic Psychology Monographs,* Vol. 55, 1957, pp. 221–285, and Lotte Bailyn, "Mass Media and Children: A Study of Exposure Habits and Cognitive Effects," *Psychological Monographs,* Vol. 71, 1959, pp. 1–48.

5. See Charles R. Wright, "Functional Analysis and Mass Communication." *Public Opinion Quarterly,* Vol. 24, 1960, pp. 603–620, and Joseph T. Klapper, *The Effects of Mass Communication,* Glencoe, III., Free Press, 1960, Chap. 1.

6. For examples of some suggestive hypotheses, see the articles in Bernard Rosenberg and David Manning White, editors, *Mass Culture,* Glencoe, Ill., Free Press, 1958. In this connection, the Committee on Communication at the University of Chicago (recently dissolved) provides an interesting historical footnote. The records of the Committee show that, originally, it was a joint venture of both humanists and social scientists. At the point where the social scientists opted for a program of research on the short-run effects of the media, the humanists dropped out.

7. For a very careful typological analysis of the concept of alienation, see Melvin Seeman, "On the Meaning of Alienation," *American Sociological Review,* Vol. 24, 1959, pp. 783–791.

8. Klapper, *op. cit.,* Chap. 7.

9. Elihu Katz and Paul F. Lazarsfeld, *Personal Influence,* Glencoe, Ill., Free Press, 1955, p. 378.

10. Matilda W. Riley and John W. Riley, Jr., "A Sociological Approach to Mass Communications Research," *Public Opinion Quarterly,* Vol. 15, 1951, pp. 444–450.

11. Eleanor E. Maccoby, "Why Children Watch TV," *Public Opinion Quarterly,* Vol. 15, 1951, pp. 421–444.

12. Leonard Pearlin, "Social and Personal Stress and Escape Television Viewing," *Public Opinion Quarterly,* Vol. 23, 1959, pp. 255–259.

13. Marvin E. Olsen, "Motion Picture Attendance and Social Isolation," *Sociological Quarterly,* Vol. 1, 1960, pp. 107–117.

14. Schramm, Lyle, and Parker, op.cit., pp. 129–131.

15. John W. C. Johnstone, "Social Structure and Patterns of Mass Media Consumption," University of Chicago, Department of Sociology, 1961, unpublished Ph.D. dissertation.

16. Eliot Freidson, "The Relations of the Social Situation of Contact to the Media in Mass Communication," *Public Opinion Quarterly,* Vol. 17, 1953, pp. 230–238.

17. Johnstone, op.cit.

18. Riley and Riley, op.cit.

19. The pioneering studies reported in W. W. Charters, *Motion Pictures and Youth,* New York, Macmillan, 1933, and in J. P. Mayer, *The Sociology of Film,* London, Faber and Faber, 1946, report on dreaming about the stars, on fan clubs, etc.

20. A recent formulation of this hypothesis is F. E. Emery, "Psychological Effects of the Western Film: A Study in Television Viewing," *Human Relations,* Vol. 12, 1959, pp. 195–214. Also see Frederick Elkin, "The Psychological Appeal of the Hollywood Western," *Journal of Educational Sociology,* Vol. 24, 1950, pp. 72–86.
21. Riley and Riley, op.cit.
22. Leo Bogart, "Adult Talk about Newspaper Comics," *American Journal of Sociology,* Vol. 61, 1955, pp. 26–30.
23. Freidson, op.cit.
24. Donald Horton and R. Richard Wohl, "Mass Communication and Para-social Interaction," *Psychiatry,* Vol. 19, 1956, pp. 215–229.
25. See Paul F. Lazarsfeld and Robert K. Merton, "Mass Communication, Popular Taste and Organized Social Action," in Wilbur Schramm, editor, *Mass Communications,* 2nd ed., Urbana, Ill., University of Illinois Press, 1961, pp. 492–513.
26. See Robert K. Merton, *Social Theory and Social Structure,* Glencoe, Ill., Free Press, 1957.
27. Schramm, Lyle, and Parker, op.cit., pp. 73–74.
28. See Roy Schafer, "Regression in the Service of the Ego," in Gardiner Lindzey, editor, *Assessment of Human Motives,* New York, Rinehart, 1958, pp. 119–148.
29. Vilhelm Aubert and Harrison White, "Sleep: A Sociological Interpretation," *Acta Sociologica,* Vol. 4, fasc. 2, pp. 46–54, and fasc. 3, pp. 1–15.

OTTO N. LARSEN

Controversies about the Mass Communication of Violence

On December 12, 1963, the following brief letter appeared in the *New York Times,* sent by a man from Nazareth, Pennsylvania:

The shooting of President Kennedy was the normal method of dealing with an opponent as taught by countless television programs. This tragedy is one of the results of the corruption of people's minds and hearts by the violence of commercial television. It must not continue.

This terse statement, perhaps cogent to some because it offers an "explanation" for an otherwise unfathomable event, is typical of an indictment frequently directed toward the media of mass communication in American society, not only by letter-writers but by men of letters from many disciplines. It says, in effect,

Reprinted by permission from *Patterns of Violence* edited by Marvin Wolfgang (Philadelphia: American Academy of Political and Social Science, 1966), pp. 37–49.

that violence is a dominant mode of mass media content. It adds that such content affects behavior. And it concludes that this calls for regulation and control. In the American system of mass communication, such indictments can have a significant social force of their own. They sensitize audience perception, generate public opinion, marshal pressures by special-interest groups, stimulate governmental investigation, and induce counteraction by the agencies of mass communication. They also raise questions of fact, problems of evidence, and matters of judgment concerning values and alternative social mechanisms for their implementation.

For these reasons, this paper attempts to assay the present state of knowledge concerning mass media violence in a context stressing the process of public indictment of the media for presenting such materials. Two concurrent but not perfectly correlated controversies will be explored: (1) the controversy over the effects of media violence and the evidence concerning such effects and (2) the controversy over the control of the portrayal of such violence.

The repeated portrayal of violence by the mass media could have many effects. One of the immediate results is the polarization of concern about such content. Thus, the body of relevant literature is mainly a compendium of lines of protest and defense, claims and counterclaims, charges and denials. To register this observation is to note more than a paucity of research. It means the presence of a public dialogue over effects and control repeated in broad form for each medium as it gains prominence and confronts decisions concerning the portrayal of violence. The pattern of this dialogue is, for the present at least, as important as the content of the competing claims. It may be said to signify the search that man is making for control mechanisms to contain the new scale that is introduced into personal and social life by the impressive technology of mass communication. In the process of examining this feature we shall naturally review conventional concerns with effects such as the alleged imprint that violent media content makes on personality, delinquency, and the like. The total effort may enhance our understanding of the functioning of mass communication in modern society generally. This, I believe, must ultimately come from continued efforts to penetrate the complexities of the reciprocal relationship between public opinion and mass communication.[1]

Controversy over Effects

I have recently had occasion to review the extensive literature on the general social effects of mass communication.[2] Rather than repeat a version of that exercise, here directed toward the specific question of the effects of violence, I shall attempt an approach employed by television when it meshes interviews with two or more public figures to simulate direct debate between them; thus I shall borrow a mass media technique to draw together the diverse appraisals of the mass media. Bernard Berelson has provided a precedent for such a procedure.[3] The manner of selection below does not warrant generalization about either the views of a given person or the discipline in which he happens to be working. The dialogue is designed merely to project significant views extant in the controversy.

The following presentation was initially developed by abstracting statements from a single publication of each of three men who have particular competence in the area: (1) Joseph T. Klapper, a Ph.D. in sociology, currently directing research for the Columbia Broadcasting System,[4] (2) Frederic Wertham, a New York psychiatrist,[5] and (3) Dallas W. Smythe, a Ph.D. in economics, formerly Chief Economist for the Federal Communications Commission and now a professor of economics.[6] Material from their publications is connected in dialogue form, with adaptations and additions to meet the requirements of this style. While the authors cite each other in their work, they by no means address each other in the manner imagined below. Accordingly, this presentation is not a stipulation of fact according to their choosing but a composite of perceived truth for our purposes. For further convenience, the dialogue will be presented as a conversation between a media-sociologist, a media-psychiatrist, and a media-economist.

Media-sociologist: The fear regarding the effects of mass media content is more frequently expressed by parents, educators, and freelance writers than by disciplined communication researchers. True, there can be no doubt that violence is frequently depicted in the media. However, the statistics of violence shine conspicuously in a standardless void. Their increasing size may attest a trend in media content, but it does not indicate that any particular effects are therefore more or less likely to occur. Actually, nothing is known about the relationship, if any, between the incidence of violence in media programs and the likelihood that it will produce effects.

Media-psychiatrist: If, as you say, there is nothing known, we are scientifically in a bad way indeed. As I see it, we are confronted in the mass media with a display to children of brutality, sadism, and violence such as the world has never seen. At the same time there is such a rise of violence among our youth that no peace corps abroad can make up for the violence corps at home. Social scientists say that the test of science is prediction, and I predicted fifteen years ago that more and more brutal violence would be committed by younger and younger age groups. Now it is a matter of common knowledge.

Media-economist: Can it be proved that particular television programs or comic books are prime causes of delinquency? The problem children you have studied appear to be media addicts who are affected by the cumulation of media violence. However, your book also seems to indicate that delinquency arises from a complex of factors, including the economic and social conditions of the environment.

Media-psychiatrist: It makes no difference in our stage of knowledge if a cause is not "immediate" but remote, not "primary" but secondary, not "direct" but indirect. What is important is that without this contributing factor the harmful effect would not have taken place, or at least not in that form. In mental life, all contributory factors have to be regarded as causal. My clinical studies of over two hundred unselected cases lead to the conclusion that children are getting more and more tele-directed. As a result there is a loss of emotional spontaneity and a distortion of natural attitudes in the direction of cynicism, greed, hostility, callousness, and insensitivity expressed in overt acts, in fantasy, and in dreams.

Media-sociologist: You mention only a few of the specific fears about media effects; some of those who fear the effects of violence seem unsure of what specific consequences might follow, only that they are undesirable. Others fear that such material elicits direct, imitative behavior — that an otherwise normal child may commit crimes after seeing them on television.

Media-psychiatrist: I have seen it in my clinical studies.

Media-sociologist: This presupposes that the media have a kind of direct, "hypodermic needle" effect. Research would not support this. Others say that media depictions of violence constitute a school for delinquency, teaching methods of crime, or that the media will have a kind of trigger effect which operates in situations of reduced moral resistance. Finally, there are even those who believe that media violence has beneficial effects by providing a kind of catharsis of anti-social drives.

Media-economist: To my knowledge there is no research evidence to support any of these charges, but my hunch would be that no child, exposed to mass media in large doses, is unaffected by it. Certainly, from our content analysis of tele-vision programs, one can conclude that, except for doctors and the unemployed, characters are highly stereotyped, with some of the stereotypes being presumptively dangerous if taken as models for viewer behavior.

Media-psychiatrist: I might point out here that although your empirical re-search may not prove that there are effects, neither does it prove that there are not. At the present time, a number of books are appearing which minimize or deny media effects and confuse the issue. So the home, which in pre-electronic times afforded the child protection, is now invaded on two fronts: by bad tele-vision programs which influence the children and by slanted books about them which influence the parents.

Media-sociologist: Let us discuss one of these books. It seems to me that *Tele-vision and the Child* by Hilde Himmelweit and associates[7] gives evidence on some of the charges we have been talking about. They studied 1,854 children in England divided into viewers and nonviewers and matched by age, sex, intelligence, social background, and other factors to determine whether observed differences were the product of viewing or were pre-existing.

Media-psychiatrist: The children were not examined. They just filled out formal questionnaires. Furthermore, when this report appeared it was already out-of-date; the British screen had not yet become littered wih dead cowboys. Moreover, it does not apply, then or now, to American children who are exposed to much more and worse screen mayhem. It is also a fallacy to think that findings are not scientific unless they can be expressed in a graph and in very large numbers. There is no substitute for a thorough clinical psychiatric examination of actual cases.

Media-economist: You are saying that you don't believe that they can general-ize their findings from a large sample to the individual, but that you can gen-eralize your results working with an individual to the larger group.

Media-sociologist: Despite your objections, let's look at some of their findings; we may even find some support for your conclusions. First, they do find that some content may be frightening, on radio as well as television.

Media-economist: We must not forget the violence in documentaries, on news broadcasts, and perhaps even in sports programs.

Media-sociologist: True. However, Himmelweit did find that real violence is less likely to frighten children than is violence in fictional programs, but, on the other hand, real violence is more widely disliked. Virtually nothing is known re-garding the duration of such fright or the ways, if any, in which it may affect children's concepts or behavior. The alleged effect on disturbed sleep, nightmares, and the like would appear to be evanescent.

Media-psychiatrist: Case histories in psychiatric literature. . . .

Media-sociologist: Let me complete the summary. Himmelweit did find that the degree to which children are disturbed appears to be related to the means by which injury is done. Shooting is not disturbing, but a knife attack may be. Violence which follows a conventional pattern, the outcome of which is predictable, such as is found in Westerns, apparently disturbs few children.

Media-psychiatrist: That pronouncement indicates the difference between the adult's offhand acceptance of what he *thinks* the child gets from television and the actual reaction of the child. It is a typical adult response, and is not how children see it. For example, the report states that if the victim who has been shot clutches at his stomach, that merely means to the child that he has been shot from the front! Many children have told me what it means to *them:* that the man is shot in the stomach because that is one of the places where it hurts most.

Media-sociologist: However, the study shows that children are apparently more sensitive to acts of verbal aggression than to actual physical violence. Sound effects are about equally as frightening as visual effects, and the child is more likely to be frightened viewing alone or with children his own age than when viewing with adults present. They also found that there was no more aggressive, maladjusted, or delinquent behavior among viewers than among nonviewers.

Media-psychiatrist: As far as negative effects are concerned, this report centers on what is frightening or disturbing to the child. From a mental health point of view, these are neither the only nor even the most important bad effects. Furthermore, the study relies on statistics based on individual answers to questions, without considering the whole child.

Media-sociologist: In general, while the media do not appear to be a crucial or primary determinant of behavioral tendencies, there are indications that violent fare may serve special functions for those who are already socially maladjusted.

Media-psychiatrist: The normal child is alleged to be invulnerable, the abnormal child vulnerable. It is not only the abnormal child, however, who can learn — and be seduced. Normal children are not inaccessible.

Media-economist: Certainly there have been studies, by Albert Bandura and others, which have shown that children in laboratory experiments exhibited greater aggression and inflicted greater punishments on others after seeing a film with violent content than control subjects who had seen a neutral film. Does this not cast doubt on the catharsis principle?

Media-sociologist: Perhaps. And while we all follow with interest the newer laboratory studies, we will also continue to be curious about what happens when laboratory studies are translated into real-life situations where influences such as social norms and parental sanctions operate. Certainly we need to know more about the duration of any immediate effects that have been observed.

Media-economist: I wonder if television crime programs and crime comics are being made scapegoats?

Media-psychiatrist: How do you mean?

Media-economist: Any review of the history of technological innovation would show that where such innovations bear on the public, they tend to become blamed for current social ills. Could it be that we are really fighting the threat to individual integrity of a technologically oriented society? Our mass media have the aspect of a one-way conveyer belt. In work, the individual has become a narrow specialist. In leisure time with the mass media he seems to become more a passive, receiving automaton. If the adult senses that political apathy and a feeling of anomie are somehow related to these threats to his autonomy, small wonder that he protests that passively sitting and watching television crime programs is not good for his child. Couldn't mass media violence also be a symptom of our general social life and not a cause?

Media-psychiatrist: Something may very well be a symptom and at the same time a cause. This is no argument. Socially, mass media violence is a symptom; individually, it may be an operative cause.

Media-economist: Possibly our concern over television and children would lead to more significant results if it were focused on the effects which are precluded because certain kinds of cultural experience, being outside the orbit of cultural industry, are not being made available to children.

Media-sociologist: Himmelweit points out that since violence programs take up a disproportionate amount of viewing time, this prevents the showing of more varied fare that could offer children a broader view of life.

Media-economist: What do we actually find on television? Do we find a world where men and women enjoy self-respect and freely accord it to others? Or does it present a world which is peopled with characters so stereotyped as to lack diversity and portrayed merely as all good or all bad? We don't know, but perhaps the intuition of sensitive laymen — such as found in Parent-Teacher Association (PTA) groups — may not be too far wide of the mark.

Media-psychiatrist: Hear! Hear!

Media-sociologist: I rest my case with need for further research. Thus far, there is little evidence that media violence is a prime mover of behavior. The content seems rather to reinforce or implement existing and otherwise induced behavioral tendencies. For the well-adjusted, it appears to be innocuous or even to be selectively perceived as socially useful. For the maladjusted, particularly the aggressively inclined and the frustrated, it appears to serve, at the very least, as a stimulant to escapist and possibly aggressive fantasy and probably to serve other functions as yet unidentified. I would also add that further information on the role of mass communication in the development of delinquency is more likely to come from the study of delinquency than from the study of mass communication.

Media-psychiatrist: We are asked to eradicate from our thinking the stereotype of the Big Media and the Little Me. This is far from being a wrong stereotype; the contrast between the immensely powerful mass media and the individual family and child is one of the most essential facts of our present existence.

The dialogue could go on, but *its inconclusiveness is enough to indicate contrasting estimates of what is known, what needs to be known, and what constitutes knowing* about the effects of mass media violence. In the face of such circumstances when confronted with the problem of selecting from alternative control mechanisms, it is prudent to subscribe to Charles Winick's conclusion that

> social scientists have generally felt that their knowledge of the effects of media is not substantial enough to permit recommendation of what ought to be proscribed, even assuming the existence of a censorship apparatus.[8]

Research is a continuous activity, and the above conclusion will not be taken as the final word in the research-policy relationship. Some additional cautions should be posted here, however. More recent and more rigorous research than that referred to above is in the direction indicating that exposure to mass media violence can directly induce aggressive behavior in both children and adults.[9] But even if future efforts substantiated such research, further work would be required to establish the social implications of such findings. The debate so far has tacitly assumed that aggressiveness of the individual is socially dysfunctional. This may be, but do we know that it is? Researchers need to consider this question.

Furthermore, in the history of each medium of mass communication, there is little evidence to support the logic that if the controversy over effects could be resolved, the problem over control might readily be solved. Indeed, folk-experience does not wait passively for technical knowledge to emerge to solve problems, but proceeds under a dynamic of its own to search for solutions. Accordingly, we suggest that in developing a strategy of research, students of effects would be well advised to broaden their conception to take into account the evolution of the transaction between media and audience. Certainly, effects do not flow only in one direction. The flow back to the media may be said to begin when someone recognizes a situation to be problematic. It comes full circle when there is an adjustment in the form of some organized regulation. We turn to a consideration of some conditions and mechanisms through which opinion is generated, expressed, and impressed in the media-audience relationship.

Controversy and Control

Paradoxically, controversy over mass communication emerges from a point of consensus bearing on the potential impact of the media: more and more people are spending more and more time in exposure to media content; this is incontrovertible. With the development and diffusion of ever more efficient technologies for the transmission of images, the world-wide opportunities for such exposure continue to accelerate. The United States continues to set the pace by creating and extending a communication system unparalleled in its magnitude.[10]

This fact of ubiquity sows the seeds of controversy. Anything so massive that compels so much attention inevitably calls forth some critical reflection on grounds of sheer quantity alone. Such reflection is quickly nourished into specific complaint when considerations of quality are coupled to the assumed potency of size. It is not the machine alone (for who has not marveled at some aspect of this complex mechanical, electrical, and organizational mix?), it is the manner in which it is operated that calls forth the critical response. A persistent feature of that operation is the portrayal of violence. It must be acknowledged that this is but a single factor contributing to dissatisfaction with the state of the communication system. Dan Lacy paints the broader picture by noting that

> the banality and emptiness of most broadcasts and films, the "slickness" of magazines, the political bias of newspapers and news magazines, the cultural and political conformity of the mass media, sex and violence in books, films and broadcasts, illiteracy and superficiality in cultural life — all are the subject of thoughtful and continuous complaint.[11]

In the American systems of mass communication, complaints, whether thoughtful or not, can be the beginning of a communicative process that may ultimately register an impact on the decision as to what content the media will offer their audience. Guided as they are by economic considerations intimately tied to audience size, the media can be acutely sensitive to audience feedback. If complaint generates controversy and if controversy generates consensus, then the probability of influence and the possibility of change is maximized. In some instances, complaint can also be effective apart from a real consensus because the media are prone to overgeneralize certain registered reactions. For these reasons it is important to attempt to identify the components and functioning of this interactive system in which complaint has such a significant potential.

Media-Audience-Critic

A first element to note is that complaint, as a forerunner to controversy, is a definition of a problem that may generate discontent, but does not uniformly arise from discontent. Since the media cater to a mass audience and attempt to satisfy the largest possible number of persons, it is not surprising that complaint does not generally emanate as a grassroots response. It is, rather, the reaction of a select, articulate minority. Bernard Berelson's characterization of the audience appraisal of television clearly represents what has been the case for each medium at the point where it begins to receive critical scrutiny.[12]

> For about fifteen years now, television has been at, or close to, the center of attention in America. The people have been watching television, and the critics, commentators, and educators have been watching the people watching television. On the whole, *the one has liked what it saw; the other, not* [italics mine].

At this point in the process, it might appear that the media, invoking their democratic calculus, would reveal little concern over the complaints of a critical minority in the face of support and approval from the vast majority of their audience. This, as we shall see, is too simple and too static a conception of the media-audience-critic relationship.

While the critics may not like what they see, they are not all of one cut, one mind, or one disposition to act. Some engage mainly in intellectual analysis of factors contributing to the decline of high culture, with resulting impressive symposia on mass media and mass society.[13] Media managers are not insensitive to such efforts but have ready defenses for deflecting the argument at this level. The words of Dr. Frank Stanton, president of the Columbia Broadcasting System, present a case in point:[14]

> Some sort of hostility on the part of the intellectuals toward the mass media is inevitable, because the intellectuals are a minority, one not really reconciled to some basic features of democratic life. They are an articulate and cantankerous minority, not readily given to examining evidence about the mass media and then arriving at conclusions, but more likely to come to conclusions and then select the evidence to support them. But they are an invaluable minority.... They probe around frontiers in their splendid sparsity, looking around occasionally to see where — how far behind — the rest

of us are. We are never going to catch up, but at least we shall always have somewhere to go.

Another set of critics is disposed to translate abstract conviction into concrete action in the court of public opinion. Whether such initiators of complaint go on to become the molders of a controversy whose pressure the media cannot ignore or deflect is contingent upon a number of factors. It will depend, first, on the nature of the media content under question, its salience to a broader public, and the relevant traditions, values, and norms concerning public display of such content.

Value Clusters

In American society, in sharp contrast to the situation in many other countries, a critic will not automatically muster support for his complaints about the portrayal of violence in the mass media. A number of value clusters are relevant here. One is the traditional aversion that Americans hold toward censorship and restriction of free expression. Another is a deep cultural commitment to violence extending back to frontier days.[15] Throughout our history a great deal of violent behavior has been positively sanctioned. Many occupations allow for and even require the use of violence.[16] Beyond that, the indicators of an abiding public fascination with violence are all around us, as witnessed in the popularity of certain athletic events, such as professional football (sometimes referred to as "Mayhem on a Sunday Afternoon"), the booming Christmas sales of toy weapons ranging from gun-shaped teething rings to simulated atom bombs, and the continued attraction of both real and fictional accounts of war and crime.[17] While the mass media may whet the appetite for such materials, any would-be critic must ultimately come to recognize that such an appetite is rooted much deeper in American experience, if not in human nature. At the same time it may be acknowledged that the presence of other value clusters (for example, concern for the welfare of children) provides a counterbalancing context receptive to criticisms directed toward mass media violence.

Opinion Leadership

Thus, the cultural context in which the media content is received sets broad limits affecting the possibility of controversy and even the shape in which it may be formed and expressed. Equally important, however, is the interpenetration and operation of the persistent action-oriented critic whose power as an opinion leader becomes manifest in terms of (1) his professional status, (2) his access to platform or medium to amplify and spread his argument, (3) his linkage to sources of organized response from voluntary associations, and (4) the ability of such organizations to mobilize community concern, political investigation, the threat of new legal sanctions, and the possibility of some form of boycott of the media by a sizable portion of the audience.

In patterned sequence, these elements have, at one time or another, emerged to direct pressures against most forms of American mass communication to influence the manner in which they portray violence and other sensitive material. A feedback chain is forged as critics speak, opinions are amplified through various media, local groups pick up the argument, voluntary associations mount crusades, legions of decency appear, clean-up campaigns are organized, distributors of media content are challenged, petitions are circulated, politicians are alerted, hearings are held, authorities testify, resolutions are passed, and government intervention is threatened. The intricate elaboration of criticism into effective public opinion, through a maze of protest, publicity, community action, legislative investigation and, finally, media reaction has been analyzed in varying degree with respect to the motion pictures,[18] the comic books,[19] and the broadcast media.[20] In each case, the feature that finally appears to compel the media to react in some visible and tangible way is the threat of restrictive laws or other intervention by governmental agencies.

Self-Regulation

In broad terms, the response of these media to the increase of public pressure has followed a similar form: after a defense of their performance in the name of a "free press," and after denouncing the evils of censorship, they take on the responsibilities of censors themselves as each develops an internal system of self-regulation. Self-regulation means that a communications industry taxes itself to establish an organization to police itself. A code of good conduct is formulated which prohibits the presentation of certain kinds of materials;[21] media content is reviewed and edited in conformity to the code before it is released; some sort of "seal of approval" is appended to symbolize this conformity; and other efforts of a public relations sort are made to head off the kind of criticism that gave rise to self-regulation in the first place. As a result, for a time at least, controversy around a particular complaint, such as the excess use of violence, may tend to subside, and a wavering equilibrium emerges between the force of public opinion and the powers of media policy, as each side of the interaction adapts itself to the other.

The above is almost precisely what happened in the case of comic books, with marked consequences for those products with a heavy violence emphasis of the "crime" and "horror" variety. This medium developed in its present form in the 1930's and grew until the early 1950's when 600 titles of all varieties filled the newsstands and sales reached over 60 million copies per month. At the peak of the dynamic opinion process outlined above, industry self-regulation was instituted in 1954. The comics code forbids the use of the words "horror" or "terror" on the cover and also places restrictions on use of the word "crime." With reference to other materials bearing on the portrayal of violence, the code, consisting of 41 specific regulations and a "catch all" provision, incudes the following restrictions:

> No comics shall explicitly present the unique details and methods of a crime.
>
> Scenes of excessive violence shall be prohibited. Scenes of brutal torture, excessive and unnecessary knife and gun play, physical agony, gory and gruesome crime shall be eliminated.
>
> No unique or unusual methods of concealing weapons shall be shown.
>
> Scenes dealing with, or instruments associated with walking dead, torture, vampires and vampirism, ghouls, cannibalism and werewolfism are prohibited.
>
> Advertising for the sale of knives, or realistic gun facsimiles is prohibited.

Appraisal

After a decade of self-regulation, the Comic Magazine Association issued a booklet reviewing its efforts.[22] While the booklet is not an unbiased appraisal, it argues:

> Besides establishing and enforcing standards more stringent than any restrictive legislation legally enforceable under the constitutional guarantees of a free press, voluntary self-regulation is effective because it brings about willing cooperation rather than the reluctant, often inadequate or belated "compliance" given to coercive laws.[23]

Then, of special relevance to the framework of the present analysis, it presents an impressive array of testimonials and commendations from church, civic, veteran, parent-teacher, business, and other organizations which leads to the conclusion that

> their comments offer substantial proof that the comic magazine industry's program of self-regulation has well accomplished its purpose of providing an effective and practical means of eliminating undesirable material from comic magazines.[24]

The battle over the content of the comic book has been a significant part of the war against violence in mass communication. It has brought to the arena of discourse, as the turmoil over the motion pictures did earlier and as current concern over television is doing, vital experience with a delicate mechanism of social control. While self-regulation appears to disarm many combatants, new issues around censorship call forth new disputes,[25] and not all of the former critics are satisfied with self-regulation as a solution to old problems. Numbered among the latter is the single most influential critic in the long controversy over comics and an imposing figure in the continuing struggle to control violence wherever portrayed in the media — Dr. Frederic Wertham, the aforementioned New York psychiatrist.

Wertham has never relented in his long campaign against the comic books.[26] His skepticism about self-regulation is indicated by a recent statement observing that "at present, with the threat of legislation receding, the number of crime comic books is again increasing by the millions." [27] If for no other reason, Wertham continues to draw sympathetic attention because his basic concern is with children. As we have seen, he asserts that from the mass media they learn that violence is a constructive, socially approved form of settling difficulties. Accordingly children should be protected, and protected not by self-regulation but by law. He insists that social control for the protection of children has nothing to do with censorship for adults, although he recognizes that to make regulations applying only to children is not easy. He then reiterates his long-standing plea for a welfare law that would control crime comic books directly packaged, displayed, advertised and sold to children under fifteen years of age, noting that similar laws concerning the sale and consumption of liquor are never termed an infringement on civil liberties or a restraint of trade.

When Wertham turns to a consideration of violence on television, his enthusiasm for legal control is tempered by the fact that many adults look at television during children's viewing time, and many children watch it outside of this period. Furthermore, he observes that no control law could be limited to television alone but would have to include the movies which are so often shown on television. Despite these difficulties, Wertham recommends two courses of action: (1) the formulation in legal terms of the permissible boundaries of the kind, quality and quantity of sadism, violence, and brutality of television shows, along with strict licensing and powers of license revocation in terms of these standards, and (2) the improvement and translation of the relevant part of the industry's code into legal terms to stimulate the industry to strengthen facilities for content analysis and to grant them sufficient powers for enforcement. He concludes that "the best efforts of the best people in television would be aided by such a law, and children would reap a special benefit." [28] And he closes with this observation: "Does the modern state need protection against the mass media? This is an issue with no easy answers. It will be debated for a long time." [29]

Wertham, a man whose critical capacities have perhaps contributed most to the controversy feeding the forces that led to self-regulation, now (in 1965) takes a somewhat equivocal stance with respect to this mechanism. He clearly does not trust it in the hands of the comic-book publishers. For television, on the other hand, he would formalize its "best" elements and buttress them with the sanctions of law. As he notes, the debate over control will go on.

Charles Winick, in a pioneering study of the activities of a program-screening department operating in television self-regulation, has sharply specified a prime requisite for the ventilation of the issue:

> A close-up examination of how self-regulation of media actually takes place might help to cast light on those shibboleths or institutions of our society whose lengthened shadows are reflected in the censor's changes and could clarify the kind of use which is being made of the censor's power. Rather than debate censorship in the abstract, an examination of how it actually works might serve to make more real the concept of censorship.[30]

Thus, concern over mass media violence moves from controversy to control and back again to controversy. Whether such cycles ultimately evolve into more satisfactory policy adjustments will depend on a better knowledge of effects, a clearer conception of alternative mechanisms of control, and a sharper understanding of how the two are linked.

Notes

1. For an example of this kind of analysis, see Herbert J. Gans, "The Creator-Audience Relationship in the Mass Media: An Analysis of Movie-Making," *Mass Culture,* ed. Bernard Rosenberg and David Manning White (Glencoe, Ill.: Free Press, 1957), pp. 315–324.
2. Otto N. Larsen, "Social Effects of Mass Communication," *Handbook of Modern Sociology,* ed. Robert E. L. Faris (Chicago: Rand, McNally, 1964), pp. 348–381.
3. Bernard Berelson, "The Great Debate on Cultural Democracy," *Studies in Public Communication,* No. 3 (Summer 1961), pp. 3–14.
4. Joseph T. Klapper, *The Effects of Mass Communication* (Glencoe, Ill.: Free Press, 1960), pp. 135–165.

5. Frederic Wertham, "The Scientific Study of Mass Media Effects," *The American Journal of Psychiatry,* 119 (October 1962), pp. 306–311.
6. Dallas W. Smythe, "Dimensions of Violence," *Audio-Visual Communications Review,* 3 (Winter 1955), pp. 58–63.
7. Hilde T. Himmelweit, A. N. Oppenheim, and Pamela Vince, *Television and the Child* (London: Oxford University Press, 1958).
8. Charles Winick, "Censor and Sensibility: A Content Analysis of the Television Censor's Comments," *Journal of Broadcasting,* 5 (Spring 1961), p. 119.
9. See, for example, Leonard D. Eron, "Relationship of TV Viewing Habits and Aggressive Behavior in Children," *Journal of Abnormal and Social Psychology,* 67 (August 1963), pp. 193–196; Leonard Berkowitz, "The Effects of Observing Violence," *Scientific American,* 210 (February 1964), pp. 35–41.
10. For details, see Dan Lacy, *Freedom and Communications* (Urbana: University of Illinois Press, 1965), p. 62.
11. Ibid.
12. In Gary A. Steiner, *The People Look at Television* (New York): Alfred A. Knopf, (1963), p. vii.
13. See, for example, Norman Jacobs (ed.), *Culture for the Millions?* (Princeton, N.J.: D. Van Nostrand, 1961).
14. Ibid., pp. 90–91.
15. A typology for the analysis of violence as part of the American social and cultural structure is presented by Walter M. Gerson, "Violence: An American Value Theme?", *Violence and the Mass Media,* ed. Otto N. Larsen (New York: Harper & Row, 1967).
16. For an examination of some complexities concerning the obvious example see, William A. Westley, "Violence and the Police," *American Journal of Sociology,* 59 (July 1953), pp. 34–41.
17. For further examples, see Roy G. Francis, "Kapow! !: An Argument and a Forecast," *Social Problems,* 12 (Winter 1965), pp. 328–335.
18. Ruth A. Inglis, *Freedom of the Movies* (Chicago: University of Chicago Press, 1947).
19. John E. Twomey, "The Citizens' Committee and Comic-Book Control: A Study of Extragovernmental Restraint," *Law and Contemporary Problems,* 20 (Autumn 1955), pp. 621–629.
20. John E. Coons (ed.), *Freedom and Responsibility in Broadcasting* (Evanston, Ill.: Northwestern University Press, 1961).
21. Codes for the American Society of Newspaper Editors, the Motion Picture Association of America, and the National Association of Broadcasters are reproduced in Wilbur Schramm (ed.), *Mass Communications* (Urbana: University of Illinois Press, 1960). The code employed by the Comics Magazine Association of America may be found in George A. Lundberg et al., *Sociology* (New York: Harper and Row, 1963), p. 239.
22. John L. Goldwater, *Americana in Four Colors* (New York: Comic Magazine Association of America, 1964).
23. Ibid., pp. 41–42.
24. Ibid., p. 49.
25. For example, John E. Twomey, "New Forms of Social Control over Mass Media Content," *Studies in Public Communication,* No. 1 (Summer 1957), pp. 38–44.
26. A prolific writer, Wertham has presented his case in many magazines and journals (and before many congressional committees), but most importantly in his book, Frederic Wertham, *Seduction of the Innocent* (New York: Rinehart, 1953).
27. Frederic Wertham, "Mass Media and Sex Deviation," *Sexual Behavior and the Law,* ed. Ralph Slovenko (Springfield, Ill.: Charles C. Thomas, 1965).
28. Ibid., p. 848.
29. Ibid.
30. Winick, op. cit.